# Economics Canada:
# Selected Readings

# Economics Canada: Selected Readings

Edited by

B.S. Keirstead,
J. R. G. Brander,
J. F. Earl
and
C. M. Waddell

Macmillan of Canada   1974

© Macmillan Company of Canada Limited 1974

ISBN 0-7705-1147-3 cloth
ISBN 0-7705-1148-1 paper
Library of Congress Catalogue Card No. 73-92685

Printed in Canada for
The Macmillan Company of Canada Limited
70 Bond Street, Toronto
M5B 1X3

to the memory of
PROFESSOR BURTON S. KEIRSTEAD
(1907-1973)

# Contents

# Preface

We believe this book is unique. It is unique in its coverage of current economic issues. Whereas most books of readings merely complement standard textbooks, ours presents a much wider range of subject matter and opinion and is intended to be provocative. The focus of the book is the Canadian economy, but in selecting pieces we did not restrict ourselves to narrow technical material. Instead, we looked for articles that dealt with the social and political dimensions of problems as well as the economic aspect.

Because this book is published by Macmillan of Canada, and one of the editors, Prof. B. S. Keirstead, was also an editor of *The Canadian Economy: Selected Readings*, students and teachers may be tempted to assume it is merely a third and revised edition. This is not so. It is an entirely new book. It is most accurately called a successor volume. We acknowledge, however, a great debt to Dr. Deutsch and Professors Levitt and Will.

The present volume departs from its predecessors in two main ways. First, the pieces included are at a slightly higher technical and intellectual level. Second, *The Canadian Economy* included only pieces by Canadians on Canadian problems. We continue the emphasis on Canadian problems, but have included a number of articles by non-Canadians. We believe the present volume will enjoy a wide readership. It includes readings suitable for a college level introductory course or for more advanced courses in Canadian economic policy and problems.

# Acknowledgements

For permission to reprint copyright material grateful acknowledgement is made to the following:

The Bank of Nova Scotia for "Foreign Investment in Canada" from *Monthly Review* of April-May, 1971 and "The Banks and the Regional Problem" from the Chairman's Report in the *Annual Report*, 1970.

Gerald K. Bouey for "What Central Banking is About": Remarks to the Canadian Club of Toronto, April 30, 1973.

*The Canadian Forum* for "Towards a New National Policy" by Eric W. Kierans in *Canadian Forum*, January-February 1972, pp. 52-55.

The Canadian Imperial Bank of Commerce for "The Next Industrial Revolution" by Athelstan Spillhaus from the Canadian Imperial Bank of Commerce *Commercial Letter*, issue No. 1, 1971.

*The Canadian Journal of Economics* for "Interprovincial Migration and Economic Adjustment" (excerpts) by Thomas J. Courchene in *Canadian Journal of Economics*, Vol. III, No. 4, November 1970, pp. 550-576; "Federal-Provincial Tax Equalization: An Evaluation" by T. J. Courchene and D. Beavis in *Canadian Journal of Economics*, Vol. VI, November 1973; "Reflections on the International Monetary System" by Wm. C. Hood in *Canadian Journal of Economics*, Vol. III, No. 4, November 1970, pp. 525-540 and "The Economics of the National Hockey League" by J. C. H. Jones in *Canadian Journal of Economics*, Vol. II, No. 1, February 1969, pp. 1-20.

The Canadian Tax Foundation for "Further Thoughts on Regional Tax Incentives" by Richard M. Bird in *Canadian Tax Journal*, Vol. XVIII, No. 6, 1970; "The Growth of Government Spending in Canada" by Richard M. Bird in *Canadian Tax Papers*, No. 51, July 1970 (excerpts); "Tax Incentives for Regional Development: A Critical Comment" by Charles E. McLure, Jr. in *Canadian Tax Journal*, Vol. XVIII, No. 6, 1970; "The Treatment of Dependants Under the Personal Income Tax" by T. Russell Robinson in *Canadian Tax Journal*, Vol. XVIII No. 1 1970; and "Fiscal Instruments and Pollution: An Evalustion of Canadian Legislation" by Leonard Waverman in *Canadian Tax Journal*, Vol. XVIII, No. 6, 1970.

Thomas J. Courchene for "Some Reflections on the Senate Hearings on Poverty," Research Report 7118, June 1971, the University of Western Ontario.

Walter L. Gordon for "Notes for Remarks at the Twenty-first Annual Meeting of the Canadian Association of Geographers," an address delivered at the 21st annual meeting of the Canadian Association of Geographers, at the University of Waterloo, June 3, 1971.

Granada Publishing Ltd., London, England for "Growthmania," Chapters 1 and 2 of *The Costs of Economic Growth,* by Ezra J. Mishan, London: The Staples Press, 1967.

Harvard University Press for "Free Trade Between the United States and Canada," Reprinted by permission of the publishers from Ronald J. Wonnacott and Paul Wonnacott, *Free Trade Between the United States and Canada,* pp. 335-40, Cambridge, Mass.: Harvard University Press, Copyright, 1967, by the President and Fellows of Harvard College.

Information Canada for "Performance and Potential" by the Northern Electric Company, originally published as "Condensation of Economic Council of Canada Report, *Performance and Potential: Mid 1950's to Mid 1970's*"; "Retail Price Indexes," from *The Consumer Price Index for Canada (1961 = 100),* Dominion Bureau of Statistics, Cat. No. 62-002, March 1972; and "A Framework for Government Decision-Making" from the Economic Council of Canada, *Eighth Annual Review,* 1971, Chapter 5, pp. 63-82. Reproduced by permission of Information Canada.

The International Monetary Fund and The World Bank Group for "The Limits to Growth: A Critique," by Mahbub UlHaq, in *Finance and Development,* Vol. 9, No. 4, December 1972, pp. 2-8.

James Lewis and Samuel, Publishers, for "Forced Growth: Government Involvement in Industrial Development," from *Forced Growth* by Philip Mathias, Chapter 1, Toronto, 1971.

Harry G. Johnson for "Problems of Canadian Nationalism" in *The Canadian Quandary,* Toronto: McGraw-Hill-Ryerson Ltd., 1963, pp. 11-21.

*The Journal of Economic Issues* for "Value Judgments and Economic Science" by Vincent J. Tarascio in *Journal of Economic Issues,* V (March 1971), pp. 98-102 and "What is Distinctive About Contemporary Capitalism?" by Benjamin N. Ward in *Journal of Economic Issues,* III (March 1969), pp. 32-48.

Lloyds Bank Limited, London, England for "Why We Need Economic Growth" by W. Beckerman in *Lloyds Bank Review,* October 1971 and "The ABC of Cost-Benefit" by E. J. Mishan in *Lloyds Bank Review,* July 1971.

Longman Group Limited, Journals Division, London, England for "The Case for Regional Policies" by Nicholas Kaldor in *Scottish Journal of Political Economy,* November 1970.

The Macmillan Company of Canada Limited, Toronto, for "Planning for Development" from *Regional Economic Policies in Canada* by T.N. Brewis, 1969, pp. 193-201 and "The Harvest of Lengthening Dependence" from *Silent Surrender* by Kari Levitt, 1970, Chapter VII.

McGraw-Hill Ryerson Limited for "The Options for Stabilization Policy in Canada," a brief presented to the Standing Senate Committee on National Finance, May 20, 1971, by Grant L. Reuber with Ronald G. Bodkin, which appears in an edited and retitled version, "Stagflation: The Canadian Experience" in *Issues in Canadian Economics* edited by Lawrence H. Officer and Lawrence B. Smith. Reprinted by permission of McGraw-Hill Ryerson Limited.

# Prologue

# ERIC W. KIERANS
# Towards a New National Policy

The Report on the "Domestic Control of the National Economic Environment" has ably described the present degree of the foreign ownership of Canada's soil, resources and industries, and the extent of the problem facing us. There is no need to repeat or summarize what is well known to all Canadians. The main recommendation puts forward the creation of a screening mechanism to judge the performance of foreign controlled firms, with the power to block additional foreign direct investment where this is judged to be in our best interests. As an interim measure, it will slow down new foreign investment but, as has been shown elsewhere, there is already a sufficiently large foreign involvement in Canada to maintain itself at a rate compounded annually that will ensure its continued domination. If the screening agency forces a fundamental re-examination of all our economic policies, then it will be a success. It must be remembered that our present condition is the result of past commercial, monetary and fiscal policies; they are the causes and if they are not changed, nothing substantial will happen to reverse present trends.

It is now fashionable to talk of an industrial strategy, a national policy that will encourage innovation, promote economic growth and employment and develop a network of Canadian technology based on certain industries. All these objectives are truly laudable and one wonders that they have to be repeated ad nauseam as some great new discovery of the source of Canada's ills. One wonders also why such a policy cannot be implemented.

The difficulty is that we have a policy, an old one to be sure, but we do not know how to get rid of it. That industrial policy goes back to 1879 and is based on the tariff. It was expanded in 1955, when we decided to seek more rapid rates of growth by the exploitation and unloading of vast quantities of our raw material and energy resources on world markets. When virtually every other nation in the developed and industrialized world follows a policy of conserving and reducing the drain on its natural resources, we encourage their consumption by outrageous tax concessions accorded to no other sector of our economy. A third element in our present industrial strategy is to imitate as closely as possible the directions of U.S. economic activity, hoping thereby to share in their prosperity. Thus, we voluntarily pursue their objectives and are rewarded with Defence Production Sharing arrangements, Auto Pact agreements and operate on the fringes of their space and satellite programmes, etc.

The Science Council of Canada concludes that "the main impediment (to a new national industrial strategy) is the poor relationship that now exists between government and industry." This is true but both parties have been committed to and benefitted from the advantages of tariff protection, resource exploitation and branch plant expansion for some considerable time. The vested interests, both governmental and industrial, are large and powerful. As Innis wrote: ''American branch factories established under the protection of the Canadian tariff and the advantages of Imperial Preference have strong vested interests in Canadian nationalism and imperial connection.'' Government planners moreover are reluctant to admit that their past policies may have been wrong.

Times have changed. The United Kingdom is joining Europe. The United States is becoming increasingly protectionist. Canada is becoming uncomfortably isolated. Suddenly, Canadians are realizing what economists have been saying all along. Imported technology and ideas do not create new comparative advantages and tariff protection does not force the pace of specialization. Our tariff walls have become a trap because our markets have been big enough to attract foreign capital with new ideas, new products and new technology.

The second element of our present industrial strategy is the emphasis on the export of natural resources. The official position of the Department of Finance is that ''there is no inherent reason why Canada cannot be a major exporter of raw materials and of manufactured goods at the same time.'' This is demonstrably false. When each of our major trading partners is searching for a balance in their merchandise trade with us, they will be striving to pay for their imports of our raw materials with their manufactured goods. An additional $1 billion export of energy resources to the United States, for example, would give us $68 million in wages and salaries. The balancing inflow of $1 billion manufactured goods could mean that we are importing anywhere from $200 million to $350 million in wages and salaries, depending on the industry. An exchange of dollars but not of employment!

The third feature of current industrial policy is the me-too-ism of the federal government's planning. So we invest in research and development on CF5's, hydrofoils, satellites and so on, all of which are more consistent with U.S. military and technological objectives than with Canadian priorities. Given the huge financial and technical resources that the United States devotes to these purposes, Canada can never be any more than a farm team, dedicated to repeating and developing what others have invented.

A new industrial strategy means that the Canadian economy must be switched into new directions. It also means that it must be switched *out of* old paths and there is the rub. The hurt to the pride of our policymakers and to the built up investment in existing industrial capacity is immediate and biting. The advantages to the Canadian people lie in the future and the long-run can always be made to appear vague and unreal. Change disrupts the status quo and the immediate disadvantages in political and electoral terms, outweigh the assurances of a more promising future.

An industrial strategy emerges from a nation's aims and objectives. It cannot exist alone and must form a part of and be fully integrated with all elements of economic policy. Nor can it be superimposed upon or melded with the old policies that it is meant to replace.

Let us assume that Canadian objectives are a more 'Just Society,' greater employment and a greater control of our economic environment. Essentially, this means that we are determined to improve, by our own policies, the quality and the standard of living of all Canadians. These objectives become ends in themselves and will not be the by-product of pursuing the aims of other nations which might be concerned with maintaining a military superiority and technological supremacy over each other. In other words, our efforts for improving the quality of life in Canada will not be hampered by the inclusion of these other objectives to the degree that obtains elsewhere.

Such objectives demand a major overhaul of our existing economic policies. All that time will permit me to do here is to indicate very briefly the direction of such changes.

## Monetary Policy

Canadian monetary policy should be strongly expansionary for many years to come. Not only do we want to expand demand to put unemployed resources to work but we will have to face the declining job opportunity trends that are clearly evident in current international trade and monetary developments. Further tight money policies can only serve to reinforce the tendencies to increasing foreign ownership since the marginal efficiency of capital worsens only for the Canadian entrepreneur and the range of investment opportunities narrows for him alone. Since the ratio of net debt to gross national product relationship is at an all-time post-war low in Canada, an expansionary monetary policy, with corresponding budgetary deficits, could be pursued for the years needed to effect a change in the directions and objectives of economic activity in Canada.

## Fiscal Policy

On the expenditure side, government spending must be directed not to copying the objectives and technology of the United States and thus becoming a pale counterfeit of that nation, but to the pursuit of the Canadian objective of improving the quality of life for our people. Thus, the federal and provincial spending power will emphasize more single-mindedly than today the objectives of eliminating poverty, reducing the burdens on the sick and the aged and financing the technology that will control and roll back the pollution of the environment and improve housing, school and hospital facilities. We can never be more than fourth or fifth rate in technologies based on force de frappe and space objectives and should reduce our present investments accordingly. While other nations invest in these objectives, Canada can make a distinctive and exportable contribution in technologies based on environmental control.

On the taxation side, we have copied, without adapting to Canadian conditions and objectives, the main features of American and British tax systems. Thus, we have a whole host of exemptions and privileges in the corporate income area that discriminate heavily against the manufacturing and service industries to the advantage of the resource industries and that favour large firms over small, despite the concession on the first $35,000 income.

If we eliminate all the concessions, depletion, accelerated depreciation, investment allowances, capital cost allowances that exceed actual funds invested by 15% to 33-1/3%, and so on, the federal government could reduce the corporate tax rate to 35% in all sectors of the economy without any loss in tax revenues. At the present time, the outrageously low effective tax rates in the resource sector direct investment into those low employment sectors and discriminate against investment in the heavier employment manufacturing and service industries. A corporate tax rate that affected equally all branches of economic activity would not distort the investment decision-making process to the extent achieved by our present system.

If the government should agree that a 35% corporate tax rate without exemption and special immunities, would yield the same revenues, I see no reason why this rate cannot be confined to wholly owned or controlled Canadian companies. Every nation favours its own citizens in one form or another and we have only to cite the most recent example, the United States investment allowance for home-made capital equipment. Let the corporate rate on foreign subsidiaries be what the rate is in the home country. If the rate is 50% in the United States or 40% in the United Kingdom, that rate shall apply to their subsidiaries operating within Canada. In no instance, however, would the rate applicable to a subsidiary be less than the 35% on Canadian companies. On the basis of existing American policy, this proposal would avoid encouragement to U.S. firms establishing in Canada to take advantage of lower corporate rates and be consistent with their DISC proposals and similar measures.

Similarly, the entire Canadian entrepreneurial community would be enlisted in the drive to halt and reverse the trend to increasing foreign ownership. This cannot be achieved by a Canada Development Corporation alone or a screening board. It requires the united efforts of all elements in the business and financial community. It is not my experience that the company with the 50% tax rate buys out the company with the 35% rate, only to lose the advantage. Rather, it is the other way round.

Such a policy would provide a clear signal of the government's determination to end the current trends to foreign control and domination of our economy, inspire Canadian businessmen to expand their own activities and buy out foreign subsidiaries and, above all, prove that we are sovereign in our own house.

## Commercial Policy

Free trade is a dogma appropriate for particular nations at particular times in their history. It is my belief that this policy would, given our present objective of reversing the present domination of our economy, be well suited to the resolution of some of our most pressing problems.

The manufacturing industry in Canada is particularly vulnerable. On the policy level, the attempt to keep out competition by tariffs turned out to be self-defeating as American, and other firms established subsidiaries inside the tariff walls. On the level of the firm, the beneficiaries of tariff protection too often felt no compulsion to keep pace with change or to develop the competitive strength to compete in world markets. As a result, we have an industry plagued with heavy over-investment and too many firms. The profits that Canadian manufacturing ought to protect by tariffs had to be shared with the foreign subsidiary. The cost of the excess capacity has been paid for by Canadian consumers through higher prices.

A tariff assures a stream of future income returns higher than would obtain under freer trade conditions. Obviously, the cost of buying out subsidiaries would be greater for Canadian firms if the tariff were to remain. A government decision to reduce tariff protection in the manufacturing industry by 10% per annum over a period of ten years would reduce the capitalized values of firms located therein. Canadian takeovers of foreign subsidiaries would not include the goodwill inherent in an outmoded tariff policy. Further, American subsidiaries, which have always better reason to locate in Europe or Latin America than Canada because of distance and transportation costs, would, again in line with current U.S. policy, be disposed to withdraw to their own borders, sell their assets to Canadian firms and attempt to export their products to us.

The main point, here, is that the market for the assets of subsidiaries located in Canada would become a buyer's market for Canadian investors and entrepreneurs, not a seller's market as it is under the umbrella of windfall profits provided by our own tariff. A 35% corporate tax rate on Canadian firms would increase the number of interested Canadian buyers; a staged removal of the tariff would greatly increase the number of anxious sellers of subsidiary operations. Canadians would be in a position to pick and choose, to refuse to pay for windfall tariff profits that would be disappearing anyway and to take advantage of a situation where the subsidiary's raison d'etre for location in Canada no longer obtains. I, myself, would commence such negotiations by offering $1 for the assets which would be $1 more than the subsidiary would obtain if it simply withdrew. Undoubtedly, one would have to go higher but, for once, the Canadian would be in the driver's seat.

Canadian firms would also lose their tariff protection and windfall gains and many would disappear. The viable firms, strongly aggressive, entrepreneurial and confident, would survive, grow and give Canada a truly competitive and expanding manufacturing sector. Canadian entrepreneurs, after a long hibernation, would be tested and there is no reason to believe that they would not make it.

## Resources

A nation's natural resources are not past production. They are the wealth of its soil and waterways. As such, they cannot be viewed in the same light as current production, to be disposed of at will by the factors that created the new goods and services. They are a trust received from the past, to be husbanded by the present and to be passed on to future generations. A generation that deliberately squanders a nation's natural wealth to enhance its own standard of living, to live high off the hog, will have much to answer for. A government that deliberately pursues a policy of selling off the natural wealth of its people to achieve short-run gains in GNP breaks faith with its own future. It reveals, by the forced sale of its assets, its inability to devise the set of objectives and policies that will increase output and distribute it more equitably on an annual basis. It admits that the standard of living depends on the selling of capital in addition to annual income.

Unfortunately, Canada decided in the late forties and early fifties, to ensure a rapid rate of growth by selling off its non-renewable resources. This policy was permanently enshrined in our tax legislation in 1955 and still survives despite the so-called tax reform bill. The current attempts of the resource industries, particularly the Mining Association of Canada, to prove their value to the Canadian economy are based on wild exaggeration and border on hysteria. Their use of the multiplier, if accepted and applied to all sectors of the economy, would force one to conclude that there were twelve to fourteen million Canadians employed in Canada instead of eight million.

A non-renewable resource policy—I am not speaking of forest products, agriculture, or hydro-electric power—should be prudent, conservative and economical in the long run. It should take account not only of our own needs but those of the generations to come. Even our own needs are not well served by the policy of resource exploitation. A billion dollars of oil and gas exports, as stated above, yields us $6 million in wages and salaries, little or no profits since they are foreign-owned and little in the way of corporate income taxes which we have given away by privilege and dispensation.

I have been constantly amazed by the violent and vehement representations of the captains of our resource industries as they fight to maintain their existing exemptions. They do their case great harm. One can accept their self-interest but they must also admit the right of governments, which have given them licenses and proprietary rights, to measure their private and immediate gains against the long run social advantage. Such firms exist, not by some divine right, but by the will of the people and the policies of governments. Intransigence and threats could easily lead to nationalization.

We should adhere to our present commitments but reduce our reliance on future resource exploitation to obtain our growth.

## Exchange Rates

It is clear that the above changes in our economic policies could not be carried through within the limits of fixed exchange rates. A change in our economic objectives to emphasize distribution and the quality of life, free trade in manufacturing, monetary expansion to expand effective demand, fiscal policy to effect a reversal of foreign ownership and control of our economy, a decline in the rate of growth of raw material exports—all will exert a great downward pressure on the value of our dollar. These needed fundamental changes in our economic aims and the orientation of our economy are too real and too deep to be contained within the usual deviations from a fixed rate. The real proof of our determination to be Canadian in fact and and masters in our own house will be our successful insistence on the need to retain a floating rate.

The relative productivities of the Canadian and American economies must differ by at least 15% simply because of the difference in size of the two markets. A proper relationship between the two currencies, based on industrial strength, might result in a value of 85¢ for the Canadian dollar. The current equality is a reflection not of comparative competitive forces but of Canadian monetary policies which have encouraged capital inflows by higher interest rates and the selling of our natural resources. Policies that reduce the value of the Canadian dollar would describe more accurately our relative industrial strengths, equalize our competitive position and defend our economy more efficiently than tariffs.

It is only in the context of an overall mix of economic policies and a declaration of basic economic objectives that one can draft an industrial policy. Such a policy comes after a society has defined its major purposes and priorities. It cannot come before. Once a society's ends are stated, the thrust of its industrial policy can be determined; those aims dictate the emphasis, whether it be civil or military efforts, a rising standard of living or concentration of wealth and industrial might, technologies that improve the environment or conquer space.

An industrial policy will be meaningless unless there is a clear definition of what Canada is, what are its aims, where it is going and how it proposes to get there. An industrial policy, a screening board and a Canada Development Corporation are, no doubt, useful — but they are only the fringes on top. A clear consensus on economic ends and the policies to achieve them are the surrey that will carry Canadians to where they want to be.

# SECTION ONE
## Introduction

BENJAMIN WARD

# What is Distinctive About Contemporary Capitalism?

Judging from recent literature, history has not dealt decisively with the old question as to the nature of capitalism. There are still those today who believe that it is the only sound and viable form of economic system, others who believe it is rotten to the core and moribund; there are still those who believe that Soviet socialism is the wave of the future, others who believe it is a deviant system associated with a middle phase of economic development, others who believe it is not essentially different from capitalism; and so on. But even if these arguments have not changed so much over the years, the world has clearly changed, and our knowledge of the operation of national economies has expanded tremendously. From the perspective of these changes, given my limited knowledge of the facts, this paper is written. Four kinds of distinctions are briefly surveyed. First there are those between the United States of sixty or eighty years ago and today, to indicate how the greatest of capitalist countries has changed with the times. Second is the extent of similarity between the United States and other developed capitalist countries, to see to what extent there is such an animal as mature capitalism. Third there is the extent of similarity among all those countries with basically capitalist institutions—that is, primary use of markets to allocate resources and substantial acceptance of the institution of private property. Finally there is the extent of diversity between capitalist and socialist countries. Armed with these lists of differences we can then return in the conclusion to the title question.

"Capitalism" and "socialism" are rather abstract terms. If they have any real significance, it should be manifest in their effects on individual and family life, and this is what we will try to evaluate. The effects will be divided into three kinds: the level of consumption, the nature of risk, and the nature of externalities experienced by average families under the various groups of régimes considered.

## The United States Then and Now

Two aspects of the contrast between this country during the last decade or two of the nineteenth century and today suggest the most relevant considerations: the changing economic situation of the individual and family, and the nature and extent of deliberate human manipulation of the economic environment.

With respect to the family the most obvious change of course is in the level of consumption of goods and leisure. With respect to such basics as food, clothing and housing the striking change is not so much quantitative as qualitative. The range and level of processing of purchased consumer goods has widened tremendously while such indicators as amount of meat products consumed per capita, the number of rooms per capita and the per capita yardage of cotton fabrics consumed have changed relatively little. A revolutionary change occurred with respect to electrical consumer durables for the home which of course did not exist in 1890. Though other furniture still constitutes the major stock of home-based movables, these appliances have revolutionized the housewife's chores. Perhaps the increase in leisure, signaled for example by the decline by about one-third in the factory work week, and the communications revolution are the changes in consumption having the most substantial impact on family life.

A fundamental if intangible part of family life is the distribution of risk over the various contingencies of human existence. Satisfactory, comprehensive data on this question are simply not available, but clearly the changes that have occurred are by no means all in the same direction. Perhaps the dominant change from the point of view of social welfare is the dramatic reduction in the risk of infant mortality to one-sixth of its former level of 16 per cent. Risks of death or impairment from illness have also declined substantially for the younger age cohorts. The risk of substantial income loss from accident has also been sharply reduced, as a result partly of increased safety measures and partly of the growth of insurance against such risks. The hundredfold increase in disbursements of life insurance companies and the very substantial government insurance programs, which in 1890 were limited almost entirely to veteran's compensation, are evidence of this change. The incidence of unemployment may not have changed substantially, but again the risk of income loss has been much reduced. Also dramatic is the increase in insurance against various risks of property loss, though it is hard to evaluate the relative uninsured risks. Risks associated with opportunity, the ability to advance in society, are especially hard to evaluate; because the economy was expanding in both periods substantial opportunities existed, and gross data indicate comparable rates of intergenerational mobility. However the quality of the opportunities was quite different with, for example, the shift from country to town generating a relatively much larger portion of migration in the earlier period. Also the very high incidence of travel casualties, thanks especially to the automobile, had no nineteenth century counterpart. It is probably a fair bet that the risk of war varies directly with the size of the armed forces; clearly it is much greater, and the risk itself a more substantial one, now than then. Perhaps in summary one might say that on the whole there has been a dramatic reduction in the income effects of divisible risks to families, the latter being risks that in principle can be shifted from the family to the group.

A third area of economically relevant change in family life is associated with externalities. Most striking here is the increase in human contacts brought about by urbanization and the transportation revolution. The average number of significant daily per capita human contacts has surely increased very substantially, as has the number of different people contacted, and the proportion of the population caught up in the urban, human-contact environment has increased several fold. One can only speculate as to the consequences of this, but it is very plausible that one consequence is "other-directedness," the increased dependence of individual criteria of choice on the behaviour and approval of others. Empathy, identification, envy and related feelings probably play a much greater role in economic choices, and the relative stranger counts for rather more than he used to in these decisions. Crowding produces increased levels of other externalities too, such as noise, pollution, aesthetic impairments, and risks to person and property, which are not effectively controlled by market relations.

Closely related to the notion of externalities is that of understanding or the "image" which individuals possess of their environment. Perhaps the most dramatic change in this regard in the last sixty to eighty years has been the increase in the proportion of the populace that has acquired a deliberative and organized interpretation of its environment. This is partly indicated by the fifteenfold increase in the proportion of seventeen year olds who are high school graduates, but also very important are curricular changes at all levels oriented toward more direct understanding of the social and physical environment and the emigration from the countryside. Equally dramatic is the consequence of the electronic communications revolution which has produced a hundredfold increase in telephones per capita, as well as generating radio and television. These devices serve to magnify contacts and, combined with the very large increases in per capita use of more conventional information sources, to present a tremendously increased body of information to the individual for processing. Higher education levels no doubt increase the processing power of individuals on the average; nevertheless, given the increased information and the greatly increased number of alternative economic choices available, a probable consequence is that far more individual resources must be devoted to relatively more deliberative economic decision-making than was the case before the turn of the century. In addition, an increased awareness of the opportunities for social control of the environment has probably made most individuals more aware of the extent to which they are manipulated by others. "Information overload," increased contacts, manipulation of feelings and attitudes—all these may have become a threat to personal autonomy of a kind and on a relative scale that has no counterpart in the earlier period.

To what extent has all this been brought under more or less deliberate and organized social control? An important factor in answering this question is the much greater importance of large scale organization today. Over half the gross national product is produced under the auspices of large scale private or public organizations. This has changed the distribution of occupations dramatically: a doubling in the proportion of professional and technical personnel in the work force since the turn of the century, a near doubling in the proportion of managers, officials and proprietors outside farming, a threefold increase in the proportion of clerical workers, an increase of about 50 per cent in the proportion of sales workers. The proportion of federal civilian employment has increased more than fourfold and the proportion of members of the armed forces more than twentyfold. All these changes are related to the increase in the scope and impact of management of people by these large organizations.

Clearly the instruments available to these organizations to manipulate people are very great. First there is the general indoctrination performed within the educational system, whose impact has presumably expanded with the increase by more than 50 per cent in the median number of years spent in school, and whose degree of uniformity as well as relevance for individual economic and social decision making may well have increased. Then there is the influence exercised through the communications media, which is clearly capable of at least affecting the proportion of the populace that makes a particular choice of goods within some product group. Then there is the indoctrination associated with the workplace, which is nearly always substantially greater than the zero associated with independent farming, and is greatest in areas like the armed forces where the relative increase in numbers is greatest.

But these are fairly direct influences. Also a whole host of indirect influences are exercised through legislative and administrative acts and by agreement among large organizations which have the effect of shaping the general environment in which we live. Monopoly was not unknown eighty years ago, but substantial control of a national market was far rarer than it is today. The government controlled so small a share of the economy that attempts to influence the economy by varying the levels of spending and taxing could not have had much impact, had they been tried. Even in monetary matters, durable banking legislation largely tied the government's hands. Redistribution efforts could at best be only marginal—in 1895 federal income tax collections amounted to $77 million. Antitrust legislation was hardly born at the federal level, and general government regulation of business activity and procedures occurred only at the margin, as with patent legislation. The armed forces were insignificant and state employment a fraction of its present size. Thus the ingredients for government control of the economy or of business hardly existed. Business collusion to control substantial portions of the economy was also infeasible except in quite limited areas, though these were features of the scene that were already undergoing rapid change.

As might be expected an increase in the ability to control has been accompanied by an increase in the understanding of instruments of control and their power. There is no need to recite a long list in this regard. Suffice it to say that at all the levels mentioned above a considerable ability exists consciously and substantially to alter the economic environment in roughly predictable ways, and much of the talent in white collar occupations is devoted to this effort. It remains an open and controversial question to what extent all these management bodies are engaged in effective collusion in this control operation, and what interests the collusion serves. It seems that management personnel in all bodies in the economy and state share a number of social traits and orientations, such as middle- to upper-class family origin and college education. It is possible that awareness of the power to manipulate tends to create elitist attitudes in the manipulators and feelings of frustration in the manipulated, with a consequent bifurcation of society which roughly coincides with relative incomes. But even the manipulators are very often manipulated, often frustrated and anxiety-ridden, and the dominance of mass culture may be sufficient to be culturally levelling rather than dividing. Also though the instruments are often powerful there is still much ignorance as to their consequences, and much ignorance as to the relevant actions contemplated by other large units. There is a great deal more deliberate coordination of actions today than in the past, but there is much blindness as to consequences as well.

In sum, Americans today live in a highly manipulated world in which both the active and the passive have a substantially greater store of information about a substantially more complex environment, in which there is much more interaction, a great threat to the autonomy of the individual, and somewhat reduced risks, except for that of general disaster, to go with their higher levels of consumption of goods and leisure. In their scope, pace, and effects on the quality of human life, these changes have perhaps had no counterpart since the rise of the first urban, river-valley civilizations. But also, in both periods of American history we were a dynamic society with great diversity in the conditions of citizens, and the signals from the environment stimulated optimism, complacency, fear, and despair in very different mixes both between and within periods.

## Developed Capitalism

The world's twelve most prosperous countries—excluding Kuwait—are the United States, Canada, the United Kingdom, Australia, New Zealand, the Scandinavian countries, the Low Countries, West Germany and France. All of these have a number of traits in common. They have basically capitalist institutions with about two-thirds to four-fifths of the national product generated by private market-oriented organizations. They all have parliamentary democracies and, relative to most of the world, open societies, though the stability of democratic institutions is not high in every case. All have relatively large levels of welfare and public consumption expenditures and employ government financial instruments both to redistribute income and to promote general economic stability and growth. Though there is a very great range of recent growth rates among these countries, all have been growing rather steadily for many decades, and all have achieved a substantial portion of their recent growth as a consequence of technical innovations. In addition there are many cultural and social traits which these countries have in common and which tend to distinguish them from the rest of the world. Finally, in terms of directions of change of the variables discussed in the last section, these economies sixty to eighty years ago probably in some real sense had more in common with the United States of that time than they do with themselves today.

It would not do to exaggerate the similarities among the ''top twelve.'' There is a variation of over 50 per cent in levels of GNP per capita and a hundredfold in population, substantial variation in the extent of nationalization of industry and public welfare programs, size of the armed forces, innovation-orientation, and quality and quantity of higher education, to mention only a few variables. However eight years ago many of the differences were relatively greater. At any rate, for our broad purposes, and particularly for purposes of contrast with nineteenth century capitalism, contemporary developing capitalist countries, and contemporary socialism, it is the similarities rather than the differences that stand out.

Are there pressures in the environment tending to push these countries toward greater similarity? Two points of evidence may be mentioned at this time: First, there is the negative indication of two countries which are among the leading candidates, in terms of GNP per capita, for entry into the top group.

These countries have neither democratic nor capitalist institutions, but it seems that their present institutions could not persist without the presence of foreign troops on their soil. They are Czechoslovakia and East Germany.

Secondly, there is the interdependence among these countries. They tend to trade much more among themselves than with others. There is much intermingling of business, with Western Europe investing perhaps half as much in the United States than the latter has in the former. Multinational businesses have become a commonplace. And political alignments tend to reflect these economic ties. The political and economic interdependence has reached the state in which changes in any of these countries tend to have significant consequences for the others. In some cases, such as the international monetary system, the interdependence is very striking. Despite the fact that each is a sovereign state the top twelve have some of the properties of a single social entity, though this strong interdependence extends at least somewhat beyond the twelve, including for example Italy. There are between 45 and 50 countries in the world today whose institutions support the preservation and growth of private property and use markets as the major allocative device, and yet which have not yet entered the charmed circle of general prosperity and modernity. In levels of GNP per capita there is a more than tenfold range among these countries, and a dozen or more of them—such as India, the Philippines and South Korea—still lie below the levels already achieved by the developed countries when their modern industrialization began. Steady growth, even with substantial aid, is problematic for most of these. Others, such as Greece, Japan and Italy, have been growing steadily and rapidly for a decade or more, can provide reasonable prosperity for a substantial fraction of their citizenry, and show signs of a capability for more or less autonomous further development.

Given a commitment to modernization, these fifty countries have one substantial advantage over their predecessors: they know what modernization is, and there already exists in the exemplars the stock of technological knowledge necessary to replicate the physical conditions of the developed countries. It is probably true that in every one of these countries a significant portion of the populace has in fact a commitment to at least some aspects of modernization.

However it is by now clear that the existence of the developed lands creates many difficulties for the latecomers. Most of these can be cast under the broad rubric of the enclave problem. Instead of moving by slow and relatively small steps into the modern world, these countries are assailed by modernity as a consequence of the revolutions in transportation and communications. At the same time the technology that is being introduced into their countries is dramatically more complex than that which has traditionally existed, and makes very different demands on the skills and understanding and even the interpersonal relations of its operators. Key jobs at least initially must often be held by foreigners, and when local nationals do take over, they have already in a fundamental sense left the world of their fathers. The new production techniques often serve the world market rather than the national one, thus further enhancing the separation; and when they do serve the national market, it is often disruptive of traditional businesses. Inevitably the enclave spills over into social and political conflict, so that modernism tends to bring a kind of brittleness to the new society, which threatens stable processes of change.

As if this were not enough, the relations among nations also create special problems for the developing lands. On the one hand there is the pattern of world trade. The developing countries tend to trade much more with the developed countries than with one another, and the dependence of any given developing country on its principal developed trading partner tends to be much greater than the dependence of a developed country on its principal developing partner. Furthermore the developing countries tend to be competitors for the developed country markets so that to an important extent an increase in exports by one is at the expense of others.

On the other hand there is the world's political structure. Economic aid is not given without strings, and trade barriers too can be varied in height to accommodate politics. Developing countries often are involved in conflicts with their neighbors, conflicts which probably tend to be magnified by domestic instability. And the greater power blocs seek to acquire and to hold allies, to the point at times of seeking the use of the armed forces of the developing countries.

Clearly the policy-makers in most developing nations continually face a very threatening world, probably a more threatening one than that of any countries in the top twelve during most of their relevant history. The ordinary citizen does not face a less threatening environment, and for most individuals there is less hope than for their nations. Not only are most of the people sunk in the most abject poverty, but the contrasts with the successful are generally relatively greater than in the developed countries. Aside from the family itself, risk-bearing institutions are much less highly developed, and where they do exist the less efficient functioning of both markets and bureaucracies tends to magnify risks associated with comparable situations. The contrasts between what one has, what one sees others to have, and what one hears of other lands, when combined with all the uncertainties of life must create very deep tensions and frustrations. The politician who offers marginal improvements will not get much of a hearing from many such people.

Finally one must emphasize the diversity among these countries. Each still retains important elements of a traditional society, often one which offered unique cultural values and orientations toward life. The range of mixes of modern elements varies greatly as do the strength and stability of political institutions and the nature and viability of secondary social groupings. Perhaps the chief common characteristic of these countries is the generally expanding enclave of modernity.

## The Soviet Union and the United States

As the leading socialist nation and one of the two most powerful nations in the world, the Soviet Union invites comparison with the United States. However, it must be borne in mind that in terms of GNP per capita she is not among the top dozen, while the United States is at the very top; also in terms of per capita consumption the Soviet Union is quite far from membership in the elite circle. In general socio-economic terms she should be included in the upper reaches of the developing nations, and this should be considered as very relevant in interpreting the comparison.

We begin with a comparison of the economic situations of families, using the framework of Section 1, and taking the Soviet Union of a decade ago as our reference point for levels of consumption. In this regard—remembering that we are concerned with marketed consumer goods, not public consumption—the Soviet citizen lives at a level that is quite comparable with that of an American citizen around 1890. If anything the comparison is more favourable to the latter. He consumed rather more meat products, less flour and potatoes, more cotton fabric and shoes, and had three times more rooms per capita. However, the Americans in 1890 lacked the new consumer durables, fabrics, and communication media available to some portion of the Soviet population. Also in dealing with averages some discount should be applied to account for the almost certainly less equal distribution of consumer goods in the United States. And in terms of rates of change of consumption levels the picture is relatively more favorable to the Soviet citizen. From 1958 to 1966 general consumption per capita increased by about 10 per cent more in the Soviet Union than in the United States, the relative gains being greatest in services and food products, with a small relative decline in non-food products.

The distribution of divisible risks to families presents quite a different picture than do consumption levels. With respect to health risks, the Soviet population appears to be in a comparable position to that of the present day American population. Indeed in terms of some indicators, such as doctors and hospital beds per capita, the Soviet Union has a slight edge. Social insurance against loss of income is in certain respects, for example, unemployment compensation and coverage of peasants, less broad than in the United States, though medical risks are far more substantially covered in the Soviet Union. State ownership entails the shifting of divisible risks away from the individual, so a simple consequence of broad social ownership is the reduction of divisible risks to individuals. However some indeterminate portion of this latter does not represent a net shift, since, for example, rationing of housing means that the destruction of a state-owned residence may cost a family substantial loss in the quality of available housing. Indeed to the extent that in other aspects of life the Soviet citizen faces a less responsive bureaucracy, his risks are increased. But clearly the general pattern of divisible economic risks to the Soviet family are much closer to the United States of today than are its levels of absorption of consumer goods.

It is very difficult to get any clear picture with respect to the comparison of externalities associated with family life in the two countries. The Soviet Union is substantially less urbanized, and private transportation and communications are far more primitive outside the cities on the average. However the consequences for the rural population are partly compensated by the effects of collectivization, which clearly increase mutual dependence and joint action. For the city dweller probably the most substantial external diseconomy stems from the crowding associated with inadequate housing. Despite its extremely laggard status, the Soviet Union and the United States in the sixties have devoted a roughly comparably proportion of their GNP to residential construction. Given the continued urbanization, the relatively low productivity of the Soviet construction industry, and the much smaller GNP per capita in the Soviet

Union, this problem promises to continue to be substantial over the near future.

With respect to pollution, the Soviets do not seem to have a particularly good record, but the lower level of economic activity probably means that this is still a relatively less serious problem than in the United States. No attempts will be made to compare the aesthetic aspects of life in the two countries, for aggregative judgments can have little meaning here. With respect to the "contacts" aspects of personal autonomy, the Soviet citizen may well have fewer than his American counterpart. However Soviet citizens are extensively schooled and indoctrinated throughout their lives with respect to the state-defined values of "Soviet man." Strict controls inhibit deviant speech and action. Clearly a substantial fraction of the populace finds the official standards unacceptable in certain respects, but they feel compelled to conform. This kind of conformity, though based on perhaps less extensive contacts than are social controls in the United States, may well be even more threatening to personal autonomy. But that is pure speculation.

With respect to the "image," the comparison also presents great difficulties. The Soviets now have roughly comparable enrollments in secondary and higher educational institutions and an intellectual "establishment" which in quality, if not in quantity, compares favourably with the United States. In certain respects, such as the number of students per teacher, they appear to be doing substantially better than the United States. Nevertheless the controls over the substance of learning and the distorted view of many aspects of the functioning of their society which the schools are required to propagate cannot but interfere with the development of an efficient image for ordinary decision-making. Economic decision-making is generally much simpler in the Soviet Union, probably even despite the decision-making costs of the empty-shelves rationing system still widely practised, and distortions of social reality are not unknown to American pedagogy. Citizens of both countries must endure a certain level of anxiety because of the conflicting signals which they receive, describing their environment, though the nature of the conflicts is very different.

With respect to the exercise of deliberate social control over this environment it is the similarities rather than the differences between the contemporary Soviet Union and United States that are most striking. It is true of course that in a sense the Soviet Union is one big centralized organization controlling in detail the lives of all its citizens. But this is a much more accurate picture of the intention than it is of the practice. There is no American counterpart to the Communist Party and its all-embracing indoctrination and control activities, and of course the openness of American society contrasts sharply with the monolithic ideology of Soviet communism. Nevertheless the Party has been rather less than fully successful in its indoctrination efforts, and Americans are subject to a good deal more ideological manipulation by school and media than we often care to admit. To some extent the very intensity of contacts creates greater problems in the United States. The Soviet Union possesses perhaps one-eighth of the telephones, still only about one-fourth of the televisions of the United States, and there is much less travel in the Soviet Union. The probably closer interfamilial contacts at home are by no means primarily oriented toward the aims of the state but are a consequence of poor housing. In their attempt to control attitudes, the Soviets have a much less sophisticated technology at their disposal, and must rely far more on the one voice with which the media speak and the urgings of Party aktivs.

Of course the instruments of economic control are very different in the two societies. Nevertheless at the enterprise level observers have often been struck by the similarities of attitudes and behavior of the key personnel. At still lower levels material incentives seem to dominate in both countries. However agriculture is a most striking and important exception to this; the similarities break down fundamentally at the city's edge.

Available statistics indicate a substantially lower productivity of labour—and of factor inputs generally—in the Soviet Union. Though comparable data are not available it seems that this cannot be attributed in any significant measure to the diversion of a substantial fraction of the labour force to the exercise of bureaucratic control over the rest of the populace. Indeed if anything the Soviets have a smaller fraction of their non-agricultural labour force engaged in white collar pursuits, which may be due to the generally lower level of economic activity.

In considering the productivity of economic instruments, the Soviets do not have a substantially greater ability to control outcomes. Their long run planning system has served as a very rough guide to the general directions of movement of the economy, but perhaps not much more so than in some capitalist countries. The system of short-run economic control has proved to be quite unwieldy, and is perhaps more a system for making ad hoc adjustments in key sectors than a procedure for generating optimal economic outcomes. And there is strong evidence that at intermediate and lower levels the interests of various groups can be brought to bear to influence outcomes, despite the monolithic front.

The Soviets are learning more about their economic system as they continue to operate. However the economy is growing and changing at the same time, and it remains a controversial question which process is proceeding most rapidly. It is frequently said that central planning worked well enough when the economic problems were simpler, but as the economy grows more complex central planning tends to work less and less well. However, much the same thing is probably also true of market economies: as they become more complex direct interdependencies tend to become more important and consequently the market too tends to work less and less well. Again it is far from clear which system becomes relatively less satisfactory, particularly when one remembers that there are probably other kinds of central planning than that practiced by the Soviets, and some of them may work better for more complex economies.

In sum, Soviet citizens, like their American counterparts, live in a highly manipulated world. They too are relatively highly educated, though in a more rigid fashion. The world they face is in many respects less complex than the American's world, except for the complexities and uncertainties that the inefficient and unresponsive Soviet bureaucracy presents. A far larger fraction of Americans are able to escape deep involvement with large bureaucracies. I suspect that, aside from the level of consumption of marketed consumer goods the typical Soviet citizen would find the contemporary United States a far more similar environment to his own than that of either the Russia or the United States of 1890.

## Developing Communism Versus Developing Capitalism

There are fourteen countries in our list of communist states: the seven Eastbloc lands, four Asian countries (China, North Korea, North Vietnam and Mongolia) and three "specials," that is, Albania, Cuba and Yugoslavia. In terms of per capita GNP they cover most of the range in the developing-capitalism spectrum. However eight of the fourteen have a per capita GNP of at least four hundred dollars, so that there is a relatively much heavier concentration of developing communist countries in the upper reaches of that spectrum. Nevertheless there has been a significant traditional-modern conflict in most of these countries during their communist periods, possibly excepting East Germany and Czechoslovakia, expressed in terms of the peasant problem.

There is also substantial variation in average growth rates among communist countries, ranging from the record rates in Rumania to apparent stagnation in Cuba. Substantial fluctuations in the rates of growth of individual countries also occur, as witness China and Czechoslovakia. Nevertheless, on the average per capita growth has tended to be higher in the communist group, than in the developing capitalist group though perhaps not substantially so. It is more generally true for the communist group that industry is the most rapidly growing sector.

The present state of the evidence permits much less confident comparisons for this section. The most obvious difference between the two groups is the relative uniformity of political system and of orientation toward economic development in the communist bloc. But when one turns to consequences of this, it is much harder to generalize. One apparently strong difference is in the area of divisible risks, where a very substantial effort toward reducing the risks of income loss from threats to health, restricted educational opportunities and the like occurs in the communist countries. Also nationalization means a substantial reduction in income inequalities. However most developing countries make some efforts in the field of risk shifting away from the family, and the concentration of power in communist countries can partially compensate the much more equal money income distribution.

A notable feature of the communist is the attempt to mobilize the entire society for the tasks of modernization. This effort clearly is at least a partial success in many countries, and its degree of success probably varies inversely with the level of income. One may suspect that this effort, combined with tight political control, reduces the indivisible risks associated with the tensions of rapid change. However experience does not speak with one voice on this matter, as China can bear witness, and the period of communist control is still rather short for definitive judgment on such a matter. Of the half dozen quite poor countries that have embraced communism, none as yet have come close to transforming its country into even the upper reaches of the developing spectrum.

Finally, the diversity in the institutions of communist states has been growing in recent years. China has embarked on at least two attempts at grand institutional transformation of its own communist system, Yugoslavia has created and operated a unique version of market socialism for more than fifteen years, and Cuba has exhibited a high degree of institutional flexibility. Experiments of lesser scope have been tried out elsewhere as well. It is still too early to tell where all this will lead, though perhaps one thing is clear: The distinguishing feature of communism has been the existence of a communist party serving as mobilizer of the masses for the tasks of modernization. When this role fades substantially, perhaps another system should be said to exist; Yugoslavia has gone farthest toward this line and perhaps has crossed it. Thus though the communist group cannot match the capitalist group in the diversity of its institutions, the difference has probably been narrowing.

## Conclusion

The various comparisons presented in the preceding sections are unfortunately for the most part rather less than perfectly grounded in the data. As we turn now to still further generalization with little or no additional empirical support the reader must be warned to be very much on his guard. A good deal of yet uncited evidence in favour of most of these statements could be brought forth. But it is not. The relevant data have not been subject to a careful and scholarly survey, and even the author would be surprised if he did not get into at least a little trouble with his interpretations. Nevertheless the function of this paper is to generalize, and so we proceed with a summary and extension of our previous remarks as to what in fact is distinctive about contemporary capitalism.

1. The developed capitalist countries today probably have more in common with each other than they did sixty to eighty years ago; indeed in important ways each of them has more in common with the others today than it has with itself eighty years ago. Changes to typical families in the direction of higher levels of consumption, greater security from many kinds of risks, more extensive interdependence with other families, and greater manipulation of attitudes and behaviour by large public and private bureaucracies are universal features of these societies.

2. The dozen or so most prosperous countries in the world today share two fundamental institutional traits, namely basically capitalist institutions and parliamentary democracy; this is much the institutionally most homogeneous of the three groups considered and there is very substantial political and economic interaction within the group. In some respects they may be considered to be a single social entity. The richest countries were also the first to set out on the path of industrialization.

3. The developing capitalist countries play the role of a sort of competitive fringe to the great collusive oligopoly of the developed. In these countries typical families are of course poorer and run much greater risks of health and substantial income loss, are less caught up in externalities of national scope, and the income is less equally distributed. The nations themselves face greater threats, both internal and external, and tend to have somewhat dependent relations with one or more of the developed countries. The more successful are doing little more than keeping pace with the growth of the developed countries; relatively speaking, most are slipping further behind.

4. Probably every developing capitalist country has some portion of one or more of its cities in which modern life styles are led. This is a social enclave of

elite families and even of some semi-elite worker families who have been co-opted into the modern sector of the economy and bureaucracy. The worldwide similarity of structures and life-styles in the modern sector probably has had no counterpart since the days of the Roman empire.

5. Socialist countries compare very poorly with developed capitalism with respect to levels of family consumption, and families tend to have less leisure. However they *are* comparable to developed capitalism, despite lower levels of GNP per capita, in the security provided families; this is particularly true of the Soviet Union. Ironically, the higher development of transport and the media in the United States may mean that its citizens on the average are subject to more intensive manipulation by the large bureaucracies than are average Soviet families.

6. There are a number of persistent institutional differences between socialist and capitalist countries: collectivized agriculture, widespread resort to direct controls over the economy, nationalization of the means of production, relatively infrequent resort to financial instruments and absence of financial markets, the ideologically oriented, one-party, authoritarian regime, the relatively closed society, and dependence on the bloc leader are all much more common and stronger features of socialist than of capitalist countries.

7. However, functionally speaking, many of the institutional differences are somewhat misleading. Because of the growing interdependence and social manipulation everywhere, the basic similarities in technology and in modern urban culture, and the great diffusive impact of modern communications, many, perhaps most participants in the modern sector have considerable similarities in orientation and even in day-to-day behaviour. The greatest distinction may well be in agriculture, but the persistence of pre-industrial culture patterns in rural areas plays quite a role in this.

8. There appears to be a sort of main line from traditional to modern, developed status, which can be characterized in terms of such broad structural changes as the shift in relative output and labour force from agriculture to manufacturing and the creation of a modern sector and its more rapid growth than the rest of the economy. Relatively rapid growth of the military sector is also frequently a part of the picture. Socialist and capitalist countries both seem to follow this path, though growth orientation is typically stronger in the socialist camp. The somewhat more rapid growth of developing socialist than developing capitalist countries is partly attributable to the relatively higher average level of output at the time most of them become socialist. However, despite its growth orientation no socialist country has very dramatically changed its relative position in the world hierarchy of prosperity since it became socialist. Capitalism exists over a greater range of this hierarchy, and no socialist country has joined the charmed circle at the top.

9. Despite the much greater and more deliberate social manipulation practiced by modern public and private bureaucracies, these bureaucracies, capitalist and socialist alike, can be viewed as being, nearly all the time, myopic scanners of their environments. Their concern is typically with making modest improvements while preserving and even enhancing the stability of existing institutions. This may be built into the institutional structure through the stabilizing of various interest groups in both types of societies, which have a greater commitment to preserving what they have than in attempting substantial

but problematic improvement. Revolutionary periods occur in both types of society from time to time, but on the whole have tended to become less frequent with time for any given social régime. There may be some sort of law that says the longer a set of institutions have lasted the greater the probability it will last a while longer.

10. Threats to the autonomy and integrity of the individual through social manipulation, both coercive and indirect, appear to be very great in the modern world, and to be growing greater in nearly all societies. There are those among socialists who believe the only answer to this threat must lie in solidarity, the development of a spirit of empathy which will give a kind of organismic status to their interdependence and presumably control it in socially and personally rewarding ways. The Chinese and Cuban leaders seem dedicated to this interpretation, at least at the moment. Elsewhere the answer apparently is thought to lie in attempts to protect the individual from the excesses of modern interaction and manipulation by providing through civil rights a check to the most destructive manifestations of bureaucratic control of the environment. This latter view appears to be widely held within the socialist camp, though apparently not so strongly by the leadership as in developed capitalism. At the moment the existence of a developmental main line, the relative homogeneity of the countries that have moved farthest along this line, and their commitment to individualism suggest the unconfident prediction that, given survival of the species and some political good fortune, something like developed capitalism will be the wave of the future for a number of presently developing countries, capitalist and socialist alike. However the rapid growth of externality problems in developed capitalism, reflected to some extent at at least in current political unrest in a number of these countries, suggests that the present socio-politico-economic régimes are deficient in important respects; and there is no experience to fall back on in predicting the future course of these countries.

### Notes

The aim of these notes is to provide the reader with some general notion as to the sources used in developing statements in the text. The emphasis is on the statistical data, and organizational assertions tend to be more intuitive and speculative. Of course the statistical data has its problems too, as witness the Czech paper, noted below, in which alternative estimates of Czech per capita national income for 1964 are cited which range from $600 to $1400.

*Section 1.* Much of the numerical data on the United States was taken from *Historical Statistics of the United States*, U. S. Department of Commerce, 1960, and the 1965, *Continuation to 1962*. See Reinhard Bendix and S. M. Lipset, *Social Mobility in Industrial Society*, Berkeley, 1959 for additional data and some developed-country comparisons. The interpretation of risk, followed throughout this paper, is not fully worked out in the text. The basic idea stems from a paper by Kenneth Arrow, "Uncertainty and the Welfare Economics of Medical Care," AER, December 1963, and from the risk sections of my *Elementary Price Theory*, Free Press, 1967. "The Image" is Kenneth Boulding's *The Image*, Ann Arbor, 1956. The share of large scale organizations in national output is something of a guess, achieved by noting that large nonfinancial corporations had about half the nonfinancial corporate assets, that financial institutions tend to be large scale, that a fair amount of smaller scale activity is in a sense organized by large scale organization through oligopoly, and that government purchases of goods and services account for about a fifth of GNP. Part 4, and especially Chapter 32 of Harold Williamson, ed., *Growth of the American Economy*, Prentice-Hall, 1951, provide comparative discussions of early market structure. On social origins of American elites see C. Wright Mills, *The Power Elite*, Oxford, 1956.

*Section 2*. General data on developed capitalism were culled from the United Nations' *Statistical Yearbook 1966*, New York, 1967, the Economic Commission for Europe's *Economic Survey of Europe*, especially those of 1959 and 1965, and Simon Kuznets, *Modern Economic Growth*, Yale, 1967.

*Section 3*. Basic data sources here were Hollis Chenery and Alan M. Strout, "Foreign Assistance and Economic Development," AID Discussion Paper No. 7, revised, June 1965, which contains data not published in their 1966 AER article; and Irma Adelman and C. T. Morris, *Society, Politics and Economic Development*, Johns Hopkins, 1967. Angus Maddison, *Economic Growth in the West*, Twentieth Century Fund, 1964, deals with GNP per capita in early stages of growth, as does Kuznets. For a development of the "brittleness" theory see Fred Riggs, *Administration in Developing Countries*, Houghton Mifflin, 1964. Kuznets discusses relative income distribution in developed and undeveloped countries.

*Section 4*. Janet Chapman's chapter in Abram Bergson and Simon Kuznets, eds., *Economic Trends in the Soviet Union*, Harvard, 1963, presents the striking data comparing 1958 Soviet Union with 1890—and 1958—United States. A 1968 Joint Committee Print, "Soviet Economic Performance: 1966-67" surveys more recent data and compares them with the U. S. Articles by D. Granick and J. Berliner in the Joint Committee's 1959, "Comparisons of the Soviet Union and the United States," discuss management similarities. On white collar comparisons see the relevant article reprinted in Alec Nove's *Was Stalin Really Necessary* and *passim* remarks in Eason's chapter in the Bergson and Kuznets volume. A more extensive interpretation of Soviet planning along these lines can be found in Chapter 4 of my *Socialist Economy*, Random House, 1967.

*Section 5*. For growth comparisons see Maurice Ernst, "Postwar Growth in Eastern Europe" in Part IV of the Joint Committee's, "New Directions in the Soviet Economy." The productivity comparisons leave much to be desired; however it is clear that measured aggregate output per unit of measured aggregate major inputs is much lower in the Soviet Union than in the United States; see for example Abram Bergson, *Economics of Soviet Planning*, Yale, 1964, Appendix. An interesting French-Czech living standard comparison by a Czech economist, I. Strup, has been translated recently in *Eastern European Economics*, Vol. 6, No. 4, Summer 1968, which puts per capita Czech consumption at less than half of French in 1964.

*Section 6*. The reader will perhaps note that there are certain similarities between the interpretation offered here and those of six authors: Galbraith, Rostow, G. Lowell Field, *Comparative Political Development*, Cornell, 1967, Branko Horvat, *Towards a Theory of Planned Economy*, Belgrad, 1964, Kenneth Boulding, *op cit.*, and Fred Riggs. I hope he will also note that there are some differences.

VINCENT J. TARASCIO

# Value Judgments and Economic Science

The problem of values and its implication for economic science has been a source of methodological controversy ever since logical positivists distinguished between positive and normative economics. A casual inspection of the literature on the subject would seem to indicate that current opinion ranges from the view that economics cannot be anything but an ethical discipline to the view that "positive" economics is independent of any ethical position or normative judgment. For instance, T. W. Hutchison (4, 14) has recently argued that Joan Robinson, G. Myrdal, and A. Smithies hold the former opinion, while G. Haberler, M. Friedman, G. Stigler, and L. Robbins are of the latter opinion. He further states that the point of view which claims that "positive" economics is independent of any ethical or normative judgments is the "orthodox" view (4, 14). Also, he takes the stance that the possible separation of "positive" economics and "normative" economics "was almost a basic tenet of the 'orthodox' methodology of economics for about a hundred years from Nassau Senior and J. S. Mill, through Cairnes, J. M. Keynes, Pareto and Max Weber, down to Robbins and Friedman" (4, 18). Finally, he tells us that there has been a recent "wave of criticism and scepticism" regarding the orthodox view. Specifically, this "recent scepticism" is said to doubt that value judgments can be completely eliminated from "Positive" economics (4, 44-45).

The major purpose of this note is to clear up a source of confusion regarding the problem of ethical neutrality which continues to persist in the literature. This confusion stems from the failure to distinguish between what I shall call *methodological* judgments and *normative* judgments. In order to make the distinction clear, I shall take up the case of Friedman, whom Hutchison calls an "orthodox" methodologist.

## Methodological and Normative Judgments

To support his claim that Friedman is an "orthodox" methodologist, Hutchison quotes from Friedman: "Positive economics is in principle independent of any particular ethical position or normative judgments" (3, 3-4). Yet Friedman admits that value judgments are involved in the choice of criteria for judging the validity of a theory, the selection and interpretation of data, the adherence to the canons of formal logic, and so forth (3, 7-16). What Friedman seems to be saying is that some value judgments are a necessary part of all positive science, while others can be dispensed with.

Here again, the vagueness of the term "values" leads to confusion. In order to attach significance to its meaning, it will be necessary to clarify whose values are referred to and which of various meanings of the term, used on different planes of discourse, are being employed.

To begin, when we speak of values, do we mean those of the observer or those he encounters in the subjects of his analysis? The latter gives rise to considerations of individual values and social choice.[1] My main concern is with value judgments as they enter scientific analysis—that is, those of the observer. Suppose we select the observer as our reference. And suppose also that we classify value judgments in terms of the various planes of scientific discourse:

> I. Methodological judgments: (a) the choice of scientific principles to be followed; (b) the scope of study; (c) the choice of methods; (d) criteria for accepting or rejecting theories; (e) professional norms; (f) theoretical assumptions; and so forth.
> II. Normative judgments: (a) personal ethics of the observer; (b) normative principles; and (c) policy views.

The crucial difference between the two types of judgments is this: judgments involved in positive economics are *methodological*, pertaining to the philosophy of science and mainly concerned with investigations into the nature of society, what is, whereas judgments in normative economics are concerned with what is best for society, what ought to be, from the observer's point of view.[2]

## The Role of Cultural Influence

Cultural influence plays a role in *both* methodological and normative judgments.[3] Indeed, if cultural influences were absent in *methodological* judgments serious questions would arise regarding the relevance of theory. And it is precisely differing cultural influences acting upon methodological judgments which caused the theoretical systems of the classicals, neo-classicals, and Keynes to differ. At the same time the development of economics as a science witnessed the attempts of economists to suppress the normative elements in their theoretical systems.

Today cultural factors are influencing intellectual thought as they have in the past. The relevance of positive economics in dealing with social problems is being increasingly questioned. In such an environment there is a tendency to become more normative-oriented. As long as the empirical and normative aspects are kept in their proper relationship, the scientific nature of the discipline can be preserved. During periods of political and social ferment, there is a temptation to suppress the positive elements so that the normative elements hold sway;[4] the eighteenth-century "heavenly city" becomes a substitute for social science. In such an environment there is also the intrusion of ideology. It is not contradiction of ideology by events that counts, but contradiction by ideals and preconceptions. As long as attitudes remain intact, no degree of historical contradiction will shatter the ideology.

If economics is to avoid such a fate, economists must make clear where the source of the problem of relevance lies, and hence where the solution to the problem lies. The problem of relevance exists not so much because economics is not normative enough but because the *methodological* judgments implicit in positive economics prevent it from dealing with many problems outside the scope of its analysis. The central issue, then, is not the inability of positive economics to study the nature of value systems but the narrow scope of economics, which precludes such studies as being outside its purview.[5]

In summary, the progress of economics as a science does not involve solely the elaboration and modification of existing theories, the development of new concepts within the framework of the existing scope of the discipline, improved techniques, or better sources of data. These factors are very important. However, there exists an additional means for progress—a widening of the scope of economics to include other social phenomena.

## Science and Ideology

The problem of ideological intrusion in economic theory becomes much more complex when the discussion is extended to social and cultural change. In particular, there remains the continuing problem of altering methodological judgments to conform with changing institutions and values. Professional training in economics is very time consuming, and individuals tend to have a psychological stake in what they have learned as well as in what they have contributed to the discipline. Hence there is often the desire to "conventionalize" thought. Such attempts have been successful in the short run, but with time either internal or external forces exert pressures for change.[6] This is what the marginalist and Keynesian revolutions were all about. But intellectual revolutions, like political revolutions, are divisive and costly; the wounds heal slowly. Also, like political revolutions, intellectual revolutions are evidences of the failure of individuals to respond successfully to a changing social and cultural environment.

### Footnotes

1. This aspect of values has been investigated by Bergson (2) and Arrow (1).

2. Both Pareto (7, p. 3) and Weber (13, p. 11) advocated the subjective minimization of ethical judgments. What they had in mind was the elimination of *normative* judgments from economic *science*, at the same time fully realizing that methodological judgments were a necessary part of positive science. As regards Weber, this fact is not understood even today. Leo Strauss (10, pp. 35-80), completely misses the point when he insists that Weber argued for a completely value-free social science. For a more detailed discussion regarding the problem of ethical neutrality see Tarascio (11, pp. 30-55).

3. The influence of culture and subjective experience upon what I have called methodological judgments has been the concern of the sociology of knowledge. In Stark's (9, p. 188) terminology the sociology of knowledge involves a study of the relationship between the "axiological layer of the mind" and the "objects of knowledge." By the axiological layer of the mind, "Stark means the prejudgments or value positions of the individual which lead him to select among objects of knowledge those elements which he feels to be important. It is out of the relationship between the objects of knowledge and the axiological system of the individual that new ideas are created, which in turn become a part of the axiological system of subsequent generations" (6, p. 79).

4. One such example is Seligman, whose critique of positive economics leads him to welcome the possibility that "all economics is apt to become normative" (8, p. 278). Seligman seems to overlook the fact that it is difficult to conceive of a normative economics without a positive economics since the distinction itself stems from positivism (unless he means by normative

economics, a kind of economic philosophy). Although Seligman points to the alleged ideological aspects of positive economics, he neglects the more serious problems of ideological intrusion associated with a purely normative system.

5. For a more detailed discussion on this point, pertaining to Pareto's sociology see (12, pp. 1-4).

6. Kuhn (5) describes the process as a displacement of one scientific paradigm, or way of seeing the world, by another fundamentally different. Since scientists are influenced by their environment, I prefer to view paradigm change as part of a more general process of cultural and social change.

### References

1. Arrow, K. *Social Choice and Individual Values*. New York: John Wiley & Sons, 1951.

2. Bergson, Abram. "A Reformulation of Certain Aspects of Welfare Economics," Q.J.E. LII (February, 1938), pp. 310-34.

3. Friedman, Milton, "The Methodology of Positive Economics," in *Essays in Positive Economics*. Chicago: University of Chicago Press, 1953, pp. 3-43.

4. Hutchison, T. W. *'Positive' Economics and Policy Objectives*. Cambridge, Mass.: Harvard University Press, 1964.

5. Kuhn, T. S. "The Structure of Scientific Revolutions," Vol. 2, no. 2, of *Foundations of the Unity of Science, International Encyclopedia of Unified Science,* Chicago, 1962, chap. ix.

6. Nabers, Lawrence. "The Positive and Genetic Approaches," in *The Structure of Economic Science,* S. R. Krupp, ed. Englewood Cliffs, N.J.: Prentice-Hall, 1966, pp. 68-82.

7. Pareto, Vilfredo. *Manuel d'economie politique*. Paris: Giard et Briere. 1909.

8. Seligman, Ben B. "Positivism and Economic Thought," *History of Political Economy* I (Fall, 1969), pp. 256-278.

9. Stark, Werner. *The Sociology of Knowledge*. London: Routledge, 1958.

10. Strauss, Leo. *National Right and History*. Chicago: University of Chicago Press, 1953.

11. Tarascio, Vincent J. *Pareto's Methodological Approach to Economics*. Chapel Hill: University of North Carolina Press, 1968.

12._____ "Paretian Welfare Theory: Some Neglected Aspects," J. P. E. 77 (Jan./Feb. 1969), pp. 1-20.

13. Weber, Max. *The Methodology of the Social Sciences*. Translated and edited by E. Shils and H. Finch. Glencoe, Ill.: The Free Press, 1949.

## PAUL M. SWEEZY
# Toward a Critique of Economics

Orthodox economics takes the existing social system for granted, much as though it were part of the natural order of things. Within this framework it searches for harmonies of interest among individuals, groups, classes, and nations; it investigates tendencies toward equilibrium; and it assumes that change is gradual and non-disruptive. I don't think I need to illustrate or support these propositions beyond reminding you that the foundation of all orthodox economics is general and/or partial equilibrium (the two, far from being incompatible, really imply each other). And as for the point about gradualism, I need only recall that printed on the title page of Alfred Marshall's *magnum opus,* the *Principles of Economics,* is the motto *natura non facit saltum* —nature makes no leaps.

It might perhaps be plausibly argued that equilibrium and gradualism provided a workable axiomatic base for a real social science at a certain time and place—the time being roughly the half century before the First World War, and the place Britain and a few other countries of advanced capitalism. (For my part, I do not believe this was true even then.) I think economics by the time of what may be called the "marginalist revolution" of the 1870s had already practically ceased to be a science and had become mainly an apologetic ideology. Putting harmony, equilibrium, and gradualism at the center of the stage was dictated not by the scientific requirement of fidelity to reality, but by the bourgeois need to prettify and justify a system which was anything but harmonious, equilibrated, and gradualistic.

It was almost at the same time as the marginalist revolution, when economics (as distinct from classical political economy) was being born as an apologetic ideology, that Karl Marx put forward a radically different and opposed mode of analyzing the dominant economic systems. In place of harmony he put conflict. In place of forces tending toward equilibrium he stressed forces tending to disrupt and transform the status quo. In place of gradualism he found qualitative discontinuity. *Natura facit salta* could well have been imprinted on the title page of *Das Kapital*.

It seems to me that from a scientific point of view the question of choosing between these two approaches—the orthodox or the Marxian—can be answered quite simply. Which more accurately reflects the fundamental characteristics of social reality which is under analysis? I have already indicated my own view that orthodox economics does not reflect that reality but rather serves as an apologetic rationalization for it. Similarly it seems to me that Marxism *does* reflect capitalist reality. Or, to put the matter in other terms, the world we live in is not one of harmonies of interest, tendencies to equilibrium, and gradual change. Rather, it is a world dominated by conflicts of interest, tendencies to disequilibrium, and recurring breaks in the continuity of development. A would-be science which starts with a false or irrelevant conception of reality cannot yield very significant results, no matter how refined and sophisticated its methods may be. The answers a scientist gets depend, first and foremost, not on the methods he uses but on the questions he asks.

This is of course not to denigrate the importance of methods and techniques of investigation. In the development of science they have probably played as important a role as basic theory. The two are in fact intimately interrelated: theory poses questions, methods are devised to answer them, the answers or lack of answers make more theory necessary, and so on *ad infinitum*.

But the scientific endeavour is really not quite so simple and straightforward as this would suggest. Some of you may be familiar with the little book by Thomas S. Kuhn, entitled *The Structure of Scientific Revolutions*,[1] which I think is very helpful in this connection. Kuhn argues that every scientific theory rests on what he calls a paradigm, which I think is very close to what I have been referring to as a conception of reality (or of some aspect of reality). Ptolemaic astronomy, for example, rested on a geocentric conception of the cosmos. The questions any science asks are fundamentally limited and conditioned by its underlying paradigm, which in time thus tends to become a hindrance rather than a stimulus to further advances. When this happens, the science in question enters into a period of crisis. The previously existing consensus among its practitioners crumbles. What is now needed is a new paradigm or, in my terminology, a new conception of reality which will once again form the basis for advance. This is often provided, as Kuhn shows in a most interesting way, by outsiders, i.e., men coming to the science from some other field where they have never learned to accept and venerate the conventional wisdom of the science with whose problems they are now concerning themselves. Moreover, as a rule the older scientists are unable to free themselves from their training and preconceptions, while the younger ones find it much easier to accept the new approaches. Gradually a new paradigm emerges and once again provides the basis for theoretical advance and for the unity of the science. In the new phase what Kuhn calls "normal science" becomes the order of the day, normal science being the posing and answering of the questions which are explicitly or implicitly allowed by the new paradigm or conception of reality.

In Kuhn's view, then, scientific advance takes place not in a straight-line, cumulative manner, starting from small beginnings and building up step-by-step and brick-by-brick to the imposing scientific edifices of today. This, incidentally, is the false idea which not only the lay public but the scientists themselves have of the process of scientific advance, a fact which Kuhn attributes in large part to the role of textbooks in the training of scientists. There are also other reasons, of course, among which I would rate as very important the tendency of scientists, in common with other bourgeois thinkers, to view all of history, and not only the history of science, in an undialectical way. The pattern of scientific advance, in Kuhn's view, is rather through the exhaustion and breakdown of paradigms, leading in sequence to crisis, revolution via the construction of a new paradigm, and advance through normal science until a new period of breakdown and crisis is reached.

It would be interesting, and very likely fruitful, to try to apply this schema to the interpretation of the history of the social sciences. But certain obvious complications come to mind. For one thing it is clear that in the social sciences a paradigm can break down not only for what may be called internal reasons—i.e., the exhaustion of the questions it permits to be asked—but also because the social reality which the paradigm reflects undergoes fundamental changes. The crisis of Ptolemaic astronomy did not arise from any change in the functioning of the heavenly bodies, but rather because the geocentric paradigm became increasingly unsatisfactory as a basis for explaining observed phenomena. In the case of social science a new dimension is added: not only the observation of phenomena but the phenomena themselves are subject to change.

Another complicating factor is that the social world involves the *interests* of individuals, groups, classes, nations, in a way that is obviously not the case with the natural world. The resistance to the abandonment of old paradigms and the adoption of new ones is therefore much more complicated and is likely to be much more stubborn in the social sciences than in the natural sciences. I believe it could be shown that one consequence of this is that revolutions in the social sciences are always associated in one way or another with political and social revolutions.

Let us now turn to a consideration of the case of orthodox economics. Here it seems to me that the underlying paradigm, along with the normal science to which it gives rise, can and should be subjected to critical attack on several grounds. As I have already suggested, this paradigm takes the existing social order for granted, which means that it assumes, implicitly if not explicitly, that the capitalist system is permanent. Further, it assumes that within this system (a) the interests of individuals, groups, and classes are harmonious or, if not harmonious, at least reconcilable; (b) tendencies to equilibrium exist and assert themselves in the long run; and (c) change is and will continue to be gradual and adaptive.

One line of attack would be that this paradigm is about a century old and that most of the basic questions it allows to be asked have long since been posed and explored by the great economists of the first and second generations—men like Menger, Wieser, Böhm-Bawerk, and Wicksell in one tradition; Walras, Pareto, and the early mathematical economists in another tradition; and Marshall, Pigou, and Keynes in still another. (The list is of course intended to be illustrative rather than exhaustive.) More recent orthodox economics, remaining within the same fundamental limits, has therefore tended, so to speak, to yield diminishing returns. It has concerned itself with smaller and decreasingly significant questions, even judging magnitude and significance by its own standards. To compensate for this trivialization of content, it has paid increasing attention to elaborating and refining its techniques. The consequence is that today we often find a truly stupefying gap between the questions posed and the techniques employed to answer them. Let me cite, only partly for your amusement, one of the more extreme examples of this disparity that I happen to have run across:

> Given a set of economic agents and a set of coalitions, a non-empty family of subsets of the first set closed under the formation of countable unions

and complements, an allocation is a countably additive function from the set of coalitions to the closed positive orthant of the commodity space. To describe preferences in this context, one can either introduce a positive, finite real measure defined on the set of coalitions and specify, for each agent, a relation of preference-or-indifference on the closed positive orthant of the commodity space, or specify, for each coalition, a relation of preference-or-indifference on the set of allocations. This article studies the extent to which these two approaches are equivalent.[2]

You will be doubtless glad to know that in his search for an answer to this momentous question the author enjoyed the support of the National Science Foundation and the Office of Naval Research.

But a much more fundamental line of attack on orthodox economics proceeds from the proposition that, whatever relative validity its underlying paradigm may have had a hundred years ago has largely disappeared as a result of intervening changes in the global structure and functioning of the capitalist system. Conflicts of interest, disruptive forces, abrupt and often violent change—these are clearly the *dominant* characteristics of capitalism on a world-wide scale today. But they are outside the self-imposed limits of orthodox economics, which is therefore condemned to increasing irrelevance and impotence.

Before I turn in conclusion to the state of Marxian economics, let me add that what I have been saying applies to economics considered as a social science, as the modern successor to classical political economy, whose task is to comprehend the *modus operandi* of the socio-economic system. I quite realize that a great deal of what is actually taught in economic departments today and is *called* economics is something entirely different. It seeks not to understand a certain aspect of reality but rather to devise ways and means of manipulating *given* institutions and variables to achieve results which for one reason or another are considered desirable. How should a corporation allocate its resources to obtain maximum profits? How should a government department weigh costs and benefits in making its decisions? How can a centrally planned society achieve a distribution of goods and services and a rate of growth in conformity with the directives of its political authorities?

Naturally, I have no objection to asking and trying to answer questions of this kind, and I suppose it is no great matter that the work is carried out in economics departments (as well as in business schools, departments of public administration, and the like). What I do object to is calling this sort of thing "science." It is no more social science than engineering is physical science. The analogy may not be perfect, but I do not think it is basically misleading either. I will only add that I think a great deal of this social "engineering" is vitiated by taking its assumptions about how economic entities and institutions work from what I consider faulty social science. Here the analogy certainly does work: engineering isn't physics or chemistry, but its success depends on making use of the scientific laws of physics and chemistry. Social engineering is in the same state of dependence, and this explains why much of it is beside the point or worse. Try, for example, to prescribe a solution for a problem involving irreconcilable conflicts of interest on the assumption of underlying harmony. This, as it happens, is being done all the time in the United States today—with respect to such problems as the racial and urban crises, relations between the advanced and underdeveloped countries, and many others.

Now in conclusion a few words about Marxian economics. Here the underlying paradigm stressing conflict, disequilibrium, and discontinuity is also about a hundred years old. Since the knowledge which it yields is totally critical of the existing society, it was naturally unacceptable to the beneficiaries of that social order—in the first instance the propertied classes which are also the possessors of political power. Marxian economics was therefore banned from all the established institutions of society such as government, schools, colleges, and universities. As a result it became the social science of the individuals and classes in revolt against the existing social order. Three points need to be emphasized here.

(1) The class character of Marxian economics in no way calls into question or impugns its scientific validity. That depends entirely on its ability to explain reality. And in this respect it seems clear, to me at any rate, that the record of Marxian economics is far better than that of orthodox economics.

(2) But it also seems to me that the record is not anywhere near as good as it could have been. There are probably several reasons for this, only one of which will be mentioned here. This is that the practice of "normal science" within the framework of the Marxian paradigm has from the beginning been extremely difficult. Excluded from universities and research institutes, Marxian economists have generally lacked the facilities, the time, and the congenial environment available to other scientists. Most of them have had to make their living at other jobs, often in the nerve-racking and fatiguing area of political activism. In these circumstances what is perhaps remarkable is that so much rather than so little has been accomplished.

(3) But why, it may be asked, have not the revolutions of the twentieth century, mostly espousing Marxism as their official ideology, not resulted in a flowering of Marxian economics (and other social sciences)? Here, I think we meet a paradox which, however, can be explained by a Marxian analysis. Revolutionary regimes so far this century have come to power in relatively backward countries and have been largely preoccupied with retaining power against internal and external enemies. In these circumstances, their attitudes toward Marxism as a social science have been ambivalent for the simple reason that it is, or is always likely to become, critical of the new social order. It follows that under revolutionary regimes, as under the previous capitalist regimes, for Marxists the practice of normal science has been difficult and often practically impossible.

I do not want to end these remarks on such a negative note. Despite all the hindrances and difficulties, I think Marxian economics has indeed made notable progress and produced important contributions to our understanding of today's world. Let me cite just one area in which I think its superiority over orthodox economics is obvious and overwhelming—in explaining what has often been called the most important problem of the twentieth century, the growing gap between a handful of advanced capitalist countries and the so-called Third World.

Orthodox economics has nothing useful to say on this subject—largely, I would argue, because it is ruled out by the underlying paradigm. And the prescriptions of orthodox economics for overcoming the gap have been proving their impotence for many years now.

For Marxian economics, on the other hand, the explanation, if not simple, is at least perfectly clear in its main outlines. This explanation, can be put schematically as follows:

(a) From the beginning, the development of today's advanced capitalist countries has been based on subjugation and exploitation of Third World countries. The latter's pre-existing societies were largely destroyed, and they were then reorganized to serve the purposes of the conquerors. The wealth transferred to the advanced countries was one of their chief sources of capital accumulation.

(b) The relations established between the two groups of countries—trade, investment, and more recently so-called aid—have been such as to promote development in the one and underdevelopment in the other.

(c) There is therefore nothing at all mysterious about either the gap or its widening. Both are the inevitable consequence of the global structure of the capitalist system.

(d) It follows that the situation can be changed and real development can take place in the Third World only if the existing pattern of relations is decisively broken. The countries of the Third World must secure control over their own economic surplus and use it not for the enrichment of others but for their own development and their own people. This means thorough-going revolution to overthrow imperialism and its local allies and agents.

Marxian economists still have a tremendous amount of work to do to explain and elucidate the many complex facets of this global process. But I suggest that in the work of such outstanding Marxists as the late Paul Baran and Andre Gunder Frank great strides have been made in recent years, and that large numbers of dedicated young social scientists, not least in the Third World itself, are not only following in their footsteps but pushing on to new frontiers.

Can anything remotely comparable be said of the contribution of orthodox economists? I think the answer is obvious. And the thought I would leave you with is that the fault lies not in any lack of talent or dedication on the part of the practitioners of orthodox economics but rather in the fundamental falsity of the conception of reality which underlies all their theoretical and empirical work.

### Footnotes

1. Thomas S. Kuhn, *The Structure of Scientific Revolutions* (Chicago: University of Chicago Press, 1962).

2. Gerald Debreau, "Preference Functions on Measure Spaces of Economic Agents," Center for Research in Management Science (Berkeley: University of California, January 1966) (mimeo).

# NORTHERN ELECTRIC
# Performance and Potential

## Introduction

During the past few years, the Canadian economy has grown somewhat less rapidly than its potential rate of growth, particularly in 1970. Unemployment has risen, and employment growth has slowed. The volume of private capital investment has increased very little since the end of the investment boom in 1966. In spite of slower growth and some increase in economic slack, price and cost advances have remained relatively high. On the other hand, Canada's international payments position has continued to be strong.

In the past, our appraisals of the performance of the economy have been included in our Annual Reviews. A year ago, we concluded that such an appraisal could be undertaken in a more useful and orderly way in a separate report this year, especially since we wished to focus attention on a broad assessment of the past decade or so.

Although this report focuses attention rather narrowly on the *performance* of the economy, we wish to emphasize strongly at the outset that *high standards of economic performance are not ends in themselves.* The ultimate purpose of achieving sustained, balanced and widely shared growth at high levels of employment is to generate the *means* for more fully satisfying the diverse needs and rising aspirations of Canadians—not only in material terms, but also in terms of a better quality of life for individuals, families, communities, and our society as a whole.

### THE SEARCH FOR BETTER ECONOMIC PERFORMANCE

Within Canada, the 1960s were years of considerable policy and institutional innovation aimed at improving both the performance and potentials of the economy. In particular, rising investment in *people* became a dominant feature of the decade, reflected especially in the very rapid growth of expenditures on education and health care. Also indicative of new initiatives were: the substantial build-up of resources for manpower and labour market programs; the evolution of a series of programs to reduce Canada's large and persistent regional disparities; new trade and other measures aimed at improving efficiencies through longer production runs in Canadian manufacturing; an attempt to moderate inflation through voluntary restraints; new steps to promote the more effective development and use of the powers of science and technology in the interests of Canada's economic and social goals; and a more explicit and co-ordinated government role, both federal and provincial, in consumer affairs. Among the institutional expressions of these initiatives were the creation of such new federal departments as Manpower and Immigration (1966), Consumer and Corporate Affairs (1967), and Regional Expansion (1969); such new agencies as the Science Council of Canada, the Science Secretariat, the Atlantic Development Council (replacing the earlier Atlantic Development Board), and the Prices and Incomes Commission; such new arrangements as the Automotive Agreement with the United States, the Program for Advancement of Industrial Technology, and the provisions under the Industrial Research and Development Incentives Act. Another highly significant development, with important implications for the evolution of planning in the federal government, was the emergence of the Treasury Board as a separate and substantially enlarged organization. Some of these developments are still very recent or are in process of change. Most of them were designed to affect the economy in the longer run, and no evaluation of their effects is attempted in this report.

In the provinces, a wide range of new steps were taken to promote improved regional economic performance. These included the great expansion of activities in education and health, the strengthening of institutional machinery for advising on economic performance and policies, the inauguration of new programs in such fields as industrial and resource development, and the establishment or expansion of provincial research councils and foundations.

In the private sector, too, the decade of the 1960s has been a period of significant changes and adjustments. Illustrative of some of the changes contributing to better performance of the economy have been the development of more widespread and sophisticated business planning in the fields of investments, marketing, manpower, and technological change, and substantial advances in the competitive capabilities of many industries.

## BASIC ISSUES IN ASSESSING PERFORMANCE

A good deal of discussion and debate about the performance of an economy still takes place on the basis of highly oversimplified (and frequently partial and inadequate, if not questionable) criteria. Faster expansion is not always better than slower expansion. Labour markets can be too tight as well as too slack. Both price increases and price declines have important roles to play in well-functioning markets. Reduced deficits or increased surpluses in a nation's balance of trade in goods and services are not necessarily "good", or the opposites necessarily "bad". The performance of an economy must, in fact, be viewed in the context of a comprehensive, complex and interrelated set of criteria which have regard to *potentials* and *goals*.

The key questions about such performance are not those which ask whether certain "performance indicators" are going up or down, or are changing rapidly or slowly. Rather, the key questions should ask what we can learn from the actual progress of the economy in relation to what might have been possible, and what advance we are making towards the objectives which we could reasonably seek to attain in the future.

In this context, the following four important points need emphasis:
— performance and potentials are interrelated;
— both may be substantially influenced by international conditions and developments;
— both need to be viewed in a long-term rather than a short-term perspec- tive; and
— both are affected by a myriad of decisions, actions, and attitudes in a modern industrial economy.

## Major Features of Performance

In 1956, there was virtually no economic slack in either Canada or the United States. Both economies were operating close to potential. In both, price increases had become troublesome. A decade later, in 1966, both economies were again operating at potential, and price increases had again emerged as a major problem.

Since 1966, the Canadian and U.S. economies have had a rather mixed pattern of similarities and differences, with perhaps more differences than in any earlier comparable periods. Strong demand pressures kept the U.S. economy pressed hard against its potentials from 1966 to 1969; only within the past year has a small amount of slack emerged. The Canadian economy remained slightly below its potentials in 1967-69, and a relatively larger degree of slack now has emerged. In this period, price and cost increases have represented a serious problem in both countries, more so in the United States. Unemployment has been more of a problem in Canada.

### THE BROAD PATTERNS OF DEMAND CHANGE

The *average* rate of growth in the *volume* of total output that it was possible to achieve over the period 1956 to 1969 without generating severe strains (that is, the average *potential* rate of growth) was about 4 3/4 per cent—somewhat less in the first part of the period and somewhat more in the latter part (mainly because of the accelerated growth in the labour force beginning early in the 1960s).

Economic developments in the United States had considerable influence on Canada's economic performance during the 1960s. Neither the pervasive slack that existed in the United States at the beginning of the 1960s nor the excessive demand and inflation that emerged in the last half of the 1960s represented ideal external conditions for the simultaneous achievement of all of Canada's basic economic goals. Thus an appraisal of Canadian economic performance as if these external conditions had been ideal is not realistic. What needs to be asked is whether Canadian performance *in the circumstances* could have been better. Because there were similarities in Canadian and U.S. performance in the period under review—as well as some notable differences—we find it useful to compare and contrast Canadian and U.S. experience in much of the analysis that follows.

## INTERNATIONAL COMPARISONS OF GROWTHS

In the slowdown after 1956, the growth of real output in Canada and the United States fell significantly behind that in continental Western Europe and Japan. The momentum of growth in North America was regained after 1961, and for a number of years output expanded at a rate comparable to European rates. Since 1966, however, there has again been some moderation in growth in both Canada and the United States in relation to various other industrial countries.

Such international growth comparisons must, however, be examined with caution; there are considerable differences in the factors affecting growth in various countries. Japan and Italy with the highest growth rates, still have the lowest average levels of output per employed person, while the United States and Canada, although they have had slower growth rates over the past 15 years, have the highest average levels of output per employed person. The faster rates of growth in output per employed person that are occurring in most other industrial countries are, however, tending to bring productivity and average real living standards in these countries closer to the levels in Canada and the United States.

## ACTUAL VERSUS POTENTIAL OUTPUT

Assessment of a country's growth performance can best be made by considering the actual level and changes in output in relation to what could have been accomplished with reasonably full and increasingly efficient use of existing resources.

For North America, potential output is usually defined as the level of output corresponding with employment of 96 to 97 per cent of the labour force—and with the economy moving along the postwar trend of productivity growth.

The potential Canadian growth *rate* over the past decade and a half has been considerably greater than that of the United States. This is entirely due to the more rapid rate of labour force growth in Canada. In fact, the percentage increase in the labour force between 1956 and 1969 was about twice as high in Canada as in the United States—41 per cent versus 21 per cent.

By 1966, the *level* of actual output was above the level of estimated potential output in Canada, but since then, actual output has remained slightly below potential. In contrast, the United States remained at or above its potential *level* for the four years 1966-69, and only during the past few quarters has actual output fallen slightly below potential.

The *level* of actual output in Canada was about 1 1/2 per cent below the estimated *level* of potential output in the three years 1967-69 inclusive. Any shortfall from an actual growth *rate* of about 5 1/4 per cent would widen this gap. The latest official forecast for 1970 suggests that real output this year will be about 3 per cent above 1969. This implies an increase in the size of the gap to close to 4 per cent of potential in 1970—in other words, actual GNP would be about $3 billion below potential GNP (in 1970 dollars). This is a measure of the gap between actual output and the output which would have been produced if unemployment had been 3.8 per cent, and if productivity had been on its postwar trend.

A widening gap between actual and potential output tends to be associated with deceleration in the rate of productivity advance, and a narrowing gap with acceleration. Between 1956 and 1961, when the gap was widening, Canadian real output per employed person grew at 1.3 per cent per year; from 1961 to 1966, when the gap was closing, the rate of real output growth per employed person rose at a rate of 3.1 per cent per year; and from 1966 to 1969, when the gap was widening again, the growth of real output per employed person fell back to 1.6 per cent per year. During periods of well-below-potential operation, capital formation also grows much more slowly or actually declines. Thus, from 1956 to 1961, business gross fixed capital formation (excluding residential construction) in constant dollars declined by 1.9 per cent per year; from 1961 to 1966, it rose by 12.0 per cent per year; and between 1966 and 1969, it declined again by 0.8 per cent per year.

## EMPLOYMENT AND UNEMPLOYMENT

Almost 1.9 million more Canadians are now employed than a decade ago — an increase of close to 30 per cent. This is substantially higher than the rate of employed growth experienced in any other industrial nation in the 1960s. This growth is mainly due to Canada's huge postwar baby boom which has led to an upsurge in the numbers of young people moving into the labour force in the 1960s; but high immigration has also been a significant contributing factor.

In the past three years, the unemployment rate in Canada has been significantly above that of the United States—on average, about 1 1/2 percentage points higher. In about half the years since 1950, the Canadian rate has been below the U.S. rate. The Canadian rate has usually been lower in prosperous periods, but higher in slack periods such as 1957-62.

## PRICES AND COSTS

Large persistent increases in general levels of prices and costs constituted one of the most serious shortfalls from good performance in the Canadian economy over the last half of the 1960s. Such increases continue to be relatively high and widespread in 1970, although some moderation in the advances of certain general price measures appears to be emerging.

Imports from the United States—which account for over 70 per cent of total Canadian goods imports—constitute one of the most clearly visible links through which U.S. price and cost developments are transmitted to the Canadian economy. Most of Canada's machinery imports are from the United States and the cost of capital goods in Canada is therefore highly sensitive to U.S. price movements. Similarly, when markets are buoyant in the United States and prices are rising, many Canadian export prices rise roughly in step with many U.S. prices. The influence of the U.S. goods prices is not confined merely to the export and import sectors. In the markets for many of the goods produced in Canada which face the threat of U.S. competition but are protected by tariffs, there is a tendency for Canadian manufacturers to establish prices a little below the U.S. price for the commodity plus the tariff. A rise in U.S. prices permits these producers to raise their prices without added risks of exposure to U.S. competition.

A further common influence on price levels in the two countries is the level of interest rates, which is an important factor in the total costs of more capital-intensive activities, including housing. The rising costs of housing and of rental accommodation in recent years has been a major contributor to the rise in the Consumer Price Index, in turn leading to escalating wage demands.

Canada and the United States have not, of course, been alone in experiencing inflationary pressures. Consumer prices, for example, have been rising considerably more rapidly in most of the major industrial countries overseas than in North America. An international comparison of consumer-price behaviour over the 1956-69 period, shows that other industrial countries, with the important exception of the Federal German Republic, generally had faster price increases than Canada and the United States over this period as a whole.

There has also been a sharp acceleration, on a worldwide basis, of prices of industrial goods moving in international trade in 1969 and 1970, after a very long period of relative stability in such prices. Canadian import prices in 1969, for example, rose at an annual rate of over 3 per cent—more than three times the average annual rate of increase over the preceding five years. Since a large proportion of these imports constitute inputs into production in Canada—the result has been some accentuation of cost increases in Canada.

Much attention has recently been focused in Canada on increases in money incomes—especially in wages, salaries, and professional fees—as a major factor contributing to sustained upward pressure on costs and prices. The factors that produce demands for larger increases in money incomes —increases that may be in excess of any possible increases in output or productivity — are not always fully recognized.

One element in this complex matter is the attempt to "catch up" with previous price increases or to offset anticipated price increases. Another element in the pressure for higher incomes—one that has tended to be underemphasized—may be increases in taxes. Indirect tax revenues (sales, excise and property taxes and customs duties) increased by about 10 per cent a year in the latter part of the 1960s, partly as a result of increased tax rates and partly as a result of increased business volume. Moreover, in recent years, partly reflecting increases in tax rates, there have been very substantial increases in income tax collections. For example, between 1965 and 1969, total revenues from direct personal taxes rose at an average annual rate of over 22 per cent. Personal income at the end of the 1960s was about two and a half times the level of the mid-1950s, while personal income taxes and employer and employee contributions to insurance and pension plans were about five times as high. More recently, these disparities have been even more marked: in 1965-69, personal income increased by about 50 per cent, while personal income tax revenues and the pension and insurance contributions more than doubled. When these rapid increases in taxes and contributions are combined with the fact that consumer prices were also rising at more than double the rate of the earlier period, the pressure on individuals to maintain their *after-tax income* positions has been very great, and there are signs that an increasing number of groups are taking not only price changes but also tax changes more explicitly into account in their approaches to income bargaining.

A number of other factors from the "cost" side have undoubtedly contributed to the upward pressures on prices in recent years. Structural changes in the economy, away from goods and towards service production and consumption, have been tending to add to price increases as a growing proportion of economic activity has been shifting into what are essentially cost-plus categories of price determination.

## THE BALANCE OF PAYMENTS

From the mid-1950s to the end of the 1960s, the current account deficit (and the net capital inflow) declined from close to 5 per cent of GNP to about 1 per cent. Changes in the merchandise trade balance mainly accounted for the large relative decline in the current account balance; the trade balance shifted from a deficit equivalent to 2 per cent of GNP in the mid-1950s to a surplus equivalent of about 2 per cent of GNP by the end of the 1960s. Apart from 1967, the services deficit remained in a range of 2 to 3 per cent of GNP. Over this period, net inflows of capital in long-term forms decreased significantly in relation to output (from about 4 per cent of GNP in the mid-1950s to about 2 per cent in the latter part of the 1960s).

From early 1969 to early 1970, virtually all of the increase in real GNP went into expanded Canadian exports. The floating of the dollar in June 1970 is attributed to Canada's decision that it would not continue to finance a very rapidly increasing volume of exchange reserves at the previous fixed rate of exchange, especially in the light of the possibility of a massive speculative inflow of capital. The huge merchandise trade surplus (about $1.3 billion in the first half of 1970) and a strong capital inflow swiftly drained away the Canadian dollar balances of the Government of Canada that were required for purchasing foreign exchange accumulating in the official reserves. Policies of restraint in Canada tended to slow the growth of imports and thus contributed to the increased trade surplus.

Whether Canada could maintain medium and longer-term balance-of-payments viability with the Canadian dollar at a level which was close to par with the U.S. dollar is an open question. The exchange rate is in fact a very important *price* in Canada's overall price system, and changes in it tend to have far-reaching consequences for many parts of the economy.

## REGIONAL DISPARITIES AND POVERTY

The emergence of some slack in the late 1960s and the development of more slack in 1970 is again being accompanied, as in earlier similar conditions, by the slower growth of employment and high unemployment rates in the lower-income regions. Employment growth in the Atlantic Provinces has averaged only 4,000 per year over the past three years (total employment in the Atlantic Provinces was 605,000 in 1969). Similarly, in this three-year period, employment growth in Quebec has averaged less than 20,000 per year (total employment in Quebec was over 2,130,000 in 1969).

Rates of unemployment have become very high in the Atlantic Provinces, Quebec and British Columbia, in all of which the unemployment rates tend to be relatively high when slack develops in the Canadian economy generally. An unusual feature in the recent pattern of increases in unemployment rates is that the Prairie Provinces, which typically have a rate below that of Ontario, had a higher rate in mid-1970. This is a reflection of special difficulties with wheat and potash marketing and problems in the construction industry. Another unusual feature is the exceptionally high rate of unemployment in British Columbia in mid-1970. This reflects, in part, the effects on the regional economy of increased industrial disputes, and perhaps also a stepped-up flow of migration to this province.

### A SUMMARY

The Council's annual appraisals of the performance of the Canadian economy have been based on a careful monitoring of underlying economic trends and developments in order to detect forces and factors actually producing, or threatening to produce, major or prolonged departures from good performance and progress in relation to the goals and potentials with which our terms of reference require us to be concerned. At the risk of considerable over-simplification, the findings of our performance appraisals may be summarized as follows:

(1) On the whole, the performance of the economy since we started to make such appraisals in 1964 has been relatively good.
(2) The glaring exception has been performance in relation to the goal of reasonable price stability. It is becoming clearer that the fundamental performance challenge here is, to some extent international in scope, and of a long-run rather than short-run nature.
(3) Over a year ago, a slowing in the rate of growth of employment brought with it a rise in the rate of unemployment to close to 5 per cent. Since then, unemployment and economic slack have emerged on a scale that has opened a significant gap between actual and potential output.
(4) While the productivity growth rate was far from steady during the 1960s, a reasonably good productivity performance has been maintained over the decade, at least in relation to Canada's historical experience.
(5) We have concluded that Canada's balance-of-payments position has remained generally strong.
(6) There was some reduction in poverty and some narrowing of regional economic disparities in the course of the 1960s.

## Demand Management

Among the most important of the decisions and policies that effect the performance of an economy are "demand-management" policies—monetary and fiscal policies.

In the case of monetary policy, there has been a growing tendency over recent years among experts to focus attention on variations in the growth rate of the supply of money as one of the most useful indicators of easy or tight policies.

In the case of fiscal policy, there are many complications in assessing its effects on demand. For instance, there is a wide variety of ways in which changing government expenditures, tax rate, tax structures, and debt management operations may affect demand that cannot all be readily encompassed in simple total measures. Also there are many ways in which government budgetary items may affect private spending. In the present "state of the art" of fiscal policy appraisal, attention is usually focused, at least initially, on the *fiscal balance* — the deficit or surplus in government accounts.

Yet discussions of fiscal policy in Canada and appraisals of its impact on the economy are frequently distorted, and sometimes misleading, owing to the use of partial and incomplete information, and to difficulties in interpreting the available information. Among the considerations frequently limiting assessments of fiscal policy are:

— the use of the federal government accounts only, leaving out of account the fiscal position of the provinces and the municipalities;
— the use of the administrative accounts of government which were designed for budgetary control purposes and not for the broad assessment of economic effects;
— the failure to take into account the transactions of the Canada and Quebec Pension Plans, which are now generating revenues well in excess of pension outlays; and
— the use of "actual" deficits or surpluses as measures of fiscal stimulus or restraint, without regard to the prevailing level of economic activity.

## THREE BUDGET CONCEPTS AND THEIR LIMITATIONS

1.   What is perhaps most frequently referred to as the "budgetary position" is the balance in the administrative budget. This presentation which is the central feature of the annual Budget Speech of the Minister of Finance, is designed essentially for administrative and control purposes.
2.   The statement of government cash transactions is more comprehensive than the administrative budget since it includes the net effects of government borrowing and lending operations as well as changes in the trust and pension accounts that affect the government's cash position. It is useful for the government's own cash management and is of considerable relevance for financial analysis.
3.   The national accounts presentation of the budget is, however, more explicitly designed to meet the needs of economic analysis. It takes a wider range of transactions into account than the administrative budget, and it excludes transactions of a purely internal bookkeeping nature. It does not, unfortunately, in its present form, cover the government's borrowing and lending operations.

## THE HIGH-EMPLOYMENT BUDGET

An illuminating approach to the assessment of fiscal policy is to look at the fiscal position that would exist at high employment. On this basis, any significant surplus would represent a restraining posture — a posture tending to hold the economy below potential. Conversely, any significant deficit on this basis would represent an expansionary posture — a posture tending to push the economy above potential.

### MONETARY POLICY

Analysis of the year-over-year changes in money supply in Canada and the United States since the latter part of the 1950s, makes clearly evident:
— the tight money policies at the end of the 1950s, just prior to the 1960-61 recession;
— the fairly stable increases in money supply over the early part of the 1960s;
— the considerable monetary expansion in the latter part of the 1960s; and
— the turn towards strong monetary restraint in 1968 and the persistence of such restraint through the early part of 1970.

### FISCAL POLICY

Looking first at the U.S. fiscal conditions, it is evident that the high-employment fiscal position:
— remained generally somewhat restraining over most of the decade 1956-66, and was fairly strongly biased against the achievement of potential output through the early years of the 1960s when there was considerable slack in the economy;
— swung strongly towards an expansionary stimulus after the mid-1960s, following the major U.S. federal tax reductions of 1964 and the large rise in defence spending with increased military involvement in Vietnam; and
— shifted back to a moderate degree of fiscal restraint following the major tax increases of 1968 and some curtailment of government spending.
The Canadian fiscal posture of all levels of government appears generally to have been more appropriate to the underlying economic conditions than that of the United States through much of the past decade. The degree of fiscal restraint in Canada since 1968, however, has been very strong — much stronger than many Canadians have realized. In fact, in 1969, such restraint appeared to have been stronger than at any time since the Korean War in the early 1950s, when total demand was clearly excessive. The analysis indicates the following:
— under conditions of slack in the late 1950s and early 1960s the fiscal position was biased in favour of a return towards full employment, or at least not biased against it;
— in the mid-1960s, there was a modest high-employment surplus, when demand was rising strongly and inflationary price and cost dangers were intensifying; and
— more recently, there has been a very large high-employment surplus. In particular, in 1969, this fiscal position was one of substantial restraint, with a strong bias towards holding the economy below potential output. The building up of such fiscal restraint in 1968 and 1969 has been the result of a major shift in the combined budgetary positions of provincial and municipal governments, as well as that of the federal government.

During 1970, the previously heavy restraint settings of both monetary and fiscal policy have been eased. Monetary expansion was resumed, and was pronounced in the second quarter in the context of the large withdrawals from federal cash balances to purchase foreign exchange at a time of upward pressure on the Canadian exchange rate. Also, the degree of fiscal restraint has been somewhat reduced through decisions to enlarge certain expenditures.

## Lessons of the 1960s

Before outlining some of the performance challenges for the 1970s and their implications for policy, it is useful to try to place in perspective some of the performance experience of the 1960s. Out of the very wide variety of lessons that might be listed, we have chosen seven for emphasis.

### BUSINESS CYCLES

The prolonged recessionless expansion of the 1960s is a fact of considerable significance, for at no other time has the economy been free for a comparable period from recurrent bouts of recession and recovery. Only a decade ago, the business cycle represented a fundamental economic phenomenon, and the analysis of business cyclical indicators was a prominent field of economic research. Economic actions of governments were mainly directed to minimize these fluctuations which were thought to originate in decisions and activities in the private sector of the economy. Governments, in other words, tended to think of their role as a "balance wheel" in the economy, adding to total demand whenever private demand weakened, and constraining total demand whenever the latter became excessive. Subsequent analysis has suggested that sometimes the actions taken had destabilizing results. Compensatory measures were in practice not always appropriate in relation to the timing and amplitude of cyclical fluctuations. Lags in the system and the difficulties involved in developing accurate forecasts sufficiently far ahead to provide an adequate basis for major policy changes, tend to make stabilization policies very difficult instruments to use effectively for offsetting short-term business fluctuations.

We have urged, because of these difficulties, that demand policies should be directed more to "steering the economy" along a smoother underlying growth path in final demand, in line with the economy's continually expanding potential. At the same time, we have also emphasized that, along with this, a wide range of complementary government and private policies are required for good performance—for example, in the fields of competition policy, mobility and training, adjustment assistance and productivity improvement. These views continue to shape our approach to the development of appropriate policy strategies for the future.

### THE COSTS OF DEPARTING FROM POTENTIAL

Another major lesson of the 1960s was the demonstration of the very heavy costs incurred in failing to keep the economy at, or close to, its potential growth path.

Moreover, such losses are cumulative for every year in which such a gap exists between actual and potential output. Nor is the loss ever made up, even when the gap is closed. Indeed, as we have already noted, such large losses may also tend to depress the future potentials of an economy for an extended period. In a society in which there is a vast and growing list of competing claims on the nation's limited resources, we must aim to avoid such low levels of performance.

There are also costs that arise from pressing an economy too hard and too fast against its rising potential. Although these are very difficult to quantify, they are nevertheless real and important, and include such things as the disruption of financial markets (especially for fixed-income obligations), the erosion of savings, the inequities imposed on people on fixed and slowly rising incomes, the possible undermining of international competitive capabilities, and the diversion of greater energies and efforts to finding methods for escaping from the adverse consequences of inflation.

## IMBALANCES AND LAGS

The past decade also demonstrated that once substantial imbalances develop in the economy, either because the economy is undershooting its potential growth path (as in 1957-61) or because of a prolonged period of growth above the potential *rate* (as in 1962-66), it takes much time and effort to get back on an appropriate growth path.

The 1960s have also brought growing awareness of the long lags that frequently exist in the response of the economy to changes in policy aimed at influencing demand conditions.

## UNEMPLOYMENT

The high unemployment of the late 1950s and early 1960s was basically the result of a lack of adequate total demand, not of technological or structural changes in the economy.

## EXPECTATIONS AND INSTABILITY

In the 1960s the role of expectations appears to have been considerably more important than many observers might have been prepared to anticipate a decade ago.

## INSTABILITY OF CONSTRUCTION

Still another major lesson of the 1960s, and a striking feature of the economy's behaviour to which the Council drew attention in its *Third Annual Review,* is the marked instability in the construction industry.

## HIGH EMPLOYMENT AND PRICE STABILITY

The experience of the early 1960s suggests that if substantial economic slack builds up in the North American economy, the rates of general price and cost increases will gradually moderate. But the experience of the mid-1960s suggests that in the process of reducing unacceptably high unemployment and moving back towards potential, a powerful expansionary momentum may be built up in the economy, with accompanying inflationary dangers in its later stages as high levels of employment are being approached.

# Challenges for the 1970s

There are many economic challenges for Canada in the 1970s. A large number of them arise from questions about how Canadians wish to make use of their growing resources to meet the future aspirations of their society.

Another group of challenges are the economic performance challenges. These arise in the context of five basic economic and social goals—full employment, a high and sustained rate of economic growth, reasonable price stability, a viable balance-of-payments position, and an equitable distribution of rising incomes. The key requirement for sustained good performance in relation to these goals is that they must be achieved concurrently, even though they are not all complementary and reinforcing.

### MEASURING UP TO POTENTIALS

To attain potential output in 1975, Gross National Product (in constant 1969 dollars) will need to rise at an average annual rate of about 5 1/2 per cent from 1969 to 1975. This would imply an increase (in terms of 1969 dollars) of over $30 billion to a level of close to $110 billion in 1975. Over the last half of the 1970s, the potential growth rate of the Canadian economy would still be high—over 5 per cent. This would imply a further increase in GNP in the latter part of the 1970s of about an equivalent real dollar magnitude, so that potential GNP by 1980 would be roughly of the order of $140 billion (in 1969 dollars).

A very large rise in employment will be needed to reach the full-employment potential of the economy by 1975—about 1.3 to 1.4 million more jobs than now exist in 1970. Moreover, over the 1975-80 period, about 1.2 million additional jobs will be required. In other words, at least 2 1/2 million net new jobs will be required in Canada over the coming decade.

A new ingredient in the challenges both for adequate job creation and for productivity growth in the 1970s will be the unprecedented flow into the labour markets of high-level manpower from the postsecondary educational systems.

The returns from the expansion in education could be substantial during the 1970s. But greater attention needs to be directed to the possibilities here, and various adjustments are needed in the private and government sectors of the economy in order to employ effectively and productively the rapidly rising volume of high-level manpower.

### PRICE STABILITY

No less important in the 1970s will be the challenge of reconciling good performance in price stability with good performance in relation to employment and growth potentials. We have never regarded full employment and price stability as "either/or" objectives. Rather, the essential challenge is to pursue both of these goals together in a balanced way and in a longer-run time perspective.

## MAINTAINING A STRONG INTERNATIONAL POSITION

The maintenance of a strong international position will also be an important performance challenge for the 1970s. Increased exports and the maintenance of adequate access to external sources of capital are needed in order to finance both the increased imports of goods and services that Canadians will demand, and increased Canadian foreign investment and aid. Canada's potential in international trade in the 1970s cannot be achieved unless producers and exporters struggle unrelentingly, with appropriate supporting government policies and programs, to enhance their competitiveness in domestic and world markets. Moreover, they may well have to do so under conditions that may not be as favourable as in the 1960s, when the substantial devaluation of the Canadian dollar was an important factor strengthening the international competitive position of many industries.

## EQUITABLE DISTRIBUTION OF RISING INCOMES

The more equitable distribution of rising incomes will undoubtedly come into greater prominence as an economic and social goal in the 1970s. In particular, the challenges of narrowing regional economic disparities and eliminating poverty clearly need, and will claim, increasing emphasis.

# Implications for Policy

We draw attention to the following major headings:
— basic strategies for policy in the early 1970s;
— longer time horizons for policy-planning;
— housing and construction;
— policy co-ordination; and
— good performance and public understanding.
   Not surprisingly, the conclusions we set out under each of these headings are often highly interdependent.

## BASIC STRATEGIES FOR POLICY IN THE EARLY 1970s

The Canadian economy has enormous potential for growth over the next few years. Any shortfall from this potential can, of course, be depicted by the experts in terms of cold, impersonal measures such as Gross National Product. But beneath this statistical veneer it means fewer jobs, lower incomes, and fewer resources to help meet our diverse and expanding aspirations. On the other side of the coin, any attempt to force the economy to operate above its potential output trend can result in a further round of inflation and other imbalances, with all their attendant inequities and dangers.

   Our recent experience reinforces the view that imbalances in one direction are very likely to breed imbalances in the other direction. With the gap between potential and actual output apparently around 4 per cent in 1970, the Council urges that:

— Policy should now be very much concerned with preventing a further build-up of economic slack.
— The public should be aware that a very critical point for demand-management policies will come after the economy begins to close the gap between actual and potential output.
— Greater recognition should be given to the fact that the problems of inflation are not simply a distasteful event of the present or recent past, but are, in part at least, a reflection of the attempts in most Western countries to run high-employment economies with inadequate emphasis on supply, structural, and other policies as essential complements to appropriate demand policies.
— Fiscal policy should aim, in the circumstances of the next few years, at achieving a small but sustained high-employment budget surplus on a national accounts basis for the government sector as a whole, including the operations of federal, provincial and municipal governments and the Canada and Quebec Pension Plans.
— The federal government and all provincial governments in Canada should give consideration to the necessity of framing fiscal policy within a well-functioning, organizational, analytical and statistical framework that provides the essential basis for fiscal co-ordination.
— Monetary policy (together with fiscal policy with which it is closely interrelated) should evolve in a way that seeks to avoid large destabilizing swings in the growth of the money supply.

## LONGER TIME HORIZONS FOR POLICY PLANNING

The powerful ''demand-regulating'' fiscal and monetary instruments could be more effective if stabilization policies were framed more explicitly within the context of long-term strategy. Visible and articulate leadership in the operation of this strategy must be provided so that the strategy can be understood by the public, and especially by those who should be conducting their own policy-planning in accordance with it.

Some major elements in the kind of long-term strategy we endorse are:

— linking more public and private decisions to a framework of potential output estimates;
— developing expenditure programs by all governments more explicitly in a longer-range context, projecting and publishing *all-government* revenues and expenditures within a framework of potential analysis for the medium term, and considering how tax and expenditure programs should be adjusted in the event of departures from potential.

## HOUSING AND CONSTRUCTION

Housing is clearly in short supply, and the need for it will be rising strongly for a long time. We endorse the current federal approach of setting housing targets and of rectifying shortfalls in private activity by providing additional government resources—especially for low-income housing.

## POLICY CO-ORDINATION

It is becoming almost trite to suggest that there continues to be a requirement in Canada for greater co-ordination of policies—within governments, between governments, and between the public and private sectors. Yet, examples of conflicts in policy, or of areas where information about programs is inadequate to support co-ordination, are not difficult to find.

Policy co-ordination—whether within governments, between governments or between the public and private sectors—requires some sort of comprehensive framework within which goals and priorities can be discussed on a national basis. And it requires better information and analysis than now exist as a basis for debating policy issues. These, as we can see them, are some of the ingredients of a better co-ordination process in Canada:

— A comprehensive framework for the discussion of goals and priorities to which both government and private decisions could be more coherently related.
— The annual preparation and publication of projections of expenditure for existing government programs (covering all levels of government) and of returns from taxes at existing rates, for at least five years ahead.
— The adoption of a common and comprehensive framework by the federal and provincial governments for evaluation of fiscal policy and government financial operations.
— Extended surveys of government and private investment intentions.
— In the case of federal-provincial relations, a further expansion of staff resources devoted to the development of information and analysis.

## GOOD PERFORMANCE AND PUBLIC UNDERSTANDING

In the final analysis, Canada's performance policies are a response to public opinion. In general, public policies cannot far outrun public understanding and acceptance. Fortunately, during the 1960s, there appears to have been greatly increased interest in public debate on economic issues in Canada. Much scope remains, however, for wider and better understanding of the goals and strategies relevant to good economic performance.

*Who,* then, has special duties to perform with respect to widening public understanding about good economic performance? The Economic Council recognizes that it has a responsibility in this area through the medium of its publications and through various other activities in which it is involved. But others also play an important role:

— the Prices and Incomes Commission;
— the Dominion Bureau of Statistics;
— the educational institutions;
— committees of the federal parliament and provincial legislatures;
— the mass media;
— the business organizations, professional associations, labour unions and other private interest groups.

## CONCLUSIONS

A major concern of this report is that the Canadian economy has fallen significantly below its potential. A quick return to potential is not feasible. But the central challenge is to begin to close the gap between actual and potential performance as soon as possible—to begin to reduce the significant human and economic costs of high unemployment—bearing in mind the need to maintain reasonable stability of prices. It is important to recognize that the present degree of slack, reflected partly in high unemployment, will tend to persist and grow until an annual rate of real growth in excess of 5 per cent is resumed.

There are some signs of firming in the North American economy as a whole. Also, demand-management policies in Canada and the United States have become less restrictive. Further, the medium-term growth potential of the Canadian economy is exceptionally large. It is important, therefore, that recent and current difficulties and problems be kept in proper perspective and that a climate be created in which decisions will be based on confidence that our economic potentials can be substantially realized in the medium-term future.

# SECTION TWO
# National Accounts

RICHARD M. BIRD

# The Growth of Government Expenditure in Canada

## A Century of Government Spending, 1867-1967

What "government" is and what "government" does have undergone striking changes during the century of Canada's existence. The most obvious of these changes has undoubtedly been the tremendous increase in the absolute size of government expenditure. In 1867, the federal government spent less than 14 million dollars. In 1967, it spent almost 9 billion dollars. Total expenditure by all levels of government in 1870 was only around 31 million dollars; by 1967 it was over 21 billion dollars.

Absolute figures alone, however, give a misleading impression of the significance of these increases in the size of government, for many other important changes also took place during this period. In particular, both prices and population increased considerably. If the dollar figures of total government expenditure are "deflated" to allow for the almost fivefold increase in the price level from 1870 to 1967, the "real" increase in expenditure declines from around 68,000% to 14,000%—which is, of course, still a very substantial increase. If a further adjustment is made for the fivefold increase in population over this period, total real government expenditure per capita in 1967 was only 26 times larger than in 1870. Finally, if the increase in real income per capita, as well as in prices and population, is taken into account, it then appears that total government expenditure as a percentage of Gross National Product (GNP) has risen only about fivefold over the last century—from around 7% of GNP in 1870[1] to 34% in 1967.

An increase of 500% may not sound as impressive (or terrible, depending on one's predilections) as one of 68,000%, but it is still a substantial increase. Furthermore, as indicated in Figures 1 and 2, this increase does not, at first glance, appear to have taken place in an orderly, regular fashion.[2] Rather, rapid increases in the relative importance of government expenditure were followed by declines and slower rises. Particularly noticeable with respect to federal expenditure is the minor peak in the early 1880s, the very rapid rise in the early years of the twentieth century—a period of new territorial acquisitions and substantial immigration—the marked peak in the World War I period, the postwar fall, and the rise in the depression. The expenditure experience of World War I was repeated during World War II, as federal expenditure first rose rapidly to a wartime peak, then declined sharply immediately after the war,

**Figure 1.**
Canada: Total Government Expenditure as a Percentage of GNE, 1867-1967

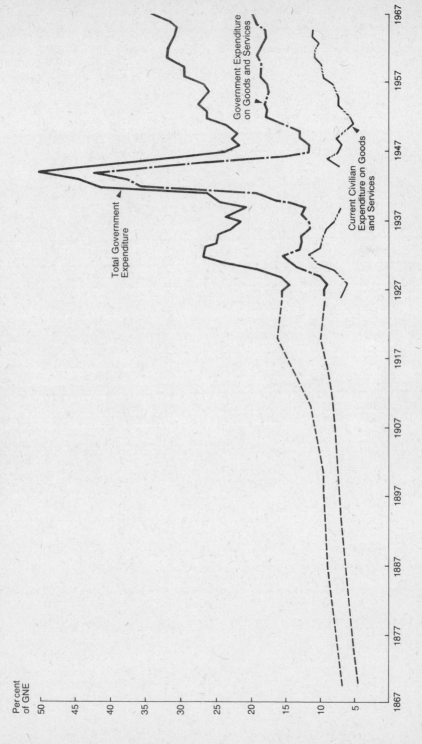

resuming a fairly steady growth since the early 1950s. Interestingly, provincial and municipal expenditure (especially the former), although strongly affected by the depression of the 1930s, grew more or less steadily and rapidly over most of the 60-year period (1906-1967) for which data are available. The behaviour of total government expenditure of course reflects the combined impact of changes in federal and in provincial-municipal expenditure, with marked peaks

## Figure 2.
Canada: Expenditure by Level of Government, 1867-1965

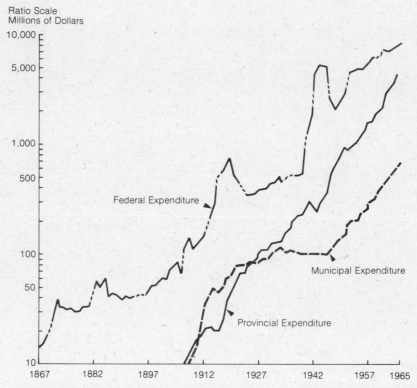

in the two world wars. The effects of the great depression are especially marked in Figure 1, which depicts the ratio of expenditure to GNP, since this ratio was sharply affected by the great fall in the level of money national income in the early 1930s.

## Is There a "Law" of Government Spending?

The marked influence of catastrophes like wars and depressions on the time pattern of the ratio of government expenditure to GNP thus seems clear.[3] Have these "great events" significantly influenced the long-term growth of the public sector in Canada? That is, if it had not been for the sharp increases in

**Figure 3.**
Canada: The Government Expenditure Ratio
and Per Capita Income, 1870-1967

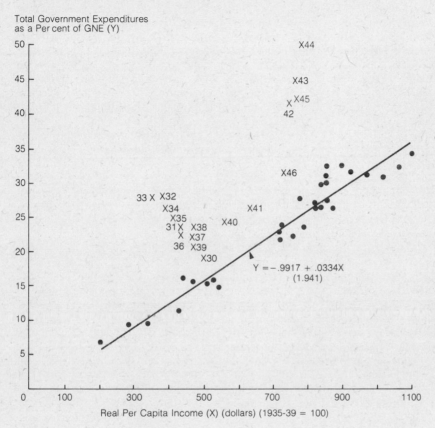

Total Government Expenditures
as a Per cent of GNE (Y)

Real Per Capita Income (X) (dollars) (1935-39 = 100)

**Source:** National Accounts (see text)

government expenditure during the wars, would government be as big as it is today?

While no question of this sort can ever be definitely answered, Figure 3 casts some interesting light on it. When, as in this chart, the available values of total government expenditure as a percentage of GNP for the period 1870-1967 are plotted against real per capita income on a scatter diagram, many of the resulting points appear to cluster around a straight line sloping upwards towards the right. The straight line drawn on Figure 3 was calculated by standard statistical procedures as the best-fitting straight line approximating the observations for all years except 1930-1946 inclusive.[4] The values for the depression and World War II years were arbitrarily omitted from this calculation as reflecting exceedingly "abnormal" periods.

The inference which the credulous reader might draw from this simple statistical manipulation is startling: the ratio of total government expenditure to GNP between 1870 and 1967 (excluding the war and depression years) appears to be largely "explained" by the level of real per capita income. War, depression, changes of government—all these, one might think, must have altered the expenditure ratio over such a long period of time. Yet these factors seem to have had slight effect compared to the influence of the increase in the real per capita income of Canadians over the past century—*and* the myriad changes in technology, knowledge, economic structure, population structure and ideology, which have caused, accompanied and followed that increase!

As the final qualifying clause indicates, the "explanation" afforded by this approach is really only a statistical association, and even statistically it is highly questionable, since much of the association between the government expenditure ratio and per capita income probably reflects common trends. There is no presumption at all that the changes in per capita income over this period were the main *cause* of the observed changes in the government expenditure ratio. Although there are some theories which suggest that a degree of causation is to be expected, on the whole, we do not as yet really have much idea of the precise nature of the casual connections, if any, between changes in the level of per capita income and changes in the relative importance of government expenditure. Indeed, these and other qualifications are so substantial that this calculation cannot be taken too seriously: it is used for illustrative purposes only.

For the sake of illustration, then, let us make the highly improbable supposition that the relationship depicted in Figure 3 has captured the "law" of government expenditure growth in Canada. When will nirvana—the day when the government expenditure ratio equals 100% of GNP—arrive? A few simple calculations suggest that this magic figure will be reached when per capita real income (in terms of 1935-39 dollars) reaches $3,024. If the rate of income growth remained near that experienced in the postwar years, this income level should be attained well before Canada celebrates its bicentennial year. As already noted, such projections are more cause for doubting the meaning and usefulness of the calculated equation than for alarm. But this absurd example does serve to raise in a dramatic way the question of whether there is some "magic ratio" of government expenditure as a proportion of national income—100%, 70%, 50%—at which disaster strikes, or at which, at the very least, there is a drastic (and unlovely?) change in our economic institutions. In the past this question has usually been raised (and debunked) under the guise of the "limit" on taxation.

One point ought to be noted immediately, however. Thus far the discussion has focused on the ratio of *total* government expenditure to GNP. In a sense, however, this ratio is misleading because it includes in its numerator substantial transfer expenditures by government which, in accordance with accepted national income accounting conventions, are not included in the denominator (GNP), because they do not represent payments for current goods and services. In 1967 these "non-exhaustive" government expenditures, which absorb no output directly, constituted 38% of total expenditures in Canada.

It is thus conceptually possible to have a government expenditure ratio (in the sense used above) of 100% and to have *no* government activities taking place at all, except the collecting of taxes and the distributing of transfer payments. However unrealistic this picture may seem, one must clearly distinguish it from the quite different case in which everyone and everything in the economy is actively employed by the government in building pyramids or missiles, depending on the century in question. It is therefore essential in analyzing trends in government expenditure always to separate exhaustive from non-exhaustive expenditure, since for most purposes the distinction is necessary to our understanding of what is really going on.

## Exhaustive and Transfer Expenditures

The relevant measure of the goods and services used up or consumed by government in the course of its own activities is "exhaustive" expenditure, that is, government expenditure on goods and services. Except for a few wartime years, exhaustive expenditure has generally been much less than total expenditure in Canada, reaching its postwar peak of 20% of GNP only in 1967. If military expenditures and government expenditures on capital account are deducted, total government current civilian expenditures on goods and services—which are probably what many people have in mind when they think, despairingly, of the "never-ending rise" of government spending—have risen only from 7.1% of GNP in 1926 to 11.2% in 1965. Over the 1926-1967 period as a whole all exhaustive expenditures rose somewhat faster than current civilian expenditures alone (from 9.4% to 19.9% of GNP), partly as a result of a tenfold rise in the importance of defence expenditures over this period, though, significantly defence spending in terms of share of GNP is now less than one-tenth its wartime peak and one-half its post-Korea peak. It will thus take much, much longer at historic rates of increase for government exhaustive expenditure to "eat up" half or all of the national product than it will take for the ratio of total expenditure to GNP to reach a level of 50% or 100%.[5]

The really rapid increase in government spending over the last 15 years has been in the non-exhaustive spending programs of government. From 1954 to 1965, for example, increases in transfers and subsidies accounted for 84% of the growth of total government expenditure in Canada, although over the longer period 1933-1965 their share of total growth was much less. The increasing size of government transfer expenditures raises a number of important questions on the nature of government activity and the reasons for expansions in transfer programs in the postwar era. These questions are particularly difficult to answer, however, because they relate primarily to the essentially ethical issue of income distribution.

For the moment, the point to be stressed is that these transfer programs should not be thought of as diverting substantial resources from private use: only exhaustive expenditures do that. On the other hand, *both* exhaustive and non-exhaustive government expenditures require financing (mostly through the tax system) and thus affect the allocation of resources in one way or another—as do many government regulatory policies which involve little or no public expenditure, though they may often require private expenditure (on septic tanks, automobile mufflers, and countless other items). The reflexive reaction of governments when electorates demand that they do something about some newly recognized problem—for example, pollution—is usually negative ("thou shalt not"), thus often increasing private rather than government outlays in the first instance, though an increase in the latter often follows soon after. The amount of government spending on a function need not reflect very accurately either the importance of the function to the community or the extent of government involvement. This raises again the question of whether there is any number which "really" tells us how important government is and what has been happening to its importance over time.

## The Measurement of Government Activity

The brief answer to this question is that there is no one magic number which measures the importance of government activity in any country at any time. Rather, there are several different numbers bearing on the relative importance of government with respect to certain features of the economy which are relevant for different purposes. The ratio of total government expenditure to GNP, for instance, is probably the most useful number to indicate roughly the relative importance of government activity, but as just pointed out it does not really measure the importance of government as a consumer of the country's economic resources. The ratio of exhaustive expenditure to GNP can perhaps serve as a measure of "government as consumer". But there is no obvious measure, on the basis of available data, of the importance of government as a producer of goods and services. Most of the ingredients of government exhaustive expenditure (other than labour) are, for example, really produced by private business firms. Government does not itself "produce" bulldozers or graders or paving machines or, for that matter, highways. The relative importance of government in total production activity as measured in the national accounts is thus less than the ratio of exhaustive expenditure to GNP would suggest.

Even the amount of current civilian government expenditure on goods and services—that is, after deducting transfers, military spending and capital expenditure—probably overestimates the share of government outlay that can properly be viewed as part of final consumption in the economy. One expert has suggested that the proportion of government expenditure constituting final production (that is, production of goods which yield utility, or a psychic income stream, directly to individuals) might perhaps be approximated as the sum of expenditure on health, education, and recreation.[6] For Canada, expenditure on health and education as a proportion of GNP rose from 3.9% in 1933 to 8.4% in 1965.[7] The remaining expenditure on goods and services by government — 10% of GNP in 1965[8]—therefore really constitutes "intermediate" production, which does not yield utility in itself but rather serves as intermediate input to government final product or to final products produced by the private sector. If 10% of measured GNP is "really" intermediate product, then GNP measured, as it is theoretically supposed to be, in terms of the value of final production is only 90% of the GNP as now recorded. Final government product constitutes almost 10% of this reduced total. These calculations are all very conjectural, of course. Nevertheless we are still probably safe in concluding that the relative importance of government final product in total production has risen in Canada over time, perhaps doubling in the last 30 years.[9]

Another serious problem in measuring government activity is that there is really for the most part no way to measure government goods and services and to value their worth in terms of some common unit such as dollars. Theoretically, of course, the value of government output (or at least, as noted above, of *final* government output) is part of GNP. In practice, since most government products are not sold in a market, there is no way to measure this output directly, so it is valued on the basis of the direct costs incurred by government. What was called above ''government as consumer'' is in this way often taken to represent ''government as producer''. Even the potentially more refined approach sketched in the previous paragraph utilizes the cost of inputs to value government output, whether final or intermediate in character. The only more direct measure of the value added to the national output by government activity that we have been able to construct—the government wage bill as a proportion of total factor income, depicted in Figure 4—still refers to the inputs used by

## Figure 4.
Canada: Measurements of Government Activity, 1926-1967

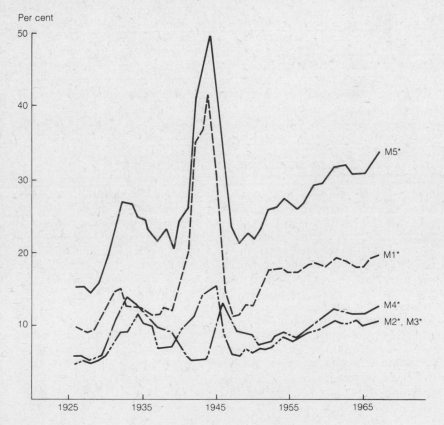

**M1\*** —Government as consumer (Total exhaustive expenditure as per cent of GNP at market prices).
**M2\* and M3\*** — Government as producer and employer (Total government wages bill as per cent of GNP at factor cost).
**M4\*** — Government as redistributor (Transfers plus interest on public debt as per cent of GNP at factor cost plus interest on public debt).
**M5\*** — Government as reallocator (Total expenditures as per cent of GNP at market prices).

government and tells us nothing directly about the output of government services. If, for example, the productivity with which government inputs are combined to produce government outputs changed over time, an increase in government consumption and expenditure might represent a decrease in government production, an increase in government production, or no change at all. There is no way to tell. There is therefore no way we can really tell whether government output has become more or less important in relation to private-sector output over time.

The productivity of some government operations has probably increased in this century as a result of improvements in technology (e.g., motorized police patrols, computerized accounting systems) and in public administration (e.g., centralized purchasing agencies, civil service training). These developments have probably more than offset the decline in the average working hours of government employees and the rise in the use of capital goods and other inputs. There is, however, no way in which we can be sure what, if anything, has really happened to government productivity—and, even more emphatically, no way of saying whether government productivity has risen more or less than that in the private sector or was higher or lower to begin with.[10] On the whole, however, we are probably quite safe in assuming that "the major factor accounting for the increase in government's use of labor and other resources has been growth in government services",[11] at least over the long run, though we cannot really *know* on the basis of any existing set of numbers whether government is "producing" more today that it did yesterday or will tomorrow.

## Government as Employer and Investor

In view of the problems in measuring government output directly and the necessarily obscure relation of government expenditure to the provision of government services, a useful supplementary approach is to focus directly on the measurement of the principal factors of production employed by government—labour and capital. In 1967, for example, all public bodies in Canada together directly employed around 900,000 people, or over 12% of the total work force. A great many others were of course employed in producing the goods and services purchased by the government from private industry—highway construction, for instance—but there is no way of telling what proportion of the labour force was thus engaged. The longest time series available on government employment relates to federal departmental employment alone (231,000 or 28% of the total in 1967): this category of employment increased more than tenfold in absolute numbers from 1912 to 1967 while population tripled in size. In 1921, federal government civilian and military employees constituted 1.4% of the total labour force; in 1967, the corresponding figure was 4.3%. The slightly different definitions used in the census indicate that departmental employment by all levels of government rose from 3% to 8% of civilian employment from 1921 to 1967.[12]

Unfortunately, there are no long-run data on total public employment in Canada, but it seems probable that public employment is relatively less important here (perhaps principally because of the smaller armed forces) than it is in the United States, where total public-sector employees constituted 12.4% of the total employed labour force as early as 1949.[13] The comparable figure for Canada in 1967, almost 20 years later, was only 11.4%. In the meantime the number of public employees in the United States has continued to rise more rapidly than population, with, for example, 3 million new state and local employees alone in the last decade.[14] Of course, the large U.S. military forces are paid much less than the market wage so that government expenditure in the United States does not appear to be as large relative to GNP as that in Canada, despite the greater public employment.

Another interesting comparison is with Japan, where central government employment as a per cent of total gainfully-occupied population rose from 0.2% in 1880 to 3.8% in 1960; total government employment in the latter year amounted to 7.1%. Over the same period, total government expenditure in Japan rose from 10.5% to 33.2% of GNP.[15] Although it is hard to make a precise comparison, it appears likely that the 1960 figures for Canada were not very different.[16] To sum up, government is thus an important employer in Canada, indeed an increasingly important one, but we seem as yet to be a long way from the completely bureaucratic state—or at least from a politically responsible one, for we have not considered at all the growing importance of large "private" business organizations and their increasing entanglement in various ways with the "public" sector.[17]

Interestingly enough, government in Canada has always been much more important as an investor than as an employer. As a percent of total investment, public investment has, as a rule, ranged from 15% to 20%, except during the depression and the war, when it became considerably more important. In 1967, government expenditure on capital account amounted to 4.5% of GNP, a proportion almost as high as its wartime peak, although current expenditure on goods and services in 1965 was less than half as high as during the war. In relation to 1926, however, both current and capital expenditures constituted twice as large a proportion of GNP in 1967.

If the very fragmentary information available on changes in government capital stock is combined with that on employment, one might perhaps infer, even without adequate capital stock data, that a dollar spent through the government has, on average, been more capital-intensive in recent years than a dollar spent outside the government. That is, the capital-labour ratio in government appears to be higher than in the private sector: in 1964-1967, for example, total government expenditure on capital account per new civilian employee was substantially greater than the equivalent incremental capital-labour ratio in the private sector.

One reason for the apparently less intensive use of labour in the government sector might be the persistent relatively higher cost of the average government employee compared to employees as a whole. But it seems unlikely that the choice of the technology of production in the public sector has in fact been much influenced by the relative prices of labour and capital (the latter surely being relatively cheaper for government than for the private sector in view of government's greater access to sources of funds), since government, by definition, has no profits to maximize in most of its operations. Perhaps a more interesting implication of these wage-bill figures is that the average cost of a federal departmental civilian employee has risen much less rapidly over the last four decades than average civilian labour cost: that is, the relative income status of the average civil servant has fallen sharply since World War I. The data do not permit us to estimate how much of this change is due to a change in the composition of government employment, but one might perhaps hazard the guess that the average composition of private employment has, as a result of changes in technology and organization, come to resemble that of government much more in 1967 than it did in 1921. For many persons, there is now probably little difference between public and private employment in terms of security, pensions, and the like. Furthermore, public-sector wages have probably adjusted more slowly than private-sector wages to changes in total productivity. In any event, as a proportion of total government expenditure, the wages bill has remained pretty close to 30% throughout the period (see Figure 5).[18]

## Figure 5.
Canada: Percentage Distribution of Government Expenditure by Economic Category, 1926-1967

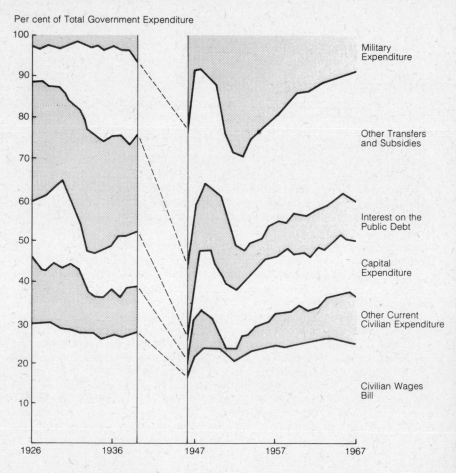

Per cent of Total Government Expenditure

Up to this point we have noted as factors potentially affecting the growth and time pattern of government expenditure the following: (1) population growth; (2) price level changes; (3) the growth of income; and (4) catastrophes such as wars and depression. It will be noted that nothing has yet been said about the political process that necessarily intervenes between, say, a change in population and a change in government expenditure. For example, at the provincial level, did the relative decline of the traditional (Liberal and Conservative) parties after World War II — a decline not reversed until the 1960s — have any discernible effect on provincial expenditure levels and patterns? Did the varying strengths of the different parties in the federal House of Commons affect expenditure in any way? Although we shall later discuss the political process in general as a factor affecting government expenditure, we have been unable to formulate any political variable in a way that seems to lend itself to meaningful use in analysis.[19] Nor do there seem to have been any very obvious changes in expenditure that can be directly connected to political changes. These and many other potentially important political questions must be left for subsequent studies.

## The Changing Composition of Public Expenditure

Moderately reliable data on the functional breakdown of government expenditure exist in general only for years since 1933. The basic trends in the changing functional composition of expenditure since that depression year seem clear (see Figure 6): over the 1933-1965 period as a whole defence accounted for 29% of the total increase in expenditure, health for 29%, education for 35%, and general government for 21%. (That these increases add up to more than 100% is explained by the fact that there were offsetting declines in debt service charges and veterans' pensions and benefits.) In the more recent 1953-1965 period, the relative importance of defence expenditure actually declined sharply, though health and, especially, education continued to account for most of the increase in total government expenditure.

The picture looks slightly different when we consider the rates of growth of expenditure on different functions relative to the rate of growth of the national income. Health then takes over the lead from education and appears to be the most rapidly expanding component of total government expenditure both over the 1933-1965 period as a whole and in the more recent 1953-1965 period. In other words, public expenditures on health grew faster than those on education, but education expenditures at the beginning of the period were so much larger than health expenditures that the *addition* to expenditures on education was nevertheless larger than the increase in health expenditures. For 1953-1965, while the elasticity with respect to national income of total government expenditure was only 1.1 (and that for defence was −1.1), the income-elasticities of the "social services", health, education and social welfare, were respectively 2.4, 2.1 and 1.3, which means, for example, that for every 1% rise in gross national expenditure, government expenditure on health in 1953-1965 rose, on average, by 2.4%.

Two features in this changing composition of public expenditure are of special interest. The first is the very erratic pattern of defence expenditure with,

**Figure 6.**
Canada: Total Government Expenditure
by Function, 1933-1965

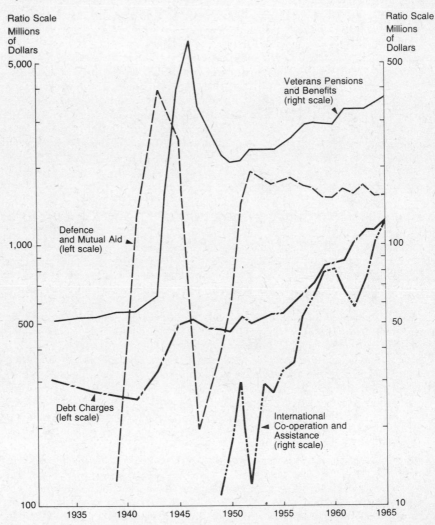

Ratio Scale
Millions
of
Dollars

Ratio Scale
Millions
of
Dollars

Veterans Pensions
and Benefits
(right scale)

Defence
and Mutual Aid
(left scale)

Debt Charges
(left scale)

International
Co-operation and
Assistance
(right scale)

as one would expect, pronounced peaks in the 1940s (World War II) and the early 1950s (post-Korea rearmament) followed by a substantial subsequent decline in both absolute and relative terms.

Even more striking is the persistent and rapid rise of government expenditure on health and education—a rise which in fact appears to have begun before 1933 and to have accelerated even further since 1965.[20] Interestingly, social

**Figure 6.**
Canada: Total Government Expenditure
by Function, 1933-1965

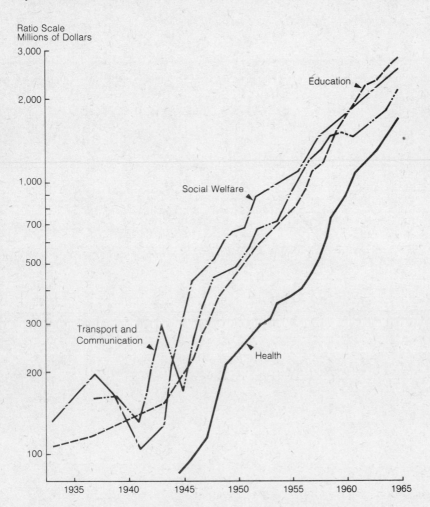

welfare expenditure—on which so much public protest about rising taxes and expenditure often seems to focus—appears, in these data, to have accounted for relatively much less of the rise in total expenditure than health and education, though in absolute terms it is still much larger than expenditure on health and around the same size as that on education.

In order to understand the considerable long-term expansion of government activity we must therefore look particularly at rising expenditure on health and education as a major contributing factor. Many possible reasons explaining the

**Figure 7.**
Canada: Expenditure by Function in
Relation to Per Capita Income, 1933-1965

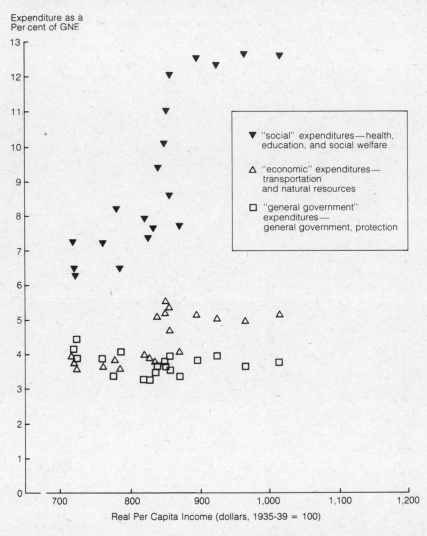

Expenditure as a
Per cent of GNE

▼ "social" expenditures—health,
education, and social welfare

△ "economic" expenditures—
transportation
and natural resources

□ "general government"
expenditures—
general government, protection

Real Per Capita Income (dollars, 1935-39 = 100)

marked upsurge of expenditure on these social services in recent decades have
been offered by different observers. A few of these arguments may be mentioned here by way of illustration.

(1) As per capita income levels rise, people will demand more of "luxuries"
such as health care and education: it is, for example, striking that the
percentage of GNP spent on "government" and "economic" services
appears to be relatively invariant to changes in per capita income, while
"social" expenditures underwent a quantum jump after World War II, as
shown in Figure 7.

(2) Expenditures on health and, especially, education may not represent simply increased "luxury" consumption expenditures, but may instead be thought of as "investment in human capital" and thus as both cause and consequence of the rising income levels and the new interest in economic growth. Educational expenditures in particular, it might be argued, are required (rather than simply made possible) by the increased complexity of modern economic life.

(3) As incomes rise, and improved communication increases the national "sense of community", one might expect more resources to be devoted to income redistribution measures—and many government expenditures on health and education can be quite properly characterized as redistribution in kind.[22]

(4) The preceding points neglect the political process through which these "demands" or "needs" are satisfied. If one takes into account the fact that politicians may think they can be re-elected most easily by "giving" something to most people, one has still another reason why public provision of health and education has become so important. In accordance with this argument, one would perhaps expect some substitution of public for private expenditures to have taken place in recent years, perhaps especially in the health field. In part, such a substitution might be taken to reflect the workings of democratic politics and in part the increased complexity of modern life and our greater interdependence, combined with the lessened ability of most individuals or families to fend for themselves in the face of adversity.

It is important to re-emphasize the very great differences in the time pattern of expenditures on different functions—differences which not only emphasize the necessity of "explaining" expenditures on different functions differently but also raise the question of whether it is useful or meaningful to discuss "the" behaviour of the undifferentiated aggregate we call "government expenditure".

## Expenditure by Economic Character

Another way of viewing the increase of government expenditure is in terms of its economic character. As noted earlier, non-exhaustive expenditures have been increasing especially rapidly in recent years, with 73% of the total expansion of government expenditure in 1953-1965 being accounted for by transfer expenditures and another 11% by subsidies. Transfers rose over this period from 12% to 17% of total personal income, while subsidies increased from 0.3% to 0.8% of total business operating revenue. By contrast, over the 1933-1965 period as a whole, current exhaustive expenditures accounted for 57% of the total increase, capital expenditures for 14%, and transfers and subsidies combined for only 21%. Some of the difference is apparently accounted for by the fact that most defence expenditure is exhaustive in nature, and the remainder arises from the understandable importance of transfers in the early 1930s: in 1933, for example, they amounted to 16% of total personal income. In any case, the more recent postwar experience again suggests the possible importance of increased redistribution intent and some of the other factors mentioned above in connection with social services as explanations of trends in government expenditure in the last two decades.

When the 1926-1967 period as a whole is viewed, as in Figure 5, perhaps the most striking change is the decline in the importance of interest on the public debt, a decline which has been almost exactly matched by the rise in the proportion of total government expenditure attributable to other transfer payments.[23] The relative importance of capital expenditures in the total expenditure budget was, by coincidence, exactly the same in 1967 as in 1926, and the slightly lesser relative importance of civilian exhaustive expenditures was offset by the increased importance of military expenditures.

## Expenditure by Level of Government

A final way of decomposing total government expenditure is by level of government. This focus is perhaps the most familiar of the three to Canadians. Most people, however, do not seem aware of the many different ways in which the degree of "centralization" or "decentralization" of the public finances can be measured. For example, the two sets of statistics available on Canadian public finance follow two quite different procedures with respect to the treatment of intergovernmental transfers. The national accounts figures treat all transfers as expenditures of the receiving government, while the public finance statistics treat only unconditional transfers as expenditures of the receiving government and consider conditional transfers to be expenditures of the donor government. As is clearly illustrated by Figure 8, just how one treats intergovernmental transfers turns out to be really quite important in determining the degree of centralization that apparently characterizes the public finances of Canada in the 1960s.

The treatment showing the greatest degree of decentralization (that is, the largest share of provincial-municipal expenditure in the total) is that used in the national accounts, which attempt to show the outlay actually made by each government for goods and services and transfer payments, regardless of the source of the funds. The rationale for this treatment is presumably the same as that for treating all expenditure by consumers as consumption expenditure regardless of the source of the funds. The dramatic change from unconditional to conditional grants which has taken place in the last decade will thus not be directly reflected in the national accounts figures. The same is true of moves in the direction of replacing conditional grants by granting "tax room" to the provinces through the opting-out procedure. This invariance to changes in institutional arrangements is presumably a good thing from the point of view of the national accounts, where one is interested in having as high a degree of intertemporal comparability in the data as possible.

On the other hand, it might be argued that having funds made available without having to "pay" the political cost of raising taxes for them, as happens with *any* kind of grant, conditional or unconditional, will tend to expand the expenditures of lower-level governments beyond the level they would otherwise attain. Furthermore, one might expect the effect on expenditure on different functions to reflect such factors as (a) the extent to which the transfer payment is tied to expenditure on the function, (b) the legal "matching" requirements for local funding of expenditure on the function, (c) the "price-elasticity" of expenditure on the function, and (d) the "income-elasticity" of

**Figure 8.**
Canada: The Centralization of
Government Expenditure, 1949-1965

Billions of Dollars
Ratio Scales

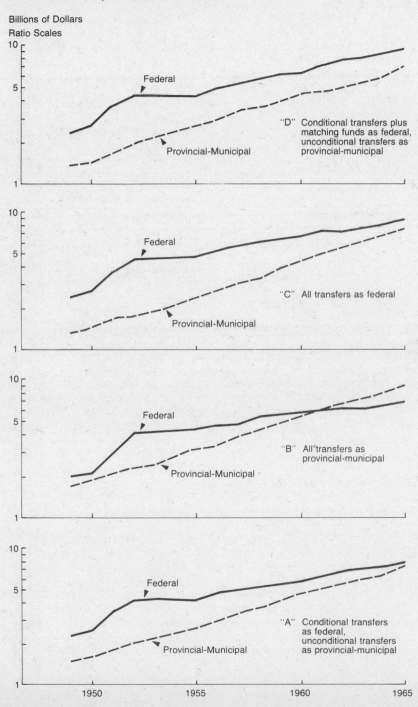

"D"  Conditional transfers plus
matching funds as federal,
unconditional transfers as
provincial-municipal

"C"  All transfers as federal

"B"  All transfers as
provincial-municipal

"A"  Conditional transfers
as federal,
unconditional transfers
as provincial-municipal

expenditure on the function. Even unconditional grants will have an income effect, so that one would expect spending on different functions to expand differently as a result of the availability of increased financing.[24] There is thus no simple answer as to the effect of different kinds of intergovernmental transfers on the level of either total spending or spending on different functions, although it is clear that there will be some such effects. The national accounts treatment dodges this entire problem by simply recording whatever expenditure actually takes place at each level of government.

Unfortunately for the cause of simplicity, for our purposes we are interested in the degree of "centralization" in the Canadian public finances. Centralization (or decentralization) is not at all a clear concept. Perhaps the most common way of measuring it is to look at the importance of the budgets of lower-level governments in the total public-sector budget. But the key question of the degree of local autonomy (or local freedom) may look quite different depending upon how we decide to calculate this ratio. All the ways of doing the requisite calculation other than that used in the national accounts hinge on questions of motivation and assumed intention and are therefore questionable.

The treatment of intergovernmental transfers in the public finance statistics, for example, is apparently intended to place the funds at the level of government which is responsible for allocating them to the function in question. If, say, a conditional grant is given by the federal government to a provincial government to be spent on education, it is taken in the public finance statistics to be equivalent to a federal expenditure on education and is therefore treated as a federal expenditure.

This treatment will, of course, indicate a lesser degree of decentralization the greater the importance of conditional grants in total intergovernmental transfers. Replacing unconditional by conditional grants will therefore increase the calculated centralization ratio. Replacing conditional grants through the opting-out procedure, on the other hand, will decrease the ratio. The degree of centralization estimated from the public finance statistics will thus be quite sensitive to the *form* of intergovernmental fiscal relations, as is clear from Figure 8. This sensitivity is a weakness of this ratio, because it is not at all obvious that changing the form of a transfer necessarily means much of a change either in the "real" degree of central vs. local power or, for that matter, in the pattern of expenditures at each level. The considerations of price and income effects mentioned above are, once again, crucially important— though, alas, completely unknown![25]

Finally, two alternative hypothetical formulations of the centralization ratio might be calculated. The first in essence considers primarily the revenue side on the grounds that "he who pays the piper calls the tune". In terms of expenditures, for instance, *all* transfers (conditional or unconditional) might be treated as donor expenditures because the donor raises the revenue in the first place.[26] The degree of centralization thus revealed would clearly be even greater than in the public finance statistics. The opting-out system introduced in 1965, however, would still lower the ratio in this measure because the revenue-raising responsibility is then transferred to the lower level of government.

A final alternative might be to treat not only the conditional transfers as donor expenditures but also *all* the matching expenditures (usually 50% of the total in most Canadian schemes)[27] as donor expenditures. The degree of decentralization is obviously at its lowest in this measure, which appears to be what some provincial premiers think is going on. Opting-out too should probably be treated as a federal expenditure in this case on the same strong assumption that the lower levels of government would not spend a cent on the aided function if it were not for the chance of cheap federal money, especially since the amount of additional tax room granted is initially calculated on the basis of the size of the expenditures in question.

This last calculation undoubtedly overstates the degree of centralization—perhaps by as much as the national accounts formulation understates it. The public finance statistics approach, being a half-way house, might seem a suitable Canadian compromise were it not for the facts that (as pointed out above) it is too sensitive to the *form* of intergovernmental fiscal relations and that there is in any case no reason to expect the substance of central-local relations to match the conditional-unconditional split.

Still another approach might be to categorize separately the open-ended matching conditional grants which have come to prominence in recent years. These very large transfers should be treated separately because it is not at all clear what they represent: more centralization or more decentralization. Partly for this reason, they seem an unneeded and confusing addition to the traditional specific grants on the one hand and block grants on the other. The spectrum of fiscal transfers goes from closed specific grants (matching only, at present) to open block grants (none at present—and probably inconceivable). A closed specific grant from the federal to the provincial governments can usefully be considered as equivalent to a federal expenditure for most intents and purposes; similarly, an unrestricted block grant is probably best treated as giving rise to provincial expenditures, except for the general *caveat* noted earlier on paying the piper. It is not at all clear what an open-ended conditional grant is. Its actual effect on expenditure patterns depends on price and income effects, political reactions and so on. Its intended effect is almost equally uncertain in most instances. On the whole, the open-ended conditional grant does not seem a very happy or necessary invention, unless, as may be true, obscurity has political virtue in its own right.

To sum up, the two treatments of intergovernmental fiscal transfers in the published financial statistics indicate different degrees of "centralization". Still other calculations are possible. None of these procedures rests on too firm a conceptual or empirical base. In short, just as was the case with the importance of government spending as a whole, there is no one magic ratio showing the degree of centralization. Different ratios are probably best for different purposes, and what seems needed to advance knowledge in this area is more thought on the purposes for which we want the knowledge. What *is* clear is that the proper interpretation of recent trends in government spending by level is *not* clear, particularly when the close relationship between changes in expenditure by function and by level of government is taken into account. One should therefore be cautious in making statements on trends in the centralization of government finance in Canada.[28]

To add to the confusion, all these aggregate comparisons of levels of government themselves conceal a great deal of diversity. In 1965, for example, per capita net general expenditure by provincial governments varied from $198 in New Brunswick to $307 in Quebec. The spread between high spenders and low spenders was marked for every function of government. This comparison is not complete, however, because of the different relative importance of provincial and municipal governments in different provinces: if both levels of government are taken into account the range in per capita total expenditure changes to from $295 in Newfoundland to $463 in British Columbia. Finally, the greatly varying extent to which expenditure on different functions in different provinces is financed from federal funds is striking.[29] Limitations of time and resources precluded further investigation of these variations in provincial-municipal expenditure in the present study. Potentially this is a fruitful field for further investigation, both of the differences in expenditure patterns among the ten provinces and also of the great variations in expenditure by the 15,000 or so local authorities (including 11,000 school boards) in Canada.

### Footnotes

1. D. G. Creighton, *British North America at Confederation*. A Study Prepared for the Royal Commission on Dominion-Provincial Relations (reprinted Ottawa: Queen's Printer, 1963), pp.66, 92. Estimated that total government expenditures in 1866, on the eve of Confederation, similarly amounted to about 7% of national income, which would suggest that Confederation had little immediate impact on the level or pattern of government spending.

2. Several of the charts accompanying this paper have been drawn on semi-logarithmic graph paper, so that the relative slopes of the lines on the graph indicate the relative rates of change of the variables being charted: in Figure 2, for example, the steeper the line, the faster the rate of increase of expenditures.

3. The data for years prior to 1926 are not sufficient to permit the depiction in detail of this time pattern for spending by all levels of government, so the inferences drawn in the text about the behaviour of government expenditure are based on data for federal expenditures alone.

4. The equation of the calculated line is:

$$Y = -.9917 + .0334X; \quad r^2 = .9391$$
$$(1.941)$$

Y is the ratio of total government expenditure to GNP, and X is per capita income in terms of 1935-1939 constant dollars.

The figure shown in parentheses below the equation is the standard error of estimate, which gives an idea of the expected dependability of estimates made on the basis of the equation. In this instance the standard error of estimate is 1.9, which means that we would expect to find about two-thirds of the observations within a band one standard error (1.9 percentage points) wide on either side of the fitted line, and 95% of the items within a wider band 3.8 percentage points on either side of the line. Finally, the coefficient of determination, $r^2 = .9391$, is shown. This figure indicates that changes in real per capita income are associated with 93.9% of the changes in the government expenditure ratio.

The data for this calculation were taken from various issues of the *National Accounts*. The implicit GNP price index in the *National Accounts* is based on 1949 = 100; it was converted arithmetically to a 1935-39 = 100 basis in order to link it with the data for earlier years taken from O.J. Firestone, *Canada's Economic Development 1867-1953* (London: Bowes & Bowes, 1958), which are not strictly comparable anyway.

The unreliability of the pre-1926 data, the lack of comparability, and the arbitrary deflation procedures necessarily employed—not to mention the various serious statistical problems inherent in correlating two long time series of this sort—all mean that this calculation must be taken with a very large grain of salt indeed. It is presented here for illustrative purposes only. A more rigorous statistical investigation of the factors "explaining" the government expenditure ratio could of course be carried out (e.g. by fitting a logarithmic relationship, by expressly allowing for the effects of depressions and wars, and so on), but it did not seem worth while proceeding along these lines, given time limitations and the general theoretical orientation of the present study.

5. As already suggested, this choice of words, while it may reflect fairly accurately what some people think of most government expenditure, prejudges, most improperly, and largely incorrectly, a complex set of issues.

6. Simon Kuznets, "Quantitative Aspects of the Economic Growth of Nations: Part VIII, The Share and Structure of Consumption", *Economic Development and Cultural Change*, X, Part 2 (January, 1962), p.9. Note that government spending on "pure" public goods, such as national defence and general government administration, is, in this formulation, really viewed as an intermediate product, presumably necessary for the economy to exist but not "consumed" in any meaningful sense by private individuals: this assumption is obviously arbitrary.

7. Expenditure on recreation is not separately available but is minor in any case. A good deal of the expenditure on health and education appears to have taken the form of transfers, but it is all considered in the text to be "final" expenditure on the assumption that the education transfers shown in these tables are spent by municipal governments (for which a similar breakdown is not available) and that the health transfers are simply the accounting form which has been chosen to achieve the desired goal of below-cost provision of health services.

8. As suggested in the previous note, the calculation by which this figure has been obtained is, in strict national accounting terms, somewhat dubious, as are those which immediately follow in the text. They serve to illustrate the point, however.

9. Kuznets, *op. cit.*, p.12, estimated for a group of high-income countries (including Canada) in the 1950s that "final" government product was around 6% of GNP (conventionally defined) on average and that the proportion had, with little doubt, risen over time.

10. There is a good discussion of all these problems in Solomon Fabricant, *The Trend of Government Activity in the United States since 1900* (New York: National Bureau of Economic Research, 1952), chap.5. One comment of Fabricant's seems as valid today as when it was written: "Our inability to obtain a more definite notion of what has happened arises not because statistical data are unpublished, but because government officials do not even collect or analyze such data. Nor can this failure, in turn, be ascribed entirely to conceptual difficulties in determining government product and government productivity. Suggested measures . . . seem hardly to have been applied. Since such data are needed for the information and education of the public and its representatives, for the more efficient control of government operations, and for sound government programming and budgeting, it is surely the responsibility of government officials to collect and analyze them" (p.110, n.41). A very few studies of public-sector productivity have subsequently been published — for example, H. D. Lytton, "Recent Productivity Trends in the Federal Government: An Exploratory Study", *Review of Economics and Statistics*, XLI (November, 1959), but I am not aware of any for Canada.

11. Fabricant, *op. cit.*, p.102.

12. The census data used for 1921 in this calculation probably understate government employment considerably, so that the rise may not have been this great in fact. On the other hand, non-departmental employment (for which there are no data) probably has grown more quickly. For a different presentation based on census data, see David A. Worton, "The Service Industries in Canada", in Victor R. Fuchs (ed.), *Production and Productivity in the Service Industries* (New York: Columbia University Press, 1969), p.243.

13. Includes government corporations and armed forces: see Fabricant, *op. cit.*, p.14, who also notes that the comparable 1920 figure in the U.S. was 6.5%, compared to perhaps 3% to 4% in Canada at that time, thus suggesting a relatively faster rise in government employment in Canada (where federal employment, civil and military, was 3.3% of the total work force in 1949 compared to 1.4% in 1921).

14. See H. H. Wellington and Ralph K. Winter, Jr., "The Limits of Collective Bargaining in Public Employment", *Yale Law Journal*, LXXVII (June, 1969), 1115; cf. Tax Foundation, Inc., *Federal Civilian Employment, Pay and Benefits* (New York, 1969), p.13.

15. See Koichi Emi, *Government Fiscal Activity and Economic Growth in Japan 1868-1960* (Tokyo: Kinokunlya Bookstore Co. Ltd., 1963), pp.5-6, 16.

16. The difficulty of working with these data is suggested by the quite different estimates for the U.S., Japan and Canada in Bruce Russett *et al.*, *World Handbook of Political and Social Indicators* (New Haven: Yale University Press, 1964), pp.70-71.

17. Although the process of entanglement has probably gone less far in Canada than in the United States (where all by now have surely heard of the famous, or infamous, "military-industrial

complex''), there is every reason to believe that the trend towards increased blurring of the line between the public and private sectors recently pointed out by Professor Galbraith (in *The New Industrial State* [Boston: Houghton Mifflin, 1967]) exists here too. It has not been possible to consider at length what, if any, merit this Galbraithian thesis has as an analytical tool in understanding the behaviour of government spending.

18. Interestingly, a similar constancy in the relative importance of personnel expenditures in Japan between 1880 and 1960 is noted in Emi, *op. cit.*, p. 7 (though the proportion fell greatly in the 1930s).

19. Admittedly, our experimentation was limited: we tried party strengths in the House of Commons, political colouration of provincial governments, and percent of popular vote in provincial elections (using data from H. S. Scarrow, *Canada Votes* [New Orleans: The Hauser Press, 1962]). Our original idea, among other things, was to measure the conservativeness of government by party affiliation as was done with some success by, for example, Elliott R. Morss, J. Eric Friedland, and Saul H. Hymans, ''Fluctuations in State Expenditures: An Econometric Analysis'', *Southern Economic Journal*, XXXIII (April, 1967), 496-517, but this turned out not to be feasible—partly because the major Canadian parties are not very different in this respect.

20. See *Government Expenditures on Health and Social Welfare, Canada 1927 to 1959* Social Security Series, Memorandum No. 16, Research and Statistics Division, Department of National Health and Welfare (Ottawa, 1961), p. 52, and John E. Osborne, ''Health Care and Social Welfare Expenditures'', *Report of Proceedings of the Twenty-first Tax Conference* (Toronto: Canadian Tax Foundation, 1960), p. 155. On education, note the data and projections (for Ontario) presented by Cicely Watson, ''Financing Education'', *ibid.*, p. 145.

21. This argument, it should be noted, does not explain why people choose to buy these ''luxuries'' through government rather than through personal expenditure on health care, for example (in education, they have little choice): in fact, there appears to have been a considerable rise in personal spending on health in recent years also, although the data are not as clear as one might wish (see John E. Osborne, ''The Economics and Costs of Health Care'', Research and Statistics memo, Department of National Health and Welfare [mimeographed, Ottawa, n.d., pp. 6-13]).

22. This comment applies even to those ''tied'' transfer expenditures referred to in note 7 above (in reference to the Kuznets definition of ''final'' government production) and to many of the ''indirect'' expenditures made through the tax system.

23. In reality, not all interest on the public debt can properly be viewed as a transfer payment. Actually, the relative rise in the importance of transfer payments may predate 1926, though the evidence for earlier years is very shaky (Firestone, *op. cit.*, p. 137).

24. A useful recent presentation of the theoretical ways in which different forms of intergovernmental fiscal transfers may affect expenditures may be found in James A. Wilde, ''The Expenditure Effects of Grant-in-Aid Programs'', *National Tax Journal*, XXI (September, 1968), pp. 340-48.

25. They are not in principle, unknowable, however; this is an important subject for further work in Canada. The only item I have found which even begins to approach the question in this way, however, contains no empirical work. (See Malcolm Martini, ''Towards a Theory of Provincial-Municipal Grants'', *Ontario Economic Review*, V, No. 9-10 [September-October 1967], pp. 5-11). Two recent useful general discussions of the federal-provincial fiscal system (Donald V. Smiley, *Conditional Grants and Canadian Federalism*, Canadian Tax Papers No. 32; [Toronto: Canadian Tax Foundation, 1963]) and John F. Graham, ''Fiscal Adjustment in a Federal Country'', in *Inter-government Fiscal Relationships*, Canadian Tax Papers No. 40. ([Toronto: Canadian Tax Foundation, 1964]) also fail to analyze the problem empirically in a way relevant to the concerns of the present study. The sole instance of Canadian empirical study on the effects of intergovernmental transfers on local expenditures of which I am aware—on provincial grants to municipalities for education in Ontario—was very brief and produced no very clear-cut results: see Gail C. A. Cook, ''Effect of Federal on Education Expenditures in Metropolitan Toronto'', Unpublished Ph.D. dissertation (University of Michigan, 1968), pp. 72-76.

26. This is equivalent to what Ratchford called the ''Revenue Basis'' for allocating intergovernmental payments, whereas the national accounts treatment is equivalent to his ''Direct Expenditures Basis''. As he noted, neither treatment is better for all purposes (B. U. Ratchford, *Public Expenditures in Australia* [Durham, N.C.: Duke University Press, 1959], p. 9).

27. This assumption is derived from the information contained in *Federal-Provincial Conditional Grant and Shared-Cost Programmes* (Ottawa: Queen's Printer, 1963) and Canadian Tax Foundation, *The National Finances 1968-69,* Chap. 8. Because the federal portion applies only to "approved costs", this assumption may overstate federal influence substantially in some fields.

28. For example, Frederic L. Pryor, "Elements of a Positive Theory of Public Expenditure", *Finanzarchiv,* N.F., Band 26 (October 1967), 414, cites Canada as showing a rising degree of centralization in the 1913-1960 period. This statement is apparently based on the public finance statistics contained in M.C. Urquhart and K.A.H. Buckley (eds.), *Historical Statistics of Canada* (Toronto: Macmillan, 1965). Most data indicate more of a trend to decentralization, at least since World War II—but this too is open to question, as already noted.

29. A great deal of further information relevant to this problem may be found in James H. Lynn, *Comparing Provincial Revenue Yields,* Canadian Tax Papers No. 47, (Toronto: Canadian Tax Foundation, 1968).

# Retail Price Indexes

## Consumer Price Index for Canada (1961 = 100)

The Consumer Price Index measures the percentage change through time in the cost of purchasing a constant "basket" of goods and services representing the purchases by a particular population group in a specified time period. The "basket" is an unchanging or equivalent quantity and quality of goods and services of items for which there is a continually measurable market price over time, corresponding to a specific quantity of the item.

The index relates to a broad but specific group of urban families and reflects the price changes experienced by that "target group". The index is unlikely to represent closely the experience of any one family within the group nor should it be expected to reflect price change for other population groups for which income, family size and place of residence are characteristically different. The target group to which the current index relates is composed of families—(a) living in cities with over 30,000 population, (b) ranging in size from two adults to two adults with four children, and (c) with annual incomes during 1957 ranging from $2,500 to $7,000. To measure the influences of price change on the cost of goods and services purchased by such families, the Consumer Price Index reflects movements of some 300 items.

The history of consumer price indexes in Canada extends back to the early 1900's and encompasses periodic revisions of index base reference periods and weighting patterns. In 1952, the time base was updated to 1949 = 100 from 1935-39 = 100 and, at the same time, weights were revised to reflect family expenditure patterns in 1947-48. A subsequent revision of weights based on 1957 expenditures was introduced at the beginning of 1961 and the time base was revised from 1949 = 100 to 1961 = 100 at the beginning of 1969.

Full details on the latest weighting patterns and time base revisions are available in the occasional paper *The Consumer Price Index for Canada (1949 = 100)—Revision based on 1957 Expenditures,* Statistics Canada Catalogue No. 62-518 and in the January 1969 issue of the monthly bulletin, Prices and Price Indexes, Catalogue No. 62-002.

# SECTION THREE
# Macroeconomic Policy

## ECONOMIC COUNCIL OF CANADA
# A Framework for Government Decision-Making

There is a compelling need to deal more effectively with the problems of contemporary society and this need is spurring the development of new approaches to government decision-making. This paper attempts to set out a framework for such decision-making.

The suggested framework places considerable emphasis on three basic elements: decision-making is essentially a process of choosing among alternatives; in order to make appropriate choices, it is essential to use the widest possible basis of relevant information and to apply the best possible analytical techniques; and the process must be one that avoids the dangers of bureaucratic and technocratic dominance by providing increased "openness" in government decision-making.

We have found it useful to view the core of this framework in terms of a highly oversimplified decision-making system, with *choices of alternatives* at these levels: policy objectives or priorities; policy or strategy; and programs or tactics. In what follows, we illustrate the alternatives faced at each level of decision-making, with particular emphasis on these basic requirements:

— the development of a monitoring system to facilitate the establishment and continued public review of policy objectives;

— the use of "feedback" mechanisms that provide for "learning by experience" and for continued reassessment and realignment of objectives, policies, and programs;

— the wider distribution of knowledge about the process and principles of decision-making, as well as the content of particular decisions;

— greater openness of government decision-making to promote increasing public understanding and involvement.

A good deal of effort in recent years has gone into making improvements at the *program* or *tactical* level of decision-making. More attention now needs to be devoted to the *higher* levels, as well as to the evolution of a more systematic approach to the whole decision-making process.

We emphasize in the strongest possible terms that progress towards improved government decision-making is *not* simply a matter of developing better information and adopting new and more sophisticated techniques. Increasingly sophisticated as they may become, better information and techniques are only aids for improving judgment. Decision-making is essentially a judgmental process. What really matters is the approach to thinking about the choices that need to be made—a continuous, conscious, and deliberate weighing of alternative actions on the broadest possible basis of knowledge and participation.

There are innumerable ways in which such a process could be fostered and promoted in the context of Canadian conditions and circumstances. Although we make some suggestions along these lines, we have not attempted to address ourselves in any comprehensive way in this Review to the complex institutional questions that could be raised.

## A System of Decision-Making

Chart 1 sets out a very simplified system or flow diagram of a central part of the decision-making process. It is a highly condensed and selective view of this system. It makes no attempt to incorporate all of the elements or the complexity of the flows. Moreover, in practice, decisions are only rarely made in the sequential fashion shown here. The three levels of decision-making are not really discrete; rather, they shade into each other.

In order to emphasize the role of analytical information in the process of choice, many other important inputs have not been shown explicitly. A complete system for the federal government, for example, would provide for inflows of information relating to the objectives, policies, and programs of provincial and municipal governments, and of foreign governments and organizations. It would also provide for good access to information from private groups—from individuals, from private organizations, and through well-functioning channels designed explicitly for consultative purposes.

More generally, in a country like Canada, policy information must flow in all directions among levels of government, and between the public and private sectors. Provincial and municipal governments, as well as private organizations, can be vitally affected by decisions, policies, and programs of the federal government; and care must be taken to provide for consultation and co-ordination. The Council recognizes, and has in the past emphasized, the importance of this aspect of decision-making, although this Review does not discuss these crucial points.

The chart is designed to focus on certain key features of a government decision-making system. First, governments are faced with the *choice of alternatives* at the levels of *objectives, policies* or *strategies* and *programs* or *tactics*. Second, analytical information is important at each level to sharpen judgments about these alternatives. Third, there is a need for on-going evaluation of programs and a continuous *feedback* of information into the decision-making process so that objectives, policies and programs can be reassessed and, if necessary, realigned in the light of *actual* results.

Finally, it is important to ensure that changes due to the impact of programs themselves on individuals and society will be systematically monitored in the decision-making process. We emphasize again that it is vitally important at all levels of "information inputs" to take account not merely of technical and analytical information, but of information in the broadest sense, including the interests of individuals and concerned groups.

**Chart 1.**
Selected Information Inputs to a Decision-Making Process

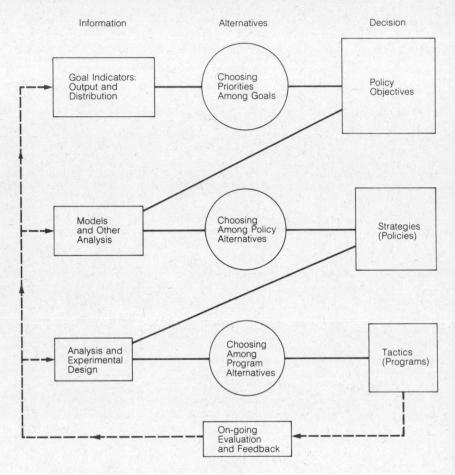

# Setting Policy Objectives

At the highest level of decision-making, the system set out in Chart 1 calls for choosing alternatives and establishing priorities from a wide variety of public concerns—to arrive at policy objectives. These objectives are *general* statements of intent directed towards achievement in particular goal areas. But to be operationally relevant, they must be more specific than the goal perceptions that prompted them. By and large, discussion about goals tends to be too vague and philosophical to provide a solid basis for identifying policy objectives.

### GOALS

Abstract goals such as freedom, equity, and justice have been articulated in many constitutions, charters, and treaties throughout history, and have reflected some of man's most noble and civilized aspirations. But while such broad generalizations may achieve wide acceptance as principles, they do not provide operational guidelines for policy formation.

The Canadian Charter of Human Rights, for example, sets out certain political, legal, and linguistic rights. This declaration is, in most respects, equivalent to an elaboration of goals. But rights, like goals, may remain only words. They do not *automatically* lead to policies that ensure their realization by all sectors of the population.

In a different area, the 1970 White Paper on *Foreign Policy for Canadians* contains a brief chapter on National Aims, which notes that "for the majority, the aim appears to be to attain the highest level of prosperity consistent with Canada's political preservation as an independent state."[1] This statement was not necessarily intended to reflect *the goal* of foreign policy, but if it were, it would pose difficult problems of interpretation. For example, is the success of a foreign aid policy measured by its contribution to *our* prosperity, and is it our present or our future prosperity? Is cultural independence a component of political independence? Is there a trade-off between less growth or income and more political independence?

These illustrations are set out here only to suggest the complexity and limitations of goal-setting. Goals that seem reasonable, desirable, and universally acceptable are almost invariably too general to provide an adequate basis for policy. As the specification of general goals into detailed objectives begins, the controversy about interpretation arises. The conflict of interest that is at the heart of the political system extends beyond the problem of elaborating the goal to everyone's or no one's satisfaction; it involves choosing among alternative goals and establishing priorities and time preferences.

> . . . there is no unit of measure that will establish the relative benefits of education against those of health or national security. . . . Choices at this high level of aggregation must be developed on the basis of public preferences that largely find their expression in the political process.[2]

The formulation of a grand design of national goals and priorities is beyond the responsibility of any single level of government. Nevertheless, highly abstract goals—in the sense of broad focal points of society's concerns—have often provided rallying points for public action. What is needed is a systematic way of channeling the energy they generate, and the aspirations they represent, into guidelines for policy.

## GOAL AREAS

Public concern is usually focused on a limited number of issues at any one point in time. Yet the process of government decision-making stretches potentially across the whole spectrum of public interest and welfare. Chart 2 illustrates the breadth of our political, economic, and social concerns, and provides a simple and admittedly arbitrary arrangement of goal areas. It is designed to include all present and future policy concerns. However, to indicate that the framework is *open-ended*—that is, to provide for concerns not yet perceived—it is deliberately entitled "Illustrative Goal Areas".

The various goal areas in the chart are intended to be readily identifiable and self-contained, although inevitably there are strong interrelationships among

# Chart 2.
## Illustrative Goal Areas

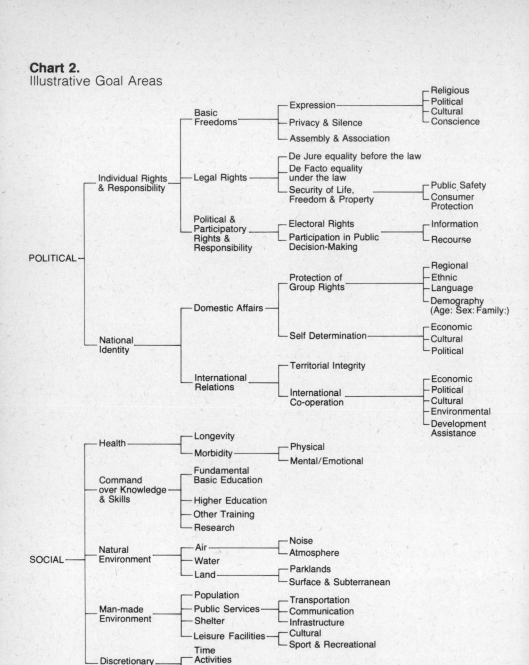

them. It is highly important that these *interrelationships* be recognized; they create a major hazard for the best policy intentions. One very good example is provided by the U.S. Interstate and Defense Highway System, which

> . . . the twenty-first century will almost certainly judge to have had more influence on the shape and development of American cities, the distribution of population within metropolitan areas and across the nation as a whole, the location of industry and various kinds of employment opportunities (and, through all these, immense influence on race relations and the welfare of black Americans) than any initiative of the middle third of the twentieth century. . . . It has been, it is, the largest public works program in history. Activities such as urban renewal, public housing, community development, and the like are reduced to mere digressions when compared to the extraordinary impact of the highway program.
> . . . Highways have never been a subject of any very great interest among persons given to writing or speculating about government. Certainly they have rarely been associated with social welfare issues, save in the early days of "getting the farmer out of the mud". . . .
> Surely it is possible to hope for something more. Government must seek out its hidden policies, raising them to a level of consciousness and acceptance—or rejection—and acknowledge the extraordinary range of contradictions that are typically encountered. (To the frequent question "Why don't government programs work?" it is often a truthful answer that they do work. It is just that so frequently the effect of a "hidden" program cancels out the avowed one.) Surely also it is possible to hope for a career civil service that is not only encouraged but required to see their activities in the largest possible scope. . . . but for many a long decade the word from the political world on high was to stick to building roads and to see that not too much sand was used in the concrete.[3]

These interrelationships, which may be complex and very powerful, are not shown by the classification used in Chart 2. A systems framework that delineated the linkages among goal areas would in theory be preferable but, by and large, the models and data essential for such an approach have not yet been developed. The categories shown in Chart 2 are elaborated merely to provide a starting point for organizing the knowledge required for the development of measures—which we will refer to as *Goal Indicators*—to serve as links between abstract goals and operational policy objectives.

## GOAL INDICATORS

During the Great Depression, Canada had widespread unemployment and a drastic decline in national production. At that time there were no comprehensive statistics of either unemployment or Gross National Product. In the absence of reliable and aggregated measures of the "slack" in the economy or the course of overall economic trends, the development of national economic policies to alleviate the severe problems of the 1930s was handicapped. It was not until after the Second World War that the national accounts were first published and comprehensive labour force and unemployment figures were regularly available in Canada. Now, of course, it would be unthinkable to develop national economic policy without reference to such measures.

The concerns of our society have greatly broadened in recent years. Economic growth and stabilization are still important but, as we have noted earlier, a variety of other issues have come to demand increasing attention. Unfortunately, the choice of objectives from almost unlimited possible goal areas requires far more than assessment by governments of electoral preferences. That kind of evaluation could be made by public opinion polls. The Gordian knot at this level of decision-making is a tangle of priorities and complex ramifications of choosing certain objectives over others.

Today's choice and ranking of alternative objectives are largely based on information about yesterday, but they will affect tomorrow. There are lags in perceiving problems, in responding to them, and in creating change. Time is a critical variable in the decision equation. While the real world situation frequently demands instant action, many of the issues facing decision-makers are here today and *not* gone tomorrow. The choice of policy objectives and success in meeting them require a longer-range view—a perspective that can only be attained by continuous monitoring of social change.

The goal areas include interests and concerns of both individuals and governments. In Canada, private decisions still govern a large share of total activity. For private industry, the market mechanism, even with its imperfections, provides some insight into "revealed" preferences, as well as guidance for resource allocation. The government sector, on the other hand, enjoys no comparable self-regulatory machinery. What is needed are more and better signposts along the route that society is following.

The Council, therefore, strongly recommends the development of a comprehensive set of statistical measures to monitor the changing conditions of our society over a broad spectrum of concerns. We have purposely rejected the term "social indicators" for these measures because of the wide variety of interpretations of that term and the increasing semantic confusion which has arisen. Instead, we call these *Goal Indicators*. We define *Goal Indicators* as quantitative-qualitative information that can be collected on a time series basis to measure a relevant and significant dimension of a specified goal area—for example, health, education, or public safety.

In a sense, we are advocating the development of an array of statistical indicators for social and political activities that would parallel some of the frequently used and widely understood measures of economic concern, such as Gross National Product and the unemployment rate. The information that now exists in many goal areas is inadequate to answer some of the simplest but most fundamental questions. How much have children learned? How many people have been lifted out of poverty? How healthy is the population? The answers to these questions will not be found in statistics about the number of teachers or doctors or about the expenditures of welfare agencies.

Major policy changes in the past have frequently come about only in response to some dramatic event like the launching of a Sputnik or to mounting evidence of such things as environmental degradation. A situation may need to develop critical proportions before it looms large enough to obtain the level of "visibility" that commands public attention. A continuous monitoring system would promote such "high visibility", help to generate concern, and lay the basis for appropriate and timely action before problems reach crisis dimensions.

For each goal area, there should be indicators of two types:
(1) *Goal Output Indicators* — to give a broad, summary view of levels of, and changes in, output;
(2) *Goal Distribution Indicators* — to show distributions of the aggregate output indicators among regions, income groups, ethnic groups, and so forth.

For example, Chart 2 indicates that the goal area "health" (which is too broad for any summary measures — at least at our present level of knowledge) consists of two rather different specific concerns: length of life, and number of days free of illness or disability. The latter in turn might be further subdivided into physical disability and mental disability. At this degree of disaggregation, the possibilities for monitoring these particular features of society become more clear. Here are some examples of *Goal Output Indicators* that might be relevant in the three subcategories of the goal area "health":

| | |
|---|---|
| Longevity | Infant mortality rate |
| | Live birth rate |
| | Death rate from: |
| |     Accidents |
| |     Degenerate diseases of old age |
| |     Acute/chronic diseases |
| Days free of physical illness or disability | Days hospitalized or abed |
| | Days off work/school |
| | Level of nutrition |
| | Level of fitness |
| Days free of mental/ emotional illness or disability | Days in psychiatric institutions |
| | Number of defective/retarded children |
| | Suicide rate |

In choosing *Goal Output Indicators* the emphasis is on measuring the "outputs" of our health and social system — infant mortality, for example, rather than expenditures on prenatal care or the number of obstetricians and pediatricians; the level of nutrition, rather than expenditures on food.

However, these summary measures are not by themselves sufficient in a highly diverse and pluralist nation. If an objective of public policy is to promote the well-being of people, one still must ask: Which people?

In general, this concern for distribution has been inadequately served by both policy and data. In the economic sphere, for example, emphasis on broad measures like Gross National Product may hide far more than it reveals. It permits, and possibly encourages, the illusion that rising income is equitably shared by all income classes, regions, or ethnic groups. More and better data are increasingly available on the subject of income distribution in Canada but, in a variety of other important public policy areas, the distributional implications are virtually unexplored.

There will be difficulties in this type of analysis, but clearly we cannot expect to achieve a higher degree of social equity in Canada without some very concentrated efforts to explore these aspects of policy. There is a real need for more and better information directing attention to inadequate housing, health, and education among minority groups; to equality of political rights; and to

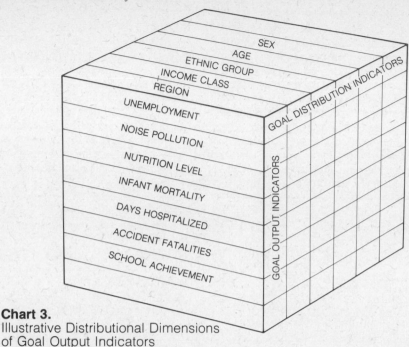

**Chart 3.**
Illustrative Distributional Dimensions
of Goal Output Indicators

greater opportunities for the upward movement of disadvantaged people on the social and economic ladders.

Moreover, for many important government programs there has been little attempt to explore what is called fiscal equity in government programs—the net balance of two vital questions: Who pays? Who benefits? For this reason we lay particular emphasis on the examination of at least some distributive aspects of manpower and education policy.

The Council urges that those goal areas in which distribution is a key concern should be monitored by *Goal Distribution Indicators.* For each *Goal Output Indicator* there are many possible distributional dimensions. Income class would be relevant for all goal areas; others, such as region and ethnicity, are of special interest to Canadians. But in particular instances, age or sex may be highly relevant. Chart 3 illustrates some of the possible distributional dimensions for a number of *Goal Output Indicators.*

Some of these indicators show that not all Canadians share in national achievements, or even have the *opportunity* to share. All public programs and policies have some distributional impact and, in some measure, have contributed to the existing pattern. Governments may attempt to alter this allocation by fiscal measures—through the selective use of revenue and expenditure powers. The income tax schedule is used not only to raise revenue, but to change the distribution of income. Public expenditures that concentrate on particular groups or sections of the population—for example, through veterans' hospitals, youth services, and legal aid programs—have a specific and intended distributional impact.

On the other hand, many policies and programs have a distributional impact, which is a side effect of actions intended to accomplish other ends. For example, monetary restraint aimed directly at moderating inflation tends to bear relatively quickly and heavily on residential construction, and more particularly on low-cost housing. Distributional side effects are far from uncommon and they can be large. Clearly, it is important to know more about effects—both intended and unintended—at the policy and the program levels of decision-making.

## SOME CHARACTERISTICS OF GOAL INDICATORS

Our primary concern here is to urge the adoption of the *principle* of developing *Goal Indicators*. Although a far-ranging discussion is under way among the experts, and there is not as yet a consensus about the specifications of such measures, we would be remiss if we did not set out what we believe should be some of their important characteristics:

— The indicators should be relatively few in number for each goal area, and each should provide a broad, summary picture of the area of concern.

— They should take the form of statistical time series that would show the state of the goal area at regular time intervals. The time interval would depend largely on the rate of change in the area under observation. A monthly measure of park and recreation facilities is unnecessary; a pollution measure every decennial census would be inadequate.

— Some experts hold that these indicators should be designed in such a way that a change in one direction can always be interpreted as a ''good'' thing; a change in the other as a ''bad'' thing. But perception of what is ''good'' or ''bad'' may vary among individuals and from one time or place to another. One has only to think of the controversy surrounding the question of population growth in developed and developing countries over the past quarter century or so. We believe simply that *Goal Indicators* should focus on the condition (and change in condition) of society and not be linked to a particular judgment of whether such a change is good or bad.

— The aim should be to measure the *real output* of the system—what the health, education, and environmental ''systems'' are actually producing; namely, states of health, levels of skill and knowledge, amount of leisure, extent of pollution, the incidence and degree of alienation, and infringement of rights and freedoms. However, in the short run, since there is not as yet even a conceptual framework for measuring real output in many areas, less adequate substitute measures or proxies will have to be developed but used cautiously as a guide to policy decisions.

Perhaps an illustration of the difficulty of choosing an output measure or even an appropriate proxy would be useful. As noted earlier, measures of output of the health system should take into account length of life and physical as well as emotional illness and distress—in other words, both the mortality and morbidity aspects of health. For this purpose, data have been developed on life expectancy free of bed-disability and institutionalization.[4] Such a measure requires some definition of a ''bed-disability-free day'', which includes or excludes from the count a day in bed with a cold, a day at home but not in bed, or a day at work with a cold (although equally severe colds may give rise to all three responses by different persons).

In the attempt to pin down an operational measure that corresponds to the conceptual framework, there will have to be compromises in the interests of feasibility. For example, given the present state of the art, it would be unreasonable to expect that the first or even the twenty-first attempt to measure illness would take account of differences in pain-threshold levels or in the behavioural response of individuals to similar illnesses.

The variety of statistical techniques that might be used to construct *Goal Distribution Indicators* will obviously complicate the task of selecting appropriate criteria. Even after some initial statistical and conceptual hurdles are passed, both the output and distribution measures will need to remain under review to ensure that they continue to be relevant—that is, to measure what needs to be measured and in the best possible way.

## POLICY OBJECTIVES AND PRIORITIES

We have argued earlier that the formulation of a grand design of national goals and priorities is beyond the responsibility of any *single* level of government. However, as the decision-making framework shown in Chart 1 suggests, at *each* level of government, a systematic effort should be made to identify the objectives of public policy. In a democratic society these choices are made through the political process, not by special interest groups or experts. But we think that the use of *Goal Output Indicators* and *Goal Distribution Indicators* offers significant possibilities for sharpening perceptions of society's needs. A monitoring system that would assist the public and the decision-maker in recognizing the issues and problems would act as an early warning system emphasizing anticipatory *action* rather than belated and often costly *reaction* to changes in society. It should help to provide a much needed bridge between the broad, abstract *goals* and *operational guidelines* for policy.

The employment of *Goal Indicators* will most certainly *not* reduce the role of judgment or compromise in choosing policy objectives and priorities. Priorities are set by the "negotiating" or political process. We hope only to add to the information content of this process. Nor should it be claimed that the use of such indicators will necessarily make judgments about priorities, or the development of consensus about choices of policy objectives, any easier. Indeed there are undoubtedly times when the identification of specific objectives may increase the clash of opinions or even paralyse action. But, in general, the risks of not bringing knowledge to bear on the choice of objectives are, we believe, much greater.

The setting of objectives is, at the political level, a question of consensus and compromise. Their selection, which involves the melding of competing claims and interests, is an expression of governments' conception of the public interest and their perception of the public will. It should permit a process of clarification of such objectives.

The reduction of regional income disparities may, for example, be said to be a national goal, but this statement is too general to provide a meaningful basis for the design of policies that can be made operational. In fact, it is clear that there are a number of possible objectives depending on our definition of "region" and "income" disparities. Narrowing regional differences may mean the differences between provinces or between smaller regions within each province. It could even relate to urban and rural differences. The narrowing of income disparities could be interpreted as the establishment of some minimum income level for individuals or families, or of similar income distributions in each region. On the other hand, it may be interpreted as a reallocation of productive and income-generating capacity of both capital and labour. These possible interpretations do not necessarily suggest different and discrete objectives; in fact, there is a significant degree of overlap. But at the next level of decision-making, the choice of alternative strategies—the relative importance of income transfer mechanisms, investment and industrial development, manpower training or mobility assistance—depends on a clear understanding of the objectives and the priorities assigned to each.

In actual practice the selection of the policy objectives takes place within the constraint of limited financial and technical resources, and in an environment of uncertainty and change. It requires a view of the problem as it exists, and as it may develop in the future; an assessment of the scope for, and prospective gains from, each additional category of expenditure; and frequently a possible trade-off between short-term and long-term results. One important function of the feedback network at that level (shown in Chart 1 and discussed later in this chapter) is to reinforce the tentative nature of objectives by providing for their continued reassessment in the light of increased knowledge and changes in the environment. The realities of uncertainty and change require this responsive dynamic approach at every level of decision-making.

## Choosing Among Policy Alternatives

Choosing a priority among a variety of goals—the first level of decision-making in our simplified system—supplies the *objective* for policy. What policy options or what broad guidelines for action are to be used to implement these objectives? The choice here is illustrated by the following example.

Many Canadians feel that the reduction, if not the elimination, of poverty is, or ought to be, a priority objective of government policy. In our *Fifth Annual Review,* we set out evidence to support the view that the distribution of income in Canada leaves a substantial number of Canadians in poverty. Generally speaking, there are two broad policy alternatives or strategies for reducing poverty—income transfers, and investment in "human" capital accompanied by efforts to open up wider income-earning opportunities for the poor. These are two very different policy options.

Transfers of income via the tax or welfare system can be provided by legislation and have a financial impact on some or all of the poverty population in a relatively short period of time. Regardless of how this redistribution is effected, there will be some side effects on incentives to work, incentives to move, and (through children) on poverty in the next generation. But there may be little direct effect on the education or skills of the labour force. The process of redistribution via income transfers will have to continue and even be increased at regular intervals to maintain the relative position of those who remain without skills and earning capacity.

Investment in human capital is a very different approach—involving the upgrading of skills and opportunities by providing training or mobility or access to improved health and housing facilities. It is concerned with developing qualities and incentives as well as providing opportunities and removing barriers. This would provide routes out of poverty into rewarding and productive employment. It is a selective approach. To succeed, there must be a real possibility that the "target population" can participate in, and gain from entering, the labour force or move to more rewarding occupations. Investment strategies are not necessarily appropriate in every poverty situation, but for those who are affected, these policies reach beyond the financial symptoms into its real causes. And some anti-poverty programs, such as housing and health facilities for the aged or disabled, reflect both transfer and investment elements.

In the short run at least, the budgetary costs of the investment approach are likely to be significantly higher than those of the transfer mechanism. Income transfers are quickly implemented, whereas the income effect of investment in human capital is largely realized over the long run.

How does one choose? The decision may depend in whole or in part on a political or value choice. But careful objective analysis can assist judgment in the selection of one or other alternative. Indeed, the first questions to be asked in deciding upon a strategy or combination of strategies are very straightforward. Who is in the poverty group? What are their characteristics? If a large proportion of those in poverty were able to enter the labour force with suitable training, more weight would be given to the investment strategy. Alternatively, if a very high proportion turned out to be in the older age group or disabled in some way, emphasis could be shifted towards the transfer strategy. The actual choice of strategy, in this case, is unlikely to be of an "either/or" variety. Any effective attack on the problem would undoubtedly require some mix of transfers and investment. But the weight placed on each would determine the general thrust or, as we have termed it, the strategy.

In many areas, particularly those relating to behavioural response and motivation, knowledge about the social system, and the impact of alternative strategies on it, is primitive. The development of models and analysis for experimentation, evaluation, and redesign of policy will involve a commitment to extending knowledge and information. The process of social change will not be unravelled easily.

To sum up, in each policy situation there are alternative ways of meeting objectives. Some of these may be politically, technologically or financially impossible, but the essence of policy formation is the selection and combination of strategies aimed at meeting objectives, while considering the widest possible range of alternatives. At some point, the "costs" of searching for alternatives will outweigh the benefits of finding the "best". An important element in these costs is the time factor—the delay in reaching and implementing decisions. This delay gives rise to uncertainties in the private sector which may impede effective decision-making.

Thus, judgment enters at every stage: what alternatives to consider; how far and how long to pursue the analysis of costs and benefits; and what interrelationships to examine. "Final answers" in the shape of formulas—simple or complex—will not replace the crucial element of judgment, nor necessarily generate creative and imaginative alternatives in the decision-making process.

## Choosing and Evaluating Programs

The third and final level of decision-making (see Chart 1) is tactical and deals with operational questions. What, in fact, is to be done? How is it to be done? What is the likely result? This is the point at which alternative programs should be designed and evaluated, resource requirements estimated, possible outcomes anticipated, and expenditures allocated through the budgetary process.

A poverty strategy, for example, becomes *operational* in the choice among alternative (but closely competing) programs that further the intended objective. The tactical alternatives in a strategy to reduce poverty are numerous, but here are a few selected examples:

— a transfer strategy might include programs like selective guaranteed income, welfare payments, unemployment insurance, and pensions;

— an investment strategy might cover programs like industrial or institutional training and retraining, basic skill upgrading, community development, provision of child care services, and social animation.

Knowledge about interrelationships and spillovers provides a better basis for designing a program network in which these effects reinforce, not impede, progress towards objectives. There is, of course, an important element of judgment here too. At some depth of analysis, almost everything can be seen to relate to everything else; at that point the analysis sinks under its own weight. Long before then, however, many simple but important interrelationships can be identified, anticipated in the design of programs, and accounted for in their evaluation.

Some may suggest that this articulation is impossible or unnecessary. But governments propose acts which, in the absence of such knowledge, must rely on traditional views, hunch or guesswork. In many instances, particularly those relating to social policy, the behavioural relationships and motivations are too complex for intuitive judgments. While the factual content of public policy and programs may not be the main or ultimate criterion of many public decisions, it can scarcely be doubted that more knowledge about how the system works would lead to better decisions.

## Learning From Experience: Feedback Mechanisms

The life of a decision-maker would certainly be a great deal easier, though perhaps far less stimulating, if society were static and unchanging. But it is not. Rather, society is constantly changing, partly as a result of decisions made by governments. In these circumstances, there is no guarantee that the anticipated or designated outcome of particular policies or programs will be attained, no matter how well designed they may be. What is required is a systematic way of learning from experience that will bridge the gap between today and tomorrow.

The system shown in Chart 1 provides for this. It shows a feedback of information into the decision-making process from on-going evaluation of programs. Where the outcome is not what was expected or wanted, the decision-maker has the opportunity to adapt or revise programs, policies, or objectives.

"Feedback" may also perform a slightly different function. Ideally, *Goal Output Indicators* and *Goal Distribution Indicators* hold, as it were, a mirror to society, and policy objectives are developed in response to perceived needs. On the basis of such objectives, strategies can then be evolved and programs designed. But program initiatives are aimed at changing some aspect of society, and this change will subsequently be reflected in the *Goal Indicators*,[5] stimulating a process of continuous reassessment and, where necessary, realignment of objectives, strategy and programs.

Systematic feedback mechanisms in major policy and program areas significantly increase the prospect of attaining policy objectives. There should therefore be legislative provisions for continuing evaluation, and for regular published reviews of the results of particular programs at stated intervals.

Much of the discussion thus far seems to suggest that we can allocate or reallocate public expenditures from scratch. Actually, in any year, the number of new policy creations is not large, and annual additions to public expenditure programs are only a small share of the total outstanding. If improvements in the decision-making process had to wait for the advent of new programs, any large impact would come only over a long period. A great deal could be done, however, to improve even incremental programs by introducing evaluation and feedback.

### Footnotes

1. Department of External Affairs, *Foreign Policy for Canadians* (Ottawa: Queen's Printer, 1970), p.10.

2. U.S. Joint Economic Committee, *The Analysis and Evaluation of Public Expenditures: The PPB System,* a compendium of papers submitted to the Subcommittee of Economy in Government, 91st Congress, 1st Session (Washington: U.S. Government Printing Office, 1969), Vol. 3, p.939.

3. Daniel P. Moynihan, "Policy vs. Program in the '70s", *The Public Interest,* No.20, (Summer, 1970), pp.94-95.

4. See, for example, U.S. Department of Health, Education and Welfare, *Toward a Social Report* (Washington: U.S. Government Printing Office, 1969), pp.99-100.

5. A *Goal Indicator* that measures the changes taking place in a particular goal area reflects all elements bearing on it, not just public policy. This raises the possibility that public policy may be credited with more or less success in generating change than is actually the case. Part of the task of analysis should, in fact, be to clarify the influences of various factors.

## E. J. MISHAN
# The A B C of Cost-Benefit

Cost-benefit analyses are in high fashion. Scarcely a week goes by without an authoritative voice asserting that, in connection with some project or other, a thorough cost-benefit study is needed. No matter how heated a controversy, a government spokesman can still the protests of the critics and be assured of a respectful silence simply by announcing that a cost-benefit analysis is in progress. The popular belief is that this novel technique provides a 'scientific' assessment of the social value of a project or at least an 'objective' assessment. True, if every benefit and every cost associated with a proposed project or investment is properly evaluated and brought into the calculus in a systematic way, the resulting sum—whether an excess of benefits over cost or the other way round—can hardly be challenged. Yet, such a statement is not much more than a tautology. The fact is that evaluating 'properly' all relevant economic data is a guiding ideal, not a current practice. For, although the procedure used in cost-benefit analysis follows certain conventions, the out-come may vary according to the economist in charge of the study, because of differences in judgment with respect both to *what* is to be included and *how* it is to be evaluated. With the passage of time, one can hope that such differences of judgment will narrow but, in the meantime, and in the absence of a consensus, the individual judgment of whoever is in charge is an important factor in the outcome.

One question that a cost-benefit study sets out to answer is whether or not a particular investment project, say project A, should be started. More generally, the question is whether a number of projects, A, B, C, D, etc. should be introduced and, if the investible funds are limited, which one, or which two or more, should be selected. Another question to which cost-benefit analysis addresses itself is that of determining the level at which a plant should operate, or the combination of outputs it should produce. I follow custom, however, in confining my attention largely to the former questions concerning the choice of investment projects.

## Costs and Benefits

In order to appreciate some of the issues raised in the technique of cost-benefit analysis, we can ask the question: Why cost-benefit analysis? Why not plain honest-to-goodness profit and loss accounting? The simple answer is that what counts as a benefit or a loss to one part of the economy—to one or more persons or groups—does not necessarily count as a benefit or loss to the economy as a whole. And in cost-benefit analysis we are concerned with the economy as a whole; with the welfare of a defined society, and not any smaller part of it. A private enterprise, or even a public enterprise, comprises only a part of the economy, often a very small part. More important, whatever the means it employs in pursuing its objectives, the private enterprise, at least, is guided by ordinary commercial criteria that require revenues to exceed costs. The fact that its activities are guided by the profit motive, however, is not to deny that a large number of people other than its shareholders benefit from it. It confers benefits on its employees, on consumers and—through the taxes it pays—on the general public. Yet, the benefits enjoyed by these others continue to exist only so long as they coincide with profits to the enterprise. Without a public subsidy the enterprise will not survive if it continues to make losses. If it is to survive as a private concern and to expand, it must, then, over a period of time, produce profits large enough either to attract investors or to finance its own expansion.

There is, of course, the metaphor of the invisible hand; the *deus ex machina* discovered by Adam Smith which directs the forces of private greed so as ultimately to confer benefits on society. And one can, indeed, lay down simple and sufficient conditions under which the uncompromising pursuit of profit acts always to serve the public interest. These conditions can be boiled down to two: that all effects relevant to the welfare of individuals be priced through the market, and that perfect competition prevail in all economic activities. Once we depart from this ideal economic setting, however, the set of outputs and prices to which the economy tends may not serve the public so well as some other set of outputs and prices. In addition to this possible misallocation of resources among the goods being produced, it is possible also that certain goods which can be economically justified do not get produced at all, while others which cannot be economically justified continue to be produced. Again, certain goods having beneficial, though unpriced, 'spill-over effects' qualify for production on economic grounds, notwithstanding which they cannot be produced at a profit. The reverse is also true, and more significant: profitable commercial activities sometimes produce noxious spill-over effects to such an extent that on a more comprehensive pricing scheme they would be unable to continue.

The economist engaged in the cost-benefit appraisal of a project is not, in essence then, asking a different sort of question than the accountant of a private firm. Rather, the same sort of question is asked about a wider group, society as a whole, and is asked more searchingly. Instead of asking whether the owners of an enterprise will be made better off by the firm's engaging in one activity rather than another, the economist asks whether *society* as a whole will be made better off by undertaking this project rather than not undertaking it, or by undertaking, instead, any of a number of other projects.

Broadly speaking, for the more precise concept of revenue to the private firm, the economist substitutes the less precise, yet meaningful, concept of *social benefit*. For the costs of the private firm, the economist will substitute the concept of *opportunity cost*—or the social value forgone when resources are moved away from other economic activities and into the construction and running of the project in question. For the profit of the firm, the economist will substitute the concept of *excess social benefit over cost*, or some related concept used in an investment criterion.

However, it cannot be stressed too strongly that the result even of an ideally conducted cost-benefit analysis does not of itself constitute a prescription for society. Since it simulates the effects of an ideal price system, an ideal cost-benefit analysis is subject also to its limitations. This means that any adopted criterion of a cost-benefit analysis requiring, as all such criteria do, that benefits exceed cost, can be vindicated only by a social judgment that an economic arrangement which *can* make everyone better off is an improvement. Such a judgment does *not* require that everyone actually be made better off, or even that nobody be made worse off. The likelihood—which, in practice, is a virtual certainty—that some people, occasionally most people, will be made worse off by introducing the investment project in question is tacitly acknowledged. A project that is adjudged feasible by reference to a cost-benefit analysis is, therefore, quite consistent with an economic arrangement which makes the rich richer and the poor poorer. It is consistent also with manifest inequity. For an enterprise that is an attractive proposition by the lights of a cost-benefit calculation may be one that offers increased profits and pleasures to one group, in the pursuit of which substantial injury may be suffered by other groups.

In order, then, for a mooted enterprise to be socially approved, it is not enough simply to show that the outcome of an ideal cost-benefit analysis is positive. It must also be shown that the resulting distributional changes are not regressive, and that no gross inequities are perpetrated.

Sophisticated cost-benefit analysis clearly requires a high order of skill in the application of quantitative techniques. More important still, it requires thorough familiarity with the economics of resource allocation. For it is more important to be measuring the right thing in a crude sort of way than to be measuring the wrong thing with impressive refinement. This dictum will be more readily appreciated after we have touched upon some of the problems that arise in the application of cost-benefit methods, problems which fall conveniently into three categories. In the largest group are the problems of designating the relevant magnitudes and evaluating them. Having evaluated the benefits and costs over time there is, secondly, the problem of choosing an investment criterion to enable us to select and rank alternative investment projects. There is, however, always some uncertainty about the expected values of future benefits and costs. This leads to the third problem: that of making allowance for uncertainty.

## What and How to Measure?

We can divide this group into four sub-groups, beginning, first, with the question of relevance.

### RELEVANCE

The treatment of direct taxation offers a simple instance. Whether a domestic enterprise is private or public, the net benefit in any year is taken to be equal *not* to net profit or net benefit, less tax, but to net social profit or benefit *before* tax. For the tax payments are simply that portion of the net benefit that is transferred, through the government machine, to the rest of the community. If, however, the enterprise is established in a foreign country the taxes paid to the foreign government *do* represent a transfer of net benefits to foreigners. Consequently, such taxes have to be deducted from the net profits or net benefits available to the home country. Moreover, if new investments in a particular foreign country have the incidental effect of lowering the rate of return there on previous investments from the home country, the losses suffered on all these older investments have to be deducted from the net profit or net benefit on the prospective new investments.

Other instances will illuminate the nature of this kind of problem. Consider investment in a railway. The rise in the rents of sites near the railway station might, on first thoughts, be regarded as one of the benefits. But the rise in such rents is nothing more than the capitalized value of the annual worth of the extra convenience provided by sites that are close to the new railway station. If the cost-benefit analysis has calculated future benefits year by year, as it ought, this increase in annual worth has already been included. Adding the rise in capital values would, therefore, amount to counting the same benefit twice, once as an annual flow and then, again, as the capital value of that flow.

Again, suppose an increase in the retail sales of a small town, the result of the movement of staff associated with the establishment of a new airport in the vicinity. The increase in profits cannot be counted as benefits of the new airport. Most, or all of it, is simply a transfer of purchasing power from one part of the country to another; in so far as sales and profits rise in the new town they fall off in other parts of the country.

## SHADOW OR ACCOUNTING PRICES

In the absence of spill-over effects (which I discuss presently) and excise taxes, a highly competitive full-employment economy would, it is believed, provide an ideal background to a cost-benefit analysis, inasmuch as the 'true' or *opportunity,* cost of all productive services would be equal to their market prices. This is valid, however, only if the owner of such services, a skilled workman, say, is indifferent as between one occupation and another. But such an assumption is too restrictive. In general, therefore, the economist will conceive of the true cost of a man's labour as equal to the value it produces in the occupation from which it is to be transferred *plus* any additional sum above his existing wage that is required to induce a worker to transfer his labour into the new project.[1] This direct method of calculation provides a guiding rule for estimating the 'shadow prices' of all productive services needed in any investment project.

It follows, therefore, that it is wrong to value productive services at their *market* prices if they are transferred from the production of goods subject to excise taxes. If, say, tax added 50 per cent to the price of a competitively-produced good, the value associated with the labour of a worker to be withdrawn from the production of this good would be 50 per cent more than his wage-rate there—at least, if we assume the labourer to be indifferent as between his present occupation and that of the investment project in question. If he is not indifferent, but prefers his existing occupation, then the premium necessary to induce him to move into the new enterpreise has (as indicated above) to be added.

Again, if a man is unemployed, his labour is not to be valued at his unemployment pay, say £10 a week, since this is not the value of his current work, but simply a transfer payment to him from the rest of the community.[2] It may be that his apparent contribution to national income is zero. However, he himself may place some value on his 'non-market activities' or, if entirely idle, he may enjoy his idleness to the extent that some minimum sum, say £12 a week, has to be paid to induce him to accept work in a new enterprise. The true cost to the economy of his work in the enterprise is this minimum sum of £12 less the £10 transfer payment, or £2. For, in agreeing to work for £12, he no longer receives his unemployment pay of £10, which now reverts to the rest of the community. Since the cost to the community of engaging his labour is only £2 a week, there is a gain if his weekly labour adds a value in excess of £2.

In general, however, new investment in one sector of the economy has repercussions in all sectors. The total numbers brought into employment as a result of this initial investment, and their costs to the economy, can be estimated, provided that the average unemployment rate for each sector and/or region is available. For there is a known relationship between the unemployment rate in a sector, and/or area, and the probability that any newly-employed labour there will come from the unemployment pool. (In the United States, for example, this probability approaches 100 per cent when the percentage unemployment in a sector or area is about 25 per cent). Investment projects which would not be economically feasible in conditions of virtually full employment may, of course, become so in conditions of low employment.

For a final example of shadow prices, consider the imports of goods by countries that are chronically short of foreign exchange. If the additional imports of some material, say copper, can be afforded *only* by relinquishing other imports to an equal value in terms of the scarce currency, the shadow price of these additional copper imports has to be taken as equal to the domestic value of the particular goods that are no longer imported. For this is the value that has to be forgone in order to obtain the additional copper. If, on the other hand, the additional copper imports are paid for by additional exports, their shadow price is the domestic value of the particular goods exported to raise the needed foreign currency.

## SPILL-OVER EFFECTS

The pricing of 'intangibles' or 'spill-over effects' can be thought of as the limiting case of a shadow price. For the market prices of spill-over effects are generally zero. In the manufacture and use of certain goods, incidental by-products are generated such as smoke, pollution, noise and so on[3] which are not recorded by the market. However, those people who have to put up with these noxious effects are not compensated in any way. It is the task of the economist, therefore, to bring them, as Pigou would have said, 'into relation with the measuring rod of money.'

The principle used is the straightforward one of accepting the scale of values of the people directly concerned. The loss of any good—including such 'free' goods as quiet, clean air, pleasant scenery, etc.—is to be valued, therefore, at the minimum sum people would be willing to accept as just compensation for their loss. These spill-over costs, together with resource costs, have to be less than the value of the total benefits if an investment is to be accepted as economically feasible.

Although the principle is straightforward enough, difficulties are encountered in obtaining reliable approximations to the value of spill-over effects. In attempting to evaluate aircraft noise, for example, the Roskill Commission made use (among other information) of replies to a questionnaire by a sample of those householders who would have to move if their neighbourhood were to be taken over for the third airport site. The key question was framed as follows:

> Suppose that your house was wanted to form part of a large development scheme and the developer offered to buy it from you, what price would be just high enough to compensate you for leaving this house (flat) and moving to another area?

A number of weaknesses are apparent in the Commission's procedure.[4] First, although 8 per cent of the householders interviewed asserted that they would not move at any price, the compensatory sum attributed to them was an arbitrary £5,000. One suspects that a good interviewer might well have elicited a finite sum from them, though one probably well in excess of £5,000. If, however, it were true only of a single case that nothing money could buy would suffice to compensate for the losses suffered in moving from the neighbourhood, then, strictly speaking, no cost-benefit analysis would admit a third London airport.

Secondly, no allowance was made for the disturbance suffered by people subjected to aerial disturbance below 35 NNI (NNI is an abbreviation for noise and number index and was developed as an index of aircraft annoyance by the Committee on the Problem of Noise). Symmetry of treatment would require that no benefits be entered for people whose enjoyment of an air journey fell below a particular point on some arbitrary index. No physical measure of pleasure is available, however, so that no matter how impulsive the decision, and no matter how marginal the benefit, each trip was valued at its full fare. Finally, the framing of the question gave the impression to householders that only a limited move was contemplated—a question of making land available for some new development. The disruption involved in parting from old friends, in changing jobs, in moving the children to new schools, may not have occurred to them. What is more, even if the purpose of the questionnaire had been made perfectly explicit, the compensatory sum required by the family would vary with circumstances about which it could not hope to have accurate information. The sum would be smallest if as quiet a neighbourhood could be found only a short distance away. It would be larger if the number of such neighbourhoods within commuting distance of work and schooling were limited. And it would be largest if no comparable neighbourhoods could be found anywhere. Again, the compensatory sum would vary according to the spread and intensity of traffic noise expected elsewhere over the future, being lower for expectations of a gradual abatement than for the reverse, and more likely, expectations. If, however, the spread of noise were expected to engulf the original neighbourhood in any case, then, with respect to the noise factor, it would not matter where the family moved, and the sum would be nil—notwithstanding which the family's welfare would decline over time, though not as a result alone of the establishment of a third London airport.

## THE PROBLEM OF CONSTRAINTS

In any cost-benefit analysis there will be a number of political or institutional conditions, more or less restrictive, which the economist has to accept. The issues they raise can be illustrated by the unlikely example of a man lawfully installing a steam hammer in his back yard. In response to the outcry, the enterprising town council hires an economist to undertake a cost-benefit study to determine whether all the houses in the neighbourhood should be sound-proofed. The total costs of the sound-proofing of all the houses affected is reckoned at £85,000. But, since the benefits over the future of the sound-proofing are reckoned to exceed £100,000, the scheme is approved.

If the economist were able to move away from his terms of reference, however, he would propose a court order preventing the operation of the steam hammer. The loss by the would-be entrepreneur might be of the order of, say, £1,000 a year or a capital value of £15,000, but the savings of the rest of the community would be £85,000. Indeed, in the absence of the court order, the council should be willing to pay the £15,000 to bribe the man not to operate his steam hammer—provided the law is able to uphold such contracts. The trouble about bribing a potential offender where the law is permissive of noise and smoke pollution is that it lends itself inadvertently to blackmail.

Consider now a more topical example: a proposal to widen a road so as to allow for three lanes of traffic each way, instead of the existing two. As before, the economist, keeping strictly to his terms of reference, may come up with a positive figure for the benefit 'enjoyed'. Allowed more latitude, however, he might point out that the traffic is already so heavy on the two-lane highway that a sizeable net gain can be achieved by a system of tolls, or taxes, calculated to reduce the traffic to an 'optimal flow'. Once the traffic approaches this level, it may transpire that an efficient public transport service is profitable and, in these new circumstances, a cost-benefit calculation can no longer justify the road-widening scheme. Moreover, the economist might wish to point out that the improvement of an existing rail service would cost much less, and yield at least as much benefit, as the road-widening scheme.

Such alternatives, however, will not emerge if the economist has to work strictly within his terms of reference or if, for political reasons, the alternatives are to be regarded as 'impractical'. Indeed, it is not too often that the economist is asked to consider all alternatives relevant to a broad problem before choosing that which offers the greatest net benefit to the community. It is more common to enlist his expertise in order to reach a decision about a particular kind of investment. Yet no matter how uneconomic they are, if political or administrative constraints are expected to remain operative during the period of time covered by the cost-benefit calculation, the economist has no choice but to accept them as part of the data.

## Criteria for Investment Projects

The benefits from an investment project by the government come to fruition over the future; and some of the costs may also be incurred over the future. In general, then, there is a distinct 'time-profile' of benefits and costs corresponding to each of the investment projects under consideration. Thus, the time-profile for one project may have large net benefits during, say, the first three years and small net benefits thereafter. For another project, the time-profile may be the reverse of this. Yet a third project may have more modest net benefits spread evenly over a longer period than the other two. For an unambiguous comparison of the value of such projects it is clearly necessary to reduce all these time-profiles to a single figure.

Of the two usual methods used, the more popular is the discounted present value (DPV) method, which consists of discounting all future benefits and outlays to a present value by means of some appropriate rate of interest. If that rate of interest were, say, 10 per cent per annum, a certain benefit valued at £1,100 next year, or one valued at £1,210 in two years' time, would have a discounted value of £1,000. The alternative method is that of calculating the internal rate of return (IRR) of the stream of future benefits and costs. The resulting figure purports to be an average rate of growth of (the present value of) the sum invested. An IRR of 15 per cent calculated for a twelve-year investment stream indicates an average annual growth rate of 15 per cent per annum of the present value of the total outlay.

An investment criterion can base itself on either of these two methods. If the DPV method is adopted, it might be thought that any public project is economically advantageous if the DPV of its benefits exceeds that of its outlays. Alternatively, if the IRR method is adopted it might be thought that any project having an IRR greater than the market rate of return should be undertaken. But it is not so simple as that. In fact, the investment criterion to be adopted depends on three related factors: on political and administrative constraints (on which I have touched earlier); on the uncertainty surrounding the size of expected future benefits and outlays (which I discuss in the following section); and on the alternative opportunities open to the investible funds which the government raises either by borrowing, by taxation or by a combination of the two.

If, say, it is decided to raise £10 millions through taxes that fall wholly on current consumption, and to spend this sum among several public projects from a list of approved investment projects, provided it is 'economically justifiable', the task of the economist is straightforward. Suppose he elects to use a DPV criterion. If there is agreement that society as a whole regards the consumption of £105 worth of goods next year as equivalent to the consumption of £100 today, he can use 5 per cent as the appropriate discount rate. Any of the approved projects is then eligible for the short list if, using this 5 per cent rate, the DPV of its benefits exceeds that of its costs. Should it happen that the total cost of the number of public projects that are eligible on this criterion exceeds the £10 millions available, the economist simply ranks the projects in descending order and goes down the list until the total outlay required does not exceed £10 millions.

If, to take another example, it were decided instead to raise the whole of the £10 millions by borrowing (the effect being supposed to reduce private investment by £10 millions) the economist may not regard any public investment as justifiable unless it can earn at least as much as is being earned by private investment. An expected yield of, say, 12 per cent in private investment then justifies his choice of 12 per cent as the appropriate discount rate. Clearly, if only a part of the £10 millions is to be raised by reducing current consumption and the remainder by reducing current private investment, the criterion has to be adapted accordingly. Finally, if there is no constraint whatever placed on the use of the £10 millions then, *no matter how the sum is raised,* the economist is justified in using a discount rate of 12 per cent. For now all, or any part of, the £10 millions made available for public projects may be invested instead in the private sector at a 12 per cent yield.

In practice, DPV is the more popular of these two methods, for two reasons: first, the use of IRR criteria occasionally produces a ranking of investment projects contrary to that produced by DPV criteria, and the logic of the DPV method appears unassailable. Secondly, a DPV criterion invariably produces a single benefit-cost ratio whereas, for some investment streams, there can apparently be more than one internal rate of return.

## Uncertainty

In the evaluation of any project there is sure to be some guesswork about the size of future costs and future benefits, arising in the main from technological innovations, shifts in demand and political changes. The problem of how to reach decisions in situations where knowledge of the past affords little guidance for the future is one that continues to attract attention.

The more familiar methods of allowing for future uncertainty may be grouped into two categories: those operating through a choice of the rate of interest in a DPV criterion; and those operating through revisions of expected future prices.

### THE RATE OF INTEREST

Since the risk of loss is not compensated by an equal chance of gain, one method is to add a percentage point or two on to a pure, or riskless, rate of interest. This was the method, for instance, that was used in evaluating the Channel tunnel project. The benefits were projected up to a 50-year period, and a 7 per cent rate of discount was adopted as being the conventional rate for long-term planning in France and Britain. There is, of course, the practical problem of discovering this riskless rate of interest, to allow for future uncertainty. Although the concept of a riskless rate of interest—one reflecting society's preference of present over future consumption—is clear, the difficulties of measuring it in an existing dynamic economy are formidable. In the event, the riskless rate of interest on long-term government bonds has been proposed as a tolerably proxy (riskless, that is, in respect of default only. Obviously, government bonds may fall in value over time, either in money or real terms without any fear of default on the nominal interest payments). This bond rate, it is acknowledged, is likely to be much lower than the current rates of return on commercial investments. But, then, a private firm is more likely to default than a central government.

While this is undoubtedly true, it may not always be relevant, which brings me to the second method of choosing the rate of interest in a DPV calculation: to adopt the rate of return in private industry as the appropriate rate of discount. As those favouring this method point out, any funds raised by the government for public projects can, in principle, at least, always be invested in private industry. Now, the riskier the type of private investment the higher, in general, is the actuarial rate of return—a result arising both from risk-aversion and tax disadvantages under the existing fiscal system. But, whatever the reasons for this higher actuarial return on risky private investment, they do not of themselves weaken the argument. If the placing of government funds in the riskier types of private investment can, in fact, realize over time these higher returns, then no public investment should be undertaken that yields rates of return below them. To the extent, however, that political constraints are imposed on the use of investible public funds, the appropriate rate of discount is below the private investment yield.[5]

## FUTURE PRICES

We can also allow for risk by estimating or guessing (in addition to the most likely future price, and quantity, of each input and output over the future) upper limits and lower limits. In this way three cost-benefit estimates are produced: a most likely, a most optimistic and a most pessimistic net benefit for each project. Although this is better than a single most likely estimate, it has the distinct disadvantage that the chance of the most likely cost-benefit occurring can turn out to be very small. One can go some way to remedy this by consulting with experts on the likelihood of each uncertain future price or quantity having different values. From such information a 'probability' table can be constructed.

This resulting 'probability' table cannot, of course, be any more accurate than the subjective estimates of the experts on which it is based. But it does bring out the full implications of these estimates, and enables us to say much more than before. In some hypothetical project, we should be able to say, for example, that there is a 90 per cent chance of the net benefit falling between £150,000 and £210,000; that there is only a $2^{1}/_{2}$ per cent chance of the net benefit being zero or negative, and so on.

If public investment in the economy is large enough to be spread over a great many projects to be undertaken within a year, then it is not unreasonable to decide each project on the basis of a single most likely cost-benefit outcome, using as discount rate the highest average rate of return accruing to risky commercial investment. Such a procedure will tend to produce for public sector investments an average rate of return above that which the same total amount of investment would have obtained if, instead, it had been invested in the private investment sector of the economy.

If, on the other hand, only a few large public investments are undertaken from time to time, it would be advisable to be guided in any decision by the sort of subjective probability table briefly described above.

## Conclusion

I conclude by summarizing the phases in a cost-benefit study in which judgments may differ. Following the order in which we have treated the subject they are to be found in the choice of which items are to be valued at market prices and which are to be valued at shadow prices; in the methods used to evaluate the shadow prices; in the range of 'intangibles' to be included in the study; in the methods used to evaluate these 'intangibles'; in the choice of an investment criterion; and in the devices used to make allowance for future uncertainty.

It must not, however, be supposed that all such sources of potential discrepancy are of equal importance, or that judgment in the above respects is evenly diffused among all economists. It is probably true to say that it is easier, at present, to secure agreement among economists on the first five of the above phases than on the last. Moreover, for many projects, the differences remaining may have little effect on the final recommendation. Nevertheless, there can be occasions where, as between one economist (or one group of economists) and another, differences in the evaluation of large public projects are critical and arise largely from differences in skill and care.

It is well to bear in mind that, in the present stage of its development, cost-benefit analysis—and, for that matter, all systems analysis—is an imperfect calculus, as much an art as a science or, more precisely, as much a matter of judgment as a technique. In many a large project it is quite possible for an economist to be swayed by prevailing fashions or the public mood or by political biases, conscious or otherwise, in favour of or against the scheme—especially in the choice of prices to be attributed to spill-over effects and in the method used to allow for uncertainty. For this reason, the interests of society are better served by making public not merely the findings of a cost-benefit study, but also the methods employed and the sources of data. Thus, although there may be good reasons for dissatisfaction with the findings of the Roskill Commission, it had the great merit of making its methods explicit.

It remains only to remind' the reader that, even if repeated scrutiny by fastidious and disinterested economists confirms the positive findings of a cost-benefit study, the question of equity remains to be debated by the public. For there is nothing in the literature of economics to support the current prejudice that considerations of equity should defer to those of allocation.

### Footnotes

1. If, instead, he prefers to work in the *new* project, we have to subtract from his value in the old occupation a sum equal to the difference between his old wage and the minimum wage he would accept to work in the new project.

2. In a popular sense, he may have 'earned' his unemployment insurance money by paying regularly his unemployment insurance premiums. But such insurance transactions are wholly 'transfer payments' within the economy.

3. Though spill-over effects can also be beneficial, their treatment is symmetric with that of adverse spill-over effects.

4. For a highly critical appraisal of the Roskill Commission's Report, the reader is referred to my paper, "What is wrong with Roskill?" in the *Journal of Transport Economics and Policy*, (September, 1970).

5. If, as is common, estimated future benefits and costs are calculated in terms of current prices, the market rate of return on private investments has to be deflated for the annual expected price rise. Expectations of a rise in prices of, say, 6 per cent per annum entail a reduction of a nominal yield of, say, 25 per cent per annum to a real yield of approximately 19 per cent per annum.

GRANT L. REUBER
AND RONALD G. BODKIN

# The Options for Stabilization Policy in Canada

## 1. Introduction[1]

At this stage in these Hearings the members of this Committee, after listening to the various views of a series of witnesses, may well feel much like Alice in Wonderland who at one point is heard to mutter "It's really dreadful the way all the creatures argue. It's enough to drive one crazy." Perhaps it would be somewhat reassuring to begin by saying that on two points at least there seems to be widespread agreement. First, the problem of reconciling full employment with stable prices is common to all industrial countries and is by no means unique to Canada—as witness the recent O.E.C.D. study on inflation.[2] Secondly, despite the ambitious claims of some commentators, no one anywhere has yet come up with a satisfactory answer to this policy dilemma, now recognized as one of the foremost issues facing many governments.

In part the differences of view about what policy should be reflect different estimates of the relative costs and benefits of rising prices versus unemployment, as well as underlying preferences. And in part these different viewpoints reflect a difference of view about the circumstances found in the country and about the empirical relationships that determine how the economy works. A host of issues arise along both of these avenues. Rather than attempt a comprehensive review of these issues, this Brief touches on three areas:

1.  The chief factors that have given rise to the recent rapid rise in prices accompanied by high levels of unemployment;
2.  The main policy options that face the country and some of the implications of each;
3.  Several associated issues that arise out of the first two questions and the questions posed by your Staff.

## 2.   Principal Factors Accounting for the Recent Rapid Rise in Prices in Combination with High and Rising Levels of Unemployment

### a)   EXCEPTIONALLY RAPID INCREASES IN THE LABOUR FORCE COMBINED WITH LABOUR MARKET IMPERFECTIONS

As the Economic Council of Canada pointed out a few years ago, the Canadian labour force has grown at an unprecedented rate since 1965 and will continue to grow very rapidly throughout the 1970s (table 1). The present rate of growth far exceeds the recent and projected growth rates in the labour forces of other industrialized countries (Charts 1 and 2). This rapid growth rate in Canada is mainly the lagged consequence of the large post-war baby boom but it has also been influenced by rising female participation in the labour force, as well as by positive net immigration. Looked at from the standpoint of job creation rather than from the standpoint of absorbing available labour supply, the Canadian economy has performed with a success that is unprecedented, at least since immediately after World War II, and that exceeds by a substantial margin the performance of the U.S. and European economies (Table 2).

*Table 1   Canada's Civilian Labour Force, 1950-1980*

|  | Average Annual Percentage Change | | | | | |
|---|---|---|---|---|---|---|
|  | 1950/5 | 1955/60 | 1960/5 | 1965/70 | 1970/5 | 1975/80 |
| Total | 1.7 | 2.7 | 2.2 | 3.2 | 2.7 | 2.3 |
| Male | 1.4 | 1.8 | 1.3 | 2.2 | 2.3 | 2.1 |
| Female | 2.7 | 5.5 | 4.6 | 5.3 | 3.6 | 2.7 |

**Source:** Economic Council of Canada, *Fourth Annual Review*, p. 72.

*Table 2   Civilian Labour Employment, 1950-1970*

|  | Average Annual Percentage Change | | | | Total Percentage Change |
|---|---|---|---|---|---|
|  | 1950/5 | 1955/60 | 1960/5 | 1965/70 | 1960/70 |
| Canada | 1.6 | 2.2 | 3.0 | 3.0 | 32.1 |
| U.S. | 1.1 | .9 | 1.6 | 2.1 | 19.5 |
| U.K. | .9 | .6 | .9 | −.6 | 2.6 |
| France | — | — | .9 | .5 [a] | 6.7 [a] |
| Germany | 2.8 | 2.3 | .6 | −.3 | 1.5 |
| Italy | — | .7 | −1.0 | −.5 | −6.6 |
| Sweden | — | — | 1.3 | .3 [b] | 7.4 [b] |

(a)  last available date 1968
(b)  last available date 1969
**Source:** OECD *Labour Force Statistics* and *General Statistics*

**Chart 1.**
Change in Civilian Labour Force in Selected Countries,
1965-1980 (Total Percentage Change)

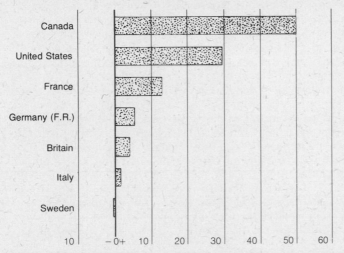

**Source:** Based on data from Demographic Trend: 1965-80 in Western Europe
and North America. Organization for Economic Co-operation and Development,
1966; and estimates by Economic Council of Canada.

**Chart 2.**
Change in Civilian Labour Force in Selected Countries,
1960-1970 (Total Percentage Change)

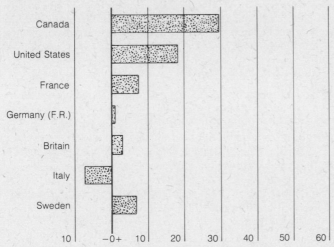

**Source:** OECD *Labour Force Statistics* and *General Statistics*.

A rapid increase in labour supply is to be welcomed on a variety of grounds, including the possibility which it opens up for more rapid increases in output because of the large increments in this fundamentally important productive resource. Moreover, with perfectly functioning labour markets little or no difficulty would arise in absorbing exceptionally large increases in labour supplies. Indeed, in a well-functioning labour market increasing labour supplies are likely to make market adjustments somewhat easier since the increments in labour supply will tend to be absorbed into growing sectors of the economy, thereby reducing the need to reallocate labour from slow-growing to fast-growing sectors in a dynamic economy. The difficulties of absorbing a rapidly growing labour force arise for the most part because labour markets are far from perfect. Among the many imperfections that are evident are various regional and occupational immobilities; inadequate information about job opportunities, restrictions on entry into various employments because of trade unions, professional and governmental barriers and regulations; labour pricing arrangements such as wage-parity and minimum wage laws; non-portable pension plan arrangements; fiscal incentives to substitute capital for labour; seniority arrangements to protect the interests of older, established workers; social welfare and other measures that undermine labour mobility and work incentives; and others.

Such imperfections become particularly serious, especially in the short-run, when the labour force grows at the rapid pace now experienced in Canada. Moreover, the effects of these imperfections are further exacerbated when aggregate demand is dampened in order to cope with inflationary pressures. Given the rapid increase in labour supplies in Canada, the anti-inflationary policies that have been followed and the imperfections found in the Canadian labour market—which may well be greater than in most other countries because of the geographic dispersion of the labour force and the importance of regional and seasonal factors—it is hardly surprising that unemployment levels in Canada have generally been higher since the 1950s than in Western Europe and the United States, where the labour force has grown more slowly and where labour markets are more homogeneous (Table 3).

### b)   EXTERNAL PRICE CHANGES

As is widely recognized, external price and wage changes, especially those in the U.S., have a fundamental influence on price and wage changes in this country. This influence arises directly through our heavy volume of foreign trade as well as through the ease with which productive factors move between Canada and the U.S. This external influence also arises indirectly through at least two channels: the first is through institutional links between businesses and trade unions in Canada and the U.S.; the second is through the influence of events in the U.S. on expectations in Canada about future trends in prices, wages and output. The first of these is obvious and has been much discussed. The second is less obvious and has received less attention but may be even more important. Available evidence suggests, for example, that expectations indices based on U.S. data are more powerful in explaining Canadian interest rates than expectations indices based on Canada data.[3]

Throughout recent history Canadian price changes have moved closely in line with international prices—particularly U.S. prices (Table 4). This has

Table 3    Unemployment Levels in Canada and Other Selected Countries
Selected Years, 1960-1970

| | 1960 | 1965 | 1966 | 1967 | 1968 | 1969 | 1970 | Correction Factor [b] |
|---|---|---|---|---|---|---|---|---|
| Canada | 7.0 | 3.9 | 3.6 | 4.1 | 4.8 | 4.7 | 5.9 | — |
| United States | 5.5 | 4.5 | 3.8 | 3.8 | 3.6 | 3.5 | 4.9 | 1.00 |
| United Kingdom | 1.7 | 1.5 | 1.6 | 2.5 | 2.5 | 2.5 | 2.7 [a] | 1.51 |
| France | — | .7 | .7 | 1.0 | 1.3 | 1.1 | — | 1.93 |
| Netherlands | 1.2 | .7 | — | 2.0 | 1.9 | 1.4 | 1.2 [a] | ? |
| Germany | 1.2 | .6 | .7 | 2.1 | 1.6 | .8 | .6 [a] | .73 |
| Sweden | 1.4 | 1.2 | 1.6 | 2.1 | 2.2 | 1.9 | 1.5 [a] | 1.20 |
| Belgium | 5.4 | 2.4 | 2.7 | 3.7 | 4.5 | 3.7 | 3.1 [a] | ? |
| Italy | 4.2 | 3.6 | 3.9 | 3.5 | 3.5 | 3.4 | 3.2 [a] | .51 |
| Japan | 1.1 | .8 | .9 | 1.2 | 1.2 | 1.1 | 1.1 [a] | 1.11 |

(a) Averages of available figures for 1970
(b) Unemployment data for Canada and the U.S. are approximately comparable; the data for other countries are not directly comparable. For a review of this matter, see Bodkin, Bond, Reuber, Robinson, *op.cit*. pp. 34-37. The correction factors shown indicate roughly the amount by which one needs to inflate or deflate reported rates in the country indicated to derive estimates comparable with Canadian rates. These correction factors were estimated by R. J. Meyers, cited by Bodkin *et al*.
**Source:** United Nations, *Monthly Bulletin of Statistics*, January 1971

Table 4    Percentage Changes in Canadian and U.S. Prices, 1965-1970

| | Percentage Change in Consumer Price Index | | Percentage Change in Implicit GNP Price Index | |
|---|---|---|---|---|
| | Can. | U.S. | Can. | U.S. |
| | (end of year) | | (av. of year) | |
| 1966/5 | 3.6 | 3.3 | 4.6 | 2.8 |
| 1967/6 | 4.1 | 3.1 | 3.4 | 3.2 |
| 1968/7 | 4.1 | 4.7 | 3.5 | 4.0 |
| 1969/8 | 4.6 | 7.9 | 4.7 | 4.7 |
| 1970/69 | 1.5 | 5.5 | 4.1 | 5.3 |
| 1970/65 | 19.1 | 26.8 | 22.0 | 21.6 |
| Annual rates | (end of quarter) | | (av. of quarter) | |
| 1968 II/I | 3.7 | 4.7 | 2.0 | 4.2 |
| III/II | 4.7 | 4.3 | 4.6 | 4.1 |
| IV/III | 4.0 | 4.9 | 3.6 | 4.4 |
| 1969 I/1968 IV | 3.0 | 6.2 | 5.8 | 4.7 |
| II/I | 8.8 | 6.4 | 8.2 | 4.8 |
| III/II | 2.2 | 5.3 | .9 | 5.5 |
| IV/III | 4.1 | 6.1 | 3.1 | 4.8 |
| 1970 I/1969 IV | 3.1 | 5.7 | 7.7 | 6.3 |
| II/I | 3.1 | 6.3 | 2.7 | 4.2 |
| III/II | .9 | 4.1 | 3.3 | 4.5 |
| IV/III | -1.2 | 5.4 | .3 | 5.8 |
| 1971 I/1970 IV | 4.6 | 1.0* | | |

*Based on February 1971 CPI

been especially true during periods when we have been on a fixed rate of foreign exchange. From 1965 to May 1970, for example, the consumer price index in Canada increased 21 per cent compared with 22 per cent in the U.S. With the adoption of a floating exchange rate in May 1970, the rigid link between Canadian and U.S. price trends was broken. Subsequently the rate appreciated by over 8 per cent. As a consequence of this, as well as strong competitive pressures in the food sector, contractionary monetary-fiscal policies and other factors, Canadian prices have risen appreciably less than U.S. prices since the spring of 1970. Unless, however, one can foresee a further significant change in the exchange rate, there is little reason to believe that after this once-for-all readjustment in relative price change has been absorbed, Canadian price changes will not again closely follow price changes in the U.S. and elsewhere. Barring truly extraordinary measures entailing substantial readjustments and economic costs, all our history indicates that it is unrealistic to believe that Canadian prices over any period of time can be expected to follow a path that differs significantly from price changes in the U.S. and other foreign countries.

### c)  POOR MARKET PERFORMANCE IN PRODUCT MARKETS

With the appearance of substantial excess capacity in the economy, one would expect prices to decline gradually in response to competition. With the major exception of the food industry, where this in fact has happened in recent months, one finds little evidence of such reductions. Indeed, throughout the period since 1968 the prices of the non-food and service components of the consumer price index have consistently continued to increase and at rates well in excess of the rates from 1960-65 (Table 5). While this phenomenon partly reflects the effect of foreign price changes and the lagged effect of earlier price and wage changes, it possibly also reflects the exercise of market power in some cases. Had producers had less market power, prices might have been more sensitive to the increased competitive pressure entailed by greater slack in the economy.

This said, one needs to add two further points however. First, producers engaged in export trade or facing import competition—which includes a majority of Canadian producers—have faced substantially greater competition since the appreciation of the exchange rate in May 1970, and this has been reinforced in some cases by tariff reductions following the Kennedy Round of tariff cuts. Secondly, corporate profits have declined substantially since 1969 and the rate of return on capital is now relatively low.[4]

The effects of market power in Canada, in both factor and product markets, are not only found in upward pressure on prices but may be even more important because of the downward rigidity in prices arising from this power. As a consequence of this downward rigidity, the resource and output reallocations required in a dynamic economy tend to raise prices as expanding industries outbid stagnant and declining industries where prices tend to remain unchanged. Although too much can be made of this phenomenon, which was first emphasized by Charles Schultze,[5] the evidence available suggests that it has been of some significance in Canada.[6] Moreover, it should be recognized

*Table 5    Percentage Change in Canadian Consumer Price Index*

|  | Total Index | Food | Goods Excl. Food | Shelter | Services Excl. Shelter |
|---|---|---|---|---|---|
| 1960/65 | 8.4 | 11.3 | 3.3 | 9.9 | 16.8 |
| 1965/66 | 3.7 | 6.4 | 2.0 | 3.1 | 4.4 |
| 1966/67 | 3.6 | 1.3 | 3.7 | 4.7 | 6.2 |
| 1967/68 | 4.1 | 3.3 | 3.7 | 6.1 | 4.4 |
| 1968/69 | 4.5 | 4.2 | 2.7 | 6.8 | 6.9 |
| 1969/70 | 3.4 | 2.3 | 2.1 | 6.5 | 5.0 |
| 1965/70 | 20.8 | 18.6 | 14.9 | 30.3 | 29.9 |

**Source:** Bank of Canada, *Statistical Summary*, March 1971 and *Statistical Summary 1969 Supplement*.

that even if there were no asymmetry in price behaviour, shifts in demand could generate increases in prices because of differing supply elasticities in various industries.[7]

### d)   RAPID GROWTH IN THE SIZE OF THE PUBLIC SECTOR

From 1965 to 1969 total government (all levels) revenues as a percentage of GNP increased from about 30$\frac{1}{2}$ per cent to 36$\frac{1}{2}$ per cent and total government expenditures (including transfer payments) from 30 per cent to over 33$\frac{1}{2}$ per cent.[8] Not only were these ratios substantially larger than at any time since World War II, but, more important, the rates of increase—20 and 12 per cent in four years—were very large by historical standards and standards in most other countries. Moreover, the projections prepared by the Economic Council suggest that further substantial increases in these ratios can be expected to at least 1975.[9]

A rapid increase in the public sector is inflationary in that it increases the marginal propensity to consume: first, because the first expenditure round through the government sector omits the bite that would be absorbed by savings in the private sector[10] and secondly, such expenditures may redistribute spending from groups with a higher propensity to save to those with a lower propensity to save. Moreover, a growing public sector may lead to a reallocation of resources from sectors where productivity growth is relatively rapid to the public sector where historically productivity growth has been very slow. Given small and gradual changes in the size of the public sector, demand management policies can adapt and compensate for these factors. This is also true with a large and rapidly growing public sector but it is likely to be much more difficult operationally, given the various factors constraining these other policies and the uncertainties about their effects. In other words, adjusting to and compensating for a large and rapidly moving element is likely to be more difficult and in practice less successful than adjusting to and compensating for a small and slowly changing element.

Another inflationary factor in the rapid growth of the public sector has been the lack of co-ordination between the demand and supply aspects of the policy.

Thus the introduction of Medicare, which greatly expanded the demand for medical services of all kinds by offering medical care to everyone at greatly reduced private cost, failed to make adequate provision for a corresponding increase in the supply of medical services. The predictable result has been a large increase in the relative prices of medical services. Many other types of policies such as those designed to support declining industries, to fund pollution control, to subsidize technology, housing and other types of investment have had a similar inflationary bias.

A further factor to be recognized in this context is that with a progressive tax system, rising prices tend to generate an ever-growing public sector.[11] This could be offset, of course, by tax reductions. Such reductions are rare, however. In situations of rising revenues and a back-log of unfilled demands for public services, recent governments have generally given priority to expenditure increases over tax reductions.

### e)   LAGS IN PRICES AND WAGES BEHIND THE APPEARANCE OF ABOVE-AVERAGE AGGREGATE DEMAND

Given some four years of above-average aggregate demand from 1963 through 1967, substantial inflationary pressures developed behind both prices and wages which have continued long after excess capacity had again appeared in the economy (Chart 3). As indicated in the recent O.E.C.D. study on inflation, price increases did not exceed their trend line until 1965 and labour's share of income, after falling below its trend line from 1962 to 1966, did not exceed its trend until after 1967. On this showing upward deviations from trend in price and labour income shares lagged some two to three years behind the appearance of above-average aggregate demand. On the basis of historical experience in Canada and elsewhere, there is every reason to expect a similar lag on the down side. Hence prices and wages have continued to rise since 1968 even though substantial excess supply has again developed in the economy. There is some evidence, however, that this lag is now gradually being exhausted and that the lagged upward pressure on prices is now becoming less.

### f)   EXCHANGE DEPRECIATION, AN UNDERVALUED EXCHANGE AND THE FAILURE TO ADOPT A FREE RATE SOONER

Early in the 1960s, Canada depreciated the exchange rate by about 11 per cent at a time when there was significant excess capacity in the economy. As this excess capacity disappeared and a high level of aggregate demand developed in subsequent years, the full inflationary impact of this devaluation was gradually transmitted throughout the economy. Moreover, the new exchange rate undervalued the Canadian dollar in terms of foreign currency, as evidenced by the continuing improvement throughout this period in the current account balance, the large increase in Canada's reserves and the upward pressure on the reserve ceiling when it was operative. This undervaluation further added to the inflationary demand pressures on the economy from 1963 onwards. In addition, because of the fixed exchange rate, international price changes were, and were expected to be fully transmitted to the Canadian economy.

# Chart 3.

## Deviations from Trend in Canadian Demand Pressures, Price Changes and Labour Income Share, 1955-1970

Real GNP
Percentage Deviation
From Trend

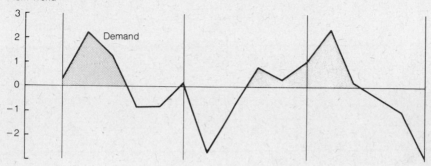

Percentage Point
Deviation From
Average Increase

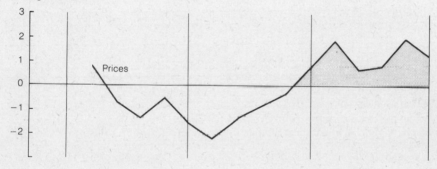

Labour Share
Percentage Point
Deviation From Trend

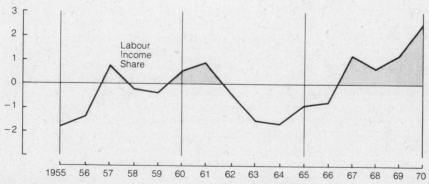

**Source:** *Inflation: The Present Problem*, OECD (Paris, Dec. 1970), p. 20.

We believe it probably was a mistake for Canada to have adopted a fixed rate in 1961 and that, having adopted it, it may have been a mistake not to have returned to a floating rate before 1970. Had we adopted a floating rate sooner, we deem it likely that we would have experienced less price inflation than we have and that our problems would now be somewhat less than they are.

### g)   MONETARY-FISCAL POLICIES

Over the period 1963 to 1968 the Federal Government can scarcely be said to have followed very active monetary and fiscal policies to combat inflation, as argued in greater detail elsewhere.[12] On the fiscal side a surplus of $625 million gradually became a deficit of $256 and $165 million in 1967 and 1968 (Table 6). A substantial surplus in 1969 was followed in 1970 by a small deficit. Other Canadian governments have had large and growing surpluses, reflecting their particular revenue and expenditure patterns and particularly the revenues generated by the Canada and Quebec pension plans. Although these surpluses have not reflected active anti-inflationary policies on the part of provincial and municipal governments, these surpluses have nonetheless served to dampen inflationary pressures.

Turning to the money supply one finds not only a very rapid increase during the period since 1965 but also wide fluctuations in the rate of increase ranging from over 20 per cent per year in mid-1968 to a net reduction in the third quarter of 1969 (Table 6). During the period of rapidly rising prices from 1965 to 1969, the money supply increased almost 55 per cent compared with a 19 per cent increase in real output. Thus $2.87 of new money was created per $1.00 of additional real output. In 1969 the increase in the money supply matched the increase in real output but in 1970—when inflation had become a major preoccupation—the rate of change in the money supply again accelerated (10.0 versus 5.6 per cent).

Nominal interest rates increased sharply between 1965 and 1969 and only recently have declined somewhat again. Real rates of interest, on the other hand, increased much less in absolute terms and at their peak probably did not exceed $5^1/2$ per cent for most borrowers.

Since 1969, as unemployed rates have risen from about $4^1/2$ per cent to almost 7 per cent both monetary and fiscal policy have been much tighter than from 1965 to 1968 when unemployment was generally well below 5 per cent.

This picture scarcely conforms with prevailing conventional notions of appropriate monetary and fiscal policy, whether inspired by Milton Friedman or Walter Heller or both. During much of this period one might have expected, by most conventional standards, changes in the money supply to at least not exceed significantly changes in real output. And, on the fiscal side, according to most conventional ideas, one would have expected to find large and growing federal surpluses deliberately designed to reduce inflationary pressure. Thus, the indictment of conventional monetary and fiscal policy can hardly be that it was tried and didn't work. Indeed, during much of this period these conventional levers appear to have been moved in the wrong direction; and to the extent that they were effective, these policies tended to enhance the upward pressure on prices rather than the other way around.

*Table 6   Selected Data on Unemployment, Output and Fiscal and Monetary Policy, 1965-1969*

| | Unemployment Percentage (seasonally adj.) [a] | Percentage Change in Real Domestic Product [a] | Net Government Savings (Dissaving) ($ millions at annual rate) [b] | | Percentage Change in Money Supply (% per year) [c] | Nominal Rates of Interest (%) [d] | | | Real Rates of Interest (%) [e] | | |
| | | | Federal | Total | | 3 mos. treas. bill | 3-5 yr. govt. bond | indus-trial bonds | 3 mos. treas. bill | 3-5 yr. govt. bond | indus-trial bonds |
|---|---|---|---|---|---|---|---|---|---|---|---|
| **Annual** | | | | | | | | | | | |
| 1965 | 3.9 | 7.1 | 625 | 325 | 11.9 | 4.0 | 4.9 | 5.7 | 1.7 | 2.6 | 3.4 |
| 1966 | 3.6 | 7.0 | 164 | 348 | 6.7 | 5.0 | 5.5 | 6.5 | 1.9 | 2.4 | 3.4 |
| 1967 | 4.1 | 3.2 | (85) | 335 | 14.0 | 4.6 | 5.6 | 7.1 | 1.1 | 2.1 | 3.6 |
| 1968 | 4.8 | 4.9 | (33) | 994 | 13.7 | 6.3 | 6.7 | 7.9 | 2.6 | 3.0 | 4.2 |
| 1969 | 4.7 | 4.6 | 773 | 2208 | 5.6 | 7.2 | 7.7 | 8.8 | 3.2 | 3.7 | 4.8 |
| 1970 | 5.9 | 2.9 | (12) | 1278 | 10.0 | 6.0 | 7.1 | 9.2 | 2.1 | 3.2 | 5.3 |
| 1970/65 | | 24.6 | | | 79.8 | | | | | | |
| **Quarterly (at annual rates)** | | | | | | | | | | | |
| 1968 I | 4.6 | 2.8 | 152 | 1380 | 9.8 | 6.7 | 6.8 | 7.7 | 3.4 | 3.5 | 4.4 |
| II | 4.9 | 8.0 | (460) | 636 | 13.6 | 6.8 | 6.9 | 8.0 | 3.4 | 3.5 | 4.6 |
| III | 5.0 | 3.8 | (68) | 708 | 18.4 | 5.7 | 6.3 | 7.9 | 2.5 | 3.1 | 4.7 |
| IV | 4.8 | 7.7 | 244 | 1252 | 9.9 | 5.8 | 6.7 | 8.1 | 1.9 | 2.8 | 4.2 |
| 1969 I | 4.4 | 7.1 | 572 | 2404 | 13.5 | 6.5 | 7.1 | 8.3 | 2.5 | 3.1 | 4.3 |
| II | 4.7 | 0.0 | 816 | 2400 | 5.7 | 6.9 | 7.5 | 8.6 | 1.3 | 1.9 | 3.0 |
| III | 4.9 | .2 | 676 | 1824 | -2.7 | 7.7 | 7.8 | 8.9 | 3.1 | 3.2 | 4.3 |
| IV | 5.0 | 7.2 | 1028 | 2204 | 5.5 | 7.7 | 8.2 | 9.1 | 3.2 | 3.7 | 4.6 |
| 1970 I | 4.9 | 2.8 | 20 | 1584 | 0.4 | 7.5 | 7.9 | 9.3 | 2.5 | 2.9 | 4.3 |
| II | 6.1 | 1.2 | (284) | 1642 | 10.8 | 6.4 | 7.3 | 9.2 | 2.8 | 3.7 | 5.6 |
| III | 6.8 | 1.5 | 276 | 1256 | 7.6 | 5.5 | 7.1 | 9.2 | 1.3 | 2.9 | 5.0 |
| IV | 6.6 | 4.7 | (60) | 660 | 19.9 | 4.6 | 6.2 | 9.0 | 1.1 | 2.7 | 5.5 |
| 1971 I | 6.1 | 1.8 [f] | | | 18.3 | 3.9 | 5.4 | 8.3 | | | |

(a)  Seasonally adjusted at annual rates

(b)  Seasonally adjusted, National Accounts

(c)  Total currency outside banks and chartered bank Canadian dollar deposits: annual, year end to year end; and quarterly, average of Wednesdays, last month of previous quarter to last month of current quarter, seasonally adjusted.

(d)  Annual or quarterly averages

(e)  Nominal rates *minus* the rate of average increase in the GNP implicit price index over the preceding three years and the current year

(f)  Based on January and February figures for 1971

No attempt will be made here to review the various factors that contributed to this situation.[13] In part, it reflected political pressures, in part a series of events beyond the control of the authorities, in part the rigid adherance to a fixed exchange rate which virtually emasculated monetary policy, and in part inadequate analysis and understanding within the government as well as without of the unfolding economic scene and the degree to which the policies being followed were inconsistent with the requirements of stabilization policy. From the standpoint of policy, the important point is not to establish with the benefit of hindsight that policy during this period might have been better but rather to ascertain what lessons might be learned from this period to improve future policy.[14]

## 3.   Policy Options

As the foregoing section implies, we fail to see why there is any great mystery about Canada's price level and unemployment experience during the 1960s. Nor is there all that much uncertainty about why prices have continued to rise since 1968 at the same time that unemployment has increased to over 6 per cent. Comments that suggest that this experience is beyond the explanatory powers of contemporary economics and illustrates the need to cast aside conventional analysis and frantically to seek out new and untried analytical techniques and policy prescriptions are largely unwarranted in our view.

In order to consider the policy options open to this country, it is necessary to have some notion of the economic environment in which stabilization policy is likely to be framed between now and, say, 1975. Three elements in the picture seem reasonably clear. First, from the demographic evidence available it is apparent the labour supply will increase at a rapid rate to 1980, though possibly not quite as rapidly as from 1965 to 1970. Secondly, the projections made by the Economic Council indicate that the size of the public sector can be expected to increase significantly to 1975, especially if new programmes are introduced to cope with such needs as pollution abatement, poverty and regional and urban development. Thirdly, external prices, and especially U.S. prices, can be expected to continue to increase at rates not far below those experienced in recent years. Strong inflationary pressures are evident at present both in Europe and Japan and even if these are reduced somewhat in the next year or so, the lagged consequences of these pressures are likely to be evident for some time to come (Table 7). The same is true of the U.S. Moreover, the prospect of a Presidential election in 1972 suggests that there will be strong political pressure to follow expansionist policies in that country, which will tend to support rising price and wage levels.

Given the continuing growth in labour supplies, continuing growth in the public sector and an inflationary world environment, it seems likely that within the framework of current policies there will be a continuing tendency for labour supplies to exceed labour demand and for Canadian prices to continue to rise over the next few years. What options are open to try to at least ameliorate these conditions?

*Table 7 Price*[a] *and Wage*[b] *Changes in Canada and Other Selected Countries, 1960-1970*

| | 1960-65 | 1965/66 | 1966/67 | 1967/68 | 1968/69 | 1969/70 |
|---|---|---|---|---|---|---|
| **CANADA** | | | | | | |
| Prices | 8.4 | 3.7 | 3.5 | 4.2 | 4.5 | 3.4 |
| Wages | 19.8 | 5.5 | 7.0 | 7.3 | 8.3 | 7.9 |
| **UNITED STATES** | | | | | | |
| Prices | 6.6 | 2.9 | 2.8 | 4.2 | 5.4 | 5.9 |
| Wages | 15.2 | 4.7 | 3.6 | 6.1 | 6.6 | 5.3 |
| **UNITED KINGDOM** | | | | | | |
| Prices | 19.0 | 3.9 | 2.49 | 4.7 | 5.5 | 5.7[c] |
| Wages | 24.6 | 6.0 | 4.33 | 8.0 | 5.8 | 3.8[c] |
| **FRANCE** | | | | | | |
| Prices | 20.3 | 2.7 | 2.7 | 4.6 | 6.4 | 4.9[c] |
| Wages | 43.5 | 5.9 | 6.0 | 12.4 | 11.3 | 8.1[c] |
| **NETHERLANDS** | | | | | | |
| Prices | 19.4 | 5.4 | 3.4 | 4.1 | 7.1 | 4.0[c] |
| Wages | 58.0 | 10.2 | 6.4 | 8.0 | 9.3 | 8.4[c] |
| **GERMANY** | | | | | | |
| Prices | 14.9 | 3.5 | 1.5 | 1.8 | 2.7 | 3.7[c] |
| Wages | 57.6 | 7.3 | 3.9 | 4.3 | 9.1 | 9.3[c] |
| **SWEDEN** | | | | | | |
| Prices | 19.6 | 6.4 | 4.3 | 1.9 | 2.7 | 6.5[c] |
| Wages | 49.4 | 7.6 | 9.5 | 6.5 | 8.1 | 11.9[c] |
| **BELGIUM** | | | | | | |
| Prices | 13.4 | 4.2 | 2.9 | 2.7 | 3.8 | 3.8[c] |
| Wages | 42.9 | 9.2 | 6.9 | 5.0 | 7.5 | 3.6[c] |
| **ITALY** | | | | | | |
| Prices | 27.1 | 2.4 | 3.2 | 1.4 | 2.6 | 4.9[c] |
| Wages | 64.1 | 3.8 | 5.2 | 3.6 | 7.5 | 17.0[c] |
| **JAPAN** | | | | | | |
| Prices | 34.0 | 5.2 | 4.0 | 5.4 | 5.2 | 7.0[c] |
| Wages | 61.8 | 11.6 | 13.2 | 14.9 | 16.4 | 2.0[c] |

(a) The C.P.I., all goods and services.

(b) An index of average hourly earning in manufacturing.

(c) 1970 figures were not available for these countries. An average of however-many monthly figures were available was used instead. The source of data was the United Nations *Monthly Bulletin of Statistics*, January 1971. The data for the CPI was consistent with the OECD data. However, excepting the U.K. and the Netherlands, the date on earnings in manufacturing were not. For other countries, this change figure is: — (the approximation for 1970) — (the U.N. data for 1969).

(d) Only two quarterly figures for 1970 were found — in OECD *General Statistics*, No. 10, 1970.

**Sources:** OECD, *Main Economic Indicators: Historical Statistics, 1959-69.*
Bank of Canada, *Statistical Summary,* March 1971.
U.S. Department of Commerce, Office of Business Economics, *Survey of Current Business,* March 1971.

## a)   LABOUR MARKET POLICIES

First and foremost, it is important that every effort be made to improve the performance of labour markets through a series of policies that make these markets more competitive and permit the absorption of increasing labour supplies more easily than at present. This issue has been much discussed over the years and has been frequently emphasized by the Economic Council.[15] Although some marginal measures have been adopted, this country has yet to adopt comprehensive labour market policies which are fully integrated with welfare and other types of policy and which will greatly improve the performance of labour markets. Without canvassing all the possibilities in detail, it is evident that measures are needed to reduce the control over labour supplies exercised by trade unions and professional organizations, to increase occupational and regional mobility through training programmes, better information and job placement services, financial assistance for moving and so forth, together with measures to increase the portability of pension and other benefits, to reduce the disincentives arising from social welfare measures to move and accept employment in another locality, to reduce present fiscal incentives to substitute capital for labour, to reduce the incidence of artificial wage levels through wage-parity arrangements and minimum wage laws. We fully recognize that implementing such changes means challenging a variety of vested interests and sacred cows. Substantial progress along these lines will call not only for technical skill but also for political courage of a very high order. On the other hand, failure to take substantial steps in this direction will imply unnecessarily high political and social as well as economic costs associated with unnecessarily high levels of unemployment.

## b)   COMPETITION POLICY

Policies to improve the efficiency of labour markets need to be accompanied by policies to increase competition and improve efficiency in product markets. The Economic Council of Canada has produced several reports on this subject within the past few years. We endorse the recommendations made in these reports and urge their speedy implementation.[16]

In this connection, we should especially like to emphasize the importance in Canada of reducing barriers to foreign trade as a means of checking price increases and reducing market power. In addition to reducing and eliminating tariffs and quotas generally, special attention might be given to liberalizing export restraint agreements, government procurement policies, aid-tying policies, and tariff and quota restrictions against low-cost imports from less-developed countries. Particular attention might also be given to tariff reductions in areas where past investigations under the Combines Investigation Act have indicated substantial elements of market power: e.g., dental supplies, matches, rubber goods, fine papers, paperboard, zinc oxide, sugar, and drugs.[17]

Such policies, as in the case of labour market policies, mean challenging various vested interests who can be expected to mount strong resistance. Nevertheless, to the extent that this resistance can be overcome, the result will be better-functioning, more competitive markets tending to produce more stable price levels.

## c) CLOSER CO-ORDINATION OF PUBLIC POLICY OUTSIDE THE REALM OF MONETARY-FISCAL POLICY WITH THE OBJECTIVES OF STABILIZATION POLICY AND INCREASED EFFICIENCY IN THE PUBLIC SECTOR

Although monetary and fiscal policy are directly concerned with stabilization policy, it is apparent that many other areas of government policy have an important impact on prices and unemployment. It is also evident that government policies in these other areas frequently are poorly co-ordinated with the objectives of stabilization policy—in many instances having an adverse influence on the effectiveness of stabilization policy.

This problem arises primarily in four areas. The first concerns income support policies, particularly in connection with food and agricultural prices. Price support policies are particularly inconsistent with the desire to stabilize the overall level of prices. Canada, fortunately, has relied mainly on a deficiency-payments approach rather than a price-support approach. Nevertheless, even a deficiency-payments approach tends to hold up prices since it is normally linked to restrictions on imports.

A second range of policies is concerned with fostering development in particular areas—e.g., research and development—or regions—e.g. DREE. Such policies have sometimes been planned and implemented with little or no attention having been given to their impact on national employment and price levels. It is not obvious, for example, that policies which subsidize technical innovations that lead to the substitution of capital for labour are in the national interest when the country has widespread unemployment. Nor is it obvious that regional development policies that subsidize sub-optimal allocations of labour and capital from a national viewpoint are in the best interest of increasing employment, raising incomes and slowing down the rate of increase of the price level. This is not to say by any means that all such development programmes are inconsistent with the aims of stabilization policy. In many cases they may in fact strongly reinforce stabilization policy. It is evident, however, that this is not always the case and that there is considerable scope for closer co-ordination of development policies with stabilization goals.

A third area is in the field of social welfare programmes, where again one can find examples of a lack of co-ordination with the aims of stabilization policy. The empirical evidence we have suggests, for example, that government transfer payments and unemployment insurance benefits inhibit labour mobility.[18] Difficulties of a different kind arise when policies such as Medicare are introduced which greatly increase the demand for services but make no provision for a corresponding increase in the supply of services, as mentioned earlier.

The fourth area relates to the need to improve efficiency in the public sector, including not only government departments but also government-related agencies such as educational and health institutions. Total employment in government and government-related agencies now accounts for about one-eighth of the civilian labour force. Although it is very difficult to measure productivity in the public sector, it seems to be generally conceded that productivity growth in the public sector, as in other service sectors, has been very slow and has been a drag on the overall growth in productivity in the country.[19] Upward pressure on prices has arisen as wage demands have out-stripped productivity gains. Given the size and growth of the public sector and its apparent low rate of productivity growth, steps to improve efficiency in the government sector are of major importance in attempting to bolster overall productivity.

We fully associate ourselves with those who have urged upon this Committee the need for greater co-ordination of Government policy. Presumably this is one of the main functions of the Economic Policy Committee of the Cabinet established in recent years. In order to advance this principle further, we suggest that consideration might be given to three specific steps.

1.   A review by the Bank of Canada and the Department of Finance of existing income, development and welfare programmes to determine their implications for stabilization and to consider how these programmes might be amended to make them more fully consistent with the goals of stabilization policy.

2.   An extension of the functions and capabilities of the Treasury Board to foster greater policy co-ordination within the Federal Government and to ensure that appropriate priority is placed on stabilization and other objectives by individual operation departments.

3.   Adoption of the principle that all departmental proposals in future should be accompanied by a careful assessment of the implications of the proposal for national and regional employment and price levels in both the short- and the long-term.

Co-ordination within the Federal Government is, of course, only part of the problem of co-ordinate public policy in this country. The other part relates to co-ordinate policy among different levels of government. This is a long-standing, widely-recognized problem to which almost everyone pays lip-service, where some progress has been made and where much more remains to be done. About all one can recommend is that everyone concerned keep soldiering on.

### d)   EXCHANGE RATE POLICY

We endorse a floating exchange rate for Canada at present, given the uncertainties in the international monetary system and the desirability for Canada to retain some freedom to follow somewhat independent monetary and fiscal policies. In saying this, we do not claim that a floating rate will make it feasible to have a price-employment experience that is totally or even largely independent of developments abroad. The claim is rather that the free rate makes it feasible to gain somewhat greater freedom in the short-run and to make adjustments to changing circumstances more smoothly.

Since 1970, of course, Canada's rate has not been completely free of intervention by the authorities. From May 1970, when we went off the fixed rate to February 1971, Canada's holdings of gold and foreign currencies increased by 13 per cent and total international reserves by 19 per cent. By intervening the authorities have prevented the rate from appreciating by as much as it would have without intervention. We question this intervention on two grounds. First, further appreciation would have served as a powerful anti-inflationary factor, both directly by placing further downward pressure on Canadian price levels and indirectly by having made it feasible to increase the money supply by less than some 15 per cent from May 1970 to February 1971, at a time when output increased a little over 3 per cent. Secondly, by allowing the rate to exceed $1.00 Canadian = $1.00 U.S., it is likely that countervailing forces would have arisen to reduce the inflow of capital and to increase the current account deficit, which would have reduced the upward pressure on the Canadian dollar.[20] By not allowing the mechanism to work to the full, in other words, we may have foregone some of the advantages of floating the rate.

It is just as mistaken to take a theological view about the floating rate as about the fixed rate. Historically, Canada has, with some exceptional periods, taken a pragmatic approach to whether we adhere to a fixed or a floating rate system. In present and foreseeable circumstances, we would argue that a floating rate which is free of intervention, except to iron out day-to-day fluctuations, will best serve the interests of stabilization policy in this country.

### e)   GENERAL MONETARY-FISCAL POLICY

All the policy options so far considered attempt to improve the trade-off relationship between price stability and full employment in the sense of making it feasible to operate the economy at lower levels of unemployment with less price inflation. Changes in monetary and fiscal policy attempt to regulate the level of economic activity. As such they determine at what point on the short-run trade-off curve the economy finds itself but also, by the manner in which they are employed, monetary and fiscal policy may affect the position of the curve itself. This may be illustrated with the aid of the accompanying figure.

**Figure 1.**

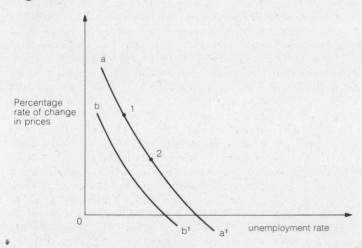

The policies discussed earlier are concerned with moving the trade-off curve closer to the origin, O. Depending on the stance adopted by monetary-fiscal policy, the economy in the short-run may in principle, be regulated to operate at point 1 or at point 2, the latter implying more unemployment and less price inflation than the former. In addition, the way in which policy is exercised may itself tend to move the curve closer to the axis, improving the trade-off relationship, or away from the axis, making things worse.

A great deal of discussion has developed regarding the stability of such a relationship as depicted in Figure 1. Leaving this aside for discussion later, we are sympathetic to the view that more stable and predictable monetary-fiscal policies that are geared to longer-term prospects and potentials may tend to improve the trade-off relationship. This does not mean that we endorse proposals to adopt automatic and rigid rules about increases in the money supply or changes in fiscal policy nor that we believe immediate circumstances can safely be ignored. There is, however, some danger of becoming too mesmerized by the immediate situation, and that by frantically adjusting in response to the changing current situation things may turn out worse than if policy were less influenced by immediate prospects and more influenced by longer-term prospects and the potential of the economy. Looking over the period from 1965 to 1971, one may argue that the large swings in fiscal and monetary policy indicated by Table 6 themselves tended to be destabilizing. Had policy been confined to a more limited range linked to longer-term employment and output prospects and potentials, the trade-off relation might now be better.

Aside from the stability of monetary and fiscal policy, there is the question of where to aim on the trade-off curve. Given the openness of the Canadian economy to external and especially U.S. price developments, it seems evident that any attempt to achieve significantly greater price stability in Canada than in the U.S. and elsewhere over any extended period of time is likely to entail very high levels of unemployment even if various policies are adopted to improve the trade-off relationship. The question then is one of preferences and weighing the *relative* costs of these high levels of unemployment against the benefits of marginally greater price stability. Although economists have been intrigued by the problem of assessing the *relative* economic costs and benefits of price inflation and unemployment and some brave attempts have been made to measure these *relative* costs and benefits,[21] the fact remains that the *relative* economic costs and benefits of price inflation and unemployment remain highly uncertain and that the *relative* social and political costs and benefits are even more uncertain.[22] As a consequence there is a considerable diversity of opinion. It is our view that when unemployment exceeds a rate of 4 to $4\frac{1}{2}$ per cent of the labour force, the combination of economic, social and political costs of unemployment outweigh the benefits resulting from the marginal gains likely to be achieved in terms of greater price stability in this country. On the other hand, historical experience suggests that when unemployment falls below 4 per cent in Canada, strong inflationary pressures develop that make it costly as well as impractical to maintain unemployment at these low levels— especially when the attempt to do so is usually followed by a swing in unemployment to levels well above 5 per cent as belated efforts are made to offset the pressures that have built up. Accordingly, we would argue that the authorities should set their eyes firmly on a target of about 4 per cent averaged out over two or three years. When unemployment is tending to fall below this level, restrictive measures should be applied even if prices are slow to reflect developing inflationary pressures; and when unemployment exceeds this level, expansionist policies should be adopted even though prices may be rising at rates comparable to those experienced in the late 1960s.

### f)  SELECTIVE FISCAL POLICIES

Historically, selective fiscal policies have usually taken the form of imposing or reducing taxes and other financial restrictions on various sectors that are assumed to be in the van of inflationary or deflationary pressures: e.g., sales and excise taxes on consumer durables, changes in house mortgage regulations, consumer credit regulations and margin requirements, changes in depreciation allowances, and so forth. Such regulations were used frequently during the 1940s and 1950s but lost favour during the 1960s. This seems to be mainly because serious doubts developed about the effectiveness of these policies, about their effects on the distribution of income and wealth and, also, because anticipations began to develop in the minds of the public, based on experience, which tended to accelerate precisely the changes that some of these measures were designed to reduce.

It is possible that we now have too great an aversion to the use of such measures and the development of new types of special fiscal measures of this kind. Among the latter are such possibilities as income tax holidays for a month or more or double taxation for a comparable period. On balance, we believe that it probably would be helpful to provide the authorities with standby authority to invoke and revoke certain types of special fiscal measures of this kind.

More recently, as part of the discussion on incomes policy, two further varieties of special fiscal measures have been receiving attention. One, which was advocated by Professor Bellan before this Committee and which in a somewhat different form has been advocated by the *Economist*[28] for the U.K., calls for a confiscatory tax to be levied against wage and salary increases which exceed a certain agreed guideline rate of increase. Thus, if the guideline rate of increase is 6 per cent, all or most earnings above this rate would be absorbed by tax, thereby totally or partially eliminating the incentive to bargain for more than a 6 per cent increase. Such a tax in our view would not only be very difficult to implement politically but also would be extremely cumbersome and difficult to administer. In particular it would be virtually impossible to separate increases in wages and salaries arising because of the greater responsibilities and output by individuals, additional hours of work or improved skills, from those increases arising because of straight-forward increases in salary and wage rates.

Another variant of this proposal has been advanced by Professor S. Weintraub, who argues for the imposition of a special corporate income tax surcharge on those firms that settle for wage and salary increases that on average exceed the announced guideline.[24] The purpose of this tax would be to increase the opportunity cost to firms of making wage and salary concessions, thereby inducing employers to resist employee demands more strongly. This tax has the merit that it is administratively feasible; any difficulties that might arise would be considerably less than those associated with a direct tax on employees. On the other hand, unless employees accepted the guideline, such a tax might have the effect of reducing the return to investors and deterring investment, either because of the increased costs of plant shutdowns and strikes or because of the increase in taxes arising from concessions to avoid a strike. And the learning process for employees could be a slow one. Moreover, such a policy would only affect groups paying corporate income taxes: it would not affect firms with zero or negative profits nor the large group of employers, employing a high proportion of the labour force, who are not subject to corporate income tax. In addition, given the ''cost-push'' hypothesis that underlies the proposal, it is difficult to see why those groups that are subject to corporate tax and have positive profits would not pass along most or all of the surtax in the form of higher prices.

The Weintraub proposal appears to Bodkin to have merit and possibly to be worthy of a trial, especially since we have so few effective weapons in this area. On the other hand, Reuber believes that it might be simpler and more effective to modify general tax rates in response to changing economic circum-stances—possibly with standby provisions being granted to the government to modify these rates quickly within a limited prescribed range on a discretionary basis without further reference to Parliament. (Note that this form of selective fiscal policy is primarily oriented unlike the Weintraub proposal, at the demand side of the economy).

In advocating standby fiscal powers to be exercised within a limited range on a discretionary basis, we are endorsing the view that on balance a well-run discretionary monetary-fiscal policy is likely to outperform a policy based on automatic rules, as suggested by some. Moreover, this suggestion together with our earlier recommendation for more stable and predictable monetary-fiscal policies rather implies an argument for greater flexibility in fiscal policy and less variability in monetary policy than we have had during the past decade. It implies furthermore that such flexibility, as is provided in both fiscal and monetary policy will be geared to longer-term prospects and potentials and not exclusively to the immediate situation.

## g)   DIRECT CONTROLS

All the options so far discussed are conventional in the sense that they are market-oriented. The main alternatives to such measures are non-market measures that attempt to exercise direct control on prices paid in product and factor markets. Proposals based on direct controls take a variety of forms and differ greatly in the range of product and factor markets to be encompassed by such controls. One such proposal has recently been placed before this Committee by Sir Roy Harrod and the arguments against such measures have also been stated before this Committee by the Chairman of the Economic Council, among others. We do not propose to review these arguments here. Suffice it to say that we seriously question the usefulness of direct controls in an open economy such as the Canadian, except perhaps on a short-term basis to meet a particular emergency such as a major war. Given what we see as a long-run problem of reconciling full employment with more stable prices, we doubt the effectiveness of such controls in achieving their objective. Furthermore, such controls in our view would mean substituting one set of policy problems for another and possibly more difficult set of policy problems. In addition, as matters stand constitutionally, it would not be feasible for the

Federal Government to impose such controls in many areas exhibiting large price and wage increases; and we can discern no disposition on the part of Provincial Governments to collaborate in implementing price and wage controls.

There are two areas, however, where the Federal Government might fairly readily impose wage and price controls: on the wages and salaries paid out of Federal Government funds and, secondly, on prices charged by regulated industries and public services.

For the Government to penalize those groups that are directly within its jurisdiction without being able to exert corresponding authority elsewhere would over time result in a deterioration in the quality of public service employees and the services provided by regulated industries. Such a deterioration would have little or no justification and we would oppose such policies.

Assuming that the constitutional obstacle could be surmounted — and that is a very big assumption — direct controls on prices and wages in our view could only be justified in industries where for political or economic reasons it proved impossible to develop reasonably competitive markets. On this basis, the case for direct controls is reduced to the classical case for regulating prices in so-called "natural" monopolies, such as public utilities — perhaps extended to what we might call "natural oligopolies". This leads into a highly complicated set of issues that cannot be pursued here. In general, the regulation of natural monopoly attempts to achieve the level of output and prices that would be justified by market-efficiency criteria rather than by monopoly criteria. But there is no suggestion even in these cases of regulating prices simply to hold prices down irrespective of economic efficiency. We would venture the judgment that there probably is limited scope in Canada for direct controls to improve successfully economic efficiency — given the openness of the economy, the competition that already exists and the possibilities of opening up markets to greater competition.

### h)  VOLUNTARY INCOMES POLICY

For reasons explained at greater length elsewhere,[25] we believe that voluntary incomes policies such as those developed by the Prices and Incomes Commission in this country and by corresponding agencies in other countries at best are ineffective and they may even be harmful from the standpoint of stabilization policy as well as other objectives of policy. Such policies, in effect, attempt to levy a voluntary tax which is used to subsidize prices. Not only does this lead to gross inequities, but also it is likely to be highly ineffective. If such taxes are to be levied, they should be universal and mandatory and it may be questioned whether the proceeds should be employed to subsidize the price of the product of the tax-payer. Moreover, such measures are naive in implying that anyone in a responsible position in either business or the trade unions would voluntarily accept them, knowing full well the influence of international prices and other influences on Canadian wages and prices as well as the high probability that many other sectors of the economy will not accept them.[26] Furthermore, such measures, by holding out the mirage of something being done, may well forestall more useful policies from being implemented and may indeed generate expectations that enhance rather than alleviate the difficulties facing the economy. Finally, by pursuing incomes policy through a vigorous public relations job, the PIC may, in effect, create "money illusion" which, far from ameliorating the adverse effects of inflation by having the public correctly anticipate it, enhances these effects by temporarily misleading the public into incorrectly anticipating more stable prices than are justified by underlying economic conditions.

Rather than rehearse these and many other arguments, it may be more interesting to refer to a recent column by Eric Jacobs commenting on the now-abandoned Prices and Incomes Board in the U.K., of which he was a member.[27] "Looking back to that June night six years ago", he concludes "it all seems a sad waste of effort." Looking at David C. Smith's review of incomes policies elsewhere, it is difficult to be more sanguine about the prospects for incomes policies in this country.[28]

## 4.   Some Related Issues

### a)   IS THERE A STABLE TRADE-OFF RELATION?

Reference was made to this question earlier. The issue is whether there exists a trade-off relationship such as depicted in Figure 1 that is stable enough to be useful for policy purposes. Suppose the Government were to aim at point 1 in the Figure, why would not the public eventually come fully to anticipate the implied rate of inflation? This in turn would result in an upward shift in the curve, leaving the rate of unemployment unchanged at its "natural" level. Thus, there would not be a long-run price-unemployment trade-off: the curve, in other words, would be vertical up and down.[29]

On theoretical grounds it is apparent that either outcome is possible. "New" neoclassical arguments, which deny the existence of a long-run trade-off, place little or no weight on market imperfections and emphasize the speed and ease with which expectations develop and markets adjust.[30] Those who believe the trade-off notion is useful for policy purposes emphasize the importance of market imperfections and argue that the relationship shifts very slowly.[31]

Empirically, the issue is also in doubt for the medium and long-term. Virtually everyone finds evidence of a short-run relationship. Virtually everyone also finds evidence of a relationship between earlier price changes and current price changes implying that expectations based on previous experience do affect current price movements. Similarly, virtually everyone finds that external price changes are a major determinant of domestic price changes in Canada and that unemployment levels affect the rate of wage change which, in turn, affects the rate of price change. What remains unclear is the speed with which expectations adjust—estimates range from less than a year to several decades—and whether, after the adjustment has been completed, the curve has become completely vertical—implying no trade-off between the level of aggregate demand and prices—or whether some slope remains —implying that there is a trade-off.[32]

Conventional policies followed in most countries since World War II imply that in their hearts the authorities in most countries also believe in a trade-off, some of their words notwithstanding. Most countries have followed aggregate demand management policies based on the view that reducing aggregate demand reduces upward pressures on prices and wages and vice versa. This approach makes little sense under the "new" neoclassical view of the trade-off since, according to this view, as people gain experience with demand management policies geared to a trade-off, their expectations will adjust. As a result, aggregate demand management policies under such a view are rendered ineffective except perhaps in the very short-run: unemployment will in any event tend to settle at its "natural" rate and money income changes will be determined by the rate of increase in the money supply.

Without pursuing this matter further, we side with those who believe there is some value from a policy standpoint in the notion of a trade-off relationship between the rate of price change and the level of aggregate demand. Without denying in any way that price expectations develop that affect current price changes, we question whether markets are so free of imperfections — such as money illusion, institutional rigidities and uncertainty — as to result in a highly unstable relationship which rapidly moves to a vertical curve. Furthermore, given the strong empirical evidence of a relationship between the level of unemployment and wage changes and between foreign price changes and domestic price changes, we question whether the curve in any event will move to a fully vertical position even if price changes are correctly anticipated.

### b) REGIONAL POLICIES AND THE REGIONAL IMPACTS OF POLICIES

From the standpoint of assisting the less prosperous regions of Canada, the most powerful policy is to maintain a high level of demand in the country nationally and low national levels of unemployment. We can think of no regional policies that will be as helpful from the standpoint both of assisting factor mobility and of maintaining strong demand for the output of these regions which, in turn, will lead to greater investment and higher incomes in these regions. Moreover, a high level of national demand is probably a prerequisite for any significant success for most types of regional policies. Without this prerequisite, most regional policies are likely to be relatively ineffective.

Although national policies designed to regulate aggregate demand are likely to have differing regional impacts, it is doubtful whether anything realistically can or should be done about redesigning aggregate monetary and fiscal policies — which already are hard-pressed to cope with national problems of aggregate demand management — to cope with regional problems as well. On the other hand, this approach does not in any way rule out specially designed programs to foster development in backward areas. Such programs, as mentioned earlier, do nevertheless have implications for national policy and need to be co-ordinated closely with national stabilization policy.

Although we have not examined regional development policies in this country in any detail, we have gained the distinct impression that they have not always been closely co-ordinated with national development objectives, that in some cases they have not been geared to development objectives at all but rather to the provision of services, income support, and the relief of poverty in the region, and that on occasion political considerations have been at least as important as economic considerations.

The unfortunate fact is that, despite much discussion and research, relatively little is known about what constitutes a good regional development policy in this country consistent with our national objectives. This is an area demanding much greater information than is now available and more intensive study.

### c)   WAGE DETERMINATION

Lurking behind much of the foregoing discussion is the sensitive but central question of what factors determine wages in Canada. In particular, to what extent does the recent rapid increase in wages and salaries reflect the play of market forces, allowing for a lag, and to what extend does it reflect labour market imperfections and/or monopoly power over the supply of labour exercised by the trade unions? The broad factual picture is reasonably clear. Canada has had unemployment rates in excess of $4^1/_2$ per cent since 1968. During the period since then wages and salaries have increased rapidly by historical standards and considerably more than productivity. These rates of increase have also been more rapid than in the U.S. and Western Europe where unemployment levels have been lower (Tables 3 and 7). A further characteristic of this period has been the rapid increase in wages in the mining and construction sectors, the latter being labour intensive compared to the manufacturing and service sectors (Table 8). Moreover, the disparity in wage changes among these sectors has been greater since 1965 than from 1960 to 1965. *Prima facie,* at least, this general picture seems inconsistent with what one would expect to find in strongly competitive labour markets. Rapidly rising wages and salaries in an open economy in the face of widespread unemployment not only make the employment situation worse but also seem to indicate serious malfunctions in the labour market.

It is widely recognized, of course, that the connection between changes in aggregate demand and wages is very loosely geared in this country because of the heterogeneous and regional nature of labour and product markets. Despite this, there is considerable evidence to indicate that wages in general and in particular industries are influenced by demand conditions.[33] Moreover, in some industries are influenced by demand contitions.[34] All the same, there is no reason to believe that the efforts of trade unions to increase wages are entirely useless. There is some fairly strong evidence for the U.S. to indicate that the main effect of their activities is to increase the wages of union members at the expense of non-union workers.[35] The extent to which union activity increases the *overall* money level of wages remains very much in doubt. In any event, the evidence is consistent with the view that unions may have succeeded in pushing up wages in some manufacturing industries and especially in the construction industries. Their power to do so in many industries seems to be relatively limited, however, when compared to the wage change experience in sectors where union power is relatively weak, e.g., the manufacturing sector versus the service sector. On the face of things, the effect of union power on wages is probably most evident in the construction sector, where wages have

Table 8    *Changes in Average Hourly Earnings — Canada 1960-1970*

|  | 1960/65 | 1965/6 | 1966/7 | 1967/8 | 1968/9 | 1969/70 | 1965/70 | 1968/70 |
|---|---|---|---|---|---|---|---|---|
| Mining | 16.3 | 7.0 | 9.2 | 8.1 | 6.8 | 13.1 | 52.7 | 20.9 |
| Manufacturing | 18.4 | 6.1 | 6.7 | 7.5 | 8.1 | 7.9 | 42.0 | 16.7 |
| Construction | 24.6 | 10.7 | 11.4 | 6.7 | 11.4 | 13.8 | 66.8 | 26.7 |
| Services [a] | 21.3 | 6.4 | 7.7 | 8.7 | 7.5 | 7.4 | 43.9 | 15.5 |

(a) Average of earnings in Urban Transit; Highway and Bridge Maintenance; Hotels, Restaurants, Taverns; and Laundries, Cleaners and Pressers.

**Source:** DBS *Review of Man-Hours and Hourly earnings, 1967-68* and *Man-Hours and Hourly Earnings*, January 1971

risen substantially more than wages in the manufacturing and services sectors, and within the manufacturing sector in such industries as automobiles, electrical apparatus, chemicals and paper.

Further evidence suggesting market imperfections and/or monopoly power is provided by studies on the effect of taxation on wage changes.[36] According to this evidence, tax increases, direct and indirect, have been partially passed on in the form of higher money wages and salaries in a number of sectors. Wage negotiations in some cases, implicitly or even explicitly, seem to be based on after-tax income.

These various pieces of evidence reinforce the notion that market imperfections and/or monopoly power are of some importance in the labour market. Precisely what these imperfections are and how best they might be reduced remains somewhat unclear, however, and warrants more attention than it has received up to now.

### d)   LAGS IN POLICY RESPONSES IN ECONOMIC RESPONSES TO POLICY CHANGES

For analytical purposes a distinction is frequently made between two types of lags: the "inside" lag—the lag between the appearance of the need for policy action and the taking of action; and the "outside" lag—the lag between the taking of action and the realization of its effects on the economy.

Given the variety of objectives to be considered by policy makers, ambiguity and uncertainty about the current state of the economy, further uncertainty about the optimum combination of policies to cope with whatever current circumstances are, and the time required to implement these policies once they are decided upon, it is evident that the "inside" lag can easily extend to a year or more, assuming, as is normally the case, that marginal adjustments are in question. Once a change in policy has been implemented a further substantial "outside" lag is likely as the effects of the change in policy gradually percolate through the economy. Hence it may be two to three years later when the effects of policy changes made in relation to initial circumstances are felt. But by this time, current circumstances are likely to be quite different and the effects of the change in policy are just as likely as not to be inappropriate as appropriate to the later-prevailing circumstances.

Reasoning along this line, some economists have argued that it is unhelpful to gear policy too closely to short-term circumstances. Instead policy should take a somewhat longer view and should rely more heavily on allowing the economy to make necessary short-term adjustments on its own.

While one may sympathize with this more relaxed and detached view of short-term stabilization policy, it is doubtful whether, in terms of practical politics, any government could pursue such a policy very far in view of the high and rising standards of policy performance demanded by the public. On past experience most governments are likely to respond because of political pressures and the question is how their policy response might be improved.

One part of the answer seems to try to limit the degree of response to some circumscribed range in order to reduce the possibility of overshooting and undershooting targets too greatly. A second part of the answer is to try to reduce the length of both the ''inside'' and ''outside'' lags of policy.

As far as the ''inside'' lag is concerned this means doing everything possible to produce more and better up-to-date economic information, improving our forecasts and our understanding of how the economy works, and establishing more closely integrated administrative arrangements to arrive at decisions more promptly. It may also mean arming the authorities with more discretionary powers—to change taxes for example—which would make it feasible to implement policy changes more quickly and directly. Even with such improvements, however, an ''inside'' lag of significant duration will remain.

Improving factor and product market performance is likely to result in a reduction in the length of the ''outside'' lag. The creation of a more stable and predictable policy-framework will have the same effect by reducing uncertainty in the minds of private decision-makers. In addition, by allowing prices, interest rates and exchange rates to respond more fully to underlying circumstances than in the past, the adjustment process is likely to be speeded up and because of this may well be less than if spread out over time through policy interference. For example, to the extent that incomes policy has an effect, it may only extend the length of the lag in the adjustment process and as a consequence make things worse. Similarly, by intervening actively in the bond and foreign exchange markets to curb other than day-to-day fluctuations in the level of interest and foreign exchange rates, the lags in the economy may simply be stretched out, which in turn may complicate things even more. But even if steps are taken to reduce the ''outside'' lag of policy, it is important to recognize that a lag of significant dimensions will necessarily remain.

### e)  CURRENT POLICY

Having said all this, one is left with the question of what to do now.

If the foregoing analysis is broadly correct, it is important that a variety of measures be adopted as soon as possible to improve market performance in labour and product markets, to improve policy co-ordination and efficiency in the public sector and other longer-term measures. However, even if effective policies are adopted in these areas, the results of such policies are likely to manifest themselves slowly. Meanwhile the Government faces the question of what to do now in terms of monetary-fiscal-exchange rate policy.

Although we have not made a detailed and careful examination of immediate term prospects, we are prepared to accept the widely-held view that the economy is again in an expansionary phase, in part because deflationary policies have been relaxed.[37] We also accept the forecast that the rate of increase in wages is likely to be somewhat less over the next few years. With no further change in policy, unemployment also seems likely to diminish but is unlikely to fall much below 5 per cent in the next year or so.

In these circumstances a case can be made for a moderately expansionary fiscal policy. We would favour implementing such a policy through reductions in personal income and especially indirect taxes for several reasons: such reductions seem likely to reduce some of the upward pressure on wages and prices; Canadian taxes at present are high by historical standards and relative to taxes in the U.S.; important tax reforms are imminent and better reforms can be more easily implemented if they are combined with tax reductions; tax reductions will add to the pool of private domestic savings and hence decrease local dependance on foreign savings, and such a reduction would offset to some extent the incidence of inflation on private incomes because of progressive income taxes.

If we assume an expansionary fiscal policy brought about by tax reductions and an orderly and consistent change in the money supply related to changes in output and unaffected by the policy changes in fiscal policy, what are the consequences likely to be for GNP and the exchange rate? The direct effect of a reduction of taxes will be to increase private spending and thence to increase imports and weaken the exchange rate. At the same time, lower taxes will increase the size of the government deficit, which will have to be financed by additional borrowing, which in turn will raise interest rates. Under a flexible exchange rate, this increase in domestic interest rates will increase capital inflows, thereby putting upward pressure on the exchange rate — in opposition to the downward pressure emanating from the expansionary expenditure effects of the tax reduction. Since, however, capital inflows are not completely elastic with respect to interest rates and are themselves sensitive to exchange rates, the expansionary effects of fiscal policy will be only partially offset: the policy, on balance, will remain expansionary.[38]

Given the countervailing monetary and expenditure effects of easier fiscal policy on the exchange rate, is the rate likely to appreciate or depreciate, assuming a given monetary policy? Though the answer is necessarily uncertain, evidence from the 1952-61 floating rate period suggests that initially the rate may tend to appreciate somewhat relative to what it would otherwise be, but that after a time the size of the expenditure effects outrun the size of the monetary effects of the tax change and the rate will tend to depreciate. Moreover, if as some evidence suggests interest rate expectations are closely geared to U.S. rates, downward pressure will be exerted on the exchange rate in the short run as well as in the long.

The practical importance of this is to suggest that it is doubtful whether one can validly argue against an expansionary fiscal policy at present on the ground that the resulting budgetary deficit will result in an increase in interest rates that, either directly or indirectly through exchange rate effects, will offset the expansionary expenditure effects of the policy, even if no adjustments are made in monetary policy.

There is, of course, no reason why within limits adjustments should not be made in monetary policy to reinforce the expansionary effects of fiscal policy. In our view, however, these adjustments should normally be more moderate than they have been in the past, as reflected by the wide range of fluctuation in the rate of increase in the money supply. In addition to establishing a more stable monetary framework, such a policy would call into play the exchange rate as a useful corrective device to regulate the level of demand and the rate of increase in domestic prices.

### Footnotes

1. We are indebted for comments and suggestions on an earlier draft of this Brief to C. S. Clark, T. J. Courchene and J. Fried, as well as to two other individuals who, because of their positions, must unfortunately remain anonymous. Sole responsibility for what is said rests, as always, with the authors.

2. *Inflation, The Present Problem,* (Paris: OECD, 1970).

3. Richard E. Caves and Grant L. Reuber, *Capital Transfers and Economic Policy: Canada, 1951-62* (Cambridge: Harvard University Press, 1971), Chap. 3; see also Stephen J. Turnovsky, "The Expectations Hypothesis and the Aggregate Wage Equation: Some Empirical Evidence for Canada," Working Paper Series 4012, University of Toronto. Turnovsky finds that U.S. expectations data are reasonable proxies for Canadian price expectations in explaining changes in Canadian wages and that they work better for Canada than for the United States (Turnovsky, p. 24).

4. According to DBS National Accounts data, corporate profits before taxes increased 9.9 per cent from 1967 to 1968, 5.5 per cent from 1968 to 1969 and decreased 6.2 per cent from 1969 to 1970.

5. Charles L. Schultze, "Recent Inflation in the United States," Study Paper No. 1, prepared for the Joint Economic Committee of the United States Congress, *Study of Employment, Growth, and Price Levels* (Washington: U.S. Government Printing Office, 1959).

6. Thomas J. Courchene, "An Analysis of the Price-Inventory Nexus with Empirical Application to the Canadian Manufacturing Sector," *International Economic Review,* X (October, 1969), pp. 359-62.

7. *Ibid.*

8. *The National Finances: 1970-71* (Toronto: Canadian Tax Foundation, 1970), pp. 9 and 13.

9. *Perspectives 1975,* Sixth Annual Review, Economic Council of Canada (Ottawa: Queen's Printer, 1969), Chap. 3.

10. In accordance with "balanced-budget" multiplier principles.

11. Indeed, one can argue that a rising rate of taxation may generate "tax-push" inflation. See John H. Hotson, "Adverse Effects of Tax and Interest Hikes as Strengthening the Case for Incomes Policies—or a Part of the Elephant," paper read to the June, 1970 meetings of the Canadian Economics Association in Winnipeg. While the argument is strongest as applied to a rising rate of indirect taxation, it can be applied, with less force, to a rising rate of taxation of personal and corporation incomes.

12. Grant L. Reuber, "Incomes Policy: Canada's Experiment with Organized Voluntarism to Curb Price Inflation," Research Report 7003, The University of Western Ontario, pp. 3-11.

13. See Reuber, *op. cit.* for a more detailed discussion of these factors.

14. Bodkin is somewhat less critical of the average degree of stimulus during the period 1965-1970, as he feels that deflationary forces were still evident in the private economy. However, he agrees with the criticisms that both monetary and fiscal policy were too variable during this period. Indeed, there is some (non-statistical) basis for believing that a steady state trade-off curve would be more favourable than those estimated from real world data by standard econometric techniques. (This argument, in fact, is developed below.)

15. Robert A. Gordon, in his book *The Goal of Full Employment,* puts heavy stress on what he calls "Manpower Policy" as a means of making the goals of full employment and stable prices more compatible.

16. Similar recommendations are contained in the OECD report on inflation, *op. cit.*, pp. 45-7.

17. Grant L. Reuber, brief presented to the Special Joint Committee of the Senate and House of Commons on Consumer Credit (Prices), February 9, 1967, Table II.

18. Thomas J. Courchene, "Interprovincial Migration and Economic Adjustment," *Canadian Journal of Economics,* III (November 1970) pp.550-576. Also, Thomas J. Courchene, "Unemployment Insurance in Canada: Some Implications of the Present System and an Evaluation of the White Paper Proposals," Research Report 7025, The University of Western Ontario.

19. Some of this apparent slow rate of productivity growth may be a difficulty in accurately measuring output growth in the service sectors, as Richard Ruggles has pointed out on several occasions.

20. For a further discussion of this mechanism, see Caves and Reuber, *op. cit.* In this context we are intrigued by the following statement by the Governor of the Bank of Canada " . . . it has been proper . . . to ease the upward pressure on the exchange rate by encouraging credit conditions in Canada which reduce the incentives for Canadian borrowers to go abroad for funds and for non-residents of Canada to employ their funds in Canada." Canadian Club of Vancouver, April 28, 1971, p. 8.

21. E.g. G. L. Reuber, "The Objectives of Monetary Policy," Working Paper prepared for the Royal Commission on Banking and Finance (Ottawa: Queen's Printer, 1962), Chap. V.

22. A few years ago, a discussion paper by a political scientist from the University of Rochester (Gerald Kramer) suggested that, in the U.S. context, the political penalties of foregone output growth and unemployment were far greater (on a per unit basis in the relevant range) than the penalties associated with a rising price level.

23. April 24, 1971.

24. Sidney Weintraub, "A Feasible Anti-Inflation Incomes Policy," *Lloyd's Bank Review* (January, 1971).

25. Reuber, "Incomes Policy," *op. cit.*

26. Leo Durocher used to say, "Nice guys finish last." The existence of voluntary incomes policies would appear to guarantee this outcome, as only the angels will accept the invitation to become the sacrificial lambs on the altar of price level stability. If intervention is decided upon, a law with mandatory provisions would seem, in our view, far more acceptable.

27. *The Sunday Times,* April 18, 1971.

28. *Incomes Policies—Some Foreign Experiences and their Relevance for Canada,* Economic Council of Canada (Ottawa: Queen's Printer, 1966).

29. A tremendous literature has developed on this issue over the years, some of which is reviewed in R. G. Bodkin, E. P. Bond, G. L. Reuber and T. R. Robinson, *Price Stability and High Employment—The Options for Canada,* Economic Council of Canada (Ottawa: Queen's Printer, 1966). Two interesting recent empirical papers relating to Canada are by Turnovsky, *op, cit.* and J. Vanderkamp, "Wage Adjustment, Productivity and Price Change Expectations," (mimeo).

30. E.g., M. Friedman, "The Role of Monetary Policy," *American Economic Review,* 58 (March, 1968).

31. Charles C. Holt, "Improving the Labour Market Trade-Off Between Inflation and Unemployment," *American Economic Review, Papers and Proceedings* LIX (May, 1969), pp. 135-146.

32. Looking at a monetarist econometric model of the U.S. economy, Andersen and Carlson, in "A Monetarist Model for Economic Stabilization," *Federal Reserve Bank of St. Louis Review,* Vol. 52, No. 4 (April, 1970), pp. 7-25, conceded that there was a short-run trade-off curve. Unlike other monetarists, however, Andersen and Carlson attempted to measure the length of time required for the economy to converge to its neo-classical growth path. The results are interesting: the various simulations suggested that such a convergence would take 19 to 35 years! In the meantime, if one opted for eventual price stability, there would be considerable foregone output and unemployment, to say nothing of induced social tensions.

33. Grant L. Reuber, "Wage Adjustments in Canadian Industry," *The Review of Economic Studies,* XXXVII (October, 1970), pp. 449-468.

34. This point has been emphasized for some time by the Economic Council of Canada.

35. Harry G. Johnson and Peter Mieszkowski, "The Effects of Unionization on the Distribution of Income: A General Equilibrium Approach," *The Quarterly Journal of Economics* LXXXIV (November, 1970), pp. 539-561.

36. D.A.L. Auld, "The Impact of Taxes on Wages and Prices in the Canadian Economy

1949-1968,'' (mimeo). See also the discussion above in Section 2d.

37. The Vice-Chairman of the Economic Council recently predicted that over the next year output is likely to increase $5^1/_2$ per cent and prices $3^1/_4$ per cent.

38. For a more detailed discussion and empirical evidence for the 1952-61 flexible rate period, see Caves and Reuber, *op. cit.,* especially Chap. 8.

## T. RUSSELL ROBINSON

# The Treatment of Dependants Under the Personal Income Tax

*It has often been pointed out that fixed exemptions do not result in horizontal equity between taxpayers. This article discusses the role of a dependants' exemption in the income tax system, and illustrates the more equitable effects of tax credits.*

## Expenses and Exemptions

The fundamental rationale for a wedge between assessed income and taxable income is that expenses clearly incurred in order to earn income should be deducted from gross income before tax is calculated. This basic principle has long been recognized by tax analysts, it is embodied in the existing tax treatment of businesses, it was espoused by the Royal Commission on taxation as a legitimate principle for personal income taxes, and it has been accepted and given very limited form in the recent White Paper on Tax Reform.

This "expense principle" may be invoked to rationalize a common exemption for the income-earner/taxpayer himself, thus giving rise to a basic exemption of the form currently used. While the expense philosophy may well justify the common exemption for the taxpayer himself, it clearly cannot be invoked to rationalize exemptions for dependants, for the care and feeding of dependants are not directly related to the earning of the income. Recognition of dependants in assessing personal income taxes must be argued on other grounds.

## Relief for Dependants as a Welfare Policy

The intention seems clear enough. As a matter of social welfare, it is generally accepted that it is desirable to afford some tax relief to taxpayers with dependants. It is also generally true that welfare policies tend (properly) to worry more about the low-income than the high-income taxpayer.

With the treatment of dependants properly viewed as a welfare policy rather than as a means to deduct expenses associated with earning income, it becomes blatantly clear that provision of a common exemption for a spouse and children has unintended and undesirable effects: (1) the tax relief is greater for the high-income than the low-income taxpayer, and the benefit is different across income classes; (2) the provision of exemptions, given the rate schedule, reduces the progressivity of the tax system relative to that achieved with the provision of uniform relief; and (3) the marginal tax rates facing taxpayers at the same total income level will be different, according to the number of dependants.

The first effect flies in the face of the underlying welfare rationale for recognition of dependants: the argument might well be that tax relief should be greater at the *lower* end of the income scale, or at the very least the same for all income earners. Who would argue that we should pay higher family allowances to the rich than the poor? Yet we are effectively doing just that by providing a fixed exemption for children. The second issue, relating to progressivity and to the total tax revenue generated from the income tax, is discussed further below. The third effect creates a differential impact on marginal net income (given equal marginal gross income) and thus creates a bias against the single or small-family taxpayers (*vis-à-vis* those with large families) in terms of the labour market in general, and in terms of the marginal decisions regarding work effort. These effects may not be very important either in terms of total work effort or employment opportunities, but it would surely be better for people with equal incomes to be faced with the same incentives, rather than with different ones depending on family size.

## Tax Credits vs. Exemptions

The introduction of an equivalent tax relief for dependants achieved by replacing exemptions with tax credits would provide a more direct and effective mechanism for achieving the welfare intentions behind recognition of dependants. Tax credits would solve the horizontal equity problem raised above, so that dependants would not be worth different amounts across the income scale. This desirable attribute alone has justified the pleas, made by the Royal Commission and by a generation of tax economists and others, for credits in place of exemptions. An additional advantage of credits is that they leave income-earners at equal income levels facing the same marginal tax rates, and thus with the same incentives with respect to marginal work effort.

It is sometimes proposed that the differential benefit accruing to high-income taxpayers as a result of fixed exemptions could be effectively taxed away again, by means of compensating upward adjustments in the tax rates. A new schedule could be designed to achieve essentially the same net tax position for some "typical" taxpayer across income levels as would be achieved with tax credits. Such an adjustment in rates would avoid the effect on progressivity (and the reduction of total revenues) over the taxpaying range of incomes which would result from an introduction or increase in exemptions taken by itself, but of course it would do nothing toward solving the horizontal equity problems, or the problem of differential incentives.

## Tax Credits vs. Exemptions: Progressivity and Total Revenues

The last comments above lead to the question of the degree of progressivity of the income tax in general, and to the related question of total revenue requirements. A switch from exemptions to credits for dependants can affect both of these, according to the amounts of credits and the extent of compensating rate adjustments. It may be useful to sort these effects out as follows.

(1) Replacement of exemptions with tax credits that have the same value for the lowest taxpaying income bracket would, taken by itself, raise more total revenue, and make the income tax more progressive.

(2) The amount of tax credit could be chosen so that *total* revenues remained constant. This would mean a higher credit than under (1). There would be taxpayers at some income level near the middle of the income range for whom the conversion to credits would leave total tax unchanged. Those with incomes above the level would receive less benefit (than under exemptions), and those below would enjoy greater benefits. While total revenue would be the same, progressivity would be increased.

(3) If both the level of total revenues *and* the overall degree of progressivity has been decided upon—say based on a tax schedule with provision for exemption—the substitution would have to be such that the total revenue collected from the group of taxpayers at *each total income level* would be maintained. (Thus the "average" tax collected at each income level would be maintained.) A new rate schedule would be needed, and it would look just like the schedule one would get by assessing the average tax collected (per taxpayer) at each income level under the existing system. Since the difference in taxes paid across taxpayers at each income level results from the existence of dependants, we may think of this "effective average" schedule as identifying the tax faced by taxpayers of average family size (in each total income class). That effective average rate schedule would, of course, be below the published schedule for a single taxpayer, and at any given income level would involve (generally) a lower "effective" marginal rate. This would be the schedule to be adopted under tax credits, with that schedule shifted vertically upward for taxpayers with "fewer-than-average" dependants, and vertically downward for taxpayers with "more-than-average" dependants.

The results of the above approach would be to equalize the tax relief for dependants across income levels, to have all taxpayers with the same total income face the same marginal rate, to generate the same total revenues and to achieve the same degree of progressivity as the existing system.[1]

## The Size of the Tax Credits

The only remaining decision would be on the size of the tax credits. The bigger they were the bigger would be the dispersion of taxes paid across family size at any given income level, and the bigger the difference in the income level at which the single versus family taxpayers started paying taxes. One could decide to maintain the same differential for the entrance to taxpaying status, and that would determine the credits. Or one could decide on the basis of what is thought to be a desirable tax relief—perhaps the effective relief for the low-income groups under the existing system, or perhaps the average tax relief which would be achieved under an exemptions system. The degree of progressivity and the total revenues would be unaffected, since we are adding and subtracting credits from our "effective average" schedule described above, so that the amount of credit could be decided as a separate question, to be judged on its own merits. Once these decisions were made, then the implied rate schedule, shorn of all credits, would be determined and used on the tax form.

The differential between credits for a spouse, other adult dependants and children would also be open for separate decision. Presumably it would be desirable to maintain differentials equivalent to the relative tax relief enjoyed by a typical family taxpayer under the existing system.

## Administration

The use of credits rather than exemptions would mean that the recognition of dependants would come at the end of the tax form (after the tax calculation, based on total assessed income minus a single "taxpayer" exemption had been made), rather than at the beginning. Apart from requiring more of the form to be filled in by those whose taxes were eliminated by dependants, there seems to be no particular difficulty at this level.

With credits a known and fixed amount, fiscal planning should be easier. Once the number of dependants associated with the taxpaying population was known, the distribution of these dependants across income classes, or changes in that distribution, would not affect total revenues. Of course, there is an effect under exemptions, which adds another, non-trivial problem to revenue projections and to assessment of incidence.

The reduction of credits according to incomes of dependants would be on a proportional basis, so that, for example, a tax credit for a spouse would be reduced to zero at the point where the spouse's income became taxable in its own right. The machinery for integrating the credit with dependants' incomes seems no more formidable than the machinery required under exemptions.

## Final Remarks

Equity in the personal income tax system was a fundamental objective of the Royal Commission on Taxation. The replacing of exemptions with tax credits was seen as an important step toward achieving equity with respect to treatment of dependants. The arguments seem conclusive. Further discussion and consideration of this particular reform proposal would seem to be highly desirable.

A further step, and one justified by the same welfare philosophy behind family allowances, would be to make tax credits for dependants "refundable", so that the poor family whose income was too low for the credit to be of full value could be paid the amount by which the credit exceeded gross tax liabilities. This way a tax credit for children of, say, $100, would be of equal value to *all* families, not just to those fortunate enough to have sufficient taxable income. After all, that is what the family allowance really is, a "refundable tax credit", by which the family's total net financial position vis-à-vis the government is reduced by [a given sum per year] per young child, regardless of income status. The form of payment is different, but the net effect is essentially the same.

If family allowances make some sense on the grounds that they at least treat children equally, independent of the income status of the parents, then refundable tax credits provide the comparable treatment within the income tax. A straight (non-refundable) tax credit is less equitable, because it does nothing for the poorest families, but it is still to be preferred over an exemption, which not only ignores the poorest families, but affords greater relief as income rises. The existence of child exemptions living side by side with family allowances is surely an anachronism, if the fundamental objectives determining treatment of dependants are to enhance social welfare and achieve equity in taxation.

### Footnote

1. It would also mean that those in any given income class who previously faced marginal rates *above* the "effective average" marginal rate for the class (e.g., the single taxpayer) would have their marginal rates lowered (to that average). Similarly, taxpayers with more-than-average number of dependants would have their marginal rates slightly raised. This is the mechanism by which neutrality with respect to marginal rates would be achieved.

## T. J. COURCHENE AND D. BEAVIS
# Federal-Provincial Tax Equalization: An Evaluation

## I. Introduction

Federal-Provincial tax equalization, authorized under the Federal Provincial Fiscal Arrangements Act, represents one of the most controversial issues in Canadian federalism. And the controversy is likely to continue since the present agreements have recently been extended through to 1974. Both net donor and beneficiary provinces appear at times to be unsatisfied. Of the donor provinces, British Columbia has been the most vocal in airing its dissatisfaction with the scheme: recently the Attorney-General of British Columbia suggested abolishing the equalization scheme and replacing it by a nation-wide negative income tax.[1] At the base of much of this dissatisfaction is the fact that these payments go unconditionally to provincial governments and not to individuals, so that their disbursement reflects the spending priorities of the recipient governments. The "have-not" or recipient provinces also from time to time express their misgivings with the details of the scheme. New Brunswick, for example, would like the scheme enlarged to include equalization of property taxes since it has now taken over this tax base from the municipalities.

The purpose of this paper is to analyze, and derive some implications from, tax equalization both for the current legislation and for several alternative schemes that have been proposed either formally or informally. Most of the paper will be devoted to an analysis of the scheme itself and not to the broader philosophical and economic underpinnings of the concept of equalization. Nonetheless, it should provide a firm background for future discussion of these more interesting and profound issues.

In outline form, the paper proceeds as follows. Section II presents alternative but equivalent versions of the present tax-equalization formula and also the actual equalization payments arising out of the Act for fiscal year 1968-1969. Section III embarks on a sensitivity analysis (on both an analytical and empirical level) of the equalization program to establish the effect on equalization payments of changes in various tax rates and tax bases for selected provinces. Also included in this section is an example of a type of provincial revenue strategy that the present formula could encourage. In Section IV we investigate some possible alternative formulations for tax equalization, including the oft-mentioned proposal of equalizing revenue to the average of the revenues of the richest three provinces rather than to the overall Canadian average. The important question of the funding of the scheme is treated in Section V. Even though this involves several strong assumptions, the inclusion of the funding provision allows us to approximate the ''net'' subsidy to each province as a result of the equalization program. Some final comments and implications complete the paper.

## II. The Equalization Formula

The most efficient approach to describing the present tax equalization formula is to quote directly from *The National Finances*:[2]

> In contrast to the equalization formula for 1962-67 which took into account only the three ''standard'' taxes and natural resource revenue, the new formula is based on the sixteen provincial revenue sources listed below:
>
> Personal income tax
> Corporation income tax
> Succession duties and shares of estate tax
> General sales tax
> Motor fuel tax
> Motor vehicle revenues
> Alcohol beverage revenues
> Forestry revenues
> Oil royalties
> Natural gas royalties
> Sales of Crown leases and reservations on oil and natural gas lands
> Other oil and gas revenues
> Metallic and non-metallic mineral revenues
> Water power rentals
> Other taxes
> Other revenues
>
> For each revenue source a base is chosen which is as close as possible to the actual base of the revenue source in all provinces. Then for each revenue source a ''national average provincial revenue rate'' is calculated by dividing the total revenue for all provinces by the total base for all provinces. This national average rate is multiplied by the base in each province and divided by the population of the province to give the per-capita yield of a ''tax'' levied at the national average rate. To obtain the equalization payment for the particular revenue source in the province the population of the province is multiplied by the difference between the per-capita yield in all provinces and the derived per-capita yield in the province at the national average rate. The total equalization payment for the province is the sum of entitlements, positive and negative, for each revenue source.
>
> There is a simpler method of calculating this payment. The percentage of total base attributed to a particular province is calculated as well as the percentage of the total population in the province. The difference between

the percentage of the base and the percentage of the population multiplied by the total revenue in all provinces from a source gives the equalization payment for the revenue source in the province. Again the total payment is the sum of payments for each source of revenue.[3]

The first method of calculation referred to in the quotation can be expressed algebraically as follows:

$$(1) \quad E_i = P_i \sum_{j=1}^{16} t_{cj} \left[ \frac{B_{cj}}{P_c} - \frac{B_{ij}}{P_i} \right]$$

where

$E_i$ = the dollar equalization payment to province i
$P_i$ = the population of province i
$t_{ij}$ = the tax rate in province i for revenue source j
$t_{cj}$ = the "national average provincial revenue rate" for tax source j. This rate is calculated for each source as the total revenue yield divided by the total base i.e.,

$$t_{cj} = \frac{\sum_{i=1}^{10} t_{ij} B_{ij}}{\sum_{i=1}^{10} B_{ij}}$$

for each source j.

$B_{ij}$ = the tax base of province i for revenue source j

$B_{cj}$ = the total tax base for Canada for revenue source j, i.e.,

$$B_{cj} = \sum_{i=1}^{10} B_{ij}$$

$P_c$ = population of Canada, i.e.,

$$P_c = \sum_{i=1}^{10} P_i$$

i = subscript referring to province
j = subscript referring to tax source

For each tax source, then, the province is entitled to a positive subsidy if its per-capita base is less than the national average per-capita base, i.e., if $\left[ \frac{B_{cj}}{P_c} - \frac{B_{ij}}{P_i} \right]$ is positive, and a negative subsidy if $\left[ \frac{B_{cj}}{P_c} - \frac{B_{ij}}{P_i} \right]$ is negative. For each tax source the dollar grant or subsidy is proportional to the national tax rate, $t_{cj}$, and, of course, the province's population. These payments are then summed over all 16 sources and if the sum, $E_i$, is positive then the value of the equalization payment to province i is $E_i$. If $E_i$ is negative, payment is set at zero.

From (1), we can take $P_i$ into the brackets yielding

$$(2) \quad E_i = \sum_{j=1}^{16} t_{cj} \left[ \frac{P_i \, B_{cj}}{P_c} - B_{ij} \right]$$

Noting that $t_{cj} = \dfrac{\sum_{i=1}^{10} t_{ij} \, B_{ij}}{\sum_{i=1}^{10} B_{ij}}$ ,

replacing $t_{cj}$ by this expression, and bringing the denominator of the expression (which equals $B_{cj}$) into the bracket yields:

$$(3) \quad E_i = \sum_{j=1}^{16} \left[ \sum_{i=1}^{10} t_{ij} \, B_{ij} \right] \left[ \frac{P_i}{P_c} - \frac{B_{ij}}{B_{cj}} \right]$$

which is the alternative formulation mentioned in the above quote. This is perhaps more obvious when it is recognized that

$$\sum_{i=1}^{10} t_{ij} \, B_{ij}$$

is the total Canadian revenue from tax source j. In words, equation (3) indicates that for each tax source j, provinces will get a positive share of total revenue for that source if their ratio of total population, $\dfrac{P_i}{P_c}$ is greater than their share of the tax base for the particular source $B_{ij}/B_{cj}$. Again, these equalization payments, positive and negative, for each source are summed for each province and a positive value of $E_i$ is the equalization payment for province i. A negative value for $E_i$ means that the payment is zero for that province.

## AN INTUITIVE VIEW OF EQUALIZATION

With a few further assumptions, we can reduce the equalization formula to a very intuitive level. Assume, first, that the total revenue, $R_i$, of each province is the sum of the province's *own* revenue plus the equalization payment it receives[4] where the former can be expressed as $\sum_{j=1}^{16} t_{ij} B_{ij}$. If we further assume that all provincial tax *rates* for a given revenue base are equal (i.e., $t_{ij} = t_{cj}$ for all i), then total revenue for province i from each source becomes

$$(4) \quad R_{ij} = P_i \left[ \left( t_{ij} \frac{B_{ij}}{P_i} \right) + t_{ij} \left( \frac{B_{cj}}{P_c} - \frac{B_{ij}}{P_i} \right) \right]$$

where the second term represents the equalization payment formula (1) above with the assumption that $t_{ij} = t_{cj}$. For the poorer provinces, this formula reduces to

$$(5) \quad R_{ij} = P_i \left( t_{ij} \frac{B_{cj}}{P_c} \right)$$

so that the have-not provinces are, in effect, able to tax the *national* average per-capita base, $\dfrac{B_{ij}}{P_c}$ rather than their *own* base $\dfrac{B_{ij}}{P_i}$. Since we are assuming that $t_{cj} = t_{ij}$ we can also interpret (5) as a national tax on a national tax base, the revenues from which are apportioned to the provinces according to their share of the population.

Naturally, to the extent that these simplifications are invalid (e.g., to the extent that the $t_{ij}$ differ from the $t_{cj}$) equation (5) will also be invalid. Nevertheless, it does provide a revealing picture of the essential principle underlying the equalization scheme.

Prior to presenting data relating to the schedule of equalization payments from fiscal years 1968-69, we should emphasize that these payments come out of general *federal* revenue and *not directly from the treasuries of Canada's richest provinces*. We shall return to the important question of the funding of the equalization scheme later in the paper.

## EQUALIZATION PAYMENTS FOR 1968-1969

Table I presents summary data relating to the level of equalization payments in 1968-69 and to total revenue for the various provinces both before and after equalization. Column (1) lists the population figures used for the calculations. Columns (2) and (3) present revenue data for "own" provincial revenues, i.e.,

$$\sum_{j=1}^{16} t_{ij} B_{ij}$$

in both dollar and per-capita terms. Alberta and British Columbia have per-capita own revenue levels substantially above levels for other provinces. Not surprisingly, the Atlantic provinces have lowest per-capita yields from their own revenue sources. Columns (4) and (5) are provincial revenues calculated by applying the national average provincial tax rate to the revenue bases in each province, i.e.,

$$\sum_{i=1}^{16} t_{cj} B_{ij} \ .$$

Differences between these two columns and columns (2) and (3) reflect differences between $t_{ij}$ and $t_{cj}$. The all-Canada figure for per-capita revenue is \$343.35. Equalization payments (following equation (1) above) are easily calculated from these data. The per-capita deficiency is equal to \$343.35

minus the relevant $\displaystyle\sum_{i=j}^{16} t_{cj} B_{ij}/P_i$ , i.e., the figures in column (5). These are

presented in column (7). Dollar values of equalization payments appear in column (6), and are the product of columns (7) and (1). Three provinces do not qualify for equalization: British Columbia, Ontario, and Alberta. Naturally, these provinces have per-capita yields at national average tax-rates that are greater than the national average, i.e., greater than \$343.35. While Quebec's equalization payment per-capita is only \$66.17, it garners substantially more than half of the total dollar value of the equalization payments because of its

Table 1  Summary Data Relating to Tax Equalization 1968-1969

| Province | Population | Own Tax Revenue¹ | | Yield at National Average Tax Rate² | | Equalization Payment | | Total Revenue | |
|---|---|---|---|---|---|---|---|---|---|
| | | ($000) | Per Capita | ($000) | Per Capita | ($000) | Per Capita % | ($000) | Per Capita % |
| | (1) | (2) | (3) | (4) | (5) | (6) | (7) | (8) | (9) |
| NFLD | 507000. | 106766. | 210.58 | 101101. | 199.41 | 72977. | 143.94 | 179743. | 354.52 |
| PEI | 110000. | 22016. | 200.15 | 21641. | 196.74 | 16127. | 146.61 | 38143. | 346.76 |
| NS | 760000. | 146304. | 192.51 | 181507. | 238.83 | 79437. | 104.52 | 225741. | 297.03 |
| NB | 624000. | 159420. | 255.48 | 143536. | 230.03 | 70713. | 113.32 | 230133. | 368.80 |
| QUE | 5927000. | 1872948. | 316.00 | 1642802. | 277.17 | 392219. | 66.17 | 2265167. | 382.18 |
| ONT | 7306000. | 2738330. | 374.81 | 2783307. | 380.96 | 0. | 0.00 | 2738330. | 374.81 |
| MAN | 971000. | 287688. | 296.28 | 286574. | 295.13 | 46816. | 48.21 | 334504. | 344.49 |
| SASK | 960000. | 322214. | 335.64 | 299305. | 311.78 | 30309. | 31.57 | 352523. | 367.21 |
| ALTA | 1526000. | 629776. | 412.70 | 803926. | 526.82 | 0. | 0.00 | 629776. | 412.70 |
| BC | 2007000. | 821146. | 409.14 | 842909. | 419.98 | 0. | 0.00 | 821146. | 409.14 |
| CAN | 20698000. | 7106608. | 343.35 | 7106608. | 343.35 | 708598. | 34.24 | 7815206. | 377.58 |

Source: Dept of Finance

1.  $\sum_{i=1}^{16} t_{ij} B_{ij}$ for the dollar column

2.  $\sum_{i=1}^{16} t_{cj} B_{ij}$, again for the dollar column

Notes: Figures in these tables may differ from actual equalization payments because of rounding error, etc. But the differences are very small.

large population. Total equalization payments amounted to slightly over $700 million in 1968-69. The final two columns of Table I present figures for total revenue (own revenue plus equalization) for each of the provinces. Looking at the per-capita data for total revenue (the last column in the table) the impact of the equalization payments is to push the revenues for all provinces except Nova Scotia well over the $300 per-capita figure. Indeed, all provinces except Nova Scotia now have revenue per capita figures above the original Canadian average figure of $343.35.

Table II presents the equalization payments that arise *from each revenue source*. The sixteen sources listed in the table correspond exactly to the sixteen sources listed in the first paragraph of this section. A positive entry in a cell implies that the province receives a positive equalization payment from that revenue source and vice versa.   Recall that one way of interpreting $E_{ij}$ is that

it is the product of the difference between $\dfrac{P_i}{P_c}$ and $\dfrac{B_{ij}}{B_{cj}}$ and the total rev-

enue from tax source j. Therefore positive entries imply that for that revenue source the particular province has a lesser share of the tax base than it does of population. When summed for each column these figures yield the totals as presented in the second last row of the table. These totals are the equalization payments for provinces whose totals are positive. Negative totals imply a zero level of equalization (see the last line of the table).

We now turn to an analysis of some of the more interesting features and implications of Canada's tax equalization plan.

## III.   A Sensitivity Analysis of the Equalization Scheme

The purpose of this section of the paper is to examine the effect on equalization payments of changes in the tax bases and tax rates of various provinces. Initially, the sensitivity analysis will be conducted on an analytical level. Later in this section, however, we shall present some empirical results for changes in specific tax bases and rates.

### CHANGING THE $t_{ij}$

For purposes of the sensitivity tests we shall again consider the total revenue accruing to province i to be the sum of the revenue from its own sources and the equalization payment; i.e.,

$$(6) \quad R_i = \sum_{j=1}^{16} t_{ij} B_{ij} + \sum_{j=1}^{16} \left[ \sum_{i=1}^{10} t_{ij} B_{ij} \right] \left[ \frac{P_i}{P_c} - \frac{B_{ij}}{B_{cj}} \right]$$

where the second term is the equalization payment adopted from equation (3). Suppose we assume that province 3 increases its tax rate on revenue source 6. Then for province 3 we have:

$$(7) \quad \frac{\partial R_3}{\partial t_{3,6}} = B_{3,6} + B_{3,6} \left[ \frac{P_3}{P_c} - \frac{B_{3,6}}{B_{c,6}} \right].$$

Table II   Equalization By Revenue Source: 1968-1969

($ ,000)

| Province / Revenue Source | NFLD | PEI | NS | NB | QUE | ONT | MAN | SASK | ALTA | BC |
|---|---|---|---|---|---|---|---|---|---|---|
| 1 | 21263. | 5065. | 21906. | 22302. | 59038. | -147083. | 11621. | 23525. | 5658. | -23294. |
| 2 | 8590. | 2326. | 12005. | 10508. | 38854. | -70121. | 4661. | 12735. | -4229. | -15328. |
| 3 | 3721. | 584. | 891. | 3624. | 3806. | -22540. | 2445. | 3972. | 4305. | -809. |
| 4 | 7708. | 1896. | 6630. | 7869. | 76302. | -53752. | 3252. | 4208. | -25025. | -29088. |
| 5 | 8597. | 562. | 5387. | 3230. | 23664. | -28600. | 3416. | -2212. | -11096. | -2947. |
| 6 | 2964. | 194. | 1857. | 1114. | 8159. | -9860. | 1178. | - 763. | -3826. | -1016. |
| 7 | 5966. | 359. | 1375. | 1392. | 44270. | -34295. | -145. | 1996. | -3400. | -17517. |
| 8 | -620. | 671. | 3978. | -897. | 8264. | 26511. | 4593. | 3626. | 4070. | -50195. |
| 9 | 2541. | 551. | 3808. | 3126. | 29701. | 36260. | 3140. | -18115. | -65505. | 4493. |
| 10 | 742. | 161. | 1112. | 907. | 8671. | 10173. | 1421. | 781. | -25067. | 899. |
| 11 | 3826. | 830. | 5736. | 4709. | 44733. | 55140. | 7215. | -1914. | -118107. | -2169. |
| 12 | 1670. | 348. | 2503. | 2055. | 19523. | 23542. | 3013. | -5549. | -42696. | -4410. |
| 13 | -4028. | 293. | 1572. | 676. | 1934. | -3215. | -570. | -506. | 3999. | -154. |
| 14 | -119. | 222. | 1316. | 768. | -7146. | 2832. | -46. | 1392. | 2747. | -1966. |
| 15 | 6877. | 1397. | 6338. | 6316. | 21966. | -40620. | 1098. | 4828. | -1221. | -6978. |
| 16 | 3281. | 667. | 3024. | 3013. | 10479. | -19379. | 524. | 2304. | -583. | -3329. |
| Total | 72977. | 16127. | 79437. | 70713. | 392219. | -274810. | 46816. | 30309. | -279977. | -153811. |
| Equalization Payments | 72,977 | 16,127 | 79,437 | 70,713 | 392,219 | 0 | 46,816 | 30,309 | 0 | 0 |

Revenues for province 3 from its own source of revenue will increase by $B_{3,6}$ times $\partial t_{3,6}$ and its equalization payment will also increase if the bracketed term is positive, i.e., if province 3 has a share of the base for revenue source 6 which is less than its share of the total population. In other words, if province 3 is a relatively poor province in terms of revenue source 6 it will garner an increase in its subsidy. If not, its subsidy will decrease. Therefore, the total change in revenue to province 3 as a result of the tax rate change will be greater than the change in its own revenue of it is a "poor" province for revenue base 6.

For the impact on the provincial revenues of other provinces as a result of a tax change in province 3 we are left only with the equalization term, i.e.,

$$(8) \quad \frac{\partial R_i}{\partial t_{3,6}} = B_{3,6} \left[ \frac{P_i}{P_c} - \frac{B_{i,6}}{B_{c,6}} \right] \text{ for } i \neq 3.$$

If province i is relatively poor in terms of base 6 (i.e., if the bracketed term is positive) then its equalization payment will increase. Otherwise it will fall, or remain at zero. Therefore, the effect of a tax rate change by province i on source j will increase the equalization payments for all provinces that are relatively "poor" in terms of revenue base j. Intuitively, this result can be explained in terms of equation (1) since an increase in the tax rate $t_{3,6}$ will increase $t_{c,6}$. These results can be generalized by replacing 3 and 6 by i and j.

## CHANGING THE $B_{ij}$

The effect on provincial equalization payments of a one unit change in $B_{ij}$ is somewhat more complicated. Assuming again that the province and base in question are 3 and 6 respectively, we have, from partially differentiating equation (6):

$$(9) \quad \frac{\partial B_3}{\partial B_{3,6}} = t_{3,6} + t_{3,6} \left[ \frac{P_3}{P_c} - \frac{B_{3,6}}{B_{c,6}} \right] - \left[ \sum_{i=1}^{10} t_{i,6} B_{i,6} \right] \left[ \frac{B_{c,6} - B_{3,6}}{(B_{c,6})^2} \right]$$

$$\text{and} \quad (10) \quad \frac{\partial B_i}{\partial B_{3,6}} = t_{3,6} \left[ \frac{P_i}{P_c} - \frac{B_{i,6}}{B_{c,6}} \right] + \left[ \sum_{i=j}^{10} t_{i,6} B_{i,6} \right] \left[ \frac{B_{i,6}}{(B_{c,6})^2} \right]; \quad i \neq 3.$$

The interpretation of (9) and (10) is quite straightforward, however. From (9), a province will naturally generate an increase in its own revenue from changing $B_{3,6}$ and this increase is represented by $t_{3,6}$ times its tax rate on revenue source 6. There are two components to the change in the equalization payments as a result of changing $B_{3,6}$ and these are represented by the last two terms of (9). As a result of changing $B_{3,6}$ there is now more total Canadian revenue associated with revenue source 6 and this will be allocated in the same manner as the previous revenue. This is captured by the middle term of (9): if province 3 has a percentage of the total base for source 6 smaller than its percentage of total population, then on this count its equalization payment will increase as a result of the change in its base, $B_{3,6}$. On the other hand, province 3 now has a larger share of the total base for source 6 than it had before the change in its base. On this count it will find that its equalization payment falls because it now is eligible for a smaller share of the total revenue $\sum\limits_{i=1}^{10} t_{i,6} B_{i,6}$ than previously. This is the third term in (9) and it must be negative, since ($B_{c,6} - B_{3,6}$) is positive. For a province which has a relatively low percentage of a particular revenue base 6, the impact on the equalization payments it receives on changing the revenue base is indeterminate. One could work out the conditions under which it will be either positive or negative, but we will defer to a numerical example on this point.

For the other provinces, any change in revenue from having province 3 alter its tax base will occur only in the equalization payments. The first term in (10) is similar to the second term in (9): a relatively rich province will lose some equalization and vice versa. The second term will always be positive and reflects the marginal decrease in the size of province j's (j ≠ 3) share of the base for revenue source 6, i.e., each of the other 9 provinces will now have a smaller $\dfrac{B_{i,6}}{B_{c,6}}$ ratio because their $B_{i,6}$ remained the same while $B_{c,6}$ increased as a result of the increase in the base province 3.

Therefore, equalization payments in *all* provinces are affected by changes in either the tax rate or tax base in a particular province. Naturally, this may not show up in the *final* values for equalization payments for the richer provinces, e.g., as a result of a tax increase in Saskatchewan, the equalization subsidy accruing to Alberta for the relevant revenue source would increase, but since the sum of all such subsidies will in all likelihood still remain negative, Alberta will still get a zero value for its final equalization payment.

Other types of experiments are also possible. For example, one could look at the impact of internal migration (or any other factor that alters $P_i$ or $\sum\limits_{i=1}^{10} P_i$) on provincial equalization payments. And the analytical solutions to some of these alternative experiments can often be quite obvious. Consider, for example, a 5% increase in all the bases (for each province and for each source). From equation (3) it is clear that the term in square brackets will remain invariant to equal percentage changes in all the bases while the term that premultiplies it will increase by 5% (assuming that tax rates are all *proportional* to income). This implies that the impact of a 5% increase in all bases is to generate a 5% increase in all equalization payments. We now turn to some numerical examples of the sensitivity of these payments to changes in both tax bases and tax rates.

## SOME NUMERICAL TESTS OF SENSITIVITY

Table III contains data relating to the impact on the equalization grants of selected changes in the rate and base parameters for various provinces. We shall restrict our comments on the results to noting a few of the more interesting findings. Detailed analysis of the Table is left to the reader. Column (1) merely recopies from Table I, for comparison purposes, the actual level of equalization payments in 1968-69. The next three columns show the impact of changes in tax rates for selected provinces—a one percentage point increase in sales tax in Nova Scotia in column (2), a one percentage point hike in Ontario's corporate income tax rate in column (3), and the imposition of a sales tax in Alberta at a 3% rate. The last row of the Table gives the change in the *own* revenue of the provinces in which the tax or base changes are made.

The result of the increase in Nova Scotia's sales tax rate results in all the provinces (except Ontario, Alberta and B.C.) increasing their equalization payment, including Nova Scotia. As a result of Ontario's corporation income tax increase (note that we are assuming an across-the-board increase in the income tax rate) total equalization payments increase by approximately $4 million (compare columns (1) and (3) for the second last row). Ontario's revenue increases by just over $28 million. Therefore, equalization payments arising out of this tax rate change amount to approximately 14% of the increase in Ontario's revenue.

Columns (4), (5), and (6), present results for changes in tax bases. A 5% increase in the tax base in Nova Scotia leads to a decrease in Nova Scotia's equalization payments, by some $1.528 million. It is extremely significant to note that its own revenue increases by only $1.467 million as a result of the sales tax base increase. Therefore, the result of a change in Nova Scotia's sales tax base is to make the provincial treasury worse off! As a result of this base change, all of the other "have-not" provinces register increases in their equalization payments, as they do for the experiments in columns (5) and (6) as well. In terms of our analytical section, this implies that equation (10) has a positive value for the "other" provinces.

As a result of having a 5% greater sales tax base, Quebec's revenue increases by nearly $30 million. Its equalization payment falls by about $15 million. As a result of the base increase, therefore, Quebec is able to garner only half of what the sales tax change would yield in the absence of an equalization scheme.

## THE ROLE FOR PROVINCIAL STRATEGIES UNDER THE EQUALIZATION SCHEME

The results we have analyzed in Table III clearly suggest that there is plenty of room for strategy on the part of the provinces with regard to their taxation programs. If a province were to raise a given amount of revenue and it is indifferent as to the revenue source from which it is to be derived, then it makes good sense for it to raise the revenue in a manner that will lead to an increase in its equalization payment. In Table II we presented a matrix of equalization payments (positive and negative) by province and source. If a province wants to increase tax rates it will also increase its overall equalization payment if it levies the increased tax on a source *for which the entry in Table II is positive*. In fact it should increase tax rates on the revenue source which has the highest positive value for $\left[ \dfrac{P_i}{P_c} - \dfrac{B_{ij}}{B_{cj}} \right]$ . To levy a tax on a revenue source for which it has

Table III  The Impact on Equalization Payments of Selected Changes in Provincial Tax Rates and Tax Bases, 1968-1969
($ ,000)

| Province | Original Equalization Payment 1968-69 | +1 percentage point in Sales tax in N.S. | +1 percentage point in Ontario Corp. income tax | +3% Sales tax in Alberta | +5% on Sales tax base in N.S. | +5% in personal income tax base in B.C. | +5% Sales tax base in Quebec | +1 percentage point in Personal income tax rate in Quebec | Increase in Water Power Rental Rate in Quebec by 44.62% |
|---|---|---|---|---|---|---|---|---|---|
| NFLD. | 72,977 | 73,016 | 73,342 | 73,301 | 73,014 | 73,178 | 73,491 | 73,153 | 72,941 |
| P.E.I. | 16,127 | 16,137 | 16,226 | 16,207 | 16,135 | 16,171 | 16,240 | 16,169 | 16,193 |
| N.S. | 79,437 | 79,471 | 79,947 | 79,716 | 77,855 | 79,740 | 80,175 | 79,619 | 79,827 |
| N.B. | 70,713 | 70,753 | 71,159 | 71,044 | 70,760 | 70,961 | 71,335 | 70,898 | 70,940 |
| Quebec | 392,219 | 392,607 | 393,870 | 395,428 | 392,682 | 394,609 | 379,237 | 392,709 | 390,103 |
| Ontario | 0 | 0 | 0 | 0 | 0 | 0 | 0 | 0 | 0 |
| Manitoba | 46,816 | 46,833 | 47,014 | 46,953 | 46,892 | 47,207 | 47,725 | 46,913 | 46,803 |
| Sask. | 30,309 | 30,330 | 30,850 | 30,486 | 30,382 | 30,693 | 31,214 | 30,504 | 30,721 |
| Alberta | 0 | 0 | 0 | 0 | 0 | 0 | 0 | 0 | 0 |
| B.C. | 0 | 0 | 0 | 0 | 0 | 0 | 0 | 0 | 0 |
| Total | 708,598 | 709,147 | 712,408 | 713,134 | 707,720 | 712,559 | 699,416 | 709,964 | 707,528 |
| Increase in Relevant Province's own Revenue | | 8,029 | 28,050 | 67,362 | 1,467 | 8,090 | 29,379 | 12,359 | 12,359 |

a negative entry in Table II (equivalently, for which $\dfrac{B_{ij}}{B_{cj}} > \dfrac{P_i}{P_c}$ ) will result in a decrease in the equalization grant.

It would have been possible to carry out extensive numerical experimentation in order to understand better the implications arising from this feature of the equalization program. We have restricted ourselves, in this paper, to two examples, the results of which appear in the last two columns of Table III. In the second last column we increased the personal income tax in Quebec by one percentage point (for all the tax brackets). This generated an increase in its *own* revenue of $12.359 million and *increased* Quebec's equalization payments by $490,000. In the last column we calculated the required percentage increase in the tax rate on the Water Power Rentals revenue source to again yield $12.359 million (i.e., 44.62%). As a result of raising an identical amount of its own revenue, the equalization payments accruing to Quebec *fall* by $2,116,000. Naturally, the Quebec entry in Table II for Water Power Rentals is negative (revenue source 14). This is a highly interesting result. The impact of the equalization plan is to bias provincial preference in the direction of raising revenues from those tax sources for which they have a relatively small share of tax base.

We now turn our attention to some proposals for modifying the current tax equalization plan.

## IV. Alternative Equalization Formulations

There are many possible ways in which the present tax equalization scheme could be altered. For purposes of this section we shall focus on only two modifications to the formula, both of which have received some attention either in the theoretical literature relating to the general topic of revenue sharing or in the public discussions relating to the Canadian equalization plan. The first modification is to replace the Canadian average provincial tax rate $t_{cj}$ in the equalization formula by the province's own tax rate $t_{ij}$. The second modification has to do with replacing the Canadian average per-capita tax base for

each source, $\dfrac{B_{cj}}{P_c}$, by an average that relates to, say, the highest five or highest three provinces. We shall deal with each of these in turn.

In his pioneering paper on revenue sharing, R. A. Musgrave[5] suggested that equalization payments to province i should reflect tax *effort* by province i. If a province wishes to receive a larger equalization payment it must be willing to subject its citizens to higher tax rates. Under the present scheme, the subsidy to province i can go up as a result of a tax increase in province j. This would be precluded under a Musgrave-type scheme. This alternative is very easily incorporated into our notational framework. Specifically, in equation (1) we replace $t_{cj}$ by $t_{ij}$ and obtain

$$(11) \quad E_i = P_i \sum_{i=1}^{16} t_{ij} \left[ \frac{B_{cj}}{P_c} - \frac{B_{ij}}{P_c} \right].$$

Thus, for a given tax source, a province with a positive value for

$\dfrac{B_{cj}}{P_c} - \dfrac{B_{ij}}{P_i}$ can increase its payment by raising its *own* tax rate on that reve-

nue source, i.e., raise $t_{ij}$. While there are some disadvantages to this formulation, it is important to note that it does have the disadvantage of encouraging *further* any strategy that might exist under the present plan. Under the philosophy embodied in (11) it is clear that the provinces would have an incentive to increase tax rates on revenue sources for which the differences between

$\dfrac{B_{cj}}{P_c} - \dfrac{B_{ij}}{P_i}$ are large and decrease the $t_{ij}$ on those sources for which this dif-

ference is smaller or negative. Much more could be said concerning this alternative to the present scheme, but we shall restrict ourselves to a few further comments later in this section when we discuss the results for 1968-69 of this and the following alternatives to the present revenue sharing plan.

## AVERAGING TO THE HIGHEST N PROVINCES

The most commonly suggested alternative to the present scheme is that revenues should be equalized, not to the Canadian average tax base for each source, but rather to the average tax base of Canada's N richest provinces where N is say 3 or perhaps 5. Unfortunately this is not a very straightforward modification because there are several ways to interpret what is meant by averaging the highest three provinces. One possibility is that for *each* tax source we choose the richest three provinces and calculate the resulting equalization payments. This would mean that the highest three provinces would differ from tax source to tax source. We rule out this interpretation because a) we feel that this is not what is generally meant by averaging to the highest three provinces, and b) the levels of equalization payments will be extremely large and it is even theoretically possible for *all* provinces to be eligible for equalization payments.

Even requiring that the same three provinces will be used for each revenue source still leaves us with at least two alternative versions, both of which appear

worthy of analysis. The first version simply involves replacing $\dfrac{B_{cj}}{P_c}$ in equa-

tion (1) by $\dfrac{B_{cj}{}^3}{P_c{}^3}$ assuming that the averaging is taking place over the top

three provinces,[6] i.e.,

$$(12) \quad E_i = P_i \sum_{i=1}^{16} t_{cj} \left[ \frac{B_{cj}{}^3}{P_c{}^3} - \frac{B_{ij}}{P_i} \right]$$

where $\dfrac{B_{cj}{}^3}{P_c{}^3} =$ the average per-capita base for the three richest provinces.

Since $\dfrac{B_{cj}{}^3}{P_c{}^3}$ will obviously be greater than $\dfrac{B_{cj}}{P_c}$ this modification will re-

sult in larger equalization payments.

This version still assumes that the per-capita deficiency is multiplied by the national average tax rate, $t_{cj}$. It is possible to argue that it is more appropriate to multiply the deficiency by the average tax rate in the *three (or more generally, the N) chosen provinces* rather than by $t_{cj}$. This would convert the formulation to:

$$(13) \quad E_i = P_i \sum_{i=1}^{16} t_{cj}^3 \left[ \frac{B_{cj}^3}{P_c^3} - \frac{B_{ij}}{P_i} \right].$$

It is not clear that (13) will result in larger overall equalization payments than will (12), i.e., it is quite possible for $t_{cj}$ to be greater than $t_{cj}^3$. We now present the impact on the equalization payments for 1968-69 of these three alternative schemes, as represented by equations (11), (12), and (13).

## RESULTS FOR THE ALTERNATIVE PROPOSALS

Table IV presents results for modifying the existing scheme along the lines of equation (12), i.e., the provinces receive a payment (positive or negative) from each source depending on the product of the national average provincial tax rate, $t_{cj}$, and the difference between the per-capita base for the top N provinces and the per-capita base for the province in question. Table IV presents figures for N = 5, 3, and 2. While it is possible to use several criteria for selecting the N provinces, our procedure was simply to use the data in column 5 of Table I to rank the provinces. On this basis (i.e., per-capita revenue yield at national average tax rates), Alberta, British Columbia, Ontario, Saskatchewan, and Manitoba, are the ordered top five richest provinces. In Table I the overall level of equalization payments is just over $700 million. As a result of averaging to the highest 5 provinces equalization payments jump to $1.282 billion (see the entry in the last row of left panel of Table IV). In Table I, the national average value of revenue per-capita (appropriately summed over the 16 revenue sources) is $343.35 per person. For N = 5 this figure (not shown) is $392.79. The interesting feature is that Ontario now is entitled to a subsidy — at the rate of $11.84 per person, or $86,470. If the averaging is carried out over the 3 highest provinces, equalization payments run to over $1^{1}/_{2}$ billion dollars — more than double the equalization in Table I (see the middle panel of Table IV). For the case where Alberta and British Columbia provide the standard (i.e., N = 2) the total value of equalization payments soars to 2.6 billion dollars. Furthermore, British Columbia now receives an equalization payment (92.6 million). Compared to the actual 1968-69 payments, this represents nearly a four-fold increase in the total equalization grants. Figures for provinces presently receiving grants do not show this large a percentage increase because part of the increases are taken up by the grants that now go to Ontario and British Columbia. Oddly enough, the figures for total revenue (i.e., own revenue plus equalization) per-capita for N = 2 (the last column) indicate that Alberta, the richest province and the only one not receiving an equalization payment ends up with the *lowest* per-capita total revenue.[7] This results because the "tax effort" (i.e., $t_{ij}$) in Alberta is the lowest of all the provinces. We leave to the reader the job of completing the analysis of Table IV.

Table IV   Equalization Payments Based on Averaging to the
Richest N Provinces

| Province | Richest 5 ($000) | $/Cap | Richest 3 ($000) | $/Cap | Richest 2 ($000) | $/ Cap |
|---|---|---|---|---|---|---|
| NFLD. | 98048. | 193.39 | 106122. | 209.31 | 135227. | 266.72 |
| P.E.I. | 21567. | 196.06 | 23318. | 211.99 | 29633. | 269.39 |
| Nova Scotia | 117019. | 153.97 | 129122. | 169.90 | 172751. | 227.30 |
| New Brunswick | 101569. | 162.77 | 111507. | 178.70 | 147329. | 236.10 |
| Quebec | 685307. | 115.62 | 779696. | 131.55 | 1119947. | 188.96 |
| Ontario | 86470. | 11.84 | 202819. | 27.76 | 622234. | 85.17 |
| Manitoba | 94832. | 97.66 | 110295. | 113.59 | 166037. | 171.00 |
| Saskatchewan | 77781. | 81.02 | 93069. | 96.95 | 148180. | 154.35 |
| Alberta | 0. | 0.00 | 0. | 0.00 | 0. | 0.00 |
| B.C. | 0. | 0.00 | 0. | 0.00 | 92612. | 46.14 |
| Canada | 1,282,591 | 392.79* | 1,555,947 | 408.72* | 2,633,950 | 468.13* |

*This is the per-capita Canadian average yield at the national average tax rate, corresponding to $343.45 in Table I.

Table V   Averaging to Highest N Provinces   Equation (3)
($ ,000)

| Province | Three Highest Provinces | Two Highest Provinces |
|---|---|---|
| NFLD | 102,408 | 124,041 |
| P.E.I. | 22,449 | 27,651 |
| N.S. | 125,048 | 163,207 |
| NB | 107,042 | 137,199 |
| Quebec | 751,264 | 1,055,500 |
| Ontario | 213,932 | 652,823 |
| Manitoba | 107,337 | 158,911 |
| Sask. | 86,516 | 136,303 |
| Alberta | 0 | 0 |
| B.C. | 0 | 95,325 |

Embodied in this table is the assumption that even though we are equalizing around the highest N provinces, it is still appropriate to use the national average provincial tax rate $t_{cj}$, for each revenue source. As mentioned above, it is also reasonable to require that this average tax rate be the average for each source of the same N provinces used in the equalization procedure. In other words, it is reasonable to use equation (13) rather than equation (12) when attempting to modify the present formula to average around the highest N provinces. The results for the equalization payments derived from applying equation (13) appear in Table V for the case of N = 3, and N = 2. The equalization payments in Table IV for N = 3 are, except for Ontario, larger than those in column (1) of Table V and the payments in Table IV for N = 2 are, except for British Columbia, larger than those in column (2) of Table V. What this suggests is that the national average tax rate $t_{cj}$ is, on average and over all revenue sources, *greater* than the average rate calculated either over the top three or top two provinces. As a result of this, equalization payments are lower for formulation (13) than for formulation (12). This should not surprise us since we noted earlier that Alberta has the lowest "tax effort".

The modification first mentioned in this section related to introducing tax effort into the equalization scheme. Specifically, the difference between the national average per-capita base and the provincial base for each source is multiplied not by $t_{cj}$ but rather by $t_{ij}$ . See equation (11). The values for equalization payments based on this formula turn out to be considerably *lower* than those from the existing scheme. Rather than presenting these results in a manner similar to the results in say, Table IV, we opted for a format that revealed the reasons why the level of equalization turns out to be lower. Refer to Table VI which gives the equalization payments by province and by source, i.e., it is identical in format to Table II. Across the bottom of Table VI are the equalization payments. Except for Saskatchewan, all provinces' subsidies would be less than they are under the present scheme. In order to see why this occurs, let us take Quebec as an example. Comparing the equalization subsidy for personal income tax (row 1) for Tables VI and II, we note that Quebec receives a greater payment under the tax effort scheme (Table VI). This is so because its tax *rate* on personal income tax is greater than the national average rate $t_{c1}$. However, for four revenue sources Quebec's subsidy is zero (revenue sources 9 to 12 which relate to oil and gas revenues) because its tax rate is zero. In turn its tax rate is zero because it probably has no tax base for these sources. Despite the fact that Quebec is a province with a relatively high "tax effort", it comes out worse under a tax effort type of scheme because the equalization payments are calculated for *each* revenue source rather than on an aggregate basis.

It should be pointed out that the results in Table VI are not too meaningful because if this particular version of an equalization program were in effect, *the provincial tax rates* $t_{ij}$ , *would probably not have the values they currently do*.


## V.   Funding the Equalization Scheme

Up to this point we have neglected entirely the fact that the scheme has to be funded. We have mentioned that the equalization payments come out of general revenue rather than from the coffers of the richer provinces. This means that the financial costs of the plan are borne by all tax-paying Canadians. And it also means that it will be fruitful to look at the costing of the equalization scheme and attempt to construct a "net benefit" to each province as a result of the total impact (costing plus payments) of the equalization scheme. The purpose of this section is to attempt such an analysis.

The first issue to be tackled is the allocation of federal revenue by province. Specifically, on average, what proportion of total federal revenue is borne by the residents of, say, Ontario? Ideally, one would like the provincial allocation for each federal revenue source. Unfortunately, such data are not presently available. The alternative we opt for is to look at the total base in each province for two of the main federal revenue sources, namely the personal income tax base and the corporate income tax base. Next we allocate to each province its

Table VI  A "Tax Effort" Approach to Equalization: Results for Formulation (11)
($ ,000)

| Province Revenue Source | NFLD. | PEI | NS | NB | QUE. | ONT. | MAN. | SASK. | ALTA. | BC |
|---|---|---|---|---|---|---|---|---|---|---|
| 1 | 19313 | 4759 | 19597 | 20966 | 67837 | -135626 | 12896 | 28384 | 5341 | -22469 |
| 2 | 9362 | 2072 | 10981 | 9133 | 47720 | -70462 | 4397 | 13949 | -3985 | 9303 |
| 3 | 2240 | 874 | 704 | 3513 | 4176 | -23793 | 1903 | 3290 | 3349 | -629 |
| 4 | 9724 | 1617 | 3704 | 8086 | 119384 | -48260 | 3399 | 4364 | 0 | -29107 |
| 5 | 10880 | 637 | 5824 | 3390 | 25462 | -29049 | 3509 | -2257 | -9655 | -2197 |
| 6 | 2741 | 137 | 1704 | 979 | 7943 | -10906 | 1071 | -676 | -6147 | -1003 |
| 7 | 12680 | 569 | 1727 | 1897 | 36806 | -33217 | -167 | 2557 | -3707 | -15592 |
| 8 | -26 | 0 | 1744 | -707 | 6553 | 23673 | 2812 | 1214 | 2747 | -60582 |
| 9 | 0 | 0 | 0 | 0 | 0 | 0 | 750 | -13196 | -70542 | 6323 |
| 10 | 0 | 0 | 0 | 0 | 0 | 5453 | 0 | 379 | -24191 | 1531 |
| 11 | 0 | 0 | 0 | 0 | 0 | 0 | 6700 | -1143 | -122254 | -2062 |
| 12 | 0 | 348 | 0 | 0 | 0 | 23542 | 3013 | -5649 | -42696 | -4410 |
| 13 | -2160 | 0 | 1505 | 183 | 2445 | -2836 | -495 | -596 | 14635 | -193 |
| 14 | -8 | 0 | 323 | 27 | -10366 | 2163 | -33 | 1055 | 1343 | -907 |
| 15 | 1497 | 257 | 1280 | 13572 | 13781 | -34537 | 811 | 4863 | -591 | -7645 |
| 16 | 4885 | 1745 | 3250 | 3714 | 6443 | -14421 | 567 | 5633 | -741 | -6599 |
| Equalization Payments | 71129 | 13014 | 52343 | 64753 | 328182 | 0 | 41135 | 42170 | 0 | 0 |

share of these taxes. These figures appear in the first column of Table VII. It is important to recognize that these ratios are only *estimates* of the provincial shares of total federal revenue. However, it is also important to note that they are probably reasonably good estimates. For example, Ontario has 45.58% of the total income tax base. It would be quite surprising indeed if the actual proportion of federal revenue collected from residents of Ontario (direct and indirect) was not within, say, 5 percentage points of 45%.

Column (2) of Table VII contains the percentage of total equalization received by each province for the 1968-69 period. Consider the province of Quebec. It receives approximately 55% of total equalization payments. But its *residents* will have to pay for about 24% of the cost of the total scheme. The net benefit to the province (treating the provincial government and the residents as a *single* entity) is the difference between these two figures or about 31% of total equalization. For Ontario, since it gets no payment, the cost to the province is about 45% of the total payment. It is even possible for a province to receive a grant and still be worse off as a result of equalization. This is nearly the case for Saskatchewan under the 1968-69 calculation. Were Saskatchewan to become somewhat better off relative to the Canadian average it is entirely feasible for its percentage of the equalization payments to fall below its share in the cost of total equalization. It is worthwhile mentioning again that the benefits of equalization go to the *province* while the cost of equalization is borne not by the province directly, but rather by the *residents* of the province. Nevertheless, it seems to us that too often public statements from various sources concerning equalization payments fail to recognize that residents of *all* provinces and not only the "have" provinces contribute to the funding of the equalization scheme.

| Table VII   Funding Estimates by Provinces | | |
|---|---|---|
| Province | Share of Total Federal Revenue Obtained from Province* | Share of 1968-69 Equalization Received by Province |
| NFLD. | 1.092 | 10.312 |
| P.E.I. | 0.185 | 2.276 |
| N.S. | 2.011 | 11.209 |
| N.B. | 1.466 | 9.978 |
| Quebec | 23.618 | 55.343 |
| Ontario | 45.581 | 0 |
| Manitoba | 3.952 | 6.606 |
| Saskatchewan | 2.866 | 4.276 |
| Alberta | 7.557 | 0 |
| B.C. | 11.676 | 0 |

*Estimated on the basis of the provincial shares of the person and corporate income tax base.

Many interesting calculations can be undertaken using these cost estimates. For example, we can investigate the net cost to British Columbia residents as a result of an increase in the tax rate in Ontario for any given revenue source. British Columbia will receive no equalization payment as a result of this tax change, but its residents will bear about 12% of the total value of the increased equalization payments resulting from the tax change in Ontario. It would be also interesting to calculate net benefits by province for the various changes in Table III. We leave this, and other such calculations, to the reader.

## VI. Conclusion

In the above sections we attempted not only to outline the present tax equalization program but as well to highlight some of its more interesting implications. In addition the paper also delved into the features of some of the possible alternatives or modifications of the present scheme. Obviously much more analysis can be done both on the current program as well as on the various suggested alternatives. However, one has to exercise some care in recommending alternatives because even slight changes in the equalization scheme can alter the conceptual underpinnings of the program. For example, as we suggested above, Musgrave would probably opt for the modification embodied in equation (11) rather than the present scheme, i.e., he would prefer rewarding "tax effort". If a province wants a larger subsidy, it has to be willing to tax its own residents more. Under this modification a "have-not" province would not garner, as it currently does, an increased subsidy simply because some *other* province increases its tax rates. Yet if the purpose of equalization is to ensure that no province has to levy unduly high tax rates in order to supply some "standard" level of services, the "tax effort" modification may not be desirable since it could encourage very high tax rates in the poorer provinces.

Nonetheless, there are a few areas in which improvements could be made.[8] Perhaps the most obvious is the incentive, under the present scheme, for provinces to tax less heavily those revenue sources with which they are relatively well-endowed and vice versa. We have no idea of the degree to which provinces react to this incentive but as our example for Quebec in Table III indicated, the dollar values involved can be quite substantial.

Finally it is important to emphasize that a complete analysis of the role of equalization payments must also encompass the myriad of other federal and provincial policies that affect the incomes both of provincial governments and the residents of the various provinces. Our goal was a more narrow one—that of evaluating in isolation some aspects of, and potential modifications to, the equalization component of the Federal-Provincial Fiscal Arrangements Act.

### Footnotes

1. "B.C. will test Ottawa in court on equalization payment issue," *The Globe and Mail* (Tuesday, February 15, 1972), p. 1.

2. Readers interested in the historical development of Federal-Provincial fiscal arrangements can consult A. Milton Moore, J. Harvey Perry and Donald I. Beach, *The Financing of Canadian Federation: The First Hundred Years* (Toronto: The Canadian Tax Foundation, 1966) or *The National Finance, 1970-71* (Toronto: The Tax Foundation, 1970), Chapter 10.

3. *The National Finances*, *op. cit.*, pp. 146-7.

4. This distorts reality in several ways. For example, revenues from federal-provincial shared-cost programmes must be added in. Furthermore, some provinces tax more than the 16 revenue sources. However, the formula can account for these provinces which tax less than the 16 sources because either the $E_{ij}$ or the $B_{ij}$ can take on a zero value.

5. R.A. Musgrave, ''Approaches to a Fiscal Theory of Political Federalism'' in *Public Finance Needs, Sources, Utilization*, National Bureau of Economic Research (Princeton: Princeton University Press, 1961), pp. 97-122.

6. The highest province is defined as that province which has the highest value for

$$\sum_{j=1}^{16} \frac{t_{cj} B_{ij}}{P_i} \text{ , etc.}$$

7. These data are not shown in the table, but are available upon request.

8. For example, it may be more costly, per capita, to provide a ''standard'' level of public goods and services. This is not brought into the equalization formula.

THOMAS J. COURCHENE
# Recent Canadian Monetary Policy
An Appraisal

Not since the late fifties and the reign of "Coynesian" economics has there been as much concern over Canadian monetary policy as there is at the present time. In part this concern stems from the central bank's current anti-inflationary policies in the face of mounting unemployment, culminating finally with the floating of the dollar. But it also reflects a more basic questioning of the operations of the Bank of Canada over the recent past. The purpose of this paper is to review the highlights of Bank policy since 1965 and to assess the appropriateness of this policy. This assessment, which proceeds on a year-to-year basis, addresses the suitability of Canadian policy both from the vantage point that Canada is able independently to chart her own policy course and then within the more realistic context of a small open economy linked to the world via a fixed exchange rate. In order to address these issues, however it is necessary to turn briefly to some institutional factors characterizing the 1965-70 period.

## I. Institutional Background

The 1967 Bank Act legislation is "by far the most momentous revision of the Bank Act" (15, p. 28) and the dominant factor altering the institutional setting of the Canadian monetary system over the 1965-69 period. From a uniform rate of 8% on all Canadian dollar deposits, the legal minimum reserve ratio was changed to 12% on demand deposits and to 4% on deposits requiring notice. Under the old Bank Act, the 8% reserve ratio could be (but never was) altered. However, the new dual rate is immutable. The secondary reserve ratio (ratio of Treasury bills, day-to-day loans, and cash in excess of the primary reserve ratio to Canadian dollar deposit liabilities) instituted via moral suasion in 1956, is now incorporated into the bank legislation. Set initially at 6%, it can be altered between zero and 12%. This switch from variability in the primary reserve ratio to variability in the secondary reserve ratio is, in our opinion, quite acceptable from the Bank's point of view since we shall later argue that the Bank calibrates monetary policy largely in terms of credit conditions rather than some monetary aggregate. Given this approach, the Bank should prefer to have a variable liquid-asset ratio since this gives it more direct control where it deems the action to be—on the asset side of the chartered-banks' balance sheets.

The second major provision of the bank legislation was to remove the 6% interest ceiling on chartered-bank loan. In theory, this has an effect very much like the lifting of Regulation "Q" would have in the U.S. Coupled with the lowered reserve requirements on notice deposits, this provided both the ability and the incentive for chartered banks to promote term deposits relative to demand deposits. Not surprisingly, Table 1 indicates that this is precisely what happened. Fixed-term personal savings deposits grew at an average annual rate of 114%. over the two-year period from mid-1967 to mid-1969 and non-chequable savings deposits at 78% per year. Chequable savings deposits declined by nearly 13% yearly. Indeed the sum of demand deposits plus chequable personal savings deposits declined over this two-year period at an annual rate of $4^1/2\%$. Other term and notice deposits (which are similar to CD's in the U.S.) exhibit an annual growth rate of only 10.8% compared to the much larger growth rates of other fixed-term deposits. This, however, is due largely to an agreement in October, 1967, among the major banks (at the implicit request of the Governor) to limit the extent to which they would attempt to attract these deposits.[1] Table 1 also indicates that for the two-year period the rate of growth of bank deposits was not at the expense of near-bank growth: trust and mortgage loan companies experienced growth rates averaging above 12% over this period compared with a 9.4% increase in the year prior to the adoption of the Bank Act.

Clearly then, the Bank Act represents a major structural change in the Canadian banking and financial milieu—a change of such magnitude that it seriously complicates the analysis of monetary policy. Take the definition of money, for example. The definition generally accepted in the past included all Canadian dollar deposits of the chartered banks. It is not at all clear that this definition is still appropriate. In addition, depending on the particular aggregate selected, the annual rate of growth in the chartered-bank component of the money supply for these two years can be well into the teens or it can be negative. As a result, several definitions will be considered, although primary emphasis is still given to formulations embodying total Canadian dollar liabilities.

In addition to Canadian dollar deposit liabilities, the chartered banks also accept foreign currency liabilities. At the end of 1969 these liabilities held by Canadian residents were in excess of three billion dollars—amounting to nearly 13% of the total of publicly-held Canadian dollar deposit liabilities. About half of these deposits were in the form of "swapped deposits."[2] No reserves are required on these foreign currency deposits. Further on the international side, accompanying Canada's fixed exchange rate was a ceiling on the level of international reserves she could hold. This ceiling, set at or near 2.6 billion (U.S.$), was the price Canada paid for being exempted from the Interest Equalization Tax (IET) provisions. In December, 1968, the ceiling was removed, but in return Canada agreed to invest all reserves in excess of working balances in non-liquid U.S. government bonds. Finally, on May 31, 1970, the Canadian dollar was set free. As we shall see, these facets of Canada's international position influenced significantly the conduct of Canadian monetary policy over the 1965-69 period. The remainder of the institutional factors are best introduced later.

Table 1   Effects of the Bank Act on Chartered Bank Deposits (in Million $)*

| Date | Demand Deposits | Other Term and Notice Deposits | Personal Savings Deposits | | | | Total Bank Deposits† | Near-Bank Deposits‡ |
|---|---|---|---|---|---|---|---|---|
| | | | Chequable | Non-Chequable | Fixed Term | Total | | |
| Aug. 9, 1967 | 5,834 | 3,280 | 8,292 | 2,035 | 987 | 11,313 | 20,427 | 5,684 |
| July, 1969 | 6,700 | 3,990 | 6,139 | 5,218 | 3,243 | 14,599 | 25,289 | 7,130 |
| Average Annual % change | 7.42 | 10.82 | -12.99 | 78.2 | 114.28 | 14.52 | 11.90 | 12.72 |

*The Bank Act became effective in mid-1967 and implementation was complete by early 1968. The August 9 data are the earliest available; 1969 data are average-of-Wednesdays figures for July.

† Excludes federal government deposits which were 760 and 876 million dollars respectively for these dates in 1967 and 1969.

‡ Trust companies and mortgage loan companies. Data are for the end of the second quarter in 1967 and 1969.

## II. Canadian Monetary Policy, 1965-70

Table 2, containing quarterly data from 1965 and some data for 1970 on various monetary and financial series, provides the statistical backdrop for most of the analysis of recent Canadian monetary policy. Several monetary aggregates appear: total publicly-held Canadian dollar deposit liabilities (column 1), total (including government) Canadian dollar liabilities (column 2),[3] and currency plus demand deposits (column 3). U.S. counterparts to two of these series are in columns 4 and 5. Regardless of which series one focuses upon, one fact is very clear; both the rate of growth and the variability in the rate of growth of money are considerably greater in Canada than in the U.S. For publicly-held bank money the quarter-to-quarter growth rate (at annual rates) is 23.2% in 1968.II and the first difference in the rate of growth reaches an astounding 22.4% from 1969.I to 1969.II.

### MONETARY INDICATORS AND BANK POLICY

It is obvious from these figures that the Bank of Canada is conducting its monetary policy is not following a money supply rule. Indeed the Governor is quite explicit on this point:

> The Bank regards its chief function in the field of monetary policy as being to help bring about the kind of credit conditions that are appropriate to domestic economic conditions and to the maintenance of the country's external financial position. By credit conditions I mean the cost and availability of money throughout the economy. . . . In the day-to-day determination of monetary policy, the central bank is not primarily influenced by considerations relating to the size of the money supply. This does not mean of course that the Bank of Canada takes no interest in, or is not influenced by, what is happening to the money supply (which in Canada is usually defined as the combined total of currency outside banks and chartered bank deposits payable in Canadian dollars). However it is a fact that we do not operate on the basis of a precise view about the appropriate trend, over some period, of total chartered bank deposits. We give priority in our thinking to the kind of credit conditions that seem to be appropriate in the prevailing circumstances. [16, pp. 10, 11, 12]
> The concept of the money supply . . . is one which I, myself, do not regard as the essential operational concept in the conduct of monetary policy. [12, p. 1034]

Canadian monetary policy is, therefore, calibrated with reference to conditions relating to nominal rates of interest and the availability of credit. That nominal rates can be a misleading indicator of monetary policy especially under conditions of inflationary expectations is well documented,[4,5] and in the analysis that follows it will become clear that calibrating monetary policy with reference to nominal interest rates was one of the major errors of Bank policy over this period.

Acheson and Chant in a recent paper (1) take this further. They suggest that over the years the Bank's focus on credit conditions in combination with its

Table 2  Quarterly Financial Data for the Period 1965-1969

Rates of Change in Various Money Aggregates

| Year Quarter | Privately Held Canadian Dollar Deposit Liabilities | Total Canadian Dollar Deposit Liabilities | Currency and Demand Deposits | Currency and Demand Deposits, U.S. | Currency and Demand Deposits and Time Deposits, U.S. | Rate of Change in Total Bank Loans | More Liquid Asset (MLA) Ratio* | Net Foreign Assets ($mill) | Resident Held Foreign Currency Liabilities | Official Holdings of Gold and U.S. Dollars | Long Term Bond Yield Canada† | Interest Rate Differential† | Real Interest Rate‡ | Unemployment Rate Quart. Av. |
|---|---|---|---|---|---|---|---|---|---|---|---|---|---|---|
| **1965:** | | | | | | | | | | | | | | |
| I | 15.2 | 15.0 | 4.9 | 2.8 | 9.2 | 15.8 | 31.67 | 12 | 1161 | 2554 | 5.04 | .89 | 3.20 | 4.1 |
| II | 14.2 | 13.4 | 11.1 | 3.2 | 7.6 | 22.9 | 30.45 | -32 | 1026 | 2480 | 5.10 | .96 | 3.24 | 4.1 |
| III | 10.6 | 14.5 | 3.2 | 5.7 | 9.8 | 20.7 | 30.54 | -83 | 1155 | 2614 | 5.30 | 1.10 | 3.24 | 3.8 |
| IV | 8.1 | 5.3 | 6.5 | 6.6 | 10.4 | 23.4 | 30.21 | -46 | 1216 | 2664 | 5.46 | 1.11 | 3.26 | 3.5 |
| Annual | 12.5 | 12.6 | 6.6 | 4.6 | 9.6 | 22.3 | | | | | | | | |
| **1966:** | | | | | | | | | | | | | | |
| I | 6.6 | 3.9 | 7.4 | 6.2 | 7.4 | 2.1 | 29.59 | -54 | 1398 | 2509 | 5.59 | 1.03 | 3.17 | 3.6 |
| II | 5.3 | 5.2 | 5.8 | 2.8 | 7.0 | 9.1 | 29.63 | -79 | 1459 | 2341 | 5.68 | 1.10 | 3.05 | 3.5 |
| III | 6.3 | 9.0 | 7.5 | 0.2 | 3.8 | 8.6 | 30.02 | -23 | 1669 | 2244 | 5.84 | 1.66 | 2.89 | 3.9 |
| IV | 6.6 | 8.2 | 10.4 | -0.4 | 1.2 | 7.7 | 30.33 | 75 | 1629 | 2236 | 5.86 | 1.16 | 2.71 | 3.6 |
| Annual | 6.4 | 6.7 | 7.8 | 2.2 | 4.9 | 6.9 | | | | | | | | |
| **1967:** | | | | | | | | | | | | | | |
| I | 19.7 | 18.7 | 17.9 | 6.6 | 12.8 | 11.6 | 30.47 | 65 | 1438 | 2203 | 5.59 | 1.15 | 2.33 | 3.8 |
| II | 11.3 | 11.2 | 3.8 | 6.4 | 11.0 | 3.9 | 30.47 | 125 | 1404 | 2169 | 5.70 | .99 | 2.35 | 4.1 |
| III | 18.6 | 18.6 | 9.4 | 8.2 | 11.0 | 22.5 | 30.31 | 161 | 1537 | 2221 | 6.03 | 1.10 | 2.52 | 4.1 |
| IV | 14.2 | 6.8 | 7.6 | 4.6 | 7.8 | 17.7 | 29.89 | 23 | 1984 | 2268 | 6.52 | 1.19 | 2.86 | 4.5 |
| Annual | 16.9 | 14.5 | 8.0 | 6.6 | 11.0 | 14.5 | | | | | | | | |
| **1968:** | | | | | | | | | | | | | | |
| I | 3.6 | 10.3 | -7.4 | 5.5 | 6.6 | 14.2 | 28.42 | 62 | 1893 | 2244 | 6.83 | 1.59 | 3.06 | 4.6 |
| II | 23.2 | 14.0 | 6.8 | 8.6 | 5.8 | 9.2 | 29.41 | 148 | 1895 | 2574 | 6.74 | 1.44 | 2.92 | 4.9 |
| III | 12.4 | 19.1 | 18.8 | 6.8 | 11.6 | 5.5 | 31.44 | 225 | 1993 | 2534 | 6.56 | 1.49 | 2.78 | 5.0 |
| IV | 11.7 | 11.1 | 8.2 | 7.1 | 12.2 | 17.1 | 30.27 | 283 | 2036 | 2826 | 7.16 | 1.74 | 3.32 | 4.8 |
| Annual | 13.8 | 14.3 | 6.6 | 7.2 | 9.3 | 12.1 | | | | | | | | |
| **1969:** | | | | | | | | | | | | | | |
| I | 18.1 | 12.8 | 7.1 | 4.1 | -0.6 | 19.6 | 28.77 | 142 | 2196 | 2779 | 7.35 | 1.47 | 3.39 | 4.4 |
| II | -4.3 | 4.8 | 8.6 | 4.4 | 0.7 | 18.1 | 27.74 | -154 | 2993 | 2623 | 7.52 | 1.60 | 3.35 | 4.7 |
| III | -5.3 | -4.4 | -5.1 | 0.0 | -6.7 | 5.8 | 27.78 | -337 | 3366 | 2539 | 7.62 | 1.48 | 3.35 | 4.9 |
| IV | 3.8 | 7.4 | 7.0 | 1.2 | 0.6 | 8.1 | 26.31 | -154 | 3260 | 2615 | 8.12 | 1.59 | 3.81 | 4.8 |
| Annual | 3.0 | 5.2 | 4.4 | 2.4 | -0.98 | 14.3 | | | | | | | | |
| **1970:** | | | | | | | | | | | | | | |
| I | 3.02 | -1.99 | 1.07 | | | -1.2 | | | | 2936 | | | | |

**Notes:** Rates of change are taken from Seasonally Adjusted Data and are at annual rates.

*This differs somewhat from the MLA ratio that the Bank of Canada publishes in its weekly Bulletin because we elect to show Net Foreign Assets separately. The MLA ratio is defined as the ratio of more liquid assets (the sum of reserves, day loans, treasury bills, loans to brokers and investment dealers, and government securities) to total major assets.

†Interest rates data are long-term government bond yields obtained from the IFS country pages for Canada and the U.S.

‡Long-Term bond rate minus the average rate of change of consumer prices over the last eight quarters.

desire to minimize debt management costs has reduced the Canadian short-term money market to the position where the chartered banks and the Bank of Canada are the only effective participants. There is clear evidence even over the past five years of this trend towards the elimination of the general public from the government securities markets. At the end of 1964 the Bank of Canada held 23.2% of the outstanding Treasury bills and the chartered banks and the general public held 60.8% and 16.0%, respectively. For December, 1969 these percentages were 16.9%, 73.8% and 9.3%, respectively.[6] The same trend shows up for marketable government bonds as well. In 1964 the public accounted for 52.5% of government bonds and the chartered banks held 25.8%, the Bank holding the remaining 21.7%. In 1969 these ratios were 43.1, 31.4, and 25.4. Quantitatively, the increase in all marketable bonds and bills from 1964 to 1969 was $2,626 million. Chartered bank holdings increased by $2,239 million, and central bank holdings by $1,001 million while holdings by the public *declined* by $614 million. The net result of the Bank's interest rate policy was that the entire government deficit over this period had to be financed via the banking system and then some![7]

This preoccupation with the cost and availability of credit has further implications. Under the lagged reserve-settlement system, reserves held at the central bank during the current month are determined by the level of deposits in the preceding month. The evidence available seems to indicate that the Bank of Canada validates the chartered-bank decisions regarding the level of deposit liabilities: central bank advances to the chartered banks and investment dealers are small, infrequent, and often not indicative of tightness when they occur, indicating that there are sufficient reserves provided for the banking *system* but that on occasion a particular bank finds itself in trouble and is forced directly, or through the investment dealers, into the Bank. There are two reasons why one would expect this response from the Bank and both relate to the role credit conditions play in the overall conduct of monetary policy. First, to fail to provide sufficient reserves would either involve the Bank in heavy rediscounting operations or result in the banking system as a whole disposing of assets. In the Governor's words the "undesirable part of . . . [this would be] the risk that it would create instability in the money market." (7 p.41) Second, the focus on credit conditions implies that the Bank is more interested in the asset side and in particular the behavior of loans than in the liability side of chartered banks' balance sheets[8] and chartered-bank lending policies appear to be rather insensitive to cash management [by the central bank, T.J.C.] except when the banks regard their holdings of liquid assets and government bonds as close to minimum levels." (7, p.9) Accordingly, it is reasonalbe to argue that the bank manages its reserves with a view more to affecting bank liquidity than bank deposits and in this way attempts to influence loan behavior. More specifically, we suggest that the Bank attaches considerable significance to the behaviour of the more-liquid-asset (MLA) ratio, defined under Table 2, so much so that for much of the 1965-69 period this ratio assumed the role both of a target and an indicator of Bank policy.[9] One implication of all this is that the chartered banking system plays a much more active role in determining the course of total bank liabilities than the traditional textbook analyses suggest. It also implies that if the Bank of Canada wishes to pursue a restrictive policy it goes about it in a very indirect manner by engaging in reserve management that serves to reduce bank liquidity in order to make it in the chartered banks' *own* interest to pursue restraint.[10]

We now turn to a year-by-year analysis of Canadian monetary policy over the 1965-69 period. Our main hypothesis is that the various factors discussed in this section in combination with the monetary discipline imposed on Canada by the fixed exchange rate account in large measure for both the size and variability of monetary growth over this period.

## 1965

From the Record:

> In the early years of the economic expansion, so long as there was a considerable amount of slack in the economy, the policy of the central bank was to allow the increasing demands for credit to be met without a tightening of credit conditions. But as the rising output of the economy began to catch up with its growing productive capacity in 1965 . . . this policy was modified and credit conditions were allowed to tighten. [16, pp.7-8.]

But from the rate of expansion of the privately-held bank money ($12^1/2\%$ in 1965) policy was anything but tight. This is especially so in comparison with 1964 when the rate of increase in bank money was about one-half the 1965 increase. In part, what the Governor means is that interest rates (Table 2, col. 11) rose somewhat in 1965 even though the "Bank of Canada resisted the downward pressure on bond prices by purchasing Government securities in the market after February 10" and "limited to about 10 basis points" (2, p. 25) the rise in Canadian rates—and in the process the money supply increased in the first quarter by over 15% at annual rates.

But there is another sense in which central bank might consider bank conditions as tightening—the MLA ratio was falling. (It averaged about 33% in 1964.) Indeed, generating a fall in this ratio was one of the principal goals of policy:

> Beginning in April the cash management of the Bank of Canada was conducted in such a way that the continued strong expansion of the chartered banks' loans brought about a further reduction in the ratio of their "more liquid" assets to total assets. [2, p.25.]

Given that the Bank wished to pursue monetary restraint, a more aggressive policy toward restricting reserves would have brought about an even greater decrease in this ratio, and with a substantially smaller increase in loans.

Why was the banking system expanding so rapidly when the announced policy of the authorities was one of restraint? Discarding the possibility that the Bank of Canada wanted this expansion, two alternatives suggest themselves. First, the combination of a fixed exchange rate and a reserve ceiling that was effective (see Table 2) seriously constrained Canadian monetary policy. A smaller degree of monetary expansion would have, in the short run, widened the Canadian-U.S. interest-rate differential and led to foreign exchange inflows above the ceiling level. Our own view is that this juxtaposition of fixed rate and fixed ceiling did indeed reduce the flexibility of Canadian monetary policy and that the policy in 1965 reflected this limitation.

However, the Governor does not feel that the ceiling poses any special restriction on the flexibility of Canadian monetary policy:

> On your more basic question . . . as to whether the combination of the fixed exchange rate and our understandings with the United States regarding the level of reserves narrows the scope for monetary policy in Canada, I think my quick reaction to that is to say that there is still enough scope to worry about . . . I think that it is the case that whatever exchange system we have in Canada, in a country where international transactions are as important as they are here, that we are bound to be influenced in the conduct of our affairs, including the conduct of monetary policy, by what is going on in other parts of the world, and particularly in the United States. [12, p. 1066.]

Later in his remarks, Governor Rasminsky stated that the reserve ceiling could be evaded by the Canadian government repurchasing its own securities in the American market and in this way use up an excess foreign exchange.[11] But in light of the concern that arose in 1968 in connection with the flexibility of Canadian monetary policy and the reserve ceiling and the pleasure expressed by the Governor upon its removal we find it difficult to visualize how Canada could have followed a policy of effective monetary constraint in 1965 without violating the ceiling requirement.

A second possibility (and one mentioned in the previous section) for the large expansion in 1965 is that the Bank's interpretation of the lagged reserve-settlement scheme allows the chartered banking system to play the dominant role in setting the level of bank liabilities. If it be the case that the Bank of Canada merely accedes, in providing reserves in the current month, to the rate of expansion set by the chartered banks in the previous month—and the evidence on borrowings mentioned above suggests that this may well be the case—then the Bank of Canada is bound to experience difficulties in regulating monetary expansion in the short run. As support for our contention that the Bank in its reserve management places major emphasis on the MLA ratio and more or less accommodates chartered-bank actions relating to rate of expansion of total bank money, we offer as evidence the following policy statement by the Governor:

> In 1964 the Bank of Canada managed the cash reserves of the chartered banks in such a way that a part of the resources needed by the banks to accommodate the large increase in their loans had to be obtained through a reduction in their holdings of government securities and other liquid assets. This reduction in bank liquidity was not such as to prevent the banks from continuing to follow strong lending policies but it brought them to a position *where their policies* could be expected to be sensitive to any appreciable further decline in the proportion of their total assets which they held in relatively liquid form. [12, p. 1014, italics added.]

This type of policy can lead to substantial "slippage" in the implementation of policy. It took until the fourth quarter of 1965 and the first quarter of 1966 for bank money and loans respectively to reflect this "tightening." Indeed, both loans and money grew at *higher* rates in 1965 than in 1964. In order to prevent the tail from wagging the dog it would appear highly desirable for the Bank to announce ahead of time what level of reserves it will make available in the following month and to allow the chartered banks to react accordingly. Such a procedure would shorten considerably the reaction time of the chartered banks to official policy, and would also serve to clarify for all sectors of the economy just what official policy is. But in order for the Bank to even consider such a policy it must be more willing than it has been in the past to tolerate interest-rate changes. A policy of maintaining interest rates at a given and stable level requires that the Bank accede to chartered-bank reserve needs and implies that the supply of money will be demand-determined.

Before one faults the Bank for inadequate implementation of its announced policy in 1965, however, there is one extenuating circumstance that must be considered. In June, 1965, the Atlantic Acceptance Corporation (a medium-sized sales-finance company) failed and many of its subsidiaries went under as well. This was a severe shock to the financial sector and the Bank reacted immediately, and successfully, to avoid a major financial panic. Part of the large rates of increase in the monetary aggregate for the second and third quarters of 1965 is undoubtedly a reflection of what the Bank considered as appropriate monetary conditions in the presence of the financial crisis: "Where . . . confidence is in danger of being seriously impaired the central bank may have to allow itself to be diverted from the pursuit of current objectives of monetary policy and give priority to measures which help to maintain confidence." [2, p.7.]

### 1966

> In the latter part of 1965 and the early part of 1966 demand pressures on the economy became particularly intense and credit conditions progressively tightened. The Bank Rate was raised in December 1965 and again in March 1966 when I stated that the "Bank's action reflected its view that in the present state of the economy some moderation of the rate of growth of over-all demand was desirable." [3, p.5.]

This view underlines the concern about inflationary dangers expressed in the 1965 *Annual Report* of the Bank released on the same day the Bank Rate was raised (March 11, 1966). Later in the year the Bank "considered that the appropriate policy was for it to offer considerable resistance to further tightening of credit conditions without, however, attempting to prevent all further upward movement in interest rates. This course involved some relaxation of the short rein it had kept on the banking system." (3, p.5) Note that the Bank is identifying rising nominal interest rates with tightening credit conditions. While it is true that nominal rates were rising, real interest rates declined continuously throughout 1966. But the availability of credit (as measured by the rate of expansion of bank money or loans) was considerably tighter than in 1965 or 1967. Nonetheless, in absolute terms the rate of monetary expansion is still considerable—well above the real growth rate of the economy. At this juncture we might note that from 1965 through 1967 the rates of expansion of Canadian money were greater than those in the U.S. (under any definition, but Table 2 presents comparable figures only for currency plus demand deposits). Under a monetary interpretation of the balance of payments, this should lead to reserve outflows and is one of the underlying causes of the foreign exchange crisis in early 1968.[12]

### 1967

> Credit conditions became very tight in 1966 [but not relative to those in the U.S., T.J.C.], and with the evidence of a slackening in the pace of economic activity I welcomed the opportunity to help bring some easing of credit conditions. [4, p.8]

Accordingly, the Bank Rate was reduced twice in the first four months of 1967. But in the spring of 1967 it became obvious that the economy was strong and expanding:

> The basic problem for monetary policy in 1967 was to decide how far to permit the very large demands for funds in capital and credit markets . . . to exert pressures on interest rates and how far to accommodate the demand by permitting increased monetary expansion. In the event, we experienced a mixture of the two—rising interest rates and considerable monetary expansion—until the closing months of the year when there was a marked slowing down in the rate of monetary growth. [4, p.9.]

Essentially, then, the central bank was "leaning against the wind" in attempting to resist interest-rate increases: "the alternative was to permit the market pressures to exert an even stronger and earlier impact on interest rates" (4, p.10). But while nominal interest rates were about 6% in the last half of 1967, real rates were less than 3%. Furthermore, the longer-run impact of this high rate of monetary expansion (nearly 17% for privately-held bank deposits) was to *increase* and not decrease nominal interest rates. In addition, the monetary expansion was quite inconsistent with the Governor's continuing deep concern in the 1967 *Annual Report* with inflationary pressures. And it is even more inconsistent with his statement: "I continue to hope that exclusive reliance will not be placed on monetary and fiscal policy to achieve this result," (i.e., better price and wage performance T.J.C.; 4, pp.7-8).[13]

The Bank Act revision which began to take effect in mid-1967 complicated considerably Bank of Canada operations. The movement of the legal reserve ratio away from 8% by ¹/₂% monthly changes to 4% for savings deposits and 12% for demand deposits "freed" large quantities of reserves and contributed to the rate of monetary expansion since considerably less than half of total bank deposits were in the 12% category. For example, one year after the implementation of the Bank Act the effective legal reserve ratio had decreased from 8% to approximately 6¹/₄%. This rigid schedule for the implementation of the reserve-requirement changes represents a tactical error on the part of those who wrote the Bank Act legislation because the Bank of Canada, in order to keep the money supply constant over the 8-month implementation period, would have had to withdraw something like 20% of existing reserves from the system. More flexibility should have been give to the Bank in the timing and introduction of these changes, especially in light of the deficit-financing required over this period (see fn. 7 above).[14]

This abrupt lowering of the reserve requirements on non-demand deposits also led chartered banks to raise deposit rates significantly in order to attract term deposits away from the near banks. A more restrictive policy towards bank reserves would have seriously affected near-bank growth. As it was, the near banks found themselves in enough trouble:

> The banks naturally took advantage of these changes to compete more aggressively for an enlarged share of the total financial business of the community. Indeed, for a period in the autumn their competition for large blocks of short-term corporate funds was so aggressive that it appeared to be uneconomic, and I felt that it threatened to introduce some instability and distortion into the financial system. I informed the banks of my view and was gratified that a more normal relationship of rates came about soon after. [4, p.9.]

This gratification took the form of persuading the five large banks to agree among themselves to limit the degree to which they would compete for these funds. In other words, they imposed upon themselves a voluntary Regulation "Q"-type restriction. One result of this was that the banks encouraged their customers to switch to foreign currency deposits where this restriction was not binding. As Table 2 indicates, these foreign currency deposits increased by approximately $450 million in the fourth quarter of 1967. The Governor's statement above that the rate of growth of monetary expansion slowed markedly in the closing months of 1967 is not true if one includes in the definition of money resident holdings of foreign as well as domestic currency liabilities of the banking system—a definition that has considerable merit in a world-economy context.

### 1968

> For the first half of 1968 the Bank gave top priority to the defence of the exchange value of the Canadian dollar. Bank Rate reached a peak of $7^{1}/_{2}\%$ in mid-March and was maintained at that level to the beginning of July. Market rates rose to the highest levels that we had ever experienced in this country up to that time. Bank liquidity declined and the rate of expansion of the banking system slowed markedly. [5, p.8.]

This last statement relating to monetary expansion is not supported by evidence in Table 2. Privately-held bank money rose in the second quarter at an annual rate of 23%! Including government deposits, the rates of increase of the banking system were 10% and 14% respectively for the first two quarters. Again the Bank is focusing on the movements in interest rates and the MLA ratio in judging the stance of monetary policy.

Once the exchange-rate crisis was over the Bank "moved to make monetary policy less restrictive and reduced the Bank Rate [in the third quarter] in three steps from $7^1/_2$ to 6%" (5, p. 8). The result was a record 19.1% increase in total private bank money following on the heels of the 23% increase in the second quarter.

These rates of increase in bank money in 1967 and 1968 are absurdly high and surely represent the low point of recent Canadian monetary policy.[15] In part, the mid-1968 increases reflect the Bank's belief that the U.S. surcharge would have a damping effect on both economies. But in large measure the Bank was again "leaning against the wind." In the Governor's words, "we had to take into account . . . the practical limitations on increases in interest rates that exist at any given time" (5, p. 9). The federal government required cash and to obtain it via bond financing to the public would have pushed rates up too high. And, the Bank argued, if rates were allowed to go that high capital would have flowed in and the government would have needed even more cash in order to buy the resulting inflows of foreign exchange. As a result the Bank of Canada permitted the chartered-banking system to purchase large quantities of federal government bonds. In turn, this increased the chartered-banks' MLA ratio by over 3% from 1968.I to 1968.III — by far the largest increase over the 1965-70 period. Given (a) that the Bank places so much emphasis on this ratio and (b) that for the first time in well over a year loan expansion was less than 10% for two successive quarters (1968.II and 1968.III), it is extremely hard to rationalize this increase in bank liquidity. But certainly it makes very evident the high priority the Bank assigns to interest-cost minimization and underscores the problem associated with calibrating monetary policy in terms of nominal interest rates. The Bank also recognized that these liquid assets were getting out of hand and "accordingly managed cash reserves in such a way that the chartered banks' holdings of such assets ceased to rise after mid-September, and the rate of expansion of the banking system was slowed" (5, p. 9). But the damage was done and was reflected in the high rates of loan expansion over the next three quarters, counteracting the Bank's attempt to pursue tight money!

The combination of the fixed exchange rate and the reserve ceiling also appears to have been a major factor in Bank policy in 1968. During the exchange-rate crisis early in the year, the Canadian-U.S. interest-rate differential was increased substantially (Table 2) and the resulting inflows of foreign exchange again threatened to push Canada's reserves through the $2.6 billion ceiling, thereby once again converting the Bank of Canada into the position of being the (unlucky) thirteenth Federal Reserve District. Appropriately enough, "increasing concern was expressed in Canada that the flexibility of Canadian monetary policy was in danger of being severely limited by a *target* level for Canadian exchange reserves" (5, p.14) and in December, after an exchange of letters between Canada and the U.S., the reserve ceiling was removed. The interest differential between Canada and the U.S. for the fourth quarter of 1968 reflects this extra degree of freedom: it is considerably larger than any previous differential and had the effect of increasing Canada's reserves well beyond the previous ceiling level.

**1969**

"Since the autumn of 1968, when it became clear that the anticipated moderation of inflationary pressures was not occurring, monetary policy has again been directed toward restraint" (6, pp. 10-11). The Bank Rate, increased in December, was raised again in February. But a first-quarter increase of 12.8% in total bank money and 18.1% in privately-held bank money hardly reflects restraint! Again the Central Bank is probably referring to the upward movements in interest rates and the falling MLA ratio. And again the Bank of Canada is allowing the chartered banks to determine the rate of growth of the banking system. In the first weeks of the second quarter the more-liquid-asset ratio fell to a "new low up to that time" (6, p. 11), but the chartered banks appeared willing to run this ratio down even lower. The Bank, not expecting this turn of events, resorted to more drastic action. In April it increased the banks' secondary reserve ratio from 7% to 8%, thus impounding about $250 million of the banks' liquid assets. In addition the Central Bank requested that the banks limit the rates they would pay on short-term, Canadian-dollar certificates of deposit. As a result privately-held bank money declined at an annual rate of over 4%. But the chartered banks were not to be outdone: faced with the prospect of losing term deposits to near banks, they began attracting foreign currency deposits to reinvest in the lucrative Euro-dollar market. Resident holdings of these deposits increased by $800 million in the second quarter of 1969 (Table 2)[16]. Redefining bank money as deposits of Canadian residents in Canadian or foreign currency results in an *increase* in privately held bank money of nearly 8% from 1969.I to 1969.II.

Chartered-bank loans increased by 18.1% in the second quarter, financed in part by drawing down net foreign assets by $300 million (Table 2), and were still increasing rapidly early in the third quarter. In addition, the first two weeks of the third quarter saw foreign currency deposits shoot up by a further $350 million. The Bank responded by placing a dollar limit on these foreign currency "swapped" deposits and by increasing further the Bank Rate. Even though the banks drew down their net foreign assets by a further $233 million the restraint was now on in full force. Loan expansion was way down in the third quarter and all monetary aggregates registered substantial declines. Real interest rates were now well above 3% and at their highest rates for the 1965-69 period.

**1970**

With unemployment remaining near 5%, monetary restraint continued, the chartered banks finally being forced to decrease loans outstanding in the first quarter of 1970 by 1.2% on an annual basis. Once again, however, Canadian monetary policy ran headlong into the realities of the fixed-exchange-rate system. Monetary restraint resulted in substantial foreign exchange inflows—over $300 million in 1970.I (Table 2). In order to sterilize these inflows the Bank had to draw down government balances at the chartered banks. This is reflected in the difference in the growth rates of the monetary aggregates—private bank money increased at an annual rate of 3.02% while total bank money declined by 1.99%. But sterilization simply kept Canadian interest rates higher than they would otherwise have been and the reserve flows began flowing in all the faster. On March 30, the Governor removed the ceiling on foreign currency "swapped deposits" hoping that they would increase and relieve the pressure on the Canadian dollar. This proved to be ineffective against the swelling inflow. From the end of March to the first week in May, government deposits at the chartered banks fell from slightly over $1 billion to $233 million, most of this decrease going to insure that the continuing foreign exchange inflow did not increase bank reserves. In order to maintain sufficient government balances to enable future sterilization the Government announced a special bond issue of $250. To insure that the banks bought this issue the Governor raised the secondary reserve ratio from 8% to 9%—enough to immobilize more than the whole of the new bond issue. When the reserve inflow continued unabated, the Bank began operating in the forward market. But this, too, offered no relief. Faced with the alternative of having to follow an expansionist monetary policy in order to maintain the par value of the Canadian dollar, the government announced (on Sunday, May 31) that the Exchange Fund would no longer maintain the value of the Canadian dollar within the IMF limits: Canada was back on a flexible rate.[17]

## III.   Résumé

From an analytical vantage point, one can indict Canadian monetary policy over this period on three counts: (i) selection of inappropriate monetary indicators, (ii) an inefficient procedure to effect desired monetary policy, and (iii) a less-than-full appreciation of the dictates underlying the fixed-rate system. We shall treat these in turn. Rates of monetary expansion well into the teens are simply not tolerable. Even policy reversals (i.e., changes in the rate of change) were above 10% on many occasions, i.e., an increase in the rate of change of privately-held bank money of over 17% from 1968.I to 1968.II followed by an 11% fall in the rate of change to 1968.III. In large measure these policies were a result of focusing on nominal rates of interest in particular and credit conditions in general as the indicators of monetary policy. "Leaning against the wind" in 1967 and 1968 served not to decrease but rather to increase interest rates and to worsen the inflation. Even the Governor now recognizes this:

> It would be a mistake to over-estimate the capacity of a central bank, by following an easy monetary policy in inflationary conditions, to bring about lower levels of interest rates that would last for any significant period of time. No doubt the central bank could, by undertaking a rapid monetary expansion, cause some temporary reduction in short-term interest rates but this would increase inflationary expectations and indeed bring about a situation that was in fact more inflationary, so that the longer-term result would almost certainly be a higher rather than a lower level of interest rates. (18, p.13.)

Recognition of this in 1965 rather than 1969 would have led to far more stability in the rates of monetary expansion and far more appropriate monetary policy!

Equally significant is the inefficient manner in which the Bank carries out its desired policy. On several occasions (e.g. 1965.I, 1969.IV) the lag between the announced policy and the reflection of this policy in the balance sheets of chartered banks is somewhere in the neighborhood of six to nine months. This unacceptably long lag arises because the Bank focuses on influencing the MLA ratio as the means of influencing chartered-bank lending activities. This is a result of the Bank's reserve-management policy which in large measure automatically validates last month's deposit liabilities, which policy in turn results from the Bank's sensitivity to interest-rate changes. The consequence of this is that for long periods of time the commercial banks are able to chart their own course of monetary expansion.[18] In addition, the MLA ratio leaves much to be desired as an indicator. For one thing the debt management policies followed during this period resulted in large upward movements in this ratio, often at times when the announced policy was one of restraint. Furthermore, it probably shares many of the defects of the "free reserves" concept. Given the current levels of interest rates and income, and the expectations regarding their future movements, there exists, for the banks, a desired MLA ratio. A different set of conditions will generate a different desired MLA ratio. Therefore a given value for the MLA ratio can be consistent with varying degrees of bank restraint. Essentially, precisely this problem occurred in 1969 when the chartered banks kept on expanding assets and liabilities even though their MLA ratio was at its historic low.[19] A far better procedure would be for the Bank of Canada to announce publicly what rate of growth of reserves it deems appropriate in the following month or months, supplemented perhaps by movements in the secondary reserve ratio to exert greater influence on the lending policies of the banks. In addition to shortening the "inside" lag of monetary policy this procedure would also clarify for the general public the current stance of monetary policy.[20]

An alternative would be to abolish the lagged reserve-settlement scheme and revert to a system where both reserves and deposits refer to the current period. Such a system seems more suited to the Canadian banking context with its oligopolistic structure and relatively stable interbank flows than to the U.S. banking setting. But even this type of system will not guarantee the Bank greater control over short-run movements in bank liabilities unless the Bank is more willing to tolerate interest-rate fluctuations.[21] It should be noted that, as of January, 1968, the chartered banks are required to satisfy the legal reserve requirement bi-weekly, although the deposit liabilities still relate to the previous month. How this modification is working out is not yet clear. On the one hand, chartered banks and dealers appear to be borrowing from the Bank more frequently and for larger amounts than was previously the case. But, on the other hand, the maximum rates of monetary expansion for the 1965-69 period have occurred under this scheme and, it should be pointed out, during periods when the Bank's announced policy was one of restraint.

## MONETARY POLICY UNDER A FIXED-RATE REGIME

Under a fixed-exchange rate the monetary policies of the smaller countries must be geared largely to balance-of-payments considerations. Given the level of income, population growth, etc., in Canada and the stance of monetary policy in the world economy, there exists a given level of monetary expansion that is consistent with a given level of international reserves. Fluctuations in reserve levels permit some flexibility in individual countries' monetary policies. But with the advent of the massive Euro-dollar market it is becoming increasingly difficult for countries to pursue independent monetary policies. The behaviour of resident-held foreign currency deposits exemplifies this well: the large increases in these deposits occurred in 1966, 1967.IV, 1969.II and 1969.IV —all periods when the Bank of Canada was actively pursuing restrictive policy! At the height of the restraint (1969.III) the Bank was forced to put a dollar ceiling on these deposits. It is interesting to note that if one defines bank money to include resident holdings of both foreign as well as Canadian dollar liabilities of the chartered banks this series exhibits considerably less variability than that of privately-held bank money.

However, fixing the quantity as well as the price of U.S. dollars effectively emasculates monetary policy. And such was Canada's predicament during most of the 1965-70 period.[22] Viewed in this light, Canada's policy with respect to monetary expansion is in part understandable. But in this broader context the Bank must bear some responsibility for Canada's adherence to the exchange rate and subsequent subjection to the wage and price spirals plaguing the international economy. And in the end we were forced to abandon the fixed-exchange rate system anyway. The appropriate time to appreciate the exchange rate (or set it free) was in 1965 or perhaps 1967 and not in 1970. With the international economy strong and inflationary expectations in their infancy in 1965, Canada, under a policy of appreciating or freeing the dollar, could have pursued a monetary policy slightly less restrictive than that of the U.S. and obtained an enviable trade-off between inflation and unemployment. As it turned out, however, the movement to a floating rate and appreciation was adopted as an emergency measure and in a time of slackening world economic activity so that in the short run at least the effect will be to gain a once-and-for-all reduction in price levels at the expense of an increase in the already high rate of unemployment.

Furthermore, it is not at all clear that Canada will enjoy many of the benefits that a flexible-exchange rate can bestow. In order to insure that the rate would not appreciate too much the Bank of Canada announced (also on May 31, 1970) a reduction in the Bank Rate, thereby easing credit conditions in Canada. In addition, the Minister of Finance suggested that the Exchange Fund would be active in maintaining the dollar at the "appropriate" level. If monetary policy is utilized to achieve and maintain a particular value for the dollar, then in effect Canada has an appreciated and not a floating exchange rate.[23] But, in theory at least, Canada now has obtained flexibility in the conduct of her monetary policy.

On these three issues, then, the Bank's performance is clearly substandard. However, to assert that monetary policy was inappropriate throughout this period may be going too far. Monetary policy is part of overall public policy and in the last analysis should be viewed in this context since the Governor is responsible to the Minister of Finance. Both fiscal policy (especially in 1967 and 1968) and the concern over regional economic disparity probably forced the Bank to be more expansionist than it otherwise would have been. And the acceptance of the reserve ceiling in return for exemption under the IET provisions was a further constraint that overall policy imposed on the conduct of monetary policy. In addition, the Bank successfully carried the Canadian economy through two crises (the domestic financial crisis in the summer of 1965 and the January, 1968, exchange-rate crisis) and to stave off a third the Bank (and Government) resorted to a flexible exchange rate. Considering that Canada is one of the most open economies in the world and the international monetary system went through its most trying period since Bretton Woods, the Bank must be given some credit for keeping the country on a relatively even keel throughout 1965-70. All things considered, however, we still contend that Canadian monetary policy over the past five years leaves much to be desired.

As a final comment we direct attention to the role of the Prices and Incomes Commission (PIC). In that the Bank proposed, helped staff, and is one of the most ardent supporters of the PIC it seems appropriate to include the operations of the PIC as reflecting, at least peripherally, the viewpoint of the Bank of Canada. One of the factors contributing to the formation of the PIC was the belief that "present policy tools are not sufficient to resolve the very real conflict that exists at the present time between the objectives of maintaining high level employment and restoring the price stability than is necessary for sustained economic growth" (11, p. 10) and that "despite large government borrowing requirements and other factors, monetary policy has played a major role in restraining growth of demand. Interest rates have risen to very high levels" (11, p. 22). But we have just demonstrated that monetary policy contributed to, rather than restrained, demand growth. It is unfortunate that the prevailing view in official Ottawa circles is that conventional macropolicy tools have done all they could to fight inflation, but their best was not enough.[24]

The Commission's role is to "*discover* the facts, *analyze* the causes, processes and consequences of inflation and to *inform* both public and government of how price stability may be achieved" (10, p.28). In its work, the PIC has been embarking on a program of voluntary wage and price controls (see Reuber [20]). As a short-run measure this may or may not be fruitful—the benefits of any shift in the Phillips curve toward a better price-unemployment trade-off must be set against the cost of potential resource misallocation. As a long-run approach to the inflation problem under a fixed-rate regime, however, it is questionable, to say the least. Canada will continue to inflate at or near the rate of inflation in the world (U.S.) economy. Now that the exchange rate is freed the PIC has, in theory, a greater role to play—for good or bad.[25]

On the role of monetary policy over the 1965-69 period and also indirectly on the role of the Prices and Incomes Commission, the last word belongs to R.A. Mundell (14, p.641, fn. 6).

When, as in 1950, Canada was faced with a situation in which the U.S. economy was involved in the Korean War and threatened by inflation, while Canada had only a year before devalued, the choice was inflation or a change in the exchange rate, and the Canadian authorities wisely chose to let the Canadian dollar appreciate rather than be forced into going along with the U.S. inflation. In [13] . . . I argued that a situation analogous to

1950 had appeared and that Canada should again let her exchange rate float upward according to free market forces. But that time the Bank opted for inflation instead.


### Footnotes

1. Interestingly enough, one of the principles underlying the Bank Act was to increase the degree of competition in the financial sector. But just three months after the provisions began to be implemented, the removal of the ceiling rate on the asset side was replaced with a Regulation "Q" type restriction on the *liability* side in order to curb the power of the banking sector relative to the near-banks.

2. Funds converted into a foreign currency, usually U.S. dollars, which have been placed on term deposit with a bank and which the bank has undertaken through a forward contract to convert back into Canadian dollars at maturity.

3. These first two series exclude currency since the Bank of Canada maintains that in its operations it does not allow a currency drain to affect the level of reserves which it deems to be appropriate. For an empirical verfication of this, see Courchene and Kelly, (8).

4. See, for example, the paper by Fand (10) and references therein.

5. While I feel that there is ample evidence to support the monetarist's contention that the money supply is a more appropriate indicator, it is important to emphasize that central bankers are quick to point out that there exist as many assessments of the current thrust of monetary policy as there are definitions of money and that these assessments can be contradictory. This is especially true for periods during which the structure of the financial sector is changing (e.g., in Canada because of the Bank Act or in the U.S. because of the effect of Regulation Q) where the various candidates for the money supply can and often do lead to divergent views on policy thrust. From a theoretical standpoint it should not matter which of the various monetary aggregates one selects as the monetary indicator provided that it incorporates in a suitable manner the behaviour of the spectrum of near monies. In terms of influencing central bank policy, developing a framework which would reconcile the conclusions one draws with respect to the stance of monetary policy from the various monetary aggregates would appear to be one of the most fruitful areas of empirical monetary research.

6. Acheson and Chant (1) interpret this development as resulting from the Bank's exercising its power of moral suasion which included, in 1956, the implementation of a secondary reserve ratio. In 1955 the general public accounted for the largest proportion of Treasury bills. Indeed, their dollar volume of bill holdings was considerably larger in 1955 than in 1969. This trend is even more disconcerting given that the express purpose of the bank legislation in the mid-fifties was to *encourage* the development of a short-term money market.

7. And these deficits (cash requirements) were large; $85 million in 1965-66; $872 million in 1966-67; $911 million in 1967-68; $1,103 million in 1968-69; $5 million in 1969-70. Source: *Budget Papers* (Ottawa: Queen's Printer, 1970), Part II.

8. Given this view, my colleague Levis Kochin points out that it is particularly appropriate that the French words in the Bank's *Statistical Summary* for assets and liabilities are, respectively, "actif" and "passif".

9. No statistics relating directly to bank liquidity appear in either the Bank's monthly or annual editions of the *Statistical Summary*. However, the *Weekly Financial Statistics* issued by the Bank give substantial emphasis to bank liquidity and the MLA ratio. In addition, the Governor's *Annual Report* always emphasizes the role of bank liquidity in influencing chartered-bank behaviour.

10. These assertions really constitute an alternative, and testable, hypothesis relating to the interaction between the Bank and the chartered banking system in the short run. However, the empirical analysis necessary to confirm or reject this hypothesis is beyond the scope of this paper. But we might note that the banking system was provided with larger reserves during 1966 than during 1965 in the sense that the *excess* reserve ratio was larger in 1966. Put another way, in 9 of the 12 months in 1966 the level of reserves held (on an average-of-Wednesdays basis) in month $t$ was above the minimum (8%) required in month $t + 1$ in order to support the deposit liabilities existing in month $t$. This was true for only six months in 1965. Yet loans and total private deposits grew at rates of 22.3% and 12.6%, respectively, in 1965 and 6.9% and 6.7% in 1966. One difference was surely that the MLA ratio was considerably larger during 1965 than 1966 (see Table 2).

11. It is appropriate to point out that the Governor is referring to the situation in 1966 rather than 1965 in these remarks. As Reuber (18) indicates the Government did repatriate $140 million of its own securities in early 1966 as a means of evading the reserve ceiling.

12. For an empirical analysis of the relationship between domestic monetary expansion and foreign exchange flows for most of the industrial countries see Courchene (9).

13. It is interesting to note that in nearly every *Annual Report* the Governor calls for some sort of commission to influence wage and price behaviour, e.g. "I hope that the public authorities will take the lead in seeking to influence the various groups in the economy who wield power to relate their demands for increases in money incomes more realistically to increase in their real output than has been the case in the past couple of years" (4, p.8). In simpler terms, Canada's Prices and Incomes Commission is the brain-child of the Bank of Canada.

14. For some further effects of this legislation on the conduct of Canadian monetary policy, see (8).

15. The Governor, too, was embarrassed by these high rates of expansion and took partial refuge in arguing strongly for a narrower definition of money, i.e., currency plus demand deposits (5, pp.9-10) which exhibits a much smaller increase over 1968.

16. Foreign currency liabilities held by both residents and non-residents increased by nearly two billion dollars in the first half of 1969.

17. The level of gold and foreign exchange was slightly over 3.4 billion dollars when Canada floated her rate—an increase of over 450 million from the end of the first quarter of 1970.

18. Indeed, given the existence of large unutilized portions of business loan authorizations and the availability of automatic personal overdrafts under schemes like "Chargex", one could argue that it is the public and not the chartered banks who control monetary expansion. We would argue, however, that if the chartered banks felt that reserves would not be forthcoming automatically to validate their increase in liabilities they would take a more restrictive approach toward these overdraft privileges.

19. It is appropriate to note that in 1969 the banks' more liquid assets embodied more "liquidity"—the ratio of bills to bonds was much greater than in earlier periods.

20. In this connection, we are sympathetic to some of the criticism levelled at the Bank of Canada in a recent paper by Acheson and Chant (1) especially with regard to the air of secrecy surrounding, and the degree of personalization (i.e., emphasis on moral suasion) governing, Bank policy.

21. In addition, the banking community would probably have to alter its attitude toward central-bank borrowing (rediscounting). Appearing before the Royal Commission on Banking and Finance in early 1963, Mr. Rasminsky stated that during his tenure as Governor (about a year and a half at the time of this statement) no bank had ever requested a second advance from the Bank in the course of any one month (7, p.49).

22. Two common fallacies need clarification at this juncture. First, it is often claimed that since the behaviour of the Canadian money supply differs from the U.S. counterpart, the Canadian position is not equivalent to being the thirteenth Federal Reserve district. But endogeneity does not require identical growth rates. If the behaviour of money in the 1st Federal Reserve district differs from that in the 12th Federal Reserve district, is the money in the 12th district exogenous? Second, a constant rate of growth of money is preferable to a variable growth rate. This is probably true for a country with a flexible exchange rate or for a country like the U.S. (with a very small foreign sector relative to the GNP) under fixed rates. But the fixed-exchange-rate system imposes a given path of monetary expansion for countries like Canada and it is far from clear that a fixed rule would be consistent with this required growth rate. However, given the erratic behaviour of the Canadian money system, it appears that from 1965-70 an expansion-to-rule policy would have been superior. The fact that the money aggregate including foreign currency deposits exhibits more stability than the Canadian dollar series suggests that Bank policy need not have been so variable.

23. The authorities would be well advised to study Mundell's assessment (12) of Canada's experience under the 1950-62 floating rate in order to avoid past mistakes. One indication of the degree to which Canada is "manoeuvering" the exchange rate is that as of the end of August the level of gold and foreign-exchange stood at 3.85 billion dollars—an increase of nearly $450 million since the advent of flexible rates.

24. Reuber (20) scores the authorities on this point.

25. It is important to note, however, that the PIC in its public statements never viewed the fixed-exchange-rate system as an obstacle in its fight against inflation.

GERALD K. BOUEY

# What Central Banking Is About

Some of you may recall that last autumn, after having accepted an invitation from your President to speak to members of your Club in the latter part of November, I subsequently asked for a postponement. A number of events of some note occurred between the date of my acceptance in August and the scheduled date in November, but the relevant one in this connection was Mr. Rasminsky's decision to retire as Governor of the Bank. The topic I had planned to use was "What can be expected of monetary policy", and suddenly I felt more like asking the question than trying to answer it. Your President was most understanding. After my appointment on February 1st he renewed the invitation and I promised to show up this time. Today I would like to say something about the way I look at central banking and in the course of doing so refer to some recent events.

Anyone taking on a job like mine is bound to notice something all too familiar about the list of major economic problems which, he is told, demand his urgent attention. The level of unemployment, the trend of prices, international monetary and trade uncertainties—surely such a list must be an out-of-date one prepared several years ago for a predecessor.

Unfortunately, the truth is that the problems central bankers have to worry about these days, whether in Canada or in other countries, are still the same hardy perennials. It's not much easier than it ever was for public policy to keep the economy expanding steadily along a satisfactory growth track. There are risks of falling off on either side—into inadequate growth and rising unemployment on the one hand, into worsening inflation on the other—and those concerned with economic policy must try to weigh these risks as best they can, knowing that the problems are not of a kind that yield to once-and-for-all solutions.

This is not the only reason why a new governor is likely to feel some trepidation. While in some quarters central banks once appeared to enjoy a quite undeserved reputation for omniscience, the opposite view—that both the motives and the competence of central banks should be regarded with suspicion—seems to have gained ground in recent years.

Up to a point, of course, it is possible even for a central banker to regard this shift in public opinion as a welcome move in the direction of realism. After all, there is no reason why those of us whose jobs involve us in the management of the nation's monetary affairs should not be expected, like anyone else, to be able to offer reasonable explanations for our actions.

On the other hand, some of us do find it a little difficult to recognize ourselves in the more extreme caricatures of central bankers that seem to be in vogue these days. Perhaps an illustration or two might help to make the point.

Some critics seem to believe that the typical central banker combines a pathological obsession for fighting inflation with a heartless disregard for the plight of the unemployed. This is alleged to be reflected in an habitual foot-dragging attitude toward monetary expansion together with continual harping on the evils of inflation.

Others suspect just the opposite—that in spite of much sanctimonious preaching against inflation central banks are in fact prime culprits in fuelling the process. Their record over the years is cited as proof that central banks can be counted on to permit a rising tide of money to finance chronic inflation, whether in response to the insatiable financial demands of governments or because of their own anxiety to avoid unpopularity.

Still others, conceding that central banks probably mean well, judge them to be merely incompetent and vacillating. According to this view, at the slightest rise in the inflation rate they jam the money tap tightly shut, and are quite surprised when this has no immediate effect on prices; later on, when the unemployment rate begins to rise, they not only fail to recognize this as being a predictable lagged effect of their own actions, but try to correct it by going to the other extreme and flooding the country with money. In this view central bankers, like the Bourbons, are incapable of learning anything from experience.

Without going so far as to claim that these caricatures are totally inaccurate, I do think that they reflect a less than perfect understanding of the problems faced by a central bank in a modern society.

Let me begin with a word about what I take to be the ultimate objectives of monetary management. My view, which is in no way new, is that the objectives of monetary policy are the same as those of public policy generally. Not only would it be presumptuous of the central bank to try to impose different goals of its own on the community, but it would also be quite unacceptable in a democratic country.

Among the most important objectives of public economic policy are sustained economic growth, high employment—that is to say, low unemployment—and reasonably stable price behaviour. These are difficult goals to achieve all at the same time, but I don't believe there is any major quarrel about them in our society. The real arguments are about what is the best strategy for achieving these objectives, and about how long a time horizon one should have in mind in weighing the consequences of alternative policy approaches.

What contribution can monetary policy make towards the achievement of these goals? We can skip the technicalities—open market operations, cash reserve management, changes in secondary reserves and in the Bank Rate. The important thing is that the central bank is a public agency with certain technical powers at its disposal, and that these powers enable it to influence credit conditions by controlling the rate of growth of the nation's privately-owned banking system.

There are two main reasons why the operations of the chartered banks have an important bearing on the functioning of our economy. The first is that bank loans and bank purchases of securities are among the major sources of financing in Canada. The second is that as a by-product of these transactions, the public comes into possession of deposit balances in bank accounts, which serve as much the most important form of money in this country.

Over the years, the amount of credit extended by the chartered banks and the amount of money in the hands of the Canadian public have grown hand in hand. At times the growth of bank credit and money holdings has been allowed to proceed quite rapidly, and at other times much less rapidly, depending on discretionary judgments of the Bank of Canada as to how to exercise its technical powers in particular situations.

The effects of these policy choices show up in various ways. The most immediate effect of a rapid rate of monetary growth is that for a time it brings about easier credit conditions than would have prevailed with slower monetary growth. The cost and availability of credit throughout the financial system are, of course, also importantly affected by changes in the underlying economic situation and in the related strength of credit demand in Canada, as well as by changes in credit conditions in other countries.

The ability of the central bank to influence credit conditions in Canada has further ramifications, since changes in the relationship between Canadian and foreign interest rate levels can affect flows of funds between Canada and other countries and can therefore affect the exchange rate for the Canadian dollar.

Of course it is not just conditions in financial markets that are influenced by Bank of Canada actions in permitting a faster or a slower rate of domestic monetary growth. The ultimate effects of the monetary policy followed — and much the most important ones — are felt in our markets for goods, services and labour. There is an important connection — though by no means an immediate or very precise relationship — between the growth of the banking system and the growth of money expenditure in the economy. It is this flow of money expenditure, of course, that enables production and employment in Canada to grow. But it is also this same flow of money expenditure that enables prices, wage rates and other money incomes to rise at the rates they do.

Monetary management is not, of course, the only influence affecting the over-all level of spending in the economy, nor is it necessarily the dominant influence. In addition to private decisions, the policy actions of governments at all levels directly affect aggregate spending in Canada through decisions taken with respect to expenditure, taxation, lending and borrowing, and so do economic and financial conditions in other countries. Major ups and downs in economic activity in Canada have always been closely related to those in the United States. One does not have to believe, however, that monetary policy is all important for the functioning of our economy in order to believe that it is nevertheless important enough to try to get it right.

So much for the nature and broad effects of the powers the central bank has to work with. How are these powers to be used in practice? This takes me back to the beginning of my remarks, where I implied that the job of a central banker is essentially a balancing act. Bearing in mind the impact of other domestic policies and of economic conditions in other countries, he wants to ensure that the banking system keeps growing at a rate high enough to enable the economy to reach — and to stay on — a sustainable path of vigorous growth at high levels of employment. On the other hand, he wants to avoid a rate of growth of the banking system so rapid that at some stage it will become virtually impossible to contain inflation while at the same time maintaining satisfactory employment growth.

In an economy suffering from abnormally high unemployment and much idle plant capacity, the main response to a strong rise in spending usually takes the form of more jobs and more output rather than a more rapid rise of costs and prices. If the growth of jobs and output is rapid enough and lasts long enough, however, in due course a stage will come where growing scarcities of the right kind of labour in the right places, together with spreading production bottlenecks, progressively alter the form of this response. In circumstances such as these, an overly rapid growth of money expenditure is increasingly likely to have as its main result a marked escalation of cost and price increases rather than further large gains in employment and output.

Indeed, if the process is allowed to continue, a point will eventually be reached where further postponement of policy measures to check the pace of spending growth in order to contain inflation will no longer be possible. Past experience in many countries shows that an unfortunate by-product of belated action to cope with a situation of this kind—once it has been allowed to get out of hand—can be a sharp slowing of economic growth and a substantial rise in unemployment. For this reason, I believe there is an important sense in which it can be said that a worsening of inflation often leads in time to a worsening of unemployment.

The operating decisions that have to be taken by the central bank necessarily involve difficult judgments about whether credit conditions are suitable, and about the degree to which the rate of growth of the banking system should be speeded up, slowed down, or maintained approximately within its existing range. Such judgments have to be made on an assessment of probabilities rather than on certain knowledge. For this reason they are bound to be provisional and subject to modification as new information and unexpected developments alter the balance of future probabilities.

An essential ingredient of judgments of this kind is an informed view not only about how the economy has been moving in the recent past and where it stands now, but also about the possible paths it might follow over periods as long as two years or more into the future under alternative policy assumptions. The need for such a long forward view about where the economy seems to be heading is a consequence of the long time lags that exist between monetary management today and its eventual impact on the future course of economic events.

Perhaps I can best illustrate the way in which the Bank of Canada approaches the decisions it has to take by outlining very briefly the basic rationale of recent monetary policy.

During 1972 the Bank of Canada permitted a further large increase of 15 per cent in the over-all size of the domestic banking system, following a 19 per cent increase in the previous year. Thus over the past two years we have had sustained monetary expansion at rates not only on the high side in relation to past Canadian experience but also distinctly higher than the recent growth rate of aggregate spending and income.

The dominant consideration underlying this expansionary policy was the obvious need for large increases in demand, output and employment for some time if the Canadian economy was to regain more satisfactory operating levels. In seeking to maintain relatively easy credit conditions, the Bank also had in mind the potential drag on economic expansion of an undue appreciation of the Canadian dollar in foreign exchange markets if too much foreign capital moved into Canada.

While giving priority to the immediate objective of reducing the margin of slack in the economy, the Bank has not been unaware of the time lags involved in the operation of monetary policy, and for some time now it has kept the liquidity of the chartered banks under close control. When the already high rate of growth in bank loans became even higher in the first three months of this year, reaching an annual rate in excess of 25 per cent, the Bank of Canada did not permit the whole of this loan expansion to be accommodated through a correspondingly faster rate of monetary growth. The resulting pressure on the liquidity of the domestic banking system, together with recent substantial increases in short-term interest rates in the United States and overseas, were the main factors that led to the recent rise in short-term interest rates in Canada, including the increase in the Bank of Canada's own lending rate.

Since a change in our Bank Rate tends to focus attention on the stance of monetary policy, I want to spend a few moments in an effort to explain as clearly as I can what our current policy is intended to achieve.

As I emphasized at the time of the Bank Rate change, substantial rates of bank loan and monetary expansion continue to be needed in order to finance vigorous growth in output and employment. There is ample evidence that the pace of economic growth in Canada since the third quarter of last year has been unusually rapid, and that we are well on our way towards the restoration of high levels of employment. Prospects that the current vigorous expansion will continue are good. There are, for example, clear signs that the pace of capital spending by Canadian business will be accelerating in the period ahead, and strongly rising demand for our exports will be an additional source of stimulus.

Looking even further ahead, however, it must be recognized that the current rate of growth in aggregate spending is too high to be sustainable over the longer run. If the economy has too much momentum when it eventually begins to bump up against its capacity limits once again, we risk a period of temporary overshoot followed by another period of slack. To guard against this danger, what will be needed at a later stage is some moderation of the rate of growth of spending.

The recent pace of bank credit extension has clearly been too rapid. Part of the increase in the demand for bank credit appears to have come from foreign corporations, which at present have an interest rate incentive to raise funds in Canada either for use abroad or to replace funds that would normally be obtained abroad. The effective interest rate paid for bank credit by large prime borrowers in the United States is currently about 8 per cent (after allowing for the widespread practice of requiring compensating deposit balances) as compared with $6^1/_2$ per cent in Canada. In view of this situation, the Bank of Canada has asked the banks to give priority in the use of their total loan resources to the credit-worthy demands of their Canadian customers rather than respond to unusual requests of the kind I have mentioned from foreign corporations or foreign-owned subsidiaries in Canada. In addition, the banks have been asked to pay particular attention to the needs of small businesses, which do not have easy access to other credit sources, and to applications for credit in the slower growth regions of the country.

I want to stress again that we are not moving to a tight money situation and that the banking system will continue to be in a position to accommodate reasonable growth in the total amount of bank lending.

I hope you will bear with me if, in concluding, I reemphasize three main points.

The first is that there are long time lags in the response of the economy to monetary management. It is true that some effects may be felt relatively quickly, but on the average the time that elapses before output and prices are affected is relatively long. Why would the Bank of Canada raise the Bank Rate when the latest unemployment figure available at the time was still as high as 5.9 per cent? (It has since come down to 5.5 per cent.) The answer is that the Bank must not only keep in mind current developments but must also look ahead to the likely situation next year and the year after.

The second point is that the demand for credit, the growth of the banking system, and the level of interest rates are all interrelated. To insist that a central bank maintain any particular level of interest rates is to insist that it abandon control over the growth of money and credit. This may seem to be an elementary point, but I sometimes have the impression that the central bank is expected to avoid both a rapid increase in the money supply and higher interest rates regardless of the strength of the demand for credit.

Finally I want to reject totally any suggestion that the Bank of Canada is somehow more concerned with price indexes than with people. As I have already stated, the Bank remains firmly committed to maintaining rates of monetary growth high enough to support a strong expansion of employment and output. But for monetary policy to go even further and promote excessive spending that will speed up the pace of inflation—inflation which in turn must eventually be brought under control with serious risk of adverse effects on employment and growth—is not my idea of the way to advance the cause of human welfare. We will do better over the longer run in terms of employment as well as in terms of our price and cost performance if we try to avoid such excesses.

Recent experience has shown how difficult it is to deal with the aftermath of periods of excessive spending through demand management policies, once inflationary expectations have become very strong. This is not, however, an argument for failing to take the necessary measures to avoid getting into such a situation in the first place.

The Bank of Canada is going to continue to pay close attention to the problem of unemployment. At the same time—although I acknowledge that living as we do in a sea of world-wide inflation greatly limits the possibilities for achieving as good a price and cost performance as we would like to see—the Bank is not going to forget about the problem of inflation.

There are many more settings on the dial of monetary policy than the extremes of very easy money and very tight money, although we seem to lack an adequate vocabulary for describing the intermediate points. The best chance of getting our policy set right is to try to strike a reasonable balance between risks that lie ahead on either side—the risks associated with too much monetary expansion or too little. But that, after all, is what central banking is about.

# The Banks and the Regional Problem

The past year has seen renewed concern about the economic differences that exist across Canada. In part this has been made more acute by the serious turn of events in Quebec, but there has also been an understandable concern, at a time when the North American economy as a whole has lost its impetus, about those regions of the country which are at the best of times slow-growth areas. In general, it is fair to say that some improvement over the past decade has been made in narrowing economic disparities, and it also appears that during the current business slowdown — which has been mild in comparison with the recognized postwar recessions — the slow-growth regions have not suffered a marked deterioration in employment and business sales. This represents some real progress towards the ultimate degree of regional balance that is sought, but a major effort is still needed.

In recognition of the public concern on this matter, we in this Bank have been making every possible effort to finance undertakings in less developed parts of the country. In more than a few cases, indeed, we have approved credits which would in all likelihood not be regarded as economic in the more prosperous regions. Even apart from these special efforts, it is probably not sufficiently understood that the branch system of banking in Canada is far from being centralized with respect to credit administration. In the case of The Bank of Nova Scotia, less than 1% of commercial loans by number now require Head Office consideration prior to approval. (In dollar terms, of course, the proportion referred to Head Office is somewhat larger. Very large loans, especially those related to the natural resource industries, require specialized skills for analysis and documentation, and these skills are necessarily concentrated in the executive offices.) The majority of loans lie within the authority of the Regional General Managers, whose motivation is to expand the business under their jurisdiction.

This is not the first time these views have been expressed in recent years, but the persistence of doubt about their validity seems to rest on the fact that regional statistics are not generally available. The reasons for the absence of published regional statistics are mainly to do with the complexities of interpreting them. Clearly in a far-flung economy such as ours, money is not always spent where it is borrowed, nor is it necessarily deposited in the places where it is saved. This applies particularly to the corporate sector, where head offices located in one region will conduct their business affairs in another. More generally, too, it is inevitable in our economy that some degree of savings will flow from one region to another. Indeed how could it be otherwise, since the projects which require heavy borrowings of funds are not generally located in the same places as the savers live. To take an extreme example, how could the Churchill Falls project, costing nearly $1 billion, be financed from local savings? Since no province or region in the country would be prepared to accept the idea that there might be a net flow of savings from its area to others, political pressures would be generated to prevent any inter-provincial flows at all. In a nutshell, every provincial government would seek to have a net inflow, creating an impossible arithmetic problem for the banks or indeed any other financial institution in the country.

## Inter-Provincial Capital Flows

The question of inter-provincial capital flows is perhaps most readily observed in the open bond markets. To begin with, most of the ten provinces have in recent years borrowed in the New York market for as much as one-quarter to one-third of their requirements. For the most part, the buyers are large United States insurance companies and pension funds which invest in fixed income securities for long terms. In this case we can clearly identify the net inflow of loanable funds, because it is originating outside the country. A very similar process takes place within Canada. Most of the insurance companies and large corporate pension funds are located in the major metropolitan areas. These institutions, as well as banks and trust companies, are the principal buyers of provincial and municipal bonds. It is quite true that these institutions operate on a nationwide scale for the most part, and therefore their resources are derived from the small savings of people who are located in the less prosperous provinces as well as in those that are better off. However, it is evident that since the greater proportion of population, especially with higher incomes, is concentrated in the better-off provinces, then on balance there is a net flow of savings through the financial institutions to the less-favoured provinces borrowing in the bond market. The same process is broadly true with respect to the general distribution of assets and liabilities of the banking system, as well as being true of the public market for provincial debentures.

The following table sets out the regional distribution of provincial and municipal securities held by The Bank of Nova Scotia at the time of writing in early December. Of course, this pattern has to be looked at in the context of the Bank's sources of deposits, since some banks emphasize one region more than another for historical reasons and other factors. A general guide to our regional pattern of business is shown by our distribution of branches, also presented in the same table. It will be seen that the regional spread of our branches is broadly similar to the regional distribution of our holdings of provincial and municipal securities. They are not identical for a variety of reasons: first, some of the provinces have not been borrowing to the same proportionate extent as others, and therefore there has not been a supply of new issues; another factor is that the individual customer relationships of the Bank happen to differ from one area to another for purely competitive business reasons; thirdly, the holdings of the Bank can change because of the buying and selling which goes on in the market place at all times; and fourthly, the distribution of deposits by region is not precisely the same as the distribution of branches.

| | Investment provincial and municipal securities | Distribution of branches by region |
|---|---|---|
| | % | % |
| Atlantic | 16.5 | 19.8 |
| Quebec | 8.5 | 9.2 |
| Ontario | 50.6 | 41.8 |
| Prairies | 16.8 | 18.3 |
| B.C. | 7.6 | 10.9 |
| | 100.0 | 100.0 |

While holdings of provincial and municipal securities are indicative of the general situation, they are only one part of our Canadian assets. Another sector of the market is the one for residential mortgages. In this sector of the market our assets are fairly heavily weighted in the rapidly growing provinces, for the obvious reason that that is where the demand for housing is strongest. Also, of course, there is some reflection of our mix of house-builder customers in different areas. The Bank of Nova Scotia has generally concentrated its residential mortgage lending in single-family dwellings, which means that with our widespread branch representation we have served the needs of smaller cities and towns as well as the metropolitan areas where apartment buildings are seen going up on every hand.

## Regional Considerations in Lending

Turning to the loan side of our business, I would like to make a few observations about the regional distribution of our commercial and industrial business, our consumer credit loans and our grain loans. Taking these in reverse order, it is self-evident that the grain loans of the banks are related almost exclusively to the three prairie provinces. In the past two years, this Bank's grain loans have varied between $60 millions and $95 millions. For the banking system as a whole, grain loans reached the exceptional figure of $1.1 billions in late 1969. At that level they constituted some 6% of all loans in Canada. The three prairie provinces account for close to 15% of the national income, and probably about the same percentage of annual savings through the banks, at least in a good crop year. It is a source of astonishment that anyone who lives in the prairie provinces should feel that a purely regional bank would better serve their interests. Last year, almost half the earning assets of an imaginary prairie regional bank would have been tied up in grain loans, and after providing for liquidity and other requirements, there would have been virtually nothing left for any other type of loan. Who would have provided funds for the oil industry, the potash industry, or the many small merchants across the provinces?

We do not claim that there is no role in Canada for regional banks, because in fact there are several regional banks and other financial institutions already, particularly in French Canada. But it is very hard to visualize how the creation of a multiplicity of regional banks would serve the interests of the public in the areas concerned. And it may be asked legitimately whether, after the creation of regional banks, it would follow that the creation of a whole flock of local and district banks would be better still. In that way it would be possible to prevent not only inter-regional and inter-provincial flows of money, but flows of money from one county to another. In time, we could succeed in creating the fragmented, insecure, and inefficient financial market which we had a century ago.

Consumer credit and loans to commercial and industrial enterprises are difficult to analyse on a regional basis with any great precision. In consumer lending, while large numbers of people are involved, there can be quite marked swings from region to region, not only reflecting economic trends over a period, but also resulting from the varying degree of competitive pressure of other financial institutions which may operate in particular parts of the country. In the last five years, our average annual rate of growth in consumer credit loans in Canada has been about 17%, and our regional growth rates have varied between about 13% and 22%, which is not a great variation considering regional differences in income, employment and comparative growth rates. Business loans, however, are extremely difficult to interpret on a regional basis, especially where larger amounts of money are involved. This, of course, is because a big percentage of such loans is made to corporations with head offices in the large urban centres; the actual business of these corporations may well be conducted in other provinces or even in slower-growth parts of the same provinces in which the head offices are located.

Another point I would like to stress is that The Bank of Nova Scotia does not discriminate between high-income and low-income regions of the country with respect to interest rates. In fact, in business loans, overall credit standards, having regard for term, risk and so on, are often more favourable in the less-developed parts of the country. However, interest rates themselves are treated on a national basis. In the residential mortgage field we have always had one national rate for NHA loans, while some years ago we took the lead in extending this practice to conventional mortgages so providing one rate of interest in all parts of the country, urban and rural, poor and rich. Lending rates on bank loans to provinces and municipalities are almost the same across the country, whereas in the open securities market this is not the case, and one finds considerable variations based on risk and market considerations.

## Special Attention to Quebec

A discussion of regional problems would not be complete without special reference to the Province of Quebec. The tragic events of 1970 have served to focus attention on the difficult set of interlocking social and economic problems with which the province is confronted. Although this Bank is generally considered to be an English-speaking institution, the fact is that we have over seventy branches in the Province of Quebec, over half of which are managed by French-speaking officers. We are actively planning the development of new branches and it is our intention to acquire and train an increasing proportion of our staff in Quebec from those of the French language. Within the past two months, we have been in the process of acquiring additional space to expand our computer facilities in Montreal, and in a short time we will be bringing our Ottawa Valley branch system within the Montreal watershed for computer purposes. We have also made a special additional allocation of funds for residential housing in Quebec, and we are searching for good commercial and consumer credit business throughout the province. We have every intention of expanding our business in the Province of Quebec, and of increasing our orientation to the French language and culture. As a national enterprise, we are very conscious of our responsibility to be able to operate in both languages when appropriate. We do not expect our staff in British Columbia to be bilingual, and the same would apply in Nova Scotia. But in most parts of the Province of Quebec, we will be devoting increasing attention to the problem of using French as a working language and of recruiting personnel from the French-speaking population. It may well be that the time of Quebec's greatest troubles is behind us, but it will be a long and difficult haul uphill to bring the economy of the province to the level where it should be.

LESTER C. THUROW

# Activities by Various Central Banks to Promote Economic and Social Welfare Programs

## The Aims, Instruments, and Independence of Central Banks

### Introduction and Summary

Although all central banks seek to regulate the supply of money and/or interest rates, the differences among central banks are as great as their similarities. These differences tend to be obscured since each country's central bank has a long history, usually springing from private ancestors. Rights, functions, and responsibilities tend to have the sanctity of time. Each country cannot imagine how anyone else could carry out central bank functions differently. Yet in fact different functions are carried out and the same functions are carried out with different instruments.

Differences among central banks raise two questions. (1) What is the optimum set of functions and instruments to delegate to central banks? (2) What is the range of functions and instruments that are actually contained within central banks? Although the first question is important, it cannot be answered without first answering the second question. Thus this analysis does not seek to determine the optimum arrangements, but merely to indicate the range of activities and the types of things that might be undertaken.

To provide an indication of the range of activities a comparative study of the central banks of Germany, France, Italy, Netherlands, India, Yugoslavia, Japan, Mexico, Sweden, Israel, and the United Kingdom was conducted.

### AIMS

Central banks in most countries designate certain sectors of the economy that are to receive favourable treatment from the central bank. This means either making loans in these favoured sectors at below market rates of interest or making credit more available in these sectors than it would be if so-called market forces were allowed to operate. In some cases this is done to aid preferentially particular sectors and in some cases this is done to offset the uneven impacts of private money markets.

## A. Preferred sectors

Since most developed countries (outside of the United States) have substantial proportions of their national output involved in international trade and since countries dislike changing exchange rates, exports almost universally receive *preferential* treatment. The Deutsche Bundesbank and the Banque de France give special rediscounting privileges to private commercial export bills; the Nederlandsche Bank and the Sveriges Riksbank in Sweden direct credit into exports; the Bank of Israel grants credits for exports at less than market rates; the Bank of England grants favourable credits for export financing.

## B. Offsetting the Uneven Impact of General Monetary Policies

Agriculture and housing typically receive favourable treatment because the impact of general credit restrictions seems to be much more severe in these sectors than in the economy in general. The Banque de France uses direct credit controls to stimulate the financing of agriculture and has special discounting provisions for agriculture and for grains stored in public storehouses; the Banco de Mexico makes low interest rate loans for housing and agriculture; the Sveriges Riksbank in Sweden regulates private banks to channel funds into housing and exempts housing from normal restrictive regulations.

## C. Social Objectives

To meet social objectives many central banks provide direct loans for state and local governments or for public agencies. Countries where the central bank fulfills this role include: Germany, France, Italy, India, and Mexico. In some, such as Italy, it even acts as a treasury for the provinces.

## D. Economic Growth

Generally central banks interpret their charge of promoting economic growth to extend far beyond general economy-wide monetary policies. In some countries this means channeling private funds into development sectors, in some countries this means direct central bank investments in private companies, and in others this means an active role in formulating and implementing national economic plans.

*(a) Channeling Private Funds* Direct credit controls are used to channel funds into industrial capital expenditures in France. The Banc d'Italia effectively uses moral suasion to give preferences to those with "sound development programs" where sound development programs mean programs that could have a large impact on economic growth. It also has and uses its power to approve or disapprove individual loans. The Banco de Mexico uses reserve requirements on private banks to direct resources into prescribed industrial securities and into loans for productive purposes. The Sveriges Riksbank in Sweden regulates private banks to channel funds into vital industries.

*(b) Public Loans and Investments* Central bank funds are sometimes invested in private companies to provide the necessary capital for economic growth. France is the principal place where this is done, but a public bank has been chartered in Italy to make investments in private firms and the Banco de Mexico invests in public corporations. Although loans are more often used in Mexico and India, the most extensive use occurs in Japan.

In Japan these loans funnel through commercial banks but are essentially loans from the central bank to industrial customers. Commercial banks borrow large sums of money from the central bank (the Nihon Ginko) and then lend these sums to industrial customers. Since many of these loans are short-term, but normally renewed, the Nihon Ginko has enormous control over the activities of industrial firms and banks. While borrowings from the central bank were almost 800 per cent of bank capital for the major banks of Japan at the end of 1968, borrowings from the Federal Reserve System in the United States were less than 2 per cent of bank capital for major American commercial banks in mid-1968. Thus the central bank has indirectly financed a sizeable part of Japan's "economic miracle."

Although Japan does not formally have central economic planning, the extensive use of loans from the central banks means that it becomes the de facto central planning agency through its decisions to make or refuse loans. Given the extent of these loans, it is not possible to decide where loans should be made without charting where the economy should go.

*(c) Economic Planning* In countries with central economic planning, central banks help both to formulate and implement plans. Often their power to make or refuse loans is the stick used to coerce firms into abiding by the central plan. In France, after the five year plan has been formulated, the central bank adjusts credit policies to accommodate the needs of the five year plan, and disperses state grants and loans to private firms made under the five year plan. The central bank becomes a central instrument in making indicative planning work.

In Sweden, National Economic Budgets are established and then the central banks, the Sveriges Riksbank, regulates private banks to channel funds in accordance with the goals set by the national economic budgets.

### E. Instruments

A wide range of instruments have evolved for achieving these specific objectives. They include special rediscounting privileges, direct loans and investments, special reserve requirements and credit ceilings, channeling of private investment funds, direct credit controls, approval over individual loans, exemptions from normal restrictive regulations, and control over non-bank financial intermediaries.

For example, the central banks in France and West Germany discount bills of more than normal duration if the bills finance preferred activities (business investment in equipment, exports, and housing in France; exports in West Germany). In Japan, there are special discount rates for bills originating in the export trade. The central bank of India has different rates for loans to different sectors, with the lowest being for agricultural operations and marketing. Permitted reserve ratios in Mexico vary according to the nature of the assets used as reserves, and access to the long-term capital market in Sweden is directly controlled by the central bank acting through a "bond queue."

### F. Other Functions

In addition, there is a wide range of other important functions that central banks undertake. The Banque de France and the Bank of England set hire-purchase (installment credit) regulations, the Banc d'Italia uses direct controls to prevent speculative inventory buildups and to prevent short term financing of long term fixed investment. The Nederlandsche Bank can delay issues of stocks and bonds, the Reserve Bank of India uses direct controls to stop the hoarding of food, the Sveriges Riksbank provides loans for home furnishings, and the Bank of England imposes credit ceilings on insurance companies, pension funds, and building societies.

## INSTRUMENTS FOR CONDUCTING GENERAL MONETARY POLICIES

Open-market operations typically are not used. This is due either to the thinness of the domestic money market or to the lack of insulation from the European money market. They are used in West Germany where the central bank announces the price at which it will buy and sell government bonds and in Israel where a market in government bonds recently has been created. Discount rates play a minor role in·short-run policies, often only as a signal of central bank intentions.

The main tool of short-run policy consists of quantitative restrictions on credit, implemented either by limitations on borrowing from the central bank or by direct limitations of commercial-bank credit. Of the countries examined, Italy, the Netherlands, and Sweden rely most heavily on direct controls on credit.

While only two countries other than the United States even use open market operations (Israel and West Germany), direct controls are used by eight other countries (France, India, Israel, Italy, Japan, Netherlands, Sweden, and West Germany) including the two other, countries that have open market operations. After direct controls, discounting provisions are the next most popular instrument with seven users (France, India, Japan, Mexico, Sweden, West Germany, and Yugoslavia) out of eleven countries in the study. Specific reserve requirements come next in the list of instruments, with five users (France, Israel, Mexico, West Germany and Yugoslavia). In addition, two countries (Italy and West Germany) use foreign exchange controls.

## INDEPENDENCE

The ability of central banks to formulate—as opposed to implement—policies vary sharply from country to country. There is no systematic pattern. The Banque de France plays an active role in formulating the French plan through its membership on the General Economic and Financing Commission of the Plan, and once this plan has been jointly agreed upon by the different members, the Banque de France plays an instrumental role in carrying out the directives of the plan. Thus the Banque de France plays a role that is very similar to that played by the Treasury Department in the United States, as part of the overall economic machinery of government.

Under the Bank of England Act of 1946, The Bank of England is subject to the dictates of the Chancellor of the Exchequer—the British Treasury Department. As a result of this Act the British Central Bank was brought under direct public control. This Act, among other things, provided that the Bank of England would carry out its functions and activities "if so authorized by the Treasury." The degree of control over the British Central Bank by the British Government is evidenced by the fact that the Chancellor of the Exchequer has the authority and responsibility for determining annually the monetary policy of the Central Bank—and therefore the British Government—for the ensuing year. In India the Bank is legally subordinate to the government.

The Bank of Japan is legally subordinated to the Ministry of Finance (the Japanese Treasury Department), but its position cannot be understood without recognizing that independence is at best a fuzzy concept in Japan where even the lines between public and private are not firmly drawn. In some sense all agencies and firms are part of a national economic plan to promote economic growth. The Bank of Japan is much more powerful than the Federal Reserve Board (it controls a major fraction of each firm's capital) and it participates along with other government agencies in policy formulation, but once these policies have been established, it has an instrumental role.

In Mexico, the Bank of Mexico is simply an agency of the government. The Secretary of Finance in the government holds veto power over almost all of the important decisions that the Board of the Bank might make. Informally it had some independence but this springs from its technical competence and prestige rather than from its legal position.

The Bank of Sweden is headed by a seven member Board of Directors. Of these, six are elected by the parliament from among its own members and one is appointed by the government. The legislators that serve on the Board of Directors are usually *not* bankers by profession. As is clear from the composition of the Bank's Board of Directors, the central bank and the government are intimately related. In staff functions, personnel actually overlap.

In Israel, the Bank of Israel is independent of the Ministry of Finance, but they work in close collaboration and adopt most decisions after previous consultation. The Governor of the Bank of Israel acts as chief economic advisor to the government and thus is a de facto part of the government.

In Yugoslavia the central bank is clearly subordinated to the government and is charged with carrying out the financial aspects of the annual social plans. Its role is instrumental and it has much less power than would be common in capitalistic societies.

Despite its government ownership, the Bank of the Netherlands is almost entirely independent of the government. It can operate without consultation with government officials, but it is obliged to comply with general directives issued by the Minister of Finance. In case of disagreement, the Bank can appeal to the government. At that point the matter is decided by the entire government.

The formulation of monetary policies in Italy formally lies with the government. In particular, policy making functions have been delegated to the Interministerial Committee for Credit and Savings. This Committee, which is composed of the Minister of the Treasury (its Chairman) and six other economic ministers, is ultimately responsible to Parliament for monetary and credit conditions. In practice the prestige of the recent governors of the Bank of Italy and the instability of Italy's governments has meant that the Bank has had a role far more important than was intended in the laws establishing it.

In West Germany the Deutsche Bundesbank is not subject to instructions from the Government, and is, according to one author, "easily the most autonomous (central bank) in the world." It is solely responsible for monetary and credit policies. It is obliged to support the general economic policy of the Government, but only to the extent that this does not interfere with the primary task of maintaining sound monetary conditions. The state derives no rights or powers as owner, but it may delay a decision for a maximum of two weeks. In turn it is obligated to invite the Bundesbank President to participate in deliberations on matters of monetary policy.

## RELATIONS WITH COMMERCIAL BANKS

Foreign central banks typically work closely with commercial banks and dictate directly the actions individual banks should take. This is facilitated by the small number of banks in many countries and by the existence of nationalized banks in others. Most of the eleven countries under consideration had nationalized banks chartered with carrying out one social purpose or another.

Thus West Germany has nineteen publicly-owned mortgage banks providing rural credit, credit for small housing units, and credit for firms too small to tap credit markets. Italy has public banks to make loans to government authorities, to own shares in private industries, and to promote housing, agriculture, public works, industrial projects, and economic growth in the south. Japan has a state bank for small businessmen and government trust funds which invest in development, exports, housing, and agriculture. Mexico has thirteen government-owned development banks for industrial development, while Sweden has state banks for housing, agriculture, small businesses, and shipping.

Since most foreign central banks are much more heavily controlled by or integrated into government policies than in the United States and face state banks in many areas, the influence of private banks' policies must correspondingly be reduced. There is much less latitude for adjusting central bank policies to the desires of the private banking community.

*Table 1  Main Policies used by Central Banks*

|  | Open-market operations | Discounts | Reserve requirements | Foreign exchange controls | Direct controls on credit |
|---|---|---|---|---|---|
| France |  | * | * |  | * |
| Great Britain | * | * |  |  | * |
| India |  | * |  |  | * |
| Israel | * |  | * |  | * |
| Italy |  |  |  | * | * |
| Japan | * | * |  |  | * |
| Mexico |  | * | * |  |  |
| Netherlands |  |  |  |  | * |
| Sweden |  | * |  |  | * |
| West Germany | * | * | * | * | * |
| Yugoslavia |  | * | * |  |  |

*Instrument in use.

# Actions Undertaken to Promote Social Welfare That Are Not Undertaken by the U.S. Federal Reserve Board

In the following lists the respective central banks will be credited with activities regardless of whether they undertake these activities directly or whether they work through intermediaries that are given favourable treatment.

If on the other hand, the country has established some public financial institution to give preferential aid to some area, but this institution does not receive preferential treatment from the central bank that activity will not be credited to the central bank. This latter set of preferential financial activities will be listed for each country, but in a list separate from that of the activities of the central bank. Public ownership of financial institutions that do not give preferential treatment will be ignored in these listings.

### A. Germany
The Deutsche Bundesbank:
1. Provides favourable export credits.
2. Gives special rediscounting privileges to prime commercial export bills.
3. Directly extends credit to state and federal agencies.
4. Stores articles of value.
5. Uses special reserve requirements to control foreign exchange flows.
6. Sets credit ceilings for individual banks to control the total supply of credit.

Other Special Financial Agencies:
1. Nineteen publicly owned mortgage banks provide rural credit and credit for building small housing units.
2. An industrial credit bank aids firms too small to tap credit markets.

### B. France
The Banque de France:
1. Makes direct equity investments in firms through an intermediary.
2. Uses direct credit controls to stimulate the financing of public works, industrial capital expenditures, local governments and agriculture.
3. Has special discounting provisions for business equipment, exports, construction of housing, and grain storage.
4. Sets hire purchase (installment and revolving credit) regulations.
5. Aids in the preparation of the national 5 year plan.
6. Adjusts credit policies to accommodate the needs of the 5 year plan.
7. Pledges itself to meet the credit needs of the 5 year plan.
8. Disperses state grants and loans made under the 5 year plan to private firms.

Other Special Public Agencies:
1. Although formally private, special government activities are used to aid banks that stimulate use of median term credit; finance public works, capital expenditures, exports, and agriculture.

### C. Italy
The Banc d'Italia:
1. Makes direct loans to the central government.
2. Acts as a treasury for the provinces.
3. Stores items of value.
4. Accepts deposits from private individuals.
5. Has special discounting for agriculture and goods stored in public storehouses.
6. Uses direct controls to prevent speculative inventory build-ups and to prevent short term financing of long term fixed investments.

7. Must approve all issues of stocks or bonds.

8. Effectively uses moral suasion to give preferences to those with "sound development programs". This is generally held to mean programs that could have a large impact on economic growth.

9. Has the power to approve or disapprove individual loans and uses this power extensively.

Other Public Financial Agencies:

1. A public bank makes loans to local government authorities.

2. A public bank owns shares in private industries.

3. Public banks exist to make loans for industrial investment, housing, agriculture and public works.

4. Special state investment agencies exist to invest in industrial projects and to promote growth in the southern part of the country.

## D. Netherlands

De Nederlandsche Bank:

1. Directs credit into exports.

2. Directly controls total lending to private businesses.

3. Can delay issues of stocks and bonds.

## E. India

The Reserve Bank of India:

1. Makes loans to state governments.

2. Gives credit to small businesses, agriculture, warehousing, the public sector, and exports.

3. Uses direct controls to stop the hoarding of food.

4. Sets loan quotas for individual private banks.

5. Makes loans for long-run industrial development.

## F. Yugoslavia

Natodna Banka Jugoslavize:

1. Directs resources into areas that will promote economic growth.

2. Controls consumers credit.

## G. Japan

Nihon Ginko:

1. Makes indirect loans to industrial firms through direct loans to commercial banks.

2. Provides loans to small businesses, exports, agriculture, and housing.

3. Has direct controls on the lending of individual banks.

Other Public Financial Agencies:

1. State bank makes loans to small businesses.

2. Government trust fund bureau makes investments and loans in development, exports, agriculture, and housing.

## H. Mexico

The Banco de Mexico:

1. Provides loans for housing, public works, exports, agriculture and industrial development.

2. Makes low interest rate loans for housing, exports, and agriculture.

3. Invests in government corporations and institutions.

4. Uses reserve requirements on private banks to direct resources into

government securities, prescribed industrial securities, and into loans for productive purposes.

Other Public Financial Agencies:

1. There are 13 government development banks for industrial development.

## I. Sweden

The Sveriges Riksbank:

1. Regulates private banks to channel funds in accordance with the goals set by the national economic budgets. Housing, vital industries, and exports are emphasized.

2. Exempts housing from normal restrictive regulations.

3. Regulates issuance of bonds.

4. Provides loans for home furnishings.

5. Finances Nobel Prize in Economics.

Other Public Financial Agencies:

1. State banks provide loans for housing, agriculture, small business, and shipping:

## J. Israel

The Bank of Israel:

1. Grants credits for exports at less than market rates.

2. Channels any necessary increases in the money supply through the government.

3. Administers state loans.

## K. The United Kingdom

The Bank of England:

1. Administers the stock that the government owns in private firms.

2. Maintains accounts for overseas central banks.

3. Exercises some control over hire purchase lending and building societies.

4. Imposes quantitative credit ceilings, but exempts exports and other preferred industries.

5. Imposes credit ceilings on insurance companies, pension funds, building societies and hire purchase houses.

6. Administers exchange controls.

7. Grants favourable credits for export financing.

# SECTION FOUR

# Economics of Canadian Social Issues (a) Poverty

T. COURCHENE

# Some Reflections on the Senate Hearings on Poverty

## Poverty: An Overview

### A. THE CONCEPT OF POVERTY

It is very clear from the various briefs to, and testimony before, the Senate Committee that poverty in Canada is a multi-dimensional problem. On a high level of generality one can talk about economic poverty, cultural poverty and social poverty. On a more specific level, one could run through a list of the characteristics of Canada's poor people and suggest that poverty embraces all these symptoms and situations. Typical of the sorts of definitions of poverty that arise from this all-embracing approach is that framed by the Department of the Secretary of State in their brief:

> Viewed as a range of what tend to be reinforcing disabilities—unemployment, inferior education, poor health, lack of motivation, unstable family life, discrimination, and so on—poverty becomes a set of conditions that renders its victims incapable of participating in our society.[1]

Indeed the thrust of many of the briefs is in the direction of arguing for an examination of the distribution of "well-being" among Canadians rather than a distribution of income in order to assess the extent of poverty in the country. To attempt such an exercise would require information on various social indicators (e.g. health care, crime statistics, pollution levels, mental stress, education levels) which combined with income data, could be used to generate some sort of "felicity index" which in turn could then be employed to assess the well-being of Canadians. While work on developing more appropriate social indicators is currently under way in Canada and while we feel that such information will be of considerable importance in this era when the emphasis is more and more on the quality of life, the proposition underlying this paper is that by far the most important characteristic and determinant of poverty is the level of income. Relatedly, the most important ingredient in a solution to the poverty problem is to raise the incomes of the poor to an "acceptable" level.

Until economic poverty is solved little can be accomplished in the way of providing solutions to the cultural and social dimensions of poverty.

Accordingly, we shall define poverty as a persistent deficiency of goods and services.[2] This deficiency is not merely with respect to some level necessary for physical survival but rather with respect to some culturally defined living standard which would take account of family size, the average level of income of Canadians, and perhaps geographical location. In attempting to lend this definition some empirical content for purposes of assessing the extent of poverty in Canada, two approaches are possible. First, "one can define the minimum income level in terms of real income and expect this definition to be revised from time to time as the overall standard of living rises".[3] This is essentially the approach taken by Miss Jenny R. Poduluk in her work on poverty in this country. In 1968 dollars, Miss Poduluk's figures are $1,800 a year for a single person, $3,000 for a family of two, $3,600 for a family of three, $4,200 for a family of four, and $4,800 for a family of five. An alternative approach, and one which the Manpower and Immigration brief finds preferable, is to define poverty in terms of a relationship to average money incomes, that is, a ratio of some measure of the average living standard. On this issue we side with Harold Shapiro who defines poverty in absolute terms and prefers to think of the relative definition (i.e. the second alternative above) more as a measure of income *inequality* than of poverty. Even if the income elasticity of the poverty line is large, it is still preferable to think of poverty in absolute terms since in Shapiro's words "there may always be some Canadians richer and better off than others but it need not follow that the poor are always with us."[4] Finally, in assessing the extent of poverty in Canada several approaches are also possible. The most common is to count the poor who are below the poverty line and express this figure as a total or as a proportion of total population on either a regional or national basis. Since all persons below the poverty line do not possess identical incomes one alternative approach would be to calculate the income deficiency, namely the amount by which a poor person's income falls below the appropriate poverty line. By summing this figure and expressing it as a percent of GNP this would provide an indication of what it would take to "lift" the poor to the poverty line.[5] Much more in the way of background research needs to be done in this whole area of estimating the extent of poverty in Canada. Obvious things like relating individuals' current incomes to their expected life-cycle earnings in order to ascertain whether current income levels actually reflect a condition of poverty have not yet been satisfactorily carried out, let alone more extensive examinations of the economic characteristics of Canada's poor.

From the very beginning of the Hearings, however, the Senate Committee itself and many of the witnesses presenting briefs opted for an alternative classification of the nation's poor. Specifically they considered the poor as falling into three broad categories:

a) persons who are unavoidably and completely outside the labour force. This category includes such groups as the disabled, the blind, the physically and mentally ill, the elderly, and the female heads of families who cannot go out to work because their children are too young. In rough figures, this category accounts for 25% of the poor.

b) the "hard-core welfarites". Accounting also for about 25% of the nation's poor, these people are not out of the labour force in the necessary and final sense of the first category, but they are for all practical purposes unemployable at the present time.

c) those who are currently in the labour force, whether unemployed or not, and whose incomes fall short of the poverty line. This group is the "working poor" and accounts for about half of the poverty problem.[6]

## B. THE COSTS OF POVERTY

Basically one can perceive three types of costs associated with poverty. First and most obvious is the *human cost* —the untold misery and suffering of those people saddled with poverty. The Hearings did much to bring out in full view to all Canadians the extent of this human cost. Second, there is the *economic* cost reckoned in terms of lost output to society. There are several measures of this economic cost. Comparison between full employment output and current output is the most obvious measure of the increased output to be gained by moving to full employment. Dr. Clarence Barber has recently put this figure at over 5 billion dollars.[7] One can take a somewhat broader view of the economic costs arising from the failure of the economy to operate at full employment levels. To the extent that as a result of poverty some persons drop out of the labour force, the appropriate economics cost is measured as the shortfall of current income from the full employment level of income where the latter is defined inclusive of all those who have the potential of being labour force participants. One could go further still and define full employment output as the level of output that would be forthcoming if the poor were allowed to acquire the earning capacity appropriate to their potential.

Finally, to the extent that the poor in Canada are provided with transfer payments of various sorts, one can speak of the *pecuniary costs* in the form of higher tax rates to the rest of society in providing these transfers. If this tax-transfer mechanism serves to decrease the level of output in the economy, part of the pecuniary cost is translated into an economic cost,[8] in addition to that mentioned above.[9]

## C. CAUSES OF POVERTY

Quite often analyses of the causes of poverty end up being a descriptive categorization of the symptoms of the poor. This was the case for many of the groups testifying before the Committee. But consistent with our earlier contention that poverty is essentially an economic problem we intend to look to the economic system to find the causes of poverty. However, we recognize fully that for poverty of the type described in category a) above the descriptive approach is most appropriate. The disadvantaged of this group are poor because they are blind, physically ill, etc. To some degree the descriptive approach to the causes of poverty is also appropriate for those persons in category b)—i.e. those potentially but not currently in the labour force. But for the bulk of those in category b) above and for the "working poor", we can, following Harry Johnson, conceive of the causes of poverty as falling into one of three broad types:

1) "poverty . . . [resulting from] failure of the economy to provide enough jobs for those able and willing to work, and *capable of earning an adequate income if allowed to work*", i.e. inadequate aggregate demand.
2) "poverty . . . [arising from] inability of individuals to contribute enough service to the productive process to earn an income above the poverty level", i.e. inadequate marginal productivity.
3) "poverty . . . [arising from] the existence of restriction of greater or lesser severity on the opportunity for individuals to participate in the productive process to the full extent of their potential"[10], i.e. discrimination.

Poverty of the first type is solely a result of unemployment or underemployment. Maintaining full employment will eliminate this type of poverty. Poverty of the second type can be eliminated by raising workers' marginal productivities. In part this could be attained by an accumulation of physical capital. More likely, however, the principal way of increasing the marginal productivity of labour is to increase the price employers are willing to pay for labour services, i.e. to increase the value of human capital. Following Thurow, we can regard the value of human capital as being divided into a price and quantity component. "Education and on-the-job experience provide the principal means for increasing the quantity or quality of an individual's capital" while "migration, improvements in information . . . . are the chief instruments to raise the price of existing human capital".[11] It is for poverty of this type that manpower programs involving retraining, placement and relocation services can and do play an important role in increasing worker marginal productivity.

As stated above, poverty of the third type is essentially the result of various types of discrimination which are more widespread than might appear at first sight.[12] One can isolate several broad types of discrimination:
a) inadequate opportunities for certain segments of society to acquire skills up to the full extent of their potential, e.g. educational and health opportunities are not available equally to the poor, markets for human capital are imperfect and discriminate against the poor, information is not as readily available to the poor.
b) monopoly power on both the demand and supply sides of the market, e.g. on the supply side unions of all types (professional, medical and labour) attempt to maintain their wages above competitive levels by imposing either quantitative or qualitative restrictions on entry; on the demand side, various types of price discrimination such as interest charges and in some cases product prices (for Negroes in the U.S., for example) have adverse effects on the poor.
c) discrimination directed against specific groups, e.g. Indians, Métis, the elderly, the uneducated, working women. This discrimination can take the form of restricting job opportunities open to them or denying them promotion or "equal pay for equal work."

On the observed association of poverty with low levels of educational attainment, Johnson suspects that "discrimination is partly responsible . . . in the sense that the requirement of educational qualifications is often less . . . that these are essential for holding a particular job . . . that they serve to narrow down the applicants that have to be considered to a manageable number''.[13]

In the process of outlining the causes of poverty we have, in fact, also set forth a framework for a solution to the poverty problem. However, it is important to recognize that raising skill levels and enacting legislation to remove elements of discrimination can never be successful in resolving the poverty issue unless there is a high demand for goods and services:

> The point is that most of the sources of poverty will gradually dissolve under the pressure of a high demand for labour, . . . The key to the solution of the poverty problem, therefore, is not simply to try to educate and train the poor up to the point where someone will find them employable at a decent wage, but to raise demand so as to make labour scarce enough for it to be privately profitable to find a way of making the poor employable at a decent wage. . . . In the absence of a policy of raising the demand for labour to the stretching point, ad hoc policies for remedying poverty by piecemeal assaults on particular poverty-associated characteristics are likely to prove both ineffective and expensive. The most effective way to attack poverty is to attack unemployment, not the symptoms of it.[14]

Now consider the situation where poverty does exist as is the case now in Canada. The force of the above argument is that the root cause of poverty lies in the economic system rather than in the personal motivation and talents of the poor themselves. If the nation feels that the unemployment rate cannot be brought down to a more appropriate level because of some alternative goal to which we aspire, say price stability, then some other alternative must be implemented to ensure that the poor are not left in desolation. This is especially true when one considers that full burden of the war on inflation falls directly on the unemployed. We have a long history of compensating the casualties of military service and it seems only reasonable that the casualties of the economic system deserve a similar consideration.[15]

This leads us directly into a discussion of methods Canada employs to compensate its economic casualties and also to one of the main purposes of the Senate Hearings — to ensure the establishment of a more effective structure of remedial measures for the nation's poor people.

## D. EXISTING POLICIES IN THE INCOME SECURITY AREA

Chart 1 presents in outline form the various income security programs available to Canadians. We shall assume familiarity with these programs. Further details are available in *Income Security for Canadians*, the recent White Paper issued by the Department of Health and Welfare. Normally when one refers to welfare or to the dole, it is the social assistance programs that one has in mind. The largest component of social assistance is the Canada Assistance Plan which is a provincial responsibility but is financed on a 50-50 basis with the federal government. It is this program which has come under most fire recently. Information relating to social assistance is often too meagre, the administration of the program often appears quite arbitrary, appeal procedures are underdeveloped, recipients often feel a stigma attached to receiving aid in this form, and funds are generally not provided in a manner that encourages self-support. Not surprisingly, most of the witnesses before the Senate Committee who were critical of the Welfare system directed their attention to this program. However, it is important to remember that the Canada Assistance Plan is only one of many elements in the overall social security structure. It is

## INSTRUMENTS OF CANADIAN INCOME SECURITY POLICY
### $4,368 Million

| GUARANTEED INCOME $263 Million | DEMOGRANTS $2,201 Million | SOCIAL INSURANCE $1,008 Million | SOCIAL ASSISTANCE $8,962 Million | |
|---|---|---|---|---|
| | | | Needs Tested | Means Tested |
| Guaranteed Income Supplement | Old Age Security $1,467 | Canada Pension Plan $ 48 | Canada Assistance Plan $678 | War Veterans' Allowances $107 |
| | Family Allowances $ 656 | Quebec Pension Plan $ 15 | Mothers' Allowances $ 28 | Blind Persons' Allowances $ 4 |
| | Youth Allowances $ 78 | Unemployment Insurance $542 | Unemployment Assistance $ 29 | Disabled Persons' Allowances $ 24 |
| | | Workmen's Compensation $185 | | Assistance for Indians and Eskimos $ 18 |
| | | Veterans' Pensions $218 | | |

Values in millions of dollars for 1969-1970

**Source:** Pages 20 and 58 of the Department of Health and Welfare White Paper, *Income Security for Canadians*, (1970).

also important to remember that social security policies are only one of the many types of government policies that have an impact in the distribution of income.

With this background we are ready to go on to the main part of the paper—some reflections both on the Senate Hearings on Poverty, and on the overall problem of poverty in Canada. However, it seems appropriate to detour a bit first and devote some attention to the concept of negative income taxation.

## E. NEGATIVE INCOME TAXATION

No current discussion of solutions to poverty can avoid introducing the concept of a guaranteed annual income or, more specifically, the negative income tax (NIT). From the outset we shall reveal our bias and suggest that we find the NIT concept to be the most appealing approach to alleviating the income deficiency of the poor. The concept is familiar enough that we do not need to go into the details of various NIT schemes. For purposes of what follows it is convenient to think of a Friedman-type plan where the exemption levels for income tax calculations set the poverty line, and the guaranteed income level is 50% of the exemption level. Note that this income guarantee need not be paid out annually but could be issued in monthly installments, for example. To ensure that the scheme meshes well with the positive side of the tax system it is convenient to have the tax rate on other income equal to the ratio of the income guarantee to the poverty line (50% in this example).

It is important to remember that a negative-income-tax scheme does *not* represent a solution to poverty. As stressed above, the solution lies in the direction of maintaining full employment, building up the earning power of individuals and ensuring equal opportunity for all to participate in the productive process. What a negative income tax does and what other welfare programs do is to treat the symptoms of poverty, namely inadequate income. Our preference for the NIT type schemes over the existing forms of social assistance relates to the following characteristics:

a) the NIT scheme would be administratively considerably more efficient than existing welfare schemes;

b) it could replace a host of current welfare legislation and, hence, rationalize welfare to the point where the system would be straightforward and well understood by all. Furthermore, it would mesh quite easily with any other income security programs that might exist alongside a NIT scheme;

c) it is efficient in the sense that families or individuals with the greatest income deficiencies will receive the largest income supplements;

d) the payments under an NIT scheme come as a right rather than a privilege. By removing the stigma attached to receiving welfare in the more traditional manner, the NIT scheme should serve to maintain human dignity which quite apart from its intrinsic value may well be of considerable importance in affecting the attitudes of the poor toward ancillary programs, such as retraining courses, which attempt to bring them more fully into the productive process.

e) the tax rate on earned income is substantially less than 100% (50% in the Friedman plan) which should have a substantial positive effect compared to the existing welfare plans on the incentive to work.

In summary, for any given sum of money allocated for supplementing deficient incomes a NIT scheme will mean that more money will reach the poor because of administrative efficiency, that the money will automatically be allocated to those in most need, and that the overall economic cost to society will be lower because the 50% tax rate on extra incomes earned should encourage persons to participate more in the labour force, thus increasing real output. To the extent that the 50% tax rate on extra income does not affect the incentive to work from what it would be in the absence of a welfare scheme, the overall pecuniary and economic cost of bringing poor peoples' incomes up to an acceptable level could be substantially less under the NIT than for any other welfare scheme.[16]

This issue of a less than confiscatory tax is exceedingly important. Under the present social assistance provided via the Canada Assistance Plan, tax on earned income is, for all intents and purposes, 100% in most provinces. Assuming that the alternative to social assistance is working at the minimum wage, this 100% tax has the objectionable feature that full-time employment at the minimum wage level is a meaningful alternative only for single individuals and small families. This is especially true when one remembers that earned income is taxable while assistance under the CAP is exempt from taxes. This situation arises because social assistance is geared to family size while the minimum wage is not. Table 1 sets out very clearly the full extent of the problem. Annual incomes at the minimum wage levels for each province are presented in column 3. Columns 5, 7, and 9 present, for each province, the levels of social assistance for families of 4, 5, and 6 persons respectively. For a family of five persons, only Quebec and British Columbia have assistance levels below the annual earnings at the minimum wage levels. Given that there are various costs associated with working in addition to the fact that earned income is taxable, it is quite clear that employment is not a meaningful alternative to welfare even at income levels considerably above the annual income equivalent of the minimum wage rate. The net result is that our present welfare system is exiling a substantial portion of the poor into the category of "hard-core welfarites", to use Senator Croll's term. Furthermore, because this built-in incentive to remain on welfare is intensified for larger families, an entire sub-generation of Canada's young people will be growing up under the stigma of welfare and with the alienation from society that a welfare sub-culture will instill. It is precisely for this type of "notch" problem that a negative income tax can make its most important contribution.

It may appear that we are offering the NIT as a panacea for the plight of Canada's poor. This is not the case. There will probably still be a role for social assistance because the level of the income guarantee under a NIT is not likely to provide enough income to maintain all families at a decent living standard. Those families headed by women will still require social assistance, as will those persons who for various reasons are irrevocably out of the labour force. The amount of additional assistance will, of course, depend on the level of the income guarantee in the negative income tax.[17] Our principal point is simply that there appears to be no viable alternative in subsidizing the incomes of the poor to a scheme which has the characteristics of the NIT.

Two of the criticisms of the NIT proposal that have been raised relate first to the fact that the proposal is very novel and no one can predict what the effect of

Table 1 Comparison of Minimum Wage Rates and Provincial Assistance Rates for families of 4, 5 and 6 persons, as at December 1, 1970.

| Province | Current Minimum Wage Rate (a) | | | Provincial Assistance Rates (b) for a Family of: | | | | | |
| | | | | 4 Persons (c) | | 5 Persons (d) | | 6 Persons | |
| | Per Hour | Per Month | Annual Wage 2080 Hours | Monthly | Annual | Monthly | Annual | Monthly | Annual |
| --- | --- | --- | --- | --- | --- | --- | --- | --- | --- |
| Newfoundland | $1.25 | $217.00 | $2,600 | $230 (f) | $2,760 | $255 (f) | $3,060 | $280 (f) | $3,360 |
| P.E.I. | 1.25 | 217.00 | 2,600 | 244 (g) | 2,928 | 270 (g) | 3,240 | 305 (g) | 3,660 |
| Nova Scotia | 1.25 (h) | 217.00 | 2,600 | 263 (i) | 3,156 | 274 (i) | 3,288 | 310 (i) | 3,720 |
| New Brunswick | 1.15 | 199.00 | 2,392 | 188 (j) | 2,256 | 202 (j) | 2,424 | 244 (j) | 2,688 |
| Quebec | 1.40 (k) | 243.00 | 2,912 | 218 (l) | 2,616 | 232 (l) | 2,784 | 243 (l) | 2,916 |
| Ontario | 1.65 | 286.00 | 3,432 | 271 | 3,252 | 303 | 3,636 | 335 | 4,020 |
| Manitoba | 1.50 | 260.00 | 3,120 | 246 | 2,952 | 267 (m) | 3,208 | 303 (m) | 3,640 |
| Saskatchewan | 1.25 | 217.00 | 2,600 | 215 (n) | 2,580 | 250 (m) | 3,000 | 275 (m) | 3,300 |
| Alberta | 1.55 | 269.00 | 3,224 | 335 (o) | 4,020 | 365 (o) | 4,380 | 395 (o) | 4,740 |
| B.C. | 1.50 | 260.00 | 3,120 | 211 (p) | 2,532 | 249 (p) | 2,988 | 287 (p) | 3,444 |

**Source:** Montly Budgets for Items of Basic Need under Provincial Social Assistance Programs Revised December 1970). Research Division, Department National Health and Welfare.

(a) Rates quoted are general minimum rates. General rates for women in 3 Atlantic provinces (Nfld., P.E.I., N.S.) are less than those for men: in Nfld. $1.00; in P.E.I. $0.95; in N.S. $1.00).

(b) Basic rates only for food, clothing and shelter. (Rent allowance note included for Nova Scotia). All provinces make provisions for increased allowances under special circumstances (e.g., special diet; increased rent where necessary). Most provinces pay medical and hospital care and also the cost of drugs where necessary. These cases should only be considered as approximations since every individual and family is different. See other footnotes.

(c) 4 persons—i.e., 2 adults and 2 children; girl 8 years and boy 13 years.

(d) 5 persons—i.e., 2 adults, and 3 children; boy 6, 1 girl 9, and boy 11.

(e) 6 persons—i.e., 2 adults and 4 children; girl 4, boys 7, 9, and girl 12.

(f) Urban rates, including fuel allowance.

(g) Urban rates.

(h) Minimum wage rate will be increased at January 1, 1971 to $1.30 for men and $1.10 for women and at July 1, 1971 to $1.35 for men and $1.20 for women.

(i) Amounts shown include approximate allowances for rent, fuel and utilities, which together could amount to a maximum of $115.00 per month. However a ceiling of $175 is set for a family receiving a provincial allowance. Supplements may be given by the municipality—e.g., in the City of Halifax approximate monthly amounts for a family of 4 would be $278.00, for a family of 5—$292.00, and for a family of 6—$315.00.

(j) Urban amounts including a maximum of $60 per month for shelter. In most cases rent is paid in full. Utilities and fuel are excluded from amounts shown above. However, these 2 items are paid on basis of actual cost.

(k) Minimum Wage Rates will be increased as follows: at May 1, 1971 to $1.45 per hour and at November 1, 1971 to $1.50 per hour.

(l) Lodging, food, clothing, personal and household expenses, urban area.

(m) Exclusive of fuel and utilities which are paid on the basis of actual cost.

(n) Amounts include $75 per month for rent. Amounts include monthly allowances of $50, $55, and $60 for rent. However, the full rent may be paid in some cases. Fuel is usually paid on the basis of actual cost and is not included in the monthly amounts of $215, $250, and $275 as shown in the above table.

(o) Set amounts are only given for food and clothing. However, it is possible for families to receive the amounts shown when rent, fuel, electricity are shown at cost, and approximately $20 per month for personal allowances is included. (As per telephone conversation with official of Department of Social Development, Alberta).

(p) Does not include coverages. An additional amount of up to 50% may be allowed for rent, or the actual rent may be paid.

introducing the scheme will be and, secondly, that in the final analysis NIT is still welfare and as such is to be avoided. We shall deal with each of these in turn.

It is true that, apart from a few pilot projects mostly in the U.S.A., the negative income tax scheme has not yet been put to the test.[18] The guaranteed income supplement for the aged (GIS) that exists as part of Canada's income security package is not really of much use in providing information for the workings of a universal scheme because it operates on a small scale and virtually all of the recipients are out of the labour force. However, there is a large scale guaranteed-income-type scheme that embodies many of the NIT characteristics—namely the revenue-equalization scheme among Canada's provinces. The scheme as described by the Minister of Finance in 1966 is as follows:

> It would provide that any province in which average provincial tax rates (not its own tax rates) would yield less revenue per capita than the yield in Canada as a whole would be entitled to an equalization payment. The payments would be arrived at in this way. We would determine . . . the tax base for each revenue source . . . and the average level of the rates or levies which the provinces generally impose. Then we would apply this average tax level to the tax base in each province . . . to find out whether the per capita yield in the province is below the national average. If the total yield of all provincial revenues, calculated in this way were to yield less than the national average in any province the Federal government would make up the difference in equalization payments.[19]

In an "aggregated"[20] fashion one can express the total revenues of province i (where all values are in per capita terms) as:

$$R_i = t_i B_i + t_c (B_c - B_i) - t_s B_i$$

where     $t_i B_i$ = province i's revenue from its own sources—equal to its average tax rate $t_i$ times its base $B_i$.

$t_c(B_c - B_i)$ = The equalization payment (defined only for the have-not provinces, i.e. only for $B_c B_i$) where $B_c$ and $t_c$ are the Canadian average tax base and tax rate respectively.

$t_s B_i$ = the payment required of province i to "pay" for the subsidies. The assumption here is that the subsidies are to be financed by assessing each province a share of the total cost in proportion to its tax base, $B_i$. Naturally, the tax rate, $t_s$ (assumed to be proportional) depends on the amount of the subsidies.

One can engage in some interesting analytics by differentiating this equation partially with respect to, for example, $B_i$, $B_j$, $t_i$, and $t_j$, noting how these changes affect the revenues of province i. This is not our concern here. Rather it is to argue that this scheme closely resembles a negative income tax with a full (100%) income guarantee, but with a substantial "work incentive". Consider what happens if province i (a have-not province) increases its tax rate, $t_i$. Its subsidy will not fall. Indeed it will increase to the extent that the increase in $t_i$ is reflected in an increase in $t_c$. Here then is a case where a poor province gets to keep all (and then some) of an increase in revenue it generates through increased tax effort (i.e., an increase in $t_i$) even though it is simultaneously receiving a subsidy from the other provinces via the federal treasury. This excursion on federal-provincial tax equalizationey have carried us somewhat afield but it does drive home the point that while the NIT scheme may appear there is a long-standing and well-accepted program in Canada that resembles very closely the essentials of negative income taxation.[21]

On the second issue as to whether or not the NIT scheme can be construed as being welfare, I think that a case can be made for NIT on the basis of equity alone. For a family of five persons, current exemptions for income tax calculation plus the $100 standard deduction amount to $3,000. The value of this exemption to a family depends on the family's total taxable income, i.e. on the marginal tax rate. For a family in the 50% bracket this exemption is worth $1,500. For a family in the 80% bracket this exemption is worth $2,400. But for a family with no income this exemption is worth nothing. Since we consider the exemption level and the progressivity of the tax system as conceptually independent matters (even with a proportional income tax the exemption level is worth nothing to a family with no income), it is not equitable to have the value of basic exemptions decided upon by the income level of the family unit. What is the basis for the government bestowing a transfer of $2,400 to the 80% bracket family, $1,500 to the 50% bracket and nothing to the zero income family? One does not have to be too much of an egalitarian to argue that if the government is in the business of bestowing gifts on families, these gifts should be available equally to all (for given family size) regardless of income. Hence the case for negative income taxes on equity grounds.

Actually, while on the subject of equity, the preferred type of negative income tax on equity grounds is similar to that proposed by James Tobin,[22] namely *refundable tax credits*. On the Canadian scene the case for tax credits over exemptions has been persuasively argued by T. Russel Robinson.[23] Basically, this latter proposal argues for a fixed dollar tax credit rather than an exemption for tax purposes. This implies that so long as units have incomes above the tax credit values, the value of these tax credits is independent of the marginal tax rate. To make the value of these tax credits equal to all regardless of income level, all that is required is that they become refundable. In Canada, family allowances are a perfect example of refundable tax credits. Rather than allowing a deduction of $550 for a dependent child, the exemption is only $300 if the child is eligible for family allowances.[24] Therefore the extra $250 exemption is replaced by an across-the-board *refundable* tax credit of $72 per year (for a young child). Whereas the $250 exemption would have meant $200 to the 80% bracket family, $125 to the 50% bracket family, and nothing to the zero income family, the $72 is given to *all* regardless of the level of family income. The equity grounds that argue for negative income taxes are the same as those underlying the family allowance payments.

## Current Federal Policy and Poverty

### A. RECENT PROPOSALS IN THE INCOME SECURITY FIELD

Up to this point in the paper we have (a) presented an overview of poverty including a section on the causes of poverty; (b) reflected our bias in arguing for a negative income tax as a solution to ameliorating the income deficiencies associated with poverty; (c) presented a very brief outline of existing government programs in the poverty-related areas; and (d) presented a résumé of some of the major issues arising from the Senate Proceedings on poverty. At this junction it is appropriate to broaden our perspective a bit and relate the foregoing analyses to current federal and provincial policies as they pertain to poverty. The present section focusses only at the federal level and deals in turn with two recent white papers on unemployment insurance and welfare policy and then the broader issue of the priority that eradication of poverty attains in the overall mix of federal economic policies.

The role that an unemployment insurance scheme might be expected to play in the set of programs in the income security field depends to a large extent on the accompanying legislation that exists in the welfare area. Consider first the case where Canada would have a guaranteed annual income of the negative income tax variety. Unlike some observers, we would still see an important role for unemployment insurance even within this context. However, its role would likely be confined almost solely to income protection, i.e. it would be primarily an *insurance* scheme rather than a welfare scheme. On the other hand, if there exists an inadequate set of complementary legislation in the welfare area one could make more of a case for using unemployment insurance as an instrument in the income support (i.e. welfare) area as well.

When the White Paper on Unemployment Insurance (*Unemployment Insurance in the 70s*) was made public there was general agreement that the forthcoming position paper on social security would move welfare policies more towards a guaranteed annual income approach or at the very least that some sort of a GAI or negative income tax would surely be the cornerstone of Canada's welfare legislation in the not-too-distant future. Accordingly, one would have expected that the unemployment insurance proposals would be such that they would pave the way for a more rationalized approach to the entire income security area. Such was not the case, however. The White Paper takes unemployment insurance far into the income support or welfare field from its traditional income protection role. The increased role for federal financing, the much-eased eligibility requirements for benefit qualification, the severing of the direct relationship between previously covered employment and the length of benefit authorization, and most importantly the special benefits for depressed areas all serve to move the proposed unemployment insurance scheme well into the welfare area and make it very difficult to integrate with any comprehensive approach to welfare.[25] One gets the distinct impression that the federal government desired to pump extra funds into the depressed areas and chose unemployment insurance as the means for the transfer because it was readily available and perhaps more importantly because it represented a constitutionally acceptable vehicle for the transfer. However, the appropriate question to ask is: given that the government wished to transfer more funds to the high unemployment areas, is the unemployment insurance program the most appropriate instrument for carrying out the transfer? In any system characterized by highly interrelated programs, it appears to us that attempting to use any one means to accomplish a multitude of ends runs into the problem of creating severe spillover effects. We would argue that such will be the case with the U.I.C. proposals. They run the risk of creating substantial distortions in resource allocation. For example, the special regional benefits will tend to encourage reverse migration and the 100% tax rate on earnings above 25% of benefits will have the effect of reducing the incentive to work on the part of the benefit recipient. Introduced within the more appropriate context of a negative income tax scheme these same transfers would have substantially ameliorated implications for resource allocation.

Turning to the White Paper on social security (*Income Security for Canadians*) our first response is that it is a severe disappointment both in terms of what it has to contribute in the way of a meaningful solution to the poverty question and in terms of what one might have expected, given the overwhelming evidence in the Senate Hearings to the effect that the present approach to Welfare in Canada is a failure. Without getting into the detailsof the proposals, the essential feature of the White Paper is to provide much increased benefits for those persons who are not actively in the labour force, e.g. the elderly and the disabled. The altering of the family allowance payments so that they taper off as family income rises does not really move very far in the direction of ameliorating the plight of working poor.[26] This is especially the case if the provincial welfare agencies take this increase into account in the assessment of needs under the Canada Assistance Plan. Oddly enough, there appears to have developed an interesting division of labour between unemployment insurance and the health and welfare department. Health and Welfare appears to be focussing on the welfare of citizens who are essentially outside the labour force while unemployment insurance is attempting through its White Paper proposals to provide relief to the working poor. In terms of our earlier analysis of the causes and solutions for poverty this division of labour is unfortunate indeed. The types of relief to the working poor through unemployment insurance schemes are simply not appropriate, and on the question of work incentives actually run counter to what we would consider to be appropriate policies.

Before taking leave of the Health and Welfare White Paper it is appropriate to point out that in many places it comes across as a poorly conceived document. The clearest example of this is the ''notch'' problem encountered by the new family allowance proposals. For a family with four children earning $10,000 a year, the family allowance payments amount to $240. The reward for earning an extra dollar of income is the loss of the entire $240. In addition, in discussing the pros and cons of a negative income tax the White Paper argues that most of the existing programs cannot be superseded by NIT because they are of a contractual nature. They then proceed to suggest that the manner in which these programs would be integrated with NIT would be to deduct from the NIT payments to poor persons any income they had coming from these contractual programs. But this seems to us to be the wrong approach. Income coming into a family from a contractual source such as Veterans' Pensions should be treated as other income, i.e. as "earned income", and the family unit would lose its NIT benefits only to the extent of 50% of this additional income (assuming that 50% is the tax on additional income under the NIT scheme).

In summary, then, the proposed federal legislation does little in the way of meaningfully attacking the most important source of poverty in the country, namely the working poor. This is the most important poverty group because numerically it is the largest group, and because the economic costs in terms of lost output are far greater for this group. The White Paper on income security practically ignores this group entirely, while the Unemployment Insurance White Paper provides considerable help to those of the working poor who are unemployed, but it is not the most appropriate vehicle for providing assistance to this group. In essence, then, Canada appears headed in the direction of maintaining its present patchwork and non-integrated approach to income security.

## B. FEDERAL PRIORITIES AND POVERTY

On a broader scale it is useful to ask what priority in overall policy formulation is assigned to the goal of eliminating poverty. One fact that stands out quite clearly is that the federal government is far more interested in the income distribution of the Canadian *provinces* than it is with the income distribution of the Canadian *people*. And perhaps this is appropriate since the Constitution assigns to the provinces the responsibility for welfare. Nevertheless, as we have seen above, the elaborate provincial tax equalization scheme ensures that each province has access to tax revenues equivalent to the Canadian average tax rate times the Canadian average tax base. In addition, the Department of Regional Economic Expansion, consolidating into this new department the activities of agencies like ARDA, FRED, ADA and ADB, is now mounting a spirited attack on regional income differentials. In terms of its long-run impact on the incomes of individual Canadians residing in the poorer provinces this approach may indeed make an important contribution to the poverty problem. But in the shorter run it is not at all clear that the result of these programs is to alter the income distribution in favour of the poverty group. Rather it may be that certain groups like industrial engineers may be among those who benefit most (as appears to be the case in New Brunswick, for example, where this group has annual incomes above the Canadian average). The point is simply that in assigning priorities between achieving more equality among Canadian individuals or among Canadian provinces, the federal government has opted for the latter.[27]

Perhaps the most controversial set of federal priorities is that reflected in Ottawa's attitude toward the unemployment-inflation issue. Canada, relative to other industrialized non-communist countries, has on the whole had higher unemployment rates and lower inflation rates.[28] We have argued above that unemployment represents a real cost in terms of lost output. Furthermore, it is a

cost in terms of foregone earnings that is borne primarily by the poor. On the other hand, inflation, of and by itself, does not represent an economic cost. Rather it is a transfer from one group of persons to another group (e.g. from creditors to debtors). It can be considered as an important economic cost only if one expects it to get out of hand and lead eventually to large-scale unemployment. Presumably the willingness of Ottawa to trade off so much unemployment in order to combat inflation reflects a two-fold belief:
a) left unattended, inflation will spiral ever upward; and
b) Canada can have a large say about the course of price behaviour independent of the international community.

We take issue with both these beliefs because we feel that within the limits of what one might call reasonable alternative policy mixes, there is little chance of Canadian inflation getting out of hand if the international (primarily the U.S.) inflation rate does not get out of hand. Essentially this implies that whereas there does exist a trade-off between unemployment and inflation *for a given rate of change in foreign prices* the most important determinant of the relationship between the rate of domestic inflation and the level of unemployment over any medium term period is the rate of foreign inflation. If one accepts this point of view then there is little justification for the current unemployment-inflation priority pursued by Ottawa. In addition, if one elevates the eradication of poverty to the level of a national goal then there is absolutely no justification at all for assigning such a high priority to curtailing inflation because the poor are affected far more by unemployment than they are by inflation.

It is worth dwelling on this point somewhat further. From time to time Ottawa has argued that inflation places a heavy burden on the poor people and is one of the major causes of poverty. The recent evidence in both Canada and the U.S.A. simply does not bear this out. Inflation may inflict some toll on the poor but ''the most obvious cost in terms of poverty that is involved in any particular combination of inflation and unemployment is that of unemployment.''[29] On this issue Arthur Okun is very clear:

> (These) substantive results reinforce other important findings from Wisconsin's Institute for Research on Poverty that inflation does not harm the poor as a group. . . . Inflation is cruel because of horizontal (not vertical) inequity. Indeed it seems to have a haphazard impact among families within the same income group which outweighs its redistribution impact among groups. For example, welfare recipients and the aged poor may be hurt by inflation even though the predominant effect on the poor is that of improved job opportunities. . . . These facts should, once and for all, stem the temptation of the political economists to invoke the plight of the poor as one of the reasons for wanting price stability. . . . And they should remind us that, when the nation is deliberately pursuing a policy of economic slowdown in order to achieve price stability, it has a special obligation to intensify other efforts to relieve the plight of the poor.[30]

In summary we assert that eradication of poverty has not assumed a very important role in the nation's preference function.

Table 2   Amounts of social allowances under GSAP for 1971, compared to the minimum income levels of the Economic Council of Canada

| Size of Family | (1) Minimum Income Levels (Economic Council of Canada)* | (2) Maximum GSAP Allowance Stage I** | (3) Break-even Point for Stage I*** | (4) Maximum GSAP Allowance Stage II** |
|---|---|---|---|---|
| Single Person | $2,045 | $1,227 | $3,143 | $2,045 |
| Two Adults | $3,408 | $2,045 | $4,480 | $3,408 |
| 2 adults, 1 child | $4,089 | $2,550 | $5,305 | $3,913 |
| 2 adults, 2 children | $4,770 | $3,055 | $6,130 | $4,418 |
| 2 adults, 3 children | $5,451 | $3,560 | $6,955 | $4,923 |
| 2 adults, 4 children | $6,132 | $4,065 | $7,780 | $5,428 |
| 2 adults, 5 children | $6,813 | $4,570 | $8,605 | $5,933 |

*1961 Economic Council figures adjusted for cost of living from 1961 to 1971.

**The allowance per child under GSAP is $505 for both Stage I and Stage II. However, there is, in addition, a family allowance of $176 per child per year. Therefore, the *total* allowance per child under the "comprehensive" GSAP plan will be $681. If this latter figure were employed in Table 2 rather than $505, the maximum GSAP allowance for Stage II would coincide with the Economic Council figures.

***The tax rate on other income for Stage I is
  —33¹/₃% on the first $2,500 of earned (assessed) income.
  —61.21% on the remaining income until the social allowance is exhausted.
The tax rate on Stage II equals 100%.

**Sources:** Chapter 5, Tome II of the Castonguay-Nepveu Report.

# Current Provincial Policies:
# The Castonguay-Nepveu Report

Quebec recently made public parts of a massive study, *La Commission d'enquête sur la Santé et le Bien-être social,* which was released under the auspices of M. Claude Castonguay, Ministère des Affaires sociales. This report (which we will refer to as the *Castonguay-Nepveu Report,* after its two Commissioners) is a very impressive document outlining wide-ranging and imaginative new proposals intended to coordinate and rationalize Quebec's health and welfare services. Our interest for purposes of this paper relates only to the welfare aspects and even more specifically to the General Social Allowance Plan (GSAP). First and foremost, GSAP is a program designed to achieve the objective of a guaranteed annual income, and the philosophy underlying GSAP is not unlike that underlying the various NIT schemes discussed above. The most novel element in the scheme is the manner in which it provides for the very difficult problem of how to adopt a guaranteed annual income plan to allow an income high enough to permit a decent living standard for those unable to

## Chart 2.

Total Income including Personal Income and Social Allowance (First and Second Stage) paid by the GSAP in Relation to Personal Income Considered and Based on the Size of the Family—1971

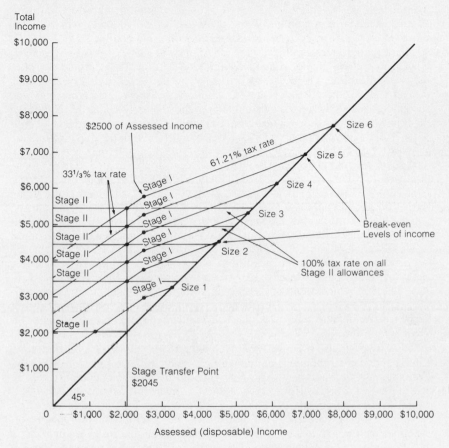

**Source:** Adjusted from Graph V.2 of Tome II *Castonguay-Nepveu Report.*

participate in the labour force and yet still maintain an incentive to work for persons in the labour force. To handle this, GSAP contains two allowance formulas, which are referred to as Stage I and Stage II. Stage II is essentially the full poverty line guarantee as defined by the Economic Council's poverty line for 1961 updated for changes in the cost of living. For one or two person households the maximum income guarantee under Stage II corresponds to the Economic Council poverty line (compare columns 4 and 1 of Table 2). For each child, the allowance increases by $505.[31] The tax rate on income earned for persons covered by Stage II is 100%, i.e. for every dollar earned the social allowance is reduced by a dollar. Since most persons covered by Stage II will be out of the labour force this confiscatory tax is deemed to be just. The Stage I allowance is set at 60% of the Stage II allowances for single persons and two-adult families. Thereafter, an allowance of $505 for each child is added to the minimum payment. These figures appear in column (2) of Table 2. The Stage I tax rate is such that the social allowance is reduced by one third of assessed income (essentially, *after tax* or *disposable* income) when this is below $2,500 and by 61.21% of assessed income beyond $2,500.

Chart 2 reproduces graphically the GSAP data in Table 2. Assessed income is measured along the horizontal axis and total income (assessed income plus the social allowance) is measured vertically. At any level of assessed income the vertical distance between the 45° line and the stage lines represents the social allowances (or negative taxes) paid to the respective families. Naturally the Stage II lines are horizontal at the maximum GSAP allowance level, (e.g. $3,913 for a family of three and $4,418 for a family of four persons), reflecting a 100% tax on any assessed income. For the kinked Stage I lines, the intercept represents the maximum GSAP allowance, e.g. approximately $3,000 for a family of four. Up to levels of assessed income of $2,500 the slope of any Stage I line is $2/3$, i.e. the tax rate on assessed income is $33^1/3\%$. Thereafter the slope is 0.3879, i.e. the tax rate on assessed income is 61.21%. For a given family size the Stage I line crosses the Stage II line at a level of assessed income equal to $1^1/2$ times the difference between the maximum guarantees of the two stages (since the retention rate is $2/3$ in this region). However, as is shown in Table 2, the differences between the maximum allowances under the two stages is *invariant* with respect to family size (excepting single persons). Specifically, it equals $1,363 which implies a cross-over point of the stage lines in Chart 2 of $2,045 (i.e. $1,363 × $3/2$). This is depicted in Chart 2 as the Stage Transfer Point[32]—the income level at which it becomes worthwhile to transfer from Stage II to Stage I.

This last point is of considerable interest. In the discussion surrounding Table I above it was pointed out that welfare payments are a function of family size whereas minimum wages are not. One unfortunate implication of this is that the work incentive (for employment at or near minimum wage levels) is diminished for large families especially if tax rates for part-time work for persons on welfare are 100% beyond some small exemption. In Table 1, for example, welfare payments for a family of six are larger, for every province, than the income that can be attained by working at the minimum wage. Under GSAP, however, the Stage Transfer Points do not depend on family size. As long as a person has the opportunity of earning above $2,045, he will be better off (abstracting from the extra expenses that might be connected with working rather than receiving welfare) under Stage I than Stage II. Furthermore, $2,045 is considerably less than the minimum wage income (expressed at an annual level assuming 2080 working hours per year) of $2,912 in Table 1 or the current minimum wage annual income in Quebec of $3,120.

Some of the more important and interesting other aspects of GSAP are the following:

— families are essentially free to choose whether they will opt for Stage I or Stage II. And they have the flexibility of being able to move back and forth between the stages as their desires and opportunities dictate.

— payments under GSAP will be at two-week intervals.

— assessed income is essentially disposable income so that it is net of personal income taxes and other compulsory contributions or costs related to employment such as social insurance plans and union and professional dues. This implies that families can at one and the same time be paying income taxes and receiving GSAP payments.

— income from assets is included in assessed income and, after a rather generous allowance, the assets themselves are included in assessed income.

— the social allowances paid under GSAP will be reduced by the full amount of benefits paid under other plans to offset an interruption in income or to provide a subsistence income, e.g. veterans' pensions, workmen's compensation, and with some modifications, unemployment insurance benefits. This ensures that GSAP will be integrated with all existing plans in social insurance areas.[33]

— family allowances are to be maintained.

The *Report* devotes considerable energy to defending the two formulae for allowances embodied in GSAP. For present purposes we note merely that it does recognize that the same objectives might well be attained by a single formula of allowances, were it not for the scarcity of resources to be redistributed. The dual formula makes it possible to introduce an incentive mechanism compatible with the break-even point lower than average income, without depriving persons unfit to work of an allowance equivalent to the maximum income level.[34]

Finally, two other recommendations are also of considerable interest. First, GSAP is to be financed out of the Quebec government's *general revenue* and second, in future, social insurance plans such as the recent unemployment insurance scheme should be limited to serving their *direct* purposes and that all governments refrain from making a permanent contribution to the financing of these social insurance plans. We shall comment on these features later.

## THE CASTONGUAY-NEPVEU REPORT AND CANADIAN WELFARE POLICY

What is the likely impact of the *Castonguay-Nepveu Report*? For several reasons we feel that it is by far the most significant public document in the welfare area today. First of all its timing could not have been better. The Canadian people have just been presented with two government White Papers in the income security area and the Senate is winding up several years of investigation on poverty. But more importantly it presents an integrated approach to ameliorating the plight of the poor, integrated in the sense that it is able to deal with both the working poor via Stage I and the families outside the labour force via Stage II and integrated also in the sense that it rationalizes not only the whole social welfare system but as well permits coordination with existing social insurance schemes. One effect of the *Castonguay-Nepveu Report* will surely be to highlight the piecemeal and fragmented approach to income security embodied in the recent federal White Papers. Implicitly it also challenges the new unemployment insurance proposals (which are moving unemployment insurance into the welfare area) by arguing that within the context of an integrated guaranteed income scheme, unemployment insurance should revert to its original goal of insuring against temporary decreases in income and, further, that it should not be publicly financed. Whether or not one agrees with all the details of GSAP or feels that the costs of such a program will be acceptable to Canadians, it is surely true it will play a very important role in future discussions and legislation in social welfare areas.

But there is another important aspect to the *Castonguay-Nepveu Report*. By producing such a well integrated and comprehensive solution to the poverty problem and a solution that calls for funding out of Quebec's general revenue it has given Quebec the initiative in the jurisdictional battle of who should be responsible for providing for a guaranteed annual income — the provinces or the federal government. If the Canadian government does not come up with some constructive counter proposal[35] it could very well be that Quebec will enact some version of GSAP, perhaps on a less grandiose scale if federal assistance in funding is not forthcoming. Then Canada must face the possibility, as the other provinces probably follow Quebec's lead, of having ten different types of negative-income-tax schemes. Our own opinion is that the recommendations of the Senate Committee embodied in the *Progress Report* are to be preferred, namely that the funding of a guaranteed income be done federally and that the provision of social services be left to the provinces. There are several advantages to having a federally run guaranteed annual income or at least a GAI into which Ottawa has a substantial input. First of all, by having a universal plan, the natural mobility of labour within the country would be facilitated. With ten provincially run GSAP-type schemes things like residence requirements, the manner in which the various schemes mesh with other existing federal legislation in the income security area as well as with the federal tax system, and the levels of the guarantee would all probably differ from province to province and serve to impede as well as distort migration flows.[36] In addition, a program like GSAP in combination with the rest of the income security legislation represents only one aspect of an integrated approach to the poverty problem. Related policies like the various retraining and relocation programs of the Manpower and Immigration Department, the regional industrial incentive policies of DREE and the overall monetary and fiscal policy must be coordinated with income security policies and this coordination is more easily attained if the federal government has some say in the running of any NIT scheme. However, it would still probably be possible to achieve the minimum degree of coordination necessary with a universally designed scheme run largely or entirely by the provinces. This leads us to the most important argument for having a considerable federal voice in a guaranteed income plan: a negative income tax integrated fully with the positive tax system provides a very convenient instrument for a stabilization policy. Loss of control of the negative range to the provinces might effectively emasculate federal stabilization policy. Hence, we anxiously await from Ottawa a constructive alternative to the *Castonguay-Nepveu Report*. Hopefully, and this brings us back to the focus of the paper, the final Report of the Senate Committee on Poverty will also take up this challenge.

### Footnotes

1. *Senate Proceedings* . . . , No. 3 (1st Session—28th Parliament), p. 97.

2. This definition is from the Brief submitted by the Department of Manpower and Immigration, *Senate Proceedings*, No. 10 (1st Session—28th Parliament), p. 365. We might note in passing that from the viewpoint of economic analysis the Manpower and Immigration Brief is really first rate.

3. *Ibid.*, p. 366.

4. Harold T. Shapiro, "Poverty—A Bourgeois Economist's View", in Officer and Smith (eds.), *Canadian Economic Problems and Policies* (Toronto: McGraw-Hill, 1970), pp. 227-8.

5. This approach is suggested in the Manpower and Immigration Brief, *op. cit.*, p. 367.

6. Perhaps the best description of these three categories (and descriptions which in part were used above) is given in the Brief by Tom Kent, Deputy Minister of Regional Economic Expansion. *Senate Proceedings* . . . , No. 17, (2nd Session—28th Parliament), pp. II. 32-II. 33.

7. C.L. Barber, "Brief to the Standing Senate Committee on National Finance" (May, 1971), p. 3.

8. The Economic Council estimates that for a man with a normal life expectancy and who marries and has a small family the total welfare payments over a period of 45 years is in the neighbourhood of $134,000.

9. In the *Sixth Annual Review* chapter on poverty, the Economic Council discusses a related type of economic cost, namely "diverted output." For example, the existence of poverty leads to the diversion of resources to deal with more sickness than would otherwise occur, more administration public welfare and assistance programs, etc. (Ottawa: Queen's Printer, 1969), Chapter 7.

10. Harry G. Johnson, "Poverty and Unemployment," in Weisbrod, B.A. (ed.) *The Economics of Poverty: An American Paradox.* (New Jersey: Prentice-Hall, 1965), p.166. Underlining is not in the original.

11. Lester C. Thurow, *Poverty and Discrimination* (Washington: The Brookings Institution, 1969), p. 69.

12. Johnson, *op. cit.*, p. 167.

13. Johnson, *op. cit.*, p. 168. Arguing as much the same grounds, Burton Weisbrod contends that the returns-to-education studies are likely to overestimate the real returns to education. (Address before the Ottawa Political Economy Club, May 18, 1971).

14. Johnson, *op. cit.*, pp.169-70. Very few of the briefs presented to the Senate Hearings were this explicit about the crucial role played by the level of aggregate demand. Two notable exceptions were the Department of Manpower and Immigration, and the Brief presented by Tom Kent, the Deputy Minister of the Department of Manpower and Immigration.

15. This sentence is adapted from Johnson, *op. cit.*, p.167. We shall return to this train of thought later.

16. Concerning the various NIT experiments in the U.S.A., Harold Watts States:

> the only prudent conclusion at this point is that no convincing evidence of differences between control and experimental (i.e. NIT) families has been found. This is a remarkable finding in itself, since there is a widespread belief that such payments will induce substantial withdrawals from work and increase in other forms of dependence . . . no significant changes (in work habits) have been found . . . but to the extent that differences appear between control and experimentals they are generally in favour of *greater* work effort for experimentals. Hence anyone who seeks to support an argument of drastic disincentive efforts cannot expect to find even weak support in the data so far. "Adjusted and Extended Preliminary Results from the Urban Graduated Work Incentive Experiment." Institute for Research on Poverty (University of Wisconsin, 1970).

17. However, the *Castonguay-Nepveu Report* does develop a NIT scheme which would in fact do away with all social assistance programmes.

18. As footnote 16 indicates, however, the prognosis is good.

19. Statement by the Honourable M.W. Sharp, Minister of Finance to the Federal-Provincial Tax Structure Committee, *Federal Provincial Tax Structure Committee*, (Ottawa: Queen's Printer, 1966), p.16.

20. Actually, the disaggregated and correct formulation is to calculate the subsidy on each of 16 revenue sources. We have aggregated them into one revenue source for each province (namely $B_i$ ) for purposes of exposition. For a rather detailed analysis of the tax-sharing formula, see D. Beavis and T. Courchene, ''An Analysis of the Federal-Provincial Tax Equalization Formula'' (University of Western Ontario) Department of Economic Research Report.

21. In passing we note that if the federal government is interested in making it ever more rewarding for the poorer provinces to increase their tax rates, the formula could be revised so that the subsidy term was of the form $t_i(B_c - B_i)$ rather than $t_c(B_c - B_i)$.

22. ''On Improving the Economic Status of the Negro,'' *Daedalus*, (Fall, 1965), pp. 878-898.

23. ''Thre Treatment of Dependents under the Personal Income Tax,'' *The Canadian Tax Journal*, Vol. XVIII (1970), pp. 44-47.

24. The current tax forms make no allusion to this possibility, but previous tax forms did.

25. For further analysis if the proposed legislation (focussing both on desirable and undesirable aspects), see T.J. Courchene, ''Unemployment Insurance in Canada: Some Implications of the Present System and an Evaluation of the White Paper Proposals,'' Research Report 7025 (University of Western Ontario Department of Economics, October 1970).

26. Recall that Ontario has suggested that selective family allowance payments by the federal government may be overstepping Ottawa's constitutional authority in this area.

27. The questions of priorities and costs in terms of lost national income is explored somewhat further elsewhere. See T.J. Courchene, ''The Role of the Provinces in Regional Economic Expansion'', paper presented to the Conference on Rural and Regional Development Issues, (Winnipeg, November 1970).

28. Brief to the Senate Meetings presented by the Department of Manpower and Immigration, *op. cit.*, p. 367.

29. *Ibid.*, p. 368.

30. Arthur M. Okun, discussant of papers on the ''Dynamics of Income Distribution'', *American Economic Review, Papers and Proceedings*, (May 1970), p. 297.

31. Note that this does *not* include the $176 family allowance payment which will still continue under GSAP. If this family allowance is added on to the data in column (4), the resulting maximum allowances coincide with the Council figures (column 1).

32. The *Castonguay-Nepveu Report* refers to this as the 'Stage Change Level.'

33. Our earlier comment on how to treat income from insurance-type plans still seems valid: we would prefer to see benefits under these schemes treated as assessed income rather than being perfect substitutes for the social allowances, since in effect they have been ''earned.''

34. Castonguay-Nepveu, *op. cit.*, p.19.

35. To argue against the *Castonguay-Nepveu Report* solely on the basis of its cost to Canadians may be constructive but it is not an alternative.

36. This is not to suggest that having a uniform benefit level for an NIT scheme throughout Canada would not also distort migration flows. The whole issue of the relationship between welfare policies and resource mobility deserves far more attention than it has been given in the past.

# (b) Pollution

# HARRY W. RICHARDSON
# Economics and the Environment

The environment is a highly fashionable subject for discussion. Yet it is easy to form the impression, particularly from newspapers, that it has only just been discovered. The truth is, of course, that the history of industrialized societies is in many respects the history of interfering with, adapting to and controlling the environment. In arguing for stronger action, we must not underrate the measures undertaken in the past, for example, to improve housing conditions and sanitation and to control harmful effluents, even in the nineteenth century. Just as there are dangers in regarding environmental issues as 'new' there are equally great dangers in distorting them out of perspective.[1] The gloomy forecasts of an environmental Armageddon are at best speculative, and at worst nonsense. A sufficient justification for treating the environment as an important public issue is that, with increasing affluence, the quality of life is becoming of greater concern to most people than multiplying their material possessions, and that in order to ensure the quality of life tomorrow we must do something about the environment today.

The purpose of this article is to show some of the difficulties that arise in attempting to apply economic analysis to environmental problems, and to point to a few solutions. First, we must delimit our field of interest. It is useful to make a distinction, if an arbitrary one, between conservation and protection. Preservation of the countryside and the rural way of life, protection of animal species in danger of extinction, and the conservation of natural resources fall within the scope of conservation. They may be important objectives; but, with the possible exception of natural resource conservation, they do not directly affect the quality of life of the mass of the people. Since the vast majority of the population of high-income, industrialized economies live in towns and cities, it is possible to justify concentration on urban problems. These include air and water-supply pollution, traffic congestion and noise, unsightly physical surroundings, derelict land, industrial smells, and the absence of easy access to outdoor recreational facilities.

It is also useful to make a distinction between positive environmental action, for example making life more aesthetically satisfying by the provision, say, of attractive city centres, and negative action, such as ensuring protection against the effects of pollutants. The former is largely a question of raising standards, especially of design; the latter implies correcting past mistakes and counteracting present tendencies inherent in the production process.

# Interdependence of Environmental Problems

Much of the literature relating to the environment is highly technical, replete with a jargon surpassing even that of the economist! At a risk of oversimplifying, technology will not be discussed here. Let us start instead with a few generalizations, concentrating for the time being on environmental pollution and nuisances rather than on aesthetics. Evidence suggests that the rates of pollution and waste creation, if unchecked, are a (probably increasing) function of the level of economic development and the rate of population growth. Moreover, since pollution is a form of congestion, it is also a function of population density, hence its importance in cities. Furthermore, 'environmental disruption' is characterized by cumulative causal sequences and interdependencies. For instance, waste products may react upon the environment so as to produce toxic effects on plant and animal life, and ultimately on human life. Protection of one environmental medium may adversely affect another: for example, the main alternative to refuse dumping is incineration which might add to air pollution. Causal chains and interdependencies of this kind are of a technological character. They do not lend themselves to economic analysis.

Nevertheless, it is possible for the economist to clothe discussion of the environment in language familiar to him. In the first place, as Marshall and Pigou demonstrated, pollution falls under the heading of *externalities,* partly because in most cases the generator of pollution does not have to pay the costs it imposes on society, partly because the media which are polluted — the air, water supply, the sea and the beach, open spaces — are public goods, that is non-marketable goods enjoyed by all. Secondly, a certain level of pollution or environmental nuisance can be tolerated without harmful effects. Each medium has its own capacity, and until the capacity level is reached pollutants will be dispersed (this is what is understood by the statement that pollution is a form of congestion). For example, vehicle exhaust fumes will do no damage in country areas, but can be a major cause of pollution in cities. The rate of pollution is determined by the total output of the polluting good, the distribution of this output among polluting agents (the amount of pollution generated may vary from one firm or household to another) and the capacity of the assimilative medium. This suggests at least three types of action to reduce environmental disruption: reducing the volume of output of the polluting good by taxation; redistributing output in favour of light polluters by either forcing heavy polluters out of business or making them switch to low-generation production methods; and investing in increases in media capacity where this is possible. Another line of action feasible in a few cases (dealing with aircraft noise may be one example) is to permit the disturbance but to recompense the victims by taxing the polluters. This compensation solution is particularly appropriate where some are polluters, but are not affected by it, while others, the public, are adversely affected by pollution but do not contribute to it.

Another general point of some importance arises out of the interdependence already mentioned. A community must be careful about the effects of protecting one medium on pollution elsewhere. If a community wishes to protect all media (air, water, land, etc.) successfully, its policy will be very expensive in terms both of capital costs and higher production costs. Moreover, it has to be recognized that a highly industrialized, densely populated economy will always generate some pollutants however much is invested in protection. In particular, the costs of controlling pollution rise disproportionately at very high levels of efficiency. For these reasons, the idea of imposing absolute standards of purity is utopian. It is much more appropriate for the goal to be the achievement of tolerable standards. A serious practical difficulty, stemming in part from cumulative causal chains and interactions, is that we do not know enough about the damage caused by particular sources of pollution. Assuming that there are limited resources available for protecting the environment we must avoid spending large sums on eliminating harmless, if unsightly, wastes while those that are potentially very harmful go unchecked.

## The Provision of Urban Beauty

Before discussing some of the difficulties involved in applying economic analysis to environmental problems and possible solutions, this is a useful point to interject some general comments on the more positive aspects of the environment, particularly in urban planning. Here the aim is not to protect nature against man but to improve upon nature by creating beauty and aesthetic pleasure. Again, this presents intractable problems for analysis, since urban beauty is a public good supplied without charge to the users. How can we apply the right kind of incentives and allocation criteria to supply such a public good in a market economy? In particular, how do urban planners know the economic value of, say, an attractive city centre? In the private market sector, the quality-versus-cost problem raises little difficulty, since consumers are usually offered a wide range of goods varying in both quality and price; and the desired combination is revealed in market decisions. But an investment decision in the public sector, such as the building of a new city centre or even a shopping precinct, may be a once-and-for-all decision, with little opportunity given for citizens to express their preferences.

In any event, what do we mean by a superior physical environment? We are unable to measure beauty, and aesthetic opinions are to a considerable extent subjective. Should we leave aesthetic judgments to the planners and urban designers, or should their schemes be heavily publicized with a view to testing the reactions of the general public? It is difficult to trade off beauty against lower costs, since urban policy makers find it hard enough to allocate their budgets between competing urban investments without taking quality differences into account. For this reason, quality is often determined residually as the best that can be afforded within a given budget. As for how to choose on aesthetic grounds between alternative schemes of equal cost, the fundamental problem is: who is going to be the arbiter of public taste? If the public itself, ways must be found for greater public participation in planning decisions. Alternatively, it might be argued that one of the functions of architects and planners is to educate the public.

## The Absence of a Market

Environmental issues are not easily handled with the traditional tools and concepts of economic theory — the price mechanism, allocation criteria, consumer sovereignty in a market system, partial-equilibrium analysis, and so on. The tell-tale references to externalities, public goods, and the absence of a market are warning signs that conventional economic analysis will not find it easy to cope. Yet, since technical solutions exist to most pollution problems, and the new troublesome nuisance that occasionally develops usually yields to a remedy in the course of time, the main obstacles to a pure environment are economic rather than technical. In short, protection of the environment is an economic problem for which economics has no ready answers.

The standard way of dealing with pollution is to treat it as an external diseconomy, to describe the appropriate pollution level as that at which the marginal social benefit of increased output of the polluting good is equal to the marginal social cost of pollution, and to prescribe some kind of policy that makes the polluter bear the marginal social costs of his actions. This type of approach might be satisfactory if these external diseconomies were aberrations from the normal functioning of the market system. However, the creation of external diseconomies, in particular waste residuals, is a general phenomenon, almost an inevitable part of production and consumption. Although the physical quantity of waste residuals and pollutants is huge (millions and millions of tons a year), it is not particularly difficult to trace the physical flows. What is awkward for economic analysis is that so many elements in the environment — the use of common property resources such as air or streams, the use of environmental media in which to get rid of wastes, and the pollutants themselves — have no price. There is no market in which they can be exchanged. From a conceptual point of view, the solution is to create an artificial market for these goods, by assigning what economists call 'shadow prices' to them. The trouble is that this means that we have to measure and assign monetary values to individual units of these 'goods'.

## Measurement Problems

The measurement problems are very serious indeed. Only a few examples can be given here to serve as illustrations. It is reasonably easy to measure the overall level of a pollutant, for example the amount of sulphur dioxide in the atmosphere. What is hard to measure is the contribution of the individual polluter. Yet quantifying this would be essential if, for example, a system of pollution charges were to be introduced. Although it may be possible to value certain kinds of pollution damage, for instance, the cost of cleaning up beaches after an oil slick, the cost of beautifying derelict tips, possibly even the increased cost of treating disease aggravated by air pollution, other kinds resist quantification. How do you value preserving open country from the invasion of power grids, the discoloration of a river by chemical effluents, the unsightliness of an urban motorway? Moreover, we are almost always concerned with estimating the impact of environmental disruption on individual human beings, and this raises additional problems. Sensitivity to the environment varies from person to person, as does adaptability to unfavourable conditions such as, for example, heavy-traffic noise. Moreover, the time-preferences of individuals vary, the most obvious difference being that between young and old, and this is important since some costly measures introduced now may not pay off for many years and some forms of pollution, as yet harmless, may have critical consequences in 10 or 20 years time.

Another implication of the failure to give environmental side-effects monetary values, and this ties in well with Professor Mishan's arguments in *The Costs of Economic Growth*, is that pollution makes nonsense of national accounting systems. The frequently wanton and profligate consumption of common property resources, the creation of huge physical quantities of waste residuals, the diffusion of pollutants and other environmental nuisances harmful to health — all these things are either inadequately or, more usually, never registered as market transactions. The consequence is that GNP is a very poor measure of growth. Indeed, if, as the evidence suggests, the social costs of environmental pollution rise relatively faster than output, GNP becomes an increasingly inadequate growth indicator. Furthermore, increases in income obtained at the expense of gross environmental disruption, destruction of amenities and accelerating absorption of natural resources are a doubtful gain. It is tempting to go to the extreme and argue that we should abandon the growth goal. A more modest and more reasonable prescription is that we should avoid 'pseudo-growth' which gives us an expansion in per capita *money* income but seriously undervalues the social costs.

## The Difficulties of Control

We could argue for years about how to incorporate environmental problems into economic theory. It is desirable that we should understand the problem of environmental pollution; but it is imperative that we should control it. Understanding will no doubt aid effective control, but even if our understanding is imperfect we should attempt control nevertheless. The reasons are the cumulative nature of many kinds of pollution and the rising costs of improving the environment over time.

If the social costs of environmental nuisances are so heavy, it is pertinent to ask why voluntary action is not taken to reduce them. Obviously, in cases where the polluters are few and the victims are many, it may involve the polluters in substantial losses to reduce their output of pollutants and they will not do so unless they are either forced to by outside forces or guided by great altruism.

There are also cases in which consumers in general are polluters and are also all adversely affected by pollution. Motor-vehicle exhaust fumes is perhaps the most notable example. At first sight, it may seem obvious that motor-vehicle owners should be happy to pay more for an anti-pollution device since the costs of such a device are by most calculations low relative to the potential benefits. However, the incentive is lacking. The individual's own contribution to pollution control is insignificant compared with the total contribution of the rest of the community. Thus, in this particular instance, the benefits of anti-pollutive devices on motor vehicles accrue from other people's devices not from one's own; on the other hand, the individual has to pay only for his own device and the costs of all the devices from which he gains benefits fall upon others. There is a strong incentive, therefore, for the individual acting alone not to install a device. Yet the fact remains that if everyone installed devices society and each individual would be better off. This can be brought about only by cooperation in which a binding obligation is undertaken by all. With a very large number of individuals, an obligation can be established only by outside intervention, in effect by the government.

In the case where producers are the polluters, there are additional considerations to be kept in mind. First, unless the producer group in question is a closed group it will be unlikely to take voluntary anti-pollution action since outside competitors would gain from any higher production costs undertaken by the group. Thus, international agreements on environmental standards can be very important as a precondition for voluntary action. Secondly, in industries where the market structure is oligopolistic there is more scope for co-operation in installing anti-pollution devices or recycling techniques, just as such a market structure facilitates price or output agreements.

Control is made more difficult by further factors. The division of the community into two groups — producers and consumers — is an oversimplification. In fact, in relation to the problems of environmental quality, society has to be subdivided into several groups. Each group has its own vested interest, and any individual may be a member of more than one group simultaneously. Appropriate groups include: taxpayers, the government, polluting consumers, victims, polluting producers, producers of commodities that cause pollution, makers of anti-pollution devices, and recycling technologists. Many of these groups may be involved in a bargaining process with each other when attempts at pollution control are introduced. Each group wishes to shift the social-cost burden of pollution onto other groups; and each member would like to shift the costs onto the other members of the same group. Similarly, each group aims at selecting the time for anti-pollution legislation that benefits it most. For example, the government ought to prefer early action, since environmental control-costs increase over time and some types of environmental nuisance could lead to irreversible changes in the biosphere.

## Ordering of Priorities

A prerequisite for effective action in the environmental field is an ordering of priorities. This, however, requires centralized co-ordination of measures of control. Despite the recent reorganization of government into the major agglomerations of the Department of the Environment and the Department for Trade and Industry, the control of environmental pollution is still diffused. The Ministry of Agriculture, the Ministry of Defence, the Home Office, the Department of Education and Science, the alkali inspectorate, and the local authorities all have environmental functions to perform. Moreover, it is unclear what degree of co-ordination exists between the branches of the super-ministries, between Transport and Local Government and Development, and between Technology and Trade, for example. This wide diffusion makes it very difficult indeed to evolve a national strategy. In particular, it is impossible to take full account of the possibly adverse effects on one medium of measures taken to protect the purity of another. If insufficient co-ordination at the national and government level rules out a comprehensive general approach, we may have to tackle environmental problems in ad hoc fashion even if this is unsound theoretically.

## Methods of Control

Laissez-faire approaches to questions of the environmental and pollution can be rejected as likely to result in a misallocation of resources, and as politically unacceptable in a society with a high and rising income. The remaining policy options include control by public investment, by introducing prohibitions and the enforcement of standards and by pricing in the form of pollution charges. The appropriate type of policy will be dictated by the nature of the environmental problem.

Environmental nuisances differ from one another in the areas over which they occur. Air pollution and traffic congestion can be coped with at the city level; water pollution and outdoor recreation resource problems usually crop up at the regional level; control of the use of pesticides and antibiotics in animal feeding needs to be decided at the national or international level; while ocean pollution can be controlled only by international agreement. In economic terms the aim should be to render internal to the unit whether it be the firm, the city, the region or the nation those costs which are at present external to it but internal to the next largest unit, that is the city, the region, the nation and the world respectively. In the case of the individual polluting firms, pollution charges can internalize the external costs by making them face up to the social costs of their decisions and providing them with some incentive to organize their businesses differently — by introducing technical changes which use low-pollutant raw materials and inputs, by investment in recycling techniques or by moving away from congested urban areas. Because an uncooperative firm might gain from the altruistic actions of others, it may be necessary to obtain cooperation at industry level.

Public investment to protect the environment usually takes the form of increasing the capacity of an environmental medium; sewage treatment plant is a typical example. Public sector investment may be especially appropriate in cases where there are substantial economies of scale in the provision of control facilities, or where the individual sources of pollution are hard to quantify, or where it is difficult to make the polluters bear the responsibility of their actions. Cost-benefit criteria may sometimes be useful in determining the appropriate level of investment; but it will often be more appropriate to use targets expressed in physical terms where the goals of environmental protection relate to safety levels of particular pollutants or to performance standards in achieving a prescribed reduction in pollution levels. With goals of this kind, which are much easier to handle than assigning monetary values to unknown 'intangibles', the role of economic analysis is to show how these goals may be achieved most efficiently.

Private investment need not be considered solely as an alternative to public investment, since some forms of environmental disturbance may be handled more simply individually while others demand collective action. The two main ways of influencing private investment are prohibitive controls and pricing. Controls can be successful in some spheres, as is shown by the relative success of the Clean Air Act of 1956, but they are in general blunt and inefficient. Banning cars from city centres, to take an extreme but frequently recommended suggestion, would help to guarantee a good environment, but the cost in terms of a less efficient allocation of resources might be very high. Congestion charges have much to be said in their favour. These raise the prices of goods that in social terms are under-priced and help to eliminate excessive production of them. If properly applied, such charges permit discrimination against heavy polluters. They encourage private firms to invest in recycling techniques or to change their production methods. They may stimulate more research into pollution abatement. They may achieve a given level of pollution control at the minimum resource cost, and thereby increase allocative efficiency. Finally, they offer some scope for the application of compensation principles via income transfers from the polluters to the victims.

The drawbacks of pollution charges are implicit in the economic analysis of pollution discussed above. Pricing prescriptions assume that the correct level and incidence of charges can be ascertained. In this case, the appropriate charge is that which makes the unit cost to the firm causing the pollution equal to the marginal social cost imposed on the community. But we have seen that these marginal social costs are in most cases difficult, perhaps impossible, to measure. Moreover, it is also necessary to be able to measure the contribution of each individual polluter; and this raises technical obstacles and administrative difficulties. Ignorance about the ultimate indirect repercussions of environmental disturbance means that pollution charges cannot at present be justified. The seriousness and reality of the environmental problem, however, provides a strong practical pretext for overriding theoretical niceties. If community goals on environmental planning relate, not to efficiency in resource allocation but to the satisfaction of human needs and improvement of the quality of life, then it may be possible to justify pollution charges at that level which brings about a desired reduction in pollution generation, induces investment in recycling and low-pollution methods of production and stimulates research into abatement techniques, even if it cannot be proved that the charges imposed match social with private costs.

## Conclusion

The upshot of this article is that economics throws some light on environmental issues but does not illuminate the darkest corners. Some of the problems are technological in nature; others can be understood by economic analysis only if we depart from pricing-allocation and equilibrium approaches. Action on environmental control must not await future breakthroughs in economic theory. We do not have to fall victim to the 'Doomsday mentality' to appreciate that the quality of our environment needs attention now. There is no reason why we should not be able to protect the environment and control the most harmful kinds of pollution provided that practical, firm and sensible measures are taken in time.

### Footnote

1. This article was written before the publication of the first report of the Royal Commission on Environmental Pollution (Cmnd. 4585, February 1971. It is encouraging to find that the Report shares this paper's stress on the need for urgent action without ringing too many alarm bells.

## LEONARD WAVERMAN

# Fiscal Instruments and Pollution: An Evaluation of Canadian Legislation

The federal and provincial governments have introduced a multitude of fiscal policies—fines, subsidies, loans and tax incentives—to induce firms and individuals to limit their pollution. Economists consider such instruments to be both less effective and more costly than a system of prices for the environmental factors. The federal government, appearing to heed economists' advice, incorporated into the Canada Water Act an effluent charge system — which was loudly condemned by provincial governments and many civic anti-pollution groups as a scheme of "licences to pollute".

This paper is intended to clarify the confusion about the nature of effluent charges.[1] First I shall discuss the nature of pollution in order to derive criteria for judging measures designed to eliminate pollution. Next I shall describe some of the existing policies for the control of water pollution, and evaluate them in terms of those criteria. Many actual policies are found to be inferior, in terms of effectiveness and cost, to a scheme of effluent charges. Tax incentives are shown to be the worst alternative to a system of charges. Finally, I consider a tax scheme that would combat pollution by making taxes similar to prices. There appears to be little merit, however, in using such a scheme: it merely renames a price system, and it obscures tax policy.

## Prices and the Environment

Much academic literature has discussed the benefits of instituting a pricing scheme for the environmental factors.[2] The major usefulness of such a scheme is that by allowing firms themselves to compare costs of reducing pollution in different ways, it ensures that an acceptable standard will be attained at the lowest possible resource cost, while at the same time guaranteeing that polluters alone, rather than the public at large, pay for clean-up costs.

The nature of pollution is that the polluter imposes some of his internal costs—namely, the cost of waste removal—on innocent third parties. The factory that pollutes the air is in essence forcing all the individuals in its locality rather than its customers to pay for its waste removal through higher cleaning costs and more respiratory illnesses. The factory itself (and those who buy its products) should bear the costs of waste removal either through installing devices that limit pollution or by paying for the right to use a public good—air—for waste removal. The solution is not so simple, however, as forcing a few factories to install abatement devices. If all pollution were the result of a readily identifiable waste product from a known source soiling clothes, remedies would be simple: insurance and the courts.[3] It is the impossibility of identifying the specific automobile (it may even be one's own) that deposits the lead on one's farm land that creates the need for public policies.[4]

The primary objective of public policy should therefore be to ensure that the amount of pollution is lowered to a socially desirable level while eliminating the imposition of costs by polluters on third parties. Fiscal instruments designed to limit pollution should therefore ensure that the polluter rather than the general public pays for clean-up costs.

If the government wanted to improve the quality of the environment, it could do so by ordering all polluters to diminish their discharge of waste by a certain percentage. While this policy would lead to the desired improvement, it would not do so at lowest possible cost. Take for example, two firms, one of which (A) discharges a highly toxic effluent, but whose cost of abatement is low, while the second firm (B) discharges an unsightly but non-toxic effluent whose costs of abatement are extremely high. Ordering both firms to reduce their pollution by the same percentage ($x\%$) is clearly not the best procedure, since it may be cheaper to remove most of the toxic waste of firm A than to remove $x\%$ of the harmless effluent of firm B. What is needed for this purpose is, first, a device to measure the costs and benefits of abatement for a single firm and, second, a comparison of the relative costs and benefits among all firms. One way of doing this might be to create a government agency to measure effluents and to suggest standards for different firms. Regulation of this sort would be very costly both in the amount of public funds needed for such a vast army of scientists and in the time it would take to arrive at a consistent policy.

Since a pricing system is used to ration other scarce resources, proposals have been made to use a pricing scheme for air and water.[5] The argument is simple: establishing a price for water would induce those firms whose per-unit clean-up costs are less than the per-unit price to install abatement devices, while firms with relatively high abatement costs would continue to dump their wastes and pay the price. The desired standard would thus be achieved in the most efficient manner.

There is no ground whatsoever for characterizing a pricing scheme for water as a licence to pollute. The price is the implicit value to society of the resource—a unit of clean water. If a firm chooses to buy this resource and use it for waste removal, to say it has acquired a licence to pollute makes no more sense than to say that purchasing a raw material input constitutes a licence to destroy.[6]

Most arguments against pricing schemes appear to reduce to arguments concerning not the *nature* of the scheme but either the expected level of the price or the federal intervention in local or provincial matters. The concern of civic anti-pollution groups over the scheme proposed in the Canada Water Act is probably justified given the ineffectual impact of government anit-pollution policies in the 1950s and 1960s (especially on industry). However, it can be quickly pointed out to these groups that effluent charges are not pollution licences, since the price for the environmental factors could be set so high that no firm would pay the price and all would install abatement devices. Therefore, much fear over the establishment of the system set forth in the Canada Water Act is not fear of the price scheme per se but fears—perhaps justifiable — that the price will be set too low.[7]

## Fiscal Instruments Presently in Force

Present federal regulation utilizes all forms of controls and inducements to promote a desirable quality of water: standards establishment (Fisheries Act, National Health Act, etc.), loans and grants (National Housing Act), tax incentives (Income Tax Act, Excise Tax Act), fines and effluent charges (Canada Water Act).[8]

### TAX INCENTIVES

Under section 1100(1) (t) of the Income Tax Regulations, assets acquired after 26 April 1965 and before the end of 1973 "primarily for the purpose of preventing, reducing, or eliminating pollution"[9] can be amortized at the accelerated rate of 50% per annum. Note that the word "primarily" suggests that new plants incorporating pollution controls as part of general production equipment would not be able to write off these pollution abatement devices at the accelerated rate.[10] Furthermore, pollution-reducing equipment that leads to the recovery of materials or by-products can utilize this provision only if these materials or by-products after 26 April 1965 "were being discarded as waste by the taxpayer, or were commonly being discarded as waste by other taxpayers who carried on operations of a type similar to the operations carried on by the taxpayer".

Under the Excise Tax Act equipment specifically used in pollution reduction, sewage disposal and water purification systems is exempt from federal sales tax.[11]

### LOANS AND SUBSIDIES

Under the National Housing Act, the Central Mortgage and Housing Corporation has since 1960 advanced two-thirds of the cost of construction of sewage treatment plants and main sanitary sewers (but not storm sewers[12]), for approved municipal projects. If the project was completed by an agreed date, 25% of the loan was forgiven. Between 1960 and 1968, $272 million was lent for 1,381 projects in 905 municipalities.[13] The increased public awareness of pollution in recent years ˙has increased the demand for these loans to the point where C.M.H.C.'s loan budget of $50 million for fiscal 1969-70 was fully committed by September 1969.

### FINES AND EFFLUENT CHARGES—
### THE CANADA WATER ACT

On 26 June 1970 Bill C-144 was enacted, "to provide for the management of water resources of Canada. . . ." The basic provisions of this Act are as follows. With respect to water either where there is a "national interest" (s.4) or, in the case of interjurisdictional waters, where water quality has become a matter of "urgent national concern" and where the province has refused to upgrade this quality of water (s.11(1)), the Minister may with the approval of the Governor in Council establish with the province (or on federal initiative alone) agencies to control the quality of specific water basins. In any federal waters, the government may also unilaterally establish such management agencies. These agencies may establish local quality standards, design and operate sewage treatment facilities, and prosecute offenders (who would be liable, on summary conviction, to fines of up to $5,000 per day). The senior governments would advise and coordinate research, while the Governor in Council may establish procedures and criteria to be followed by each agency in setting quality levels, fees, etc.

While economists cannot pronounce judgments on the constitutionality of the Canada Water Act, they can offer opinions on the need for federal supervision.[14] As Richard Bird and I have argued elsewhere,[15] water pollution is essentially of a local or provincial nature (since water basins are essentially local or provincial); the sole reason for federal involvement is the competition between municipalities and provinces for the fiscal dollar. The imposition of necessary standards or taxes to control pollution reduces the desirability of any one municipality or region for industrial location as compared to municipalities or regions that have no such pollution control. Thus, few areas will on their own initiative introduce strong anti-pollution laws unless other areas do so first. Hence the need for federal legislation, to ensure that while pollution controls vary somewhat among areas to reflect local needs and desires, no one area becomes a pollution haven to the detriment of the tax base in all other areas. This need is answered by the Canada Water Act.

Effluent charges are mentioned in a few sections of the Canada Water Act. "Except in quantities and under conditions prescribed . . . including the payment of any effluent discharge fee prescribed therefore, no person shall deposit . . . waste of any type in any waters comprising a water quality management area . . . " (s.8). Later sections authorize the agency to recommend such effluent fees (13(1) (iv)) and collect effluent charges (13(3) (c)), and authorize the Governor in Council to prescribe effluent charges (16(2) (d)). Nowhere in the Act is there any mention of *how* these charges are to be set.

## Provincial Fiscal Instruments

Every province has some agency that is responsible for water quality in that province. Few provinces have, however, established significant fiscal programs for the elimination of water pollution. Only Ontario and Quebec offer tax relief in the form of accelerated capital cost allowances.

### PRESENT MEASURES IN ONTARIO

As an example of advanced provincial assistance, the schemes of the Province of Ontario will be briefly outlined.

### Tax Relief

The federal provision of accelerated depreciation has been approved and is duplicated under Ontario income tax jurisdiction.

### Grants and Subsidies

(a) In 1967 the Province instituted a system of tax expenditure grants equal to the Ontario sales tax on approved abatement equipment installed by industries and municipalities. (Expected cost for fiscal 1970-71 is $2 million.)

(b) In 1969, the Ontario Water Resources Commission began a program of subsidizing the costs of sewage or water treatment plants for an area where the per-capita costs of such a project were greater than the provincial average of $120.00 per capita for sewage plants and $100.00 per capita for water systems. The subsidy is up to 50% of per-capita costs in excess of these averages.

(c) Also in 1969, the O.W.R.C. began to subsidize 15% of the cost of projects whose capacity was greater than the present needs of the area.

### Loans

The major agency concerned with water pollution in Ontario is the Ontario Water Resources Commission, established in 1956 to improve water quality. Besides setting standards and approving all sewage gathering and treatment and water treatment systems in the province, the agency has promoted water quality by borrowing funds on provincial credit and allocating these funds to municipalities. By 1969, $1.2 billion had been lent to municipalities.[16] In addition, the agency has constructed 333 water and sewage projects under provincial ownership and operation. Municipalities are charged the cost of such projects according to their use.[17]

### Water Use Charges

Effluent charges relate to the reduction *in quality* of the water resulting from the waste flow. Many provinces presently have in force charges relating to the *quantity* of water used by the firm.[18] While these charges are uncoordinated among provinces, and probably do not reflect the true value of water to society (few charges have for example, been increased in the last decade), their existence provides a base on which to build a full effluent charge system.

Four provinces—Alberta, British Columbia, Nova Scotia and Saskatchewan—levy a single non-recurring charge when they license the right to use water. Eight provinces (all except Prince Edward Island and New Brunswick) and the federal government (Yukon and the Northwest Territories) levy an annual fee for the use of water in the production of hydro-electric energy. These annual fees vary among provinces but are related to the installed capacity of the hydro plant. While five provinces—Nova Scotia, Quebec, Newfoundland, Saskatchewan and British Columbia—also charge an annual fee for water usage, only the charges of the last two provinces[19] are designed to reflect the quality and quantity of water used.[20] Charges for the use of a public resource—water — are therefore not something new to Canada (in fact, British Columbia first assessed water fees in 1859).

# The Impact of Fiscal Instruments— in Theory

The nature of pollution is that costs are imposed on those who desire neither the pollution nor the concomitant good produced. Any scheme is therefore to be condemned that either continues to allow third parties to bear the producer's internal costs or merely transfers these costs to the public purse, rather than forcing the absorption of real costs by the polluter. As will be shown below, tax incentives and subsidies are not adequate answers to the pollution problem since they do not force the producer to pay all his relevant costs.[21]

## TAX INCENTIVES

Tax incentives are in many ways the worst alternative to pricing schemes since their true cost is hidden and they distort firms' investment decisions.

The usual incentive policy, accelerated depreciation, has often been labelled by members of the business establishment merely an interest-free loan. This label is misleading, since accelerated depreciation provisions can have five substantial misallocative effects. First, if the resulting loss in tax revenue is compensated for by increasing taxes on those who do not pollute, then accelerated depreciation involves subsidization of polluters by non-polluters. Second, accelerated depreciation is available to all (at least to all those with profits) regardless of credit rating and regardless of the value to society of the project being undertaken. Third, the true costs to society of this policy are never made public.[22] In addition to these faults, accelerated depreciation provisions are applicable to capital assets in place and thus create incentives to invest in capital-intensive abatement techniques that qualify for tax treatment although less capital-intensive techniques may be less costly.[23] Finally, the effect of accelerated depreciation provisions and therefore their incentive depends on the tax rate of the firm—that is, on its profits. The provision is of no use to firms making losses and it is therefore useful (in the short run) to those who can best afford abatement investment without the program.

The remission of sales and excise taxes is really only a token measure.[24] These remissions, however, have this much to be said for them: the imposition of such taxes on intermediate goods is inefficient, and the effect of the provision is not dependent on the firm's profits.[25] However, the remission of taxes on equipment but not building materials again may bias the firm's choice of pollution abatement method.

An investment credit (not used in Canada) avoids some of the undesirable features of tax incentives since the amount of aid is not related to the level of profits of the firm. However, an investment credit is related to initial investment expenditures and thus creates the incentive to substitute original capital in place for operating costs (substitution of capital for labour). Moreover, the general public still foots the bill. No tax incentive scheme or subsidy forces the polluter to directly pay for the damages he is causing.

## SUBSIDIES AND GRANTS

Direct federal public grants to cover investment or operating costs for either municipal or industrial pollution control are unwarranted: there is no reason why the resident of some mountain resort should subsidize those living or producing in our smog-shrouded metropolises. Those responsible for polluting the air and water, be they residents of some urban megalopolis or owners of a mine in Alberta, should not expect the public at large to help clean up local pollution.

The argument mentioned above that municipalities and even provinces have little incentive to introduce strong pollution laws unilaterally (especially for industry) is not an argument for federal aid but only for the federal establishment of fairly uniform laws.[26]

### LOANS

While no good reason can be found for the provision of subsidies to municipalities or industries to reduce their pollution, there may be very good reasons for providing temporary loan assistance on the introduction of anti-pollution laws. The capital requirements of many firms and local governments will be greatly increased with the establishment of strict standards. If imperfections in the capital market make it difficult for firms or municipalities to get funds, then there may be good reason for the provincial or federal government to float or guarantee bond issues for pollution control purposes. Such federal provision will reduce the cost to the smaller borrowers both through the reduction of risk yielded by the federal signature and through reductions in the transaction costs of one large issue as compared to floating a large number of smaller bond issues. Loans from federal or provincial sources thus alleviate the short-run dislocations of new strict pollution laws without removing the necessity of the polluter's bearing the full costs of its operations in the long run. Furthermore, loan programs can be run at little cost (other than accounting) to the federal authorities. If some subsidy is thought politically expedient, then either the interest or some portion of the principal can be forgiven in special cases. At least with this type of subsidy the exact costs to the granting authority are known.

## Evaluation of Existing Policies

Present policies are a mixture of loans, loans with grant provisions, tax incentives, simple standard establishment, and, under the Canada Water Act, effluent charges (of which no example exists at the moment). The loan provisions of federal agencies such as the Central Mortgage and Housing Corporation, which administers the provisions of the National Housing Act, and provincial agencies such as the Ontario Water Resources Board are for the most part excellent, for they attempt to minimize the cost of funds to municipalities. However, certain policies of each of these agencies are inequitable. Under N.H.A. rules, if the sewer or the treatment plant is completed by a given date then 25% of the loan is forgiven. This is inequitable to municipalities that cannot meet N.H.A. requirements for a loan. The O.W.R.C. in 1969 decided to subsidize the costs of sewage treatment for municipalities where the expected per-capita cost of constructing and operating treatment plants is above the provincial average of $120.00 per capita. The program will be used to subsidize the resort areas of Port Carling ($135.00 per capita) and Haliburton ($150.00 per capita); it is estimated that by 1976, $89 million will be spent in this way.[27] That the residents of ·Sudbury or Niagara Falls should have to subsidize vacationers in resort areas seems a better example of perverse distributive effects than of equity.

The reliance on accelerated depreciation provisions in the federal, Ontario and Quebec income tax statutes must be condemned for the reasons discussed above: the provisions are inefficient, costly and misallocative of resources. They create an incentive to invest in capital-intensive abatement techniques. Furthermore, Regulation 1100(1)(t) as presently written allows the accelerated depreciation of structures built *primarily* for reducing pollution. It is often cheaper to change the production process itself than to add on capital-intensive controls at the end of the process.[28] Under present legislation, firms are induced to add on such features rather than change the production machinery.

The effluent charge scheme proposed in Alberta, should not expect the public principle, and it is difficult to argue against such good principles. But there is no information on how the price is set, how it will be changed and how it will vary among various water basins. Judgment on the impact of the charge system must therefore be reserved until more information is available on the mechanism that will be used to establish the specific prices.

## A Tax Scheme to Limit Pollution

While the use of tax incentives is an inefficient means of combating pollution, tax policy can be useful if it can be altered so as to be more like a price system. A tax based on the toxic content of effluence would have the same effect on the producer as a price for using the resource, if the tax varied with the reduction in quality of the environment resulting from the discharge.[29] It may even be politically advantageous to utilize such a tax scheme rather than a price system since it is highly unlikely that anyone will call a tax a licence to pollute.[30] Furthermore, the tax could probably be administered by existing bureaucracies and machinery rather than requiring a new set of branches to administer effluent charges.

A form of pollution not discussed in this paper is the waste content of final consumption rather than the toxic element in producer's waste discharge. Charging for air or water will of course not limit the plastic containers, aluminum cans and non-returnable bottles used by consumers. This solid waste could be limited by introducing a tax on the waste content of production at either the producer's or the consumer's level.[31] Raising the price of these materials will limit their use.[32]

There are a number of important reasons, however, why I feel that the problem of pollution control should be left entirely out of the tax sphere, even though, as was suggested above, tax policy could be a powerful tool. Primarily, tax policy is designed to transfer purchasing power from the private sector to the public sector. Introducing these types of corrective tax measures confuses tax policy needlessly. Furthermore, if effluent charges are disguised as taxes, then businessmen may get the idea that with the return of prosperity, taxes, including air and water taxes, should be reduced. Also, the government could start to think of the tax as primarily for revenue-producing purposes and attempt to adjust it for that purpose rather than for pollution control. Air and water are truly scarce resources and should be priced. To disguise these necessary prices in tax schedules defeats one of the purposes of the price—informing everyone that clean air and clean water are not available for the taking.

We are all concerned about reducing pollution. Let us not, in our haste to improve the quality of our lives, however, impose unnecessarily harsh standards on firms (for example, reduce all effluence by 80%) or subsidize polluters out of the public purse. To establish realistic standards and force those who use the public's air and water to pay for that right can most easily and efficiently be done by the government's establishing effluent charges. Rather than criticizing such a scheme, the public should ensure that the prices for the environmental factors are set high enough and that the subsidization of pollution abatement is stopped.

### Footnotes

1. This paper concentrates on the problem of restricting water pollution, although the discussion of policies can be generalized to include other pollution problems as well.

2. See, for example, J.H. Dales, *Pollution, Property and Prices* (Toronto: University of Toronto Press, 1968); A.V. Kneese and B.T. Bower, *Managing Water Quality: Economics, Technology, Institutions* (Baltimore: Johns Hopkins Press, 1968, for Resources of the Future, Inc.); and L. Waverman, "Pollution: A Problem in Economics," in L.H. Officer and L.B. Smith (eds.), *Canadian Economic Problems and Policies* (Toronto: McGraw-Hill of Canada Ltd., 1970).

3. In fact, the courts and insurance are used when the source of the pollution is identifiable. The Electric Reduction Company at Port Maitland, Ontario, has been sued by individuals in the area for fluoride pollution. Oil tankers carry insurance for third-party liability in case of break-up and resulting pollution.

4. In economists' terminology, air and water are to a large extent collective goods subject to technological external diseconomies.

5. Dales, *Pollution, Property and Prices*; and Kneese and Bower, *Managing Water Quality*. There are differences in the proposals of spokesmen such as Dales and Kneese. Dales suggests that the government establish the desirable level of pollution and auction off pollution rights to the highest bidder. Kneese's schemes are more conventional and are described below.

6. The information package accompanying the Canada Water Act attempts to falsely legitimize effluent charges by suggesting that the funds acquired will be used to install governmental clean-up projects. The proper price should be set so as to produce the socially desirable use of water; earmarking of the funds from selling water is immaterial, except as a political selling point.

7. The price very likely will be too low in the short run. The method of choosing the proper price is to set a rate, determine firms' reactions and the resulting level of pollution, then adjust the price up or down, to more closely approach the desired pollution level. Given the facts of political life, it is probable that an initial price will be too low.

There is a great similarity between a pricing scheme and a system of fines. A fine creates a uniform price to be paid no matter how grossly a firm over-pollutes, and a zero price if the firm meets the standard. Fines are clearly inferior to per-unit prices if the fine is for the mere offence of polluting (as it is today) rather than for the volume of pollution (a price). If fines are graduated in accordance with the amount by which a standard is exceeded, then they will amount to prices.

8. A concise summary of existing legislation is given in the Canadian Council of Resource Ministers, *A Digest of Environmental Pollution Legislation in Canada (Air, Water and Soil)*, (September 1967); and Systems Research Group, *Canadian Legislation Pertaining to Environmental Quality Management*, Working Paper No. 3 (Toronto, 1970). A complete analysis of the legislation affecting the Great Lakes Basin is given in H. Landis, "Legal Controls of Pollution in the Great Lakes Basin," *Canadian Bar Review* (March 1970).

Other federal instruments have been the Winter Works program (Ontario, for example, received $3,900,000 between 1961 and 1965 under this program) and Special Orders in Council specifying payment for victims of pollution.

9. Income Tax Regulations, Schedule B, Class 24.

10. At least, this is an economist's interpretation of the Act.

11. For example, Schedule III, Part XII(i)(e) of the Act exempts "goods for use as part of sewerage and drainage systems."

12. This omission is questionable. Studies in the United States (e.g. American Chemical Society, *Cleaning our Environment: The Chemical Basis for Action* (Washington, D.C.: 1969), p. 120) have shown the runoffs from combined and separate storm sewers to have significant pollution effects. It appears this is a problem in Toronto, which otherwise has one the best municipal systems.

13. The average project was therefore just under $200,000 and the average loan to a municipality was approximately $300,000. Assuming all projects to have finished on time, the total grant by C.M.H.C. was $68,000,000 or roughly $50,000 per project and $750,000 per municipality.

14. Landis, in "Legal Controls of Pollutions", presents exceptionally well argued views both on the unconstitutionality of the Act and on the existence of federal waters. In addition he shows how conflicts may arise if both provincial and federal laws are enacted.

15. R.M. Bird and L. Waverman, "Some Fiscal Aspects of Controlling Industrial Water Pollution", Institute for the Quantitative Analysis of Social and Economic Policy, Working Paper #7005. Also to be published in D. Auld (ed.), *Pollution Dollars and Sense* (Toronto: University of Toronto Press, Spring 1971).

16. From data for 1956-1964, one-third of OWRC loans were earmarked for water supply and purification projects rather than for sewage treatment and disposal (J.A. Vance *et al.*, "The Diverse Effects of Water Pollution on the Economy of Domestic and Municipal Water Users," Background Paper A 4-1-5, Canadian Council of Resource Ministers, 1966). Therefore, $800,000,000 was lent for pollution control purposes.

17. For example, the Lake Huron Water Supply System, begun in 1964, controls, operates and sells water to customers (mainly the City of London) at cost.

18. Canadian Council of Resource Ministers, *Environmental Pollution Legislation in Canada*.

19. Saskatchewan's fees were first introduced in 1968.

20. This does not imply that other provinces do not control effluents. They establish standards but do not use effluent charges.

21. Bird and Waverman, "Some Fiscal Aspects of Controlling Pollution"; R.W. Judy, "Economic Incentives and Environmental Control", Paper presented to the International Symposium on Environmental Disruption in the Modern World, (Tokyo, March 1970); and M.J. Roberts, "River Basin Authorities: A National Solution to Water Pollution", *Harvard Law Review*, Vol. 83, 1970.

22. Ontario estimated the costs of accelerated depreciation at $2-$3 million for fiscal 1970-71 (Budget Speech). The costs to the federal authorities are probably $25-$40 million (assuming Ontario has one-third of polluting industry and federal tax revenue is four times provincial revenue).

23. For example, land-intensive techniques such as treatment lagoons may be dropped in favour of capital-intensive schemes.

24. Again, probably in the order of $2 million for Ontario, and $10 million federally.

25. Taxing capital goods confuses incidence unnecessarily.

26. Bird and Waverman, "Some Fiscal Aspects of Controlling Pollution."
There may be firms that prefer to shut down rather than meet the standard. This is no reason to subsidize those firms that threaten to go under. For example, monetary policy increasing the cost of capital forces some firms into bankruptcy. Should these firms be able to receive federal assistance when federal monetary policy leads to higher interest rates? This would negate one purpose of the policy.

27. Ontario Budget, 1970.

28. Roberts, "River Basin Authorities."

29. Of course, such a tax scheme would be most difficult to design.

30. Which of course points up the inherent irrationality of labelling effluent charges licences to pollute.

31. Senator William Proxmire, as reported in the *New York Times*, (8 May 1970). (See "Wanton Waste Makes Woeful Expense", in the last issue of the *Journal*, p.441 -Ed.).

32. If society feels that some specific form of solid waste is clearly undesirable, then society can ban that product.

# (c) Planning and Regional Development

## NICHOLAS KALDOR
# The Case for Regional Policies

In Britain, as in other countries, we have become acutely aware in recent years of the existence of a 'regional' problem—the problem, that is, of different regions growing at uneven rates; with some regions developing relatively fast and others tending to be left behind. In some ways this problem of fast and slow growing regions has not led to the same kind of inequalities in regional standards of living, in culture or in social structure, in the case of Britain as in some other countries—such as Italy, the United States or France. And in general, the problem of regional inequalities within countries is not nearly so acute as that between the rich and poor countries of the world—with differences in living standards in the ratio of 20:1, or even 50:1 as between the so-called 'advanced' countries and the 'developing' countries. Yet, as investigations by Kuznets and others have shown, the tremendous differences that now divide the rich and poor nations are comparatively recent in origin. They are the cumulative result of persistent differences in growth rates that went on over periods that may appear long in terms of a life-span, but which are relatively short in terms of recorded human history—not more than a few centuries, in fact. Two hundred, or two-hundred-and-fifty years ago, the differences in living standards, or in the 'stage' of both economic and cultural development of different countries, or parts of the globe, were very much smaller than they are today.

The primary question that needs to be considered is what *causes* these differences in 'regional' growth rates—whether the term 'regional' is applied to different countries (or even groups of countries) or different areas within the same country. The two questions are not, of course, identical; but up to a point, I am sure that it would be illuminating to consider them as if they were, and apply the same analytical technique to both.

In some ways an analysis of the strictly 'regional' problem (within a common political area) is more difficult. There is first of all the question of how to define a 'region' within a political area—a problem that does not arise when political boundaries, however arbitrary they may be from an economic or social point of view, are treated as a given fact one need not enquire about. There is in fact, no unique way of defining what constitutes a 'region'—there are innumerable ways; the most that one can say is that some ways of drawing such boundary lines are more sensible than others; and given the fact that this is so, the exact demarcation of a 'region' may not make too much difference to the subsequent analysis.

248

Another aspect in which the analysis of 'region' within a country is more difficult is in terms of the identification of the fate of an area with the fate of its inhabitants. The mobility of both labour and capital within countries tends to be considerably greater than between countries—even though economists, in their desire for clear-cut assumptions on which to build, tended to over-estimate the one and to under-estimate the other. (There is only an imperfect mobility within countries, and there is also some mobility between them.)

Finally, a region which is part of a 'nation' or a 'country' tends to have common political institutions, a common taxing and spending authority and a common currency—all of which have important implications on the manner in which its external economic relations are conducted.

## The Role of 'Resource Endowment'

But subject to these differences, what can we say about the causes of divergent regional growth rates—whether inter-nationally or intra-nationally? If one refers to classical or neo-classical economic theory, the common explanation is in terms of various factors—summed up under the term 'resource endowment'—which are themselves unexplained. Some areas are favoured by climate or geology; by the ability, vitality, ingenuity of their inhabitants, and by their thriftiness, and these innate advantages may be enhanced by good political and social institutions. Beyond suggesting that the right kind of human material is fostered by a temperate climate—in zones which are neither too hot nor too cold—and all of this owes a great deal to historical accidents and to luck, the theories which explain riches or poverty in terms of 'resource endowment' do not really have anything much to offer by way of explanation.

Nevertheless one must agree that they go as far as it is possible to go in explaining that part of economic growth—and until fairly recently this was much the most important part—which consisted of 'land based' economic activities, such as agriculture or mineral exploitation. These are clearly conditioned by climatic and geologic factors—the suitability of soil, rainfall, the availability of minerals, and so on. These provide the natural explanation why some areas are more densely settled than others; and why the comparative advantage in procuring different products (and which settles the nature of their external trading relations) should differ as between one area and another. No sophisticated explanation is needed why it is better for some areas to grow wheat and for others bananas: or why some areas which are lucky in possessing things with a fast-growing demand (such as oil or uranium) are fortunate, from the point of view of their growth-potential, in relation to others which possess minerals with a slow-growing or declining demand—coal, for example. We would all agree that some part of the interregional specialisation and the division of labour can be adequately accounted for by such factors.

It is when we come to comparative advantages in relation to processing activities (as distinct from land-based activities) that this kind of approach is likely to yield question-begging results. The prevailing distribution of real income in the world—the comparative riches or poverty of nations, or regions—is largely to be explained, not by 'natural' factors, but by the unequal incidence of development in industrial activities. The 'advanced', high-income areas are invariably those which possess a highly developed modern industry. In relation to differences in industrial development, explanations in terms of 'resource endowment' do not get us very far. One can, and does say, that industrial production requires a great deal of capital—both in terms of plant and machinery, and of human skills, resulting from education—but in explaining such differences in 'capital endowment' it is difficult to separate cause from effect. It is as sensible—or perhaps more sensible—to say that capital accumulation results from economic development as that it is a cause of development. Anyhow, the two proceed side by side. Accumulation is largely financed out of business profits; the growth of demand in turn is largely responsible for providing both the inducements to invest capital in industry and also the means of financing it.

We cannot therefore say that industries will be located in regions which are 'well endowed' with capital resources for reasons other than industrial development itself. It was not the result of the peculiar thriftiness of the inhabitants of a region, or of a particularly high degree of initial inequality in the distribution of income which 'induced' a high savings-ratio, that some regions became rich while others remained poor. The capital needed for industrialisation was largely provided by the very same individuals who acquired wealth as a result of the process of development, and not prior to it. The great captains of industry, like Henry Ford or Nuffield were not recruited from the wealthy classes—they started as 'small men'.

Nor is there a satisfactory 'location theory' which is capable of explaining the geographic distribution of industrial activities. The only relevant factor which is considered in this connection is that of transport costs. But transport cost advantages can only help to explain location in those particular activities which convert bulky goods—where transport costs are an important element, and where processing itself greatly reduces the weight of the materials processed. If say, two tons of coal and four tons of iron are needed to make a ton of steel, it is better to locate steel plants near the coal mines and the iron ore deposits; and if these are themselves situated at some distance from each other, it is best to locate the steel plants near both places, in proportions determined by the relative weight of the two materials per unit of finished product—i.e., in this example, two-thirds of the plants near the iron ore, and one-third near the coal mines—since this arrangement would alone ensure full utilization of transport capacity in both directions.

But where the effect of processing in reducing bulk is not so important, the location of the processing activity may be a matter of indifference—whether it is near the source of the materials, near the market for the products, or anywhere in between. It is often suggested that such 'footloose' industries tend naturally to develop near the market for their products. But this again is a question-begging proposition. Great urban conurbations are normally large centres of industrial activity—the 'markets' are there where the 'industry' is. The engineering industry in this country is highly concentrated in and around Birmingham—it is also a great 'market' for engineering goods of various kinds. But it does not explain why either of these should be located there, rather than in some other place, say Leeds or Sheffield.

# The Principle of 'Cumulative Causation'

To explain why certain regions have become highly industrialised, while others have not we must introduce quite different kinds of considerations—what Mydral (1957) called the principle of 'circular and cumulative causation'. This is nothing else but the existence of increasing returns to scale—using that term in the broadest sense—in processing activities. These are not just the economies of large-scale production, commonly considered, but the cumulative advantages accruing from the growth of industry itself—the development of skill and know-how; the opportunities for easy communication of ideas and experience; the opportunity of ever-increasing differentiation of processes and of specialisation in human activities. As Allyn Young (1928) pointed out in a famous paper, Adam Smith's principle of the 'division of labour' operates through the constant sub-division of industries, the emergence of new kinds of specialized firms, of steadily increasing differentiation—more than through the expansion in the size of the individual plant or the individual firm.

Thus the fact that in all known historical cases the development of manufacturing industries was closely associated with urbanisation must have deep-seated causes which are unlikely to be rendered inoperative by the invention of some new technology or new source of power. Their broad effect is a strong positive association between the growth of productivity and efficiency and the rate of growth in the scale of activities—the so-called Verdoorn Law. One aspect of this is that as communication between different regions becomes more intensified (with improvements in transport and in marketing organisation), the region that is initially more developed industrially may gain from the progressive opening of trade at the expense of the less developed region whose development will be inhibited by it. Whereas in the classical case—which abstracts from increasing returns—the opening of trade between two regions will necessarily be beneficial to both (even though the gains may not be equally divided between them) and specialisation through trade will necessarily serve to reduce the differences in comparative costs in the two areas, in the case of the 'opening of trade' in industrial products the differences in comparative costs may be enlarged, and not reduced, as a result of trade; and the trade may injure one region to the greater benefit of the other. This will be so if one assumes two regions, initially isolated from one another, with each having both an agricultural area and an industrial and market centre; with the size of agricultural production being mainly determined by soil and climate, and the state of technology; and the size of industrial production mainly depending on the demand for industrial products derived from the agricultural sector. When trade is opened up between them, the region with the more developed industry will be able to supply the needs of the agricultural area of the other region on more favourable terms: with the result that the industrial centre of the second region will lose its market, and will tend to be eliminated—without any compensating advantage to the inhabitants of that region in terms of increased agricultural output.

Another aspect of asymmetry between 'land-based' and 'processing' activities (which is basically due to economies of large-scale production) is that in industrial production, contractual costs form an important independent element in price-formation; competition is necessarily imperfect; the sellers are price-makers, rather than price-takers. Whereas in agricultural production it is prices that are derived from, or dependent on, contractual incomes (i.e. on the level of wages).

As a result, the 'exchange process'—the nature of the adjustment mechanism in inter-regional trade flows and money flows—operates differently in the two cases. In the case of trade between agricultural regions, the classical theory of the adjustment process is more nearly applicable. The price of agricultural commodities rises or falls automatically with changes in the balance of supply and demand; these price changes in individual markets will automatically tend to maintain the balance in trade flows between areas, both through the income effects and the substitution effects of price changes. Where the goods produced by the different regions are fairly close substitutes to one another, a relatively modest change in price—in the 'terms of trade'—will be sufficient to offset the effects of changes in either supply or demand schedules as may result from crop failures, the uneven incidence of technological improvements, or any other 'exogenous' cause. If the goods produced by the different regions are complements rather than substitutes to each other, the adjustment process may involve far greater changes in the terms of trade of the two areas, and would thus operate mainly through the 'income effects'. But in either case, the very process which secures an equilibrium between the supply and demand in each individual market through the medium of price changes will also ensure balance between sales and purchases of each region.

In the case of industrial activities ('manufactures') the impact effect of exogenous changes in demand will be on production rather than on prices. 'Supply', at any rate long-run supply, is normally in excess of demand—in the sense that producers would be willing to produce more, and to sell more, at the prevailing price (or even at a lower price) in response to an increased flow of orders. In this situation the adjustment process operates in a different manner—through the so-called 'foreign trade multiplier'. Any exogenous change in the demand for the products of a region from outside will set up multiplier effects in terms of local production and employment which in turn will adjust imports to the change in exports; on certain assumptions, this adjustment will alone suffice to keep the trade flows in balance.[1]

Some time ago Hicks (1950, p. 62) coined the phrase 'super-multiplier' to cover the effects of changes of demand on investment, as well as on consumption; and he showed that on certain assumptions, both the rate of growth of induced investment, and the rate of growth of consumption, become attuned to the rate of growth of the autonomous component of demand, so that the growth in an autonomous demand-factor will govern the rate of growth of the economy as a whole.

From the point of view of any particular region, the 'autonomous component of demand' is the demand emanating from *outside* the region; and Hicks's notion of the 'super-multiplier' can be applied so as to express the doctrine of the foreign trade multiplier in a dynamic setting. So expressed, the doctrine asserts that the rate of economic development of a region is fundamentally governed by the rate of growth of its exports. For the growth of exports, via the 'accelerator', will govern the rate of growth of industrial capacity, as well as the rate of growth of consumption; it will also serve to adjust (again under rather severe simplifying assumptions) both the level, and the rate of growth, of imports to that of exports.

The behaviour of exports on the other hand will depend both on an exogenous factor—the rate of growth of world demand for the products of the region; and on an 'endogenous' or quasi-endogenous factor—on the movement of the 'efficiency wages' in the region relative to other producing regions, which will determine whether the region's share in the total (overall) market is increasing or diminishing. The movement of 'efficiency wages' (a phrase coined by Keynes) is the resultant of two elements—the relative movement of money wages and that of productivity. If this relationship (the index of money wages divided by the index of productivity) moves in favour of an area it will gain in 'competitiveness' and *vice versa*.

As regards the movement of money wages the one uncontroversial proposition that one can advance is that given *some* mobility of labour, there is a limit to the differences in the levels of wages prevailing between industrial regions, or between different industries of a region. Indeed, it is a well known fact that whilst the general level of money wages may rise at highly variable rates at different times, the pay differentials between different types of workers, or between workers doing the same job in different areas, are remarkably constant. This may be the result partly of the mobility of labour but also of the strong pressures associated with collective bargaining for the maintenance of traditional comparabilities.[2] But this means that the rates of growth of money wages in different regions will tend to be much the same, even when the rates of growth in employment differ markedly. On the other hand, under the Verdoorn Law, the rates of growth of productivity will be the higher, the higher the rates of growth of output, and differences in the rates of productivity growth will tend to exceed the associated differences in the rates of growth of employments.[3] Hence differences in the rates of productivity growth are not likely to be compensated by equivalent differences in the rates of increase in money wages.

In other words, 'efficiency wages' will tend to fall in regions (and in the particular industries of regions) where productivity rises faster than the average. It is for this reason that relatively fast growing areas tend to acquire a cumulative competitive advantage over a relatively slow growing area; 'efficiency wages' will, in the natural course of events, tend to fall in the former, relatively to the latter—even when they tend to rise in both areas in absolute terms.

It is through this mechanism that the process of 'cumulative causation' works; and both comparative success and comparative failure have self-reinforcing effects in terms of industrial development. Just because the induced changes in wages increases are not sufficient to offset the differences in productivity increases, the comparative costs of production in fast growing areas tend to fall in time relatively to those in slow growing areas; and thereby enhance the competitive advantage of the former at the expense of the latter.

I am sure that this principle of cumulative causation—which explains the unequal regional incidence of industrial development by endogenous factors resulting from the process of historical development itself rather than by exogenous differences in 'resource endowment'— is an essential one for the understanding of the diverse trends of development as between different regions. In reality, the influences and cross-currents resulting from processes of development are far more complex. The intensification of trade resulting from technological improvements in transport or the reduction of artificial barriers (such as tariffs between regions) has important diffusion effects as well as important concentration effects. The increase in production and income in one region will, as such, stimulate the demand for 'complementary' products of other regions; and just as, in terms of micro-economics, falling costs generally lead to oligopoly rather than monopoly, so the principle of cumulative causation leads to the concentration of industrial development in a number of successful regions and not of a single region. These 'successful' regions in turn may hold each other in balance through increasing specialisation between them — some area becomes more prominent in some industries and another area in some other industries.

Actually, in terms of national areas, Kuznets found that different industrialised countries are remarkably similar in industrial structure, at similar stages of industrial development. The tremendous increase in international trade in industrial products between highly industrialised countries since the Second World War was more the reflection of specialisation within industries than that between industries: it was mainly in parts and components and machinery for industrial use. For example, in the case of the motor car industry, whilst most developed countries have a developed and highly competitive motor car industry (and are large net exporters) there has been a huge increase in international trade in motor car components — with some countries supplying some part of a carburetor to everybody, and some other country doing the same for some other part of the engine, or the carburetor.

There are also important diseconomies resulting from excessive rates of growth in industrial activities in particular areas: the growing areas will tend to have fast rates of population growth (mainly as a result of immigration) with the associated environmental problems in housing, public services, congestion, and so on, and these at some stage should serve to offset the technological economies resulting from faster growth. But as is well known, many of these diseconomies are external to the individual producer and may not therefore be adequately reflected in the movement of money costs and prices. A counterpart to this are external economies in the slow growing or declining regions — in terms of unemployment of labour, or an under-utilised social infrastructure, which again tend to be external to the firm and hence inadequately reflected in selling costs or prices. There is some presumption therefore for supposing that, if left to market processes alone, tendencies to regional concentration of industrial activities will proceed farther than they would have done if 'private costs' were equal to 'social cost' (in the Pigovian sense) and all economies and diseconomies of production were adequately reflected in the movement of money costs and prices.

## Regions and Countries

It is time now that we consider some of the basic differences in the mode of operation of this principle — i.e. of 'cumulative causation' as between different regions of a single country and as between different political areas.

There is, first of all, the fact that the inter-regional mobility of labour is very much greater than the international mobility of labour. As a result differences in regional growth rates cannot cause differences in living standards of the same order as have emerged in the last few centuries between more distant regions, separated by political and cultural barriers. Real earnings no doubt improve faster in the areas of immigration rather than in areas of emigration, but the very fact of easy migration limits the extent to which differences in regional growth rates will be associated with divergent movements in earnings per head. The fact that trade unions are nation-wide and collective bargains in most countries are on a national basis, is a further reason why the movement of real earnings in various regions broadly tends to keep in step.

A second, and even more important fact is that a region which forms part of a political community, with a common scale of public services and a common basis of taxation, automatically gets 'aid' whenever its trading relations with the rest of the country deteriorate. There is an important built-in fiscal stabilizer which arrests the operation of the export-multiplier: since taxes paid to the Central Government vary with the level of local incomes and expenditure, whilst public expenditures do not (indeed they may vary in an offsetting direction through public works, unemployment benefit, etc.), any deterioration in the export-import balance tends to be retarded (and ultimately arrested) by the change in the region's fiscal balance—in the relation between what it contributes to the central Exchequer and what it receives from it.

This 'built-in' fiscal stabiliser—i.e. that a fall in exogenous demand leads to an increase in the public sector deficit, and thereby moderates the effect of the former on employment and incomes—operates of course on the national level as much as on the regional level; and it is one of the main reasons why a fall in exports does not generate a sufficient fall in the level of incomes to maintain equilibrium in the balance of payments through the adjustment in imports. But the important difference is that in the case of the region the change in the local fiscal balance is externally financed; in the case of the nation the balance of payments deficit causes a fall in reserves, or requires 'compensatory finance' from abroad, which is by no means 'automatic'.

This seems to me the main reason why there appears to be no counterpart to the 'balance-of-payments problem' on the regional level. It is often suggested, by the 'monetary school' that the reason why a country with a separate currency gets into balance of payments difficulties, whilst a region never does, is because in the one case the 'local money supply' is reduced in consequence of an excess of imports over exports; in the other case the monetary authorities offset the effects of the adverse balance on current account by 'domestic credit expansion'—by replacing the outflow of money (resulting from the excess of imports) with 'new' money. In my view this way of looking at the problem is putting the cart before the horse. The 'replacement of the money' is simply a facet of the fact that the foreign trade multiplier is arrested in its operation through the induced fiscal deficit—possibly aggravated also by the fall in private saving in relation to private domestic investment (though in practice the latter factor may be quantitatively of less importance, since the foreign-trade multiplier will tend to induce a reduction in local investment, and not only in local savings). But exactly the same thing happens at the regional level—with the outflowing money being (at least partially) replaced by a larger net inflow from the Exchequer, which is a direct consequence of the 'outflow'; but since it happens automatically as part of the natural order of things nobody kicks up a fuss, or even takes notice of it.

In these ways 'regions' are in a more favourable position than 'countries'. On the other hand sovereign political areas can take various measures to offset the effect of an unfavourable trend in their 'efficiency wages' which is not open to a 'region'—i.e. by diverting demand from foreign goods to home goods, through varying forms of protection (tariffs and non-tariff barriers, such as preferences given in public contracts) and occasionally also—though usually only very belatedly, in extremities—through adjustment of the exchange rate.

Of these two instruments for counteracting adverse trends in 'efficiency wages'—protection and devaluation—the latter is undoubtedly greatly superior to the former. Devaluation, as has often been pointed out, is nothing else but a combination of a uniform *ad-valorem* duty on all imports and uniform *ad-valorem* subsidy on exports. The combination of the two allows the adjustment in 'competitiveness' to take place under conditions which give the maximum scope for obtaining the advantages of economies of scale through international specialisation. Protection on the other hand tends to reduce international specialisation, and forces each region to spread its industrial activities over a wider range of activities on a smaller scale, instead of a narrower range on a larger scale. The effects of protection in inhibiting the growth of industrial efficiency is likely to be the greater the smaller the GNP (or rather the gross industrial product) of the protected area. It is no accident that all the prosperous small countries of the world—such as the Scandinavian countries or Switzerland—are (comparatively speaking) 'free traders'. They have modest tariffs, and a very high ratio of trade in manufactures (both exports and imports) to their total output or consumption.

It has sometimes been suggested—not perhaps very seriously—that some of the development areas of the U.K.—such as Scotland or Northern Ireland—would be better off with a separate currency with an adjustable exchange rate vis-à-vis the rest of the U.K. For the reason mentioned earlier, I do not think this would be a suitable remedy. However, we have now introduced a new instrument in the U.K.—R.E.P.— which potentially could give the same advantages as devaluation for counteracting any adverse trend in 'efficiency wages', but with the added advantage that the cost of the consequent deterioration in the terms of trade (the cost of selling exports at lower prices in terms of imports) is not borne by the region, but by the U.K. taxpaying community as a whole.

For this same reason, perhaps, the drawback of R.E.P. as an instrument is that it would be politically very difficult to introduce it on a scale that could make it really effective. The present R.E.P. is equivalent to a 5-6 per cent reduction in the 'efficiency wages' in the manufacturing sector of the development areas. Since 'value added by regional manufacturing' is no more than a quarter, or perhaps a third, of the total cost of regional export-commodities (the rest consist of goods and services embodied that are mainly produced outside the region) the effect of a 6 per cent R.E.P. is no more than that of a 2 per cent devaluation (for the U.K. as a whole). It thus could have only one-fifth of the effect on 'regional competitiveness' which the recent U.K. devaluation had on the U.K.'s competitiveness in relation to the rest of the world.

Development Area policy comprises a host of other measures as well, of which the differential investment grant is the most costly and the most prominent. In my view investment grants as an instrument are less effective for the purpose of countering adverse trends in competitiveness than subsidies on wages (and not only because they stimulate the wrong kind of industries—those that are specially capital intensive) but I would agree that this is an issue that requires closer investigation than it has yet received.

I should like to end by mentioning one other possibility. Given the limitation on the scope of development expenditures by the natural disinclination of the Central Government (or the Parliament at Westminster) to spend huge sums in subsidising particular regions, isn't there a case for supplementing Central Government sources from local sources—through more local fiscal autonomy? For example, if it was found (and agreed) that R.E.P. is an efficacious way of subsidising regional exports (I suppose this is far from agreed at the moment) and that this may have dramatic effects in terms of enhanced regional development in the long run, would it not be in the interest of the regions to supplement the centrally financed R.E.P. by the proceeds, say, of a local sales tax? Perhaps this is a dangerous suggestion since in practice the growth of locally financed subsidies might simply be offset by lesser subsidies from the Centre. It would be less 'dangerous' however, if it was the Central Government which offered to raise the level of such subsidies—R.E.P. or even investment grants—on condition that a proportion of the cost should be raised by local taxation. Clearly, far more could be spent for the benefit of particular areas, if the areas themselves would make a greater, or a more distinct, contribution to the cost of such benefits. But these are thoughts for the distant future; long before they become practical politics we shall be deeply involved in the same kind of issues in connection with our negotiations to enter the Common Market.

### Footnotes

1. The necessary assumptions are that all other sources of demand except exports are endogenous, rather than exogenous—i.e., that both Government expenditure and business investment play a passive role, the former being confined by revenue from taxation, and the latter by savings out of business profits.

2. It has also been true in an international context that the comparative differences in the rates of growth of money wages in the different industrial countries had been smaller (in the post-war period at any rate) than the differences in the rates of productivity growth in the manufacturing industries of those countries, though the reasons why this has been so are not as yet well understood (cf. e.g. Kaldor (1960), paras.22-23 and Table 1).

3. Recent empirical analyses of productivity growth in manufacturing industry suggest that a 1 per cent increase in the growth of output is associated with a 0.6 per cent increase in productivity and a 0.4 per cent increase in employment (cf. e.g.: United Nations, 1970).

# MAURICE ZINKIN
# A Child's Guide to Planning

This coherence of forecasts over the whole range of the organisation is at the base of the next use of the word 'planning'. When the literature talks of corporate planning it very frequently has in mind, above all, the search for new opportunities, whether the expansion of a present product range or diversification into totally new lines, and the development of strategies for the exploitation of these opportunities.

Any such plan requires as pre-conditions, first, that coherent forecasts be made of what will happen to the business if it continues on its present lines and, secondly, that these forecasts be found to be in some way inconsistent or inadequate.

Let us take inconsistency first. The forecasts may reveal that the business will generate much more cash than the present lines require; or that there will be a top management of an ability to produce more decisions than the present lines need; or that the present lines are going to decline in the market, leaving many assets from the sales force to the factories under-employed.

These inconsistencies can sometimes be solved by liquidation of the excess assets—the cash is distributed in bigger dividends, some of the top managers seek other jobs, the excess salesmen are dismissed; but usually such liquidation involves the organisation in the loss of one of its major assets, the team of people and machines, ideas and experience which the firm has built up over time. Therefore, most firms will prefer an attempt to diversify to a partial liquidation, nor is this an irrational decision. In most countries the shareholder pays less tax on a capital gain than on a bigger dividend. The manager's remuneration depends to a considerable extent on the size of his business. The redundant employee may have to accept a worse job. Everybody's interests tend to work together to make growth the preferred choice.

Growth is, however, only a sensible choice, if it can be achieved at an adequate rate of return. At the heart, therefore, of planning is the definition of what one is trying to do and the minimum conditions under which one will do it. Once these are decided there has to be a process of search for those opportunities which will satisfy the objectives and fulfil the conditions. It is this process of search which is often referred to as planning. The planners, whether they be a corporate planning department of the Board or a single entrepreneur, forecast the environment, social and economic, in which the firm will be operating and try and detect in their environment an opportunity for expansion which has not already been detected by so many others that it will not be profitable—a condition which is often forgotten.

The opportunity may be provided by a change in taste, pop records, for instance; or by a growth in affluence, the need for more housing, for instance; or by a technical innovation, the computer, for instance. Wherever it lies, the term 'planning' is somewhat misleading as a description of the process of detecting it. There is more intuition than planning about it. Intuition will operate, however, much more successfully if the ground has first been thoroughly covered. One's feeling for how people will spend more money if they have more may be superb, but before one exercises it, it is a good idea to get as good a forecast as one can of whether they will in fact have more money and, if so, how much. Profitable growth depends on judgment, the judgment which can put together an understanding of the firm and what it can do, of the environment and the way in which it is changing, and of the public and what they may need. Within the limits of what the human brain can absorb, the more one knows about the firm and the public, the better one's judgment is likely to be; but in the end the flash of inspiration which says that people will be willing to fly or to use deodorants is of the same nature as that which shot Archimedes out of his bath. It is inspiration, but inspiration based on cogitation, often long, over fact thoroughly collected and fully assimilated.

Whether one decides to grow or not, and what risks one decides to take in doing so, depends very largely upon one's objectives. One may wish to be rich or one may wish to have a quiet life, one may wish to build up a firm which will be a power in the land or one may wish to keep it to a size where one's not too clever son can still be Chairman. This choice of objectives is also very often called planning, though it is planning only in the sense that the laying down of objectives implies that they will be mutually consistent and that some attempt will be made to achieve them. It is no good, for example, laying down objectives both of 12 per cent after tax and of total risklessness. One does not get 12 per cent after tax for operations without risk. Equally, it is no good laying down objectives and then not enforcing them. It is useless, for example, to lay down an objective of 12 per cent after tax on the basis that one is good at enterprises involving risk, and then accepting a large number of propositions which offer very considerably less than 12 per cent on the basis that they are riskless.

When all the other meanings of the world 'planning' have been gone through, when the forecasts have been made, the inspirations undergone and the objectives laid down, there still remains the last, the old-fashioned use of the word 'planning,' the meaning in which most people have been planning for most of history. To plan in this sense means simply to arrange for implementation, to lay down the way in which one is going to do what one has decided to do and how one is going to make sure that it is, in fact, done.

In this meaning of the word 'planning,' plans proliferate. One makes a plan to go to the theatre, one then has to find a free evening which is also a free evening for the people with whom one wishes to go, one must then find out whether one's own free evening is one on which the theatre has seats free, one must then ensure that one's cash flow is such that one can pay for the seats. Finally, one must lay down a timetable by which one gets to the theatre before the curtain goes up, and one must consider whether one's comfort will be greater if one eats before or after the play. If the objective one has laid down for oneself is to get married, the planning process is even more complicated. There is the need to search the environment to find a suitable partner, there is the need to consider what product-plus will make one acceptable to the partner and there are then all the networks required to get everybody to the wedding ceremony at the right time, to ensure that a house is bought and a mortgage obtained before rather than after the couple start family life together, and so on.

Implementation planning, therefore, is something to which we are all accustomed in our daily lives. It is very questionable whether the launch of any new product involves planning more complicated than is required for a perfectly normal couple to get married. The only reason why one tends to think of it as more complicated is that most people stop at one marriage, whilst most brands go on through a series of re-launches.

It is, of course, not only the marketing side of businesses which has to make implementation plans nearly as complicated as those people make in their private lives. Production has to be scheduled, routes have to be chosen for distribution vehicles, inventories have to be kept at required levels, the gimmicks for promotions have to be ordered in good time, and so on. Every business has an endless series of routines of about the level of complication of arranging to go to the theatre. Every now and then, when a factory has to be built, a new product launched, or perhaps a new sales force obtained, they almost reach the level of complication of bringing up a child.

The difference between private life and business life is that businesses live in a competitive world in a way in which married couples and parents do not. It is considered positively meritorious for others to take one's business away from one by offering better services, cheaper prices. Our children are never offered the option of more generous or more understanding parents, and society still frowns on others offering to one's wife too wide a choice of alternative husbands.

This does not, however, change the essential nature of implementation planning. It only means that businesses can afford fewer mistakes. They have to operate to a higher level of accuracy than private individuals. It is this need for a higher level of accuracy which produces all the mystique in modern discussions of planning, all the genuflections to the computer without which no article can be considered modern. What most planning procedures and computer programmes do is to make rigorous a process which has always gone on in a rough and ready way. The computer is very rarely more than 5 per cent better than an average stock clerk, perhaps 10 per cent if the stock clerk was really not very good; and one may doubt whether the stock clerk was more than about 5 per cent better than the average housewife, who day in day out has quite a difficult inventory problem to solve.

What the computer does do which is new is to enable one to make one's planning more complex and yet to keep it rigorous. When the planning is done by people with pencil and paper, it has to be cut down so as to make the calculations manageable. It is, therefore, split into sub-routines; somebody calculates how the promotion will be sold to different customers and somebody else how the machines to produce it will be scheduled. A third person adjusts stocks, and yet a fourth routes vehicles. The computer enables one to put all these sub-routines together, so that the whole process can be done in one and all the interactions of one part of it on another can be taken into account. If the system has been properly analysed and the programmes properly written, the computer will produce a valuable increase in accuracy; but unless the firm was very badly run before, the increase will not be greater than the increase a housewife achieves when she learns to balance the economies of buying bigger packages against the cost of a deep freeze. Indeed, probably the most valuable result of putting one's planning on a computer is that everything has to be spelled out for a computer. It makes no assumptions for itself. Managers are, therefore, compelled to define what it is they expect to happen and the assumptions which make them expect it. In theory they both could, and should, do this without a computer; in practice one often has to buy the computer before one can force them to go through the mental agony.

If one splits up planning into these different meanings, one sees that it is, in fact, nothing new. Alexander the Great and the Prophet Moses must have planned in all these ways. If our computers and our text books of corporate planning enable us to come somewhere near their success, we will have every reason to be satisfied with ourselves.

F. T. WALTON

# The Formulation of Regional Economic Objectives[1]

During the past decade a new dimension has been added to Canadian economic policy. It has been increasingly recognized that the future development of the Canadian economy must be based upon, or at least allow for, a greater degree of positive participation by all the major economic regions of the country. Indeed, the Prime Minister has gone so far as to suggest that a failure to do something about reducing "regional disparities" is just as likely to break up the federation as a failure to resolve the matter of national unity.[2]

The addition of regional considerations to Canadian economic discussion and policy-making is the result of a variety of influences. One factor has been a slow, but increasing, realization that the resource boom of the 1950s, which supported a rapid rate of national growth, contributed very little either to reducing "regional disparities" or to laying the basis for the future development of viable economic activity in the lagging regions of the country. This is especially true of the Atlantic Region. It is not surprising, therefore, that the Atlantic Provinces Economic Council should have been the first group to draw national attention to this lack of full regional participation in Canadian growth. More recently, the Economic Council of Canada, on the basis of their staff studies, have put the same point on a more general basis by documenting the lack of convergence over time in the degree of interregional income disparity, when such convergence has characterised the United States experience over the same historical period. The conclusion which emerges from the recognition that rapid national growth is not a sufficient means of ensuring full regional participation or of reducing interregional income disparity is, of course, that special policies and programs are required for this purpose. Both APEC and ECOC have been advocates of the addition of such policies to existing frameworks, although with a difference in emphasis. The regional group has promoted programs to develop the Atlantic Provinces, while the national body has been concerned mainly with introducing regional objectives at the federal level which would also have a built-in consistency with national economic goals.

A second factor, although related to this failure of rapid national growth to solve regional economic problems, has not been so clearly or generally recognized. I believe, however, it is even more important. It is also more fundamental. It is the change in the general circumstances within which Canadian economic policy must be determined in the future, from those which prevailed during the post-Korean War resource boom and, to some extent, throughout the whole postwar period. During the 1950s, we in Canada had few fundamental economic decisions to make for ourselves, and even less opportunity to make them. The essential policy problem was how best to meet the substantial demand for our raw materials and to facilitate their movement to largely external markets. The task for us was not so much to define those sectors (or those areas) where development ought to occur in order to be consistent with national goals and priorities, but rather to find ways and means in which to take advantage of the large and growing—and clearly expressed—United States demand for our raw materials and natural resources. In a sense the policy choice was so obvious as to require neither definition nor discussion. It was also so lucrative an opportunity as to rule out any serious attempt to suggest alternatives. So we geared ourselves up to accommodate the external demand for our natural resources, because that way lay growth, development and a higher standard of living.

I have no quarrel with the policy choice implicit in Canada's response to the conditions which existed a decade or so ago. I merely wish to point out that these circumstances enabled Canadian policy-makers to deal mainly in terms of the programs and projects required to execute a policy which was already exogenously determined. So the nation built the St. Lawrence Seaway and roads to resources, facilitated substantial immigration and as much inter-provincial migration as could be managed in spite of a slow rate of labour force growth, and "managed" the economy through the use of Keynesian monetary and fiscal policies. The "learning experience" gained by the policymakers during this interval thus not only excluded any consideration of regional economic problems, but also—and much more importantly—omitted any serious concern with defining national economic goals and deciding themselves, on the basis of these, what policy should be adopted to promote future development and growth. It was perhaps partly for this reason that Canada did not really recover from the 1957-58 recession until it had become a 1957-61 interlude of stagnation.

The resource boom, incidentally, improved the credibility of the Canadian conventional wisdom that natural resources are the major determinant of both the pace and the location of economic development. They certainly were during the 1950s, but I doubt if that brief experience in one country adequately supports the general conclusion so often drawn by Canadian economists that the natural resource potential of any area largely determines its future economic prospects. Yet an assessment of such potential is the point of departure usually adopted in the attempt to ameliorate the economic conditions of any area within Canada, regardless of the nature of the problem to be solved.

The main point I wish to make here, however, is that we now find ourselves as a country with new problems and much less obvious challenges than those we faced in the 1950s. Moreover, the successful resolution of these problems requires that national policy be carefully determined, simply because the choice is neither so obvious nor so uncomplicated as responding to strong American demand for raw materials. Yet the lack of any real experience of this new environment for policy-making may well lead to our retaining certain popular myths or to our inadequately recognizing the policy parameters which now prevail, and could result in a failure to cope with the challenges, or to take advantage of the opportunities, before us.

The regional problem is but one of the considerations to be taken into account in any determination of Canadian economic policy. But it is imperative that it be introduced at the objective-setting and policy determination stages and taken adequately into account there. There is little point in adding a few, relatively minor regional development programs or projects—which may nevertheless be very costly indeed—at the last stage in the goals-policy-programs and projects sequence, if the national policy is so defined as to omit or effectively rule out any chance of their being successful. If regional problems are to be successfully tackled in Canada, they must become a matter of national economic priority and receive consideration in the goal-setting and policy determination process at the national level.

This is not to suggest that the whole burden of solving regional economic problems lies with the federal government. The Provinces will continue to have important responsibilities for various aspects of regional development, which should not be exercised with only regional problems in mind. Perhaps one of the first steps Provinces can usefully take is to accept that their various expenditure programmes should be consistent with the attainment of national economic objectives and priorities.

Against this general, perhaps sweeping background, the purpose of this paper is a limited one. It is to comment on the objectives which regional economic policy at the national level should seek to achieve, and to consider how we in Canada ought to approach the definition of such regional objectives at the present time.

In Canada the term "regional disparities" formerly meant various statistical measures used in support of the case for special policies to improve economic conditions in the lagging Atlantic Region. It referred not only to lower per capita income, but also to higher unemployment, greater unemployment, lower productivity, lower investment per capita, and so on. Since the Economic Council of Canada undertook its examination of regional economic considerations three years ago, the term has come to connote interregional income disparity. From this it is but a short step to defining the Canadian regional problem as regional income per capita below (or above?) the national average. Once the problem is defined for policy purposes in this way, the obvious (but not necessarily correct) conclusion then is that the objective of regional policy should be to eliminate—or reduce—this "gap".

In this particular context the most important single influence has been Chernick's excellent study for the Economic Council.[3] It is a systematic, careful, thorough examination of trends in provincial personal income per capita over the whole period for which such data are available, which also takes due account of the limitations of both the data and the interpretations that can be placed on their movement over time. The most striking observation Chernick makes, is the dissimilarity of historical experience between Canada and the United States, already noted.

Not so surprisingly, however, Chernick's qualifications do not all survive the process of transplantation of his findings into other publications. In the Economic Council's own Second Annual Review, the contrast between Canadian and American experience with interregional income disparity is used rather forcefully to suggest either the relative peculiarity of Canadian conditions, or a failure adequately to match the American performance, or both. And this without any effective demonstration of the comparability of Canadian and American experience in this respect since 1926, let alone an explanation of the factors accounting for the dissimilarity beyond noting an association, in the American case, "with the regional dispersal of growth capacity so as to embrace southern areas which traditionally had been outside the mainstream of economic advance."[4] At least this appears consistent with the Economic Council's general tendency to regard the United States not only as its main source of economic methodology, but also as the only other national economy with which Canada should be compared.

There is some evidence that the Atlantic Development Board has gone further and accepted the elimination of the disparity between national per capita income and per capita income in its "constituency," the Atlantic Provinces, as the main objective to be achieved through the "plan" it is currently formulating. If so, it is apparently without any published substantiation that this choice of policy objective is suitable, feasible or necessary.

The participants in the current election campaign are inclined not only to consider elimination of the "gap" between national and regional per capita income as the proper objective for Canadian regional policy, but also are in some danger of expecting the "gap" to disappear quite quickly and dramatically once they have an opportunity to implement the changes in regional programs, and agencies, which they apparently have in mind. I do not consider this state of affairs a function of naive or excessive political aspirations. I believe, rather, it reflects the general lack of attention to regional problems in this country in the past, as well as the inadequate interest of Canadian economists in developing a theoretical basis for policy to achieve "regional" objectives.

Let us suppose, for the sake of illustrating this point, that elimination of the "income gap" is a suitable objective for regional policy. Then the relevant question would become, how should policy be designed in order to best achieve this objective? Before we could answer that important, and nagging question, there would be a number of more specific questions to be considered.

The first set of these concern the nature of the indicator being used as the target variable. Elimination of the "income gap" is most frequently interpreted to mean seeking a zero value for the difference between two variables, namely, personal income per capita in Canada and personal income per capita in any (and every?) major Canadian region. Thus policy affecting any single region would be concerned with the influence it has, or can have, on *two* variables.

Further complexity is introduced with a recognition that income per capita is a ratio between total personal income and total population in each geographic entity being considered. Thus the policy variable comprehends not "gap", not more or less comparable measures, but *four* significant and separate variables each subject to direct and indirect policy influence, namely:

Personal Income, Canada
Population, Canada
Personal Income, Region
Population, Region

Nor is there any basis for supposing that policy which affects any one of these will at the same time affect the others, in a way and to a degree that is entirely consistent with narrowing our ''income gap.'' The degree of complexity to be attached to our single target variables becomes even greater, of course, if we extend the system to include all five major economic regions, and not just one as above.

While public policy does influence the population variables, we may treat it for present purposes as simply a means of standardising regions and countries for comparative purposes. This would make personal income the more important variable for regional policy to influence—at least directly. Therefore, the second set of questions concerns the adequacy of the Personal Income measure for use as a target variable in regional policy formulation.

Here it should be noted that personal income has come into use for making interregional comparisons, and before that for measuring the performance of an individual regional economy over time, because it is the best measure of aggregate economic activity at the regional level which is available from the D.B.S. National Accounts. The fact is that personal income is essentially a proxy for gross regional product or (net) regional income. If either of these other measures were available, it would soon be substituted for personal income as a means of assessing and comparing economic performance in the several major regions of the Canadian economy.

In this reasoning I have been supposing that regional policy is mainly concerned with accelerating regional economic development. I recognize this view may not be generally held. It is possible to take the position that regional policy amounts to reducing the per capita ''income gap'' by whatever means seems to be appropriate or feasible. Thus reduction of interregional income disparities may be approached as a development objective, or as a welfare objective, or both. This is due to the composite nature of the personal income measure, which includes both components whose size is determined by the economic status or performance of the region concerned, as in the case of salaries and wages, and components whose size is determined by other factors (including the lack of economic performance within the region concerned) as in the case of government transfer payments. Obviously, policy can seek to eliminate the ''income gap'' by increasing the flow of transfer payments to the less prosperous regions; or policy can pursue the same objective by stimulating the economic development of these regions. The choice between these two alternatives will determine whether regional policy is to be development-oriented or welfare-oriented. It is a fundamental decision in the regional policy making process.

For practical purposes the choice can never be quite so clear cut. Some mix of development and welfare objectives will be necessary. That can readily be admitted.

What should not be ruled out, however, is some attempt to elaborate alternative policy models to be used as aids in determining the character and emphasis of regional policy. If we assume, for example, that regional policy is to be development-oriented, increased transfer payments are eliminated as a proper means of closing the interregional ''income gap.'' Then attention would be focussed on discovering methods of increasing economic activity in the less prosperous regions in order to raise personal income there. The policy problem would then consist in maximising regional "earned" income over time, or in other words, to accelerating the economic development of particular regions. At this point we might as well substitute gross regional product as the target variable for regional policy. Then we can go on to elaborate a policy model for each region setting out the interrelationship among such regional variables as output, income, employment, investment and so on, and indicating which of these can and should be influenced by various possible programs and projects which might be introduced as part of regional policy. There would remain, of course, the necessary task of reconciling regional policy, thus determined, with policy to achieve national economic objectives.

To summarize, I have argued in this section that elimination or reduction of the interregional "income gap" is not a meaningful basis for devising regional policy for essentially four reasons:

(1) The "income gap" implicitly refers to two geographic entities for which policy ought to be devised separately (and then reconciled).
(2) The personal income numerator in the two figures (personal income/population) compared to measure the "gap", is an imperfect measure of economic status or performance at both the national and regional levels. A better target variable for regional economic development policy would be gross regional product (GDP) or (net) regional income.
(3) Since economic policy in Canada is already explicitly concerned with achieving various national economic objectives, the proper focus in regional policy formulation will be on various aggregate variables for each region including, but not restricted to, regional personal income.
(4) On the assumption that regional policy is to be development-oriented rather than welfare-oriented, the main need is to elaborate a policy model showing the interrelationships among various economic variables, such as employment, output and investment, in *each* region. Such a policy model would become the basis for setting objectives and formulating policy suited to their achievement in each region. Five such models would not be a substitute for, but a complement to, a similar model elaborated for the national economy. The national model and the five regional ones would also have to be used together as part of the same process of national-regional objective-setting and national-regional policy formulation.

It would be helpful if there were a ready body of economic theory on which the formulators of Canadian regional policy could draw for assistance. It is fairly obvious, however, that when the policy problem is defined as the narrowing of the "income gap", there is no branch of economic theory capable of immediate use as a basis for policy-making. A general equilibrium framework, perhaps emphasizing the interaction of disparate income levels on the population denominators, is perhaps the nearest thing we might expect. Such a model would imply a welfare orientation. But the main trouble with this approach is that it leaves unanswered the questions, most pertinent in a policy sense, of how the personal income and population variables in the region and in the nation, are to be influenced. The model, even if applicable, requires more detailed specification.

If, however, the policy problem is essentially to stimulate the development of less prosperous regions, the concern would be with the economic development of regions. Two parts of the field, thus defined, may be broadly distinguished, namely, the study of past development in each region and the problems to which it has given rise; and the direction, character, rate and manner of future development which should be fostered. Both have been largely neglected by Canadian economists; but it is future development, with its more immediate relevance for policy, with which we are mainly concerned here.

What basis exists in economic theory for regional economic development?

It should perhaps be noted that economic theory is not itself a coherent, interrelated whole. There is, for example, the well-known general distinction between macroeconomics and microeconomics. Of these two, it seems to me that macroeconomics is more relevant to regional policy than microeconomics because policy for regional economic development—as distinct from programs of projects intended to serve the same purpose—must be based on a proper understanding of the ''macro'' variables affecting each regional economy. The point has already been made that regional income, regional output, regional employment and regional capital investment are the relevant variables. What we are after is something at the regional level that meets the criteria Ackley has suggested as most significant in making Keynesian models usable for macro policy purposes, —the number of variables is small enough to be manageable, hypotheses are (mostly) framed in terms that permit empirical testing and measurement, and among variables isolated are those which are strategic at least for the traditional instruments of monetary and fiscal policy.[5] The difference would be, however, that the strategic variables might encompass more than simply those which can be influenced by traditional monetary and fiscal policy.

Regional economic development may be related in some, usually relevant way to most branches of economic theory. Regions trade with one another, hence some of the theorems of international trade theory may be applied to regions without significant loss of validity.[6] Theories of economic development may also be applied to regions as well as to countries providing the regions are big enough—a criterion which each of Canada's major economic regions more or less satisfies. Income and employment levels are presumably determined for regions by the same sort of factors in the short run that neo-Keynesian theory teaches us to observe at the national level. One must follow Meyer's dictum,[7] however, and avoid defining regional economic development so as to make all of economic theory directly relevant in one way or another to regional policy.

It would be most helpful to have a theory of regional economic development. We do not. A general theory of regional development capable of explaining different sorts of circumstances and of prescribing various suitable lines of policy to meet them, would offer the most skilled theoretical economist a substantial challenge. That such a theory has not emerged to date is perhaps largely due to the greater preoccupation of regional practitioners, whether economists or not, with solving practical problems in this relatively new field of public policy.

However that may be, we are left with considering what theoretical structure may be developed for regional policy from the main, conventional branches of economic theory. Which of these are more important than others? Which offer the greatest promise for empirical testing and/or further refinement? Above all, can they somehow be integrated in a general theory of regional economic development? The answers to these profound questions lie beyond the scope of this paper; but some general observations may be in order.

I have already noted the rather tenuous link drawn between postwar British regional policy and the national full-employment objective. The significant point here perhaps is that no theoretical bridge has been created between the attainment of higher employment in Britain's less prosperous regions and the redistribution of industry policy which is the main means employed in seeking this regional objective. There has been a noticeable leap from the contention that higher regional employment contributes to full employment nationally (or to faster national growth), to analysing, in rather practical terms, the factors which influence a firm's decision to locate or expand its production facilities. In other words, the question of whether the redistribution of industry among British regions is the best, or indeed the only, means of reducing regional unemployment, has never really been explored. That Britain has a regional policy, but no theoretical framework within which the policy is devised, assessed and reformulated, is underlined by the Board of Trade's recent decision — after twenty years — to sponsor an examination of how well the regional policy has worked!

Keynesian theory itself is concerned with short-run income and employment determination. It is thus of little direct relevance for regional economic development which is, presumably, a long-term process.[8]

Contemporary theories of growth have developed from Keynesian theory in an attempt to prescribe methods of achieving steady state growth. As Hirschman has shown, they do not take us very far towards a proper understanding of the regional development process because they do not come to grips with the real factors which can be influenced by policy action to encourage development.[9] Thus there is little available in economic growth theory, as narrowly defined, which might be adapted and used as a theoretical basis for regional policy formulation.

Regional economic development may also, of course, be considered simply as a particular case of economic development. Little has suggested that there are broadly two types of economic development theory: that concerned with explaining the genesis of progress, or the lack of it and the subsequent course of growth; and that concerned with planning growth, hence with breaking the bottlenecks to a forced, more or less state-directed, process of growth.[10] Much of the substance of economic development theory of both types may be applied equally well to lagging regions. The difference, however, is that a region is a part of a national economy and not dependent, therefore, to the same extent upon savings within the region or foreign capital to overcome balance of payments difficulties. The region may instead be able to draw on a flow of investment funds from its national government or, in some cases, by private firms headquartered elsewhere within the same country, without the same restrictions as would be imposed by having its own external equilibrium to maintain.

The inadequacy of economic development theory for adaptation to regions, however, is due to the same sort of reason as the shortcomings of growth theory. There is as yet no single general theory of economic development which is widely accepted. Nor perhaps should we expect one ever to emerge. Economic development is a complex, long-term process in which many factors, not all economic, interact: to expect to find a single theory capable of comprehending all such factors and of being applied to all sorts of development situations would appear, to say the least, unrealistic. At any rate, while many of the factors in development are common to regions and countries, the existing state of economic development theory is too unsettled to allow regional economic development to find a readily applicable junior version therein.

This brief, cursory review of Keynesian income and employment theory, growth theories, and development theory has shown that none in its present state provides a ready guide for regional economic development. Perhaps this only reveals the lack of perfection in these branches of general economic theory. It certainly leaves a clear field for regional economic development to find its own theory based on its own peculiar characteristics and capable of dealing with its own special problems. It leaves a corresponding need to develop a special-purpose theoretical basis for regional policy models and regional policy making.

What conclusions should we draw for Canadian regional policy in the light of the discussion above?

Perhaps the place to begin is by noting that a couple of preliminary, but fundamental, concessions must be made about regional policy. It would be well, first, to recognize that the regional problem is apt to remain a permanent feature of the Canadian economy. There is little point in continuing to expect its solution to be quickly accomplished by a regional spending agency like the Atlantic Development Board[11] or by a half-baked program such as that administered by the Area Development Agency. The problem is more deep-rooted and must be tackled with appropriate adjustments in basic policy, and not merely with programs and projects haphazardly added as, in effect, minor adjustments at the fringes. It is much easier to direct the course of the ship from the bridge than from the engine-room! What is required is basically a commitment to designing and pursuing regional policy, especially on the part of the federal government. The second preliminary but fundamental adjustment required in the conventional way of approaching the regional problem would be to drop the use of "gaps" when the time comes to set regional objectives (for national policy) and to elaborate the regional element of total national policy as part of a coherent whole. The attempt to define the regional problem narrowly as a gap between national and regional values—whether for unemployment rates as in Britain, or per capita income levels as in Canada—is both misleading and inappropriate. It is misleading because it makes the problem seem all too simple; it is inappropriate because it does not provide a helpful framework for policy-making.

With "gaps" set aside, the next step would then seem to be for regional policy makers to consider each of Canada's major economic regions separately and individually at first. This would by no means rule out reconciling regional policy thus determined with national economic objectives; indeed I would regard such reconciliation as part and parcel of the same process of formulating overall economic policy for the whole country, and the next necessary step in that process. The virtue of adopting this individual-region approach would be that policy can then be formulated initially in terms of the macroeconomic variables affecting each regional economy; and this is absolutely necessary if we are to have regional *policy* and not just programs and projects. In this there is no need to be excessively bothered by the bogey of provincialism, first because the Provinces do have powers to influence long-term regional development which may be more telling than those available to Ottawa, and there is no point in ignoring this possibility; secondly, because the Provinces have a concomitant responsibility for considering national economic objectives and priorities, the exercise of which cannot be policed but should be encouraged. In this regard it is just possible too that by having the Provinces play an effective part in regional-national policy formulation, Canada may find a means to greater conformity with the United States experience of converging regional income levels. A renewed, and more purposive, interest in regional policy making on the part of the Provinces may become an effective substitute for the market economy response, or whatever, which brought Southern regions of the U.S. within what the Economic Council has termed "the mainstream of economic advance."

In pursuing this sort of approach, it would be desirable for the federal government and the Province(s) concerned to collaborate in the elaboration of a macroeconomic model for each region to be used as a basis for designing policy to stimulate the region's economic development. In this a number of specific further needs may be cited, although none should be accepted as a sufficient reason for postponing the design of regional policy in the manner suggested here. Regional accounts are the best point of departure for designing regional policy models, and work on improving them should be accelerated; meanwhile, greater use can be made of the regional data that are available. Also, much more study of past movements in such regional macro variables is warranted: Chernick's study has demonstrated the possibilities with the data on per capita income,[12] but the analysis on this front should also be extended to make regional economic history a less neglected field of study and research in Canada. Again, however, the desirability of more historical research need not postpone work on devising suitable regional policy.

In this there is a particular need for those designing the regional models to bear in mind that certain, broader types of policy can be used to influence the regional macro variables more or less directly. Such policy, moreover, is capable of implementation by both Ottawa and the Provinces. There is no real need to rely entirely on programs and projects, especially if a minor policy adjustment may achieve the same result more easily, or less expensively, or even less obtrusively.[13]

Related to the consideration of how policy might be used to affect the macro variables in the individual region, is the whole question of how the region has responded to past policy influences. We know very little about how past policy—whether by design or accident—has influenced regional development in Canada. This field is ripe for investigation, and should not go unexplored much longer. It is not at all helpful, for example, to assume that the Atlantic Provinces' economy has failed to respond to market influences, when it may well be that the effect of federal and provincial economic policy generally has been to erode market influences entirely.

If increased emphasis on the macro variables for regional policy making is suitable, then it gives rise to a corresponding need for much more study of the theoretical aspect involved. Probably the most critical requirement of all is to develop a theoretical framework for Canadian regional policy. As latecomers to this branch of economic policy, we in Canada have the advantage of being able to avoid some of the mistakes others have made elsewhere. Designing a suitable theoretical framework early enough to lay a useful basis for regional policy is one such opportunity afforded us and we could, if we wished, co-operate in this with British economists who are setting out to examine such possibilities in their own country. In view of the present need, and considering also the likelihood of considerable further development of the Canadian economy over the next several decades in which all regions may participate, and which might make Canada an interesting laboratory for testing various regional policy models[14], I should think regional economic development might now become a respectable field even for Canadian academic economists!

Finally, we need to adopt an increased willingness to observe and to analyse the experience of other countries, over that so far displayed by some of our prominent regional practitioners. It is true that we would look long and hard before we would find another country similar to Canada in all respects. But we should be prepared to go deeper, and to get behind institutional differences and immediate circumstances in order to discover the essential similarities as well as the essential differences, for example, between the British regional problem and our own. In this search for essential points of comparison, I believe a greater concentration on the macroeconomic variables affecting each region, and the policy required to influence such variables, can provide the means of considerable illumination.

### Footnotes

1. This paper is based partly on research carried out in the University of Glasgow while I was a lecturer in Political Economy there from 1965 to 1967. This work was greatly stimulated by the guidance of Professor Thomas Wilson, and assisted materially by a Predoctoral Fellowship awarded me by the Canada Council. I am also grateful for helpful comments on an earlier draft to Professor W. Y. Smith, Professor H. K. Larsen, Mr. Arthur C. Parks, Mr. D. J. McDonald and Mr. J. F. O'Sullivan.

2. In an interview with Peter Newman, Mr. Trudeau commented, "The second threat (to Canadian unity) is if the underdevelopment of the Atlantic Provinces is not corrected—not by charity or by subsidies but by helping them become areas of economic growth—then the unity of the country is almost as surely destroyed as it would be by the French-English confrontation." (Saint John, N.B.: *Telegraph-Journal*, April 27, 1968).

3. S. E. Chernick, *Interregional Disparities in Income*, Staff Study No. 14, Economic Council of Canada (Ottawa: Queen's Printer, August 1966).

4. Economic Council of Canada, Second Annual Review, *Towards Sustained and Balanced Economic Growth*, (Ottawa: Queen's Printer, December 1965), p.103.

5. Ackley, Gardner, *Macroeconomic Theory* (New York: Macmillan, 1961), chapter XV.

6. Ohlin attempted to formulate an economic theory specifically about regions within the framework of international trade theory in his *Interregional and International Trade* (Harvard, 1933).

7. John R. Meyer, "Regional Economics: A Survey," (AER, March 1963), p. 20 viz., "An almost unavoidable temptation . . . is to assert that it (regional economics) is simply *all* of economics scaled down to whatever level is required to adequately measure or forecast economic activity for a specific geographic area."

8. A by-product of the association between Keynesian theory and regional policy in Britain has been the study of regional "multipliers". For a stimulating discussion of work in this field, see T. Wilson, "The Regional Multiplier—A Critique," forthcoming.

9. A. O. Hirschman, *The Strategy of Economic Development,* chapter 2.

10. I. M. D. Little and J. M. Clifford, *International Aid,* London: George Allen & Unwin, 1965).

11. See Royal Commission on Canada's Economic Prospects, *Final Report,* (Ottawa: Queen's Printer, 1957), chapter 19, where it was suggested that the provision of basic capital facilities, or infrastructure, over a relatively short period, would enable the Atlantic Region to achieve self-sustaining development and thereby overcome the region's economic difficulties.

12. See also Marvin McInnis, "The Trend of Regional Income Differentials in Canada," *CJE,* I, No.2, (May 1968), pp. 440-470.

13. This would not rule out the use of various programs and projects as supplementary means of seeking to achieve the regional (or the national) objectives. Indeed, such "micro-policies" would doubtless continue to be necessary although the need for them would be reduced in accordance with the success achieved through an improved manipulation of the macro-variables.

14. The fact that we have only five or six major economic regions, and a federal system of government, means that each regional economy can be influenced by the policy of the national government and at least one provincial (regional) government. This distinguishes us in a significant way from both the Western European and U.S. economies.

PHILIP MATHIAS

# Forced growth: Government involvement in industrial development

*Forcing: the process of hastening growth of a plant by an artificial environment and the application of growth-promoting substances obtained from external sources. A forced plant tends to be less robust.*

In the late 1950s, there appeared in Canada a strong "development psychology" among both federal and provincial governments, and lots of hard cash was set aside for programs of assistance to companies prepared to build manufacturing plants in areas of high unemployment or low wages.

At the provincial level, new lending agencies like the Manitoba Development Fund and Nova Scotia's Industrial Estates Ltd. were born, and endowed with the power to borrow large sums of money for assistance programs.

At the federal level, the 1960s brought many major assistance programs such as the Agricultural Rehabilitation and Development Act (ARDA), the Fund for Regional Economic Development (FRED), the Area Development Agency (ADA) and the Atlantic Development Board (ADB).

During the decade, billions of dollars of capital was spent by federal and provincial governments to persuade anyone, from major international corporations to penniless promoters, to build large industrial plants in places in which they would not normally locate. Fish plants were built in the Maritimes and pulp and paper plants in the northern Prairies. A chemical plant in underdeveloped Manitoba established a struggling subsidiary in underdeveloped New Brunswick. An electronics firm uprooted its plant in Ontario to qualify for assistance in Nova Scotia. A small money-losing shipyard moved from New Brunswick, one region of high unemployment, to another, Prince Edward Island. The assistance programs were undoubtedly a success in that much valuable industry did settle in the underdeveloped parts of Canada. But they were only a partial success. A large number of the major manufacturing plants that were built with the help of government money gave rise to widespread contention that the money had not been wisely used.

Many important issues intrude into the development question: foreign ownership, public ownership, the justifiable cost of creating a job, the adequacy of the province as a political unit responsible for resource development, and even the validity of spending large sums of money on development at all. A few of these projects of the 1960s have brought out some of the most crucial dilemmas Canada faces in her economic and social life today.

Before these dilemmas can be examined, the question must first be asked: Why bother to develop the remote parts of Canada at all?

From an economic point of view, the importance of development varies from region to region. In the unpopulated parts of the Northwest Territories, for instance, development simply brings into use the local resources and generates revenue for the several levels of government. There may be no society in the region for it to affect. The same is true of vast regions of Labrador and the northern parts of the Prairie Provinces. But in the more populated southern Prairies, in Quebec and in the Maritimes, industrial development is needed to end poverty and redress social disorders created by sweeping changes in the economic patterns of the country. Many of the places that need industrial development in Canada are old centres of industry or commerce that have been bypassed by new technology or changes in the economy.

In the 1800s, the Maritimes were busy centres of shipbuilding, immigration and transportation. With the development of the steam-driven vessel and the emergence of Ontario as the industrial heart of Canada, the Maritimes started an economic slide from which they have never recovered.

Like the Maritimes in miniature, the city of The Pas in northern Manitoba grew as a railway distribution centre for trappers and the smaller towns of northern Manitoba. It was bypassed when an air service was started to Thompson, an important mining centre farther north. The same sort of thing has happened to Winnipeg, which used to be an important distribution centre for western Canada. This role has diminished, though Winnipeg has managed to build other economic functions in its place.

The regions that have fallen into decline after a commercial heyday suffer special forms of social distress. One of the most serious is the constant drain of the young and the educated away into southern Ontario and British Columbia, where they have better chances of employment. In the period 1946-66, 30% of all the migration that occurred in Canada consisted of movement away from Saskatchewan and 20% consisted of net migration away from Nova Scotia. The only regions enjoying a net gain in population were Ontario, Alberta, and British Columbia. The net result of the population movements is to improve the labour forces of Ontario and British Columbia and to reduce their quality in such provinces as Saskatchewan and Newfoundland. According to the 1966 census, men between the ages of 20 and 44 comprised 17% of the total population in Ontario, whereas in industry-poor Prince Edward Island they comprised only 14% of the population.

Such depletion of the labour force has two effects. It becomes more difficult for industry to find suitable labour in a depleted region, and the market for locally produced consumer products diminishes, making it even less attractive for certain industries to locate there.

Many people in these regions can leave and seek their fortunes elsewhere, but there are some that cannot, such as the Indians, who often have special problems related to discrimination and an inability to understand the demands of an industrial society. The highest populations of Indians are in the two underdeveloped Prairie Provinces of Manitoba and Saskatchewan, where they represent more than 3% of the population. In Ontario and Quebec, Indian people comprise less than 1% of the population. Emigration of part of the working force from provinces like Saskatchewan increases the proportion of the less fortunate within the population, and these become a greater responsibility to the underdeveloped provinces. Industry has to be brought to these people who cannot move away to Ontario and British Columbia.

As well as high unemployment in the underdeveloped regions of Canada, there is also a markedly lower level of wages in the jobs that are available in these places. The personal disposable income per capita in Ontario in 1968 was $2,520 a year, 13% above the national average, and the highest in Canada. In Newfoundland, on the other hand, personal disposable income was $1,280 per capita, about half of Ontario's. Weekly earnings in Newfoundland averaged $99.15, considerably lower than the Ontario average of $113.52.

These disparities of income and opportunity in the underdeveloped regions tend to disturb national harmony. The people of the Prairies believe their economic misfortunes are partly due to discrimination against them by Ottawa and the Canadian business establishment in Ontario. The election of the Liberal Government of Robert Bourassa in Quebec in the turbulent times of 1970 on a platform of economic progress demonstrates that even cultural troubles can be partly soothed by economic remedies.

As well as economic, humanitarian and political reasons for industrial development, there may be important cultural reasons. In many, many things Canadian, there appears to be a powerful centrifugal force at work. The population hugs the border with the United States, and the eastern and western sea coasts. Industry is even less well distributed. Most of it is in the "golden horseshoe" around international Lake Ontario and in the Pacific rim provinces of Alberta and British Columbia. This centrifugal tendency is also evident in culture. Many Canadians of even second and third generation like to preserve their identity by remaining partly British, French, Ukrainian or perhaps Mennonite.

The result is a "cultural mosaic," which many Canadians proudly distinguish from the "melting pot." But there seems to be little Canadian cultural cement between the ethnic tiles of the mosaic, and so it might perhaps be reasonable to look for the cement in such places as Vermilion, Alberta, and St. Jones Without, Newfoundland, which are not subject to the same international influences as Toronto and Winnipeg. Industrial development in these places might help Canada to become a more homogeneous nation with the distinct personality so many Canadians seek.

The first major development program instituted by the federal government in the 1960s was the Agricultural Rehabilitation and Development Act (ARDA). Its primary purpose, initially, was to help impoverished farmers by improving their land, relocating them off marginal land, and increasing output. ARDA later turned its attention to basic deficiencies in farm structure and organization, and from there to a "total approach" to resource development, involving the expenditure of several hundreds of millions of dollars on mining, fishing and industry, to help rural areas break out of poverty.

Other federal programs were subject to the same continual change as the ARDA program, and some confusion and lack of enthusiasm developed among the civil servants administering these programs in Ottawa.

In 1962, the Atlantic Development Board (ADB) was created to advise the Atlantic Provinces on the best ways to attract development. In 1963, the Board was provided with funds totalling $100 million to implement an overall plan for the Atlantic Provinces and to build up the region's infrastructure: roads, electric power, services at industrial sites, etc. The Atlantic Provinces have the lowest incomes in Canada and the highest unemployment. In 1968, the average personal income in Newfoundland was only 55% of the Canadian average. In Prince Edward Island, it was 63% of the average, in Nova Scotia 78%, and in New Brunswick 71%. On the Prairies, average personal income in 1968 was closer to the Canadian average, the lowest being Saskatchewan's at 90% of the national average. Unemployment in Newfoundland often runs at two or three times the national average and the seasonal swings in employment are extreme. When the Atlantic Development Board had spent all of its $200 million, it resumed the role of an advisory body.

In 1963, the federal government formed the Area Development Agency (ADA) to "encourage industrial development in areas of chronic unemployment on a planned basis." In July 1965, ADA was provided with what became its main development instrument—generous incentive grants provided by the Area Development Incentives Act. Under a program that lasted until March 31, 1971, ADA offered cash grants to secondary industry establishing in designated areas, which contained most of Canada's chronic unemployment and low-income regions. The program provided for cash grants of up to $5 million to be made to any company building new manufacturing or processing facilities in these areas or to firms that were engaged in expansion.

In late 1967, doubts were raised about the effectiveness of some of the federal government's programs. An Economic Council of Canada study prepared by research economists of the Canadian Centre for Community Studies declared that the hundreds of millions of dollars being paid out under ARDA, the Prairie Farm Rehabilitation Act (PFRA), and the Maritimes Marshland Rehabilitation Act (MMRA) were not producing a net benefit to the economy. The PFRA alone had spent about $300 million in the previous 30 years on soil and water conservation and projects to stabilize the Prairie economy. The Economic Council study said: "From the hundreds of projects listed in the ARDA catalogue, it would not be difficult to pick out many in which the taxpayer pays one dollar so that the farmer somewhere in the fringe area can make 50 cents." Talks between Ottawa and the provinces got under way within a few months of the report to change the thrust of the ARDA agreement.

As well as grants, the federal government has used tax relief incentives to encourage development. In the budget of 1963, Finance Minister Walter Gordon introduced generous tax incentives for companies locating in the designated areas of ADA. Initially these incentives were to expire in December 1965. They consisted of a three-year tax holiday and provision for write-off of up to 50% of the depreciable value of machinery in any one year and of 20% of the depreciable value of buildings. Normal rates of depreciating machinery and buildings for tax purposes are 20% and 5% or 10%. The benefit of rapid write-off is that it heavily reduces taxes in the early years so that an early, high return on investment can be achieved. The quick profits can be reinvested and made productive in other plants.

These generous write-off and tax incentives had a powerful effect, and undoubtedly contributed to the capital expansion boom of 1966-67. Large numbers of pulp and paper mills were built in remote places like Lac Quévillon and Portage du Fort, Quebec, in order to qualify for the incentives, though these mills were also built as a competitive reaction to expansion triggered in British Columbia by provincial policies of the time.

The most flexible and probably the most valuable federal assistance plan was launched in mid-1969, when the federal government introduced a new incentive grant scheme to combat regional disparity, under which the maximum grant to an individual applicant was raised from the $5 million stipulated by the ADA program to $12 million. The regions in which these grants were available included most of the Maritime Provinces, eastern Quebec, a broad region stretching across Ontario at the same latitude as Winnipeg, the southern quarter of Manitoba, strips of Alberta and Saskatchewan to the south of Regina and Calgary, and the southeastern corner of British Columbia. The regions designated by the Department of Regional Economic Expansion have been fixed for three years, to July 1, 1972. Before that date, there is to be a review after consultation with the provinces.

The amount of assistance dispensed by Ottawa under the new scheme has been doubled to $100 million a year, and the amounts available to individual companies have also been increased. There are two qualifications: the amount paid on any plant may not be more than $30,000 per new job created nor more than 50% of the capital employed in the operation. The new program has also been streamlined and made much more flexible than the old.

In the late 1950s and early 1960s, many provincial agencies for attracting industry were created. The most controversial have been the Manitoba Development Fund (MDF) and Nova Scotia's Industrial Estates Ltd. (IEL). Both IEL and MDF were made responsible to a board of directors which, though appointed by the Government, was not directly responsible to the Government for the activities of the corporation. The directors were all members of the business establishment. Both corporations were headed by drum-beating promoters, Rex Grose and Bob Manuge, tough, hard-working salesmen who would travel around the world to personally persuade business tycoons to come to Nova Scotia or Manitoba. The style was the same; some critics called it "twanging the old-boy network," an activity facilitated by having leaders of the business community on the boards of directors. Manuge and Grose would both work out "deals" with companies they felt they could persuade to come to their province, offering incentives that were often not made fully public.

The more secretive of these two Crown corporations was the Manitoba Development Fund, which was enjoined by law not to make public the details of loans made to companies settling in the province. This provision gave the Fund considerable freedom to offer loans of magnitude that might have raised controversy had the details been made public. Under the Development Corporation Act passed in 1970, the NDP government of Premier Ed Schreyer changed the name of the MDF to the Manitoba Development Corporation (MDC). MDC now makes details of its loans public and is empowered to take equity in a corporation to which it grants assistance. The taking of equity will enable the MDC to share in the management and the profits of the assisted company. In some cases, the old MDF lent 80% of a plant's cost without participating in the ownership or profits of the company through its equity. In

1971, in a move suggesting a similar restructuring, Nova Scotia's Industrial Estates Ltd. was subjected to a searching investigation by the new Liberal Government of Premier Gerald Regan, who wanted a detached cost benefit analysis of its 13-year record.

Unlike the Manitoba Development Fund, which borrowed money on the market against MDF bonds guaranteed by the Government, the Saskatchewan Economic Development Corp. (Sedco), another provincial lending agency, borrows from the Saskatchewan treasury against Sedco securities. Sedco also keeps the details of its loans secret, but there has been no major controversy over Sedco, which has always been much less in the limelight than the Manitoba Development Fund. In Saskatchewan, under the Liberal government of Premier Ross Thatcher, development decisions have been taken openly by the Premier. In Manitoba, the previous Progressive Conservative governments claimed the MDF made its decisions independent of Cabinet control.

The provincial lending agencies make it much easier for local companies to borrow development capital. As the agency is on the spot, the borrower can call at the head office and present his case much more convincingly in person. The agency can also appraise an enterprise in terms of local conditions and can call on the expertise of government officials who are well acquainted with the local economy. Managerial ability of a prospective borrower can be more easily gauged by a face-to-face interview. Some government agencies also say that they can make a loan much more quickly than most commercial institutions. These factors tend to overcome the disadvantage felt by Prairie or Maritime companies trying to deal with the local branches of a bank that has its head office in remote Ontario.

But the greatest service the provincial lending agencies provide is that they act as lenders of last resort and will usually take a greater risk than a commercial lender.

On the other hand, there are indications that the provincial lending agencies suffer from parochialism and a very limiting form of penny-pinching. In several of the controversial projects that went ahead in Manitoba, Nova Scotia and Prince Edward Island in the 1960s, there is evidence that few people on the staff of the provincial lending agency or in the civil service had the expertise to really assess whether a given project was a valid economic proposition or contained a reasonable financing agreement. In Manitoba, a provincial civil servant with a little paper mill expertise would have been able to tell very quickly that the capital cost figures quoted for the ''$100 million'' paper and lumber complex at The Pas were too high according to ordinary standards. Shocked by the quantity of money absorbed by the Churchill Forest Industries paper complex at The Pas, Premier Schreyer's government has appointed a pulp and paper engineer to the staff of the Manitoba Development Corporation.

Another clear case where provincial authorities were not able to handle the technical side of a project is the heavy water plant in Glace Bay, Nova Scotia.

The financing of the Prince Albert pulp mill in Saskatchewan, financed with the help of the Saskatchewan government and controlled by the New York based firm of Parsons & Whittemore, involves a finely calculated distribution of risks and profits between the Government and its entrepreneur partner and contains many precautions for protecting the Government's interests. But some of the misleading information that has found its way into the press suggests that few officials of the Saskatchewan Government understand the complicated financing of the Prince Albert mill. The agreement appears to have been designed by Parsons & Whittemore, a company which has accumulated much expertise in paper industry matters and world markets. What sort of agreement, though, might have been drawn up if Saskatchewan had entered into partnership with a company less scrupulous and less expert than Parsons & Whittemore?

The lack of the proper experts in provincial governments is attributable to a misguided search for economy and the few occasions in the past when an expert on, say, heavy water production might be needed by a provincial government. But it is also partly due to the ease with which a government can call upon the services of independent consultants for a particular project without incurring the expense of employing them permanently. However, this involves another set of problems, as Manitoba has discovered in its experience with the pulp and paper mill at The Pas. It is generally admitted that an independent consultant may be subject to pressure to provide its client with the sort of advice he would like to hear, rather than the sort of advice he should get.

The drift of Canada's poorer provinces towards larger units may tend to remove some of these shortcomings. In late 1970, a report was published recommending that the Maritime Provinces join to form a single regional government. The Prairie Premiers, in the same period, were also developing joint policies on universities and other regional matters. Bigger "provinces" would be able to hire more experts and economists to evaluate proposals from companies asking assistance and to work out more of the sophisticated and imaginative deals that are needed to attract industry and make it viable.

Another advantage of the larger units would be a reduction in competition between the provinces for development industries.

Such competition has tended to increase the price that is ultimately paid for the prize by the winner. Before it settled in Manitoba, the Churchill Forest Industries group was holding talks with the government of Quebec over the possibility of building a paper mill there. Undoubtedly, the price Manitoba paid for the Churchill Forest Industries complex was affected by the need to attract it away from Quebec. In early 1970, the Michelin tire group of France decided to build three plants costing $100 million in Nova Scotia, but only after a period of fierce competition between Nova Scotia and Quebec to capture them. The intrigue behind the scenes even involved pressure by Charles de Gaulle on the Michelin company in favour of a Quebec location. Michelin stubbornly stuck to its decision to locate the plants in Nova Scotia, and is receiving $50 million assistance.

Competition for development also taxes the facilities and patience of Canada's commercial counsellors in the embassies abroad. Some say there is a continual stream of industrial commissioners from the cities and the provinces through the embassies. They ask that thousands of leaflets be distributed and that the special advantages of their particular city or region be extolled to local industrialists who might be interested in expansion in North America.

A provincial government that has decided to offer assistance to promote local industry would appear to have a choice of three partners in development—a

Canadian company, a Crown corporation or a foreign-owned company. But in reality the province is often left with little alternative but to go along with a foreign-owned company, distressing though the implications may be for long-term control of the Canadian economy. Canadian companies may not have the resources or the imagination or even sometimes the inclination to build a major plant where an underdeveloped province needs it. Before Saskatchewan entered into an agreement with Parsons & Whittemore Inc. of New York for a pulp mill at Meadow Lake, it asked for proposals from major Canadian pulp and paper companies and received none.

Crown corporations are usually not acceptable—even to a New Democratic party government. Manitoba's NDP government, elected in 1969, had to tread cautiously over the use of Crown corporations for development for fear of frightening away businesses that might have been thinking of coming to Manitoba. Besides, a Crown-owned paper company, for example, would find it difficult to compete in the North American market, where all other companies are in the private sector.

At first glance there would appear to be many Canadian precedents for the creation of Crown-owned development corporations. But in fact, few of Canada's Crown corporations are inspired by the need to create jobs for the unemployed or to help the unfortunate. Provincial ownership of Canada's power generation and distribution facilities is as much for the benefit of free-enterprise industry which needs a reliable power source as it is for the domestic user. Other Crown corporations have been set up for special historical reasons. Canadian National Railway Co. was formed by the merger of several private railroads in northern Canada that were unable to operate profitably but were needed for development of such places as Sudbury and Timmins. Air Canada was created because there was not sufficient private capital to set up a Canadian-owned airline. Polymer Corp., the rubber producer in Sarnia, was formed during World War II because Canada needed a rubber producer in a hurry. From time to time, there have been movements to have these companies transferred back into the realm of private enterprise and out of the hands of government ownership, rather than to make more Crown corporations.

But there are precedents for province-owned development corporations even in non-socialist governments. Liberal Premier Jean Lesage's Quebec government (1960-66) set up, in 1964, Sidbec, the province-owned steel mill, after unsuccessfully talking to big steel companies in the private sector.

The shunning of "socialism" has driven several provincial governments into arrangements in which they have paid all or most of the expenses of establishing a plant, using a promoter or a company as a "private enterprise" front that gave the project political respectability. In the Churchill Forest Industries forest-products complex at The Pas, Manitoba, and in the Gulf Garden Foods fish plant in Prince Edward Island, the provincial governments put up almost all the money, and the profits—if any had been generated—would have gone entirely to the promoters.

If neither a Canadian partner nor a Crown corporation is available to develop a particular resource, a province is left with the choice of not developing and leaving its people unemployed or taking a foreign partner. The passage into US hands of an established Canadian company like Ryerson Press, Toronto, in late

1970 may be deplorable, but different standards of judgment must surely be applied to concessions made to foreign interests in underdeveloped regions. Two heavy water plants give a pungent commentary. Near the provincially owned heavy water plant at Glace Bay—a $120 million disaster—is a smart new heavy water plant being operated efficiently by the Canadian subsidiary of a major US company, General Electric Co. For its fish plant, Prince Edward Island would have done better to bring in a competent US company like the food, chemicals and packaging conglomerate W. R. Grace & Co., rather than to pour $10 million into the hands of a virtually unknown Canadian promoter. The pulp mills built in Saskatchewan by Parsons & Whittemore may be financed in a way that is favourable to the American company, but what real alternative was available to the Government of Saskatchewan to diversify its wheat and potash economy?

The most successful development is the mighty Churchill Falls in Labrador by a largely British-owned consortium. Newfoundland will reap nothing but profit from Churchill Falls, though its development was agonizing at times. The creation of Saskatchewan's two pulp mills will also probably prove a success, though the assumption by the province of a risk of about $150 million has been necessary and the deal is rather generous to the private partner. Into Prince Edward Island's fish plant, Manitoba's forest-product complex, and Nova Scotia's heavy-water plant, about $220 million of precious public funds have been poured. Only one of the plants—the fish plant—is close to proving it can operate normally and at full capacity.

T. BREWIS
# Planning for Development

## The Concept and Growth of Planning

One of the notable features of the post-war economic scene has been the widespread adoption of economic plans. Before the Second World War the Soviet Union was almost alone in the world in the planning of its economy, but the scene has now changed to such an extent that countries which do not have some kind of a program as a framework for development may well be in the minority. Admittedly, the nature and extent of planning differ widely from one country to another. The Soviet methods of planning have little in common with those of, say, France. None the less, the disposition of countries to prepare economic plans of one form or another is not only widespread but seemingly increasing.

At an early stage in the operation of the World Bank, it became apparent that if aid to the less developed countries was to be effective, it would need to be integrated with various government policies to form a coherent framework; since then, the Bank has assisted a great many countries to prepare comprehensive development programs. The experience gained by the Bank in working with underdeveloped countries is not without relevance to a discussion of the development of depressed areas in the wealthier countries. In both the less and the more developed countries the provision of individual assistance on a project by project basis is open to criticism. To achieve maximum results, projects have to be related to each other and formulated in the context of other institutional developments.

In preparing a plan, the desirable lines of development are clarified, and the very act of preparing one is a useful exercise in itself, for it focuses attention on the objectives and problems to be overcome, the information required, and the prerequisites for fulfilment. It is the purpose of planning to ensure coherence and co-ordination. Failing these, waste and dislocation are likely to result. Though development planning is primarily concerned with the economic sphere, it is likely to affect political, social, and administrative spheres as well, for these are all interrelated. In some cases social attitudes may be one of the greatest impediments to economic change.

In Canada the subject of planning has been brought to the fore not only as a result of rural development under the FRED legislation and through the functions of the Atlantic Development Board but also, as noted in the following chapter, through the planning operations of certain provincial governments.

However, it was not until the 1960s that regional planning evoked any significant interest in Canada, and considerable doubt remains in many quarters as to its nature, purpose, and wisdom.

It is the intention of this paper to touch very briefly on the planning process which is of increasing concern to some of the provinces. The term "planning" conveys different things to different people. In common usage it covers a wide spectrum from the detailed and comprehensive direction of an entire economy by a government to the lesser efforts of public or private agencies to co-ordinate various aspects of economic policy. In the view of one writer on the subject, economic planning is a "comprehensive and co-ordinated social action to guide the future course of the economy".[1] The Atlantic Development Board for its part regards planning as the formulation of a comprehensive set of mutually consistent policy proposals, arranged in order of priority, scheduled over a period of time, and directed toward the attainment of given objectives. In the present context, regional economic planning is understood to mean the establishment of specific regional economic objectives couched in operational terms and the selection and implementation of measures to achieve them.

Planning for regional development has much in common with planning for development at the national level, but there are various issues which, at least in Canada, can largely be disregarded in planning at the regional level. Among these are the international balance of payments and its impact on national price levels and credit conditions. On the other hand, interregional flows of labour, goods, and capital are of particular importance in regional planning. A reduction in unemployment in the Atlantic provinces may influence levels of migration materially, and the increased incomes that result may lead to a rise in "imports" from other parts of the country, with repercussions on the interregional flow of funds. At the moment very little is known about these interregional relationships in Canada, but discussion and experience in other countries leaves little doubt of their importance. We know, for instance, that the movement of workers to and from Northern Ireland is greatly influenced by the relative availability of jobs in England. Improved conditions in Northern Ireland lead to a reduction in the exodus of workers and to some extent there is a reverse flow, so that unemployment diminishes less than would otherwise be the case. Similarly, when the labour market is very tight in England, English firms tend to expand their operations in Northern Ireland; then when the pressures slacken they tend to reduce them. The same kind of pattern may well operate in the Atlantic provinces.

The size of the region selected for planning is itself a matter of crucial importance—the smaller the area selected, the more important the flows into and out of the area are likely to be. Thus a major investment in a small area may lead to a heavy influx of workers from outside so that there is virtually no change in the employment situation of workers who are long-time residents of the area.

A distinction needs to be drawn between the plan itself and the process involved in its preparation. The plan is the end product. Unless the information on which it is based has been adequately prepared, it is unlikely to be of much use and may indeed prove detrimental to development. Since the information that ideally one might wish to have is never likely to be complete, at some stage enquiry has to give way to decisions. The enquiry stage can be so prolonged that the plan itself is unduly delayed. This appears to have been the case with the Atlantic Development Board. Detailed studies extending over several years have still to find their expression in a plan for the Atlantic region. Several factors have accounted for the delay, among them an earlier lack of interest at the political level.

Before continuing with a discussion of the actual process of planning, it may be helpful to note the meaning of certain expressions commonly used in planning terminology. A "comprehensive rural development" is, to quote from the FRED legislation, "a program, consisting of several development projects, that is designed to promote the social and economic development of a special rural development area and to increase income and employment opportunities and raise living standards in the area, and that makes provision for participation by residents of the area in the carrying out of the program".[2] The Agreement Covering a Comprehensive Rural Development Plan for the Interlake Area of Manitoba[3] defines "development strategy" as the means by which the objectives of the Agreement will be promoted in the Special Rural Development Area; "plan" as the over-all design for implementing the rural development strategy; "program" as a definite course of intended proceedings for a major operation within the plan; and "project" as an undertaking with specific objectives that forms a self-contained unit within a program.

## The Process of Planning

Action has to be taken on several fronts in the preparation of a plan. One of these is the collection of information which will serve as the basis for establishing clearly defined objectives. Such information will include data on resources; on the labour force, its size, composition, rate of growth, and skills; on the economic structure of the region; on the various types of economic activity, primary, secondary, and tertiary, and the changes that are occurring therein; and especially on potentialities for growth. Much of this information is unlikely to be available and will have to be collected.[4]

Typically, the planning process begins with the furnishing of certain estimates at the macro level, and this is accompanied by more detailed projections for individual industries and sectors. Thus, assuming the objective is to provide employment for the expected growth in the labour force of the region over a specified period of time, required output can be calculated in aggregative terms, using a national accounts type of framework. The probable deficiency in output needed to achieve the requisite level of employment can then be ascertained on the basis of past and current growth trends and productivity. The magnitude of the gap will suggest an objective in aggregative terms and alternative ways of closing it can be examined. Along with this, the potentiality of specific industries can be explored in detail, and in the light of the projections estimates can be made of future total output and employment. Here there is often a temptation to review the potential largely from the standpoint of supply and to give insufficient thought to possible changes in demand which are equally deserving of attention. But even granting this qualification, the summing of the sectoral data will still not be an adequate exercise in itself, for the sectors are interrelated, and the assumptions regarding potential output in one will have implications for others. Adjustments must be made on this account, and upon their completion the detailed industry estimates will permit a refining of the estimates made at the macro level.

The determination of general goals, such as the reduction of income disparities and unemployment, may be taken at an early stage; but without a clear awareness of the potentialities of the region it is unwise to be too specific, for the costs of attaining such goals may prove to be excessive. There is no point in establishing targets without regard for the costs of their attainment. For example, it may appear possible to raise per capita incomes in the employed labour force by increased investment, but increases in labour productivity and wages associated with larger capital inputs may lead to a reduction in the number of workers required. To increase local employment substantially at the same time as incomes are raised nearer national levels might thus involve extensive intervention on the part of the federal government, more perhaps than is considered justifiable or politically feasible. Objectives, in short, should not be spelled out in detail until their implications are clear; but until they are spelled out they cannot form an adequate basis for a plan. As an illustration, a general goal to reduce income disparities between the Atlantic region and the rest of the country, without stating the amount by which they are to be reduced or the time period involved, is not sufficient, though it can serve as a starting point.

The time period over which the plan is to be fulfilled must also be decided. There is something to be said for setting up both a long-run plan, which will make it easier to maintain a sense of direction, and a short-run plan, which will indicate the immediate steps to be undertaken. Ideally, the short-run plan should be tied in with the preparation of the annual budgets at the provincial level to ensure effective implementation and avoid conflict.

Inevitably there will be developments that were not foreseen or correctly appraised at the outset, and for this reason some flexibility has to be maintained. To allow for these, the plan should be kept under constant review and modified in accordance with the need for change. A static plan will quickly become obsolete. A compromise must be struck, however, between excessive change on the one hand and undue inflexibility on the other.

Target rates for the growth of the more important sectors of the economy, based on past trends and an evaluation of future possibilities should be established. There will undoubtedly be differences of opinion as to what constitutes a feasible rate of growth for various sectors of the economy, and an indication of the range of opinion is desirable. The estimates can then be reviewed at the over-all planning stage, and the interrelationship of the various sectors can be examined with a view to avoiding inconsistencies between them. For example, if a recommended rate of development of a particular industry calls for a certain input of skilled labour, the supply must be adequate. This may in turn have implications for the construction of technical schools and the training of instructors.

For certain purposes and for larger regions, it would be helpful to have an input-output table prepared, so that the implications of expansion in one industry can be traced through to every other, but the construction of such tables is a demanding undertaking and the manpower available for such a task is in very limited supply.[5] Such tables, moreover, need to be kept up to date. This is of increasing importance when significant changes are contemplated in the structure of a region, that will result in new relationships between industries. An industry might continue to draw upon local supplies until it reaches a certain size, then turn to outside suppliers. Alternatively, an industry might attract new sources of local supply as it grows, decreasing its dependence on imports from outside. Once the market reaches a certain size, new plants may be attracted which would formerly have found it unprofitable to operate there. The more rapidly a region grows, the more likely are inter-industry relationships to shift. A mere projection of past relationships may thus prove seriously misleading.

Account should also be taken of changes in consumption patterns, which are to be expected as incomes rise. In some cases these will lead to an expansion in local purchases, in other cases to the opposite, as where consumers turn to larger urban centres which offer a wider range of choice of superior goods. There are, in short, non-linearities in production and consumption.

Having something in common with input-output analysis is industrial-complex analysis. The limitations of input-output studies have encouraged a related but quite distinct approach to the subject of inter-industry relationships, and it has important implications for those engaged in regional planning. Specific inter-industry connections may be essential to profitable production, and important external economies may emerge as development takes place. Although it has features in common with the input-output matrix, industrial-complex analysis has certain advantages from the standpoint of those engaged in efforts to encourage regional growth. This kind of analysis outlines in more detail than is possible in an input-output table the relationships existing within a relatively narrow range of activities, and it does not have to depend on the historical evidence of past inter-industry coefficients. What it loses in breadth, it gains in depth and flexibility.[6]

## The Strategy of Development

As mentioned above, one of the major functions of the planning process is to make as clear as possible the relative advantages and disadvantages of alternative courses of action, so that the strategy of development can be decided upon. To achieve economies of scale, it may seem wise to encourage the re-structuring of certain industries and the re-grouping of population in new urban centres. Various ways of accomplishing this are likely to present themselves and a choice between them will need to be made. But it is necessary not only to decide where the main thrusts of policy are to be directed and the form they should take but also to ensure that the machinery for implementation is adequate. This last is of particular importance. The administrative machinery for the fulfilment of development plans is often weak. Development planning is a new art and traditional practices have to be designed and refashioned to accomplish it.

Given the limitations of staff and data as well as the need to obtain public understanding and support, there is likely to be merit in keeping the plan fairly simple, concentrating on those areas where agreement can most easily be reached and where the powers to implement change are likely to be most readily available. This will frequently be in the area of public investment, and a useful first step is often the co-ordination of various public investment expenditures. It is not uncommon to find expenditures are being undertaken by a number of bodies with different objectives. Changes in the private sector are likely to be less amenable to public influence, but much will depend on how closely the government and the private sector have co-operated in arriving at decisions on how to develop a region. There are occasions when sanctions may be necessary, but as a general rule it is preferable to avoid these and create conditions which ensure that the incentives offered by the private sector harmonize with the public interest. In a democratic society public support for the plan is indispensable. Without it the whole process is likely to be in vain.

### Footnotes

1. H. E. English, "The Nature of Democratic Economic Planning," *Canadian Public Administration,* VIII, No. 2 (June 1965), p. 125. This volume of the journal and Vol. IX, No. 2 (June 1966) contain a number of contributions on the subject of planning, including regional planning. See also T. N. Brewis and Gilles Paquet, "Regional Development and Planning in Canada: an Exploratory Essay," a paper presented to the annual meeting of the Canadian Political Science Association in Ottawa, June 1967, *Canadian Public Administration,* XI, No. 2 (Summer 1968), pp. 123-62. Several enlightening papers on the subject of planning in Canada have been prepared by the Policy and Planning Directorate of ARDA, containing observations arising out of experience. See for example, *ARDA and Poverty: Lessons in Developmental Planning* by Leonard D. Poetschke, a mimeographed paper prepared for presentation at the Canadian Agricultural Economic Society Annual Meeting in Hamilton, Ontario, June 25, 1968.

2. Bill c. 151 p. 2, para. 5(a).

3. Department of Forestry and Rural Development, *op. cit.,* p.8.

4. There have been many works in recent years on the subject of planning. A good brief introduction to the subject is Jan Tinbergen's *The Design of Development,* a publication of the Economic Development Institute, International Bank for Reconstruction and Development (Baltimore, Md.: Johns Hopkins Press, 1958). A more technical study is J. R. Boudeville's *Problems of Regional Economic Planning* (Edinburgh: The University Press, 1966). See also W. Arthur Lewis, *Development Planning: The Essentials of Economic Policy* (London: Allen & Unwin, 1966).

5. Input-output analysis is a powerful analytical tool in the study of economic development, showing in detail how changes in one or more sectors of the economy will affect the total economy. For an excellent introduction to the subject see William H. Miernyk, *The Elements of Input-Output Analysis* (New York: Random House, 1965). In Canada quantitative data on the economic relationship between regions in the form of input-output tables have only recently become available. The input-output study of the Atlantic provinces, which was completed under the direction of Kari Levitt, extended over several years and was completed only a short time ago.

6. An analysis along these lines is currently being undertaken for the government of New Brunswick.

# CHARLES E. McLURE, JR.

# Tax Incentives for Regional Development: A Critical Comment

*The problem of raising the income level of inhabitants of depressed regions is a chronic one in Canada, and one to which there is no final solution. There are, however, various ways of attempting a solution. These ways may be said to polarize on incentives tied to capital and incentives tied to labour. And Professors McLure and Bird are at opposite poles. All that an editor can add is that obviously there is much to be said on both sides. . . .*

## 1. Introduction

In a paper presented to the 1968 Conference of the Canadian Tax Foundation Professor Richard Bird questioned the wisdom of basing tax incentives (or subsidies) for regional economic development upon labour input rather than upon capital input.[1] Bird's argument can be summarized by the following quotation from his paper:

> This panel is concerned with policies aimed at reducing "regional dispar-ity", that is, the spread between average per capita incomes in different regions of the country. These income differences in large part reflect differences in the productivity of labour. If we assume for the purpose of the present argument that labour in the poor regions is not to be moved to the rich regions, then the only direct way to reduce the regional productiv-ity differential, and thus the regional income disparity, is to increase the capital-labour ratio in the poor regions. In terms of this analysis, then, any subsidies or incentives should be aimed primarily at producing the highest possible inflow of capital into the poor regions per dollar of public expenditure on the subsidy. . . .
> . . . the crucial purpose of regional tax incentive policy is to induce *more* capital to flow into the region and, for a given revenue cost . . . this end can be achieved more effectively with incentives focused on capital rather than on labour or on production. (pp. 193, 198-9; italics in original.)

The purpose of the present critical comment is to question the validity of Bird's argument. Incentives related to the use of capital are likely to be more efficient in attracting capital to the depressed region than incentives tied to labour. But attracting capital to the region is likely to be only a proximate goal, the final objective being to raise the income level of inhabitants of the depressed region,[2] and in general it is neither necessary nor sufficient for the achievement of this ultimate goal to attract capital to the region.

Section 2 below compares capital and labour incentives as means of raising incomes in the depressed region.[3] It is concluded that in general capital subsidies cannot be more effective than labour subsidies in raising the wage rate or employment level in the depressed region. Section 3 discusses briefly considerations that qualify this conclusion. Though they play no part in Bird's argument for a capital subsidy, there may be good reasons for favouring incentives tied to capital rather than to labour.

## 2. The Factor Proportions Argument

Geographic immobility of labour is at the heart of the case for tax incentives for economic development. Either because labour is unable to earn a socially acceptable wage even if fully employed or because there exists regional unemployment (or underemployment), regional incentives are advocated. Raising the wage rate or the level of employment in the region appears to be the goal of policy, and is accepted in what follows.

### THE FULL-EMPLOYMENT CASE

If labour is fully employed in the depressed region, but unable to earn an "adequate" wage, public policy presumably would aim at raising the wage rate. A subsidy based on the wage bill would do so directly. It would attract no capital to the region, and therefore it would have no effect upon output, the capital-labour ratio, or the productivity of labour; it would simply raise wages directly by the amount of the subsidy. Because labour is immobile, such a subsidy would be analytically equivalent to the classical tax on land.

The method by which a capital subsidy would raise the wage rate, if indeed it did so, would be quite different. In general such a subsidy can be expected to attract capital to the region and thus to raise the region's capital-labour ratio, as Bird has indicated. But this is not enough to guarantee that the wage rate would rise as a result of the subsidy. Suppose that demand for the output of the region is quite insensitive to price. Then the increased output resulting from the augmentation of the capital stock in the region would drive down the average price of the region's products. It is quite possible for this depressing effect on the wage rate resulting from lower product prices to outweigh the positive influence resulting from the rise in the amount of capital per man in the region, especially if capital can easily be substituted for labour in the industries of the depressed region.

Naturally, this perverse effect need not occur. If the depressed region's products are fairly good substitutes for those produced in the rest of the nation and capital cannot easily be substituted for labour, the capital subsidy would raise the wage rate, as Bird assumes. But on the basis of the static considerations fundamental to Bird's arguments, the capital subsidy cannot raise the wage rate by more than an equally expensive subsidy to labour.[4]

## THE UNEMPLOYMENT OR UNDEREMPLOYMENT CASE

In many developing countries the existence of a traditional sector in which workers can receive incomes greater than their potential wages in the advanced sector in effect places a floor under the wage rate.[5] The result is underemployment, often on a regional scale, and the goal of public policy can be taken as increasing employment in the depressed region's industrial sector.

As in the full-employment case, the ''regional problem'' can ordinarily be eased by stimulating investment in the depressed region. But again, attracting capital to the region is an inefficient (and potentially perverse) means of achieving the ultimate objective of reducing underemployment. As before, the capital subsidy can be expected to result in a reduction in the average price of the region's products and increased consumption of them. Ordinarily more labour would be required to produce the increased output. But what if demand is fairly insensitive to price and capital is easily substituted for labour in the production process? In such a case the substitution of capital for labour induced by the subsidy could outweigh the effect of the small increase in the output of the region, and underemployment could be aggravated by the capital subsidy. As before, this perverse result need not occur. But (in the static world of this analysis) a subsidy to capital can never create more employment than an equally expensive subsidy based on the wage bill. Clearly if underemployment or unemployment exists because the wage rate cannot fall (to the level of the marginal revenue product of labour at full employment), the most efficient way to solve this aspect of the regional problem is to use a labour subsidy to break through the wage floor.[6]

## 3. Qualifying Remarks

The previous discussion was entirely in terms of factor proportions. This orientation seems appropriate both as a starting point in the analysis of regional subsidies and because this is the context of Bird's criticism of my proposals for Colombia.[7] But it is necessary at least to mention some considerations that could alter the conclusions of the previous section.

The savings rate, the rate of technological change, the extent of economies external to individual firms but realizable to the region as a whole, etc. may be greater in capital-intensive than labour-intensive industries.[8] Moreover, processes that are initially labour-saving may ultimately prove to be capital-saving.[9] Closely related are the possibilities of inducing an increase in the available quantity of capital and entrepreneurship by creating a shortage of these scarce inputs, of economizing on scarce entrepreneurial and managerial talents by using machine-paced production processes, of focusing upon the production of new products which are capital-intensive rather than duplicating productive capacity in existing labour-intensive industries, and of taking advantage of backward and forward linkages in spurring economic development.[10] For any of these reasons it may be advisable to rely on capital-oriented subsidies rather than labour-oriented ones. But careful analysis is required in each instance to determine that such dynamic considerations outweigh the static arguments of the previous section. Contrary to Bird's opinion, capital subsidies are generally inferior to labour subsidies on the basis of these static considerations.

### Footnotes

1. Richard M. Bird, "Tax Incentives for Regional Development," *Report, 1968 Conference, Canadian Tax Foundation*, pp. 192-9. The policy recommendations for Colombia which Bird was criticizing are contained in my "Tax Incentives for Colombia," in which Malcolm Gillis (ed.), *Fiscal Reform for Colombia: The Final Report and Staff Papers of Colombian Commission for Tax Reform*. Harvard Law School International Program in Taxation, forthcoming. The argument of the present paper is developed at greater length and more rigorously in "The Design of Regional Tax Incentives for Colombia," another chapter of mine in the same volume. It should be noted that I did *not* recommend a labour subsidy for Colombia, as Bird intimates. Rather, I argued that any subsidy or tax incentive should be adopted only after an examination of the regional problem that was beyond the capability of the Commission staff, but that if a regional tax incentive were adopted it should not be tied to investment in the depressed region.

2. This is only one of a number of goals that might be set for regional policy; see Richard M. Bird, "The Need for Regional Policy in a Common Market," *Scottish Journal of Political Economy* (November 1965), pp. 225-42, and "Tax-Subsidy Policies for Regional Development," *National Tax Journal* (June 1966), pp.113-24, for a more exhaustive discussion of the need for policies for regional economic development. The goal of increasing labour income in the depressed region is accepted as the basis of the analysis that follows.

3. A subsidy based on value added need not be considered explicitly, since it is formally equivalent to an ad-valorem subsidy on both factors.

4. It can be argued, perhaps correctly, that the dole represented by the labour subsidy will have little tendency to reduce the regional disparities over time, whereas the capital subsidy will tend to reduce them; these dynamic considerations are discussed in section 3 below.

5. Other potentially important reasons for a floor on wages are minimum wage legislation, union demands, conventional ideas of what constitutes a "just" wage, etc. Bird, in "Tax Incentives for Regional Development," p.198, dismisses this case with the assertion that "low labour productivity rather than high unemployment is in fact the principal factor underlying regional income disparities and therefore the appropriate focus for tax incentive policy. Tax incentives which explicitly encourage the employment of more low-wage, low-skill labour thus have no place in regional development policy." But in Colombia, as in other developing countries, the probable existence of dualism in the depressed region makes the analysis of the underemployment case highly relevant, as Bird admits parenthetically in footnote 17, p.198.
The best known expositions of the dual economy hypothesis are W. Arthur Lewis, "Economic Development with Unlimited Supplies of Labour," *The Manchester School* (May 1954), pp.139-91, and Gustav Ranis and John C. Fei, "A Theory of Economic Development," *American Economic Review* (September 1961), pp.533-65. John E. Moes, in *Local Subsidies for Industry* (Chapel Hill: University of North Carolina Press, 1962), also considers the possibility that in the Southern United States a dual economy may exist.

6. N. Cuthbert and W. Black, in "Regional Policy Re-examined," *Scottish Journal of Political Economy* (February 1964), pp.1-16, recognize this in the following comment on the Report of the Joint Working Party on the Economy of Northern Ireland:

> One advantage of a wages subsidy which the Working Party might have stressed is that it could be used to offset the tendency for grants calculated on the basis of capital employed to be particularly attractive to firms in which the ratio of capital to labour is high. The report reiterates the desirability of attracting labour-intensive industries but it does not give sufficient weight to the fact that it may be possible to make the Province more attractive to labour-intensive industries by basing subsidies on labour costs alone as well as capital costs.

7. This is especially true for a country such as Colombia which must import most of its severely scarce capital subject to tight balance-of-payments constraints. It is anomalous that Bird should argue for under-pricing capital in a regional context while arguing persuasively against doing so in *Taxation and Development: Lessons from the Colombian Experience* (Cambridge, Mass: Harvard University Press, 1970), pp. 124-31.

8. W. Galenson and H. Leibenstein, "Investment Criteria, Productivity, and Economic Development," *Quarterly Journal of Economics* (August 1955), pp.343-70; Harvey Leibenstein, "Technical Progress, the Production Function, and Dualism," *Banca Nazionale del Lavoro Quarterly Review,* (December 1960), pp. 345-60; and A. Gershenkron, *Economic Backwardness in Historical Perspective* (Cambridge, Mass. Harvard University Press, 1962).

9. Henry J. Bruton, "Growth Models and Underdeveloped Economies," *Journal of Political Economy* (August 1955), pp. 322-36.

10. Albert O. Hirschman, *The Strategy of Economic Development* (New Haven: Yale University Press, 1958), *passim*. Bird, in "The Need for Regional Policy in a Common Market," has also discussed many of these factors in regional development. In "Industrial Development in the Brazilian Northeast and the Tax Credit Scheme of Article 34/18," *Journal of Development Studies* (October 1968), pp.5-28, Hirschman recognizes the factor proportions argument but emphasizes the linkage effects of capital-oriented subsidies. He writes of the tax credit system for development of the Brazilian Northeast:

> The obvious objection to it is that it cheapens the cost of capital, or, at the least, that it increases the availability of capital to entrepreneurs so that the industries which are being established in the Northeast are likely to be more capital-intensive and less labor-intensive that they might be under a "neutral" incentive system.... It is my impression that the capital-bias... has not led to serious distortions in the technologies of firms that chose to become established in the Northeast....With or without Art. #34/18, firms tend to use the latest technology without too much adaptation in the labour-intensive direction.... The projects subsidized by the 34/18 mechanism... are bringing a more diversified and sophisticated industrial structure to the Northeast, with sharply increased representation of industries that are both dynamic and rich in linkage effects. The (labor/capital) ratio, which is characteristic of industrial investment in Brazil in general, does not take into account the activities that will spring up to service these 34/18 industries. It is precisely in these service industries that the labour/capital ratio is much higher than in the more basic industries that comprise the 34/18-induced industrialization. Hirschman, pp.23, 15, 18.

## RICHARD M. BIRD

# Further Thoughts on Regional Tax Incentives

... Audi alteram partem. *Here is Professor Bird's answer to Professor McLure's comment.*[1]

Economics is both an art and a science. Academic economists often tend to stress the latter, and more pragmatically-oriented economists in government or business the former, but in fact both aspects are clearly essential ingredients in the formulation of sound advice on economic policy. The "scientific" aspect of economics in part consists in rigorously deducing conclusions from stated premises and in clothing these bare theoretical bones with appropriate quantitative magnitudes. The art lies mainly in knowing how to apply the knowledge thus derived to the real world (and also in manipulating the available numbers to answer the questions that analysis suggests are important, although we shall refer no more to this problem in the present note). The old cliché to the effect that where there are two economists, there are at least three opinions about every economic question is thus misleading. Trained economists are usually in full agreement on the "scientific" or logical aspects of the question at hand, so apparent disagreements generally reflect differing appraisals of the realism and relevance of the piece of analysis in question in the particular real world situation. Reasonable men, even economists, can and do disagree on these matters.

Charles McLure's commentary[1] on my 1968 paper on the design of regional tax incentives illustrates the soundness of these aphorisms. There is, I believe, no fundamental disagreement between us on the outcome of the particular analysis in question, but we do differ to some extent in our understanding of the appropriate objectives of regional policy and in the degree of our belief in the direct applicability of the theoretical analysis to the problem in hand. In view of the growing importance of regional problems and policies in Canada at the present time, I am happy to seize the occasion of McLure's thoughtful critique to clarify these points of apparent difference as well as to elaborate the main points in my original paper.[2]

The next section of this note, then, confirms our fundamental analytical agreement, and points out an apparent difference in our conceptions of the objectives of regional incentive policy. The paper concludes with a few brief reflections about regional policy which are, I believe, too important to be lost sight of even in a discussion as narrowly focused on the merits of particular tax incentives as the present one.[3]

# The Analysis of Regional Tax Incentives: Objectives and Mechanics

Professor McLure and I are clearly in full agreement that one cannot really design an appropriate tax incentive policy unless one has a clear understanding of what the objectives of this policy are. I suspect that we might also agree that in fact it is virtually impossible, in any country, to satisfy this simple requirement. Whether because of the political virtues of calculated ambiguity, or because the issues have not been thought through, it is always exceedingly difficult to determine the aims of official regional policy.[4] It is in part for this reason that both McLure and I simply *assumed* a single objective of incentive policy in order to be able to analyze the efficacy of different means of attaining that objective through tax incentives. In my own case at least, I also think the objective chosen is important in Canadian regional policy, and rightly so, as argued below, but the main reason for thus limiting the analysis was to make it tractable, as was made clear in the introduction to the earlier paper.

Unfortunately, it appears we have each assumed a different objective, and this in large part explains why we reach different conclusions on the appropriate form of regional tax incentives. The ultimate objective I assumed was that incentives should increase the productivity of labour in the poor region.[5] The proximate way to achieve this end, I said, was by increasing the capital-labour ratio, which can, as McLure agrees (see his section 2), be done most efficiently by attracting capital to the region. There is thus no disagreement between us on this point: to quote McLure, "incentives related to the use of capital are likely to be more efficient in attracting capital to the depressed region than incentives tied to labour."

The disagreement arises rather from McLure's contention that this is the wrong objective and therefore the wrong policy. The actual ultimate objective, he assumes, is to increase labour income in the depressed region, and he demonstrates, in an analytically impeccable manner,[6] that it is conceivable that capital subsidies will not be more efficient in raising the wage rate (or employment) than (presumably equal-cost) wage subsidies. More than this, however, McLure argues that it is even possible for a "perverse result" to occur, with a capital subsidy actually *reducing* labour income in the depressed region.

There are thus three points at issue in this discussion, none of them trivial: first, the appropriate objective of regional incentive policy, second, the likelihood of perverse outcomes from capital subsidies and, third, the applicability of this discussion to Canada. I shall take up each of these points briefly.

As already suggested, the choice of objective in these analyses is basically arbitrary, owing to our ignorance of the nature of the problem and the intentions of public policies regarding it. There are only three points that may be worth making in this connection. The first is that raising labour income is *not* the same as raising labour productivity.[7] McLure is not really wrong when he reads my original paper as being aimed at raising labour incomes and then criticizes my analysis on this ground, because my exposition in the introduction to that paper was too compressed to be clear, but it should be clear from the present discussion that these two objectives are in fact different. The second point is that (as also noted above) we are in full agreement on the correctness of my analysis that capital subsidies are more efficient in obtaining *my* objective. Finally, although I confess this too was not obvious in the original paper, what I had in mind in emphasizing the need to improve labour productivity as I did throughout the paper (after the introduction) were precisely the kinds of generally unquantifiable dynamic considerations cited in the last section of McLure's paper.[8] I am the first to admit that a great deal more thought and research is needed on the problem of the appropriate objectives of regional policy (and I hope the present exchange stimulates more people to labour at this task), but I remain convinced both of the usefulness of considering the effects of incentive policies on regional productivity differentials and of the correctness of my original analysis in this respect.

Turning now to McLure's assumed objective of increasing labour *incomes,* I have already noted my general concurrence with his formal statement of the analysis in this case. There are, however, two points that might be made in this connection, one primarily theoretical and one mainly empirical. The first, to which I alluded in my original paper, is that, in principle, subsidies to labour will not induce producers to utilize more labour-intensive techniques.[9] The argument that labour subsidies will create more employment than capital subsidies is thus weakened, although it remains true that capital subsidies will induce producers to use more capital-intensive techniques and that the final outcome depends on the extent to which the capital goods employed in the poor region are produced in that region. Since in the case of the Atlantic provinces capital goods are usually imported, I doubt if this point is particularly significant in the present context.

More important, however, is the dependence of McLure's "perverse" result (where capital subsidies depress employment or wage rates) on the relative size of the elasticity of demand for output and the elasticity of substitution of factor inputs. To get away from the jargon, the "perverse" case depends entirely on the assumption that (to quote McLure) "the increased output resulting from the augmentation of the capital stock in the region would drive down the average price of the region's products." The likelihood of this result is thus a matter for empirical investigation. In the absence of any facts on the relevant magnitudes, my contention would be that in the case of the Atlantic provinces, which are relatively small in relation to the rest of Canada, this perverse outcome is most improbable. The consideration of the relative size of the poor and the rich regions may well be reinforced by the marketing practices of the multi-regional companies responsible for many regional exports, although to my knowledge this subject has never been studied. In short, the intriguingly "perverse" effect of capital subsidies in reducing labour income, on which McLure lays such stress, is, I believe, unlikely to be of any significance in the Canadian context.

## The Analysis of Regional Tax Incentives: Limitations

The final question I would like to consider briefly concerns the applicability of any of this analysis in the context of Canadian regional problems, notably in the Atlantic provinces (and eastern Quebec).[10] The first thing to be said in this connection is that we are both right (or wrong) and relevant (or irrelevant). Take your choice. This outcome is a familiar one in economic analysis: "it all depends" — in this instance on one's beliefs as to what we are trying to do in regional policy in Canada and/or what we should be trying to do, as well as, to a lesser extent, on the unknown magnitudes of some key factors in the analysis.

A more general comment that should be made is that one must be very careful in applying to the complexity of the real world such simple arguments as both McLure and I have put forward. The simplified approach of economists to complex problems has proved to have great power as an analytical tool and has, to date, put us well ahead of all the other social sciences in terms of social relevance and utility. But like all sharp tools, economic analysis can hurt the unwary user. In this instance, a perfect example is afforded by the "qualifying remarks" that appear at the end of McLure's paper. I do not *know* any more about these things than he does — perhaps even less — but I am, as suggested earlier, inclined to give them more weight than McLure does.

Further, I am not prepared to accept the implication of his concluding statement that the burden of proof always lies with those who think these vague and unquantifiable effects are significant, and that in the absence of conclusive proof to the contrary, the clear, simple arguments of static economic analysis must be presumed to win the day. Life is not this simple. There can be, I contend, absolutely no such presumption that the (potentially) quantifiable outweighs the unquantifiable. It is unfortunate that this is so, because it gives so much leeway to charlatans and vested interests — and in no field are there more examples of both than in regional policy — but that, I am afraid, is the way it is, and wishing will not make it different.

The main argument of this comment may now be briefly restated by way of summary: (1) I do not accept McLure's conclusion that "capital subsidies are generally inferior to labour subsidies on the basis of these static considerations", because the objectives we are considering are different. Without specifying the objective one cannot analyze the efficacy of policies, and in the present state of the art we do not know with certainty what the relevant objectives are. I have also questioned in part the validity of his analysis with respect to his own objective, at least in the Canadian context. Finally, I have suggested that at the present state of our knowledge there is more "art" than "science" in regional economic policy, and probably rightly so, since "science" in its present state leaves out what may be (we simply do not know) the most important aspects of the problem.

This last statement leads me to two final points which I think badly need emphasis in this entire discussion. (I suspect Professor McLure would agree with both of these points, although I have not had the benefit of discussion with him on them.) The less important point is that, as stated in my original paper, tax incentives are, as a rule, among the least efficient policy instruments and should be resorted to only after much soul-searching and for reasons thought to be overwhelmingly important. The fact that I have now discussed regional tax incentives in two papers does *not* mean I am recommending them in Canada at the present time or even that I am fond of them in any circumstances.

The more important point, however, and one that cannot be stressed too much, is that it is simply not possible to design sensible regional policies unless one knows exactly what one is trying to do. The real problem in the entire area of regional policy is that no one is apparently very certain what the aim of the policy is or should be. In this situation all economists can do is either to postulate some objective and run it through the analytical machine (as McLure and I have been doing) or, probably more usefully, to attempt to study the realities of the regional situation in order to be able to perform such professional analysis competently when asked to do so—as well as, one would hope, to aid in the formulation of a meaningful regional policy in the first place. It is depressing to end with a plea for more relevant research in so hackneyed an area as regional differentials in Canada, but that is precisely where I must end. For without clear ideas of the nature of the problem one cannot go about remedying it. Solutions follow problems, not precede them. It is thus probably premature to introduce still more policy correctives designed to overcome ''the'' regional problem in Canada without more understanding of it than we yet have.

### Footnotes

1. See the preceding article.

2. See Richard M. Bird, ''Tax Incentives for Regional Development,'' *Report of Proceedings of the Twenty-First Tax Conference* (Toronto: Canadian Tax Foundation, 1968), pp. 192-99. Also available as No.8, Reprint Series, Institute for Policy Analysis, University of Toronto.

3. To clear away some underbrush, I should perhaps note that in part McLure's first footnote is somewhat misleading, since at the time of writing the earlier paper I had in fact not seen one of the papers on Colombia he mentions there and had only glanced at a summary of the other. My remarks were thus based primarily on verbal discussion and hence may well have slightly misinterpreted his position. If so, I regret the misunderstanding. The main point I would like to make, however, is that my comments were *not* intended as a criticism of his position for Colombia but rather to demonstrate their inapplicability to Canada. As will be seen, I still stand by this conclusion.

A second apology should really be made to all readers of the original paper. To my surprise, on rereading that paper, I find I never said specifically that I was considering the case of the Atlantic region of Canada, which I was. This oversight can be explained only by the haste with which the original paper was prepared (in about a week, to replace a scheduled panelist who became ill) and by the fact that I probably assumed that everyone in my audience would recognize what I was talking about. This inexcusable display of hubris on my part has now received its just reward. The present note can thus be read in part as a clarification of the 1968 paper, as well as a response to the main thrust of McLure's comment, and a restatement of what I consider to be some of the important issues in respect to regional incentive policy.

4. In addition to my earlier papers which McLure cites in his footnote 2, and which refer mainly to experience in Europe and in the less-developed countries, this statement receives support from extensive research on Canadian regional problems now being carried out as part of his doctoral dissertation at the University of Toronto by J. H. Lynn.

5. McLure's distinction between the full-employment and unemployment cases should have been made in my previous paper which was (as noted in footnote 5, p. 193) concerned only with the former case. I am now more inclined to see the situation in the Atlantic provinces as containing elements of both cases.

6. As is only to be expected from the author of a fine exposition of the implications of neoclassical capital theory for regional policy. See his ''Taxation, Substitution, and Industrial Location,'' *Journal of Political Economy*, LXXVIII (January-February 1970), pp.112-32. The mathematically sophisticated will benefit by consulting both this paper and his ''Design of Regional Tax Incentives for Colombia'' (cited in the first footnote of his comment). Others should be warned that this entire discussion (on both our parts) is being conducted in terms of a heroically simplified model of reality, a point to which I shall return later.

7. Nor, incidentally, is it the same as raising the income level of the inhabitants of the depressed region, which might, for example, perhaps be done most efficiently either by direct transfer payments to the individuals in question or—if (as is probably true) the short-run benefits from this approach are considered insufficient to offset its long-run detrimental effects—by transferring to

them ownership rights to capital (and natural resources). That no one would take the latter suggestion seriously is an interesting comment on prevailing social philosophy.

8. In addition to the references to my earlier work and to the Hirschman paper which McLure cites, the reader is referred to my "Regional Policies in a Common Market," in Carl S. Shoup (ed.), *Fiscal Harmonization in Common Markets* (New York: Columbia University Press, 1967), I, pp. 385-456, for a fuller treatment of these aspects of the problem.

9. See p.198 of the 1968 paper. Note that this point is especially relevant to the passage from Cuthbert and Black cited approvingly in McLure's footnote 6. Recently I ran across formidable support for this view in Paul A. Samuelson, "A New Theorem on Nonsubstitution," *Collected Economic Papers* (Cambridge, Mass.: The M.I.T. Press, 1966), I, pp. 520-36. Of course the underlying economic model is greatly simplified, but so is that in all this discussion.

Incidentally, at the risk of still more self-advertisement than is already inherent in the nature of the present exchange, I would like to call the attention of readers, especially any near the seats of power, to three suggestions in my original paper which I still think deserve more attention than they have received: (1) the argument for a general "start-up" incentive (p.199): (2) the suggestion that there may be increasing returns to scale for incentives (p. 196); and (3) the contention that incentives must be made available to multi-regional firms if they are to be effective (pp. 196-7).

10. In order not to confuse matters still further, I shall confine my comments on Colombia to this footnote and to one point. McLure's suggestion in his footnote 7 that I am inconsistent in arguing one way in my book on Colombia and the other way when it comes to regional incentives. It is quite true that I am superficially inconsistent in this respect: but (apart from reflecting my basic sympathy with the dictum that "consistency is the hobgoblin of little minds") the explanation for the different conclusions lies in the completely different analytical frameworks assumed in the two cases. I see no inconsistency in stating that I am 99% in agreement with McLure's forthcoming analysis of Colombian tax incentives — which is, unsurprisingly, in agreement in about the same proportion with my own previously-published work on that country (which did not deal at all with *regional* tax incentives.) But as I have tried to show in the present comment, this fact has nothing to do with the present discussion, where one may legitimately dispute the appropriateness of my assumed policy objective but not the correctness of my results, given the objective.

# Improper Location of Industry

Because of Canada's large size and the peculiar distribution of its population, the geographic location of plants can be of great importance. The difficult task of picking the right location is often made much more difficult by regional incentives to locate in a particular area. In many of these areas the ability of a plant to compete is considerably reduced.

This is particularly true when a government-subsidized industry, located in a less-developed province, further divides an already fragmented market. The intensified competition that results can harm, or even destroy, both the new company and long-established companies. In the long run, establishing non-viable industries does not provide employment, but simply moves unemployment from province to province.

There is a place for small-scale manufacturing in the less-developed provinces, as the success of many companies attests. Manufacturing industry is not, however, the ultimate solution to the development of these areas, since it fails to make use of their inherent advantages. Where manufacturing is clearly not viable, government subsidies should be used to develop resource-based and service employment.

THOMAS J. COURCHENE

# Interprovincial Migration and Economic Adjustment

## Introduction

Problems relating to regional economic disparity are becoming more and more the focal point of Canadian economic policy. Not only do these regional disparities evoke policy measures directed specifically toward regions, but their presence also impinges on the types of policies that can be prescribed for other economic ills. For example, the current overriding concern with inflation cannot be viewed without reference to regional disparities. With inflation proceeding at a rate of 4 per cent in 1968, for example, appropriate monetary and fiscal policy might call for a curtailing of aggregate demand. But with unemployment rates already well over 7 per cent in the Atlantic region such a policy would push unemployment rates to an unacceptable level in this region (if indeed they are not already at an unacceptable level). In a recent article McInnis highlighted the seriousness of this regional disparity:

> Over the period 1926-1962 taken as a whole, the level of variability of relative per capita income among regions has been approximately constant. Furthermore, over the long term, there has been little change in the relative positions of the individual regions. On the basis of this evidence the trend of regional income differentials in Canada appears to have been roughly a constant; there has been neither convergence nor divergence.[1]

This raises several important questions: what are the avenues through which regional adjustment proceeds? How adequate are these channels? What is and what ought to be the role of government (provincial and federal) in the adjustment process? While an analysis of the channels and adequacy of regional adjustment is beyond our scope, it is, nevertheless, the appropriate context within which to investigate interprovincial migration—the purpose of this paper. As interesting as a study of migration of and by itself may be, throughout this paper the analysis of migration will be considered as a means toward achieving a more important goal, namely economic adjustment or the efficient allocation of resources. For this reason we shall, where possible, focus on movements of the labour force rather than the entire population, precisely because the former is more relevant to economic adjustment.

In a country as large and diverse as is Canada it would be surprising indeed if the process of general economic growth did not imply differences in the rates of growth in different regions. Changes in the structure of consumer demand, changes in technology and the discovery of new sources of natural resources are bound to have differential impacts on regional economic growth. In order that economic adjustment proceed, resources will have to be reallocated geographically. Furthermore, the regional rates of population growth may be such as to contribute further to the adjustment problem. Since labour is the most important factor of production (in the sense that it accounts for roughly two-thirds of the cost of producing the flow of final goods and services) it is not unreasonable to expect it to bear the lion's share of the adjustment.[2] Labour-force adjustment takes place at all levels—local, intraprovincial, interprovincial, and international. In this paper our focus is on interprovincial migration only, even though the intraprovincial movements, for example, are considerably greater in magnitude.[3] In this sense our analysis presents, at best, only a partial picture of the role of migration in economic adjustment.[4]

## Labour force migration: some theoretical issues

Basic to the theory relating to interprovincial labour-force migration is the idea that labour is a factor of production. Efficient allocation of resources requires factors seeking out those opportunities in which their return (appropriately defined) is greatest. If there is no cost to relocating, then focusing on the differential returns of various jobs is sufficient to determine the direction of factor mobility. But there are costs to mobility and especially to interprovincial mobility since this involves geographical dislocation. Therefore factors will tend to move where their net return (benefits minus costs) is greatest. Alternatively we can, following Sjaastad[5], treat migration as an investment in human capital where the costs of this investment are the present value of foregone earnings plus any money and non-money costs directly associated with migration and the return to the investment is simply the discounted present value of future earnings arising from migration. Naturally, investment in human capital in the form of migration should proceed if the present value of returns exceeds this cost.

As stated, both these approaches to migration amount to not much more than economic truisms. Most of this section will be devoted to isolating variables that can be expected to impinge on either the costs associated with, or returns derived from, migration, thus converting the underlying theory into a series of testable hypotheses. Except for the age-related hypotheses which fit more naturally into the human-capital framework, the hypotheses that follow are consistent with either approach. Some of these hypotheses will not be very novel. For example, the hypotheses that inter-provincial mobility is positively related to differential provincial incomes and negatively related to distance have already received impressive empirical support.[6] Indeed, Vanderkamp's theoretical analysis is cast in a benefit-cost framework and the present paper can be viewed as an extension of his work.

Since wages are the return to labour, the prime determinant of labour-force migration on the benefit side should be relative wage rates in the various provinces. However, we do not attempt to construct a representative wage rate at a provincial level. Rather, we utilize income data to approximate the average yearly earnings per worker. In a study for the Economic Council, Denton[7] develops what we consider to be an appropriate proxy for wage income, namely earned income per employed person. Earned income is defined as those portions of provincial personal income associated with employment, i.e., labour income, military pay and allowances, and the net income of unincorporated business proprietors, including farmers. This total is divided by the labour force less the yearly average number of unemployed persons. In other words, if the average unemployment rate in province $i$ is 4 per cent, the denominator, i.e., employed persons, equals 96 per cent of the labour force. Notationally, we shall refer to this as $Y/E$ where $Y$ is earned income and $E$ is the average number of employed persons. Letting $i$ represent the sending province and $j$ represent the receiving province, we have:

*Hypothesis I:* Migration from province $i$ to $j$ will be positively related to $(Y_j/E_j)/(Y_i/E_i)$, i.e., to relative labour incomes.

Based on the work of Vanderkamp[8] there is considerable evidence to suggest that the earned-income-per-employed-person variables ought to be included *separately* in a regression equation. Specifically, Vandercamp argues that, given $Y_j/E_j$ , a lower level of $Y_i/E_i$ might not increase migration from $i$ to $j$[9]. On the one hand a decrease in $Y_i/E_i$ will increase the relative wage differential and on this count stimulate migration, but on the other hand it will also lower the general level of income in region $i$ and tend to make people less able to bear the cost of job relocation. We view this argument as a capital-market-distortion argument. One could argue that if capital markets were perfect the potential migrant would be able to borrow to finance this investment, and there would be no reason to act differently toward an increase in $Y_j/E_j$ than toward a decrease in $Y_i/E_i$. But the markets for human capital are far from perfect. Accordingly we formulate:

*Hypothesis II:* An increase in $Y_j/E_j$ will increase the rate of migration from $i$ to $j$. A decrease in $Y_i/E_i$ will also lead to movements from $i$ to $j$ . In absolute value, however, the coefficient for $Y_j/E_j$ will be larger than for $Y_i/E_i$ . Some of the empirical work in this paper will relate to hypothesis I and some to hypothesis II.

By themselves, relative wages (represented by $(Y_j/E_j)/(Y_i/E_i)$) do not capture adequately the economic attraction of the various provinces. For example, British Columbia has the highest level of earned income per employed worker in Canada. However, it also has one of the highest rates of unemployment in Canada. It is important that this latter variable be allowed to influence interprovincial migration. *Ceteris paribus*, the greater the unemployment rate in the receiving province, $U_j$ the smaller will be the migration flow to $j$. Accordingly:

*Hypothesis III:* Migration from $i$ to $j$ will be negatively related to the unemployment rate in the receiving province $U_j$.

Analogously, for any given level of $Y_i/E_i$ the greater the unemployment rate in the sending region, $U_i$, the greater will be the outmigration rate from that region. It may be true that an increase in unemployment also serves to inhibit migration because the potential migrant (if unemployed) may be deprived of a source of income to finance the direct costs of moving. However, the indirect cost of moving (i.e., the foregone earnings) is zero so that the net return to investment is all the higher. Since the latter effect will, in our opinion, prevail, we formulate:

*Hypothesis IV:* Migration from $i$ to $j$ will be positively related to $U_i$.

Focusing still on the benefit side, we want to incorporate into the analysis the level of *unearned* income per member of the labour force. In this paper we are not interested in non-labour incomes such as dividend income, even though it is obvious that these will affect the decision to migrate. Rather, we are interested in the government-transfer type of unearned income. Within this framework we specify three different types of variables. The first focuses on location-oriented subsidies or transfers only. As a proxy for this we utilize, for each province, the sum of statutory subsidies, equalization and stabilization payments, and the Atlantic Provinces Adjustment Grant under the Federal-Provincial tax-sharing arrangements. Notationally we refer to these as $TG$. Although these transfers do not go directly to persons, but rather to provincial governments, they represent benefits to residents in the sense that their tax burdens are reduced accordingly.[10] We scale these transfers to each province, $TG_i$ by the provincial labour force, $L_i$. The greater the level of these transfers per labour force, $TG_i/L_i$, the smaller will be outmigration from province $i$.

*Hypothesis V:* Migration from $i$ to $j$ is negatively related to the level of inter-governmental transfer payments per worker of sending region, $TG_i/L_i$.

Since the level of these transfers is generally inversely related to the level of per capita income of the provinces, it is quite possible that they will have some effect in decreasing the provincial disparity in $Y_i/E_i$ . If this is the case, then the effect of transfers will be captured indirectly in the relative wage variables (assuming hypothesis I is verified). Hypothesis V seeks a direct test of the impact of $TG_i/L_i$

For the time series data set relating to migration of family allowance recipients we employ total federal transfer to province $i$, notationally $TT_i$, rather than $TG_i$.[11] Because of the differing income levels in the various provinces a given dollar transfer of funds per member of the labour force will be "worth" more to a low income province than to a high income province. Accordingly we scaled $TT_i$ not by $L_i$ but by $Y_i$ so that the transfer variable becomes relative transfers, i.e. $TT_i/Y_i$. For the family allowance data set, then, hypothesis V will read: Migration from $i$ to $j$ is negatively related to the relative transfers to province $i$, $TT_i/Y_i$.

Thus far we have been assuming that the opportunity cost of being unemployed is the wage rate. But in reality the opportunity cost is the wage rate minus the benefit rate under the unemployment insurance programme. The larger are the rates of unemployment compensation, the lower will be the cost of being out of work and the less the tendency to migrate. Accordingly:

*Hypothesis VI:* The greater the level of unemployment insurance benefits in province $i$, i.e., $UT_i/Y_i$, the smaller will be the outmigration from $i$.[12]

In summary then, outmigration from province $i$ is hypothesized to be positively related to the rate of unemployment in province $i$ (hypothesis IV), and negatively related to the rate of unemployment compensation in province $i$ (hypothesis VI).

Turning now to the *cost* side of interprovincial migration, distance is the principal variable we employ to represent the direct money costs involved in migration. Nearly all empirical studies find a negative correlation between the rate of migration and the distance moved, other things being held constant. In addition, nearly all the studies indicate that the marginal cost of each additional mile implied by the regression equations far exceeds the actual transportation cost for an additional mile. This implies that distance serves as a proxy for other costs, money and non-money, that are likely to be associated with distance (e.g., the cost of returning home for a visit or in case of an emergency increases with distance; information concerning job opportunities probably declines with distance; the greater the distance, the greater the degree to which family, community, and cultural ties will have to be broken).

*Hypothesis VII* then, is: The rate of migration from $i$ to $j$ is negatively related to distance from $i$ to $j$, $D_{ij}$.

Migration from province $i$ to $j$ is positively related to the education level in province $i$. This is *Hypothesis VIII*.

Sufficient evidence already exists on the positive contribution of education to migration[13] so that we need not defend hypothesis VIII. But we can carry the analysis somewhat further. It has become standard procedure in migration studies to focus on the income-distance trade-off, i.e., the ratio of $(Y_j/E_j)/(Y_i/E_i)$ to $D_{ij}$. Education tends to encourage migration because it increases the benefits as well as decreases the costs of moving. For example, insofar as more education provides the potential migrant with greater knowledge concerning employment opportunities in other provinces, education serves to increase the benefits of migration. Another way of stating this is that geographic size of the labour market increases with increasing education. But insofar as any cultural or provincial ties lessen with greater education, or the risk of becoming unemployed after moving decreases with greater education, it can be considered as reducing migration cost. In other words, the greater information that accompanies greater education provides the potential migrant with more knowledge of $Y_j/E_j$ and also serves to decrease the information and other costs associated with distance. Accordingly, we propose:

*Hypothesis IX:* The greater the level of education, the greater will be the income-distance trade-off.

A subset of the census data kindly supplied by Dr. Leroy Stone permits us to develop hypotheses relating to age and migration. Viewing migration as an investment in human capital, and taking a life-span earnings as the relevant return, it is clear that for a given income differential the benefits from migration will be greater the younger the migrant (assuming, of course, that our relative income variables are decent proxies for relative life-span earnings between $i$ and $j$). In addition the costs of moving are likely to increase with age. On this point Schwartz notes:

A few cost elements which vary systematically with age are the following:
1. All the cost elements which are associated with the size of family (and size of family is clearly a function of age). . . .

2.The cost of losing the experience in giving up past "on the job training." . . . and the cost of new training.

3. The psychic cost which is also probably a function of age.[14]

Assuming that income differentials represent the primary returns to migration and distance reflects the primary cost, this leads us to formulate:

*Hypothesis X:* The impact of provincial income differentials on migration is negatively related to the age of the migrant.

*Hypothesis XI:* The impact of distance on migration is positively related to the age of the migrant.

We now turn to some determinants of migration not based directly on optimum resource allocation grounds. In a related study, McInnis[15] suggests that for some provinces the movement of people from rural to urban centres takes the form of interprovincial migration. In particular, he is referring to the prairie provinces and PEI. We generalize this observation and assume that the process of urbanization is likely to cross interprovincial boundaries for those provinces which are largely "rural." Specifically, we assume that the percentage of the labour force employed in agriculture is a good proxy for the degree to which a province can be classified as "rural," and formulate:

*Hypothesis XII:* The rate of migration from $i$ to $j$ is positively related to the percentage of labour force of province $i$ that is employed in agriculture.

The remaining variables that we consider are more on the cultural level. Previous studies, e.g., Stone,[16] have shown that the Quebec labour force is considerably less mobile than that for the rest of Canada. Viewed somewhat differently, the above variables will overestimate outmigration from Quebec. The combination of cultural, language, and religious elements are probably at the base of this phenomenon. But even this low outmigration may be consistent with a human capital approach. As Becker[17] suggests "if specific ( . . . that is, to the firms, industries or countries [provinces]in question) training were important, differences in earnings would be a misleading estimate of what migrants could receive." At any rate, we allow for this by including a dummy variable for outmigration from Quebec. Relatedly, the migration from the four Atlantic provinces to Ontario is far greater (based on the regression results that follow) than the simple cost-benefit model we specify would indicate. In large measure, this results again because reasons of a cultural-language nature inhibit their migration to Quebec. This effect too will be allowed for by the use of a dummy variable, i.e., the dummy variable will have 5 observations equal to unity and the remaining 85 will be zero. Four of these values of unity will relate to outmigration from each of the Atlantic provinces to Ontario while the fifth will relate to outmigration from New Brunswick to Quebec, once again capturing a non-economic (language) motive for migration. The third and final dummy variable we employ is to take account of the tremendous outmigration from Saskatchewan to Alberta—over 4 per cent of the Saskatchewan labour force moved to Alberta during the 1956-61 period (Table A-I). All of the dummy variables enter the equation as intercept dummies. A more realistic use of these variables would surely have been to allow them to enter the equations as slope dummies. But the primary purpose of including them was to increase the explanatory power of the various models so more sophisticated specifications were not, in our opinion, warranted. We hasten to add that none of the

Table A-I   Outmigration Rates for Canadian Labour Force, 1956-1961

| From | Nfld. | PEI | NS | NB | Que. | Ont. | Man. | Sask. | Alta. | BC | Total |
|---|---|---|---|---|---|---|---|---|---|---|---|
| Newfoundland | 0 | 0.0002800 | 0.007710 | 0.002990 | 0.006250 | 0.02466 | 0.001020 | 0.0009900 | 0.001940 | 0.002010 | 0.04785 |
| Prince Edward Island | 0.002980 | 0 | 0.01457 | 0.01260 | 0.007430 | 0.04478 | 0.001940 | 0.0007800 | 0.005610 | 0.003850 | 0.09454 |
| Nova Scotia | 0.002270 | 0.002280 | 0 | 0.01393 | 0.008900 | 0.04333 | 0.002530 | 0.0008400 | 0.003920 | 0.006220 | 0.08192 |
| New Brunswick | 0.001590 | 0.001730 | 0.01003 | 0 | 0.02472 | 0.03652 | 0.001470 | 0.0005300 | 0.002900 | 0.002490 | 0.08198 |
| Quebec | 0.0001900 | 0.0001000 | 0.0007400 | 0.0009300 | 0 | 0.01398 | 0.0005800 | 0.0002500 | 0.0009300 | 0.001250 | 0.01895 |
| Ontario | 0.0003400 | 0.0002100 | 0.001740 | 0.001210 | 0.007450 | 0 | 0.002890 | 0.001120 | 0.002920 | 0.003440 | 0.02132 |
| Manitoba | 0.0003200 | 0.0001900 | 0.001510 | 0.001290 | 0.004280 | 0.02632 | 0 | 0.01093 | 0.01541 | 0.01569 | 0.07882 |
| Saskatchewan | 0.0001000 | 0.0001700 | 0.0006800 | 0.0003000 | 0.001500 | 0.01326 | 0.01578 | 0 | 0.04073 | 0.02319 | 0.09571 |
| Alberta | 0.0001600 | 0.0001100 | 0.0006500 | 0.0004500 | 0.002710 | 0.01220 | 0.004990 | 0.008690 | 0 | 0.02490 | 0.05486 |
| British Columbia | 0.0001500 | 0.0000500 | 0.001470 | 0.0005800 | 0.002550 | 0.01316 | 0.003990 | 0.004640 | 0.01710 | 0 | 0.04369 |

**Source:** 1961 Census of Canada, Bulletin 4.1—10, Table J.4 and J.1.

Table A-II   Interprovincial Migration Flows: 1956-1961

| From | Nfld. | PEI | NS | NB | Que. | Ont. | Man. | Sask. | Alta. | BC | Total outflow | Net outflow | Net outflow/ labour force (per cent) |
|---|---|---|---|---|---|---|---|---|---|---|---|---|---|
| Newfoundland | 0 | 29 | 808 | 314 | 655 | 2604 | 108 | 105 | 205 | 212 | 5040 | 2782 | 0.026 |
| Prince Edward Island | 95 | 0 | 465 | 402 | 237 | 1429 | 62 | 25 | 179 | 123 | 3017 | 1348 | 0.042 |
| Nova Scotia | 500 | 502 | 0 | 3064 | 1959 | 9529 | 557 | 185 | 863 | 1368 | 18527 | 8506 | 0.039 |
| New Brunswick | 268 | 291 | 1686 | 0 | 4155 | 6137 | 248 | 90 | 489 | 419 | 13783 | 4621 | 0.027 |
| Quebec | 324 | 166 | 1226 | 1548 | 0 | 23300 | 970 | 417 | 1556 | 2078 | 31585 | 2844 | 0.002 |
| Ontario | 779 | 487 | 4030 | 2796 | 17242 | 0 | 6686 | 2593 | 6759 | 7954 | 49326 | −19134 | −0.008 |
| Manitoba | 104 | 63 | 488 | 418 | 1384 | 8517 | 0 | 3538 | 4988 | 5079 | 24579 | 6566 | 0.020 |
| Saskatchewan | 32 | 52 | 211 | 93 | 465 | 4106 | 4889 | 0 | 12617 | 7182 | 29647 | 16121 | 0.052 |
| Alberta | 76 | 53 | 307 | 212 | 1262 | 5684 | 2326 | 4050 | 0 | 11598 | 25568 | −11387 | −0.024 |
| British Columbia | 80 | 26 | 800 | 315 | 1382 | 7154 | 2167 | 2523 | 9299 | 0 | 23746 | −12267 | −0.023 |
| Total Inflow | 2258 | 1669 | 10021 | 9162 | 28741 | 68460 | 18013 | 13526 | 36955 | 36013 | | | |

**Source:** DBS, Census of Canada, *1961*, Bulletin 4.1-10, Tables J.4 and J.1.

conclusions reached in this paper is affected by the inclusion of these dummy variables.

The two remaining issues that we wish to address require data for several years; so they relate only to the family allowance data set. Firstly, is the time pattern of migration becoming more responsive to such variables as sending and receiving region income? Casual empiricism suggests that information regarding employment opportunities and incomes in other provinces is increasing over time. In addition, transportation costs are declining, at least relative to incomes. We propose:

*Hypothesis XIII:* Interprovincial migration is proceeding with increasing efficiency over time.

The remaining area for investigation is the response of migration to the level of over-all economic activity, represented by the Canadian unemployment rate. In a previous study Vanderkamp suggests that "unemployment has a significantly negative effect on the volume of mobility between regions" and further that "this relationship is not adequately captured by regional unemployment differentials."[18] This is *hypothesis XIV*.

## THE FORM OF THE ESTIMATING EQUATION

What is the appropriate dependent variable in an interprovincial migration analysis? Should one focus on gross or net flows? Should the flows be in absolute terms or in rates? From the manner in which the various hypotheses are phrased, it should be clear to the reader that we intend to focus on the *outflows* from each province to every other province. Moreover, since we are interested in isolating the determinants of migration it is appropriate to focus on the *gross* outflow from each province because it is in the province of departure that decisions to leave are taken.[19]

Rather than use the absolute gross outflow, we divide this outflow by the relevant parent population in province *i* (labour force for the census data and family allowance population for the data set on family allowance migration). Again, one can quarrel with this procedure. Vanderkamp, for example, divides the gross outflow from *i* to *j* by the *sum* of the parent population in *i* and *j*. In a study of US migration Schwartz[20] concludes that both these polar cases are deficient but, if one has to choose, standardization by the parent population of the sending province is preferable. The dependent variable, then, is the rate of outflow from each province to every other province. Intuitively, it appears to us to be more satisfactory than the Vanderkamp procedure.[21]

For most of the empirical section we employ the simplest types of models—all variables enter in a linear or log-linear fashion. Because the census data, when classified by age, involve cells with zero gross outflows for certain provinces the linear version is used almost exclusively for this data set. The log-linear specification of the model is employed for the family allowance transfer data set. For both data sets, however, we include results obtained from other specifications including that employed by Vanderkamp.

## Footnotes

1. M. McInnis, "The Trend of Regional Income Differentials in Canada," *Canadian Journal of Economics,* I, No. 2 (may 1968), pp. 440-70.

2. Adjustment of course need not imply geographical mobility. Occupational mobility and skill-upgrading of labour are also important facets of the adjustment process.

3. For an excellent study of intraprovincial mobility of the Canadian population which focuses on cultural and demographic, as well as economic motives, see L. O. Stone, *Migration in Canada, Regional Aspects,* 1961 Census of Canada Monograph, DBS (Ottawa, 1969).

4. Even at the level of interprovincial mobility we are neglecting emigration and immigration. For some aspects of immigration and adjustment the reader can consult L. Parai, *Immigration and Emigration of Professional and Skilled Manpower during the Post-War Period.* Special Study No. 1, (Ottawa: Economic Council of Canada, 1965).

5. L. Sjaastad, "The Costs and Returns of Human Migration," *Journal of Political Economy,* LXX, No. 5 (October 1962), supplement.

6. See John Vanderkamp, "Migration Flows and their Determinants, and the Effects of Return Migration," Discussion Paper 22, Department of Economics, University of British Columbia (July 1969)

7. F. T. Denton, *An Analysis of Interregional Differences in Manpower Utilization and Earning,* Staff Study No. 15 (Ottawa: Economic Council of Canada, 1966).

8. Vanderkamp, "Migration Flows."

9. Indeed, Vanderkamp's empirical results suggest that a decrease in $Y_i/E_i$ will *decrease* migration from $i$ to $j$ (*ibid.*, Table 1).

10. A more complete analysis would, of course, include relative tax rates in the various provinces as a determinant of interprovincial migration. This, too, is beyond the scope of this paper.

11. Reserach on the two data sets was separated in time by several months. Data on total transfers were obtained after the section IV empirical work was completed, but prior to the research on the family allowance data. No attempt was made to incorporate $TG_i/L_i$ into the section V equations.

12. A detailed analysis of the relationship between unemployment insurance payments and interprovincial migration is the subject of a separate paper: T. J. Courchene, "Unemployment Transfers and Interprovincial Migration" (mimeo, 1969). We shall touch on this hypothesis only very briefly in this paper, and only in connection with the family allowance data set. Note that we again scale unemployment transfers by income in province $i$, $T_i$ rather than by labour force, $L_i$. Results of equations embodying $UT_i/L_i$ are available as *ibid*.

13. For example, see A. Schwartz, "Migration and Life Span Earnings," unpublished Ph.D. thesis, Department of Economics, University of Chicago (1968) for the contribution of education to U.S. migration, and Stone, *Migration in Canada* for the influence of education on intraprovincial population movements. Note that while we shall measure education in terms of formal schooling, it may well be a proxy for skill level. We make no attempt to distinguish between these two.

14. Schwartz, "Migration and Life Span Earnings," pp. 56-7.

15. M. McInnis, "Provincial Migration and Differential Economic Opportunity," in Stone, *Migration in Canada,* chap. 5.

16. Stone, *Migration in Canada.*

17. G. S. Becker, *Human Capital* (New York, 1964), pp. 28-9.

18. John Vanderkamp, "Interregional Mobility in Canada: A Study of the Time Pattern of Migration," *Canadian Journal of Economics,* I, No. 3 (August 1968), p. 595.

19. Vanderkamp, "Migration Flows," also focuses on gross outflows. However, McInnis, "Provincial Migration," in his analysis of 1961 census data, employs net migration as the dependent variable. By his own admission his results are not very encouraging. In part, we feel that this can be traced to the choice of net migration as the dependent variable. Note that McInnis also uses population movements while we have argued that labour-force data are more appropriate (where available) for a study of migration as an economic variable.

20. Schwartz, "Migration and Life Span Earnings," Appendix I.

21. Consider two provinces $i$ and $j$ where $j$ has a labour force ten times as large as that of $i$. Assume also that 9 per cent of Province $i$'s labour force migrates to $j$ and 1 per cent of $j$'s labour

force migrates to $i$. Under our procedure, the rates of migration for $i$ and $j$ would simply be 9 per cent and 1 per cent respectively. Under the Vanderkamp formulation the migration from $i$ to $j$ would be 0.8 per cent while that from $j$ to $i$ would be 0.9 per cent. (Both these numbers are rounded). In other words, despite Vanderkamp's attempt to avoid the use of net migration, his procedure would show a greater per cent flow from $j$ to $i$ than from $i$ to $j$ precisely because the *net* flow from $j$ to $i$ is positive.

# (d) Economic Growth

# EZRA J. MISHAN
# Growthmania

## I

Revolutions from below break out not when material circumstances are oppressive but, according to a popular historical generalization, when they are improving and hope of a better life is in the air. So long as toil and hardship was the rule for the mass of people over countless centuries, so long as economic activity was viewed as a daily struggle against the niggardliness of nature, men were resigned to eke out a living by the sweat of their brows untroubled by visions of ease and plenty. And although economic growth was not unheard of before this century—certainly the eighteenth century economists had a lively awareness of the opportunities for economic expansion, through innovation, through trade and through the division of labour—it was not until the recent post-war recovery turned into a period of sustained economic advance for the West, and the latest products of technological innovation were everywhere visible, and audible, that countries rich and poor became aware of a new phenomenon in the calendar of events, since watched everywhere with intentness and anxiety, the growth index.[1] While his father thought himself fortunate to be decently employed, the European worker today expresses resentment if his attention is drawn to any lag of his earnings behind those of other occupations. If, before the war, the nation was thankful for a prosperous year, today we are urged to chafe and fret on discovering that other nations have done perhaps better yet.

Indeed with the establishment of the National Economic Development Council in 1962 economic growth has become an official feature of the Establishment. To be *with* growth is manifestly to be 'with it' and, like speed itself, the faster the better. And if NEDC, or 'Neddy' as it is affectionately called, is to be superseded, it will be only to make way for larger and more forceful neddies. In the meantime every businessman, politician, city editor or writer, impatient to acquire a reputation for economic sagacity and no-nonsense realism is busy shouting giddy-up in several of two-score different ways. If the country was ever uncertain of the ends it should pursue, that day has passed. There may be doubts among philosophers and heart-searchings among poets, but to the multitude the kingdom of God is to be realized here, and now, on this earth; and it is to be realized via technological innovation, and at an exponential rate. Its universal appeal exceeds that of the brotherhood of man, indeed it comprehends it. For as we become richer, surely we shall remedy all social evils; heal the sick, comfort the aged and exhilarate the young. One has only to think with sublime credulity of the opportunities to be opened to us by the harvest of increasing wealth: universal adult education, free art and entertainment, frequent visits to the moon, a domesticated robot in every home and, therefore, woman forever freed from drudgery; for the common man, a lifetime of leisure to pursue culture and pleasure (or, rather, to absorb them from the TV screen); for the scientists, ample funds to devise increasingly powerful and ingenious computers so that we may have yet more time for culture and pleasure and scientific discovery.

Here, then, is the panacea to be held with a fervour, indeed with a piety, that silences thought. What conceivable alternative could there be to economic growth? Explicit references to it are hardly necessary. When the Prime Minister talks with exaltation of a 'sense of national purpose' it goes without saying that he is inspired by a vision, a cornucopia of burgeoning indices.

But to be tediously logical about it, there is an alternative to the post-war growth-rush as an overriding objective of economic policy: the simple alternative, that is, of not rushing for growth. The alternative is intended to be taken seriously. One may concede the importance of economic growth in an indigent society, in a country with an outsize population wherein the mass of people struggle for bare subsistence. But despite ministerial twaddle about the efforts we must make to 'survive in a competitive world', Britain is just not that sort of country. Irrespective of its 'disappointing' rate of growth, or the present position of the gold reserves, it may be reasonably regarded, in view of its productive capacity and skills, as one of the more affluent societies of the West, a country with a wide margin of choice in its policy objectives. And it is palpably absurd to continue talking, and acting, as if our survival—or our economic health'—depended upon that extra one or two per cent growth. At the risk of offending financial journalists and other fastidious scrutinizers of economic statistics, whose spirits have been trained to soar or sink on detecting a half per cent swing in any index, I must voice the view that the near-exclusive concern with industrial growth is, in the present condition of Britain, unimaginative and unworthy.

The reader, however, may be more inclined to concede this point and to ponder on a more discriminating criterion of economic policy if he is reminded of some of the less laudable consequences of economic growth over the last twenty years.

Undergraduate economists learn in their first year that the private enterprise system is a marvellous mechanism. By their third year, it is to be hoped, they have come to learn also that there is a great deal it cannot do, and much that it does very badly. For today's generation in particular, it is a fact of experience that within the span of a few years the unlimited marketing of new technological products can result in a cumulative reduction of the pleasure once freely enjoyed by the citizen. If there is one clear policy alternative to pressing on regardless, it is the policy of seeking immediate remedies against the rapid spread of disamenities that now beset the daily lives of ordinary people. More positively, there is the alternative policy of transferring resources from industrial production to the more urgent task of transforming the physical environment in which we live into something less fit for machines, perhaps, but more fit for human beings.

Since I shall illustrate particular abuses of unchecked commercialism in later chapters and criticize them on grounds familiar to economists, I refrain from elaboration at this point. However, it is impossible not to dwell for a moment on the most notorious by-product of industrialization the world has ever known: the appalling traffic congestion in our towns, cities and suburbs. It is at this phenomenon that our political leaders should look for a really outstanding example of post-war growth. One consequence is that the pleasures of strolling along the streets of a city are more of a memory than a current pastime. Lorries, motorcycles and taxis belching fumes, filth and stench, snarling engines and unabating visual disturbance have compounded to make movement through the city an ordeal for the pedestrian at the same time as the mutual strangulation of the traffic makes it a purgatory for motorists. The formula of mend-and-make-do followed by successive transport ministers is culminating in a maze of one-way streets, peppered with parking meters, with massive signs, detours, and weirdly shaped junctions and circuses across which traffic pours from several directions, while penned-in pedestrians jostle each other along narrow pavements. Towns and cities have been rapidly transmogrified into roaring workshops, the authorities watching anxiously as the traffic builds up with no policy other than that of spreading the rash of parking meters to discourage the traffic on the one hand, and, on the other, to accommodate it by road-widening, tunnelling, bridging and patching up here and there; perverting every principle of amenity a city can offer in the attempt to force through it the growing traffic. This 'policy' — apparently justified by reckoning as social benefits any increase in the volume of traffic and any increase in its average speed — would, if it were pursued more ruthlessly, result inevitably in a Los Angeles-type solution in which the greater part of the metropolis is converted to road space; in effect a city buried under roads and freeways. The once-mooted alternative, a Buchanan-type plan — 'traffic architecture' based on the principle of multi-level separating of motorized traffic and pedestrians — may be an improvement compared with the present drift into chaos, but it would take decades to implement, would cost the earth, and would apparently remove us from contact with it. The more radical solution of prohibiting private traffic from town and city centres, resorts, and places of recreation, can be confidently expected to meet with the organized hostility of the motoring interests and 'friends of freedom'. Yet, short of dismembering our towns and cities, there is no feasible alternative to increasing constraints on the freedom of private vehicles.

## II

Other disagreeable features may be mentioned in passing, many of them the result either of wide-eyed enterprise or of myopic municipalities, such as the post-war 'development' blight, the erosion of the countryside, the 'uglification' of coastal towns, the pollution of the air[2] and of rivers with chemical wastes, the accumulation of thick oils on our coastal waters, the sewage poisoning our beaches, the destruction of wild life by indiscriminate use of pesticides, the change-over from animal farming to animal factories, and, visible to all who have eyes to see, a rich heritage of natural beauty being wantonly and systematically destroyed — a heritage that cannot be restored in our lifetime.

To preserve what little is left will require major legislation and strong powers of enforcement. But one cannot hope for these without a complete break with the parochial school of economics that has paralysed the mind of all governing authorities since the industrial revolution. It will require a new vision of the purposes of life to stand up to the inevitable protests of commerce, of industry, and of the financial journalists, protests that employment, expansion, exports—key words in the vocabulary of the parochial school—will be jeopardized if enterprise is not permitted to develop where profits are highest.

Our political leaders, all of them, have visited the United States, and all of them seem to have learned the wrong things. They have been impressed by the efficient organization of industry, the high productivity, the extent of automation, and the new one-plane, two-yacht, three-car, four-television-set family. The spreading suburban wilderness, the near traffic paralysis, the mixture of pandemonium and desolation in the cities, a sense of spiritual despair scarcely concealed by the frantic pace of life—such phenomena, not being readily quantifiable, and having no discernible impact on the gold reserves, are obviously not regarded as agenda.

Indeed, the jockeying among party leaders for recognition as the agents of modernization, of the new, the bigger and better, is one of the sadder facts of the post-war world, in particular as their claim to the title rests almost wholly on a propensity to keep their eyes glued to the speedometer without regard to the direction taken. Our environment is sinking fast into a welter of disamenities, yet the most vocal part of the community cannot raise their eyes from the trade figures to remark the painful event. Too many of us try not to notice it, or if occasionally we feel sick or exasperated we tend to shrug in resignation. We hear a lot about the 'cost of progress', and since the productivity figures over the years tend to rise we assume that on balance, and in some sense, we must be better off.

### III

In the endeavour to arrest this mass flight from reality into statistics, I hope to persuade the reader that the chief sources of social welfare are not to be found in economic growth *per se,* but in a far more selective form of development which must include a radical reshaping of our physical environment with the needs of pleasant living, and not the needs of traffic or industry, foremost in mind. Indeed, in the later chapters I shall argue that the social process by which technological advance is accommodated is, in any case, almost certain to reduce our sources of gratification in life. Before launching into these main themes, however, something must be said about two things: (1) that myth which persuades us that, as a nation, we have no real choice; that living in the twentieth century we are compelled to do all sorts of things we might otherwise not wish to do, and (2) as a particular instance of the no-choice myth, to consider Britain's foreign trade. Since childhood, all too many of us have lived in awe of the balance of payments, and now that growth is all the rage, indeed an imperative, we have unthinkingly come to link faster growth with an improved balance of payments. We ought first, therefore, to examine briefly the much misunderstood relation between economic growth and the balance of payments, after which we should reconsider a traditional belief in the importance of a large volume of foreign trade.

Enough will be said, I hope, to indicate that there is a great deal more choice in matters of foreign trade than is usually conveyed by the newspapers, at least enough to free us from the imagined compulsion of having to expand rapidly, and from popular fears of 'not surviving', or 'being left behind in the race', or 'stagnating in an amiable backwater', *ad nauseam*. Having pushed aside such matters, we are free to extend the rationale of the market mechanism in order to explain how the persistence of commercial habits of thought are responsible for the creation of so much 'diswelfare'. We may then move on to consider the principles that should inform the policies of any government that is at all concerned with the well-being of ordinary people.

## The No-choice Myth

### I

Let us begin by being platitudinous to the point of remarking that of three possible goals of long-term policy (1) economic growth, (2) a more equitable distribution of the national product, and (3) improved allocation of our national resources, all three play some part in the complex of existing economic policy. Differences of opinion may therefore be attributed to differences in emphasis. For many years now the emphasis has been almost entirely on growth, whereas one of the themes of this essay is that it ought to be almost entirely on improving the allocation of our existing resources. It is the task of these first chapters to persuade the reader of the urgent need for this shift in priorities.

Before inspecting these long-term goals more closely, let us distinguish them from the perennial concerns of the day-to-day running of the country which too often appear wholly to absorb the energies of the government. These routine preoccupations, which go to fill the financial columns of our newspapers and are the subject of innumerable reports, are three in number: (*a*) the maintenance of a high level of employment, (*b*) the stabilization of the level of prices, and (*c*) the promotion of a favourable balance of payments. In so far as we succeed in these objectives we refer to the economy as 'healthy' or, better yet, 'sound'. Certainly it would be reckless to ignore the indices of the current performance of the economy. Any time that (*a*) a large proportion of the voluntary labour force is without employment, or (*b*) an initially suppressed inflation has slipped its restraints and a distrust of the currency is spreading, or (*c*) there is no reasonable prospect of paying for the inflow of goods from abroad, a sense of crisis impends and there is warrant enough for temporarily overlooking long-term goals in the immediate attempt to return the economy to a more acceptable norm in any of these respects. The economy may be likened to an engine whose smooth functioning is indicated by governors labelled 'employment', 'price stability' and 'balance of payments'. Obviously any poor performance calls for repairs; and it is the task of a good mechanic to avoid breakdowns and ensure the good condition of the engine. But keeping the engine trouble-free is not an end in itself. The engine drives a vehicle, and the speed of the vehicle to some extent, and the direction it takes, to a greater extent—long-term policies—are what really matter.

Since national self-castigation, in all economic matters at least, has been in high fashion since the war, one must risk the charge of unpardonable complacency by the reflection that our post-war record has been good enough compared with those of other countries. We have enjoyed a very high level of employment (some economists would say too high) and though in consequence prices have indeed risen they have not risen at a dangerous speed. The balance of payments position, though frequently troublesome, is not intractable and may be resolved by a variety of measures none of which is likely to cause any great hardship. Our growth rates, as we all know, appear near the bottom of the international league table. But if we can bear to live with this mortifying fact,[3] we can still live comfortably. None the less, the attention paid to these popular indicators of 'economic health' is excessive when compared with any critical analysis of our long-term plans. An explanation of the popularity of this sort of 'index economics', especially among financial journalists, may well be that an aptitude for summarizing official figures, for the uttering of grave warnings whenever there is a down-turn in the graphs, is not a difficult one to pick up.

The knowledge that several hundred financial journalists and government officials pursue this hobby—tabulate figures (to the nearest million), construct charts, and spin endless columns of verbal statistics—is something we might continue to put up with were it not for the fact that the fascination with index economics detracts attention from the broader aims of economic policy, and tends to become a substitute for them. We become so preoccupied with the ups and downs of the indices that we fail to raise our sights to the larger issues that confront us. Continuously arguing about and tinkering with the economic engine, we have only afterthoughts to spare for the rapid and visible changes taking place about us. In the event, there is no general awareness by the public of the range of significant social choices facing it.

Admittedly the economic engine has not been turning very smoothly for some time, but the trouble is, in the last resort, more political than economic.

In a bid to capture public support successive governments have gone out of their way, over the last fifteen years, to implant expectations of rising incomes and opportunities. More recently, official support of arbitrary growth targets has as much as invited annual wage-claims by the trade unions. Having so assiduously sown the seeds of rising expectations we are reaping the harvest of rising prices. A slow but uninterrupted inflation over the last quarter of a century has imparted to the economy a psychological momentum: workers, managers, bankers, professional men, shareholders, all anticipate rising incomes and prices to continue over the future notwithstanding anything governments may do.

The political commitment to a fixed parity for sterling and to support for a level of employment that is evidently well within the inflationary zone, however, makes it risky for governments to do the obvious things—introduce effective flexibility into the price of sterling and into monetary policy. They have turned, instead, with singular lack of success, to increased reliance on fancy fiscal measures, to dramatic announcements of changes in Bank rate, and to brave but ineffectual ministerial speeches exhorting us to work harder and export more, all of which give greater impetus to the preoccupation with index economics and to dilletantism among financial journalists.

I cannot see this country in the near future freeing itself from the exhausting preoccupation with the internal and external value of its currency, and from drifting from one petty crisis to another—and, therefore, among the endless bickering and hullabaloo, neglecting the growing disamenities about us and the consequent urgency of revising our long-term economic policy to deal with them—(1) unless the Government is ready to make more frequent and more drastic changes in the money supply, and to accustom businessmen to respond without consternation to wider and more frequent movements in Bank rate and security prices;[4] (2) unless the Government is prepared to see the employment figure decline below the 98 per cent level;[5] and (3) unless the government is prepared to promote flexibility in the price of sterling to enable us to determine our domestic policy, primarily and for all times, by reference to the domestic situation and not, as at present, primarily by reference to the state of our foreign exchange reserves.

It does not seem self-evident to me that if the need for these measures were put fairly to the public they would be rejected. But even if they were received, initially, with ill grace, they should—at least if we believe in their efficacy—be brought continuously to the attention of the public. In view of this desideratum it is discouraging, though perhaps not surprising, to observe that whenever the economist gets too close to the machinery of government he is all too prone to talk the language of 'political feasibility'. In order to avoid frustration he may learn to advocate only those measures he believes stand some chance of acceptance. This implies, however, failure to advocate technically efficient measures for fear of being ignored by governments whose range of policies is limited by party ideology, financial shibboleths and public prejudice. But once the economist succumbs to the easy habit of making only those recommendations that accord with 'political realities' he soons finds himself in the uncomfortable position of using his authority to sanction the political fashions of the day.

## II

There is, however, one more reason why we have failed to take the straightforward measures referred to, preferring instead to tinker with a ragbag of fiscal devices, and this is the popular belief that faster growth is the real solution to our chronic economic infirmities. If only we can 'get Britain moving', presumably at the official $3^1/_2$ per cent growth rate, inflation would cease to plague us and our balance of payments problems would cease. Indeed, there is a two-way connection here: if faster economic growth is believed by some to enable us to overcome the problems posed by excess imports and rising prices, the same people are also apt to believe that success in increasing exports and stabilizing prices improves the prospects for economic growth. Thus, if we are all of us opposed to 'stop-go' policies, it is not because the excitement is too much for us; not even because they cause great hardship in themselves, but because these periodic reversals of monetary and fiscal measures taken by successive governments are believed to be detrimental to sustained economic growth. If we worry about creeping inflation, it is not so much because of its inequitable distributional effects as for fear of losing exports. And, as indicated, there are many who believe that increased exports is both a pre-condition and an effect of increased economic growth.

This is the circle of reasoning within which we have been confined during the last decade or so and which is predominant in official quarters. It is a circle of reasoning that seems to leave us little choice. We appear to be caught in a treadmill, wherein we must press harder if we are to 'keep up in the race', or even to survive. Yet, if the truth must be told, there is no economic warrant for such constricting beliefs. We have only ourselves to blame if our no-nonsense patriots have mesmerized us over the years into this unrelenting frame of mind.

With the rapid growth in the popular channels of communication it is more true than ever before that the sheer weight of reiteration rather than the power of reason influences the attitude of the public. A simple term such as 'growth potential' is loaded with compulsion: it suggests that waste is incurred whenever we fail, as invariably we do, to realize this potential growth. It is a term apt to the technocratic view of things, that envisages the country as some sort of vast powerhouse with every grown man and woman a potential unit of input to be harnessed to a generating system from which flows this vital stuff called industrial output. And since this stuff can be measured statistically as GNP (Gross National Product), it follows that the more of it the better. Viewed as powerhouses for producing GNP, certain countries appear to perform better than Britain. It is obvious, therefore, that we must make every endeavour to catch up. Moreover, other countries use more engineers and more PhD's per million of population than we do. Also they have a higher productivity. It follows that we *need x* per cent more engineers and *y* per cent more PhD's. To continue, steel output could, if we tried hard, rise to *z* million tons by 1970, as much *per capita* as the US has now. In consequence, we *need* to expand steel capacity at *w* per cent per annum. Again, in order for every family in Britain to have its own motor-car by 1975 we need to expand the motor-car industry at *v* per cent per annum. With such 'needs of industry' to be met we shall require increased commercial transport and, therefore, increased imports of fuel. Consequently we *need* to work harder in order to pay for our *needs*. And so we go on, slipping from implicit choices to explicit imperatives.

It would be futile, of course, to suggest that we should be thinking about the possibilities of reducing the working day. After all, in the US, where productivity per man-hour is said to be about twice our own, people do not appear to be enjoying more leisure.[6] How could we possibly hope to compete in world markets? What choice have we but to return to the treadmill?

This is a sad state for any nation to be in, and in an affluent society surpassingly strange. Having come this far into the twentieth century with economists interpreting the alleged increase in our real income as 'enrichment' or, more sagaciously, as 'an extension of the area of choice', and then to be told almost daily that we have no choice; that if we are to pay our way in the world we must work harder than ever. This is enough surely to tax the credulity of any being whose judgement has not yet been swept away by torrents of economic exhortation.

But of course we have a choice, a wide range of choice! The main purpose of this essay is to uncover the kinds of choices that face us, or any modern community, and to make it apparent that the so-called policy of economic growth as popularly understood is hardly more than a policy of drifting quickly—of snatching at any technological innovation that proves marketable with scant respect for the social consequences.

In the formulation of the ends of economic policy the word *need* is not to be invoked. Markets do not *need* to expand—although, of course, businessmen dearly like to see them expand (whether through increasing *per capita* income, increasing domestic population or increased immigration). It is quite possible to arrange things so as to produce a good deal fewer gadgets and instead to enjoy more leisure. And, although blasphemous to utter, it is also possible to train fewer scientists and engineers without our perishing from the face of the earth. Nor do we *need* to capture world markets in the hope of being able to lower costs; or to lower costs in the hope of capturing world markets. We can, while acting as rational beings, deliberately choose to reduce our foreign trade and in some lines, therefore, to produce smaller quantities at a somewhat higher cost. We can even decide to reduce the strains of competition and opt for an easier life. All these choices and many others can be translated into perfectly practicable alternatives whenever public opinion is ready to consider them. And I have no objection to our bright young men dubbing all suggested alternatives to the sweat-and-strain doctrine as 'irresponsible' provided they agree to use the word *want* instead of *need*. This simple switch of words will serve to remind us that policies radically different from those we habitually pursue are actually open to us all the time—though some people may well feel uncertain of, or disapprove of, some of their consequences.

### Footnotes

1. Like a national flag and a national airline, a national plan for economic growth is deemed an essential item in the paraphernalia of every new nation state.

2. According to Professor L.J. Battan, of Arizona, *The Unclean Sky: A Meteorologist Looks at Air Pollution*, the air above is treated as a vast sewer. Gases have been poured into the atmosphere in the mistaken belief that the wind, like a river, would not only carry the wastes away but somehow purify them in the process. As a result, some ten million tons of solid pollutants are now floating around in the sky. There is, however, a limit to what the finite atmosphere can safely disperse: what goes up must eventually come down.

3. Not every kind of growth index, however, would place Britain near the bottom of the list. Much would depend upon the base period adopted, the length of the period chosen, the goods included and their relative weights in the index. If frequent tea-breaks and other manifestations of disguised leisure are regarded as *goods*—and economics suggests they be so regarded—their conceivable quantification and inclusion in any index of output per capita might go some way to enhance Britain's comparative performance.

4. There is one non-political argument against the vigorous use of monetary policy—a policy that entails more frequent and more drastic (though less dramatic) changes in Bank rate and also in the supply of money—vigorous enough to exert the required pressure notwithstanding the high liquidity of the private sector: the instability argument. If monetary policy is used as timidly as it is currently being used, then it will continue to be ineffective. If, on the other hand, the measures taken are drastic enough to be effective they will, it is suggested, be too effective; i.e. once the pressure begins to tell it will send the economy into a downward spin. The strong measures required to correct this downward movement will, in its turn 'overshoot the mark' and send the economy soaring into inflation.

If this were a fact of economic life we might well despair of deflecting the economy from the path of perpetual inflation. But though it is a common view, and one that lends support to those who would avoid politically unpopular measures, there is just no evidence to support it. Indeed, in an economy in which changes in Bank rate and in the money supply are infrequent and limited, the data necessary for testing this peculiar instability hypothesis do not exist. In these frustrating circumstances there is much to be said for bolder experiments with monetary measures.

5. We may have to learn to live with the unpalatable social fact that (at least in a non-totalitarian society) price stability requires $x$ per cent unemployment on the average, where $x$ is greater than two. This may not be unbearable if the turnover of the unemployed pool is fairly rapid and, also, if substantial increases in unemployment pay come into force.

6. In this connection see T. Scitovsky "What Price Economic Progress," *Yale Review*, 1959, reprinted in *Papers on Welfare and Growth* (London: Allen & Unwin, 1964).

# ANTHONY CROSLAND
# The Anti-growth Heresy

All social democratic ideals fundamentally relate to how we distribute our wealth and allocate our resources: that is what socialism is about, and what divides the Left from the Right. We shall not get the allocation we want without a certain view of taxation and public expenditure, and of social control and collective responsibility. And we shall not get that without a healthy rate of economic growth.

I start, therefore, with the question of growth, and a confession of personal error. Looking back, I was too complacent about growth in *The Future of Socialism* (though I had learned my error by the time I wrote *The Conservative Enemy*). I accepted the then-official projections which forecast a nearly stationary population; hence, like others at the time, I did not foresee the huge demands on our resources for housing, education and health which a rising population brings in its train. And I did not anticipate that successive governments would be so eccentric as to use periodic bouts of deflation—that is, deliberate *reductions* in growth—as almost their only means of regulating the economy.

In the event, Britain's record of economic growth has been lamentable. The facts are dreary and familiar. Over the years we have grown at only half the rate of most other advanced industrial countries. We have been successively overtaken in average living standards by Sweden, Australia, Canada, Germany, France, Switzerland, New Zealand, Denmark, Norway, Holland and Belgium. By 1980, on present trends, we shall have been overtaken by Japan (spectacularly) and Finland, and possibly by Austria and Italy. And our performance is not improving. Our annual growth-rate over the last five years of 2.2 per cent was lower than in the previous decade. (This alone is almost sufficient explanation of Labour's defeat last June.)

This wretched showing, for which all of us who were in government must share responsibility, exacts a calamitous cost in terms of welfare, both public and private. Certainly we cannot even approach our basic objectives with the present rate of growth. These objectives require a redistribution of wealth and resources: and we shall not get this unless our *total* resources are growing rapidly.

I do not, of course, mean that rapid growth will automatically produce a transfer of resources of the kind we want; whether it does or not will depend on the social and political values of the country concerned. But I do assert dogmatically that, in a democracy, low or zero growth wholly excludes the possibility. For any substantial transfer then involves not merely a relative but an *absolute* decline in the real incomes of the better-off half of the population (which incidentally includes large numbers of working-class voters); and this they will frustrate. They will protect their real incomes initially by enforcing compensating claims for higher money incomes and so creating a violent wage inflation, and ultimately by using the ballot box to elect a different and more lenient government. In a utopia (or a dictatorship) perhaps we might transfer more of a near-static gross national product towards 8 million pensioners and better housing and clearing up pollution. In the rough democratic world in which we live, we cannot.

The point is illustrated by our own recent experience. The transfer of resources which we want inevitably requires high taxation and public expenditure. But the popular mood is one of intense resentment of high taxation and of certain forms of public spending such as family allowances and supplementary benefits. This mood unquestionably inhibited the Labour government from doing many of the things that it wished to do.

Now the mood is no doubt partly due to myth and ignorance: I cannot convince any of my constituents that they are not paying a marginal (if not an average!) rate of income tax of 8s 3d in the pound. But it is also due to a harsh reality, the reality of slow growth. People will never like paying taxes: we all want, and reasonably so, more money to spend on ourselves and our families. But we like it even less when, as has been the case over the last five years, our personal spending (as measured by consumption per head) has risen by little more than 1 per cent a year. This was a stingy enough increase anyway: moreover it wholly failed to match the expectations created in the 1950s when, for a variety of partly fortuitous reasons, there was a rapid and sustained increase in consumption per head. People had come to expect that this would continue. When it did not, and growth slowed down, a mood of frustration set in which gave rise not only to the present exceptional resentment of high taxation, but also to the present exceptional pressure for higher wages. And, of course, it cost Labour the last election.

British experience is confirmed by experience abroad. The Organisation for Economic Cooperation and Development, after studying the matter, recently concluded that 'the growth rate of government spending . . . tends to be highest in countries where output growth is highest.' It is to the lasting credit of the Labour government that for a considerable time it resisted this tendency, and increased the share of public expenditure in gross national product, even though growth was slow. But more recently the trend re-asserted itself, and Labour reined back hard on public spending as the election grew nearer. We may now take it as certain that rapid growth is an essential condition of any significant reallocation of resources. (It is also desirable, of course, for other reasons.) Growth alone can give us the elbow-room we need, and remove the present dispiriting constriction on almost any form of public spending.

Nevertheless, as soon as we claim for growth a higher priority than it has had, we run into some well-entrenched opposition. Moreover we find that some of our supporters are ill-equipped for the argument. On the one hand there is now a positive anti-growth lobby among the environmentalists. On the other hand many of those who currently preach growth make it sound altogether too easy: they want the end but ignore the means.

I start with the opposition. More and more people are arguing that growth has too high a priority already, and are warning us of its cost in terms of pollution and threats to the environment. The Duke of Edinburgh remarks scathingly that 'gross national product is rapidly assuming the religious significance of a graven image'; anti-growth economists on both Right and Left like Professors Mishan and Galbraith are amongst the most revered pundits of the day; and doomwatch journalists have had the run of their lives in the last 12 months.

We must treat any argument based on the environment with instinctive sympathy and deadly seriousness. There are very real costs to economic growth. Higher production means more pollution of every kind: more smoke, noise, pesticides, effluent, garbage. Higher living standards, and particularly the demand for more space and more mobility, must mean more encroachment on the countryside. Urban clearance will threaten historic buildings, urban roads will ruin existing houses, redevelopment will destroy traditional patterns of living. And these are not costs simply in terms of aristocratic amenity. Working-class people are becoming more and more concerned, from the inhabitants of Acklam Road to the millions of Tangiers. One also notes the growing interest of local Labour Parties in questions of the environment.

It follows that we must not become growth extremists, maniacally fixed on index numbers of production and seizing on any technological innovation regardless of social (or, in the case of Concorde, even economic) cost.

Japan is an example of a country which, having single-mindedly pursued the goal of quantitative growth, is now counting the environmental cost and finding it extremely heavy.

Our task is to ensure that growth really does lead to an increase in welfare, remembering that welfare consists not only of the quantity of goods and services which we produce, but also of the quality of the environment in which we consume them. We are therefore concerned, here as in other fields, with the quality and composition of the growth. We must continuously bring the environmental argument into the balance-sheet: and we must devote part of the growth to combating its costs.

It can be done, given the will and the right priorities. We know the technical answers to most forms of pollution. We can, in the long run, produce quieter aircraft-engines, pollution-free cars, clean rivers, safe pesticides and effective waste disposal. Sensible planning can conserve the countryside even in the face of more people with more cars and more leisure. And urban planning can, in theory at least, protect the urban environment; though in practice it often fails to do so owing to the low taste and filthy greed of private property developers and the unimaginative inhumanity of some local councils.

It will require high public expenditure, more rigorous and imaginative planning, and an inflexible determination to impose on both industry and consumer the full costs of the pollution which they create. It will, in other words, involve an allocation of resources which is not determined by market forces but reflects our social priorities.

But none of this is an argument against the growth which we desperately need; it is an argument for discriminating growth and for applying its fruits intelligently. To say that we must meticulously attend to the environmental case does not mean that we must go to the other extreme and wholly neglect the economic case. Here we must beware of some of our friends: parts of the conservationist lobby would do precisely this.

Their approach is hostile to growth in principle and indifferent to the needs of ordinary people. It has a manifest class bias, and reflects a set of middle- and upper-class value judgments. Its champions are often kindly and dedicated people. But they are affluent and fundamentally, though of course not consciously, they want to kick the ladder down behind them. They are highly selective in their concern, being militant mainly about threats to rural peace and wildlife and well loved beauty spots; they are little concerned with the far more desperate problem of the urban environment in which 80 per cent of our fellow citizens live.

Being ignorant of the need for growth and the plight of ordinary people, they cannot see that there is even a conflict of interest over a reservoir on Dartmoor, potash mining in Yorkshire, or the acquisition of rural land for overspill housing. The fact that Plymouth is an intermediate area with above-average unemployment, that potash mining will increase national prosperity, that overspill housing may relieve the misery of thousands of slum families — these facts are not even put into the balance sheet. The economic argument is totally ignored: preservation of the status quo is the sole *desideratum*. Sometimes, of course, they are splendidly right, and we *should* override the economic argument (as we did in the case of Swincombe and as the US Senate did with their supersonic jet). But what is not tolerable is to pretend that it does not exist.

At the extreme the approach becomes comical, as when Mishan proposes towns where only horses and horse-drawn vehicles would be admitted, and a ban on all international air travel. No doubt such hairshirt solutions would be good for our health; they obviously appeal to lean and fit professors. But it is easy to see what the result would be. To quote Mishan: 'With more leisurely travel restored, one could confidently expect an enormous reduction in the demand for foreign travel.' Yes, indeed. The rich would proceed in leisurely fashion across Europe to the Mediterranean beauty spots where they would park their Rolls-Royces and take to a boat or horse-drawn vehicle. As for my constituents, who have only a fortnight's holiday, let them eat cake in Blackpool.

This attitude is no doubt natural. Affluence is obviously more agreeable when it is a minority condition. Driving round the country was much pleasanter when the roads were nearly empty. For the minority, Venice and Majorca have been ruined since the hoi polloi invaded in their charter flights and the local peasantry bought noisy Vespas. And a rural retreat was safer and more serene before demands for lower housing densities began to decant the urban masses into the countryside.

But of course the approach is unacceptable. My working-class constituents have their own version of the environment, which is equally valid and which calls for economic growth. They want lower housing densities and better schools and hospitals. They want washing machines and refrigerators to relieve domestic drudgery. They want cars, and the freedom they give on weekends and holidays. And they want package tour holidays to Majorca, even if this means more noise of night flights and eating fish and chips on previously secluded beaches — why should they too not enjoy the sun? And they want these things not (as Galbraith implies) because their minds have been brain-washed and their tastes contrived by advertising, but because the things are desirable in themselves. It is reasonable to argue that these consumer pleasures should take second place to more urgent social claims: it is neither reasonable nor attractive to treat them with lofty condescension and disdain. Those enjoying an above-average standard of living should be chary of admonishing those less fortunate on the perils of material riches.

Since we have many less fortunate citizens, we cannot accept a view of the environment which is essentially élitist, protectionist and anti-growth. We must make our own value judgment based on socialist objectives; and that judgment must be that growth is vital, and that its benefits will far outweigh its costs.

In fact the anti-growth approach is not only unacceptable in terms of values: it is absurd in terms of the environment itself, however narrowly defined. For the greater part of the environmental problem stems not from present or future growth, but from past growth. It is largely a backlog problem, the legacy of 100 years of unplanned growth. It is a problem of *existing* slum housing, polluted rivers, derelict land and belching factories.

Even if we to stop all further growth tomorrow we should still need to spend huge additional sums on coping with pollution; it will, for example, cost hundreds of millions of pounds to clean our rivers of their present pollution. We have no chance of finding these huge sums from a near-static gross national product, any more than we could find the extra sums we want for health or education or any of our other goals. Growth is the essential pre-condition.

# JOHN KENNETH GALBRAITH
# Galbraith Answers Crosland

Some seven years ago—as my partner in wickedness Dr. Mishan has recently reminded us—Mr. Anthony Crosland wrote that 'greedy men, abetted by a complacent government, are prowling over Britain and devastating it.' He might have added that they were so prowling, as also in my own country, not in the name of enlightened self-interest, which until a few years previously had provided the rationalisation for all profitable plunder, but in the name of healthy economic growth.

Now in his Fabian pamphlet, *A Social Democratic Britain,* while still protesting that amenity, where *really* important, must have priority over growth, Mr. Crosland concludes that the true enemies of progress and social democracy are those of us who question the priority commonly accorded to economic expansion. I do not plead guilty. Since Mr. Crosland skilfully compresses much error in small space let me deal similarly with the truth in numbered points.

(1) The conflict between growth and environment that concerns Mr. Crosland is specific. Mining versus a national park, the people and a Norman church versus Cublington, the Indians and caribou versus the Alaskan pipeline, petrol stations (of possibly the most repulsive architecture since before the pyramids) as opposed to pleasant roadsides. The marginal cost of substitution is usually low. The effect of these specific conflicts on gross national product, even if decided overwhelmingly in favour of amenity, would, I am persuaded, be *comparatively* slight. For in their effect on growth they must be compared with the consequences of trying to control the economy through monetary and fiscal policy (with the need, recurrently, to bring all growth to a stop or, as now in the United States, to put it in reverse). This effect on economic growth is incomparably greater.

(2) With the enhanced vision that comes to all of us when we are out of office Mr. Crosland now accepts the need for wage and price controls (an incomes policy) as an alternative to stop-and-go economic policy. (These controls do not, of course, replace the orthodox measures. They supplement them and allow them to be much less depressive. Fiscal and monetary restraints must, on occasion, be Draconian if they are the sole reliance.) I have been arguing tediously for such a comprehensive policy for at least a decade. One wonders about the grace of a new convert to growth (as one goes about getting it in a practical way) stigmatising an old advocate as anti-growth.

(3) I have argued that many of our wants are induced by advertising. That they are so contrived is part of the case for not according the private sector

production that supplies them automatic priority. Mr. Crosland (perhaps speaking carelessly) denies that advertising has such function. If Mr. Crosland is right what in Heaven's name are advertisements for, *The Times* In Memoriam column possibly apart?

(4) Mr. Crosland suggests that those of us who wish to weigh economic growth against other considerations have a class bias. We've made it; we want to kick down the ladder for those that come behind. We are too selfish to see that they, too, want to louse things up, I'm experienced in this argument: in revising *The Affluent Society* a few years ago I was moved to pay tribute to an 'especially percipient' type of critic who had discovered that my 'social vision was being clouded by too much income.' But here Mr. Crosland is merely being silly. It is one test of an economist's competence that he provide himself, non-larcenously, with whatever money he needs. This I did years ago. But, if anything, this qualifies me to talk about socially damaging production and consumption. Overwhelmingly it is the production and consumption of the well-to-do and rich which cause the trouble. As Mr. Crosland knows, they consume disproportionately to their numbers. And it is their automobiles in the central cities, their jets over Kew, their SST, their highway through black Washington, DC, their lush offal on the New York upper East Side which assault the environment. The New York air and streets suddenly became quite tolerable a few weeks back when the taxis went on strike. It's the well-to-do who ride the cabs. The proletariat ride the subway. I wouldn't dream of denying Mr. Crosland's constituents a holiday in the sun. Nor would others who are sensibly concerned with conservation.

(5) Finally, in the United States, as is now sadly evident, economic growth does little for those at the bottom of the economic pyramid. They lack the education, skills, work discipline, often the health, that allow them to participate effectively in the economy and therewith in the increasing income that growth provides. Growth only helps those who have a foothold in the system and it helps most those who have the most. Moreover the impression on the liberal Left that economic growth would solve the problem of poverty was (and remains) an excuse for eliding the action—federal aid to education, civil equality, help for women who head families, health insurance, a guaranteed income, all supported by much more strongly redistributive taxation—that is a remedy. In our case, anyhow, those who put their faith in economic growth were displaying the class hypocrisy Mr. Crosland assails. They still are.

MAHBUB ULHAQ
# The Limits to Growth: A Critique

The basic thesis in the *Limits* is a simple one—and for that very reason it has a powerful appeal. It derives its conviction from the simple notion that infinite growth is impossible on a finite planet. It lends an air of frightening urgency to this notion by contending that the limits to growth are already being reached and that mankind is destined for catastrophe during the next 100 years unless this growth is stopped right away.

The basic thesis of the *Limits to Growth* model breaks down into the following major themes:

(1) Many critical variables in our global society—particularly population and industrial production—have been growing at a constant percentage rate so that, by now, the absolute increase each year is extremely large. Such increases will become increasingly unmanageable unless deliberate action is taken to prevent such exponential growth.

(2) However, physical resources—particularly cultivable land and nonrenewable minerals—and the earth's capacity to "absorb" pollution are finite. Sooner or later the exponential growth in population and industrial production will bump into this physical ceiling and, instead of staying at the ceiling, will then plunge downward with a sudden and uncontrollable decline in both population and industrial capacity.

(3) Since technological progress cannot expand all physical resources indefinitely, it would be better to establish conscious limits on our future growth rather than to let nature establish them for us in catastrophic fashion.

The authors concede that more optimistic alternative assumptions can be built into the model but they contend that this merely postpones the problem by a few decades so that it would be better to err on the side of action now rather than later. They are also conscious of some of the problems that zero growth rates may raise for the world. They hint at policies of income redistribution between the rich and the poor nations as well as within these nations; and they plead for a change in the composition of production away from industrial output and toward the social services. Unfortunately, many of the redeeming qualifications that the authors mention are not pursued by them and are generally lost in their anxiety to make their predictions as dramatic as possible.

## The Basic Assumptions

Any study of the *Limits* model clearly must start with a critical examination of the assumptions that went into the model of the world economy on which it is based; it is a truism that a model is just as good as the assumptions built into it. Our investigations showed that many assumptions in the model were not scientifically established and that the use of data was often careless and casual. This was particularly true of the assumptions regarding nonrenewable resources and pollution. We also found that, contrary to the protestations of the authors, the model was fairly sensitive to the choice of these assumptions, and that reasonable adjustments in the assumptions regarding population, nonrenewable resources, and pollution could postpone the predicted catastrophe by another 100 to 200 years even if one accepted the general methodology of the model. And in this context an additional 100 years might be as vital as an additional second might be to a car driver in a traffic emergency—it could transform the whole situation.

## POPULATION

The *Limits* model is right in postulating that world population has been growing exponentially in the last century and that, if the present rate of growth continues, today's population of 3.6 billion will double in the next 35 years. However, while such medium-term assumptions are fairly sound, the model does not do justice to a number of demographic factors that are likely to come into play in the long run, and which may even be significant in the short run.

To begin with, some of the recent demographic trends indicate that fertility has already started to decline in a number of countries. Of the 66 countries for which accurate data are available, as many as 56 show a decline. Most demographers are agreed by now that the 1970s will see the population growth rate reach a plateau so that by 1980 population growth rates will tend to decline, slowly at first and rapidly thereafter.

Furthermore, one of the major features in the population model of the *Limits* is that fertility and mortality levels are determined largely by economic factors, such as the level of industrial production and the output of services. Population growth in the *Limits* model can only be reduced by increasing per capita industrial production. This in turn increases the output of services, including education, which both permits the growth of family planning services and creates the climate for their use to be effective. Little attention is given to the possibility—considered realistic by many demographers—that population growth may be checked by family planning even at low levels of income.

No one will deny that continued population growth at the present rate is a serious matter which should engage the urgent attention of humanity. The question is not whether population growth can continue unchecked forever; it simply cannot. The real issue is how to arrest it through deliberate policies of population planning, and through technological breakthroughs in population control methods suitable for use in the poor nations.

We should not, however, play down the population problem as presented in the *Limits* model. Even if population control efforts are successful, the world will still be left with a substantial population problem in both absolute numbers and scope for future growth. The long time lags involved in demographic change ensure that population growth would continue for several generations after balance had been achieved between mortality and fertility. Any prognostication about the future, therefore, must take into account the inevitability of a world population several times larger than the present 3.6 billion.

## NONRENEWABLE RESOURCES

A number of assumptions have been made about nonrenewable resources which turn out, on close examination, to be characterized by the same rather dramatic gloom with which *Limits* views population. The figures on reserves of nonrenewable resources generally come from the U.S. Bureau of Mines, but the Bureau warns that 80 per cent of their reserve estimates have a confidence level of less than 65 per cent; *Limits* ignores this important reservation. Moreover, some of the reserve estimates—particularly for the communist countries—are extremely old or incomplete; some estimates for Mainland China, for example, go back to 1913! Again, reserve estimates have been revised frequently over time and are likely to change again in our own lifetime; between 1954 and 1966, the reserve estimates for one of the largest resources, iron ore, rose by about five times. It is estimated by the Bureau of Mines that even these reserves can be doubled at a price 30 to 40 per cent higher than the current price. Similarly, the reserve estimates for copper today are 3.5 times their level in 1935 and it is estimated that they could be more than doubled again if the price were three times higher. The *Limits* authors allow for such contingencies by assuming that reserves could increase by five times over the next 100 years. This assumption has appeared generous to many who have been alarmed by the sweeping prognostications of *Limits* but it is in fact extremely—and many experts would say almost irrationally—conservative.

It can, of course, be objected that reliance on such illustrations of how the world's resource base has expanded shows an unjustified and adventuresome confidence in history. However, this can no more be faulted than the use of history in the *Limits* study which only looks at the story of irrationality, waste, and neglect.

The pessimism of the assumptions on nonrenewable resources becomes even more evident if one considers that the concept of resources itself is a dynamic one: many things *become* resources over time. The expansion of the last 100 years could not have been sustained without the new resources of petroleum, aluminum, and atomic energy. What are tomorrow's possibilities?

As an immediate example, there exists the imminent potential for exploiting resources on the seabed. Reserves of nodular materials—the most promising underwater source of minerals—distributed over the ocean floor are estimated at levels sufficient to sustain a mining rate of 400 million tons a year for virtually an unlimited period of time. If only 100 million tons of nodules are recovered every year—a target which appears to be within reach in the next 10 to 20 years—it would add to the annual production of copper, nickel, manganese, and cobalt to the extent of roughly one fourth, three times, six times, and twelve times, respectively, compared to the current free-world production levels. And the present production cost estimates are a fraction of current prices—$1/5$ for copper, $1/13$ for nickel, $1/24$ for cobalt. These estimates—like all such estimates—are very tentative; but there is a good deal of evidence that exploitation of seabed resources is fast becoming a real possibility.

If certain resources are likely to become scarcer—or, to use the jargon of the economists, if supply inelasticities are likely to develop—it is a scientific and intellectual service to humanity to draw attention to those resources and to the time period over which they may vanish, given current usage and the present state of knowledge. Research into these areas is, therefore, both useful and vital. But it is quite another thing to argue that no amount of research, no technological breakthroughs, will extend the lifetime of these resources indefinitely or to pretend that supply inelasticities will afflict all natural resources in the same manner and at the same time in an aggregate model. While identification of specific supply inelasticities in advance of time is a definite service, sweeping generalizations about complete disappearance of all nonrenewable resources at a particular point of time in the future is mere intellectual fantasy.

It should also be remembered that the waste of natural resources is a function of both their seeming abundance and of public attitudes. It is quite possible—and indeed probable—that with either of the above factors changing, resources can be conserved without undue pain. For the major flaw of today's pattern of consumption is not really that we consume too many final goods and services, but that we use our resource inputs extremely inefficiently. If certain resources become more scarce and their relative price increases, there will be a powerful incentive for their more efficient use—a factor that *Limits* completely ignores, as it ignores similarly potent positive factors throughout. For instance, energy can be much more economically used. There is scope for smaller cars with weaker engines, public rather than private transport, increasing efficiency in burning fuels and in generating and distributing electricity, and improved design of aircraft engines and bodies.

Looking at the problem, as *Limits to Growth* has done, in terms of quantifying the life expectancy of resources as presently constituted, we conclude that these are sufficient to last very much longer than stipulated. It is not a question of expecting natural resources to accommodate forever our current patterns of growth, production, and consumption; clearly, they will not. But we are confident that natural resources will last long enough to allow us time to make deliberate adjustments in the way we use them so that resource needs can be met indefinitely. We have seen no convincing evidence to suggest that mankind faces a final curtain about 100 years from now through depletion of nonrenewable resources.

## POLLUTION

The assumptions regarding pollution are the weakest part of the model of world economic activity on which *Limits* is based. In many instances they are not established on any scientific basis. We still know so little about the generation and absorption of pollution, and about the effects of pollution, that definite functions are very hard to establish.

Our examination of the relationships between pollution and economic growth began with a study of the model developed in the book *World Dynamics*.[1] We did this because the *Limits* model was not available to us at that time. This indirect examination was justified because the *Limits* model treats pollution in much the same way that *World Dynamics* does. The main differences are that *Limits* allows for a time lag between the generation of pollution and its effects and also for pollution resulting from agricultural development. However, these differences are hardly important for the main argument of the *Limits* model.

Although little is known about the generation of pollution, it is simply claimed in the *World Dynamics* model that it rises at the same speed as the growth in capital stock per capita. As natural resources are used, progressively more capital must be applied to extract a given amount of final output—because of the necessity of using increasing amounts of energy in production as resources are either consumed or disposed of. Hence pollution grows to increasingly higher levels. In fact, the prediction of a pollution catastrophe depends on the value of the ratio assumed in the model between the pollution level and capital stock per capita. It appears from our study, however, that if the assumed value could be reduced by $5/8$—an adjustment well within the error range of the data—the prediction of catastrophe would be completely erased. Since data on actual relationships between pollution and capital stock are sparse, there is no particular reason to favour one value for the ratio rather than another.

Again, in discussing the earth's capacity to absorb pollutants, the *World Dynamics* model assumes, entirely arbitrarily, that the world's overall capacity to absorb pollution is four times the present annual level and that pollution levels beyond certain limits will start affecting human mortality. While it may be true that accumulating pollution levels may destroy present concepts of living during the next 100 years, there is little evidence that life itself will be destroyed.

Furthermore, the authors do not fully consider that higher levels of industrial development will allow societies to devote additional resources to taking care of the pollution problem without sacrificing continued economic growth. It has been estimated, for example, that the United States could spend $16 billion a year, or about one third the annual increase in its gross national product, and achieve a substantial reduction in pollution over the next six years. Despite this, the United States could still increase its per capita consumption by another $900 over this period. Similarly, it has been calculated that about 80-90 per cent of present pollution can be removed at a relatively low cost: the cost increases would be about 5 per cent for industrial waste; 2 per cent for thermal electricity; and 10 per cent for automobiles.

Despite such objections to the *Limits* model, it should not be thought that pollution is of little global concern or that it is unrelated to economic growth. It is simply that information of the kind given above—which is extremely pertinent to the *Limits* projections—illustrates that pollution build-up and world collapse is *not necessarily inevitable even with continued economic growth*.

In general, however, the assumptions of the model regarding population, depletion of nonrenewable resources, and pollution generation and absorption should not be taken lightly. However, more study and research is needed to establish more reasonable parameters for these three critical variables in a long-term model.

## Nature of the Model

From an analysis of the basic assumptions of the model, we turned to its essential nature and methodology. Here we found that our analysis was handicapped by the extreme aggregation found in the model. The whole world is treated as one and homogenous even when it is clear that the real world is characterized by vast differences in income and consumption patterns: for instance, the per capita income levels in developed countries are 14 times those in the developing countries; and the style of development, the patterns of growth, and the composition of consumption demand vary widely in different parts of the world.

The highly aggregate nature of the model raises a number of difficulties in analysis. For one thing, it is not clear how seriously one can take averages of various variables which are widely dissimilar. For another, it makes any plausible interpretation of the model very difficult. There is only one aggregate natural resource or one aggregate pollutant, keeping one guessing as to how representative its behaviour is of the real world which is marked by much greater diversity, complexity, and substitutability.

More important, it is not possible to get any useful policy guidance from such an aggregate view of the world. The real world is divided politically into a number of nation states and economically into developed and developing countries. They do not all behave similarly nor are they affected in the same manner. Thus, if natural resources are being progressively depleted, this may raise their price and benefit the producing countries which are mostly in the developing world. The transfer of resources from the rich to the poor nations in such a situation may well alter the overall pattern of growth rates. Such natural checks and balances arise in the real world but they are not allowed for in the *Limits* aggregate world model which moves only in one direction—toward disaster.

Before we can arrive at any useful or relevant conclusion, a minimum condition is to construct at least a ''two-world'' model, distinguishing between the developed and the developing world. Without a greater degree of disaggregation there is a great danger that the model may become a caricature of the real world rather than a mere abstraction.

The methodology used in the model further helps us along the road to disaster. It does not allow for economic costs and prices nor for conscious choices made by society; there are no real corrective mechanisms—only physical engineering relationships. The world keeps on proceeding in its merry way—frittering away its resources, populating itself endlessly, accumulating pollution—until one fine morning it hits disaster.

Is this a realistic abstraction from the world as we know it? In the real world, there is not one nonrenewable resource but many. They do not suddenly disappear collectively but become more and more scarce individually. As each resource becomes more scarce, price signals flash and alarm bells ring all over the world. This directs technological research into them; possibilities of substitution are explored; conscious choices are made by society to economize on them, to do without them, or to enlarge their exploitation by using marginal reserves or by recycling at a higher price. In other words, corrective mechanisms start working. Similarly, it is hard to believe that a pollution crisis can sneak upon humanity as insidiously as the model implies. Even a modest level of pollution would mean that even though the world average of persistent pollutants were still quite low and not yet obnoxious to human health, some particular localities would be suffering to a point at which corrective action would have to be taken—London, for example, introduced legislation to help purify its air and eliminate the deadly ''pea-soup'' fogs.

Humanity faces these problems one by one, every year in every era, and keeps making its quiet adjustments. It does not keep accumulating them indefinitely until they make catastrophe inevitable. One does not have to believe in the invisible hand to subscribe to such a view of society. One has merely to believe in human sanity and its instinct for self-preservation. While the model itself contains hardly any mention of conscious corrective mechanisms, in a larger sense its very appearance can be regarded as part of the corrective mechanism which societies devise in response to major problems.

One of the most curious parts of the model is its treatment of the role of technology. In an age of the most dramatic technological progress, the authors contend that there cannot be a continuation of such rapid progress in the future. And this is merely an assumption, not a proven thesis. The model *assumes* that certain things in this world—population, capital stock, pollution—will grow at exponential rates; but it *assumes* that certain other things—specifically technology to enlarge the resource base and to fight pollution—will not grow exponentially. Any such model is inherently unstable and we should not be surprised if it leads to disaster.

The authors' assumptions are, however, scarcely realistic since man so far has continuously proved his ability to extend the physical limits of this planet through constant innovations and technological progress. There is no reason to think that technological innovations in conserving, recycling, and discovering new resources, and in combating pollution will stop simply because by their very nature we cannot predict them in advance.

## POLICY IMPLICATIONS OF THE MODEL

The policy implications which flow from the *Limits* model are the least stressed and the least developed part of the book. Yet, it is these policy implications that have attracted the greatest attention since the book has appeared. The major policy conclusion from the model is the prescription of a zero growth rate, both in population and in material production. But that prescription is not logically derived from the model. Even if one accepts some of the premises of the authors about certain physical limits to further unchecked growth, it is not clear from their work why the world must immediately move in 1975 to zero growth rates. Since the model is excessively aggregated, the authors are in no position to discuss various alternative choices which are still open to society even if physical limits to growth are conceded.

There is first the choice between development and defense. Presently, about $200 billion is being spent on defense, which is one of the major users of world resources and generators of pollution. If society is really concerned about resource constraints, could it not consciously choose to devote less resources to defense and more to development? Again, there is the choice of patterns of growth. If natural resources become more scarce, could society not decide to have a different pattern of consumption—based on more services and leisure—which is less resource-consuming? Finally, if the rich nations were to stop growing, the growth of the developing world could well proceed without putting major pressures on global physical limits, whatever these may be. These are some of the real choices that humanity faces at present and a good deal of debate is centering on them. But these choices can hardly be considered in the context of the *Limits* model which is sweeping in its overall policy prescriptions.

Another area of policy concern is world income distribution. If we were to accept, as the authors do, the thesis that the world cannot be "saved" except through zero growth rates, we must also demonstrate that world income redistribution on a massive scale is possible. Otherwise, freezing the present world income distribution would not "save" the world; it would only bring about a confrontation between the haves and the have-nots. The *Limits* recognizes this but skips the issue rather lightly as if it were a mere irritant. It does not address itself to the basic issue; how is such a redistribution to be brought about in a stagnant world? Through negative growth rates in the developed world and positive growth rates in the developing countries? Through a mass immigration of the populations of the developing countries into the developed world? Through a massive transfer of resources under a world income tax? And what is the realism of all this in a world that is rather reluctant to transfer even 1 per cent of its gross national product in the form of development assistance? While income redistribution is a desirable objective and must be pursued with full vigor, we must recognize that it is going to be even more difficult to achieve — both within and between nations — if there is no prospect of future growth and various groups fight to keep their share in a stagnant world.

The basic weakness of the *Limits to Growth* thesis is not so much that it is alarmist but that it is complacent. It is alarmist about the physical limits which may in practice be extended by continued technological progress, but complacent about the social and political problems which its own prescriptions would only exacerbate. Yet it is such problems which are probably the most serious obstacles in the way of enjoyment of the earth's resources by all its population. The industrialized countries may be able to accept a target of zero growth as a disagreeable, yet perhaps morally bracing, regime for their own citizens. For the developing world, however, zero growth offers only a prospect of despair and world income redistribution is merely a wistful dream.

The shock waves generated by the *Limits* will do good if they start some serious academic work on the long-range issues of global survival. To the extent that they divert effort from the grave but probably soluble problems of our own day to plans for dealing with spectres in the future, they can only do harm.

**Footnote**

1. Jay W. Forrester, *World Dynamics* (Cambridge, Mass: Wright-Allen Press, 1971).

W. BECKERMAN

# Why We Need Economic Growth

In recent years there has been an increasing tendency to doubt whether faster economic growth should be an important objective of economic policy. These doubts, which were greatly stimulated by J. K. Galbraith's book *The Affluent Society* and more recently by Mishan's *The Costs of Economic Growth*,[1] have provided important correctives to the 'growth at any price' school of thought. Nevertheless, correcting one over-simplified extreme does not mean advocating the opposite. It may well be that exaggeration in a good cause, or in opposition to a bad cause, is practical politics in the wicked world we live in, but the question of the desirability of economic growth is a complex one and exaggeration in either direction does not help to unravel the complications. Today, when there is great interest in some of the relationships between economic growth and the environment, it is important to try to sort out which aspects of the growth issue fall within the competence of economists, what the economists can say about them and what they would need to know in order to say more. This is a very tall order and here I can try to meet only a small part of it.

## The Economist's Contribution to the Debate

Questions such as 'will faster economic growth make society happier?' are not the sort of questions that economists, in their professional capacity, are equipped to answer. The economist can have authoritative views on certain aspects of economic growth, such as its relationship to the rate of investment, since this is essentially about how the economic world actually operates. He cannot, however, say anything in his professional capacity about any connection between growth and happiness, and he never will. No science can tell us whether modern man is happier than mankind 100 years ago, or even ten years ago. The concept of happiness is one for which there can be no scientific objective measure, although this does not preclude the possibility of experiments to check whether people *believe* they are happier.

The economist can go beyond simple positive statements about the way economies operate and advise as to whether certain choices are 'good' or 'bad' *for the chooser* (not the economist), provided he has all the necessary information. For example, he can say whether society *should* choose a higher rate of investment in order to obtain higher growth, provided he knows both the effect of investment on growth and society's preferences as between present and future consumption. But he has no special authority in his professional capacity to say what these preferences *ought* to be. No question involving choice, whether between growth and happiness, or between roads and schools or between apples and pears, can be answered without reference to a value system—a set of preference patterns—and no amount of knowledge of the technical relation between the alternatives (how much of one has to be sacrificed to get more of the other) provides the economist with any objective or special insight into what is a 'good' preference pattern. Furthermore, whilst the economist may be able to advise on whether a certain choice is appropriate to the chooser's preferences, this does not mean that he can guarantee the chooser that he will be 'happier' as a result, unless happiness is defined to be commensurate with the sort of 'optimization procedure' that economists deal with.

This brings us to consider in slightly more detail what contribution the economist can make to the question of whether society is making the best choice between economic growth and the 'quality of life' and what sort of information he needs in order to make a greater contribution.[2]

First, as indicated above, the economist knows that choice involves a value system and a 'model' of the way the economy works, that is, a set of technical relationships between the parts of the economy. Thus, when he finds a fellow economist suggesting that society should sacrifice economic growth in the interests of other objectives, or when he finds the standard politician saying the opposite, the economist will know that such different conclusions should, in principle, be the product either of different value judgements or of different 'models' of how the relevant parts of the economic universe work, and he will seek to identify and bring into the light these two sources of difference.

Secondly, the economist should be particularly alert to the folly of all-or-nothing solutions—of adopting single objectives. It is just as illogical to decide that economic growth should get absolute priority over other objectives, or that preservation of environment should get absolute priority, as to decide that the only objective of policy is price stability or a balance-of-payments surplus. The economist knows that the 'best' choice invariably requires some combination of objectives.

Thirdly, the economist is likely to have some specialist knowledge about the particular 'model' of the economy that is relevant to the choice between economic growth and whatever else it is that is being weighed against it in the scales. This may be important in order to help people to match these technical relationships against their own value systems and to identify what value judgements are relevant. For example, it may be important to know exactly *who* is likely to lose from growth and *who* might stand to gain, and this will depend on some positive economic analysis of how growth affects different groups in society.

The economist's technical contribution may also include the logical implications of certain possible situations, such as the analysis of the way in which 'external costs' of producing certain goods (e.g. the classic example of smoke from factory chimneys) may induce a divergence between private interests and the economic welfare of society defined in a certain manner. Economists may also have a particular responsibility to point out that increases in national product, which has been measured according to their definitions, may fail to lead to increases in welfare defined more widely.

Although some of the contributions to the debate made by modern critics of economic growth had already been either discussed or mentioned by other economists, such as Pigou, long ago, they have still tended to be overlooked in nearly all discussion of practical economic policy issues. Galbraith's and Mishan's forcible reminders were, consequently, by no means superfluous. Nevertheless, a lot more thought needs to be given to the relationship between economic growth, on the one hand, and welfare or the environment on the other. If we are concerned with the welfare of the population as a whole, we need to be sure that we are not attributing to the population as a whole a system of preferences that is, in fact, that of only a minority. And we also need to ask how far we can really generalize about the technical relationships in the economy that are relevant to the question of whether growth conflicts with welfare because of its effect on the environment.

In the rest of this paper, therefore, I shall discuss i) the value judgments that have influenced some of the currently fashionable hostility to economic growth, and how far these are likely to be shared by the majority of the population; ii) a more technical aspect of the relationship between growth, as conventionally measured, and economic welfare: namely, that which arises on account of the existence of the famous 'externalities'; and iii) the extent to which the desirability of faster growth is connected with the speed at which other countries are growing.

## Value Judgements and Some Effects of Growth

As Mr. Klappholz rightly points out in his introduction to one of Dr. Mishan's books, the validity of a person's arguments does not depend on the purity of his motives for putting them forward.[3] Their validity is entirely a matter of whether the logic is straight and the facts are right. But the social sciences are not concerned only with the validity of people's arguments; they are concerned also with explaining why people behave as they do and hence with why they believe what they believe. Furthermore, in this particular case, some understanding of the way that different groups and classes in the community have different interests in the apparent conflict between economic growth and the 'quality of life' helps to keep the environmental issue in perspective.

In earlier times opposition to economic growth was relatively quiet and passive. This was probably because much of it came *not* from those who were loudest in proclaiming their moral superiority and their emancipation from the soul-destroying aspirations of a materialist society, but from those whose privileges would be threatened by economic growth. In the words of W. H. Auden: 'A childhood of love and good things to eat: why should he not hate change?'[4] Growth inevitably involves change and with change there is always the risk that some established privileges will be destroyed. The servants will get uppity and the lower orders will disturb the seclusion of those parts of the world that have previously been reserved to the rich. The poor have little to lose and so have no particular incentive to be anti-growth.

Recently, however, the anti-growth movement seems to be composed largely of people who are concerned with the harm—both physical and spiritual—that is done to the quality of life by the unchecked pursuit of the profit motive and of those who are increasingly appalled by the worst manifestations of contemporary society. Thus, we have arrived at the strange situation where those who had long been against growth, if passively, because it might threaten their privileges, should now find vocal and self-righteous support from those who usually claim to be concerned with the underdog. Those people who are in the latter category would do well, therefore, to ask themselves how it is that they have finished up in the same camp as the others. And they should remember that it is all very well for the better-off sections of the community in one of the richer countries of the world, already equipped with motor cars and consumer durables and whose lives are thereby less constrained by immobility and household drudgery, to attack the current pre-occupation with these goods but, as Anthony Crosland pointed out a long time ago, 'Generally, those enjoying an above-average standard of living should be rather chary of admonishing those less fortunate on the perils of material riches.'[5]

As regards the contribution to the debate made by Dr. Mishan, it is probably well known that one of the major themes of *The Costs of Economic Growth* (as he says himself) is the 'externality argument'. This is the discussion of the way in which certain forms of production and consumption impose costs, like smoke or polluted water from factories, on people other than those carrying out these activities. One of the developments which seems to disturb Mishan most is air travel. This not only imposes external costs in the form of noise, but also leads to an overcrowding of hitherto pleasant holiday retreats, thereby reducing the pleasure obtained previously by the small minority able to seek out these retreats. What had hitherto been quiet Greek islands full of charm and local character have now been transformed into coarse versions of Blackpool or Miami Beach, where all the hotels are more or less the same and where one meets the same people that one met back home. The mystery of travel to foreign parts has been destroyed, the world made narrower and its variety shattered by the advent of cheap fast jet travel.

Now all this may well be true, but to propose, as Mishan does, an international ban on all air travel cannot possibly be justified on these grounds alone. It may be perfectly feasible for a small *élite* to make their way slowly to Delphi by road and mule but, for the average American secretary or Lancashire textile worker, with only two weeks' paid holiday, it is quite out of the question. To presume that the benefits obtained by thousands or millions of such people from their packaged tours, parked in tourist reservations among the identical cement blocks of modern hotels, would be less than the loss incurred by a much smaller number of people on account of the disruption of their solitude is either a reflection of a value judgment or an unsubstantiated guess about the facts. I suspect that it is the former and that the presumption reflects what many of Mishan's disciples would describe as 'bourgeois' values: namely, those of the middle-class middle-aged, with enough time and money to go a little way off the beaten track but not quite rich enough to be protected from the masses on their own yachts or private islands.

## Growth and Externalities[6]

As pointed out above, the second half of any problem of economic choice is the relevant 'model' of the economy. There are many features of the economy which may be relevant to the choice between growth and welfare. Here, however, I wish to concentrate mainly on one such feature which is very much in fashion nowadays: the existence of 'externalities', such as smoke from factory chimneys, noise from jet planes, pollution of rivers and beaches and so on. These have come to the forefront of the debate about economic growth largely because the public is becoming increasingly anxious, and rightly so, about pollution and the absence of a system of property rights (e.g. to clean air or water) that would mitigate the damage from these 'externalities'. Also, the emphasis given by Dr. Mishan to externalities in the context of his attack on growth suggests that they are responsible for a conflict between growth and welfare. But to conclude that such a conflict follows from the existence of external diseconomies requires various assumptions, which are not explicitly set out by Mishan, let alone by the paler and more popular varieties of anti-growth literature, and which do not, in fact, necessarily hold in the real world.

The whole problem of 'externalities' or 'spill-over effects' arises because some forms of production or consumption impose costs or disadvantages on people other than those responsible for the production or consumption concerned. These are called 'external' costs, and where they exist the free market mechanism will not, unless special measures are adopted, lead to the socially desirable level of output of the goods and services concerned. For example, suppose that the production of steel results in the emission of smoke from the chimneys of steelworks and that this smoke imposes certain costs, in the form of laundry charges or re-painting of houses, on people who live nearby. The steel industry will not normally include these external costs in its calculations of how much steel it should produce and it is obvious that it will tend to produce more steel than if it *did* have to bear these costs. In the jargon of economics, 'output will be pushed beyond the social optimum.' There will be some excess output, the costs of which exceed the value society places on this excess output. Thus, the welfare of the community will be less than it would have been if steel output had been kept to the lower (social optimum) or 'ideal' level.

Now, although Mishan never explicitly says so, the only reasonable interpretation one can place on the emphasis he gives to these external costs in his attack on economic growth is that growth must lead to an increase in the extent to which there is a divergence from the ideal output. If there is no connection between economic growth and the degree of divergence from this ideal pattern of output it is difficult to see why about a quarter of his book on the costs of growth is devoted to the way that externalities lead to such a divergence. But, in fact, he does not demonstrate anywhere why economic growth should mean an increase in this divergence; he merely discusses the way in which economic growth leads to an increase in external costs. However, that is not the same thing as an increase in the divergence from an ideal output, let alone a reduction, on balance, in the community's welfare. For, although growth may lead to a rise in social costs, some gains are likely to be secured.

That growth or, more particularly, an increase in output of the type discussed above will lead to an increase in external social costs is highly likely and in many instances inevitable. If there are more factories producing smoke from chimneys, more external costs are imposed on society. But an increase in external costs is no more reason for preventing the growth of the industry or industries concerned than is an increase in the private costs of the industry. External costs are no more 'costly' *per se* than internal costs. The conventional private costs that firms do include in their calculations reflect ultimately the labour costs — the boredom of work, the loneliness of thought and the sacrifice of leisure — embodied in the goods and services normally included in a firm's costs of production. One would not argue that output should not be allowed to expand because it would be associated with an increase in normal internal costs.

What matters is whether more output leads to a greater divergence from the ideal level and, if this is the case, whether that implies some reduction in welfare.

As regards the former, the presumption that greater output leads to a greater divergence from the ideal level holds only if, say, the costs of pollution per unit of output of the product responsible rise as output increases. Of course, this may well be the case with most kinds of pollution but not with others, where the reverse may apply. But secondly, and more important, even if it were true that for most products the pollution costs per unit of output rose with higher output, it would still not follow that the community would be worse off. Even if the degree to which actual output departs from the ideal rises with economic growth, this merely means that actual output in the economy as a whole, and economic welfare as a whole, falls further and further below the maximum feasible level of economic welfare. This still does not mean that economic welfare actually declines.

The need to make rather sweeping assumptions in order to deduce a general correlation between economic growth and reduction of welfare on account of externalities also applies to the effect of increases in certain kinds of consumption, such as the travel and tourism problem.

In the case of tourism, what happens presumably is that with a rise in the number of tourists the benefits to the people who first went to the places in question begin to diminish, since these become spoilt by *hoi polloi*, the extra noise and so on. It is true, therefore, that these pioneers will not enjoy their holidays as much as they did originally. But, even if this is the case, it does not necessarily follow that all tourists will feel as dissatisfied. Other tourists and newcomers may well have the time of their lives. It will still be true that the volume of tourism exceeds the ideal level but that does not tell us whether such excess rises with economic growth and the demand for travel; let alone how much enjoyment the great majority of people get from their holidays. After all, millions of people now go to the Costa Brava or the Côte d'Azur or Rhodes and presumably some of them *must* consider it worth more than the cost of going there, since it is highly unlikely that a modest rise in the price of travel to these places would make all the tourists vanish overnight. For some people a particular resort may be ruined altogether, but all the newcomers are enjoying themselves, and even some of the earlier tourists may admit to having an agreeable time.

In short, the mere fact that external costs may rise with economic growth does not mean that growth leads to a rise in the extent by which actual output of any polluting or congesting activity exceeds the ideal level. And, secondly, even in the cases where it does, there is still no presumption that total welfare must decline. The community may still be better off even if the gap between actual and potential welfare is increasing.

If one is prepared to make the assumption that, after a point, the curve of external costs per unit of output rises more and more sharply, then it is true that, *eventually*, a point must be reached where further growth and increases in demand lead to a fall in welfare. And there is a good *prima facie* reason for thinking that, at some point or other, this must be the case. For example, most, and possibly all, forms of pollution are essentially reductions in some scarce resource, such as pure water or clean air. The less one has of something like this, the more one values what is left. Hence, even if the pollution of water in terms of the usual physical characteristics, per unit of industrial output, did not increase with the rise in industrial output, it would still be true that, as clean water became scarcer, the value of a unit of the remaining clean water would rise. (After all, the sheikh whose Cadillac breaks down in the desert and who is dying of thirst will willingly give up his car to any Bedouin who will give him a drink of water in exchange.) But even if we accept that, in principle, the curves of external costs per unit of output must be of this shape, we still cannot say that society has *now* reached the point where the rise in such costs per unit of output has become so great that further increases in output must lead to a fall in net welfare, unless we know whereabouts we are on the relevant curve.

Another aspect of the whole question, however, is the assumptions that have to be made about the extent to which external costs *per unit of output* shift. It may well be that the real trouble with externalities is not so much that output will not be fixed at ideal points, given these externalities, but that there is no incentive at all to producers to adopt techniques of production that *cut* pollution costs per unit of output. But, as usual, once changes in technique over time are brought into the picture, there is virtually no basis for any valid generalizations. It may well be that in some cases economic growth and changes in technique lead to increases in external costs per unit of output. But equally there may be cases of decreases. For example, there has been a large improvement over the last few years in the degree of air pollution in this country, in spite of increases in output. This is partly the result of legislation, but it is also partly the result of changes in techniques leading to a switch, in industry and in homes, from coal to other forms of fuel that produce much less smoke and sulphur dioxide per unit of output of the product provided.

Thus, the range of assumptions that needs to be made in order to establish that we have reached a situation in which the costs of growth in the aggregate more than offset the benefits seems to be considerable, though it might not prove too difficult to establish that there is some rough evidence for some of these assumptions.

## Growth, Satisfactions and Relative Incomes

A completely different line of attack employed by Mishan on the desirability of economic growth *per se* is based on two further propositions. First, he argues that, in so far as needs and desires increase together with the satisfactions of existing needs and desires, economic growth does not really make people any better off. Secondly, there is the claim that welfare, widely defined, is, anyway, a matter of one's relative income, not absolute income, so that an increase in national income cannot make people taken as a whole any better off, though it may, of course, lead to a redistribution of income, with some people relatively better off but others worse off.

The former proposition, which need not detain us long, is that higher incomes lead merely to increased wants, so that the gap between wants and their satisfactions may be as great as ever, or even increase. This raises philosophical issues and possibly interesting questions about the correct use of certain words, such as 'pain' or 'pleasure'. Propositions about the extent to which increases in 'pain' in the form of unsatisfied wants have just offset the increases in 'pleasure' from increased satisfaction of other wants may be interesting and important subjects for speculation. However, they are not propositions which economists are particularly well qualified to evaluate.

Of far greater importance, in my view, is the attack on growth based on the so-called 'relative income hypothesis', namely:

> the hypothesis that what matters more to a person in a high consumption society is not his absolute real income, his command over material goods, but his position in the income structure of society . . . the more truth there is in this relative income hypothesis—and one can hardly deny the increasing emphasis on status and income-position in the affluent society—the more futile as a means of increasing social welfare is the official policy of economic growth.[7]

Now, it is true that taking one country in isolation, then, in so far as there is some truth in the relative income hypothesis (which is probably only partially true), it would be pointless to raise the total income of the country. Either nobody is any better off relatively or some are better off but this is cancelled out by others being worse off. But the great weakness of this argument as an attack on the desirability of growth in any one country is that it ignores the existence of other countries. And if other countries are taken into account then the relative income hypothesis, far from being an anti-growth argument, could become a very powerful argument in favour of faster growth. Hence, the people whose views place them anywhere in the range from extremely anti-growth to just worried about the pattern of growth lest it be, on balance, undesirable, should beware of using this line of argument.

For, if other countries are also growing, then, failure by any given country to follow suit would mean that the *relative* income of the given country would decline, so that the 'welfare' of its inhabitants would diminish. It should be noted that anybody adopting this position would be playing the game by the Mishan rules, and not questioning how sensible it is for people to be influenced by their relative incomes, rather than by their absolute incomes. Anyway, it is not for economists in their professional capacity to pass judgements on people's preferences, except to comment on their internal consistency.

Furthermore, it is arguable that it is less irrational for a nation to be concerned with its relative income than for an individual. For it is not simply a matter of decline in national dignity if we all finish up, in ten or twenty years' time, as waiters in tourist hotels administering to the needs of the millions of rich, visiting foreigners from all parts of the world, or if we all have to dress up in some sort of archaic national costume and study folk-dancing to amuse the tourists. Nor is it even a matter of most of the male population between the ages of twenty and fifty going abroad to earn much higher incomes in the factories of Japan or Italy or Argentina. There is the danger that it could lead to one's industries and one's whole economy coming more or less under foreign control, which, in the end, could mean that one's society would also come under the control of interests that could hardly be expected to give the social welfare of the inhabitants of the country concerned a very high priority. How far this danger is a real one depends, of course, on the correct 'model' of the economy.

The implications, then, of the relative income hypothesis when the existence of other countries is taken into account are as follows. First, account would have to be taken of the prospective growth rates of these other countries in deciding how much priority should be given to growth. Secondly, the relative income hypothesis would mean that efforts to accelerate growth could be justified even if our ideal growth rate, in the absence of this hypothesis, were lower than that of other countries. As a result, some of the more popular arguments in favour of higher growth, especially when these take the form of arguments for more investment in order to 'catch up' with other countries' rates of investment and growth, which are quite foolish as they stand, can be cloaked with more intellectual respectability than they really deserve.

For example, the standard popular argument that we must invest more 'in order not to fall behind other countries' is quite absurd without the relative income hypothesis. For the best or 'optimum' rate of investment is that at which the rate of return on marginal investment just equals the rate at which society discounts the value of future consumption. Otherwise, the sacrifice of present consumption entailed by the investment may have a higher (or lower) present value than the present value of the extra consumption that will be enjoyed in the future as a result of the investment. Clearly, different countries may have different rates of return on investment and different rates of time preference. Hence, what is the best rate of investment for one country need not be the same for another. The rate in Germany, say, may be higher than it is in Britain or Spain. Further, the Germans may well be investing more than they should (in the jargon, 'beyond their optimum rate'), so it would be even more absurd for us to invest more simply because they are doing so.

But once the relative income hypothesis is accepted all this changes. Of course, in attacking the obsession with international league tables of growth rates Dr. Mishan is essentially saying that it is foolish for the relative income of a country, *vis-à-vis* other countries, to enter into its over-all sense of 'welfare'. But in that case either he should say that it is less foolish for relative incomes to affect an individual's welfare or he must say that, although individuals *ought* to be concerned only with their absolute incomes, it is still foolish for them to want more absolute incomes!

The significance of the likely levels of consumption in other countries may be seen more clearly if we look at some actual figures of how relative levels of 'real' consumption (i.e. allowing for differences in price levels) are likely to develop over the next few years on the basis of some recent projections, as shown in the table opposite. This shows estimates of relative levels of 'real' consumption per head in various countries in 1962/63, together with the changes in consumption between then and 1968 and projections of growth rates over the next decade as estimated by the OECD. Figures like these are obviously subject to a considerable margin of error and they should properly be regarded as indicating no more than orders of magnitude.

Taking them at their face value, these estimates suggest that by about 1978 real consumption per head will exceed the British level by about 20 per cent in Germany and Switzerland, 30 per cent in France and by nearly 60 per cent in Japan (i.e. about the amount by which the USA exceeded the British level in 1962/63). The Japanese figure may seem astonishing, but one should not forget the power of compound interest. As recently as 1962/63 the Japanese level was about only two-thirds of our own, but over the seven years 1963-1970 Japanese GNP per head has nearly doubled, whilst that of the UK has risen by less than a quarter. And if it should be thought that the growth rate officially projected for Japan is implausible it should be remembered that over the last few years the *actual* Japanese growth rate of about 11 per cent a year has exceeded by a considerable margin the earlier official Japanese projection of around 8 per cent a year.

In the context of the relative income hypothesis, the implication of these figures for the desirability of growth now becomes rather complicated. It will clearly depend partly on whose growth one is talking about—which country—and partly on how far people cease to be dazzled by relative levels of national product and growth rates. As regards the former, the point is that the countries that are presently growing very rapidly may be growing faster than their ideal rates. For they may be sacrificing too much present consumption in the interests of greater future consumption, having failed to take account of the future excess of their consumption levels over those of the slow-growing countries. For example, perhaps the Japanese would be better advised to relax a bit and stop investing about a third of their national product, since they are going to be richer (per head) than most of the world in a few years' time anyway.

Unfortunately, this line of argument would only make it more difficult to persuade people of the second, and more important, point: that they should not take account of other people's incomes. But, as indicated above, whilst it may be easy to see the futility of worrying about other people's incomes at a personal and individual level, it is not so simple a matter at the national level, given the world that we live in. This brings us back to where we began: the need to clarify our value judgments. Many of the people who are most concerned with the deterioration of the environment are also those who are most apprehensive of the consequences of this country's economic strength being completely over-shadowed by that of countries where the importance attached to economic growth relative to other aspects of welfare is even greater than here. Such people might be forced, however reluctantly, to accept a certain amount of growth, despite its costs, to preserve economic independence. On the other hand, there might be better and cheaper ways of preserving such independence. But, whatever the answer, the choice is surely a complicated one, and no purpose is served by over-simplification.

*Indices of 'Real' Consumption per head in Selected Countries, relative to the UK, in 1962/63, 1968 and 1978.*

| | Index of 'real' consumption per head in 1962/63 (UK=100) (a) | Increase in 'real' consumption per head 1962/3-1968 (b) % | Index or 'real' consumption per head in 1968 (UK=100) (c) | Projected increase in 'real' consumption per head 1968-1978 (d) % | Index of estimated 'real' consumption per head in 1978 (UK=100) |
|---|---|---|---|---|---|
| Austria | 72 | +21 | 78 | + 48 | 85 |
| Belgium/ Luxembourg | 85 | +17 | 89 | + 50 | 100 |
| Canada | 126 | +20 | 136 | + 30 | 130 |
| Denmark | 104 | +16 | 109 | + 44 | 120 |
| France | 93 | +25 | 104 | + 69 | 130 |
| Germany | 94 | +21 | 103 | + 54 | 120 |
| Italy | 56 | +25 | 63 | + 59 | 75 |
| Japan | 65 | +50 | 88 | +136 | 160 |
| Netherlands | 77 | +26 | 87 | + 41 | 90 |
| Norway | 97 | +18 | 103 | + 49 | 115 |
| Spain | 45 | +32 | 53 | + 58 (e) | 65 |
| Sweden | 130 | +19 | 140 | + 37 | 145 |
| Switzerland | 116 | +13 | 118 | + 32 | 120 |
| UK | 100 | +11 | 100 | + 33 | 100 |
| USA | 162 | +23 | 179 | + 34 | 180 |

(a) derived from Beckerman and Bacon, 'The International Distribution of Incomes', Table 4, in *Unfashionable Economics*, edited by Paul Streeten, Weidenfeld and Nicolson, 1970. By 'real' is meant that allowance is made for differences in relative price levels — i.e. for the internal purchasing power of currencies.

(b) OECD National Accounts Statistics.

(c) col 1) adjusted by col 2) and then expressed as index of UK in 1968.

(d) OECD *The Outlook for Economic Growth*, Paris 1970, Table 2. I have assumed that the volume of consumption per head will change more or less in line, over the period 1968 to 1978, with the projected rate of growth of GNP per employed person given for the period 1970-1980 in this publication.

(e) Assuming Spanish growth per head over next ten years about equal to that of 1958-1968.

## Conclusion

In this article I have tried to draw attention to a few issues involved in the question of how far economic growth is desirable. I have no doubt that there are many other complications and I do not suppose that I have selected the most important ones. First, I have suggested that we should clarify the value judgments lying behind our views on growth, and check how far they are likely to be shared by the majority of the population. In this connection I have stressed that economists, in their professional capacity, have no more status than anybody else and so have no special qualifications for saying whether economic growth is good or bad. Secondly, I have argued that some technical relationships between growth and welfare defined more widely — those arising out of externalities in general and pollution in particular — are more complicated than might appear at first sight and that special assumptions are needed in order to establish that growth is bad for welfare on this particular score. Finally, I have discussed the extent to which the 'relative income hypothesis' implies that there is little point in economic growth, and I have suggested that this hypothesis might, in fact, have quite the opposite implication.

Thus, the only clear conclusion that emerges from all this is the obvious one that the desirability of growth is a very complicated issue. Economic growth has its advantages and disadvantages, and its pursuit raises all sorts of difficult problems for society. This has probably always been the case and, though there is no evidence that human beings ever completely solve any of their problems, they do make progress in some of them. To adopt a simple extreme position in favour of, or against, economic growth *per se* is, of course, the easiest solution. We need not bother then about collecting evidence, or trying to devise and introduce appropriate policies to minimize the conflict between economic growth and welfare. But it is not the best solution.

### Footnotes

1. E.J. Mishan, *The Costs of Economic Growth* (London: Staples Press, 1967).

2. The following few paragraphs present the 'official' party line about the role of the economist as the detached adviser on optimal strategies for somebody else's value judgments. Personally, I don't subscribe to this doctrine, and I regard the economist as a special kind of propagandist. But if this were made widely known our propaganda would be less effective, which is why I make this point in a footnote where nobody is likely to read it.

3. E.J. Mishan, *21 Popular Economic Fallacies* (London: Allen Lane, The Penguin Press, 1969), p. 27.

4. W.H. Auden, *Profile*.

5. C.A.R. Crosland, *The Future of Socialism* (Jonathan Cape, 1956), abridged and revised paperback edition (1964), p. 222.

6. This is the most heavily abridged section of my British Association paper. The reader interested in some of the technicalities behind the conclusions postulated here should refer to the complete paper (see footnote to p.1).

7. Mishan, *The Costs of Economic Growth*, p.120.

# SECTION FIVE
# The Services Sector

DAVID A. WORTON
# The Service Industries in Canada, 1946-66

## Introduction

The subject of this paper reflects the increasing concern being felt over the paradox demonstrated in the growing importance of the service industries and the simultaneous existence of glaring gaps in our theoretical and empirical knowledge of this sector. Although the trends that have shaped the present industrial structures of the developed economies of the world are both long-standing and, in certain superficial respects, even obvious, their measurement and systematic analysis is a comparatively recent phenomenon.[1] The inventory of published work which has slowly accumulated owes much to the National Bureau of Economic Research's series during the 1950s on production, employment, and productivity in American industry. The contributions by Barger and Stigler,[2] for instance, may be noted as direct antecedents of the Bureau's current program of research aimed specifically toward the service industries.[3]

Canadian data on the industrial distribution of national product and the labour force have been used in comparative international studies of the structural changes accompanying economic growth,[4] but the record of indigenous research is a meager one. Some studies parallel to the NBER series exist in the background studies prepared a decade ago for the Royal Commission on Canada's Economic Prospects and in its own assessment of "the probable economic development of Canada and the problems to which such development appears likely to give rise."[5] Special mention may be made of the study by Hood and Scott, who, with sectoral projections of employment, productivity, and output, and the historical analysis underlying them, clearly established the growing importance of the service industries in Canada and tentatively estimated the measure of their potential contribution to the key growth variables.

Despite the clear indication thus provided of pressing research needs in the area of services, there has been since that time only fragmentary reporting of their role in the structural evolution of the Canadian economy; certainly there have been no basic studies to identify, measure, and explain the factors which might be at work in it. The objectives of this paper are: first, to repair the purely descriptive aspects of this deficiency with up-to-date and, to some extent, new statistical material; and, second, to make a start on the analytical task by testing Fuchs' major findings at the aggregate level against these data. Two other "country" papers[6] have already drawn on the Fuchs-Denison methodology.

Some Canadian evidence should therefore be helpful in broadening the international perspective. From a purely domestic point of view, a survey of the service industries as a whole and their interrelations with other major sectors of the economy has been shown by Fuchs to be a necessary preliminary to more detailed studies.

Comparisons between Canada and the United States can hardly be avoided but, because of the aggregative nature of the data used for both countries and the attendant simplifications of methodology, the scope for useful conclusions is somewhat limited. It might, for instance, seem that the service sector in Canada has developed along lines similar to that of the United States, but not to the same extent, so that historical experience in the United States could provide some basis for anticipating the future course of events in Canada. In fact, any rigorous comparative study would require not only a much more detailed analysis of the basic economic statistics of what Stigler has graphically called "the promiscuous ensemble of the service industries"[7] but also the assembly of a very wide range of supplementary information. For although the parallel growth of the Canadian and U.S. economies suggests certain common developments (such as the spread of education, better medical services, and the growth of government functions), there must be considered against this the many influences (geographic, political, cultural, and social as well as purely economic) that qualify this broad picture of similarity and interdependence. As Stigler put it:

> ... those forces which we have found to be directly related to employment in the service industries are not in general perfectly, or indeed always highly, correlated with rising real income or any other index of economic development. We must therefore expect to find large national differences in the roles and rate of growth of the service industries: as between two countries with equal real incomes, the service industries will be larger ... the greater the urbanization, the higher the level of education, the lower the degree of inequality of income distribution, the larger the relative numbers of children and aged in the population and so forth.[8]

One obstacle to comparisons between the Canadian findings of this paper and those of Fuchs arises from the difference in sector definitions. Those used here follow the classification system presently in use by the Dominion Bureau of Statistics for its measures of real output by industry of origin,[9] which treats transportation, storage, and communication as service industries. The goods sector thus comprises: agriculture; forestry, fishing, and trapping; mining, quarrying, and oil wells; manufacturing; construction; and public utility operations. The service sector comprises transportation, storage, and communication; trade; finance, insurance, and real estate; community, recreation, business and personal services; and public administration and defense. This definition underlies most analytical usage in Canada and was, in particular, adopted as the basis for the official measures of productivity change in the goods and service sectors, although in this case service is actually restricted to the commercial service industries.[10] Hood and Scott also treated transportation, storage, and communication as a service industry, but within a more detailed framework, in which the goods sector was divided into agriculture, resource industries, primary and secondary manufacturing, and construction.

The analysis of productivity differentials between the goods and service sectors that is central to this paper is primarily based on the DBS measures, which have been privately extended to include the noncommercial industries. For full sector comparisons, the definitions used here differ from Fuchs' only as noted. For a modified goods sector analogous to Fuchs' "goods," the official productivity data for the nonagricultural goods industries were used, and to approximate "service," those for the commercial service industries were used.

In the analysis of long-term trends in the industrial distribution of the labour force, the supporting tabular material shows data for the Fuchs, as well as the Canadian, definition of the service sector.

Two other points of a technical nature should also be made. First, while many of the primary statistical series of DBS now reflect the 1960 Standard Industrial Classification, derived aggregates such as industry distributions of current and constant dollar gross domestic product are still generally being compiled on the 1948 basis. Hence, the Census and Labor Force Survey data of Tables 1 and 3, respectively, are the only exceptions to the consistent use of the old classification basis. It may be noted, incidentally, that the new classification favours the service sector slightly at the expense of goods since one of its more important effects is the transfer of establishments primarily engaged in repair work from manufacturing to retail trade and various other service industries.

The second point concerns the comparability of the current and constant dollar distributions of GDP. With the major exception of their labour income component, which is assembled from establishment data, current dollar distributions are classified on a company basis, while the constant dollar distributions are wholly on an establishment basis. Classification differences between the two series reflect the extensive degree of vertical integration between the resource industries and manufacturing and, to a certain extent, trade. They are quite important in industries such as forestry and mining, but the distorting effect on a "goods" and "service" comparison is probably not significant.

## Historical Labour Force Trends

As implied in the introductory comments, a major task of this paper must be to establish the extent to which Canadian experience confirms Fuchs' findings for the United States: that employment has been rising at an appreciably faster rate in the service industries than in the goods industries since 1929 and, in particular, that "virtually all of the net growth of employment in the United States in the postwar period has occurred in the service sector."[11] For this purpose, decennial census distributions by industry of the experienced labour force[12] from 1931 forward have mainly been used, together with some adjusted U.S. Census data for 1950 and 1960.

The Bank of Montreal's analysis of changes in the industrial structure of the Canadian and United States economies, which extended back to 1881, will first be briefly recalled. Despite the technical difficulties of such an extended comparison, an unmistakably clear outline emerges of a radical transformation during this period.

In Canada in 1881 less than one in five persons in the labour force was employed within the service industries, including transportation and public utilities, while one-half of the labour force was engaged in the primary industries of agriculture, forestry and fishing. Manufacturing accounted for one person in eight.

There has been a gradual shift over the intervening years so that in 1951 nearly half of the labour force was in the service industries and agriculture accounted for only one person in five, almost a complete reversal of the positions in 1881. Manufacturing employed one person in five instead of one person in eight while the construction group has lost ground . . .

This rising trend, important though it has been, has still not carried the service industries to the relatively important position they have attained in the United States. Similar employment shifts have occurred in the U.S., . . . but service industries occupied nearly 52% of the U.S. labour force in 1950 in comparison with 45% in Canada, a figure reached by the U.S. some 20 years ago. In the U.S. the proportion employed in agriculture in the 1880's was the same as in Canada, viz. 50%, but by the early 1950's had fallen to 12% — much lower than the 19% in Canada.[13]

This broad picture can be brought up to date and given further precision by a consideration of Tables 1 to 5. Table 1 shows that, on the basis of the Fuchs definition, the service sector grew by 143 per cent between 1931 and 1961, thus increasing its share of the experienced labour force from 31 to 46 per cent, while the broader definition allowed for a slightly smaller increase of 131 per cent and a change in share from 39 to 54 per cent.

The United States data of Table 2 are, of course, both conceptually and statistically different from those on which Fuchs based the statement that "we are the first nation in the history of the world in which more than half of the employed population is not involved in the production of food, clothing, houses, automobiles, and other tangible goods."[14] Fuchs' data are also more up to date. However, the fact that the 1960 distribution identifies only 48 per cent of the labour force with his definition of the service sector (although 55 per cent in the broader definition) is not nearly so remarkable as the very close correspondence between these percentages and those which result from the proximate Canadian data. What emerges here is that the lag in the relative development of the Canadian service sector, which Tables 1 and 2 show as still being quite important at the beginning of the 1950s, was substantially eliminated in a single decade.

A more detailed examination of the changing growth rates which gave rise to this phenomenon is facilitated by a rough updating of the data of Table 1. For this purpose, monthly estimates of the industrial distribution of the employed portion of the civilian labour force, adjusted for armed forces employment, must be used. It will be seen that the two alternative tabulations for 1961, provided by Tables 1 and 3, differ not only in absolute numbers but also in their percentage distribution between the various industries. The use of slightly different reference dates is part of the explanation, but more important are the sampling variability of the monthly labour force survey estimates and the differences in the form of questions used — particularly with respect to agricultural employment. Also, the data of Table 3 refer only to the employed portion of the labour force and there was a high rate of unemployment in mid-1961.

Table 1  Census Distributions of the Experienced Labour Force by Industry, Canada, 1931-1961 (thousands of persons)

| Industry | 1931 (a) | | 1941 (b) | | 1951 | | 1961 | |
|---|---|---|---|---|---|---|---|---|
| | Number | Percentage of Total | Number | Percentage of Total | Number | Percentage of Total | Number | Percentage of Total |
| Trade | 421 * | 10.7 | 496 | 11.0 | 746 | 14.1 | 991 | 15.3 |
| Finance, insurance, and real estate | 92 | 2.3 | 90 | 2.0 | 144 | 2.7 | 229 | 3.5 |
| Public administration and defense | 95 | 2.4 | 431 | 9.6 | 301 | 5.7 | 480 | 7.4 |
| Community, recreation, business and personal services | 608 | 15.5 | 685 | 15.2 | 791 | 15.0 | 1,261 | 19.5 |
| Service industries, total—Fuchs definition | 1,216 | 31.0 | 1,701 | 37.8 | 1,982 | 37.6 | 2,960 | 45.8 |
| Transportation, storage, and communication | 297 | 7.6 | 288 | 6.4 | 450 | 8.5 | 531 | 8.2 |
| Service industries, total | 1,513 | 38.6 | 1,989 | 44.2 | 2,432 | 46.1 | 3,491 | 54.1 |
| Agriculture | 1,124 | 28.7 | 1,074 | 23.9 | 824 | 15.6 | 641 | 9.9 |
| Forestry, fishing, and trapping | 98 | 2.5 | 144 | 3.2 | 180 | 3.4 | 143 | 2.2 |
| Mining, quarrying, and oil wells | 72 | 1.8 | 93 | 2.1 | 104 | 2.0 | 120 | 1.9 |
| Manufacturing | 671 | 17.1 | 906 | 20.1 | 1,302 | 24.7 | 1,405 | 21.8 |
| Construction | 250 | 6.4 | 220 | 4.9 | 319 | 6.0 | 430 | 6.7 |
| Electric, gas, and water utilities | 25 | 0.6 | 26 | 0.6 | 49 | 0.9 | 70 | 1.1 |
| Goods industries, total | 2,240 | 57.1 | 2,463 | 54.8 | 2,778 | 52.7 | 2,809 | 43.5 |
| Industry unspecified or undefined | 169 | 4.3 | 46 | 1.0 | 67 | 1.3 | 158 | 2.4 |
| Total employed, all industries | 3,922 | 100.0 | 4,498 | 100.0 | 5,277 | 100.0 | 6,458 | 100.0 |

NOTE: Figures may not add due to rounding.

Source: 1941, 1951, and 1961 data—DBS Catalogue No. 94-551, 1961 Census of Canada, Bulletin SL-1. Labour Force —Occupation and Industry Trends, Ottawa, 1966, Table 12; 1931 data—Ninth Census of Canada, 1951, Report No. SP-8, Occupation and Industry Trends in Canada, Ottawa, 1954, Tables 10 and 11.

(a) For rough conformity with the later figures, which reflect the 1960 Standard Industrial Classification, those of 1931 were adjusted as follows: post office transferred from public administration and defence to transportation, storage, and communication; auto repairs, watch and jewelry repairs transferred from manufacturing to trade; boot and shoe repairs, blacksmithing transferred from manufacturing to community, recreation, business, and personal services; dairies transferred from retail trade to manufacturing.

(b) Persons in active service on June 2, 1941, who were excluded from the published 1941 figures, have been included here.

*Table 2   Census Distributions of the Experienced Labour Force by Industry, United States, 1950 and 1960 (thousands of persons)*

| Industry (Canadian Designation) | 1950 | | 1960 | |
|---|---|---|---|---|
| | Number | Percentage of Total | Number | Percentage of Total |
| Trade | 9,788 | 16.2 | 10,960 | 15.7 |
| Finance, insurance, and real estate | 1,954 | 3.2 | 2,749 | 3.9 |
| Public administration and defense | 3,267 | 5.4 | 4,619 | 6.6 |
| Community, recreation, business and personal services | 11,524 | 19.1 | 15,429 | 22.1 |
| Service industries, total—Fuchs definition | 26,533 | 44.0 | 33,757 | 48.4 |
| Transportation, storage, and communication | 4,267 | 7.1 | 4,284 | 6.1 |
| Service industries, total | 30,800 | 51.1 | 38,041 | 54.6 |
| Agriculture | 7,048 | 11.7 | 4,415 | 6.3 |
| Forestry, fishing, and trapping | 133 | 0.2 | 104 | 0.1 |
| Mining, quarrying, and oil wells | 970 | 1.6 | 714 | 1.0 |
| Manufacturing | 15,307 | 25.4 | 18,536 | 26.6 |
| Construction | 3,764 | 6.2 | 4,302 | 6.2 |
| Electric, gas, and water utilities | 692 | 1.1 | 765 | 1.1 |
| Goods industries, total | 27,914 | 46.3 | 28,836 | 41.4 |
| Industry not reported | 1,543 | 2.6 | 2,847 | 4.1 |
| Total employed, all industries | 60,256 | 100.0 | 69,723 | 100.0 |

NOTE: Figures may not add due to rounding.
**Source:** U.S. Bureau of the Census, *Census of Population: 1960*, Volume I—Characteristics of the Population, Part 1—U.S. Summary, Washington, D.C., 1964, Tables 83 and 210. Civilian labour force distributions of Table 210 rearranged to conform with 1960 Canadian S.I.C. as far as permitted by the 149 category level of classification, and Armed Forces added (Table 83). Principal internal changes to Table 210 were: postal service transferred from public administration and defense to transportation, storage, and communication; sanitary services from electric, gas, and water utilities to public administration and defense; eating and drinking places from trade to community, recreation, business and personal services; and automobile repair service and garages from community, recreation, business and personal services to trade.

Even discounting the greater sampling variability at the industry level, these data cannot be used to approximate labour force growth by industry because of the different over-all rates of unemployment between the two periods and the lack of published data on its detailed incidence.

These objections are less important for comparisons at the sector and total levels, and the data of Table 3 can therefore be taken as a fairly reliable indication that the accelerated development of the service industries during the 1950s has not carried through as strongly to the present time. Nevertheless, the percentage of the employed labour force classified in Fuchs' service sector in mid-1966 leaves no doubt that Canada's formal qualifications for admission to the hitherto exclusive club of "service economies" must by now be firmly established!

A somewhat sharper picture of the differential growth of the goods and service sectors in Canada emerges from Table 4, which is essentially a comparison of average annual rates of growth by industry and sector between 1931 and 1961 with those of the 1951-61 sub-period. Separate growth rates for the

*Table 3   Distributions of the Employed Labour Force by Industry, Canada, 1961 and 1966 (thousands of persons)*

| | 1961 | | 1966 | |
| Industry | Number | Percentage of Total | Number | Percentage of Total |
| --- | --- | --- | --- | --- |
| Trade | 1,012 | 16.1 | 1,172 | 16.0 |
| Finance, insurance, and real estate | 242 | 3.9 | 301 | 4.1 |
| Public administration and defense | 500 | 8.0 | 540 | 7.4 |
| Community, recreation, business and personal services | 1,190 | 19.0 | 1,631 | 22.3 |
| Service industries, total—Fuchs definition | 2,944 | 46.9 | 3,644 | 49.7 |
| Transportation, storage, and communication | 502 | 8.0 | 538 | 7.3 |
| Service industries, total | 3,446 | 54.9 | 4,182 | 57.1 |
| Agriculture | 723 | 11.5 | 583 | 8.0 |
| Forestry, fishing, and trapping | 105 | 1.7 | 110 | 1.5 |
| Mining, quarrying, and oil wells | 76 | 1.2 | 122 | 1.7 |
| Manufacturing | 1,453 | 23.1 | 1,737 | 23.7 |
| Construction | 406 | 6.5 | 516 | 7.0 |
| Electric, gas, and water utilities | 70 | 1.1 | 75 | 1.0 |
| Goods industries, total | 2,833 | 45.1 | 3,143 | 42.9 |
| Total employed, all industries | 6,279 | 100.0 | 7,325 | 100.0 |
| Unemployed (a) | 410 | | 238 | |
| Total labour force | 6,689 | | 7,563 | |

NOTE: Figures may not add due to rounding.

**Source:** Dominion Bureau of Statistics, Special Surveys Division, *Special Tables 1 and 3(c)*, supplementing DBS Catalogue No. 71-001, *The Labour Force*, Ottawa, monthly. 1961 data were calculated as the average of the employed civilian labour force estimates by industry for the survey weeks of May 20, 1961 and June 17, 1961 for rough conformity with Census of Population reference data. A similar procedure was followed in 1966 using the survey weeks of May 21, 1966 and June 18, 1966. Annual averages of Armed Forces employment were added to the civilian labour force data in both years.

(a)  Unemployed were 6.1 per cent of the total labour force in 1961 and 3.1 per cent in 1966.

two earlier decades as well might have added to the usefulness of the table in some respects, but for the purpose of sector comparisons, the disproportionate importance of public administration and defense in 1941 would have been a distorting influence. Corresponding U.S. growth rates between 1950 and 1960 are also included, as well as some rough estimates at the sector and total levels for 1961-66, the derivation of which is described in the table.

Over the entire period from 1931 to 1961, the average rate of growth of the total experienced labour force was 1.7 per cent per annum, with services (our definition) and goods increasing at markedly different rates of 2.8 per cent and 0.8 per cent, respectively. Between 1951 and 1961, the over-all rate of growth was somewhat higher, at 2.0 per cent, and the disparity between the sectoral rates enormously greater. During this decade then, there can be no doubt that Canadian experience parallels Fuchs' finding that the service sector absorbed virtually all of the net postwar growth of employment in the United States. However, the data for 1961-66 suggest that there has been in recent years a

*Table 4* *Average Annual Rates of Growth of the Experienced Labour Force by Industry, Canada, 1931-66, and United States 1950-60*

| Industry | Canada | | | United States |
|---|---|---|---|---|
| | 1931-61 | 1951-61 | 1961-66 (a) | 1950-60 |
| Trade | 2.9 | 2.9 | n.a. | 1.1 |
| Finance, insurance, and real estate | 3.1 | 4.7 | n.a. | 3.5 |
| Public administration and defense | 5.5 | 4.8 | n.a. | 3.5 |
| Community, recreation, business and personal services | 2.5 | 4.8 | n.a. | 3.0 |
| Service industries, total— Fuchs definition | 3.0 | 4.1 | 3.7 | 2.4 |
| Transportation, storage, and communication | 2.0 | 1.7 | n.a. | 0.0 |
| Service industries, total | 2.8 | 3.7 | 3.3 | 2.1 |
| Agriculture | —1.9 | —2.5 | n.a. | —4.6 |
| Forestry, fishing, and trapping | 1.2 | —2.3 | n.a. | —2.4 |
| Mining, quarrying, and oil wells | 1.7 | 1.4 | n.a. | —3.0 |
| Manufacturing | 2.5 | 0.8 | n.a. | 1.9 |
| Construction | 1.8 | 3.0 | n.a. | 1.3 |
| Electric, gas, and water utilities | 3.5 | 3.6 | n.a. | 1.0 |
| Goods industries, total | 0.8 | 0.1 | 1.5 | 0.3 |
| Total employed, all industries | 1.7 | 2.0 | 2.5 | 1.5 |

**Source:** Tables 1, 2, and 3.

n.a.=not applicable.

(a) 1961-66 growth rates are based on the data of Table 3, with the unemployed being prorated between sectors according to the percentage distribution in each year of the employed labor force. If, as seems probable, this procedure overstates the actual number of unemployed in services and understates the number in goods in both years, the growth rates in services and goods will be respectively understated and overstated because of the higher over-all rate of unemployment in 1961.

distinct moderation of this accelerated development of services and a return to something like the longer-term trend. Of the increase in total employment of 1,046 thousands during this period, shown by Table 3, the goods sector accounted for approximately 30 per cent, in contrast with a corresponding percentage for 1951-61 of less than 3 per cent, as calculated from the labour force distributions of Table 1.

The decline in the relative importance of the goods sector between 1931 and 1961 is virtually all accounted for by agriculture, whose share in the experienced labour force fell from 28.7 to 9.9 per cent. It was also the only industry in which the labour force declined in absolute terms over the period as a whole, although the combination of forestry, fishing, and trapping experienced a significant decline between 1951 and 1961. Actually, as may be seen from Table 1, the nonagricultural goods industries gained slightly in relative importance by 1961, their successive percentage of the total labour force at the decennial intervals being 28.4, 30.9, 37.1, and 33.6. Within this particular aggregate, the dominant component of manufacturing also experienced a moderate over-all gain in relative importance—from 17.1 to 21.8 per cent—with the residual industries holding more or less constant.

United States experience between 1950 and 1960 was broadly consistent with this general pattern. The decline in the percentage share of the experienced labour force classified to the goods sector was almost wholly matched by a corresponding decline in agriculture, leaving the relative importance of goods industries less agriculture virtually unchanged at 35.1 per cent. While manufacturing in Canada lost some ground during the 1950s, there was a small increase in its relative importance in the United States.

The contribution that agricultural shifts made to the changing industrial distribution of the North American labour force was thus an extremely important one. It is illustrated in Table 5, which adds the decrease in agriculture to the increase in the total experienced labour force and distributes this amount between the service and goods sectors and a residual category of unclassified changes. What emerges on the source side of the equation for Canada is the record of a substantial contribution of shifts from agriculture to the growth of the non-agricultural labour force since 1931. In recent years, this has been somewhat lower than the average for the 1931-61 period although, as may be seen from Table 1, the latter figure conceals important variations in agriculture's contribution during the 1931-41 and 1941-51 decades. Shifts from agriculture played an even greater part in the growth of the nonagricultural labour force of the United States between 1950 and 1960, and the data used in the Bank of Montreal study[15] indicate that, in contrast to the situation in Canada, the relative contribution of agriculture was very similar in the two preceding decades.

The disposition of these increases in the Canadian nonagricultural labour force shows a roughly two to one relationship between the service and goods shares over the entire period from 1931 to 1961, with the service sector increasing its share considerably during the 1950s and then reverting more recently to the long-term average pattern. In the United States during the 1950s, the service sector accounted for an appreciably lower share of the increase in the nonagricultural labour force than in Canada, although comparisons are difficult because of the magnitude of the ''industry unspecified or undefined'' category in both countries. Rough calculations with the Bank of Montreal data,[16] however, indicate that the thirty year average shares of services and nonagricultural goods in the increase of the nonagricultural labour force were, at approximately 62 and 32 per cent, quite close to the corresponding figures for Canada.

Before concluding this general review of historical trends in the industrial composition of the Canadian labour force, two points relating to the future sources of growth in the nonagricultural labour force will be briefly touched upon. The first is the extent to which shifts out of agricultural labour might continue to make a significant contribution. Table 1 shows that, although agriculture's percentage of the total experienced labour force decreased in each of the three decades covered, the absolute decline was not important until some time after 1941. This can probably be explained, first of all, by the diminished employment opportunities outside of agriculture during the depression years and, secondly, by the emphasis on agricultural production during World War II. Average annual rates of decrease during the 1941-51 and 1951-61 periods were, at 2.6 and 2.5 per cent, respectively, virtually identical, while the data of Table 3, in spite of their dubious value for growth rate calculations, suggest a marked increase since 1961 in this rate of decline. These trends are in keeping with the almost universal tendency among industrially advanced countries for

*Table 5 Changes in the Experienced Labour Force and Its Disposition between Sectors, Canada, 1931-66, and United States, 1950-1960 (thousands of persons)*

| Source and Disposition of Change | Canada | | | | | | United States 1950-60 | |
| --- | --- | --- | --- | --- | --- | --- | --- | --- |
| | 1931-61 | | 1951-61 | | 1961-66 (a) | | | |
| | Number | Percentage of Total | Number | Percentage of Total | Number | Percentage of Total | Number | Percentage of Total |
| Increase in total experienced labour force | 2,536 | 84.0 | 1,181 | 86.6 | 1,046 | 88.2 | 9,467 | 78.2 |
| Decrease in agriculture | 483 | 16.0 | 183 | 13.4 | 140 | 11.8 | 2,633 | 21.8 |
| Increase in nonagricultural labour force | 3,019 | 100.0 | 1,364 | 100.0 | 1,186 | 100.0 | 12,100 | 100.0 |
| Net increase in service sector | 1,978 | 65.5 | 1,059 | 77.6 | 736 | 62.1 | 7,241 | 59.8 |
| Net increase in nonagricultural goods sector | 1,052 | 34.8 | 214 | 15.7 | 450 | 37.9 | 3,555 | 29.4 |
| Increase or decrease (—) in "industry unspecified or undefined" (b) | —11 | —0.3 | 91 | 6.7 | n.r. | n.r. | 1,304 | 10.8 |

**Source:** Tables 1-3.

n.r. = not relevant.

(a) 1961-66 data cover employed labour force only.

(b) "Industry unspecified or undefined" may include some persons identified with agriculture.

progressively greater agricultural outputs to be produced with a declining labour force as the result of farm mechanization and related technological developments as well as changes in the organization of agricultural production.

Given the very large decline in the absolute number of persons engaged in agriculture which has already taken place since 1941— something in the order of 50 per cent according to the figures of Tables 1 and 3, the intuitive reaction is that the scope for further absolute decreases might be somewhat limited. However, some calculations in a study prepared for the first annual review of the Economic Council of Canada,[17] based in part on the assumption of a continuation in the trend towards the decreasing relative importance of marginal farms,[18] estimated that an annual decrease in the agricultural labor force of about 2.3 per cent per annum could occur between 1963 and 1970. The rough data of Table 3 suggest that this rate had been considerably exceeded up to 1966, and the most recent projections of potential employment by the Council show a revision of the estimated rate of decline in agriculture to 3.1 per cent per annum.[19]

The second point concerns the future rate of growth of the total labour force. The average rate of increase from 1951 to 1966 was, according to the figures used here, approximately 2.2 per cent per annum. Again drawing upon the projections of the Economic Council of Canada, an annual average percentage increase of 3.2 between 1965 and 1970 is anticipated.[20] This rate of growth is as high as almost any ever attained in Canada's history and is far in excess of the recent and current growth rates in the labour forces of other industrial countries.

The potential disposition of this large and continuing influx of new workers will be importantly determined by the incidence among them of the basic demographic characteristics (age, sex, and education), for which Fuchs has shown there are marked differences between sectors in the United States. Some historical Canadian evidence on the industrial distribution of these characteristics is considered later in the paper. At this point, it may be noted that, on an over-all basis, rising female participation rates are expected by the Economic Council of Canada to make the female component of future labour force growth particularly large. Out of the projected 1.2 million additions from 1965 to 1970, it is estimated that some 620,000 will be females. An equally significant prospect is the anticipated large upsurge in the labour force of males under 25, which is expected to be 250,000 during the same period.

## Reasons for the Relative Growth of Service Employment—the Income Elasticity Hypothesis

Before considering possible explanations for the long-standing and persistent tendency toward the relative growth of service employment, the relevant data for 1946 to 1966, the period of main concern in this paper, may be briefly summarized. Table 6 shows the changing relative importance of the goods and service industries as illustrated by the three variables of employment,[21] production in current dollars, and real or constant dollar output. On the basis of full sector definitions, the relative proportions of employment accounted for by goods and services were virtually reversed between 1946 and 1966, with goods declining from 58.8 to 42.0 per cent and services increasing from 41.2 to 58.0

Table 6   Per Cent of Employment, Value of Production, and Real Output in the Goods and Service Sectors, and the Growth Rates by Sector, Canada, 1946 and 1966.

| | Percentage of Total | | Growth Rate (per cent per annum) |
|---|---|---|---|
| | 1946 | 1966 | 1946-66 |
| Total economy | | | |
| Goods sector | | | |
| Employment | 58.8 | 42.0 | 0.3 |
| Value of GDP | 51.2 | 46.3 | 7.5 |
| Real output | 52.1 | 56.2 | 5.1 |
| Service sector | | | |
| Employment | 41.2 | 58.0 | 3.8 |
| Value of GDP | 48.8 | 53.7 | 8.5 |
| Real output | 47.9 | 43.8 | 4.3 |
| | | | |
| Commercial nonagricultural economy | | | |
| Nonagricultural goods sector | | | |
| Employment | 54.0 | 47.8 | 2.2 |
| Value of GDP | 50.4 | 48.6 | 8.2 |
| Real output | 50.8 | 57.2 | 5.8 |
| Commercial service sector | | | |
| Employment | 46.0 | 52.2 | 3.4 |
| Value of GDP | 49.6 | 51.4 | 8.6 |
| Real output | 49.2 | 42.8 | 4.5 |

Note:   All measures shown here are based on data classified according to the 1948 SIC. Additional estimation was necessary to derive all three sets of figures for the commercial service sector. It is technically incorrect to use real output data for share analysis since the per cent distribution in any year will depend upon the weights used. The use of any set of fixed weights, however, ensures that the differential between the sector growth rates is carried through, to a greater or lesser degree, into the sector shares. All growth rates were calculated by compounding between initial and terminal years. While acceptable for the purposes of this table, where the emphasis is on *differential* rates of growth between sectors, tests have shown that this procedure frequently overstates—and sometimes importantly—the results derived by least squares of logarithms method over this period.

Source:   Employment data—Worksheets underlying index numbers of employment published in DBS Catalogue No. 14-201, *Aggregate Productivity Trends*, Ottawa, 1967, supplemented by data for the noncommercial industries from the DBS Special Surveys Division, as noted in Table 3; Gross Domestic Product data—DBS Catalogue No. 13-502, *National Accounts, Income and Expenditure, 1926-56*, Ottawa, 1958, and DBS Catalogue No. 13-201, *National Accounts, Income and Expenditure*, Ottawa, annual; Real output data—DBS Catalogue No. 61-505, *Indexes of Real Domestic Product by Industry of Origin, 1935-61*, Ottawa, 1963, and DBS Catalogue No. 61-005, *Annual Supplement to the Monthly Index of Industrial Production*, Ottawa, May 1967.

per cent. This reflects the marked differential in the growth rates of employment in the two sectors, which were 0.3 and 3.8 per cent per annum for goods and services, respectively. There were parallel, though much less pronounced, shifts in current dollar production during the same period. The share of the service sector in the value of gross domestic product increased from 48.8 to 53.7 per cent as the result of a growth rate 1.0 per cent higher than in the goods sector.

Within the commercial nonagricultural economy, employment also grew faster in services than in goods. The disparity between the two growth rates was smaller than in the full sector comparison, however, and this resulted in a more moderate increase in the service sector's share of employment, from 46.0 to 52.2 per cent. This mainly reflects the exclusion of agriculture from the comparison, since employment in the commercial service sector grew only slightly more slowly than in the full service sector. There was also an increase in service's share of current dollar production, from 49.6 to 51.4 per cent, which, as in the case of the full sector comparison, was a good deal smaller than the corresponding gain in employment.

A completely different picture emerges when changes in the share of real output and sector growth rates are considered. Within the total economy, the service sector's share of real output *decreased* from 47.9 to 43.8 per cent, and the commercial service sector lost even more ground within the commercial nonagricultural economy with a decrease from 49.2 to 42.8 per cent. The corresponding growth rate differentials (service minus goods) were −0.8 and −1.3 per cent per annum.

When these figures are considered in relation to the current dollar data, it is evident that there was in Canada a very marked rise in service prices relative to those of goods during the postwar period. Furthermore, as Table 7 shows, sector differentials in the rate of growth of the implicit price deflator between current and constant dollar output are not affected by changes in the sector definition used. Prices in the industries excluded from the restricted sector comparisons, namely agriculture and noncommercial services, must therefore have risen at about the same rate as those in the nonagricultural goods and commercial service industries, respectively.

Postwar United States experience appears to have been quite different. As in Canada, the implicit price deflator for the service sector as a whole grew faster than that for total goods, although the differential was only two-thirds of the corresponding Canadian figure. However, the implicit price deflator for the excluded goods industries, namely agriculture, forestry and fisheries, and government enterprise, apparently declined, while that for real estate, households and institutions, and general government combined seems to have grown at an appreciably faster rate than in the remainder of the service sector. Consequently, for sector comparisons other than goods and service, differentials in the rate of growth of the implicit price deflator were much smaller than in Canada and even, in the extreme case of "goods" and "service", virtually nonexistent.

It is true, of course, that the United States data of Table 7 are based on different sector definitions than those underlying the Canadian data and relate to a shorter time period that excludes the sustained high growth of the 1960s. Questions can also be raised about the validity of some of the basic data and whether the distribution, direction, and magnitude of possible bias is similar for both countries. Taking the data at their face value, however, it is difficult to escape the conclusion that the rise in the price of services relative to goods during the postwar period, although common to both countries, has been greater and more pervasive in Canada than in the United States.

As will be shown below, this point has an important bearing on the first hypothesis considered by Fuchs as a possible explanation for the differential growth of employment in the two sectors, namely that the increase in the service sector's share of total employment may be due in some part to a higher income elasticity of demand for services than for goods. The essence of this

*Table 7   Rates of Growth of Employment, Value of Production, Real Output, and Implicit Price Deflator, in the Goods and Service Sectors, with Sector Differentials, Canada and United States (per cent per annum)*

| Sector | Canada, 1946-1966 | | | | United States, 1947-1961 | | | |
|---|---|---|---|---|---|---|---|---|
| | Employment | GDP | Real Output | Implicit Price Deflator | Employment | GDP | Real Output | Implicit Price Deflator |
| Goods | 0.3 | 7.5 | 5.1 | 2.4 | —0.1 | 5.0 | 2.9 | 2.1 |
| "Goods" | 2.2 | 8.2 | 5.8 | 2.4 | 0.4 | 5.7 | 3.1 | 2.6 |
| Service | 3.8 | 8.5 | 4.3 | 4.2 | 2.3 | 6.7 | 3.4 | 3.3 |
| "Service" | 3.4 | 8.6 | 4.5 | 4.1 | 1.9 | 5.8 | 3.0 | 2.8 |
| Sector differential: | | | | | | | | |
| Service—goods | 3.5 | 1.0 | —0.8 | 1.8 | 2.4 | 1.7 | 0.5 | 1.2 |
| Service—"goods" | 1.6 | 0.3 | —1.5 | 1.8 | 1.9 | 1.0 | 0.3 | 0.7 |
| "Service"—goods | 3.1 | 1.1 | —0.6 | 1.7 | 2.0 | 0.8 | 0.1 | 0.7 |
| "Service"—"goods" | 1.2 | 0.4 | —1.3 | 1.7 | 1.5 | 0.1 | —0.1 | 0.2 |

**Note:**   Although Fuchs' terminology of "goods" and "service" is applied here to the Canadian data, the sector definitions underlying the latter are those outlined in the introduction and used in Table 6 and elsewhere.

**Source:**  Canadian data—Table 6; U.S. data—Fuchs, *Productivity Trends in the Goods and Service Sectors, op. cit.*, Table A-2.

hypothesis is that, as income per capita rises and a certain standard of goods consumption is achieved, further increments in income tend to be channelled in greater proportion toward spending on additional services rather than on additional goods. Of course, demand is affected by a great many factors other than income—changes in relative prices, quite obviously, as well as those in tastes and technology, and also institutional factors such as the distribution of income and the degree of urbanization. There can also be significant differences between the short-run and long-run effects of income and price changes since current consumption decisions are importantly influenced by past behaviour as manifested in established habit patterns and stocks of durable goods.[22] Even relatively sophisticated econometric techniques cannot separate out more than a few of these numerous and interrelated effects simultaneously, so that inconsistencies between the results of different partial approaches can occur quite frequently. The best-known work in this area is based on consumer expenditure data only[23] and therefore cannot explain the quite different factors which determine expenditures in other important areas of final demand.

Fuchs' principal approach to the testing of the income elasticity hypothesis was therefore an indirect one. Notwithstanding the fact that many industries produce intermediate as well as final outputs, he argued that, if the rise in real income per capita between 1929 and 1963 had in fact resulted in a more elastic demand for services than for goods, it ought to be reflected in a more rapid rise in real output for the service sector relative to the goods sector. Accordingly, his conclusion that the income elasticity effect was not a major part of the explanation for the growth in the service sector's share of total employment rested heavily on the fact that differential rates of change of real output between the two sectors were very small relative to those for employment.

Fuchs used two alternative sets of differential rates of change of real output for comparison with those of employment on the assumption that distributions by sector of GDP in current dollars on the one hand, and those of constant dollar product on the other, are indicative of the limits of possible measurement biases in the growth of service output relative to that of goods.[24] The use of the former measure eliminates the effect of differential price change since prices are deemed to have changed at the same rate in both sectors. When constant dollar measures are used, allowance has to be made for the possibility of a shift to goods resulting from the price effect. Sector differentials (service minus goods) in the rate of growth of the implicit price deflator between 1929 and 1963 were positive but relatively small, so that the price effect did not appear to be of major importance.

United States data for the period 1947 to 1961, as summarized in Table 7, do not present such a uniform picture as those analyzed by Fuchs because of the marked disparity in the growth of both current and constant dollar output between those industries subtracted for the purpose of the restricted sector comparisons and their parent aggregates. If attention is confined to the core sectors of ''service'' and ''goods'', however, it is quite clear from the relationship between the output and employment differentials that Fuchs' more broadly based conclusion about relative income elasticities is not invalidated by more recent experience.

In some respects, the postwar Canadian data seem easier to assess. Differentials between service and goods output based on the current dollar measure, in which the direction of probable bias is favourable to services, are uniformly small in relation to the employment differentials for all four comparisons. Again, the constant dollar output measures show that goods output increased faster than service output in each case. The data also indicate that agricultural output grew less rapidly than in the remaining goods industries, which, in conjunction with the apparently negligible change in the implicit price deflator for agriculture, tends to confirm the generally accepted view that the income elasticity of demand for agricultural products is low.

However, the use of bracketing assumptions to assess the possible magnitude of relative changes in output as indicators of underlying income elasticities of demand depends, for its efficacy, on a fairly narrow spread between their limits, i.e., on moderate differentials between the rates of growth of the implicit price deflators for each sector. In the Canadian case, these differentials are so pervasively large that they put the assessment of the probable price effect, which runs counter to the income effect, outside the range of unsupported judgment.

A question which is perhaps more relevant in the present context, and to which the data used here can supply a much firmer answer, is whether the service industries in Canada face demand schedules that are more elastic in total than those for goods. A more rapid rise of real output in the service sector than in the goods sector would clearly indicate a stronger elasticity of response to the combined effect of changes in income, relative prices, the degree of urbanization, and other relevant factors mentioned earlier. That this has almost certainly not happened is evident from the sector differentials in the rate of growth of real output shown in Table 7, even when allowance is made for any reasonable margin of error in their calculation.

Some corroboration of this conclusion may be sought in an examination of the relative growth of rough end-use demand series for goods and services which can be developed by expanding national accounts distributions of personal expenditures on consumer goods and services to include other categories of final demand.[25] These are current dollar data which cannot be converted into real terms because of the inability to make a corresponding separation of the implicit price deflator for Gross National Expenditure into its goods and service components. Moreover, these classifications reflect the embodiment of service outputs in final demand for goods, and vice versa. Nevertheless, the comparison provides an interesting supplement to that based on output data, and what emerges, on the basis of compound rates between terminal years, is that the average rate of growth of "Demand for Canadian Services," at 8.7 per cent, was slightly higher than that of "Demand for Canadian Goods," at 8.1 per cent, between 1946 and 1966. Bearing in mind, however, the marked differential between the implicit price deflator for GDP goods and GDP services, it seems almost certain that the rate of growth of final demand for Canadian services in real terms—as the result of income elasticity and all other influences—was lower than that for goods.

In summary then, it can be said that, while the data considered here do not permit any firm conclusions about sector differentials in income elasticity as such, the sharply differing rates of employment growth between the goods and service sectors in Canada during the postwar years cannot be explained by differences in the rates of growth of sector outputs or of final demand for their products. Indeed, even after allowance for the imperfections of many of the underlying statistics, the evidence clearly suggests that output grew faster in the goods than in the service sector, even though goods employment grew more slowly. The explanation must therefore lie in the differential rate of growth of output per person employed, and this in turn raises a fresh set of questions as to what factors might have been responsible for the differing productivity performance of the two sectors.

## Reasons for the Relative Growth of Service Employment—Changes in Productivity

That output per person employed grew much faster in goods than in services, regardless of how the sectors are defined, is clear beyond doubt from the rough data of Table 8.

Table 8   Average Annual Rates of Growth of Output per Person Employed, Goods and Service Sectors, Canada, 1946-66 (per cent per annum)

| Sector Definitions | Goods | Service | Differential (G—S) |
|---|---|---|---|
| Goods and service | 4.8 | 0.5 | 4.3 |
| Nonagricultural goods and service | 3.6 | 0.5 | 3.1 |
| Goods and commercial service | 4.8 | 1.1 | 3.7 |
| Nonagricultural goods and commercial service | 3.6 | 1.1 | 2.5 |

Source: Table 6.

The evidence of the preceding section also indicates that this differential change of output per person employed is the principal explanation for the much more rapid rise of employment in the service sector between 1946 and 1966. This in itself, however, is not a particularly illuminating conclusion. The well-established character of the differential has most certainly had and will continue to have implications just beginning to be perceived, which go much further and deeper than the superficial effect on head-counts of employment.[26] The first step toward an understanding of how the structure and workings of the Canadian economy might be affected by this phenomenon must clearly be an attempt, however tentative, to disentangle some of the factors responsible for the slower growth of output per person employed in the service industries.

Fuchs' work suggests that at least four measurable factors have been involved in the U.S. situation. These are a more rapid decline in hours worked per man in the service industries, the differential effect of intrasector shifts in the relative importance of industries with different levels of productivity, a slower rise in the quality of the work force in the service industries, and a less rapid growth in the amount of capital employed per worker.

In this section, the procedures followed by Fuchs to estimate the effects of these factors[27] are retraced with Canadian data. As noted in the introduction, the analysis is essentially based on the official DBS measures of real output per person employed and per man-hour recently developed for the goods and

*Table 9   Rates of Growth of Output, Input, and Productivity, Goods and Service Sectors, Canada, 1946-66 (per cent per annum)*

|  | Goods | Nonagri-cultural Goods | Service | Commercial Service |
|---|---|---|---|---|
| Real output | 4.67 | 5.33 | 4.24 | 4.28 |
| Employment | — 0.09 | 1.43 | 3.79 | 3.10 |
| Man-hours | — 0.73 | 1.04 | 3.06 | 2.39 |
| Output per person employed | 4.76 | 3.84 | 0.44 | 1.14 |
| Output per man-hour | 5.43 | 4.24 | 1.15 | 1.84 |
| Labor income | 6.74 | 6.85 | 8.67 | 8.49 |
| GDP, current dollars | 6.19 | 7.06 | 8.36 | 8.19 |

**Note:**   All growth rates were calculated by the least squares of logarithms method. The productivity growth rates were derived from time series of output per unit of labour input rather than by subtraction of the growth rates of the components.

**Source:** Output, employment, man-hours, and productivity growth rates—DBS Catalogue No. 14-201, *Aggregate Productivity Trends, 1946-66*, supplemented by private estimates from published sources for the noncommercial industries; growth rates of labour income and gross domestic product in current dollars calculated from published series in DBS Catalogue Nos. 13-502 and 13-201, *National Accounts, Income and Expenditure* with private adjustments for coverage in the case of the commercial service sector.

service sectors of the commercial economy, which have been privately extended to include the non-commercial industries. The component data are shown in Table 9 together with certain other relevant input measures, to be discussed later in this section.

As well as reflecting more precise methods of calculation than have hitherto been used in the paper, the official productivity measures embody a number of refinements and developments on the labour input side.[28] There are two major sources of employment statistics for the commercial economy, the monthly household-based labour force survey and the monthly establishment-based employment survey. In view of their different basic purposes, they vary in coverage, concept, and methods, and neither is completely suitable in its published form for productivity measurement purposes. In order to overcome these difficulties, a composite series of persons employed was developed, using elements from these and certain supplementary sources. After the necessary conceptual and statistical adjustments, this provides a reasonably consistent match for the real output measures. Most of the employment data for paid workers originate from establishment surveys, while the labour force survey is the source of data relating to the self-employed and unpaid family workers.

The quantities to be explained, namely sector differentials in the growth rates of output per person employed in Canada between 1946 and 1966 for the various alternative comparisons of goods and services, are shown in Table 10, together with estimates for the specified explanatory variables. Roughly corresponding measures for the United States, covering the period 1947 to 1961, are also included for comparative purposes. Fuchs' analysis of the United States data between 1929 and 1961 did not cover the subperiods explicitly but, as he suggested, there are important differences between them, both in the magnitudes of the productivity differentials and the explanatory variables, so that the more recent experience is what is relevant here.

Table 10 *Explanation of Output Per Person Employed Differentials Between Goods and Service Sectors, Canada and United States (per cent per annum)*

| | Canada, 1946-1966 | | | | United States, 1947-1966 | | | |
|---|---|---|---|---|---|---|---|---|
| | Goods Minus Service | Goods Minus Comm. Service | Nonag. Goods Minus Service | Nonag. Goods Minus Comm. Service | Goods Minus Service | Goods Minus "Service" | "Goods" Minus Service | "Goods" Minus "Service" |
| Differentials in growth rate of output per person employed (goods minus service) | 4.32 | 3.62 | 3.40 | 2.70 | 1.94 | 1.88 | 1.59 | 1.53 |
| Accounted for by differentials in Rate of decrease of average hours worked | 0.07 | 0.05 | 0.33 | 0.31 | 0.07 | 0.06 | 0.09 | 0.08 |
| Effects of intrasector shifts | 0.60 | 0.40 | 0.17 | −0.03 | 0.40 [a] | 0.26 [a] | 0.14 [a] | 0.00 [a] |
| Rate of growth of labour quality | 2.08 | 1.57 | 0.31 | −0.21 | 0.79 | 0.95 | 0.66 | 0.82 |
| Rate of growth of capital input | −0.23 | −0.24 | 0.49 | 0.47 | −0.06 | 0.25 | 0.21 | 0.52 |
| Leaving Unaccounted residual (errors, technological change, economies of scale, etc.) | 1.80 | 1.84 | 2.10 | 2.16 | 0.74 | 0.36 | 0.49 | 0.11 |
| Percentage of O/PE unexplained | 42 | 51 | 62 | 80 | 38 | 19 | 31 | 7 |

**Note:** All calculations within sectors are by division of component growth rates plus 100 rather than by subtraction.
**Source:** Canadian data—Table 9 and shift calculations re-referred to in text; U.S. data—Fuchs, *Productivity Trends in the Goods and Service Sectors, op. cit.*, Table A-2. Canadian sector definitions—see pp. (4 and 5); U.S. sector definitions—see *ibid.*, p. 3.
(a) Estimate, calculated from shift differentials reported by Fuchs for 1929-61 and Canadian data for 1946-66.

*Table 11    Growth Rates of Output Per Person Employed, Goods and Service Sectors, Canada and United States, 1946-66 (per cent per annum)*

|  | Canada | United States |
|---|---|---|
| Goods | 4.76 | |
| Nonagricultural goods | 3.84 | |
| Service | 0.44 | |
| Commercial service | 1.14 | |
| Goods | | 3.03 |
| ''Goods'' | | 2.68 |
| Service | | 1.09 |
| ''Service'' | | 1.15 |

**Note:**    All calculations are by division of component growth rates plus 100.
**Source:** Canadian data—Table 9; U.S. data—Fuchs, *Productivity Trends in the Goods and Service Sectors, op. cit.,* Table A-2.

The largest Canadian differential in output per person emerges from a comparison of the full goods and service sectors. As Table 11 shows, the exclusion of the noncommercial industries appreciably raises the rate of growth of output per person employed in service and the exclusion of agriculture lowers it in goods, thereby reducing the differential in the modified sector comparisons. As the result of parallel though less pronounced influences, the relationship between the U.S. differentials shows a similar pattern. In absolute terms, however, the latter are much smaller than the corresponding Canadian measures, mainly because the rate of growth of output per person employed was higher in the Canadian than in the U.S. goods industries. For instance, as may be seen from Table 11, the 2.38 percentage points of difference between the two differentials for the full goods and service comparison are accounted for by differences of 1.73 between the goods components (Canada minus U.S.) and 0.65 between the service components (U.S. minus Canada).

There are considerable variations in the extent to which the output per person employed differentials can be accounted for by the explanatory variables, both internationally and within each country. The lowest Canadian percentage of unexplained differential is higher than the highest United States percentage. Again, the spread between these percentages is large for both the U.S. and Canadian data and runs in opposite directions, with the fully restricted goods and service comparison faring worst in the Canadian case but best in the U.S. Attention must now be turned to a detailed examination of the postwar behaviour in Canada of these explanatory variables, whose differing importance in individual sector comparisons has produced the widely differing results just noted.

## DIFFERENTIAL CHANGES IN AVERAGE HOURS WORKED

In assessing the contribution of this factor to the sector differentials in output per person employed, the different nature of the Canadian and U.S. employment data must be remembered. As indicated earlier,[29] Fuchs uses an employment series which excludes unpaid family workers and converts part-time employees to full-time equivalents. Thus, the most important influences on the differential rates of change of average hours worked in the

United States, shown in Table 10, are presumably long-term changes in the workweek of full-time employees in the two sectors. The Canadian employment concept includes part-time workers, both paid and unpaid, so that any average hours worked measure reflects not only the trend of hours worked by full-time employees but also the effect of changes in the relative importance of part-time employees. Comparisons of the Canadian and U.S. sector differentials in average hours worked cannot therefore be particularly meaningful.

There is a striking difference in the size of the average hours worked differential between the sector comparisons based on total goods and those involving nonagricultural goods. This is due to the very large shift of employment out of agriculture between 1946 and 1966 and the fact that the level of average hours worked in agriculture was markedly higher than that in the nonagricultural goods industries during the whole of this period. As Table 9 shows, the combined effect of these two influences is to raise the rate of growth of man-hours more than that of employment when the transition is made from goods to nonagricultural goods, with the result that the rate of decrease of average hours worked is smaller in the latter sector than in the former.

The differentials in the rate of decrease of average hours worked for the two comparisons involving nonagricultural goods are therefore larger than those which are based on the full goods sector, but they must be interpreted with caution because of the part-time effect referred to above. Tests with the source data[30] of the average hours component of the man-hours used in the official productivity measures for the goods and service sectors between 1959 and 1966 indicate that, while the average hours worked by all persons employed in services declined appreciably relative to the corresponding nonagricultural goods measure (an annual growth rate of $-0.76$ per cent compared with $-0.13$ per cent), changes in the average hours worked by persons employed for thirty-five hours or more in each survey week were quite similar in both sectors (actually an increase of 0.27 per cent per annum in nonagricultural goods and of 0.21 per annum in services).

Thus the differentials of 0.33 and 0.31 per cent per annum shown in Table 10 can probably be attributed for the most part to a steady growth in the importance of part-time employment in the service industries during the postwar years. To the extent that this trend is likely to persist — and there is no evidence to suggest otherwise during the forseeable future[31] — such differentials will continue to provide an important part of the explanation for the disparity in output per person employed between the nonagricultural goods and service sectors.

## THE EFFECTS OF INTRASECTOR SHIFT DIFFERENTIALS

These were estimated for the Canadian data in the same manner as Fuchs'. Rates of change of output per person employed for each component industry within a particular sector were weighted by the average of their shares of output and the appropriate inputs in 1946 and 1966. Because of the conceptual ambiguity of such a cross-weighting technique, it seemed desirable to test whether the four standardization procedures would have yielded results of different sign if used separately. With minor exceptions, all the alternative fixed-weight measures of productivity growth, and therefore their averages within a sector, were lower than the corresponding growth rates inclusive of shift effects.

The individual sector shift effects were 0.58 per cent for goods, 0.15 per cent for nonagricultural goods, −0.02 per cent for service, and 0.18 per cent for commercial service, all on a per annum basis. The pure effect of the diminishing importance during the period in question of agriculture, where the level of output per person employed was lower than in most other goods industries, was thus 0.43 per cent per annum. This is the major component of the first two shift differentials shown in Table 10. For the comparison between the two restricted sectors, nonagricultural goods and commercial service, the two shift effects virtually neutralize each other, and the nonagricultural goods minus service differential is mostly accounted for by the modest shift effect within nonagricultural goods, since that within the full service sector was negligible.

No comparison can be made with the shift differentials for the United States which are shown in Table 10. These were estimated on the basis of Fuchs' calculations for goods minus service and "goods" minus "service" for the period 1929-61[32] in conjunction with the relationship between the four Canadian differentials for the postwar years, and were only included for the purpose of calculating an approximate measure of the unexplained residual in Table 10.

## DIFFERENTIAL CHANGES IN LABOUR QUALITY

In order to compensate for the heterogeneous character of conventional man-hours data, Fuchs used labour compensation as a standardized measure of labour input. The crucial assumption here is that,

> if . . . the price of labour (adjusted for quality, effort, and so forth) changes at the same rate in all branches of the economy, then the change in total labour compensation in a particular industry relative to the change in the economy as a whole is equal to the change in labour input in that industry relative to the change in labour input for the economy as a whole.[33]

It then follows that relative quality changes between industries or sectors can be inferred from differentials in the rates of change of compensation per man-hour. On this basis, Fuchs established that there had been a significantly faster growth of labour quality in the goods as compared with the service industries for both the full and restricted sectors over the entire period from 1929 to 1961, a conclusion which the more recent U.S. experience also supports, as may be seen from Table 10. He next discussed a number of other factors which might have had some bearing on this differential, such as the incidence of unionization, the effects of nonpecuniary advantages and differential industry rates of growth, as well as the one which probably strikes closest to the central assumption, i.e., whether, given the existence of sector differentials in educational attainment, there might have been pronounced differences in wage trends for workers with different amounts of formal schooling. In respect to the factors expressly considered, Fuchs was of the opinion that they did not seem sufficiently important to invalidate the observed results.

He then went on to consider whether, on the basis of sector differentials in labour force characteristics such as age, sex, color, and education—variables that can be related to earnings[34]— there existed any independent evidence which would verify his inferences about differential quality change. The details of this analysis will not be repeated here, but the over-all thrust of the data considered was that there had been a distinct tendency over the period in question for workers in the goods sector to become progressively more concentrated in the "high quality" groupings with respect to the characteristics examined.

The Canadian results shown in Table 10 are therefore surprising if some parallel with those of the U.S. is looked for. The range of the four alternative differentials in compensation per man-hour is extremely broad, with that for goods minus service looking perhaps too good to be true while, at the other extreme, it is quite remarkable that the rate of growth of labour quality which the indicator in question represents should appear to be faster in commercial service than in nonagricultural goods. However, as the preceding discussion on differential changes in average hours worked will perhaps have suggested, the disparity between the results of the comparisons based on the full goods sector and those involving nonagricultural goods is mostly accounted for on the man-hours side of the calculation. Average hours worked in agriculture are considerably higher than in nonagricultural goods, and the very sharp decline of employment in that industry over the period in question reduced the rate of growth of man-hours from 1.04 per cent per annum in nonagricultural goods to −0.73 per cent in the total goods sector.

Perhaps the most obvious comment on these results is that the quality of the basic data may simply not be adequate to support the calculation of meaningful second-order differences. For example, a 5 per cent range of error in the growth rates of labour income and man-hours would be sufficient to yield sector differentials in compensation per man-hour as wide apart as 0.72 and −1.13 per cent in the case of non-agricultural goods and commercial service, and an even greater latitude could exist for any estimates including agriculture.

Before assigning a major share of the blame to data deficiencies, however, it should be pointed out that the compensation data used in the numerators of the sectoral indicators of changes in labour quality analyzed here relate only to paid workers and are thus inconsistent with the man-hour measures used in the denominator which cover the self-employed as well. Fuchs acknowledged a similar problem[35] but was apparently able to ignore it. Labour-type income of the self-employed in Canada forms part of the national accounts categories of "accrued net income of farm operators from farm production" and "net income of nonfarm unincorporated business," and a very large proportion of the latter originates in the service industries.

There is, of course, no unique way of separating out such income, and the procedure, followed in Table 12, of assuming that it accounts for the entire amount reported under these headings may be just as unsatisfactory as ignoring it altogether. It cannot even be claimed that these two crude alternatives provide limiting values for the sector differentials, since there are feasible combinations of the distribution of self-employed labour income by industry and changes

Table 12    Alternative Estimates of the Differential Rates of Growth of Labour Quality and Capital Input, Goods and Service Sectors, Canada, 1946-66 (per cent per annum)

|  | Goods Minus Service | Goods Minus Commercial Service | Nonagri- cultural Goods Minus Service | Nonagri- cultural Goods Minus Commercial Service |
|---|---|---|---|---|
| Labour quality | 1.30 | 0.93 | 0.49 | 0.12 |
| Capital input | 0.49 | 0.35 | 0.30 | 0.16 |

**Source:** Table 9. Sector labour income measures have been modified by the inclusion of accrued net income of farm operators from farm production and net income of non-farm unincorporated business from DBS Catalogue Nos. 13-502 and 13-201, *National Accounts, Income and Expenditure*, Table 24.

over time in its relative importance which could yield results falling outside such limits. However, the modified sector differentials of compensation per man-hour shown in the first row of Table 12 certainly look more reasonable, and labour-type income may very well be a sufficiently high and stable proportion of total unincorporated business income so that the assumption underlying the results of Table 12 is a better approximation of reality than that on which the Table 10 results are based. At any rate, there is scope for further investigation here and a more sophisticated attempt to calculate valid measures of labour compensation by sectors.

It may be noted incidentally that the procedure for modifying the sector differentials in compensation per man-hour just discussed also yields revised estimates of the differential rates of growth of capital input, since labour compensation is the denominator in the calculation of the latter measure. What the procedure amounts to in effect is a reallocation between the two explanatory variables of the differential growth of current dollar GDP per man-hour, so that the unexplained portion of the differential rate of growth of output per person employed remains unchanged. The revised estimates for the differential growth of capital input will be evaluated at a later stage in the paper.

The ambiguous nature of the results arrived at by the calculation of compensation per man-hour differentials from Canadian data underlines even more firmly than in the U.S. case the need for an independent assessment of the quality effect, as well as an investigation of the factors which might distort its reflection in unit compensation differentials.

Some impressions of the changing incidence by sector of what Fuchs has identified as "high quality" demographic characteristics can be derived fairly readily from decennial census and labour force survey sources. However, the association of these characteristics with earnings data by industry cannot at the present time be taken very far because of the limited cross-classifications which are readily available at this level. Given the appropriate detail, standardized measures of labour input by industry, based on earnings-weighted distributions of significant combinations of characteristics, could be prepared. This is a possibility that can perhaps be anticipated with more confidence than that of

*Table 13   Civilian Labour Force Employment and Growth, by Sex, Service and Goods Sectors, Canada, 1946-66*

|  | Per Cent Distribution | | Annual Growth Rate |
|  | 1946 | 1966 |  |
|---|---|---|---|
| Services |  |  |  |
| Men | 64.9 | 57.9 | 3.4 |
| Women | 35.1 | 42.1 | 4.9 |
| Total | 100.0 | 100.0 | 3.9 |
| Goods |  |  |  |
| Men | 85.3 | 84.4 | 0.5 |
| Women | 14.7 | 15.6 | 0.9 |
| Total | 100.0 | 100.0 | 0.6 |
| Total |  |  |  |
| Men | 77.3 | 69.7 | 1.6 |
| Women | 22.7 | 30.3 | 3.6 |
| Total | 100.0 | 100.0 | 2.2 |

**Note:**   1966 data adjusted to conform with the 1948 SIC. Growth rates compounded between terminal years.
**Source:** DBS, Special Surveys Division, Special Table 3(c), supplementing DBS Catalgoue No. 71-001, *The Labour Force*, Ottawa, monthly.

making allowance for the effects of other influences on earning capacity, but both of them must be left open for further study and data development.

On the first point, a Canadian study[36] has shown that educational attainments among women in the general population are somewhat higher than among men for similar age groups, mainly because a higher proportion of females have completed high school. In 1965, the proportion of females 25 years of age and over with high school graduation was 18.5 per cent, while for males the proportion was a little less than 13 per cent. The increasing proportion of women in the labour force, particularly in the service sector, might therefore have been expected to raise the average educational, and thus the quality, level of persons employed in the service industries. As Table 13 shows, about 42 per cent of employment in the service sector in 1966 was accounted for by women, compared with 35 per cent in 1946, and the growth rate of women in services has been close to 5 per cent per annum.

However, Census data suggest that the educational differential in favour of women has been diminishing. This is indicated by the figures of Table 14. Between 1951 and 1961, the educational status of males clearly rose faster than that of females. Indeed, the proportion of females with 9-12 years of schooling declined a little, while that of males with 13 or more years of schooling increased faster than the proportion of females in this category.

Thus, the evidence of Table 14 suggests that, in Canada, the quality of the male labour force, which currently accounts for some 85 per cent of total employment in the goods sector, has been rising faster than the quality of the female labour force, which is heavily concentrated in the service sector. The

*Table 14 Per Cent Distribution of the Civilian Male and Female Labour Force by Years of Schooling, Canada, 1951 and 1961*

| | Per Cent Share | |
| Years of Schooling | 1951 | 1961 |
|---|---|---|
| Females | | |
| 0-4 | 3.0 | 3.6 |
| 5-8 | 31.0 | 26.3 |
| 9-12 | 52.7 | 51.6 |
| 13+ | 13.3 | 18.5 |
| Total | 100.0 | 100.0 |
| Males | | |
| 0-4 | 8.3 | 7.1 |
| 5-8 | 46.7 | 37.3 |
| 9-12 | 35.6 | 40.1 |
| 13+ | 9.4 | 15.5 |
| Total | 100.0 | 100.0 |
| Both sexes | | |
| 0-4 | 7.1 | 6.2 |
| 5-8 | 43.2 | 34.3 |
| 9-12 | 39.3 | 43.2 |
| 13+ | 10.3 | 16.3 |
| Total | 100.0 | 100.0 |

**Note:** 1951 concept—"number of years attended"; 1961 concept—"highest grade attended." 1951 Census includes 14 year olds.

**Source:** 1951 data—Dominion Bureau of Statistics, *Ninth Census of Canada, 1951, Vol. IV—Labour Force, Occupations and Industries*, Table 19. 1961 data—1961 Census, unpublished (available on request).

joint effect of shifts in the sectoral distribution of the two characteristics of education and sex comes out more directly in Table 15. The percentage of the total labour force in goods industries with 9 or more years of schooling rose from 37 per cent in 1951 to 47 per cent in 1961, while the corresponding percentage in the service industries, although much higher in both years, showed only a small increase. Changes between 1951 and 1961 for the nonagricultural goods and commercial service sectors were of the same general order, but the absolute levels of educational attainment were markedly different. The exclusion of agriculture increases the quality of the goods labour force, while the exclusion from services of the non-commercial industries results in a decrease of average quality.

Table 15 also shows changes in the percentage of the labour force in both sectors falling into what is generally thought of as the higher quality age group. In summarizing his impressions of similar data, Fuchs comments that "the service-sector work force has been increasingly drawn from females, non-whites, the young, and the old,..."[37] As far as age is concerned, this tendency was not pronounced in the United States in recent years; in Canada, the opposite was the case. The proportion of the sector labour force between the ages of 25 and 64 actually increased for both variants of the two sectors, although the increase was smaller in services than in goods.

*Table 15   Education and Age Characteristics of the Labour Force, Goods and Service Sectors, Canada, 1951 and 1961 (per cent of sector labour force)*

|  | Goods | Service | Nonagri-cultural Goods | Commercial Service |
|---|---|---|---|---|
| 1951 |  |  |  |  |
| Ages 25 to 64 | 72.2 | 71.3 | 73.0 | 71.2 |
| 9 years or more of schooling | 36.7 | 64.0 | 42.0 | 59.2 |
| 1961 |  |  |  |  |
| Ages 25 to 64 | 77.8 | 74.8 | 78.9 | 75.2 |
| 9 years of more of schooling | 46.9 | 69.4 | 51.2 | 65.4 |

**Note:**   1951 data roughly adjusted to conformity with the 1960 SIC. The conceptual difference of the schooling question noted in Table 14 applies here.
**Source:** Same as Table 14.

## DIFFERENCES IN THE RATE OF GROWTH OF CAPITAL INPUTS

An extension of the assumption underlying Fuchs' estimates of relative changes between sectors in standardized labour inputs permits the derivation of a rough measure of that part of the differential change in output per person employed attributable to changes in the rate of growth of capital per person employed. Just as relative changes in labour compensation were used to estimate relative changes in quality-adjusted labour input, so, on the assumption that "the price of a composite unit of factor input (land, labour, and capital) has changed at the same rate in all branches of the economy,"[38] relative changes in total factor input were equated with relative changes in total compensation, as measured by current dollar gross product. Thus, the differential rate of growth of capital per unit of labour input emerges residually by subtracting the differential in the growth of output per unit of total factor input from that of output per unit of labour input or, more simply, by calculating differentials in the rate of growth of total compensation per unit of labour compensation.

Table 10 suggests that, on the basis described, there was in Canada during the postwar years a faster rate of growth of capital inputs in nonagricultural goods than in services, but that when the goods sector is broadened to include agriculture, this differential is reversed. These results bear little obvious relationship to those for the United States where three comparisons out of four show capital inputs to have grown faster in goods than in services, the exception being goods minus service where there was a slight margin in favour of services.

The modification of the underlying labour compensation series along the lines indicated earlier produces the alternative Canadian differentials shown in the second row of Table 12. It is again difficult to assess whether these are more realistic than the original results of Table 10. To the extent that the revised labour quality differentials represent an improvement, then, given the validity

*Table 16   Growth Rates of Total Compensation Per Unit of Labour Compensation, Goods and Service Sectors, Canada and United States (per cent per annum)*

|  | Canada, 1946-66 | | United States, 1947-61 |
|  | Original | Revised |  |
|---|---|---|---|
| Goods | —0.52 | 0.67 |  |
| Nonagricultural goods | 0.20 | 0.48 |  |
| Service | —0.29 | 0.18 |  |
| Commercial service | —0.28 | 0.32 |  |
| Goods |  |  | —0.28 |
| "Goods" |  |  | —0.01 |
| Service |  |  | —0.22 |
| "Service" |  |  | —0.53 |

**Note:**   All calculations are by division of component growth rates plus 100.
**Source:** Canadian data—same as Table 12; U.S. data—Fuchs, *Productivity Trends in the Goods and Service Sectors, op. cit.*, Table A-2.

of the underlying assumption that the price of a composite unit of factor input has changed at the same rates in all industries, there ought to be a parallel improvement in the indicators of the differential growth of capital inputs. One obvious point is that the alternative measures reverse fhe sign of the differential in the comparisons involving the full goods sector where there is no intuitive reason to suppose that the inclusion of agriculture would change the results so drastically from those of the comparisons based on nonagricultural goods.

A further difficulty of the Table 10 results is brought out in Table 16. This shows the components of the sector differentials which are seen to be largely derived as differences between negative values of the total compensation per unit of labour compensation measure. It is not, of course, a sine qua non that a positive sector differential be derived as a subtraction of positive quantities since, in a purely arithmetic sense, it can just as well represent a less rapid decline in capital input relative to labour as a more rapid increase. However, the former proposition is again intuitively difficult to accept and the alternative results shown in Table 12 have at least the merit of not depending upon such an interpretation.

As in the case of the labour quality differentials, some independent evidence must be sought and, for this purpose, differential changes in direct capital-labour ratios may be used. Official statistics of fixed capital stocks are not yet available for all industries in the economy,[39] but private estimates by Hood and Scott[40] permit rough estimates to be made of the differential changes in capital-labour ratios between the goods and service sectors up to 1955.

Table 17 shows that the capital-labour ratio increased between 1946 and 1955 for each variant of the goods and service sectors and that the increases in goods were much greater than those in services. Furthermore, the measure for the full goods sector increased more than that for nonagricultural goods and there was a similar disparity between commercial service and the full service sector. These findings are more consistent with the revised than with the original growth rates of total compensation per unit of labour compensation

*Table 17    Changes in the Net Stock of Capital and Employment, Goods and Service Sectors, Canada, 1946-55*

|  | 1946 | 1955 | Per Cent Change |
|---|---|---|---|
| Total goods |  |  |  |
| Value of net stock of capital (in millions of 1949 dollars) | 7,731.8 | 15,770.5 | 104.0 |
| Index of persons employed (1949=100) | 95.9 | 98.0 | 2.2 |
| Capital-labour ratio | — | — | 99.6 |
| Nonagricultural goods |  |  |  |
| Value of net stock of capital (in millions of 1949 dollars) | 6,468.6 | 12,950.8 | 100.2 |
| Index of persons employed (1949=100) | 87.7 | 111.6 | 27.3 |
| Capital-labour ratio | — | — | 57.3 |
| Service |  |  |  |
| Value of net stock of capital (in millions of 1949 dollars) | 11,925.8 | 18,203.0 | 52.6 |
| Index of persons employed (1949=100) | 92.0 | 130.4 | 41.8 |
| Capital-labour ratio | — | — | 10.8 |
| Commercial service |  |  |  |
| Value of net stock of capital (in millions of 1949 dollars) | 5,654.9 | 8,968.3 | 58.6 |
| Index of persons employed (1949=100) | 86.0 | 117.0 | 36.0 |
| Capital-labour ratio | — | — | 16.6 |

**Source:** Capital stock data—Hood and Scott, *op. cit.,* Table 6B3; index numbers of persons employed—same as Table 6.

(shown in Table 16) and thus, in spite of the shorter time period covered, tend to support the alternative estimates of the contribution of changes in relative capital-labour proportions to differential output per person employed in Table 12.

A rather oblique indication that the trend toward increasing capital intensity in the goods industries relative to services (indicated by Table 17) has continued to more recent times is provided by the growth of capital and repair expenditures in the goods and service sectors relative to that of employment between 1955 and 1965. Rough calculations indicate that the proportions between the two were in the order of 26:1 and 6:1 for goods and nonagricultural goods, but only about 2:1 for both the service and commercial service sectors. Even allowing for the fact that these ratios have an upward bias because of the price inflation in the current dollar expenditure data used, they provide further support for the proposition that part of the explanation for the lower rate of growth of output per person employed in the service industries is the fact that capital per person employed has risen more slowly than in the goods sector.

## Summary and Conclusions

This paper has attempted, first of all, to delineate the broad changes which have taken place in the industrial distribution of the Canadian labour force since 1931. What has emerged quite unmistakably is the picture of a steady increase in the proportion accounted for by the service industries, the cumulative effect of which has been a virtual reversal of the relative importance of the goods and service industries as they stood at the beginning of the period. This shift gathered momentum in the 1950s and has continued with somewhat diminished force in more recent years. A striking fact about this increase in the relative importance of the service industries is that it was, in effect, achieved at the expense of agriculture, which lost ground steadily in relative terms and, since the Second World War, in an absolute sense as well.

Whether this shift of employment to the service sector will continue in the future and, if so, to what extent are questions to which no answers were attempted. It was noted, however, that a significant proportion of the new additions to the labour force during the next few years was expected to be distinguished by the kind of demographic characteristics which are becoming increasingly identified with employment in the service industries. Any systematic assessment of future employment trends must really start from the demand side, and the most promising approach would seem to be through an over-all projection exercise, based on an up-to-date input-output table, of the kind which has recently been attempted in the United States as part of the Federal Interagency Growth Study Project.[41]

In considering what might have been responsible for the relatively faster growth of employment in the service industries, it was concluded that the pure effect of a higher income elasticity of demand for services than for goods was difficult to identify, but that the total influence from the demand side could not have been a substantial factor. Rather, the main explanation lies in a much lower rate of increase of output per person employed in the service sector than in goods. The reasons for this difference are extremely difficult to quantify, but the evidence examined, both direct and indirect, suggests that all of the four factors explicitly considered by Fuchs have also been operative in Canada in varying degrees according to which particular sector comparison is made.

Thus, it is fairly certain that part of the differential in output per person employed is accounted for by a faster rate of decrease of average hours worked in services than in goods, although it will be recalled that this effect is mainly the result of a growth of part-time employment in services which has had no significant parallel in the goods sector. Shifts in the relative importance within sectors of industries having different levels of productivity appeared to be of about the same magnitude in both the nonagricultural goods and commercial service sectors and therefore contributed nothing to the explanation of the basic productivity differential. On the other hand, important shift differentials emerged when the goods sector including agriculture was compared with services.

The results obtained when assessing the importance of differential rates of change in labour quality and of physical capital per worker on the basis of Fuchs' proxy measures for total labour input and total factor input were somewhat ambiguous in nature, because of the difficulty of developing a valid measure for total labour input which embraces all classes of workers. However, the limited supplementary evidence which was considered suggested that Fuchs' general conclusions on these points were probably valid for postwar Canadian experience also, and it gave some support to the results derived by the direct method on the basis of the alternative measures of the growth of total labour input which were presented.

Some comments were made earlier on the adequacy of presently available data when used in the context of what appears to be a simple analytical framework, but which is in fact extremely rigorous in the demands which it makes on data. It may never be possible to distinguish clearly between the effects of deficiencies in the data and those of the methodology itself, but the air could clear somewhat with a reworking of the relevant calculations when the forthcoming historical revisions to the Canadian national accounts and the next stage in the updating of the real domestic product measures are completed.[42] A similar reworking of the U.S. analysis, on the basis of comparable revisions of the source data which were recently completed,[43] should also be carried out. Canada-U.S. comparisons on a more consistent basis for sector definitions and time periods covered could then be an extremely useful way of looking more closely at the basic methodology which has not so far been subjected to much critical scrutiny.

During the next few years, further developments in the area of real output measures, labour statistics, and capital stock estimates are planned in Canada which will gradually improve the basis for analyzing differential productivity trends in the goods and service sectors. However, it is difficult to be optimistic about even long-term prospects in some of the more intractable areas of real output measurement in the service sector. It is often said that, because output in the non-commercial industries is measured by labour inputs, changes in output per person employed are zero by definition. In fact, because of the many diverse measures of labour input used on the output side which are not consistent with the labour force employment series generally used in the denominator, negative productivity change invariably results, as may be readily inferred from the difference between the service and commercial service measures of output per person employed shown in Table 9. It may be desirable in future analyses of differential productivity change to inpute some more realistic measure to this difficult sector of the economy. Even the assumption of zero productivity change would result in a significant narrowing of the goods minus service differential.

### Footnotes

1. Colin Clark's *The Conditions of Economic Progress*, 1st edition (London, 1940) is generally recognized as the first empirical study of comprehensive scope.

2. Harold Barger, *The Transportation Industries, 1889-1946: A Study of Output, Employment, and Productivity* (New York: NBER, 1951), and *Distribution's Place in the American Economy since 1869* (Princeton for NBER, 1955); George J. Stigler, *Trends in Employment in the Service Industries* (Princeton for NBER, 1956).

3. In the context of this paper, specific mention may be made of Victor R. Fuchs' *Productivity Trends in the Goods and Service Sectors, 1929-61: A Preliminary Survey*, Occasional Papers 89 (New York: NBER, 1964) and *The Growing Importance of the Service Industries*, Occasional Paper 96, (New York: NBER, 1965). Other studies, both completed and in progress, are listed in *Contributions to Economic Knowledge Through Research*, 47th Annual Report (New York: NBER, June 1967).

4. See, for example, Simon Kuznets, "Quantitative Aspects of the Economic Growth of Nations, II, Industrial Distribution of National Product and Labor Force," *Economic Development and Cultural Change*, Supplement to Vol.V, No.4 (July 1957) and *Modern Economic Growth: Rate, Structure and Spread* (New Haven and London, 1966).

5. Bank of Montreal, *The Service Industries*; J.C. Lessard, *Transportation in Canada*; W.C. Hood and Anthony Scott, *Output, Labour and Capital in the Canadian Economy; Final Report*; Ottawa, 1956-57.

6. B.M. Deakin and K.D. George, "Productivity Trends in the Service Industries, 1948-63," *London and Cambridge Economic Bulletin*, No.53 (March 1965); J.A. Dowie, "Productivity Growth in Goods and Services: Australia, U.S.A., U.K.," *The Economic Record* (December 1966).

7. *Op. cit.*, p.166.

8. *Op. cit.*, pp.165-166.

9. See DBS Catalogue No.61-505, *Indexes of Real Domestic Product by Industry of Origin, 1935-61* (Ottawa, 1963) and DBS Catalogue No.61-005, *Annual Supplement to the Monthly Index of Industrial Production* (Ottawa, annual).

10. DBS Catalogue No.14-201, *Aggregate Productivity Trends* (Ottawa, 1967). The noncommercial exclusions comprise public administration and defense, education, hospitals, religion, other community services not elsewhere classified, and domestic service.

11. *The Growing Importance of the Service Industries*, p.1.

12. Census industry and occupation data before 1951 were based on the "gainfully employed" concept rather than the "labour force" concept. This may affect comparability over time in the industries where part-time female labour is important. For an explanation of the difference between these concepts, see Dominion Bureau of Statistics, *Ninth Census of Canada, 1951, Report No. SP-8, Occupations and Industry Trends in Canada* (Ottawa, 1954).

13. Bank of Montreal, *op. cit.*, p.4.

14. *The Growing Importance of the Service Industries*, p.1. The series used was "Number of Persons Engaged in Production," published by the Office of Business Economics of the Department of Commerce. It excludes unpaid family workers and converts part-time employees to full-time equivalents.

15. Bank of Montreal, *op. cit.*, Table 1, pp.5-6. These data actually combine agriculture with forestry and fishing, but the latter industries comprise only a small proportion of the total.

16. *Ibid.* Public utilities were included with transportation and classified in the service sector, but their relative importance was slight.

17. John Dawson, *Changes in Agriculture to 1970*, Staff Study No.11 prepared for the Economic Council of Canada (Ottawa, 1965), pp.23-24.

18. Defined, for this purpose, as those with annual sales of less than $2,500 per farm.

19. Economic Council of Canada, *Fourth Annual Review, The Canadian Economy from the 1960's to the 1970's* (Ottawa, September 1967), Table 4-1.

20. *Ibid.*, Table 3-12 and related discussion.

21. From this point forward, the employment series mainly used is that underlying the official DBS productivity estimates, as noted in Table 6. See also the next section of this paper for a brief resume of its derivation.

22. H.S. Houthakker and Lester D. Taylor, *Consumer Demand in the United States, 1929-1970* (Cambridge, Mass., 1966), pp.8-9.

23. See, for example, Kuznets, *Modern Economic Growth: Rate, Structure and Spread*, Table 5-10, and also Houthakker and Taylor, *op. cit.*

24. Fuchs, *The Growing Importance of the Service Industries*, Table 6 and related discussion.

25. For the source material of these calculations, see DBS Catalogue No.13-502, *National Accounts, Income and Expenditure, 1926-56*, (Ottawa, 1958) and DBS Catalogue No.13-201, *National Accounts, Income and Expenditure* (Ottawa, annual), Tables 1, 2, 19, and 55.

26. See, for instance, Fuchs, *The Growing Importance of the Service Industries*, pp. 14-24, for a discussion of some of the economic implications.

27. The results of his calculations are summarized in Tables 2 to 4 in *Productivity Trends in the Goods and Service Sectors*.

28. See also DBS Catalogue No.14-501, *Indexes of Output per Person Employed and per Man-Hour in Canada, Commercial Nonagricultural Industries, 1947-63* (Ottawa, 1965).

29. See footnote 14.

30. Labour force distributions of employment by intervals of hours worked.

31. On the contrary, given the greater opportunities for part-time employment which the service sector provides, and the attraction of such employment for female participants, the high proportion of females expected in the projected additions to the labour force by 1970 makes it possible that the trend will be even more pronounced.

32. See Fuchs, *Productivity Trends in the Goods and Service Sectors*, Table 4. Differential shift effects were found to account for about one-fifth of the sector differential in output per man in the

full sector comparison — largely because of agriculture, but were of negligible importance in the case of the modified sector comparison.

33. *Ibid.*, p.8.

34. For some recent Canadian tabulations of earnings by sex, age, and selected levels of schooling, see DBS Catalogue No.91-510, *Earnings and Education*, by J.R. Podoluk (Ottawa, 1965), Table 6.

35. *Productivity Trends in the Goods and Service Sectors*, p.9.

36. DBS Catalogue No.71-505, Frank J. Whittingham, *Educational Attainment of the Canadian Population and Labour Force: 1960-1965*, Special Labour Force Studies No.1 (Ottawa, October 1966), p.7 and Table 2.

37. *Productivity Trends in the Goods and Service Sectors*, p.30 and Table 10.

38. *Ibid.*, pp.9-10.

39. See, however, DBS Catalogue Nos. 13-522 and 13-523, *Fixed Capital Flows and Stocks—Manufacturing, Canada, 1926-60* (Ottawa, August 1966).

40. Hood and Scott, *op. cit.*, Table 6B3.

41. See *Manpower Report of the President and a Report on Manpower Requirements, Resources, Utilization, and Training by the United States Department of Labor*, transmitted to Congress, Washington, D.C., March 1966.

42. See comments in the May 1966 and May 1967 issues of DBS Catalogue No.61-005, *Annual Supplement to the Monthly Index of Industrial Production.*

43. See "The National Income and Product Accounts of the United States: Revised Estimates, 1929-64," *Survey of Current Business*, Vol.45, No.8 (August 1965); and "Revised Estimates of GNP by Major Industries", *Survey of Current Business*, Vol.47, No.4 (April 1967).

## J.C.H. JONES

# The Economics of the National Hockey League

Recently there have been attempts to bring the NHL under the Combines Act.[1] These resulted from the NHL's failure to grant Vancouver and Quebec City franchises in the expanded league, and from the refusal to allow a former player to "retire" to join the Canadian National (amateur) Team. Consequently, on the assumption that such actions demonstrate that the NHL is a business like any other business and thus, presumably, should be treated like any other business, it must fall under the Act.[2] Alternatively, it has long been argued by team owners that their prime interest is in "love of the game"[3] and not in a purely business venture. It is the purpose of this paper to show that, given the unique features of professional sport, the conduct of the NHL can be explained without any behavioural assumption of "love," by the application of basic microtheory based on a profit-maximizing hypothesis. This is done by constructing a theoretical model of the NHL and testing the implications of the model against its actual conduct.

## I The theoretical framework

The unique feature of professional sport is that in the sporting production function no club[4] in and of itself produces a saleable output (a game), only an input (the arena and/or the team). Therefore, each club must form a coalition with another club to produce a revenue-generating output. Total revenue is the product of number of games, number of seats sold, and average price per seat. Given that a coalition between at least two clubs is necessary, when the number of clubs exceeds two a super coalition of clubs (a formal organization, the league) is more effective and efficient in performing certain joint functions, for instance, distributing the group product (scheduling), and dealing with the relationships between clubs and between the group and other groups.

Given mutual dependence, let us assume the following. First, the optimum goal of each club is to maximize profits. Second, the league desires to maximize the material welfare of its member clubs and therefore its optimum goal is that the clubs act so as to maximize joint profits. In an oligopoly situation neither optimum will be attained. Instead, because of the opposing forces which simultaneously move the clubs between the two optima, a qualified joint profit maximizing position will be achieved.[5] In this case the position will be one which is compatible with maintaining the viability—that is, the survival—of the league.[6] Given mutual dependence, a club cannot survive if all other clubs do not survive. Hence, the actions of each club must be constrained by the operational necessity of maintaining the league. Thus, the "equilibrium" position for the group is one in which the clubs are earning profits that are sufficient to keep them in the league and so preserve the viability of that organization.

Subject to the constraints that the league remain viable and that the institutional framework is given and does not change throughout the analysis,[7] let us assume that each club wishes to maximize profits. So, with output given, each club attempts to maximize revenue and minimize costs. In these circumstances we would expect the following.

On the revenue side, though the demand for the output is a function of the usual variables[8] (tastes, prices, incomes, quality, substitutes, etc.) the most interesting feature of the sporting demand function is *competition* between teams. Thus, other things being equal, the greater the degree of competition the larger the crowds and, hence, the greater the revenue. The degree of competition can be measured by the degree of uncertainty over the outcome of the game, so that the greater the uncertainty the larger the "gate." However, when uncertainty disappears and the result can be predicted with a high probability of success, attendance suffers. Consequently, mutual dependence is not confined solely to producing a game but also to producing a crowd, because the revenue of every club depends on the performance of *both* teams. Clear superiority or inferiority affects the gate of both teams because it reduces uncertainty. Therefore, for the league as a whole the greater the uncertainty of the outcome (the closer the teams are in rank standing, the "better balanced" the league), the greater the aggregate attendance. Hence, the aim being to maximize revenue we would expect that, in contrast to most oligopolistic situations, the group wishes to promote competitive equality between clubs.

However, for each club to accept unequivocally joint profit maximization as furthering its own aim of profit maximization it must be assumed that collusion is complete,[9] and that no club has any incentive for winning continually. If these two latter requirements are not met, the desire to maximize uncertainty will no longer be paramount. If for instance the incentive to win exists, clubs will desire to increase the certainty of winning the game, rather than the uncertainty of its outcome.

This gives rise to two conflicts—first, between optimum group and club objectives and the means by which they may be achieved; and second, between clubs. If there are consistent winners and losers, the non-attainment of goals by losers will result in pressure to improve their positions. This inter-club conflict could result in warfare which might destroy the league as a viable organization, so worsening the position of every club. Therefore we would expect a solution compatible with preserving the viability of the league. Although it will not be one which results either in joint profit maximization for the group or attempted profit maximization for each club, it will ensure group "equilibrium."

On the supply side, the single most important input is the human one—the players. This is the major element promoting uncertainty over the outcome of the game. Hence we would expect that most moves by the group to improve inter-club competition would involve some means of redistributing or equalizing this element. In addition, the players distinguish NHL hockey on a quality basis from all other hockey. That is, NHL hockey is superior to all other hockey because its inputs are superior. Therefore, one would expect the NHL to attempt to obtain the best players available, vis-à-vis other competitive leagues. Finally, in the cause of minimizing the cost of this input we would expect the group to minimize inter-club competition for factors.

Consequently, if the foregoing is correct we would expect that: (1) the league attempts to promote competitive equality between clubs primarily through the redistribution of players; (2) should collusion be incomplete then solutions other than (1) will be adopted in order to maintain group stability; (3) the group will attempt to employ the best players available so as to differentiate their product from other similar products; (4) they will attempt to accomplish (3) at minimum cost. In order to see if these predictions are borne out by the actual behaviour of the NHL the remainder of the paper is divided into: a brief outline of the pertinent organizational characteristics of the NHL and testing propositions (1) and (2); an examination of (3) and (4); and application of the theory to those 1966 issues which gave rise to the policy questions—the NHL expansion and the new professional-amateur hockey agreement.

## II Demand and revenue

The organization of the NHL is defined by the following structural characteristics. The National Hockey League is made up of six clubs (in Canada, Toronto and Montreal, and in the United States, Boston, Chicago, Detroit, and New York), each of which holds a franchise which allows commercial exploitation of NHL hockey in a defined spatial area (the city in which the club is located plus a radius of 50 miles of the corporate limit). This monopoly right is marketable as the franchise may be sold and/or moved subject to the agreement of three-quarters of the remaining league clubs. Each club is selling a highly differentiated product (NHL hockey) and entry is completely blocked unless the group decides to admit new clubs. The league itself is governed by one representative from each club (Board of Governors) and a president who supervises its day-to-day operations. Its function, aside from providing a formal channel of communication, is chiefly administrative; the president is merely the agent of the owners having nothing more than control over the ''morals of the game.''[10] The intra-league relationships are explicitly defined by the league constitution and by-laws, although a considerable degree of latitude is allowed each club in its own spatial market area. For instance, each club is allowed to set its own admission prices, and negotiate TV and radio contracts; each team participates in 70 games, 35 at home and the same number ''on the road''; the revenue from any game goes entirely to the home club and, assuming no TV receipts, depends on the number of paid admissions; and, any game is sold at a variety of different prices which, depending on one's view of the relationship between the seat and the view of the game, can be considered either product differentiation or price discrimination.

## PROPOSITION 1. PLAYER REDISTRIBUTION AND COMPETITIVE EQUALITY

The data necessary to test statistically the relationship between attendance and uncertainty as specified by the model are unfortunately unavailable.[11] However, it seems that, in order to attempt to ensure a degree of uncertainty the NHL clubs have adopted a system of what could be called co-operative "handicapping," the object of which is to try to ensure that individual clubs do not accumulate all the best players and so destroy inter-club competition. The more obvious examples are as follows: (1) each club is allowed a maximum number of players under contract—a "reserve list" of 30 players plus 3 goalkeepers, and out of these 33 a NHL "protected list" of 18 plus 2 goalkeepers. Any player not on a "protected list" but on a reserve list who is under contract to a NHL club can be "drafted" (claimed) by another NHL club for a fixed draft price of $30,000 (1967); (2) any NHL draft is based on the *last* club in the league having first pick of all non-protected players. Then it is the turn of the fifth club and so on in inverse order of league standing; (3) during the course of a season a club may wish to assign a player to a club outside the NHL. This the club cannot do unless all clubs in the league agree, in effect "waiving" him through the league. If any other league club wants the player on waivers it may claim him at the predetermined waiver price. Again, the team ranked last in the league at the time waivers were asked has first choice.

Such handicapping is necessary because complete collusion does not exist. Although the clubs have solved many of the problems which disrupt typical oligopolistic arrangements—particularly, each club sets its own prices in its own monopolistic spatial area—collusion is still incomplete because playing talent is distributed unequally and there is incentive to win.

## PROPOSITION 2. COMPETITIVE EQUALITY AND GROUP STABILITY

If playing talent were not unequally distributed we would expect every game to end in a tie, or each team to win exactly half its games, or each club to win the league championship one-sixth of the time (preferably once every six years). None of these hypotheses is supported by the facts. For instance, in the twenty seasons from 1946-47 to 1965-66, Montreal finished first nine times and second seven; Detroit finished first nine times, second twice, and from 1948-49 to 1956-57 finished first every year except one, when they finished second. At the other end of the scale, during the same time span, Boston finished last five times, and fifth four times, the highest finish being second in 1948-49 and 1958-59; Chicago finished last nine times and fifth twice; New York finished last four times and fifth ten times; Toronto finished first twice, second five times and last only once. Thus, given the unequal distribution of ability, maximum uncertainty cannot result.

At the same time there is an incentive to *win*. The first four ranked teams in the league compete for the Stanley Cup, a post-regular season finale which increases the revenue of these clubs. In addition, given the degree of uncertainty, a winning club draws larger crowds than a losing one. This latter point has been frequently noted[12] and Chicago is often cited as the prime

*Table I    Paid attendance as a percentage of maximum seating capacity and Final rank in League for Chicago Black Hawks, 1946-1947 to 1966-1967*

| Season | Final rank in League | Paid attendance as a percentage of maximum seating capacity* |
|--------|--------------------|------------------------------------------------------|
| 1946-47 | 6 | 85 |
| 1947-48 | 6 | 84 |
| 1948-49 | 5 | 81 |
| 1949-50 | 6 | 67 |
| 1950-51 | 6 | 44 |
| 1951-52 | 6 | 26 |
| 1952-53 | 4 | 47 |
| 1953-54 | 6 | 24 |
| 1954-55 | 6 | 23 |
| 1955-56 | 6 | 26 |
| 1956-57 | 6 | 22 |
| 1957-58 | 5 | 35 |
| 1958-59 | 3 | 44 |
| 1959-60 | 3 | 49 |
| 1960-61 | 3 | 60 |
| 1961-62 | 3 | 70 |
| 1962-63 | 2 | 92 |
| 1963-64 | 2 | 99 |
| 1964-65 | 3 | 100 |
| 1965-66 | 2 | 105 |
| 1966-67 | 1 | 103 |

**Source:** Estimated from figures supplied by the NHL.
*Where the figures exceed 100 this means that all seats were sold and the remainder of the crowd utilized standing room.

example. Despite the lack of data necessary to estimate accurately the demand function, there does appear to be a correlation between Chicago's performance (winning or losing) and attendance. This is shown in Table I. Following the Second World War attendance was high but fell consistently as the club's record of futility continued (1946-47 to 1951-52). In 1952-53 the club made the "play-offs" and attendance rose but fell again as the club reverted to last place. In 1957-58 the team finally escaped last place and attendance increased. By 1958-59 they reached the play-offs and since then have never finished lower than third—a situation reflected in the club's attendance figures.

The upshot of incomplete collusion is conflict between optimum group goals and club goals, and between club goals. These conflicts could destroy the league so there must be some solution other than maximizing uncertainty. If we assume that the game results are not rigged in advance, two solutions (or some combination of the two) suggest themselves.

First, let there be a system of side payments whereby winners compensate losers. This could take the form either of profit redistribution or redistribution of that element which primarily promotes the uncertainty—the players. For instance, at the end of each season profits could be redistributed or the best players from the winning clubs could be transferred to the losing clubs. If a financial side payment were adopted the object would be to attempt to retain the club goal and achieve a form of joint profit maximization without maximizing uncertainty. Yet this would only ensure a more or less equal profit distribution because, unless it is assumed that the demand curve facing the individual club is quite inelastic, group revenue would fall as the degree of certainty increased. This, however, ignores all the difficulties which arise in practice when group revenue is shared.[13] With player redistribution, the objective would be to maximize uncertainty by moving closer to the optimum group goal. In effect, this would completely subordinate club objectives to the group which, as long as there is any incentive to win at all, would be alien to the club. However, the draft and waiver system is a "human" side payment which goes part way towards solving the conflict problem by moving closer to the group goal of maximizing uncertainty. Nevertheless, it does not go all the way.[14]

Second, the objectives of the clubs must undergo some reassessment because they are unattainable simultaneously, and joint profit maximization requires complete adherence to group objectives. Consequently, there must be recourse to a second-best solution which ensures group stability even though it represents a non-optimum situation from the point of view of each club. To deny this is to ignore the implications of the fact that each club is mutually dependent on another club. Thus, although the best of all worlds for the club is the certainty of victory, because of mutual dependence such victory may be a pyrrhic one at the gate. Hence for every club the minimum of all possible acceptable solutions is not to be a consistent loser; but the minimum of all possible maximum solutions is to qualify for the Stanley Cup play-offs. In other words, in the NHL a "winning club" is one which makes the Stanley Cup play-offs which means finishing ranked in the first four in the league. From this point of view, the league championship is nothing more than a 210 game elimination contest to decide which clubs have the distinction of playing off for "The World's Hockey Championship."[15]

The fact that there are *four* winners resolves much inter-club conflict by increasing the chance that each club has of "winning." However, the clubs are not totally indifferent about their position in the first four rankings because the first- and second-place clubs play off against the third- and fourth-place clubs and have the home ice advantage for four out of the seven games. Thus, we have competition for "league standing." This tends to spread the degree of competition among more teams in the league.

At the same time, although the probability of winning the Stanley Cup is a positive function of league standing—since 1946-47 the league winner has won the trophy ten times, the runner-up six times, the third-place team three times, and the fourth, twice—the league winner has in fact only won it less than 50 per cent of the time. Hence the degree of uncertainty over which is the superior team increases with the addition of the play-offs.

If this argument is correct one would expect to see the influence of striving to reach the play-offs reflected in attendance figures. Again, although total statistical information is imperfect, this would appear to be the case. For example, since 1948-49 Montreal has never played to less than 100 per cent of seating capacity. But during that time it has never been out of the play-offs and has won eight Stanley Cups—five in a row.[16] Since 1946-47 Toronto has never played to less than 100 per cent of seating capacity. However, it has failed to make the play-offs only twice and has won seven Stanley Cups. Since 1946-47 Detroit has only missed the play-offs once and although it only reached 100 per cent of seating capacity [in 1968] attendance has been very stable, never falling below 72 per cent of capacity.

When a club does not achieve its minimum objectives it will create pressure to change more fundamentally the rules of conduct which govern intra-league relationships. For instance, some clubs may not make the play-offs for a long period of time. Or again, the waiver rule may not fulfil its purpose because, as waivers can be withdrawn, they may be a search for market information as a prelude to trading. Then, if the league is to remain viable more drastic changes will have to be made. The two most notable examples concern the introduction of: (1) the original intra-league draft in 1954 and (2) the universal amateur (Junior) draft in 1962.

(1) In the late forties and early fifties there were in effect two divisions in the NHL: Detroit, Montreal, and Toronto — whose successes were reflected at the gate; and Boston, New York, and Chicago who had difficulty winning and drawing crowds. Chicago was about to drop out of the league. However, James D. Norris was "urged" to buy the club by the Board of Governors of the NHL even though he already had an interest in the New York Rangers (and holding an interest in more than one club was illegal under the NHL constitution). Norris agreed to buy the franchise,[17] but the problem was the quality of the players. Norris attempted to buy players from the "have" clubs but their owners would not co-operate. The upshot was that in 1954 a draft rule was adopted by the NHL clubs over the protests of Montreal against whose highly productive farm system it was directed.[18]

Under this system each club was only permitted to "protect" a maximum of 18 players and two goalkeepers. Beyond this number a player under contract to any NHL club could be drafted for $15,000. This innovation assured the league as a whole of a pool of professional talent no matter how unproductive the individual farm systems might be, and went some way towards satisfying the weaker teams.

(2) The introduction of the amateur draft arose out of the Shock incident. In the early sixties Boston was consistently last in the league. To try to rectify the situation Boston attempted to buy the best Junior prospect in Ontario and Quebec. This involved Boston in a price war with other NHL clubs over Ron Shock. Boston apparently won out with a bonus of $10,000 and signified their willingness to repeat the process with other juniors.[19] Such financial competition was averted when the clubs agreed to establish the universal amateur draft whereby weaker teams could draft two players from their competitors' sponsored teams at a fixed price ($3,000). Once again, there was a pronounced shift in league policy to counteract the pressure placed on it by one club.

Both these examples illustrate two striking facts. First, both moves were in the direction of increasing the competitiveness of all clubs. Secondly, despite potential and actual conflict the inter-club agreement is stable over time. Although most of the conditions for stable collusion are present — small numbers and a formal organization make policing easier, markets are spatially separated, there is no unilateral price policy, and there is group control over new innovations and entrants—the factor which distinguishes the professional sporting leagues from other oligopolistic coteries is *mutual dependence*. Once the implications of this are grasped the only factors that can destroy the group are: shifts in the demand for the product which forces withdrawal of the league or clubs; ignoring mutual dependence so that one or two teams become so superior as to reduce uncertainty to zero; the wish of members of the group to dissolve the league;[20] or competition from some other group which sells a generically similar product.

Thus, on the revenue side the model appears to explain the activities of the NHL quite well.

## III Supply and cost

On the supply side the model implied that the NHL would attempt to employ the best players available vis-à-vis other leagues so as to differentiate their product, and that they would do so at the minimum possible costs. The league largely succeeds in the former through its monopsonistic power in the labour market, the result being that NHL sells a superior product and simultaneously keeps out potential entrants. However, although inter-club competition for players is reduced almost to zero, it is not certain that clubs maximize rents by forcing wages to opportunity costs because the lack of information allows only a highly speculative conclusion.

### PROPOSITION 3. LABOUR MARKET CONTROL AND INTER-CLUB COMPETITION

The monopsonistic position of the NHL and its clubs is based on the standard player's contract and the protected list, on ownership of and affiliation agreements with, minor professional league clubs, and on the CAHA-NHL agreement which gives the NHL control of amateur hockey. The result is that the hockey labour market can be considered to be vertically integrated (see Figure 1). It may be roughly divided into three stages pyramidically:[21] at the apex stands the NHL; one stage further back, the minor professional leagues; finally at the base the amateur leagues which are themselves vertically integrated on an age basis (see Figure 1, n. 2). Each of these stages may be thought of as adding *quality* to the input so that the NHL ultimately ends up with the superior player. Thus, in contrast to vertical integration in product markets, the NHL is not interested in the minor league outputs as inputs in the NHL, but only in the fact that by producing outputs the minor leagues add quality (seasoning) to their inputs which in turn become NHL inputs. Nevertheless, control over outputs does give the NHL clubs direct control over inputs.

Broadly, the vertical system works as follows: NHL clubs own and control clubs in the minor professional leagues and, through the ''sponsorship'' and ''affiliation'' system, amateur clubs (Figure 1, col. (1)). At the amateur level, in order to play in Juvenile or Junior clubs players have signed ''option'' agreements (col. (3)), which gives the professional club ownership of amateur playing rights and the right to require the players to sign a professional contract

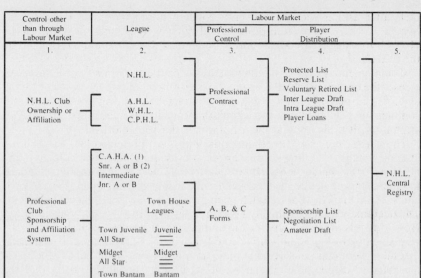

Figure 1   Vertical Integration in the Hockey Market

(1)  The administrative breakdown into branches is shown in Table III.
(2)  The age limits for the competitive categories are Senior and Intermediate (no limit), Junior (under 20), Juvenile (under 18), Midget (under 16), Bantam (under 14), Pee Wee (not shown, under 12).

when requested to do so. All professional players are tied to the NHL club by the contract (col. (3)), and are distributed among teams and leagues according to distribution lists (col. (4)). The whole distribution system is run by the NHL Central Registry (col. (5)), an arm of the league charged with keeping track of and co-ordinating all changes in player distribution.

The major bases of monopsony power and their influence on inter-club competition for players are as follows.

(i) *Standard professional contract*[22]: Although the club that signs a player has prior monopsonistic claim to his services (up to the limit imposed by the protected list), in effect he becomes part of the professional hockey player pool because he can be traded, drafted, or assigned to another club.[23] The monopsonistic status of the club is determined by the "assignment,"[24] and "option" clauses of the contract. The former clearly spells out that the player has no control over where and for whom he plays professional hockey. Failure to report to the club to which he may be sold or transferred, means suspension. This in turn means, not only that he cannot play for any other professional club, but that, as the CAHA recognizes all professional suspensions, he cannot play amateur hockey. Thus there is no way he can earn a living by playing hockey other than with an NHL sponsored club. Indeed, once a contract has been signed there are only two ways he can escape the NHL and still play hockey. First, he may no longer have the ability to remain in professional hockey so that, after asking waivers, the club concerned can terminate the contract. Second, he may retire from professional hockey by placing his name on the club's "voluntary retired list" and with the club's *permission* be reinstated by the CAHA.[25]

Complementing the assignment clauses is the "option" or "reserve" clause, the burden of which is to put the onus of contract renewal solely on the club.[26] The player cannot break the contract by refusing to sign and still continue to play hockey, and although provision is made for compulsory arbitration, it turns out that the arbitrator is the league president.

The "reserve clause" in conjunction with the "protected list" produces a system which, according to the league president, is the most effective and efficient for producing competitive equality.[27] The argument usually advanced to support this contention is that because the league is made up of rich and poor clubs, if the market were free rich teams would bid away all the choice talent. The outcome would presumably be a diminution of the necessary uncertainty. However, this argument ignores the mutual dependence which must exist, the fact there has not been competitive equality in the NHL for the last 20 years, and that the cost of entry ensures that there are no rich and poor clubs. Moreover, the equality of competition can be brought about equally well by the free market.[28] But the reserve rule makes it cheaper. Clearly, the reserve clause is an element of market control which stops the player from selling his services to the highest bidder. This is perfectly consistent with the club wishing to minimize cost.

(ii) *The minor professional leagues:* In their organizational set-up, distribution lists, and in the rules governing inter-club conduct, the minors are almost exact replicas of the NHL. The single most pertinent fact is that they operate as a farm system for developing NHL players. They are dominated by the NHL either through direct NHL club ownership, affiliation agreements with NHL clubs, or the "joint affiliation agreement"[29] between the NHL and the minor leagues.

The degree of ownership integration varies with each NHL club—on the one hand, each owns a CPHL team, on the other, in 1966 only Toronto was fully integrated by ownership of Rochester, Victoria, and Tulsa.[30] But every NHL club either through ownership or affiliation is represented in each league (see Table II). Broadly speaking "affiliation" defines a relationship between minor and major club whereby the NHL club loans players to the minor club (or provides other financial assistance), and the minor clubs allow the NHL clubs to use spaces on their lists.[31] From the point of view of control, the key element in the agreement is that, in contrast to NHL clubs, minor clubs can transfer players directly to the NHL without first obtaining waivers from clubs in their own league. In addition, should the farm system of a particular NHL club fail to produce sufficient talent, minor league players may be drafted (for inter-league draft, see Figure 1, col. (4)).

These relationships ensure that the distribution of professional playing talent is in the hands of the NHL and so automatically precludes the minor leagues from challenging the position of the NHL.

(iii) *The amateur leagues:* The main factors giving the NHL effective control of amateur hockey are the following three points from the CAHA-NHL agreement.[32]

First, the CAHA recognizes the NHL as the sole and exclusive governing body and bargaining authority for professional hockey.

*Table II   The Ownership and Affiliate Relationship between the Professional Leagues and Clubs, and their Junior Sponsored Clubs (as of January 1967)*

| Leagues | Professional and Junior Clubs | | | | | | | | |
|---|---|---|---|---|---|---|---|---|---|
| NHL<br>JUNIOR* | Boston<br>Estevan<br>Niagara Falls | Chicago<br>St. Catharines<br>Dixie Beehive | Detroit<br>Weyburn<br>Hamilton | Montreal<br>Montreal<br>Peterboro | New York<br>Kitchener<br>Burlington | Toronto<br>Marlboros<br>Ottawa | | | |
| CPHL†<br>JUNIOR* | Oklahoma<br>Winnipeg Braves<br>Winnipeg Warriors | St. Louis<br>Sudbury<br>Moose Jaw | Memphis<br>Edmonton Oil Kings<br>Edmonton Canadians | Houston<br>Chatham<br>Lachine Maroons | Omaha<br>Brandon<br>North Bay | Tulsa<br>Markham<br>London | | | |
| AHL‡<br>JUNIOR* | Hershey<br>Oshawa<br>Winnipeg Monarchs | Buffalo<br>Sarnia | Pittsburgh<br>Stratford<br>(& minor assoc.)<br>St. Jerome<br>(& minor assoc.) | Quebec<br>Regina Pats<br>Quebec | Baltimore<br>Kitchener | Rochester<br>Cornwall<br>Trois Rivières | Providence<br>Nationale<br>Maisonneuve | Cleveland<br>Kirkland<br>Verdun<br>Maple Leafs | Springfield |
| WHL‡<br>JUNIOR* | San Francisco<br>Shawinigan<br>Waterloo<br>(& whole assoc.) | Portland<br>Flin Flon | Los Angeles<br>Saskatoon<br>Sorel Hawks | Seattle<br>Ft. William<br>Hull | Vancouver<br>Winnipeg Rangers<br>Kingston Frontenacs | Victoria<br>Calgary Buffalos<br>Melville (Sask.) | | | |

*Junior A and B.

†Each club is owned by the NHL club vertically above it.

‡The clubs in this league have working agreements with more than one NHL club.

*Table III   Number of Sponsored Junior Teams and all Junior Teams in each CAHA Branch (as of January 1967)*

| Branch | Number of Junior A teams | Number of other Junior teams | Number of sponsored teams |
|---|---|---|---|
| British Columbia* | 10 | 13 | 0 |
| Alberta* | 6 | 8 | 3 |
| Saskatchewan* | 6 | 6 | 6 |
| Manitoba* | 6 | 7 | 6 |
| Thunder Bay† | 8 | 0 | 1 |
| Ontario Hockey Assoc.‡ | 13 | 111 | 11A+9B |
| Ottawa and District. | 10 | 20 | 2 |
| Quebec‖ | 18 | 66 | 11 |
| Maritimes# | 12 | 0 | 1 |
| Newfoundland* | 7 | 0 | 0 |
| Canada | 96 | 231 | 50 |

*Branch covers the entire province.

†North-West Ontario, west of the 85th Meridian.

‡Ontario (excluding Thunder Bay, and Ottawa and District) plus the counties of Temiscamingue, Rouyn, Noranda, Abitibi East, and Abitibi West in Quebec.

That part of Ontario east of and including the counties of Leeds, Lanark, and Renfrew, plus the counties of Pontiac, Hull, Gatineau, and Papineau in Quebec.

‖Quebec (excluding those parts of Quebec in Ontario Hockey Association and Ottawa and District).

#New Brunswick, Nova Scotia, and Prince Edward Island.

Second, the NHL obtains direct access to the labour market through the sponsorship system. Sponsorship means the exclusive right of *a professional* team to direct the affairs of any two amateur teams.[33] However, due to ownership and affiliation at the minor professional level, the NHL club really directs eight or more amateur clubs. Taking Toronto as an example, this can be illustrated by Table II. Toronto directly sponsors two Junior teams, the Marlboros and Ottawa. But in 1966 through its ownership of Tulsa, Rochester, and Victoria it sponsored Junior teams in Markham, London, Cornwall, Trois Rivières, Calgary, and Melville.

In addition to the NHL, two sponsored clubs rule, the CAHA definition of a *club* includes Senior, Intermediate, Junior or Juvenile, Midget and Bantam teams, so that sponsorship can give rise to a chain of affiliates which increase the degree of vertical integration (See Figure 1, col. (2)).[34]

Table III, in conjunction with Table II, shows that there is geographical concentration of sponsorships in Ontario and Quebec, and in the large metropolitan centres throughout the country. This means that there has been considerable player mobility which has led to wholesale special exceptions to CAHA rules concerning inter- and intra-branch transfers.

Third, control of individual players is extended by use of "try out" ("A" form) and "option" ("B" and "C" forms) agreements, which attempt to bind amateurs to a particular professional club when they have reached sixteen years of age.[35] While the A form merely gives negotiation rights, the B and C forms give the club an exclusive continuing option on the player's services both amateur and professional. Indeed, when a C form has been signed the player is a professional. As it is in the signing of amateurs that the greatest competition occurs between NHL clubs, the sponsorship list, the universal amateur draft (see section II) and the negotiation list attempt to circumscribe this. The former is analagous to the protected list and the latter makes for orderly negotiation.

Finally, a series of minor points reinforce NHL control. These include the CAHA's adoption (with minor changes) of NHL playing rules, acceptance of the voluntary retired list, and agreement that no amateur club can bind a player with a reserve clause. The total outcome is that the amateur-professional relationship is the same as exists between professional leagues—domination by the NHL.

The total outcome is likely to be that, as the model forecasts, the NHL does employ the superior players vis-à-vis other competitive leagues.

## PROPOSITION 4. MONOPSONY POWER AND PLAYER COSTS

Given the monopsony power of the NHL and its clubs, is it exercised so that player costs are minimized? Because there is no information available on wages, what follows must be regarded as highly speculative.

In general there are two extreme views on the subject of wages of professional athletes and their opportunity costs. One suggests that given the monopsony power of most major league clubs in any sport—football, baseball, or basketball—there is no reason for wages to be above opportunity cost. The other view points out that the large sums paid to professional athletes are bound to be above their opportunity cost—where else could Willie Mays make $125,000 or Wilt Chamberlain $250,000—which suggests that monopsony power is illusionary.

Hockey would appear to fall into the first category because there is no reason why wages should be above opportunity costs.[36] With NHL control over entry, competition from any other league which could increase factor cost (as the American Football League did for the National Football League) is absent. Thus, the only way wages could rise above opportunity costs would be through inter-club competition. But the option clause, protected list, and voluntary retired list, severely limit such rivalry. Competition is a factor in signing amateurs (e.g., the Shock incident) prior to option agreements, but again negotiation and sponsorship lists are confining factors.[37]

Nevertheless, the annual rash of prolonged barn painting and other assorted reasons for "holding out" suggests that the process of wage determination is more a matter of bilateral bargaining than the straight application of monopsony theory. The situation is indeed a bargaining one due to two factors. First, given that the demand for any input is wholly a derived demand, as the club desires to win, it is not completely indifferent over whether the player performs for the team or not. Thus if the club has to pay more for a winning team than a losing team it will do so. Second, if attendance is a function not only of the performance of the teams but also of individual stars (irrespective of the performance of the team) then once again the club would be willing to pay above opportunity cost. Of course both factors assume that the human inputs are heterogeneous and there is no possibility of substitution at a lower wage. The upshot is that monopsony power is not absolute. It is true that each club has the power to drive wages to opportunity costs and, coupled with the threat of suspension which automatically disbars a player from organized hockey, make this stick. But, given that winning is important and the "superstar" effect does exist, the player may be able to bargain his wage above pure opportunity cost.

The bargaining range is set by value product and opportunity cost. Where the wage actually falls within this range depends on the bargaining strength of the player and the extent to which the team is ready to enforce the rules and regulations. If the player is extremely valuable to the team in that there are no good substitutes, he may be able to bargain for a wage significantly above his opportunity cost. There is no doubt, for instance, that certain "superstars" make large salaries because of their ability to draw crowds, and therefore make important contributions to the gate. For example, although in the 1966-67 season Chicago finished first in the league for the first time ever, attendance was lower than in 1965-66 when the club finished second. Although we would have expected the reverse to be true, the statistics ignore one qualitative factor—in 1965-66 Bobby Hull broke the 50-goal record. Similarly, in 1965-66 Boston finished fifth rather than last and, as expected, attendance increased. In 1966-67 they reverted to last, but attendance increased. One of the major reasons was the play of Bobby Orr. Yet it is doubtful if either of the above players received his value product.[38]

However, what about the player whose ability is not unique and for whom there are reasonably good substitutes? His salary may be above his opportunity costs if there are substantial external benefits to winning or if there is group bargaining. In the first case, consider how much is a winning Montreal team worth to its owners, Molson Brewery? If the external benefits are strong then the club may give a player a substantial portion of his rent for a winning team.

In the second case, although group bargaining by players can be very effective because the game depends on the labour input, it requires that the players' group be sufficiently inclusive (the four professional leagues) so that substitution is impossible. Under these circumstances the players' union was effective in raising both salaries and fringe benefits for *all* players during the fifties. The same is apparently true of the new association formed in 1967.

However, given the NHL view of what constitutes arbitration, and the monopsonistic power of the clubs, it would be very strange if the wages of all players were too far above their opportunity costs. While the club may not push salaries to their lowest levels—even on the basis of wishing to maintain player morale[39]—there is certainly no reason to believe that the converse is true. Thus, although the clubs may fail to minimize player costs in line with their monopsony power, this is not due to any benevolent use of their power but rather to the fact that such power is not absolute. Consequently, if we take into account the need to win, the heterogeneity of inputs, strengths and weaknesses in the bargaining process, the need to ensure player morale, etc., we could conclude that the clubs are minimizing player costs. However, it must be stressed that as we have no data this conclusion is highly conjectural.

Nevertheless, on balance we are probably justified in saying that on the supply side the implications of the model have been largely borne out.

# IV Expansion and the new agreement with the CAHA

The foregoing analysis dealt with the NHL as it existed prior to the 1967-68 season. In 1966 two events occurred which changed its character—the league expanded by granting franchises to Los Angeles, San Francisco, Philadelphia, Pittsburgh, Minneapolis, and St. Louis; and the NHL-CAHA agreement was rewritten. Do either of these changes invalidate the above analysis? The answer is no, and both changes can be explained by using the same hypothesis, that the clubs are interdependent profit maximizers.

Why did the league expand? The answer is primarily associated with the revenue which can be obtained from increasing the extent of the market through television.[40]

Over the period 1960-61 to 1965-66, all NHL clubs were consistently playing at or moving towards, capacity. By 1965-66, Chicago and Montreal were over 100 per cent of seating capacity. Toronto had dropped below capacity for the first time in memory, while Detroit, New York, and Boston were playing at 96, 80, and 85 per cent of seating capacity respectively.[41] When full capacity attendance is achieved, revenue can be increased by boosting the size of the arena, increasing the number of games, and/or increasing ticket prices. However, if we make the reasonable assumption that there is a ceiling on arena size, number of games and ticket prices, then there is a limit to the extent that the local market can be increased. This revenue ceiling can be removed by use of television at either a local or national level.

If there is positive excess demand in the local market it can be met either by closed circuit TV or local commercial stations. Commercial TV is probably the best way of attracting the marginal viewer, providing that the substitutability between "live" and TV hockey is relatively small. If it is not, the club runs the possibility of losing a large portion of its "live" audience, so that total net revenue may not increase. Indeed most clubs who have used TV to expand their local markets have gone to closed circuit television because it appears to offer less of the "substitutability" drawbacks associated with commercial TV.

On the other hand, when commercial TV is used the object is usually expansion in other than local markets. To reduce the danger for substitutability there are usually local blackouts when the local team plays at home. When there is no blackout, revenue may fall. For instance, in the 1956-57 season Boston had four out of ten games carried nationally by CBS, playing New York twice, Detroit once, and Montreal once. The average "live" gate from these four games was $14,892 compared with $24,910 per game "for non-televised engagements against the same clubs." For these games the Bruins received $10,000 from CBS, therefore ending with a revenue loss of $1,018.[42] Yet Montreal and Toronto have never suffered the same fate and consistently play to over 100 per cent of seating capacity.

However, US national network TV does pay the most money for televising sport. Thus, if a team is playing to capacity crowds and is already utilizing closed circuit television, a national TV contract appears very profitable. But the prerequisite for a national contract is a national market. The expansion placed teams in the remaining major US television markets (excluding the south). The NHL did obtain a national TV contract from CBS.[43]

Thus, solely on the basis of television it is possible to explain the distribution of new franchises and why Vancouver and Quebec City were omitted. The Canadian TV hockey market is already dominated by Montreal and Toronto. What advantages would accrue to Toronto and Montreal if expansion took place in Vancouver and Quebec City? As it was predictable that new teams would be inferior to Montreal and Toronto, it is doubtful if either the CBC or CTV could have been persuaded to substantially increase their price to accommodate two new teams. At the same time the addition of the Canadian cities was not necessary to get an American TV contract.[44]

Given the expansion, the basic model can also help explain in more detail the "stocking" of the new teams, and the formation of the new NHL division.

With the degree of control over players it was obvious that the new clubs would have to stock their teams from the rosters of the existing clubs.[45] If the maximum amount of competition was the league objective, this could only be promoted by a draft which allowed no protection of any player by any club. However, given the incentive to win, such a move would obviously not appeal to the existing clubs. Hence, no open draft.

In 1966, following pressure from various sources to take amateur hockey out of professional hands, the CAHA-NHL agreement was rewritten. However, although the new agreement appears to be more palatable the NHL has in fact retained the same degree of monopsonistic control at possibly a cheaper price. The main provisions of the new agreement are as follows.[46]

The NHL will terminate all sponsorship of amateur clubs. All amateurs will only be drafted when they reach 21 years of age and the "try-out" and "option" agreements will be discontinued. The NHL will pay a set amount to the CAHA for each player drafted. Finally, a player development fund will be set up, financed by the NHL, to develop hockey players.

What advantages does this arrangement have from the point of view of the NHL? First, although it appears to give control of amateur hockey back to the CAHA and so dispel most of the public outcry over professional control, it really only makes this control more indirect. For instance, despite the loss of sponsorships and A, B, and C forms, etc., the NHL has the *exclusive* right to draft all amateurs who will still (according to the agreement) be playing under NHL rules. The purpose of the option agreements, sponsorship lists, etc. was to reduce inter-club competition for players; this purpose is *retained* by the new universal draft. In fact, it is probably retained at a cheaper price than would otherwise have had to be paid. With six new clubs entering the league there would have been extreme competition for players. This would have resulted in increased prices for players and increased costs of setting up amateur farm systems. With the new agreement all such cost disappears.

Second, financial control still rests with the NHL through control of the Joint Development Committee, which approves all payments to the CAHA leagues. As there is no information on how much it cost the NHL clubs to run their amateur farm systems, one cannot judge how adequate the amount of money invested by the NHL under this new arrangement is. However, it is doubtful that even by doubling the size of the NHL the funds going to amateur hockey will be doubled. Thus, there is again a potential cost saving to every club.

Third, ultimate control still resides with the NHL because if it is not satisfied with the number of or calibre of players developed, the CAHA has agreed to implement a program of accelerated player development.

Thus, in any weighing of costs and benefits it appears as if the NHL has increased its benefits at a lower cost.

## V Conclusion

Given the fact that the evidence appears to accord with what the model predicts we can justifiably say that the conduct of the NHL can be explained by the model. However, whether the model provides any indelible guides to public policy is another matter. The NHL clearly possesses monopoly and monopsony power, and if the possession of market power is enough to warrant application of the Combines Act then the NHL is liable. But as the Act presently stands there is some doubt as to whether any liability exists, because professional sport is considered a *service*, and *services* are immune from prosecution under the Act.[47] Whether it is desirable that the NHL be placed under the Act (irrespective of its market power) is another matter. Perhaps there are wider questions of the public interest which are not represented by the Act. Nevertheless, what is clear is that a complete reappraisal of the Combines Act vis-à-vis professional sport should be undertaken.

### Footnotes

1. See Bill C-132, first reading Feb. 25, 1966.

2. See, for example, remarks of Mr. Ron Basford, who introduced C-132, in *Commons Debates*, June 13, 1966, 6364.

3. See, for instance, statements by Mr. James D. Norris at *Celler Hearings*, 2978, and more recently by Clarence Campbell, quoted in Jack Olsen, "Private Game: No Admittance," *Sports Illustrated*, April 1965, 69.

4. Throughout the paper the following definitions hold: *Club*, an input made up of human and physical capital; i.e., the team (a collection of players), the coach, and the management represent the human capital; the arena and equipment are the physical capital.

5. See W. Fellner, *Competition among the Few* (New York, 1965), esp. Chap.1.

6. For a good discussion of the criterion of viability and survival and its implications for prediction and the explanation of economic behaviour see Armen A. Alchian, "Uncertainty, Evolution and Economic Theory," *Journal of Political Economy*, LVIII (1950).

7. Given are: the number of teams, the number of games, arena seating capacity, the production function and the techniques specifying how the inputs should be combined (i.e. game rules) including number of players, size of ice surface, size of goal, etc.—in short, all factors considered in the Constitution, By-Laws, and Playing Rules of the NHL.

8. Though no attempt is made here to specify all the factors which could affect attendance, the following are mentioned because they are more or less unique to hockey (although analagous factors are found in other sports): (1) the drawing power of a particular "super-star" (e.g., Richard, Howe, Hull) or team irrespective of the projected outcome of the game. It is interesting to note that when exhibitions are staged between NHL and minor league clubs (when the outcome of the game is not important), very often the ability of a particular star or the NHL team is heavily stressed in pre-game advertising; (2) the *style* of hockey played—defensive, offensive, the likelihood of fights, etc. Clarence Campbell, for instance, has said that offensive style hockey which increases scoring has a positive effect on attendance (see Paul Deacon, "Thinner Ice for Pro Hockey," *Financial Post*, April 19, 1952). Certainly over the years the rule changes have attempted to make hockey a faster, more wide open game, for example, the forward pass, the red line, etc.; (3) the selling job that radio, TV, and newspaper sports writers do for hockey, sometimes called the

"fourth estate benefit" (see W.C. Neale, "The Peculiar Economics of Professional Sport," *Quarterly Journal of Economics*, LXXVIII February 1964, 3); (4) whether the game is played during the weekend or mid-week; (5) parking and the weather; (6) in Toronto and Montreal "conspicuous consumption," and when Toronto plays Montreal—ethnic considerations.

9. See W.J. Fellner, *Competition among the Few*, pp.131-2.

10. See statement of Clarence Campbell at *Kefauver Hearings,* 504. This emphasizes that "franchises" in hockey are different from those granted to automobile or farm implement dealers, for example. Here the franchise controls the central organization.

11. However, the case has been succinctly stated by Conn Smythe: "New York and Boston keep drawing because there are only six teams in the league . . . so you've always got an attraction coming in. But if you had two more teams that couldn't win games it would be different. If you had four rotten teams in the league you'd have a hell of a time getting people in the rink. They wouldn't buy season tickets for 35 games a year knowing that they had to take 15 or 20 lousy games." Quoted in Jack Olsen, "Private Game; No Admittance," p.66.

12. See Paul Deacon, "Thinner Ice for Pro Hockey?"

13. Financial side payments are practised with varying degrees of complaint from the member clubs by the Canadian Football League.

14. Inter-club trades could be considered a form of side payment especially if they are motivated by the desire to strengthen weaker clubs. For instance, over the years there has been a noticeable tendency for winning teams to avoid trading with each other and to trade with losing teams.

15. See *National Hockey League Guide 1966-67*, p.26. This should not be confused with the World Championships sponsored by the International Amateur Hockey Association.

16. The Montreal example is similar to that of Chicago except that in Chicago capacity has not changed but in Montreal it has as follows: 1946, 9600; 1949-50, 12,400; 1950-51, 13,201; 1951-52, 13,307; 1953-54, 13,488; 1954-55, 13,531; 1959-60, 13,708; 1960-61, 13,728; 1966-67, 14,097. Data supplied by the Montreal Club.

17. See *Celler Hearings*, 2972-77.

18. Frank J. Selke, *Behind the Cheering* (Toronto, 1962), p.137.

19. See Dick Beddoes, "N.H.L. Brand on the Young," *Globe and Mail*, April 26, 1966.

20. The NHL was formed when the National Hockey Association was dissolved to "freeze out . . . Eddie Livingston whose team . . . had somehow got under the skin of the boys from Ottawa and Montreal." Selke, *Behind the Cheering*, p.56.

21. Throughout the paper "professional hockey" means those clubs whose players have signed a Standard Player's Contract and covers the NHL and the "minors," i.e., the American Hockey League (AHL), Western Hockey League (WHL) and Central Professional Hockey League (CPHL). Any club whose players have not signed such a contract are considered "amateurs," nominally controlled by the Canadian Amateur Hockey Association (CAHA).

22. The author was unable to obtain an up-to-date Player's Contract, but current information suggests that it has changed very little for ten years (this applies both to content and numbering of the clauses). All references are to the 1958 version found following p. 790, *Kefauver Hearings*.

23. See *Celler Hearings*, 2987.

24. See particularly clauses 11, 6, and 18.

25. NHL By-Laws Section 8 (5) and (6).

26. Clause 17.

27. Clarence Campbell, *Kefauver Hearings*, 506.

28. See S. Rottenberg "The Baseball Players' Labor Market," *Journal of Political Economy*, LXIV, p.256. It should be noted that the parallels between baseball and hockey are *very* close, and in fact the rules and regulations governing the NHL "evolved out of the experience of baseball." *Celler Hearings*, 2982.

29. *Celler Hearings*, 3112-24. This agreement was drawn between the NHL, AHL, WHL, and the Quebec Hockey League. Since then the Quebec League has gone out of existence but available evidence suggests that things have not changed significantly with the addition of the CPHL, especially as all the clubs in this league are directly owned by NHL clubs.

30. During the 1965-66 fiscal year Toronto sold its interest in Rochester, and at the end of the 1966-67 season the Victoria franchise was moved to Phoenix and sold to local interests.

31. See the "Joint Affiliation Agreement," clause 4, *Celler Hearings*, 3114.

32. See *C.A.H.A. Hockey Rules 1954-1955*, pp.67-70, which contains a synopsis of the CAHA-NHL agreement. Although a new agreement came into effect in 1958, the *Report on Amateur Hockey in Canada by the Hockey Study Committee of the National Advisory Council on Fitness and Amateur Sport* (Ottawa, January 1967) suggests that no major changes took place in 1958. It should be noted that the NHL acts for *all* professional hockey leagues when dealing with the CAHA, *Celler Hearings*, 3121.

33. See NHL By-Laws in *Celler Hearings*, 3054-58, and the "Joint Affiliation Agreement", 3115.

34. See *Report on Amateur Hockey in Canada*, 13-14.

35. For copies of the agreements see either *Celler Hearings*, 3079-82, or *CAHA Hockey Rules*, 1954-55, pp.71-77.

36. Although it would be interesting to compare the wages and working conditions of hockey players with other professional sports, lack of data precludes this.

37. Signing amateurs can be expensive as the following shows. "Detroit, Chicago, New York, Montreal, Toronto scrambled for Frank Mahovlich when he was a 14 year old playing for Schumacher. Leafs got him. They paid him $1,000 to sign a Junior B certificate; $1,300 a year for tuition, laundry money and three trips home each of the 5 years he was at St. Michael's College; $1,000 to the scout who signed him to a "C" form, $10,000 bonus to the "Big M" to turn professional; $10,000 for his first year's salary." G.E. Mortimore, "What Happened to Hockey", *Globe and Mail*, n.d., p.22.

38. Rottenberg argues that the only circumstance in which a player would receive his full value is if all players on the team insisted on receiving theirs. Then rents would be zero. "The Baseball Players' Labor Market," p.253.

39. *Ibid*.

40. One additional reason for expansion can usually be found in the desire of the established clubs to blockade entry. For instance, the New York Mets received a franchise in the National Baseball League only after the formation of a third major baseball league was seriously mooted (see Jimmy Breslin *Can't Anybody Here Play This Game* [New York, 1963], pp.47-9). However, considering NHL expansion, the formation of a major rival league was not considered a serious possibility.

41. Calculated from figures supplied by the NHL.

42. This example was taken from "Big Troubles Ahead for the N.H.L.," *Financial Post*, Nov. 30, 1957.

43. CBS is to pay the NHL a total of $3.6 million over three years; $600,000 the first year (the old teams are to share this equally among themselves); $1,200,000 the second year and $1,800,000 the third (in the last two years the money is to be split 12 ways). Reported by the CP, *Victoria Daily Times*, Sept. 23, 1966.

44. However, Vancouver could have had a franchise if the city had sold to Stafford Smythe (principal owner of Toronto Maple Leafs) and associates a downtown block for $1. Smythe would then have provided a team and an arena. Whatever one thinks of the move and no matter how sympathetic one is to Vancouver's drive for major league status, this proposal was a massive attempt at using full line forcing!

45. This was also an opportunity for the existing teams to reap a little extra reward. For $2 million per club the new teams were allowed to draft 20 players each, owned by the old clubs.

46. For a detailed list of provisions see *Report on Amateur Hockey in Canada*, pp.19-26.

47. See *Commons Debates*, Feb. 23, 1966, 1670; *Report of the Director of Investigation and Research*, March 1966, 7; Combines Investigation Act; D.H.W. Henry, "Developments and Proceedings Under the Combines Investigation Act for the Year Ended March 31, 1967," *The Antitrust Bulletin*, XII (Fall 1967).

# SECTION SIX
# Canada and Foreign Ownership

# HARRY G. JOHNSON
# Problems of Canadian Nationalism

My subject is Canadian nationalism. This is not a subject in which I have a long-established scholarly interest. The growth of nationalist sentiment in Canada during the past five years or so has, however, forced itself on my attention through my professional interests in international trade and monetary policy, as well as through my general interests as a Canadian citizen. As a Canadian, I have been disturbed because nationalism in its recent form seems to me to appeal to, and to reinforce, the most undesirable features of the Canadian national character. In these I include not only the mean and underhanded anti-Americanism which serves many Canadians as an excuse for their failure to accomplish anything worthy of genuine national pride, but also what I think of, perhaps unfairly, as the small-town pettiness of outlook that is the shadow side of many Canadian virtues. As an economist, I have been even more disturbed by the protectionist and anti-foreign investment proposals which have been associated with nationalist sentiment. It is not just that these proposals seem to be attempting to enlist, by specious reasoning, the support of a confused nationalist sentiment for measures whose chief effect will be to increase the profits and power of particular interests at the expense of the community. Much more serious is that these proposals seem to me to be running in the precisely opposite direction to the kinds of policies Canada should be pursuing to make the most of her opportunities in the emerging world economy. What is also serious, the emphasis that has been placed on foreign competition and American investment in Canada as the causes of Canada's recent economic difficulties has served to distract the attention of the general public—though not of the professional economists—from the fact that these difficulties are in large part attributable to an inept and perhaps wilful—certainly unnecessary—failure of those in charge of Canadian economic policy to take appropriate remedial measures. Thus, far from contributing to the growth of a stronger, more independent, and identity-conscious nation, Canadian nationalism as it has developed in recent years has been diverting Canada into a narrow and garbage-cluttered cul-de-sac.

## I

As I understand it, the nationalist position is that Canadian national identity and independence—frail plants of a very recent growth—are being threatened by insidious influences emanating from the United States, influences both cultural and economic, which if not resisted will inevitably lead to the absorp-

tion of Canada by the United States, culturally and economically if not politically. Further, it is argued, these influences should be resisted by using
government action to foster forces Canadian and frustrate forces American,
because forces Canadian are by definition valuable and ought to be protected
and promoted. By implication forces American are not valuable, though
nationalists often try to avoid saying so specifically.

The nationalist position seems to me to beg a number of questions which can
conveniently be grouped into questions of fact and questions of logic, or
(perhaps better) questions of democratic theory. The first question of fact
concerns the meaning and extent of the national identity and independence that
are alleged to be threatened. It seems to me that on this question the nationalists
often tend both to underestimate the extent to which there exists a Canadian
national identity, and to confuse independence in the sense of having the power
to take independent action with something quite different— "independence"
in the sense of choosing to take action different from the actions of other countries, usually the United States. So far as national identity is concerned, I have
no doubts at all that a Canadian is an animal recognizably distinct from an
American, not just in the way he pronounces "out" or "about" or "twenty"
but also in his attitudes and general character. My confidence on this score is the
result of having observed Canadians in different international contexts, and
listened to people of other nationalities discussing Canadian character and
behaviour. I won't say that the qualities I think of as typically Canadian are
altogether admirable—in addition to seriousness and a fairly high level of
competence, they include a certain provinciality of outlook, signs of inferiority
feeling, and a tendency at meetings either to orate at a high moral level or to
keep quiet and then grumble afterwards about not being listened to—but they
are recognizable as a distinct national mixture. So far as national independence
is concerned, both my brief acquaintance with Canadian constitutional history
and my observation of the Canadian role in international affairs give me no
cause to doubt that Canada is an independent country in the only reasonable
meaning I can give to that word. I do not think that Canadian independence is
impaired in any way when Canada's political leadership decides that Canada's
best interests lie in supporting policies initiated by the United States; and I
cannot understand the belief of various Canadians I know that Canadian
independence can only be demonstrated by opposing American policies. It also
seems to me that in many cases—for example, on the question of recognizing
the People's Republic of China—Canadians fall into the immature habit (or
perhaps adopt the debating trick) of blaming Canadian policies of which they
disapprove on American domination when the plain truth is that the alternatives
they desire are simply unpopular in Canada.

The second question of fact is how, precisely, Canadian identity and independence are threatened by the United States. With respect to the threat to
national identity, the nationalist usually points to the consumption of American
goods and the practice of the American standard of life in Canada, and to the
wide circulation of American communications media in Canada. This is not a
convincing argument, especially to an economist. What the nationalist sees as a
"penetration" of Canada by the United States, the economist sees as an
expression of the preferences of an opulent society. That the taste for

American-type goods, ways of life, and communications and advertising methods has been spreading rapidly all over the world as incomes have risen, and that they have been instituted in countries subject to very little direct American influence, make it difficult to argue that American penetration and not simply affluence is the explanation. One may deplore many features of the affluent American style of life, but I do not think one can deny either that it is what people want to buy, or that it does contribute to human comfort and pleasure. Nor do I believe that the deplorable aspects could be removed by forcing people to buy Canadian goods and magazines instead of American—the Canadian producers would simply produce the same types of goods, and probably not as well. In support of this prediction, one needs only to refer to the extent to which Canadian popular magazines have altered their formats, and especially their writing styles, in imitation of American popular magazines.

With respect to the threat to Canadian independence, the nationalist usually points to the proportion of imports from the United States, and of American ownership of Canadian enterprises, as if these themselves were a proof of "domination" by the United States; in some ways, on the contrary, they represent Canadian exploitation of the United States. For example, the half-billion or so dollars of corporate income taxes that Canada collects from American direct investments here comes more or less directly at the expense of the United States Treasury; and the United States government has heavily subsidized Canadian resource development through the depletion allowances. Aside altogether from that sort of question, neither imports of American goods nor imports of American capital acquire voting rights in Canada, so Canadian independence as embodied in the sovereignty of Parliament can hardly be threatened that way; and it is very hard to see why the economic dependence of the United States on Canada which is the other side of Canadian economic dependence on the United States—that is, the interdependence between the two—should make the American Government more rather than less anxious to put pressure on Canada.

I now turn to questions of logic. The fundamental questions about the nationalist position, it seems to me, concern the validity of the assertion that closer economic relations with the United States, through mutual trade and through American investment in Canada, mean that Canada must inevitably be absorbed by the United States, and the implications of the conclusion that the trend towards closer integration with the United States should accordingly be halted and if possible reversed. So far as the assertion of inevitable absorption is concerned, I have never been able to understand the logic of it. It seems to me to assume a degree of economic determinism in politics going far beyond anything the facts of history would warrant. Nations have in the past practised free trade, or at least had lower barriers to trade than they now have, without losing their national identity or feeling an overwhelming urge to submerge themselves in political union with a larger country. If it were true that economic integration leads to a loss of identity, how could one explain the survival of minority and regional groups inside national boundaries, such as the Scotch and Welsh in the United Kingdom or the French Canadians and Nova Scotians in Canada? I would be very surprised indeed if closer economic integration between the

United States and Canada, arrived at as a result of the voluntary processes of profit-seeking trade and investment, led to a Canadian demand for political integration; rather, I would expect that closer economic integration, by enabling Canadians to achieve a standard of living closer to that of the United States, would make them better able and more willing to use the political sovereignty of their country to pursue political and social policies appropriate to their own conceptions and requirements.

But supposing that the development of closer economic ties with the United States might lead Canadians eventually to desire a political union with the United States, is this a valid reason for trying to prevent by government intervention now the formation of these closer economic ties? The belief that it is seems to me to raise some very thorny questions in the theory of political democracy, because it implies the proposition that the present generation is entitled to arrange things so as to preclude the possibility of a situation arising in which a future generation may decide, for reasons which seem sufficient to it, on a course of action which the present generation, ignorant of those reasons and anyway dead and gone by then, would not approve of if it were thrust on them at this time. In other words, it implies that future generations should not be trusted to decide what is good for them, and that the present generation has the right to choose for all future generations. It seems to me that this is an unreasonable arrogation of authority, and that the present generation, whatever it decides for itself, has no right to try to limit the freedom of future generations by depriving them of the opportunity to choose. The argument for frustrating future generations becomes particularly irrational when it is used as an argument for frustrating the present generation as well.

The nationalist position raises another important question of political theory, in connection with its contention that it is desirable to support things Canadian and repress things American in the interests of Canadian national excellence. This contention, which is intimately bound up with the sentiment of anti-Americanism, seems to me thoroughly to confuse legitimate nationalism and chauvinism. By legitimate nationalism I mean the pride that a citizen can rightfully take in the achievements of his own country, and the obligation he should assume to strive to make that country a better place to live in. Chauvinism is the perversion of nationalism into the assumption by the citizen that his country has superior accomplishments by virtue of its being his country, and that because it is his country it is *ipso facto* already the best place to live in. Contemporary Canadian nationalism seems to me to be riddled with chauvinism in its constant harping on the idea of Canadian-ness rather than goodness as the objective, and its assumption that if you make things more Canadian you automatically make them better. There are, in my view, a great many accomplishments that Canadians can and should be proud of; but they should be proud of them because they are accomplishments, not simply because they are Canadian. There are also some things in Canada that Canadians should be ashamed of, and could do something about—slums, town planning, water pollution, technological unemployment, race discrimination in immigration policy, to name a few—things for which Canadian responsibility has not proved a guarantee of superiority. I would be wholeheartedly in favour of any form of Canadian nationalism that sought to raise Canadian standards in areas such as these; on the grounds that present conditions are not good enough for Canada; but since Canadians themselves are responsible for present conditions, I do not find much cheer in the simple panacea of more Canadian-ness.

This brings me to the question of anti-American feeling in Canada, a feeling which has always been a latent component of the Canadian national character but which seems to have become particularly virulent in recent years. This is a subject on which the Canadian talent for genteel hypocrisy comes to its finest flower, with eminent Canadians loudly expressing their admiration and warm friendship for the American people while advocating schemes for depriving some of them of control of their property, and professional explainers of Canada to the Americans begging the Americans not to be offended by the nasty anti-American remarks they are about to hear, because we're just having a friendly argument among ourselves, and really we love them.

It is this two-faced character of anti-Americanism in Canada—the desire to enjoy the emotional jag of indulging in hatred, envy and greed while maintaining the pretense that one is being very restrained and reasonable and that Americans not only should not be offended but should in fact approve—that I find particularly repugnant to me as a Canadian. It seems to be a characteristic which distinguishes Canadian anti-Americanism, to its discredit, from anti-Americanism elsewhere in the world; and, paradoxically enough, it seems to confirm what it seeks to deny, the similarity of Canadians to Americans, for the desire to be loved in spite of one's obnoxious behaviour is a deeply ingrained American characteristic. I suspect that it derives, at least in part, from an inner recognition that anti-Americanism is an unreasonable and somewhat shameful sentiment; certainly, when one delves into the things that nationalists complain of about American influences in Canada, one runs into signs of such awareness. One sign is the tendency of nationalists to rest their case on elaborate hypothetical arguments, the gist of which is that there is nothing very tangible to complain about in American behaviour in Canada at present, but that circumstances might arise in which Americans in Canada might do something that Canadians would disapprove of—it being assumed without question that Canadians would never do anything that Canadians would disapprove of. Another sign is the tendency, which one can observe most easily in the speeches of the present Governor of the Bank of Canada,[1] for arguments which begin with strongly anti-American statements to degenerate into preaching at Canadians about their lack of enterprise, thrift, resolution, and other American virtues.

Anti-Americanism in Canada rests almost entirely on assertions convincing only to those already convinced. Yet is is a latent element in the Canadian national character, apparently always available for mobilization. The question about it which puzzles me, and which seems to me more worth consideration than the particular issues on which anti-Americanism focuses from time to time, is why Canadians have this propensity for anti-American sentiment. I would suggest that it is closely connected with a certain immaturity in the Canadian national character, expressed in the unwillingness to accept the fact that Canada is, except from the geographical point of view, a small country. Unlike the citizens of other small countries bordering on large countries, Canadians are not prepared to content themselves with the advantages that can be derived from small size, but set themselves the impossible aspiration of equalling the United States, and, still more impossible, of getting the United States to treat them as equals. In the nature of things such aspirations are doomed to disappointment; and their disappointment almost inevitably curdles into resentment against the United States for its effortless imperviousness to the Canadian challenge, a resentment which subsides whenever Canada seems to be progressing more rapidly than the United States, but flares up whenever Canada runs into heavy weather. Thus anti-Americanism becomes a way of evading recognition of the inconsistency between Canadian aspirations and Canadian possibilities, and finding emotional consolation for inevitable failure. It is a poor kind of consolation, and a destructive one; and it diverts Canadian energies into a rather unattractive mixture of bombast and self-pity. This is regrettable, because there is nothing wrong with being a small nation. Canada, as a small but rich American nation, has an important and worthy role to play in world affairs, a role which Canadian statesmen and officials have understood and lived up to most effectively on various occasions; but it cannot be played effectively by Canadians consumed with jealousy of the United States.

## II

The economic measures advocated by the nationlists fall into two categorles: increased protection for Canadian secondary industry, and the forced insertion of Canadians into the ownership and management of American enterprises in Canada. On both these matters the Government has already made some moves in the nationalist direction. I have three reasons for doubting that the advocacy of these measures is in the Canadian national interest.

In the first place, it is extremely questionable whether these measures will produce the benefits to the Canadian people that are claimed for them. They are more likely to have the effect of benefiting particular groups of Canadians at the national expense. The arguments that have been trotted out for protectionism are the customary old fallacies: the nation will become richer by subsidizing inefficient high-cost production of goods that could be purchased more cheaply by exports; Canadian production will become large-scale and efficient if only the market it serves is made small enough and oligopolistic enough by high tariffs; inability to compete in free competition with foreigners demonstrates superior potential efficiency justifying a concealed public subsidy; without protection Canadian industry would disappear completely and everyone would be out of work. The arguments for "Canadianizing" the ownership and management of American enterprises rest on the doubtful assumption that it is the function of share-holders, directors and managers rather than of Parliament to see that business is conducted in the national interest, and that to be a Canadian is sufficient to guarantee competence and devotion in this endeavour; or they rest on the doubtful proposition that American companies consistently refuse to maximize their profits by employing competent people, because those people happen to be Canadians. It is also hard to understand how one will become the master in one's own house by becoming a dividend-receiver or major-domo in someone else's house.

The most predictable effect of higher protection is that Canadians in the protected industries will have higher incomes, or be able to get away with a less efficient performance, than they otherwise would, and this at the expense of the general Canadian community. The most predictable effect of Canadianization of American subsidiaries is that some Canadian capitalists will obtain higher dividend and directorship incomes than their enterprise and business knowledge hitherto entitled them to, and that some Canadian employees of American firms will be paid more than their competence hitherto justified, at the cost of some discouragement to American investment in Canada and some reduction in the efficiency of the operations of already established enterprises. These effects may be thought desirable in themselves, especially by the beneficiary Canadians. But they do not necessarily carry with them the national benefits that protectionists allege they will; and there is a serious danger that by concentrating their case on the emotionally appealing but economically unsubstantiated arguments for protection the nationalists will persuade the public into accepting policies which yield profits to some Canadians but a loss to the country.

Not only is it very doubtful whether protectionism and "Canadianization" will produce the national benefits claimed for them; the philosophy of economic nationalism which they represent seems to be the opposite of what is called for if Canada is to make the most of her opportunities in the modern international economy. That economy is characterized by the rapid spread and progressive development of industrial production, which demands efficiency and flexibility if a country is to compete on the world market. It is also characterized by the belief on the part of the major industrial countries of Europe and many of the underdeveloped countries that the small size of their national markets prevents them from reaping the full potential gains of industrial development; hence their desire and willingness to expand their markets by entering into arrangements for free trade areas and common markets. Both the spread of industrialization and the formation of larger trading groups offer a threat and a challenge to the advanced economies of North America—Canada and the United States—which were shielded from keen international competition from the war until just a few years ago. The alternatives are to face the challenge confidently, actively joining in the process of extending the area of international competition; or to retreat from international competition into protectionism. Protectionism is the natural first choice of a private enterprise system which has gone soft from easy living in a period of boom, but its likely effects would be to impair the vigour and efficiency of Canadian industry, impede adjustment to the new circumstances of international competition, and in the long run retard the rate of economic growth. There are good reasons for believing that much of Canadian industry could adjust to and hold its own in modern international competition—it has more capital, skill and modern technology at its disposal than many of its emerging competitors—and if the protectionist argument that what restrains Canadian industry is the small size of the Canadian market is valid, it suggests that Canada would gain in efficiency from the greater access to large foreign markets that participation in freer trade arrangements would entail. In short, the situation of increasing international competition which has helped to give rise to demands for protection offers great opportunities to Canada, opportunities to which protectionism seeks to shut the door. This is not to say that Canada could avail herself of those opportunities without strains of adjustment; but wise policy would seem to consist in taking measures to facilitate adjustment, rather than in attempting to prevent it.

My third reason for believing that the advocacy of protectionist and Canadianization measures has not been in the Canadian national interest is that, by attributing the high unemployment of the past few years to the absence of sufficient tariff protection and to American investment in Canada, the nationalists have helped to divert attention from the fact that the depressed condition of the Canadian economy is to a substantial extent the result of the economic policies pursued by the Government and the Bank of Canada. In so doing, the nationalists have helped the authorities to evade a searching public discussion of those policies, which would have been a much more useful contribution to the growth of Canadian national independence than the fostering of anti-American sentiment could ever be.

I do not wish to elaborate the theory of economic policy in the Canadian economy, or to repeat the criticisms which eminent Canadian economists have made of the policy of the Government and the speeches of the present Governor of the Bank of Canada. It is well known to all that the Governor would rather coin reproving phrases than print the money that would reduce unemployment to a tolerable level, and that on matters of economic principle Mr. Coyne has a habit of coming down tails. There is, perhaps, some scope for arguing seriously that it is desirable to prolong and intensify a severe recession in order to restrain an extremely mild upward movement of prices. But it is an almost incredible failure of leadership that while such a policy is being pursued, a Government which owns the central bank should seek to disclaim responsibility for monetary policy; that the Governor of a Bank which commands as good economic advice as any central bank in the world should attempt to deny that the Bank could or should alleviate unemployment, using arguments which even the most generous-minded economists find hard to credit; and that, while basing his policy on the overriding need to prevent inflation he should appear to endorse protectionist methods of raising employment which, if applied, would in all probability have a more inflationary effect than would monetary expansion. It is equally incredible that a country which had the intelligence to adopt a floating exchange rate, and so free itself from the conflict between internal and external balance which has long hobbled the policy of Britain and is now hampering that of the United States, should be floundering in worse straits than either of them, and instead of courageously using its freedom should be blaming its troubles on its less foresighted neighbour. Canada has had a golden opportunity to show her capacity for intelligent economic policy in the past few years, by using the freedom of her floating exchange rate to avoid the loss of economic impetus that has afflicted the United States; if she has instead chosen to fritter it away, it is Canadians who must bear the responsibility—and Canadian nationalism which has helped to disguise that fact from the Canadian people.

### Footnote

1. This was written before June 1961, when the controversy over Mr. James Coyne became public knowledge.

## THE BANK OF NOVA SCOTIA
# Foreign Investment in Canada

Judged in its broadest context, foreign investment has played a major role in the economic development of Canada. The use of foreign capital and in many cases the related introduction of foreign know-how and technology have provided a higher level of Canadian output and incomes than would have been possible if this country had relied solely on domestic sources of savings and investment. Yet foreign investment comes in a variety of forms, which in turn carry varying implications and raise differing sorts of questions. Many of the issues involved are quite complex, and all the more so because they extend beyond purely economic bounds. In the past few years, a growing volume of study and research on the subject has been proceeding;[1] this paper attempts to outline some of this material, focussing on some of the problems as well as the benefits which arise out of foreign investment.

## Some Historical Perspective

It is no coincidence that the periods of fastest Canadian growth have also been marked by heavy inflows of foreign capital. For Canada's part, there has been a clear need for a high rate of capital formation to provide not only an infrastructure for the economy—for example, British financing for the railways before the First World War—but also the means of developing the country's massive natural resources and a manufacturing base. To the outsider, Canada has quite plainly offered investment opportunities which appeared to be equalled in few other places. Both these closely related factors have shaped the overall course of foreign investment, and between 1926 (the first year of reliable estimates) and the end of 1970, Canada's gross long-term investment liabilities to non-residents grew from $6 billions to almost $44 billions.

The combination of investment requirements and investment opportunities over these years has produced not only fluctuations in capital flows but also a considerable change of pattern. Since the 1920s there has been a steady expansion of U.S. direct investment in controlled companies in Canada, partly to develop new-found resources and partly as a means of getting around the Canadian tariff, while the two marked surges of post-war capital investment in Canada—in the mid-1950s and mid-1960s—were facilitated in large degree by direct participation of foreign companies as well as by bond and equity financing abroad (portfolio investment). By the end of 1970, the book value of total foreign direct investment in Canada had increased to over $25 billions (of which nearly four-fifths was owned by U.S. residents), portfolio investments had risen to about $16 billions, and other foreign holdings of real estate, mortgages etc., to about $2.7 billions (see Chart).

# Foreign Long-Term Investments in Canada

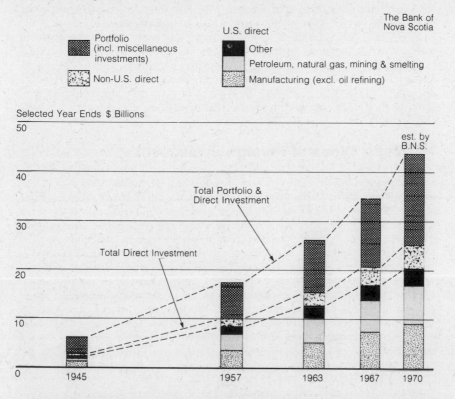

Portfolio (incl. miscellaneous investments)

Non-U.S. direct

U.S. direct

Other

Petroleum, natural gas, mining & smelting

Manufacturing (excl. oil refining)

The Bank of Nova Scotia

Selected Year Ends $ Billions

est. by B.N.S.

Total Portfolio & Direct Investment

Total Direct Investment

50

40

30

20

10

0

1945    1957    1963    1967    1970

The determinants of investment flows are, of course, subject to continual change. Within the last 10 years, the growth of the Canadian economy and the significant move towards a greater liberalization of world trade have improved the market environment for manufacturing companies in particular and have begun to lessen the inducements for operating small-scale replicas of U.S. firms behind the Canadian tariff. Of major importance, too, have been the attempts to rationalize production and trade flows in certain industries—most notably the automobile industry, where the Auto Pact brought a massive round of new investment in more specialized and efficient Canadian productive facilities as well as an expansion of automotive trade.

While the pattern of investment opportunities thus has been changing in recent years, Canada's requirements for foreign capital have also been subject to new considerations. Since 1966, Canada's balance of payments on current account has undergone a major improvement, swinging from an average annual deficit of $1.1 billions in 1965 and 1966 to a surplus last year of slightly more than that amount. While due account has to be taken of the specially favourable factors which have been affecting this country's trade position—including the sluggish course of business investment—there is not doubt that over the recent period the shortfall in Canadian savings has been nothing like as large as in much of its past history. On a ''net'' basis—taking account of the entire flow of both short-term and long-term capital into and out of Canada—greater scope is thus being opened for Canadian investments abroad, especially by larger Canadian companies capable of extending their productive activities on a wider international basis.[2] One of the most striking developments of the past ten years, indeed, has been the rising prominence of the so-called multinational company with operations spread out in a goodly number of countries. Extension of such companies into other parts of the world has, on the one hand, introduced a new and significant dimension to the questions relating to foreign investment in Canada. But it has likewise opened up new horizons for Canadians in their own approach to corporate growth and to relevant economic policies.

## Major Types of Foreign Investment

Approximately one-third of Canada's foreign long-term liabilities consists of *portfolio investment*. This type of indebtedness arises when non-residents purchase long-term bonds of Canadian governments and corporations or make minority investments in Canadian equity shares. In the case of foreign bond issues, the major source of portfolio investment, the initiative typically is taken by the Canadian borrower, and reflects a desire on his part to take advantage of the lower interest rates and broader capital markets of other countries. In recent years the total borrowing requirements of Canadian provinces and provincial agencies have increased persistently; and, to avoid undue drawings upon domestic capital markets as well as possibly to secure lower interest costs, provinces have borrowed substantial amounts in the New York market, and some also in Europe. Over the past four years, in addition, there has been a sizeable volume of corporate borrowing abroad, the most notable being the spaced-out drawings of close to $500 millions for financing of the huge Churchill Falls power project.

All told, new issues of Canadian securities in foreign markets averaged $1.4 billions per year over the period from 1963 to 1970. In 1968 and 1969 they ran to nearly $2 billions a year, and even after allowing for retirements net issues were about $1.6 billions. In the past year, however, the marked easing of borrowing conditions in Canada, combined with a government request to avoid foreign financing if possible, has brought a sharp reduction in the volume of new foreign issues, and there may well be less reliance on this kind of financing in the years ahead.

Despite the substantial volume of foreign portfolio financing over the past four years, the flow of foreign *direct investment* has remained the most dynamic element in the growth of Canada's gross long-term investment liabilities. At the end of 1970 estimated total direct investment in Canada at somewhat over $25 billions, accounted for roughly 60% of total foreign long-term investment. This kind of investment, involving foreign control over physical (as opposed to financial) assets, has been the major source of concern among many of the critics of foreign investment in Canada. Unlike portfolio funds, direct investment involves the import of a "package" which may include capital but also encompasses such factors as technology, risk-taking ability, management know-how and market access. Capital will usually be part of the direct investment package and, at times, access to capital is itself the main element in the

Sources of Funds used by Affiliates of U.S. Companies in Canada
(U.S. $ millions)

|  | 1963 | 1964 | 1965 | 1967 | 1968 |
|---|---|---|---|---|---|
| Internally-generated funds |  |  |  |  |  |
| Retained earnings* | 336 | 497 | 373 | 444 | 529 |
| Depreciation and depletion allowances | 552 | 623 | 681 | 800 | 864 |
| Sub-total | 888 | 1,120 | 1,054 | 1,244 | 1,393 |
| External funds |  |  |  |  |  |
| Funds from U.S. | 168 | 156 | 551 | 242 | 127 |
| Funds obtained outside U.S.** | 241 | 307 | 497 | 423 | 539 |
| Other sources and adjustments | 29 | 88 | 75 | 138 | 53 |
| Sub-total | 438 | 551 | 1,123 | 803 | 719 |
| Total Funds Used | 1,326 | 1,671 | 2,177 | 2,047 | 2,112 |

**Note:** *Retained earnings run around half of total net income of the companies concerned.
\*\*Mainly funds secured in Canada including funds from issues of securities, loans from financial institutions, and trade credits.
**Source:** Survey of Current Business, Nov. 1970, U.S. Department of Commerce. Based on reports from large U.S. companies accounting for the major share of foreign investment in the manufacturing, petroleum and mining industries. Data available only for the years shown.

whole process; but direct investment can also proceed without any cross-border movement of capital at all, as occurs when foreign corporations increase their control over assets through an investment in kind or a reinvestment of subsidiary earnings. As may be seen in the accompanying table, funds from the United States actually supplied a relatively small proportion of the total financing needs of U.S.-controlled companies in Canada between 1963 and 1968. Over 60% of the funds used for the expansion of these firms in the indicated years was, indeed, "internally generated" by the affiliates themselves in the form of retained earnings and depreciation and depletion allowances. Of the "external" supplies of financing coming other than from the United States the most important have been through direct borrowings in Canada, either by security issues, by bank loans, or by short-term trade credits.

## Direct Investment—Economic Costs and Benefits

Direct investment essentially involves moves by a parent corporation to apply its special advantages in the form of technology, finance or market connections to factors present in a foreign country, such as plentiful natural resources, lower wage levels or a protected local market. The decision to extend production across national boundaries proceeds from the calculation that the corporation's unique advantages will more than offset disadvantages relative to local firms more familiar with the local environment and all its legal, political and social overtones; it also implies a judgment that the corporation could not achieve results as good or better (from its point of view) through such alternative routes as the sale or leasing of production and patent rights, licensing or joint venture arrangements. For the recipient or host economy, the decision by a foreign corporation to produce within its borders will in most instances contribute to a higher level of capital formation and employment. Even where there is no local shortage of savings, the operation of foreign subsidiaries provides stimulating influences not only through the continued chanelling of advanced technical know-how and strong risk-taking capacity in the companies directly concerned but also through the secondary effects on domestic sales and incomes and through the diffusion of technical and managerial skills to local companies.

Foreign direct investment in Canada's resource-based industries has generally fitted into this classic mould. In the forest and mineral developments of the 1920s and 1930s, and in the great postwar expansion in oil and gas, iron ore and other resources as well, direct long-term market outlets, ready access to needed large amounts of capital and advanced technical know-how and experience all had a part to play. It should be clear also that these developments in turn contributed greatly to the strengthening and deepening of the whole Canadian economy through this period, extending added stimulus to the growth of local population and markets and thereby inducing enlargement of other service and secondary industries.

On occasion, excessive bunching of such developments has tended to accentuate upward pressures on Canadian costs and prices and thus to raise problems for less vigorous sectors of the economy. Concern on such grounds is clearly evident in some current discussions of Canadian policies with respect to the development and movement of oil and gas from Alaska and the Canadian Arctic. Yet in being alert to such potential problems it would be foolish to ignore the undeniable long-term benefits of efficient production in lines where Canada does have recognizable comparative advantages.

Foreign direct investment has also, of course, played a major role in the development of Canadian secondary industries, beginning again as early as the 1920s. Such investment, however, has in large part been of a "defensive" type, undertaken not to increase the return available but to forestall loss of markets or of profits in trying to sell over the Canadian tariff (and in the 1930s into Commonwealth preferential countries as well).

While tariff barriers thus were a crucial factor in attracting foreign manufacturing subsidiaries into Canada, the tariff levels in turn have hampered the effective performance of such companies and of Canadian manufacturing in general. Since it took a tariff in the first instance to induce the foreign companies to establish production facilities in Canada, it should not be too surprising that the subsidiary companies would tend to be less efficient than their parents. But because of the nature of the U.S. production and marketing system, and the heavy reliance on brand names and advertising, Canada in general attracted not isolated U.S. producers but virtually the whole range of major companies in particular industries—so establishing the pattern of too many plants producing too many product items with unduly short production runs and unduly high production costs. Studies in recent years have widely documented the nature of these problems, and have examined them also in relation to Canada's anti-combines legislation, and other aspects of the Canadian industrial environment. While some subsidiary companies in fact have been able to achieve high standards of performance, in general it has been found that their operations tend to parallel the shortcomings of domestically-controlled firms. The inherent advantages of the parent companies, thus, have not been as fully transmitted and diffused through the Canadian economy as might be desired; and consumers have not seen all the benefits that could result in terms of price or product quality. Yet even with these quite evident limitations, which the Canadian government has been seeking to remedy (as in the Auto Pact), there is little doubt that, in general, direct foreign investment has made a substantial contribution to the productivity of Canadian factors of production and, thereby, to the pace of overall Canadian economic growth.

The financial cost to Canada for the use of direct investment lies in the profits accruing to non-residents. High profits themselves need not be indicative of an excessive rate of return and may simply be a reflection of efficient operations. It is only where a firm is being subsidized by being permitted to earn monopoly profits that the host country need be concerned. In any case, available data for much of the 1960s show that the before-tax profits of foreign-owned firms in Canada, as a percentage of equity, averaged only slightly higher than those of domestic firms. Canada, moreover, participates in the profits of foreign-owned firms through taxation. The real financial cost of direct investment, therefore, declines as Canadian corporate and withholding taxes rise and as the authorities improve their surveillance of interfirm pricing (in particular, the prices set on raw material exports to the parent). The after-tax rate of return on U.S. direct investment in Canada, averaging about 8% for 1967-69, has been substantially below the average return on all U.S. overseas investment, and in fact in most countries would be considered a reasonable payment merely for the services of long-term debt funds.

As noted in the table showing the financing of U.S. subsidiary companies in Canada, roughly half the profits of these companies are reinvested in Canada—a significantly higher proportion than is true of such firms in other countries. While the percentage has remained relatively unchanged over the years, the actual amounts of dividends paid out have of course increased in line with the greater absolute amount of direct investment in Canada; between 1950 and 1970, for example, total outward transfers have increased from $366 millions to $780 millions. Some concern has been expressed about the implications of these rising outflows for the long-term health of Canada's balance of payments. In fact, however, foreign direct investments have contributed both to growth in export earnings and to displacement of imports, and there is no evidence to suggest that these trade effects have in any way been insufficient to cover the growing volume of dividend payments. This is not to deny that the presence of foreign-controlled companies in Canada increases the risk of occasional instability in Canada's foreign exchange position. But such instability arises essentially from unfavourable patterns of events or misdirected policy developments, and foreign-controlled corporations are only one (though an important one) of the channels for destabilizing movements of funds.

One final cost of direct investment, the degree of which is difficult to gauge, is its effect in reducing the incentives to improve skills and technology in Canada. The ease of importing such foreign capabilities (and the pull also which the United States has on talented and educated Canadians) has undoubtedly hampered the local development of entrepreneurial talents and discouraged domestic research and development. But while such impediments may be significant, it is still open to Canadians to seek to improve their capabilities in these respects.

## Broad Policy Issues

Much of the expressed concern about foreign investment in Canada has focussed on the large size of many of the foreign corporations that have established subsidiary operations in Canada, on their dominant position in many
important industries, and on potential conflicts of interest in the exercise of
their decision-making power.

In fact, as the C.A.L.U.R.A. returns[3] show, Canadian industries run the
gamut from close to 100% control by non-residents (as in petroleum refining) to
a near-zero element in many services and utilities. Successive governments
have decided that certain "key sectors" of the economy — such as press and
communications, air and rail transportation, financial institutions and, most
recently, the uranium industry — should be subject to direct limitations on the
extent of non-resident participation. Beyond this, various public regulatory
authorities establish and administer a wide range of operational standards for
vital industries, whether they be domestically or foreign controlled; these
include such matters as forest management standards, provincial mineral regulations and conservation quotas for oil and gas. In important industries, also,
operational conditions are much influenced by cross-border agreements
worked out by the U.S. and Canadian governments. In all of these respects,
there is a continuing challenge to find ways of best serving the national interest.

A more direct, but still rather general, aspect of government policies related
to foreign investment lies in the so-called problem of extra-territoriality — i.e.
in the extension of foreign laws and regulations to subsidiary operations in
Canada. Most prominent in this respect have been some of the U.S. balance-
of-payments guidelines of recent years, U.S. anti-trust laws, and the U.S.
regulations on trade with communist countries. Essentially what is involved
here is a matter of conflicting political jurisdictions, and such problems are
becoming of wide international interest with the spreading operations of
multi-national corporations. Thus far, however, the only approach open to the
Canadian government is to be ready to introduce new national laws or administrative steps in instances where this is needed to countervail against the
intrusion of U.S. law.

Probably one of the most significant direct problems arising out of the
operation of major U.S.-controlled companies in Canada relates to the size of
many of these companies and to their predominant position in important and
(very often) the fastest-growing segments of Canadian industry. Though there
is little if any evidence to support suggestions of undue political influence,
especially in any combined way, the relative size of the companies involved
does frequently add a complicating dimension to the pursuance of national
objectives, and in some cases, too, there may well be difficulties in reconciling
the specific interests of a subsidiary in Canada with the broad international
interests of a multi-national organization. In general, however, these problems
have been far from unmanageable, and for the most part they have represented
just one aspect of the broader challenge to maximize the benefits, while also as
much as possible limiting the costs, of foreign investment.

On this broad question of the performance of foreign-controlled companies,
much study has been pursued in recent years especially by Professor A. E.

Safarian of the University of Toronto. From his work Safarian concludes that "where behaviour that has been defined as undesirable by public authorities does appear, it can often be related more closely to aspects of the economic environment of the subsidiary, and only distantly, if at all, to the fact of foreign ownership." In other words, it is aspects of the national industrial climate, and not location of ownership, that constitute the main impediment to good economic performance.

On one other source of concern — that is, the predominant position of large non-resident companies in fast-growing sections of the economy — the constructive response surely lies not in choking off the benefits to be secured through efficient expansion of such companies but in fostering more competitive market conditions in Canada and in seeking to strengthen the capacity of Canadian enterprises to participate in new areas of growth and development. Studies made by the Economic Council of Canada have pointed up the extent to which this country has lagged the United States in levels of educational attainment and managerial training as well as in effective local application of technological research. In these and other aspects of the question, the major challenge is to set realistic and balanced policy objectives, and to develop practical means of working towards them.

### Footnotes

1. See especially Task Force Report on Foreign Ownership and the Structure of Canadian Industry, prepared for Privy Council Office, January 1968; A. E. Sefarian "The Performance of Foreign-Owned Firms in Canada," for Canadian-American Committee, May 1969; Sidney E. Rolfe, "The International Corporation," for International Chamber of Commerce, Spring 1969; and C. P. Kindleberger *American Business Abroad* (Yale University Press, 1969)

2. Along with the (approx.) $44 billions of long-term foreign investment into Canada at the end of 1970, other items mainly short-term in character raised total Canadian external liabilities to about $49 billions. At the same time, Canadian assets in foreign countries totalled about $21 billions (the major components being over $11 billions of long-term investment, close to $5 billions of official exchange reserves, and substantial private holdings of short-term investments).

3. Corporations and Labour Unions Returns Act.

KARI LEVITT

# The Harvest of Lengthening Dependence

## Profile of a Rich, Industrialized, Underdeveloped Economy

In spite of Canada's high income and high degree of industrialization, the country has not shared in the recent world trend towards an increase in the importance of trade in relation to domestic production. In consequence, Canada's trade as a percentage of that of industrial countries dropped from 9.6 per cent in 1953 to 7.2 per cent in 1965 and her commodity terms of trade declined from 101 in 1954 to 97 in 1965. The deterioration in terms of trade for all underdeveloped countries over the same period was from 109 to 97. In developed countries the corresponding improvement in terms of trade was from 96 to 104.[1] The reasons for these trends are to be found in the high proportion of primary or crudely processed materials in Canada's exports and the correspondingly high proportion of finished manufacturers in her imports. Canadian exports are heavily concentrated in a few product lines. These are either pure raw materials such as wheat, iron and other metallic ores, petroleum and natural gas, or crudely processed manufactures such as woodpulp, newsprint, lumber, flour, aluminum, copper and metal alloys, and primary iron and steel products.

In a study of thirteen industrialized countries of the Western world it was found that end-products accounted for 60 per cent of exports. For Canada the comparable ratio was only 19 per cent. Although there has been an increase of 12 per cent in the share of highly manufactured goods in Canada's exports in the last decade, the increase for other relatively small industrialized countries[2] over the same period was 37 per cent.[3] In 1954 Canada was exceeded only by New Zealand in value of trade per head. By 1964 Canada ranked eighth, exceeded by Belgium, Luxembourg, Holland, Switzerland, Denmark, Norway and Trinidad-Tobago, in that order. In none of those countries, with the exception of the last-mentioned, do crudely processed materials account for as high a percentage of exports as they do in Canada.

Recent trends in Canada's imports are equally suggestive of structural underdevelopment. The share of consumer goods in imports rose from 29 per cent in the mid-fifties to 34 per cent in the mid-sixties, mainly due to increased imports of automobiles and new-technology manufactures. End products increased their share in imports from 50 per cent to 54 per cent over the same decade. The indication is that technological advance of a type that results in new products not produced in Canada, together with imitative demand by consumers and producers, are an important factor in explaining Canadian import patterns. It should be noted that the heavy inflow of direct investment to Canada's manufacturing industries has coincided with a rise in manufactured imports relative to domestic production. This ratio rose from 18 per cent in 1954 to 21 per cent in 1965, reversing a contrary trend in operation since the mid-1920s.[4] It is well known that world trade in highly manufactured goods is rising more rapidly than trade in industrial raw materials and primary products. Canada appears unable to share in the gains which these trends offer to other industrialized countries.[5]

While there has been an increase in the export of manufactured goods in recent years, this has been strongly related to the implementation of the Defence Production Sharing Agreements of 1959 and the automobile agreements of 1963. The proportion of highly processed exports which fluctuated between 11 per cent and 14 per cent in the 1950s had risen to 19 per cent in 1965. Inedible end products rose from less than 8 per cent of total Canadian exports in 1959-60 to a level of 15 per cent in 1965. Most of the expansion took place in the U.S. market.

While the devaluation of 1962 undoubtedly resulted in some increase in commercial exports, the bilateral arrangements between the governments of Canada and the United States accounted for the greater part of the increase. These special arrangements are a manifestation of increasing corporate and governmental integration between the two countries. The industries directly involved are the automobile, aircraft, electrical, chemical and machinery industries — all heavily controlled by U.S. capital. Increased export sales to the United States have been gained at the expense of economic and political vulnerability.

The Defence Production Sharing Agreements, whereby Canadian firms are permitted to bid on equal terms with U.S. firms for American war contracts, accounted for $260 million of Canada's exports in 1965, or 30 per cent of all Canadian inedible end-product exports to the U.S. In 1966, U.S. defence contracts placed in Canada had increased to $317 million. Although these sales are small in relation to total Canadian production, the concentration of employment exposes Canadians to the possibility of severe unemployment in given areas in the event of the termination of these agreements. As the Canadian Minister of External Affairs explained: "Think of the impossible position we would be in if the Defence Production Sharing Agreements were abrogated . . . to pull out would be to endanger our economy and safety." It should be noted that the foreign exchange earned by these defence exports is pre-empted by the undertaking of the Canadian government to purchase American war supplies. Thus in 1966 Canadian defence purchases in the U.S. amounted to $332.6 million.

Of greater importance than the defence arrangements are the automobile agreements which lifted exports of cars and parts to the U.S. from a level of $36 million in 1963 to $231 million in 1965 and to $2,428 million in 1968. The *quid pro quo* for these automobile exports, however, has taken the form of increased imports by the automotive corporations involved, and the balance of commodity trade in cars and parts with the U.S. remains in deficit. This deficit rose from

$551 million in 1963 to $714 million in 1965, and has since declined to $343 millions in 1968.

The expansion of normal commercial sales of highly manufactured goods abroad has thus been extremely modest. This is so in spite of efforts to promote exports, including the provision of export credit, the work of the Export Finance Corporation, the promotional efforts of the Department of Trade and Commerce, and strings on foreign aid which sometimes require 80 to 90 per cent Canadian content.

## Research and Development

The difficulties of expanding commercial manufactured exports are compounded by the low level of industrial research and development expenditures in Canada and their high concentration in industries which service the special requirements of the U.S. defence department. Canadian expenditures on research and development are smaller, in relation to its GNP (1.1 per cent) than that of industrial countries of Western Europe—West Germany (1.3 per cent), France (1.5 per cent), the U.K. (2.2 per cent), and very much smaller than expenditures in the U.S.A. (3.1 per cent).

What is more, in Canada 79 per cent of such research is performed by government and only 12 per cent in the business sector compared with the United States where, even though much of the work is done under government contracts, 71 per cent is carried on by industry. Comparable figures for West Germany, France and the United Kingdom are 61 per cent, 48 per cent and 71 per cent.[6] The bulk of industrial research expenses in the U.S. are, however, subsidized by public funds. The situation in Canada was summed up by Dr. Steacie, president of the National Research Council in the following words: "Because of the financial relationship between Canadian and American firms, most Canadian plants are essentially branch plants, and research is normally done by the parent organization outside the country. As a result Canadian industry has been largely dependent on research done in the U.S. and Britain."[7]

The most recent survey conducted by the Dominion Bureau of Statistics reported a total of $264 million spent on industrial research and development. Thirteen firms accounted for half of these expenditures and they were heavily concentrated in the electrical, aircraft and chemical industries. The electrical products and aircraft industries accounted for 47 per cent of total research and development expenditure and these same industries received 83 per cent of federal funds granted to industry for research. Four companies alone received 55 per cent of total federal support. We already observed that Canadian government subsidies to industry are heavily directed towards industries in which foreign firms predominate and which are heavily engaged in defence production. The huge utility industry is, by contrast, according to the Dominion Bureau of Statistics' report, entirely self-financing as regards research.

Industrial research in Canada is strongly biased towards applied rather than basic work. The Dominion Bureau of Statistics survey reports that only 356 of 6,367 trained scientists and engineers engaged in R and D in Canadian industry in 1965 were doing basic research.[8] Information compiled by Professor Wilkinson shows the lower levels of R and D expenditures in almost every industry in Canada as compared with the U.S.

*Table 1   R and D Expenditures as Percentages of Manufacturing Industry Sales, Canada and the United States*

| Industry | R and D as Percentages of Sales Canada, 1963 Intramural and Extramural (a) | United States 1962 |
|---|---|---|
| Aircraft | 10.09 | 27.2 |
| Drugs and pharmaceuticals | 3.92 | 4.4 |
| Scientific and professional equipment | 3.19 | 7.1 |
| Electrical products | 2.58 | 7.3 |
| Other chemical products | 1.53 | 3.8 |
| Petroleum and coal products | 1.17 | 0.9 |
| Machinery | 1.04 | 3.2 |
| Pulp and Paper | 0.72 | 0.1 |
| Primary metals (non-ferrous) | 0.86 | 0.8 |
| Rubber | 1.50 | 1.4 (b) |
| Primary metals (ferrous) | 0.33 | 0.5 |
| Non-metallic mineral products | 0.35 | 1.1 |
| Textiles | 0.26 | 0.2 |
| Metal fabricating | 0.22 | 0.8 |
| Other manufacturing | 0.11 (c) | 0.4 (d) |
| Food and beverages | 0.10 | 0.2 (e) |
| Other transportation equipment | 0.06 | 2.8 |
| Furniture and fixtures | 0.05 | 0.1 |
| Wood | 0.02 | 0.1 |
| Average, all manufacturing | 0.7 | 2.0 |

(a) Intramural refers to expenditure on R and D within the firm.
    Extramural refers to outlays for research and development performed outside the reporting firms, and primarily outside the country.
(b) Includes plastics.
(c) Includes tobacco and products, leather, clothing and knitting mills, and miscellaneous manufacturing.
(d) Covers same industries as in note (c), plus printing and publishing.
(e) Food only.
**Sources:** Canadian data: Dominion Bureau of Statistics, *Daily Bulletin Supplement* — 3: "Industrial Research and Development Expenditures in Canda, 1965," April 12, 1967, Table 2; and *Manufacturing Industries of Canada: Section A*, 1963. U.S. data: Gruber, Mehta, and Vernon, "The R and D Factor in International Trade and International Investment of United States Industries," *Journal of Political Economy*, February, 1967, p. 23, Table 1.
Reproduced from Wilkinson, *op. cit.* p. 122.

The comparison is interesting because there is evidence of a strong correlation between R and D expenditures on the one hand, and success in the export of manufactured products on the other. Gruber, Mehta and Vernon, following the hypothesis suggested by Professor Vernon in his article on "International Investment and International Trade in the Product Cycle,"[9] offer impressive statistical evidence that American strength in the export of manufactured goods does not lie in a greater abundance of capital, but rather in the ability to develop new products and cost-saving processes. Initiatives in R and D thus yield an oligopoly position in supplying foreign markets to countries which have the capacity to innovate. Their results are summed up in Table 2.

*Table 2   Relationship between Research Effort and Export Performance of 19 U.S. Manufacturing Industries*

|  | Research Effort | | Export Performance | |
|---|---|---|---|---|
|  | Total R & D expenditures as a percentage of sales | Scientists & Engineers in R & D as a percentage of total employment | Exports as a percentage of sales | Excess of exports over imports as a percentage of sales |
| Transportation equipment | 10.0 | 3.4 | 5.5 | 4.1 |
| Electrical machinery | 7.3 | 3.6 | 4.1 | 2.9 |
| Instruments | 7.1 | 3.4 | 6.7 | 3.2 |
| Chemicals | 3.9 | 4.1 | 6.2 | 4.5 |
| Machines (non-electrical) | 3.2 | 1.4 | 13.3 | 11.4 |
| Five (above) industries with highest research effort | 6.3 | 3.2 | 7.2 | 5.2 |
| Fourteen other U.S. industries | 0.5 | 0.4 | 1.8 | —1.1 |

**Source:** Gruber, Mehta and Vernon, *op. cit.*

In this analysis comprising nineteen industries, the five most research-intensive ones accounted for 89 per cent of total R and D expenditures, 78 per cent of company-financed R and D expenditures, and employed 85 per cent of industrial scientists and engineers. While their sales were only 39 per cent of the total sales of all nineteen industries, they accounted for 72 per cent of the exports. The study debunks a widely held belief that high-technology industries are, to use economists' jargon, capital-intensive, and consequently that countries in which capital is cheap relative to labour enjoy a "comparative advantage" in such industries. The correlation to this proposition of course is that countries in which capital is relatively scarce should not attempt to develop such industries.

The Gruber-Mehta-Vernon study found that labour costs form a larger percentage of value added in the five most research-intensive industries (24.7 per cent) than in the fourteen others (17.2 per cent). Correspondingly, the capital component of cost measured in terms of depreciation as a percentage of value added is smaller in the five most research-intensive industries (4.3 per cent) than in the other fourteen (5.3 per cent). Net fixed assets as a percentage of value added is also lower in the five leading industries (31 per cent) than in the other fourteen (41 per cent). The picture is completed by the observation of the authors that:

> Industries with comparatively high export sales of products involving scientific and technical aspects in their sales and servicing will have a high propensity to invest in manufacturing subsidiaries in the markets they serve and that in these "oligopoly industries" therefore, individual firms are likely to consider foreign investments as important forestalling tactics

to cut off market pre-emption by others. And they are likely to feel obliged to counter an investment by others with an investment of their own.

While Canadian industry is basically derivative and imitative, there exist the proverbial exceptions. These consist of cases where indigenous Canadian R and D has been a vital factor in gaining export markets. The list is familiar because it is pitifully short. It includes Canadian developments in nuclear power plants, telecommunication systems, the STOL aircraft developed by De Havilland for bush mining and explorational landing fields, the air navigational devices of Canadian Marconi and Computing Devices of Canada, and products pioneered by the Polymer Crown Corporation. The Canadian steel industry, primarily Stelco, has, as previously mentioned, maintained its world-wide reputation for innovation. The list, however short, belies the negative attitude of many experts that Canada is too deficient in technical skills to develop its own products.

A tragic feature of Canada's technological hinterland status is the frustration experienced by her scientists, many of whom sooner or later depart in search of more challenging work in the United States. In the words of a Canadian scientist:

> It is well known that many a Canadian scientist in the U.S. would happily return to the land of his birth and early nurture if the same scientific opportunities existed here. But there is the rub—the same opportunities do not exist in Canada; partly this is to be expected from the disparate populations of the two nations, but partly it arises as a concommitant of Canada's satellite role in economic affairs . . . not only are opportunities lacking in Canada, but the organization of science in Canada . . . and our attitudes toward it, are largely fashioned in the U.S. . . . It is one thing to learn something from the American way of doing things, but complete integration into the American way stifles development of a distinctive Canadian style and a distinctive Canadian attitude about science, particularly with regard to its cultural values in society.[10]

Another measure of the technological dependence of Canadian industry is the nationality of patent applicants. Here we find that 95 per cent of all patents taken out in Canada over the period 1957-61 were by foreign applicants, with 65 to 70 per cent by U.S. applicants. This is probably the most remarkable single statistic of technological dependence. The proportion of foreign applicants for patents is much higher for Canada than for any other developed country. Similar figures for other industrial countries were 80 per cent for Belgium, 70 per cent for Scandinavian countries, 59 per cent for France, 47 per cent for the United Kingdom and 32 per cent for West Germany.[11]

## The "Miniature Replica" Effect

The effect of branch-plant economy on the structure of domestic industry is by now well established: too many firms producing too many product lines at high unit cost. When branch plants enter a tariff-protected market in which consumer tastes approximate those of the metropolitan economy we get what Dr.

English has named the "miniature replica" effects.[12] The spill-over of advertising and other corporate overheads related to product-differentiation and promotion make it profitable for foreign companies to assemble or sell a large range of their products in the hinterland. In many instances the international corporation does not enjoy a technical superiority as much as a marketing advantage arising from the familiarity of the consumer with the trade marks and brand names of its products. As Safarian has observed, "the great majority of the companies are a small fraction of the parent in size yet they are producing almost the full range of the identical or slightly modified products of the parent. Not surprisingly their unit costs are in most cases higher than those of the parent on major comparable products."[13] The case best documented is that of the refrigerator industry. Here it has been estimated that the Canadian market of 400,000 per annum could be efficiently served by two plants. In fact there are nine plants, and seven of these are U.S.-controlled branch plants. In 1966 these accounted for 80-85 per cent of refrigerator production, compared with 71 per cent in 1960. These Canadian subsidiaries almost duplicate in number the plants producing refrigerators for the much larger American market. All of them operate well below optimum size.[14]

It is not true that the Canadian domestic market is too small to support a diversified manufacturing industry. Rather the combination of tariff protection and branch-plant organization has resulted in the inefficient production of too many similar products. The manufacturing industry catering to the domestic market, both foreign and locally-controlled, tends to be inefficient. Safarian's original study and the more recent investigations he undertook as a member of the Watkins team found that the nationality of ownership is irrelevant to economic performance. Foreign-controlled subsidiaries are no more efficient than locally-controlled firms. Nor are they less efficient. The evidence suggests that the key to efficiency in Canadian industry lies in rationalization, specialization, and innovation. Economic policies designed to this end would require a reduction of Canadian tariffs, the planned rationalization of select sectors of the manufacturing industry by means which include the takeover of redundant branch plants, and a large increase in research and development expenditures in high-technology industries catering to commercial markets. It requires above all a rejection on the part of Canadians of the branch-plant mentality which breeds a debilitating attitude of complacent incompetence and resignation to perpetual dependence on external initiatives.

## Canadian Savings and the Growth of U.S. Subsidiaries

There is a widely held belief that Canada needs foreign investment because the country is "capital-hungry" and domestic savings are inadequate to finance expansion. While it may be advantageous to borrow portfolio capital, which does not transfer control, there is no conclusive case for the view that foreign direct investment constitutes the only way in which sufficient savings can be mobilized. Nor can a convincing case be made for the view that direct investment is necessary because entrepreneurial opportunities cannot be exploited without it.

In fact the inflow of direct investment funds constitutes a small fraction of total gross national saving in Canada. In 1965, for example, which was a year of relatively heavy foreign direct capital investment, the flow of new funds into Canadian subsidiaries was $500 million, or less than 5 per cent of total Canadian domestic savings, which exceeded $10 billion in that year. Indeed, these new funds are a minor source of finance for expansion by the subsidiaries; the major portion is provided by the re-investment of profit, by depreciation and depletion allowances, and by borrowings from Canadian financial institutions.

Over the years 1957 to 1965, 85 per cent of the funds used to expand U.S.-controlled industry in Canada was provided from Canadian domestic savings. More specifically, U.S. subsidiaries in Canada obtained 73 per cent of their funds from retained earnings and depreciation, and a further 12 per cent from other Canadian sources, and only 15 per cent from the United States. While the mining industry received 19 per cent of total funds from the U.S. and the petroleum industry 22 per cent, manufacturing branch plants obtained only 9 per cent from the U.S. throughout the period.[15] In the year 1964, for example, of a total investment of $2,557 million by U.S. subsidiaries in Canada, $1,244 million was financed from retained earnings, $764 million from depreciation allowances, $423 million from Canadian and third-country borrowing and only $126 million from funds from the United States. Of the funds obtained in Canada, only $71 million was issue of equity stock. The Dominion Bureau of Statistics has estimated that, in the nineteen-year period 1946-64, the accumulation of undistributed earnings added $5.2 billion, or 40 per cent, to the increase in Canadian external indebtedness. Well over half of these reinvestments accrued to manufacturing subsidiaries.[16]

We have estimated that the gross internal savings of foreign-controlled firms constitute about 15 per cent of total annual Canadian domestic savings. The proportion of profit which is ploughed back is much higher in the branch-plant sector than in the rest of the Canadian economy. Thus about one-third of total Canadian retained earnings accrued to foreign-controlled companies. These internal savings are pre-empted for investment in the concerns in which they are generated. If the parent companies do not wish to re-invest subsidiary profits, they can and do transfer funds out of the country. Such funds, whether re-invested or transferred, are not available to finance the expansion of other sectors of the Canadian economy.

The Canadian Department of Trade and Commerce study revealed a similar pattern of financing. In 1965 a total of $1.8 billion was available to foreign-owned subsidiaries for investment expenditures. Of this amount, $1.2 billion was generated within the subsidiaries by retained earnings and depreciation. The remaining $658 million was raised from sources external to the subsidiaries: $274 million in loans from parents; $113 million in equity holdings by parents; $254 million in bank loans and long-term borrowing; and only $37 million in equity holdings by independent shareholders.[17]

The shortage of finance is at least in part the result of branch-plant economy. Contrary to common belief, Canadian savings are not low, nor is the Canadian investor averse to taking risks. Despite lower average incomes in Canada, the rate of personal savings is substantially higher than that in the United States. In 1967 Canadians saved about 9 per cent of disposable after-tax income compared with a rate of 7 per cent in the United States. What is more, the average

Canadian is more inclined to invest his savings in equity stock than his U.S. counterpart. Thus interest income forms a larger proportion of total investment income in the United States than in Canada, despite the fact that interest rates are lower there.[18] There appears to be no shortage of demand for equity investments in Canada—only a shortage of available stock.

For these reasons Canadian financial institutions have, in recent years, greatly increased their holdings of foreign equities. As recently as 1960, major Canadian financial institutions held only 10 per cent of their stock portfolios in foreign equities; the proportion had risen to 24 per cent by 1966. The trend was most pronounced in mutual funds which held 17 per cent of equity holdings abroad in 1962, 35 per cent in 1966, and 53 per cent in 1967. Most of the foreign stock portfolios of the major Canadian financial institutions are in industries which are not listed on the Canadian market. Over 40 per cent is invested in office equipment and airline stock, and about 35 per cent in electrical and electronics, drug and cosmetics, automotive, aerospace, photography and rubber stocks. The York University study points out that ''if suitable Canadian stock issues do not become available, there is some likelihood that half the equity holdings of these institutions may soon be in foreign equities, a proportion already exceeded by the mutual funds.''

While the trend towards internal financing and reliance on banks' trade credit and the bond market is creating a general scarcity of equity issues, the proportion of listed equities which are ''locked in'' is substantially higher in Canada (30 per cent), as compared with the United States (10 per cent). The total annual demand for additional equities in Canada has been estimated to be almost double the supply provided through new Canadian issues. The meagre supply of Canadian equities results from the fact that so many Canadian corporations are private companies, and even where they are public a very substantial portion (40 per cent) of listed Canadian equities are held as direct investments by non-residents.

There is a lack neither of savings nor of opportunities for profitable economic activity. Canada provides the classical case of a rich underdeveloped economy in which the capital market is too narrow to channel local savings into local investments. A substantial volume of trading in Canadian shares takes place on U.S. exchanges and large blocks of Canadian shares are held as direct investments for the purpose of guaranteeing control. While fifteen stock exchanges in the United States increased the volume of trading in equities by 171 per cent between 1962 and 1967, the six exchanges in Canada increased trading volume by only 38 per cent. A comparison of the industry-composition of listings of the Toronto Stock Exchange with the New York Stock Exchange underlined the difference between a metropolitan and hinterland economy: 25 per cent of TSE listings represent mining stocks, compared with 3 per cent of New York listings, while very little automobile, chemical, electrical and electronic stock is traded in Toronto.

On the assumption that Canadian financial institutions may find it necessary to invest half their total equity portfolios in foreign equities, the York University study estimated that, by the early 1970s they could hold $5 billion in foreign equities. Not only are the Americans buying up Canadian industry with Canadians savings, but they have in effect mobilized Canadian savings to assist in the expansion of the U.S. based multinational corporations. As Professor Conway suggests:

> The sizable outflows of Canadian institutional and private capital coupled with the substantial direct investment holdings of Canadian equities by non-residents raises questions. If Canadian money must go abroad for suitable equity vehicles while non-resident capital in the form of direct investment creates such vehicles based on viable enterprises in Canada, possibly some additional effort must be made by the investment community towards encouraging a climate where Canadian entrepreneurs and financiers undertake to create more domestic investment vehicles which will attract domestic capital.[19]

Evidently, barriers to the expansion of Canadian enterprise do not lie in a global shortage of savings but rather in the structure of the goods and capital markets which places the independent enterprise at a disadvantage with respect to the branch plants. Frequently the former do not have access to sales outlets because markets are firmly controlled by existing corporations.[20] The capital market places the foreign branch plant at a decisive advantage in obtaining funds. Although it typically relies on internally-generated capital, large expansion can be financed by transfers from parents and affiliates in the form of loans or equity purchase by the parent. Here the small branch plant enjoys a strong advantage *vis-à-vis* the small independent firm.

The Royal Commission on Banking and Finance, 1964, noted that small independent Canadian-owned firms appear to have more difficulty at all times in obtaining long-term finance than do those which are subsidiaries of large and well-financed Canadian or American corporations. It is interesting to note that more than one-third of Canadian-controlled firms with assets under $1 million reporting to a CMA questionnaire reported sources of long-term capital as inadequate. This compares to one out of twenty-nine non-resident firms in the same size category.[21]

The authors of the Watkins Report suggest that the only way Canadian savings seeking equity investment can be channelled into Canadian industry is by incentives that would make all large private companies in Canada offer equity shares. Many, although not all, of these are wholly-owned subsidiaries of foreign corporations, such as British Petroleum, General Motors, General Foods, IBM, Canadian International Paper, and many others. It is doubtful how many of these firms would respond because, as the authors of the Report themselves admit "the commitment of some firms to the wholly-owned subsidiary is too strong to be shaken by any feasible set of incentives."[22] It is estimated that a 25 per cent minority share in all corporations with assets over $25 million or more amount to $3.5 billion or $4.5 billion at a minimum. Even if some of the capital so raised were transferred abroad, there would be an increase in Canadian minority participation, and a reduction in the long-run drain of dividends abroad.

Apart from the fact that U.S. subsidiaries have shown little enthusiasm for selling any part of their equity to Canadians, there remains an obvious need to develop new Canadian-controlled enterprises. To this end the Watkins Report recommended the implementation of the Canada Development Corporation proposed by Walter Gordon years ago. This corporation would be a large quasi-public holding company with entrepreneurial and managerial functions. It might organize and participate in consortia of investors, both domestic and foreign, so that large projects beyond the capacity of a single institution could be undertaken under Canadian control. There would presumably be emphasis on joint ventures, on rental of foreign licences and patents, where necessary, and on arrangements in which controlling interests would remain Canadian.

Other instruments of policy, including those proposed by the authors of the Watkins Report, can be devised without difficulty. The real question is whether there exists the will to regain control over the economy. This is not a question which economists can answer. This fact does not, however, relieve them of the responsibility of asking it.

## Political Disintegration

The most bitter harvest of increasing dependence and diminishing control may yet be reaped in the form of the internal political balkanization of Canada and its piecemeal absorption into the American imperial system. The final outcome of a branch-plant society is a merging of value systems and a meshing of corporate and technocratic elites which must ultimately call into question English Canada's willingness to pay the price of continued independence.

The ruling elite which founded Canada a hundred years ago were nationalists. But they were never called upon to pay. There was, in the days of Macdonald's National Policy, no conflict between the pecuniary interests of the dominant classes and their nationalism. Circumstances were such that they could enjoy both wealth and power. Power was exercised within a political framework which granted to the central government wide rights of control over the population. In distinction to the open frontier lawlessness of American democracy, Canada was an ordered, stable, conservative and authoritarian society, based on transplanted British institutions. Canada's constitution was appropriately enacted by the British Parliament, on the initiative of a group of colonial politicians, venerably depicted as the "Fathers of Confederation," who could evade the necessity of seeking the popular consensus which they could never have obtained. The arrangements were quite compatible with the interests of the bureaucratic clerical elite of French Canada. Between these groups, there was no serious conflict of interest or of outlook. The elite of English Canada was defined by their rejection of American democracy. The elite of French Canada was in effective control of a national community which had been by-passed by the French Revolution. Canada has been, from its foundation in 1867, a conservative society.

Hitched to an east-west spine of trade and investment, the Canadian nation found strength to resist American annexationist pressures in the might of the pound sterling and in British imperial power. For decades Canadian politicians refined the techniques of compromise and survival. Externally, they man-oeuvred between the British and the American metropolis. Internally, French-Canadian national survival was guaranteed by the powers exercised by the Catholic Church and the isolation of French Canada from modernizing influences. Members of the French-Canadian elite were integrated into the political structure on the terms of the English-Canadian elite, which controlled the economic structure. There developed over these years, a sense of Canadian national identity, corresponding to the conservative character of the nation under construction. Canadian patriotism *vis-à-vis* the United States was defined in terms of loyalty to the British monarchy.

The passing of time has eliminated Britain as a significant factor in Canadian politics. The problems are more difficult than they were in 1867 and the structures appropriate a hundred years ago are plainly obsolete today. The English-Canadian elite are no longer sure where they are going. Compromise and accommodation are useful political techniques for a small or middle power that knows what it wants, and can navigate the cross-currents created by stronger external powers. But compromise and accommodation as an operating philosophy of a community that does not know what it wants, in a situation in which the current runs powerfully in one direction, can lead only to drift and eventually to disintegration. The performance of Prime Minister Pearson and his administration bears witness.

The crisis of Canada's national existence is expressed in three distinct, but related confrontations: Canada versus the United States; Ottawa versus the provinces; and English Canada versus French Canada. Our theme is the effect of the new mercantilist links with the American empire on each of these conflicts, and the interplay of these relationships on Canada's chances of survival.

It is clearly no longer in the interests of the economically powerful to be nationalists. As George Grant has said: "Most of them made more money by being the representatives of American capitalism and setting up branch plants . . . Capitalism is, after all, a way of life based on the principle that the most important activity is profit-making. That activity led the wealthy in the direction of continentalism."[23] In the National Policy era Canadian business could enjoy both wealth and power. The former was always primary; power was mainly a means to wealth. If today wealth comes more easily without power, no tears are shed. In the words of E. P. Taylor, "Canadian nationalism? How old-fashioned can you get?"

While economic factors are quick to act on the orientation of the business class, the erosion of the value system, which was formed during the nation-building phase of Canada's history, is a slower process. Although branch-plant industry, branch-plant trade unions, branch-plant culture and branch-plant universities are undermining traditional Canadian values, yet these values persist. Respect for law and order, regard for civil rights, abhorrence of mob rule and gangsterism (whether practised at the bottom or the top of the social scale), and traditional respect for Ottawa as the national government of the country are still deeply felt in English Canada. These are the elements of English-Canadian patriotism and they define the English Canadian, as distinct from the American. This value system is as real as the branch plants. It is the source which nourishes English-Canadian nationalism, and it is reinforced by every action of the United States which violates these values.

Whereas these values were created by the older Canadian elite, which shaped the nation, the existing business class cannot give effective expression to Canadian nationalism because it has been absorbed into the world of corporate empire. It rejected John Diefenbaker because he is a nationalist; it rejected

Walter Gordon for the same reason. Grant has observed that the power of the American government to control Canada lies not so much in its ability to exert direct pressure as in the fact that the dominant classes in Canada see themselves at one with continentalism.[24]

The effect of the American corporate presence on relations between central and provincial governments is clear; the linear transcontinental axis, which once integrated the nation under an active and strong central government, has largely disintegrated. The new pattern of north-south trade and investment based on resource-development and branch-plant manufacturing, does not require a strong central government. The central government is left to manage the old infra-structure of communications and commercial institutions carried over from the previous era. However, new public expenditures are typically regional—hydroelectric schemes, highways, schools, hospitals and the like. The system of fiscal redistribution conflicts with the economic interests of the richer and more fortunate provinces. The federal function of providing for the defence of the nation is not sufficiently urgent to offset the shift of so many other functions to the regional level. Furthermore, a considerable part of the prosperity of defence work originates from the United States government, and is strongly regional in its impact on employment and income.

Political fragmentation along regional lines serves the interests of the international corporations. While the Ottawa mandarins ponder how to emasculate the Canada Development Corporation, the provinces have been forced to create their own development agencies. Recent efforts to launch regional development policies at the federal level have produced a bureaucratic structure whose organizational sophistication far out-distances that of the policies which have to date been announced by Ottawa.

In the absence of effective federal initiatives to provide the means of mobilizing and directing Canada's resources towards the elimination of regional disparities, the provinces will reinforce the continentalist trend by joining the competitive scramble for foreign investment. They opposed the rationalization of the fiscal structure proposed by the Carter Commission and the government White Paper on taxation; they pressured the federal government into begging exemption from the U.S. interest equalization tax. They may be expected to oppose each and every measure devised to control the terms on which foreign capital may enter Canada. In the absence of effective leadership by Ottawa they reinforce the continentalism of big business by dismembering the federal structure of Canada.

The relationship between English Canada and Quebec is a special one. Quebec is both a province within Confederation and the *patrie* of the French-Canadian nation. The demand for more autonomy by the province of Quebec thus has a dual character. In part, it resembles demands for increased provincial powers expressed by all the larger provinces, in part, it is the political form in which the desire for self-determination of French Canada expresses itself.

Clearly, there can be no national equality for French Canada without power over economic decisions. In the area of public policy, we thus have the demand for a larger share of revenue, and for a voice in tariff, monetary and immigration policy. For French Canada, more economic power for the government of Quebec is crucial, because the provincial public sector is the only effective lever by which French Canadians can influence decisions affecting their lives. While the English-Canadian elite is rapidly relinquishing economic control to the American corporations, the French-Canadian elite urgently desires entry into private corporate power. Such entry is highly restricted at present, and the situation has been fully documented by John Porter in his book *The Vertical Mosaic*. Yet national equality requires that economic decisions affecting Quebec must be made by French Canadians, not by English-Canadian or American corporations. Nothing less can assure the continued existence of a French-speaking community on the North American continent.

For French Canada, modernization has meant not only dislocation and disruption of settled routines but also incorporation into the industrial system, and the new humiliation of daily dictation by the anglophone. This is as true for the miner, the factory worker, the sales clerk, as it is for the professional and middle classes. Whereas the latter may have an educational advantage in terms of ability to function in the language of those who hold economic power, the humiliation is greater rather than less. Their education and their wider horizons enable them to articulate the frustrations of the French-Canadian community in Canada. The island of anglophone privilege which extends from McGill University and Westmount to the western edge of Montreal and which controls much of the commercial and industrial life of the French-speaking province, acts as a constant abrasive to these frustrations. This experience is unknown to the English Canadian. It is unknown also to the immigrant, who chose to leave his native land to come to North America. In this sense the so-called "ethnic groups" are assimilated and become an integral part of English Canada.

The experience of linguistic domination also explains the lack of discrimination in French-Canadian resentment between English-Canadian and American domination. It is interesting that public opinion polls constantly show less concern about American domination in Quebec than anywhere else in Canada, and no less a politician than René Lévesque does not appear to fear the consequences of "liberating" Quebec from the domination by the English-Canadian financial elite with the help of more powerful American capital. What difference, after all, to the French-Canadian worker in Arvida, whether orders are received in English from a foreman employed by a Canadian company like Alcan, or an American company, like Union Carbide?

The French-Canadian middle class is comprised of self-employed professionals, small businessmen and bureaucratically-employed technocrats. No private French-Canadian entrepreneurial group can effectively challenge the powers of the anglophone corporations. The logic leads from nationalism to state entrepreneurship. This was the policy which guided the more radical elements of the Lesage administration during the so-called Quiet Revolution. It was symbolized by the creation of Hydro-Quebec as the first step to a more extensive expansion of the public sector into the resource industries of the province.

In such a confrontation with the corporation, the advantage which French Canada has over English Canada is a more clearly defined sense of national purpose and a greater confidence in its ability to achieve its objective. That objective is to build, in North America, a modern French-speaking society in which the population can enjoy both prosperity and dignity. If this can be achieved in union with English Canada, so much the better. If English Canada makes this impossible, there is every indication that, eventually, Quebec will secede. If there is an economic price to be paid for control by French Canadians over the terms on which their daily lives are lived, an increasing minority seems ready to pay it. Nationalism and separatism have struck a chord because the population of Quebec is Quebecois in the sense in which no resident of Ontario is Ontarian.

Those who view Quebec separatism as the main threat to Canada's survival, might ask themselves why French Canadians should remain within Confederation when the dominant English-Canadian majority appear to put such a low value on Canada's national independence? What is being offered? To wander hand-in-hand, biculturally and bilingually, into the gravitational orbit of the American empire? Is it any wonder that some Quebeckers believe that separation might offer a better chance for cultural survival in North America? At worst, Quebec would have its own *Roi nègre* to administer the French marches of the Empire, while the Ottawa bureaucrats are presiding over the English marches.

The "continentalist" orientation is fundamentally destructive of Canadian unity because it rejects the maintenance of a national community as an end in itself. The value system by which a nation is ultimately defined is put up for sale. In every "cost benefit" calculation concerning the gains and losses from the continued U.S. presence within the Canadian economy, there is an implicit price tag on national values and beliefs. The American corporations which reach forward to control the markets they presume to serve homogenize the culture of the inhabitants. Continentalism extends the American melting-pot philosophy into Canada. Bilingualism and biculturalism, even if it were to be translated from a pious wish to reality, is no defence to this process of seduction. By the intake of branch-plant factories and the associated branch-plant culture, national values in the hinterland are shaped in the image of the metropolis. When the process is complete there remains, as Gad Horowitz has suggested, no reason to regain control.

The process is far advanced. What is in question today is the will of English Canada to survive as a distinct national community on the North American continent. If the will is waning, if English Canada is succumbing to a sort of national death-wish in relation to the United States, why should Quebec, and in particular the young people now pouring out of schools and universities, wish to remain junior partners in this sad venture?

Writing in 1960, before the consequences of Canada's branch-plant status were as apparent as they are today, Professor Aitken summed up the dilemma in the following words:

> No one doubts that American investment has accelerated the pace of economic development in Canada; . . . but it seems also likely to convert Canada into a hinterland of United States industry. . . . To each spurt of expansion there is a corresponding shrinkage in Canada's freedom of action, in its self-reliance, and in its ability to chart its own course for the future.[25]

The focus of decision-making has been transferred from Canada, where in the past it was subject to strong direction by the federal government, to the board rooms of huge U.S. corporations, operating on a world scale and each charting its own future under the protection of its metropolitan government. An increasing number of English Canadians (and undoubtedly the majority of her academic economists) do not care who charts the course so long as income continues to grow. An able young English-Canadian economist recently dismissed as "pernicious" the argument that American corporate control constitutes a constraint on Canadian decision-making, with a reference to Buridan's ass which starved because it could not choose between two piles of hay. "He did achieve the goal of preserving the freedom to choose, but at what a price!" The preservation of freedom, we are told, is a means to an end. As such it should not be elevated to the status of a goal. Not even economists can put a value on a means, so that we are asked to pay a price to achieve something whose worth can never be assessed. Very few of us are willing to pay an infinite price for anything—and certainly not for such poor excuses for a national objective.

Because freedom is priceless, it is worthless. A strange conclusion even for an economist. The logic, of course, is flawless. "Maîtres chez nous," in French, or in English, is plainly asinine; it is a "non-goal." The rational Canadian presumably will not lift his head from the trough for long enough to explore unknown pastures in search of greener grass. He will eat whatever hay is dished up, secure in the knowledge that he is getting the same all-American grub—albeit a somewhat smaller ration.

The attitude of the Quebec technocrats presents a striking contrast. Confident in their ability to chart their own course, French Canadians are asserting their determination to control their economy—including the right to make their own mistakes. In the words of one of Quebec's leading economists:

> French Canadians in Quebec can set themselves concrete objectives, achieve them fully, partially, or even fail to meet them, like any other people. . . . When a society has been for so long in search of fulfilment and has found it within itself, it is very unlikely that it can be distracted from this purpose.[26]

The dominant Protestant culture of English Canada resists the idea that a nation, like a family, is more than an aggregation of individuals; that it is a community shaped by common cultural and historic experiences. More particularly it does not seem to understand that the experiences shared by English and French Canadians have left a very different imprint on the consciousness of the two national communities. Instead of an outward-looking and self-confident sense of national purpose, English Canada has at times exhibited an angry reaction to the fact that French Canadians do not want equality on the terms set down by the dominant English-Canadian elite. The effort to head off French-Canadian self-assertion with a bilingual federal civil service and French schools in English Canada has little appeal in Quebec, while causing considerable dissension in some areas of English Canada. The refusal of Ottawa to recognize French Canada as a nation, and its insistence on the ten provinces concept of Confederation has led to the balkanization of the country, as the pressures applied by Quebec are used as a lever to escalate the fiscal demands of all the provinces at the expense of effective central government. As René Lévesque put it, there must be more to English Canadian nationalism than just "holding on to Quebec." If there isn't, then "it's cheaper cars and cigarettes for you all, and U.S. citizenship—along with the fading away of a growing (even though 'branch-plant') economy and its managerial society; and the draft, and present and future Vietnams and a share in the terrific agony the American society is inflicting upon itself."[27]

The refusal of the dominant English-speaking community to recognize explicitly the national aspirations of Quebec is propelling the fragmentation of the country to the point of piecemeal absorption into the American empire. Under these conditions it becomes increasingly difficult to repatriate the focus of decision-making, or to implement the "new national policies" suggested by Professor Watkins and his associates.

The obstinate refusal of Ottawa to accommodate the demands of Quebec for national equality within a Canadian partnership of two nations is pushing nationalist forces in the French province to seek their own independent hinterland relationship with the United States, on the theory propounded by an economist close to René Lévesque and the Parti Québécois that "we have no choice but to strike our own bargain with American capital." As Peter Regenstreif reported in January 1969, Quebeckers are selling out and Americans, who regard the province as a relatively safe place in comparison with really troubled areas of the world, are buying in. The Quebec economy is becoming ever more Americanized in the process.[28]

One is entitled to doubt the wisdom of exchanging domination by St. James Street for domination by Wall Street and the American corporations. The tragedy, however, is that the root of this dilemma rests in the failure of Ottawa to accommodate the special fiscal needs of Quebec within the framework of a national policy aimed at making all Canadians masters of their own house. The advent of Trudeau promised to rescue the federal government from the all-time low in prestige and power associated with the Diefenbaker and Pearson eras. In spite of the flair of the new prime minister for projecting the image of revitalization, the pattern of subservience to Washington continues. The erosion of Canadian sovereignty and national unity has not been arrested by proclamations of bilingualism and biculturalism and a "get tough with the provinces" policy.

The ambivalence of English Canada concerning the reality of the nations as a community underlies the difficulties of communication with Quebec. Sadly, this same ambivalence renders English Canada so vulnerable to the disintegrating forces of continentalism. If national purpose is nothing more than a cumulation of individual purpose, and if individual purpose consists essentially of more money, more leisure and more consumer goods, then why trouble about Canada's loss of independence? And yet English Canada is deeply troubled.

The "foreign investment" issue in Canadian politics will remain unresolved until English Canada redefines its goals as a national community. As Horowitz asked: "Control our economy for what?" That question, in the end, is one which individuals must answer. Dwelling in the web of the new mercantilism of the great corporations, Canadians will have to decide what value they place on living in a human community that they can control and handle. For French Canada that community appears to be Quebec. From the desire to control their environment arises the demand for effective political and economic power.

The Harvest of Lengthening Dependence 437

In English Canada there exists the possibility that the cultural integration into continental American life has proceeded to the point where Canada no longer is a meaningful national community. Yet here there is the possibility that the current reaction among the younger generation against domination by the efficiency-mongers of big business, big government or big anybody may revive the "conserving" nationalism which derives from the desire to control and shape the conditions of life within a community. Only the emergence of a new value system within English Canada can ensure the continued existence of a nation here.

### Footnotes

1. International Monetary Fund, *International Financial Statistics,* Supplement to 1966-67 issues; and United Nations *Yearbook of International Trade Statistics,* various years.
2. The small industrial countries here are Austria, Belgium, Luxembourg, Denmark, Netherlands, Norway and Sweden.
3. M. G. Clark, *Canada and World Trade,* Staff Study No.7, Economic Council of Canada, Ottawa, 1964.
4. Wilkinson, *op. cit.,* chapter 3.
5. If Canadian trade follows this pattern (and it promises to do so) then total imports which are heavily concentrated on highly processed commodities will tend to rise more rapidly than will total exports, which are largely raw and crudely processed materials. *Ibid.,* p.44.
6. See Gruber, Mehta and Vernon, *op. cit.,* p.26.
7. Dr. E. W. R. Steacie, president of the National Research Council. Statement to the Royal Commission on Canada's Economic Prospects, quoted in Safarian, *op. cit.,* p.171.
8. D.B.S. Industrial Research and Development Expenditure in Canada, Dec. 1967. See pp.15&16 and 38-40.
9. Raymond Vernon, *op. cit.*
10. L. E. H. Trainor, "Americanization of Canada—A Scientist's Viewpoint." (Mimeo).
11. C. Freeman and A. Young, *The Research and Development Efforts in Western Europe, North America and the Soviet Union* (Paris, O.E.C.D., 1965). For comment by Watkins and associates, see *Foreign Ownership,* p.97.
12. H. E. English, "Industrial Structure in Canada's International Competitive Position," The Canadian Trade Committee, Montreal, June 1964.
13. Safarian, *op.cit.,* p.305.
14. *Foreign Ownership,* pp.154-55.
15. *Sources of Funds of Direct U.S. Investments in Canadian Manufacturing Mining and Petroleum.*

|  | percentage | | | | | | | | average |
|---|---|---|---|---|---|---|---|---|---|
|  | 1957 | 1958 | 1959 | 1960 | 1961 | 1962 | 1963 | 1964 | 1957 1964 |
| Funds from the U.S. | 26 | 25 | 20 | 21 | 13 | 10 | 8 | 5 | 15 |
| Re-invested profit | 35 | 32 | 39 | 45 | 41 | 43 | 45 | 49 | 42 |
| Depreciation | 26 | 30 | 30 | 35 | 34 | 32 | 33 | 30 | 31 |
| Funds from Canada | 13 | 14 | 11 | —1 | 12 | 15 | 14 | 17 | 12 |

**Source:** *U.S. Survey of Current Business,* various issues.

16. D.B.S., *The Canadian Balance of International Payments: A compendium of statistics from 1964 to 1965.*
17. *Foreign-Owned Subsidiaries in Canada, op.cit.,* section 3.
18. G. R. Conway, "The Supply of, and Demand for, Canadian Equities," *op.cit.*
19. *Ibid.,* p.44.
20. In the primary resource field industries, a guaranteed long-term market in the parent for at least part of the subsidiary's output has often been the critical factor in the decision to exploit the

resource, sometimes much more important than the supply of capital or of technology. *Foreign Ownership*, p.76.

21. Report of the Royal Commission on Banking and Finance, Ottawa, 1964, pp.87-88.

22. *Foreign Ownership*, pp.291, 412.

23. George Grant, *Lament for a Nation*, p.47.

24. *Ibid.*, p.41.

25. Hugh G. J. Aitken, *American Capital and Canadian Resources*, pp.112-113, 114.

26. Jacques Parizeau, quoted by René Lévesque in *The Star Weekly Magazine*, Toronto, January 20, 1968.

27. *Ibid.*, Lévesque.

28. Peter Regenstreif, *Montreal Star*, January 18, 1969.

## WALTER L. GORDON
# Notes for Remarks at the Twenty-first Annual Meeting of the Canadian Association of Geographers

The main theme of the discussion today is the Economic Relationships among Europe, Canada and the United States. As I interpret it, my part in the program is to describe what has been happening to Canada, what in practical terms Canadians can do about it, and then to make a few very tentative remarks about Canada's present and potential relationships with Europe.

Back in the nineteen twenties and thirties, Canadians of my generation were concerned about our colonial relationship with Britain. We were disturbed primarily by the fact that we had little freedom when it came to foreign policy. Canada followed Britain into World War I almost automatically. We did the same thing, subject only to the formality of a parliamentary vote, in World War II. Our first diplomatic mission was not established in Washington until 1926. Prior to that, our relations with the United States were conducted through the British Embassy. Now, of course, all that is over. We are as free of British influence, diplomatic or otherwise, as we are of any other country, apart of course from the United States.

Towards the end of World War II, Canadian politicians and senior civil servants began to develop economic policies designed to provide the jobs that would be needed when the men serving in our armed forces were demobilized. Perhaps inevitably, they looked for leadership and assistance to enterprising Americans and American corporations. The Honourable C. D. Howe who had established a tremendous reputation as the wartime boss of Canadian industry, was especially active in his encouragement to American business leaders to establish themselves in Canada. In addition, the Prime Minister, the Right Honourable W. L. Mackenzie King, authorized secret negotiations with Washington looking towards some kind of economic union between Canada and the U.S.A. At the last minute, Mr. King, a politician to his fingertips, called the whole thing off. After his death, it was discovered that he had been a long-time believer in the occult. It is at least open to surmise, therefore, that during one of his seances, he was reminded, perhaps by Sir Wilfrid Laurier himself, about what happened in the 1911 general election which was fought on the subject of reciprocity! You will remember that Sir Wilfrid was defeated.

But, despite Mr. King's withdrawal from any formal proposal linking Canada's and the United States' economies, massive inflows of U.S. capital continued to be welcomed for the development of our resources and the acquisition of our business enterprises. We had won our freedom from British colonialism only to embark upon a course that would make us an economic satellite of the United States within a decade or two. Few Canadians realized what was happening. It was evident that our country was being developed much more quickly than would have been possible without massive inflows of foreign capital and the managerial and other skills, the technology and the access to markets that came with it. Our standard of living was improving rapidly. Our politicians, our civil servants, our leading bankers and industrialists, most of the economists in our universities, all seemed to preach the benefits and the virtues of "continentalism". Anyone who questioned this "conventional wisdom" was ridiculed as being some kind of chauvinistic nut.

What has been the result? In a word, it is the very considerable integration of the Canadian economy with that of the United States. Two-thirds of our exports, largely industrial raw materials, go to that country. About seventy per cent of our imports, mostly finished goods, come from there. A goodly proportion of this trade takes place between U.S. parent corporations and their wholly-owned Canadian subsidiaries. It is estimated that between 6,000 and 8,000 Canadian companies are controlled abroad mostly by American corporations. Of greater significance is the fact that the larger and more enterprising companies in most of the more dynamic Canadian industries are controlled by foreigners, mostly by Americans.

Americans have invested many billions of dollars in Canada and a large part of this is represented by the value of direct investments in those Canadian companies that are subsidiaries of U.S. corporations. Undoubtedly, these investments have appreciated considerably above their original cost. And because in most cases the profits are being plowed back and reinvested, the total amount is increasing all the time.

The exact amount of these investments is difficult to evaluate. What is important from the Canadian point of view are the percentages of key Canadian industries that are controlled by foreigners, mostly by Americans. Here are some of them:

— 60% of all manufacturing companies.
— 60% of all mining enterprises.
— 85% of the primary metal smelting and refining industries.
— Over 90% of petroleum refining.
— About 80% of the oil and gas industry, including exploration and development.
— 95% of the automobile industry.
— 90% of the rubber industry.
— 75% of the chemical industry.
— 75% of electrical apparatus.
— 90% of the computer industry. ... and so on.

While I cannot vouch for the complete exactness of the percentages I have quoted, they should be sufficiently accurate for purposes of illustration. Let us think about their implications.

Every one of our integrated oil companies, that is, the oil companies that do everything from exploration and development through to the retail sales of gasoline, are internationally controlled, nearly all of them by American parent corporations. To many Canadians, it does not make sense that so much of an industry of this importance should be controlled by people or by corporations who live outside our borders.

Much the same thing is true in the case of our mining industry, another dynamic sector of the economy.

Again, if we take *all* the manufacturing industries in Canada, we find that some 60 per cent of them are controlled by foreigners, mostly again by enterprising Americans. Moreover, all or nearly all the larger and more dynamic manufacturing concerns are subsidiaries of large American corporations. This is true, for example, in the automobile industry. General Motors, Ford and Chrysler account for about 95 per cent of all the automotive vehicles produced in Canada—as they do in the United States. But Canada, despite her relatively modest population, ranks very high in the list of nations when it comes to the use or consumption of automotive vehicles. Some Canadians wonder whether it would not make sense for us to begin to establish an automobile industry of our own. The Japanese have done this with great success and so, of course, have the Germans and Italians.

No other developed country in the world has allowed so much of its industry to be controlled abroad. Many Canadians believe the time has come when this trend should be reversed.

The facts I have mentioned should be enough to demonstrate the extent to which the trade, business, financial and economic affairs of Canada are intertwined with those of the United States. As a result, our levels of production, employment and prices depend very largely upon what goes on in that country.

Any discussion of this process of integration of the Canadian economy with that of the United States is now being confused by the mystique of the so-called "multinational corporations"—the new and very effective technique of modern imperialism. It is suggested that within a few short years, some 500 of these great enterprises will account for not less than half the total output of the Western world. It is suggested further that these few corporations will be free for all practical purposes of government control. It is implied by those who are critical of governments and of government intervention and who at the same time tend to admire the big and powerful in the private sector, that this state of affairs will be good for everyone. I submit that this is nonsense. Certainly, it is nonsense for anyone who believes in democracy and freedom and who tends to question the inherent altruism of business corporations including the altruism of the larger or multinational ones.

When an heretical viewpoint of this kind is asserted, the apologists for the multinational corporations suggest vaguely that if some controls over their activities are thought to be desirable, these should be developed by some kind of international organization. But just how this could be worked out in practice is anything but clear. The world is still organized under a system of nation states. This may not be an ideal system. But unless and until some kind of world government evolves, it would seem to be the system we shall be living under for quite some time. It is conceivable that after a devastating world war from which few, if any, people would survive, the "victorious" super power could bring about some kind of world government by force. But short of that, it would seem to be wishful thinking of the most naive kind to assume that a form of world government with sufficient strength to police and control 500 of the world's most powerful corporations will arise for many years to come.

Most—but not all—of these multinational corporations are very large American companies with subsidiaries in one or more other countries. Inevitably, this means that the people who direct the operations of the parent companies, mostly located in the United States, make the ultimate decisions that will affect the lives of their employees in other countries and to some extent the economies of those countries. These policies include decisions respecting the expansion or contraction of production, the location of new plants, export policy, wage policies and so on, in the "host countries".

A few months ago, Mr. Henry Ford, on landing in Britain, was reported as saying his company would make no more investments there if his 30,000 or more employees in that country were "unrealistic" in their wage demands. Six weeks ago, Mr. Leonard Woodcock, the President of the United Automobile Workers of America, was reported as saying in Toronto that political pressure would be brought to bear in Washington to discontinue the Canadian-American auto pact if the wages paid in Canadian automobile plants were not increased to U.S. levels. There are some who may think wage levels in Britain are too high and therefore that Mr. Ford's threat was quite in order. There are others who may think wage levels in Canadian automobile plants are too low and therefore that Mr. Woodcock's threat was understandable.

But the question to be asked is whether two Americans, both of whom are very powerful in their respective realms, should be in positions to influence the course of economic events in Britain or in Canada. I think not. On the contrary, I submit it is high time that the mystique of the multinational corporation and all the unfettered power that goes with it should be debunked.

Pending the evolution of world government—and I have expressed doubts about this occurring at any early date—each national state, the so-called host countries, should control its own economy. This means each host country should exert whatever controls it thinks desirable and expedient over the business organizations and the trade unions within its borders including, in particular, the operations of subsidiary companies of foreign parent corporations and the local branches of international trade unions. I shall make some suggestions in this regard, insofar as Canada is concerned, a little later on.

Some people believe that the process of integration of the Canadian with the U.S. economy has gone too far to be reversed. Amaury de Riencourt had this to say in discussing the takeover of Canadian business and Canadian resources by Americans in *The American Empire* which was published in 1968:

> . . . But any practical steps to halt the trend or reverse it would lead to such a drastic fall in the Canadian standard of living that they could never be tolerated.
>
> The violent reaction to Canadian Finance Minister Walter Gordon's mild attempt to do so in 1963 illustrates the stark impossibility of resisting this wholesale takeover: 'So devastatingly hostile was the reaction that the effect on the government in the interval was almost traumatic,' states an

expert on Canadian affairs. What is clear is that an increasingly large proportion of Canadian businessmen are merely employees of American companies headquartered in New York, Detroit, or Chicago. And these American companies, parents of Canadian subsidiaries, owe their first allegiance to American, not Canadian, legislation and interests. As a result, no Canadian subsidiary dares contravene the United States' anti-trust laws or the Trading with the Enemy Act. Inevitably, unobtrusively, American legislation applies in Canada in an extraterritorial way. It is also obvious that if the international market for goods produced on both sides of the border were to shrink substantially, American companies would probably not hesitate to close down their operations in Canada so as to maintain full production in the United States.

Those who believe that there is no threat to Canadian independence point to the fact that the United States was developed out of British capital in the nineteenth century. But that capital was in the form of redeemable bonds, whereas United States investments in Canada are in the form of outright ownership of subsidiaries. American investments, again, are controlling investments, providing not only the financial resources but the technical skills, the managerial know-how, the research and development, and the overall business policy. Furthermore, not only are a majority of the large Canadian corporations American-owned but they also happen to be in the most dynamic sectors of the economy. . . .

Mr. de Riencourt is quite wrong in his assertion that steps to halt or reverse the present trend would lead to a drastic fall in Canadian living standards. If Canadian policy was clearly stated and fairly administered and if the necessary measures were applied gradually over a period of years, there is no reason why there should be any drop in Canadian living standards. On the contrary, we could achieve a degree of insurance, which we have not at present, against a future disruption of our economy and a possible fall in living standards resulting from policy decisions taken in another country. But Mr. de Riencourt's pessimistic view is an example of what one international observer believes has happened and is still happening to Canada.

George Ball, who was Under Secretary of State in the Kennedy and Johnson administrations, in his book *The Discipline of Power* also published in 1968, had this to say:

Canada, I have long believed, is fighting a rearguard action against the inevitable. Living next to our nation, with a population ten times as large as theirs and a gross national product fourteen times as great, the Canadians recognize their need for United States capital; but at the same time they are determined to maintain their economic and political independence. Their position is understandable, and the desire to maintain their national integrity is a worthy objective. But the Canadians pay heavily for it and, over the years, I do not believe they will succeed in reconciling the intrinsic contradiction of their position. I wonder, for example, if the Canadian people will be prepared indefinitely to accept, for the psychic satisfaction of maintaining a separate national and political identity, a per capita income less than three-fourths of ours. The struggle is bound to be a difficult one—and I suspect, over the years, a losing one. Meanwhile there is danger that the efforts of successive Canadian governments to prevent United States economic domination will drive them toward increasingly restrictive nationalistic measures that are good neither for Canada nor for the health of the whole trading world.

Thus, while I can understand the motivating assumptions of the Canadian position, I cannot predict a long life expectancy for her present policies. The great land mass to the south exerts an enormous gravitational attraction while at the same time tending to repel, and even without the divisive element of a second culture in Quebec, the resultant strains and pressures are hard to endure. Sooner or later, commercial imperatives will bring about free movement of all goods back and forth across our long border; and when that occurs, or even before it does, it will become unmistakably clear that countries with economies so inextricably intertwined must also have free movement of the other vital factors of production—capital, services and labour. The result will inevitably be substantial economic integration, which will require for its full realization a progressively expanding area of common political decision.

It is no secret that Mr. Ball's views were shared by a number of somewhat less senior, but nevertheless influential, officials in Washington. No doubt these officials would feel insulted if they were to be compared with the more outspoken advocates of imperialism of another age. And yet, their objectives are essentially the same. Empire-building is a disease that is still common.

In 1965, George Grant, the distinguished Professor of Religion and an Associate Professor of Political Economy at McMaster University, wrote a short but highly disturbing book about Canada's plight. It was a cry from the heart which he entitled *Lament for a Nation*. Let me quote one paragraph from a book that made a profound impression.

Canada has ceased to be a nation, but its formal political existence will not end quickly. Our social and economic blending into the empire will continue apace, but political union will probably be delayed. Some international catastrophe or great shift of power might speed up this process. Its slowness does not depend only on the fact that large numbers of Canadians do not want it, but also on sheer lethargy. Changes require decisions, and it is much easier for practising politicians to continue with traditional structures. The dominant forces in the Republic do not need to incorporate us. A branch-plant satellite, which has shown in the past that it will not insist on any difficulties in foreign or defence policy, is a pleasant arrangement for one's northern frontier. The pin-pricks of disagreement are a small price to pay. If the negotiations for union include Quebec, there will be strong elements in the United States that will dislike their admission. The kindest of all God's dispensations is that individuals cannot predict the future in detail. Nevertheless, the formal end of Canada may be prefaced by a period during which the government of the United States has to resist the strong desire of English-speaking Canadians to be annexed.

At the time, it was difficult to disagree with Grant's despondency. But thanks in part to him, a new generation of Canadians, and some older ones, have woken up to what has happened and is still happening to their country, not only in the economic field, but in the cultural and social fields as well.

Undoubtedly, this current feeling of concern lest Canada be absorbed by the United States is due partly to a feeling of dismay, revulsion might be a better word, about what has been happening in the United States. Canadians, like many people in the United States especially many young people, want no part of what is going on in Vietnam. They are disgusted by the cruelties, the decimation of the civilian population, the devastation of the countryside, and also by the deliberate falsehoods of top military and civilian leaders in their attempts to explain actions that cannot be justified when performed by a civilized and normally humanitarian people. Moreover, while Canadians sympathize with their American friends about the social problems the latter must contend with, including the threat of escalating tenseness between blacks and whites, they do not wish to be drawn into what could become a very serious internal conflict.

It is more difficult to pinpoint differences in values and in attitudes to life between Canadians and Americans, but such differences do exist. For example, Canadians have accepted a mixed enterprise economy with more intervention by governments in the daily conduct of their lives. There is not the same veneration of Big Business here—or of big businessmen for that matter—and a little less preoccupation with material things than is the case across the line. Whatever it is, an increasing number of Canadians want their country to remain free and independent so that they can develop their own sense of values, their own attitudes to life and their relationships with the world at large in their own way. Fortunately, Canadians are strong enough and affluent enough to do this if they have sufficient will.

The Committee for an Independent Canada was formed to provide a focus for Canadians who are concerned about our gradual loss of independence—or, if you will, at the increasingly dominant influence of the United States on all phases of our lives. It is a grass-roots, non-partisan movement with very little money and a limited, volunteer organization. But it is catching on. There are now some thirty-five sub-committees established in most of the larger population centres from one end of Canada to the other. When Claude Ryan, the editor of *Le Devoir,* became co-Chairman of the Committee some eight or nine months ago, he felt—we all felt—this was a cause in which all Canadians, French and English-speaking, could participate and share. I still believe this to be true despite the crisis of last October.

The Committee in its Statement of Purpose, covers a variety of subjects including cultural and social matters as well as economic. However, today I shall mention only its objectives in the economic field.

In the first place, it recommends the establishment of a federal agency to supervise the conduct of foreign-controlled companies in Canada and to review proposals for new investments in Canada by foreigners including proposals to acquire existing Canadian companies.

This proposal is not new. It has been recommended on previous occasions both by a group of independent university economists who were requested by the government to study the whole question in 1967 and, more recently, by a Committee of the House of Commons.

If such an agency is established—and I am sufficiently optimistic to believe it will be—it would presumably review transactions between Canadian subsidiary companies and their foreign parent corporations. In particular, it might be expected to review the prices paid by the Canadian subsidiaries for parts and components imported from their foreign parents and to examine the possibilities of having alternative sources of supply established in Canada thus providing more jobs at home. The agency would presumably review the prices charged by Canadian companies for exports of industrial raw materials to their foreign parent corporations and, at the same time, examine the possibilities of these materials being processed to a greater extent in Canada. I expect also that any such federal agency would wish to know whether Canadian subsidiaries of foreign concerns were restricted in any way from exporting their products to any other countries in the world.

I presume that in the case of proposed takeovers of Canadian companies, the federal agency would assess the advantages, if any, which would accrue from such proposals. If the agency were not convinced that it would be in the best interests of Canada for more of our companies to be controlled abroad, then presumably it would not give its approval. On the other hand, if Americans or people from other countries came forward with proposals for some new development which would provide employment opportunities in Canada, then I would assume that the federal agency would approve. It might suggest that it would be in everyone's best interests for the proposed new development to be sponsored not solely by a single foreign source, but in partnership with some Canadian group, including perhaps the newly proposed Canada Development Corporation. But I doubt whether such a joint venture approach should be insisted upon in all cases.

Neither the Committee for an Independent Canada nor, to my knowledge, any other responsible group or individual has ever advocated shutting off all foreign capital inflows into Canada. All we say is that foreign investments in Canada should be subject to some form of Canadian control as is the case in such countries as Japan, Sweden and Mexico, for example. If we could be as successful in developing our economy in the next 25 years as Japan has been in her remarkable recovery since the war, I am sure we would all be more than satisfied.

The Committee for an Independent Canada was among those who recommended the establishment of the Canada Development Corporation which is designed to channel Canadian savings into new developments of various kinds.

The Committee has also proposed that the government should implement policies designed to increase the proportion of Canadian ownership but it has not suggested what such policies should be.

Speaking personally, I would like to see it stipulated that the senior executive officers and a large majority of the directors of all Canadian companies over a certain size should be Canadian citizens, resident in Canada. I would also be in favour of a policy statement — to go into effect gradually over a period of years — which would require all large Canadian companies to be 51 per cent owned by Canadians. Perhaps this should apply only to those companies in those industries like the petroleum and automobile industries that are monopolistic or oligopolistic in structure. It is bad enough for certain Canadian industries to be oligopolistic in structure, like the banking industry, for example, where the three largest banks exert such a dominating influence. It is even worse in those industries where one or two subsidiaries of foreign parent companies set the pace including the prices to be charged consumers of their products. This is true in automobiles where General Motors wields a more or less monopolistic influence, in the computer industry which is dominated by IBM, in the oil industry where Imperial Oil exerts a powerful influence, and so on.

There would need to be provision for exceptions and in some cases for an extension of time before the requirement for Canadian ownership would become effective and any such provision should probably exclude the thousands of small companies in Canada that are controlled abroad.

What I believe we should be aiming at is to break up the existing foreign-parent wholly-owned-Canadian-subsidiary-company relationships in the case of the larger companies in Canada.

There are those who say that Canada could not afford, even over a period of years, to acquire control of the larger companies that at present are subsidiaries of foreign parent companies. This may have been true at one time but, if so, it is true no longer. We enjoyed a favourable balance of some $1,300 million on current account in our balance of payments in 1970. It is anticipated that we shall have a favourable balance in 1971 and for several years to come. As a result of our favourable trading balance and of continuing inflows on capital account, Canada's exchange reserves have increased by more than two billion dollars in the last three years.

Moreover, according to studies made for the Toronto Stock Exchange, accumulated savings in pension funds, etc., available for investment in common stocks are expected to increase at an appreciable rate. The trouble at the moment is the shortage of Canadian common stocks available to meet this anticipated demand—due to the fact that so many of our larger companies are wholly-owned subsidiaries of foreign parent corporations.

Because of these various factors and the fact we can and should expect a continued inflow of foreign capital, Canadians are in an excellent position to begin acquiring a greater degree of ownership and control of our principal companies. All we need is the vision and the determination to take advantage of this situation.

There are those who fear that any interference with the free flow of capital in or out of Canada would be dangerous. They fear that inflows of foreign capital would stop and therefore that our more dynamic industries would cease to grow. I suggest that such fears are grossly exaggerated. It is inconceivable that this would happen if we approach the problem sensibly and fairly.

We all know that most of the current increase in foreign ownership in Canada is accounted for by the retained earnings of existing Canadian companies which are controlled abroad or by their borrowings in Canada.

Moreover, let me repeat that the Committee for an Independent Canada is not opposed and has never been opposed to capital inflows from abroad. All we say is that such capital inflows should come here on Canadian terms. Arrangements along these lines have worked well in other countries. They should work equally well in Canada.

Canadians should not—and I am quite confident Canadians will not wish to—isolate themselves from the United States in any way. Despite some differences and despite our feelings about remaining independent, the Americans are our neighbours and our friends. Moreover, it would be the height of folly to shut ourselves off from the greatest market in the world.

But in addition to our many associations with the United States and the American people, we have strong cultural and social, as well as trading, ties with Europe and we should do all we can to strengthen them. In the past, our principal relationships were with Britain and with France. But more recently, the Canadian population has been enriched by thousands of immigrants from Italy, from Germany and, in fact, from every country in Western Europe (and from the countries of Eastern Europe as well). Canadians wish to do everything within their power to maintain and to strengthen these relationships both in the cultural and in the economic fields. It would be a tragedy for us if, with the advent of the European Common Market, our ties with the countries of our forbears should be weakened. We must do everything we possibly can to see this does not happen. We must strive to increase the volume and the variety of our trade with all European countries. We must encourage an increasing flow of visitors in both directions. And we must encourage contacts of all kinds in the cultural field. If Canadians can accomplish these objectives, we shall have a better chance of escaping absorption by a friendly but sometimes overpowering neighbour.

I should like to close by quoting a paragraph from Claude Julien's book *Canada: Europe's Last Chance* —

> In Victoria, as in Ottawa or Montreal, there are Canadians of both linguistic groups who feel really Canadian, that is, very different from both the 'mother country' and the powerful neighbour to the south. They carry inside them a vision of a North American country linked with Europe and with the United States, but free in its own movements — original because it is founded on two cultures and the rejection of the melting-pot; open to the Commonwealth countries with whom they share old ties and to the French-speaking countries with whom they are forming new ties; accepted by newly independent countries because Canada was never a colonizer; and tolerated or respected by Communist countries because Canada is occidental without ever having become aggressive.
> Canadians who look at their country in this way are still too rare. ...

That is true, but let us hope that more of us are at long last beginning to wake up.

# International Trade and the International Monetary System

## WM. C. HOOD

# Reflections on the International Monetary System

In choosing my topic for this evening I am somewhat constrained. If I choose to speak on current economic policy which in fact commands all of my attention these days, I run certain risks. Really, I decided not to run these risks when I assumed my present post. I could preach to you about the state of the profession. But I know you will be pleased that I would rather not.

There really is only one course I should like to take tonight. I should like to share with you my reflections on the international monetary system which I have been able to observe recently at pretty close range. I shall not purport to offer any fresh prescriptions or panaceas. Rather, I shall reflect upon what can be a rather technical subject in a non-technical way in the hope of placing some recent developments and current prospects in a useful perspective.

I propose to group my remarks on the international monetary system under two main headings — how it works and how it may evolve. But before embarking upon that programme, perhaps I should begin with a brief statement of what it is.

## I    What is it?

A basic feature of the present-day international monetary system concerns the arrangement governing the rates at which domestic monies of individual countries may be exchanged for one another. This arrangement is in fact an undertaking by signatories of the Articles of the International Monetary Fund to restrict the variations of the spot rates of exchange of their currencies for currencies of other signatories taking place within their borders to a range of one percentage point either side of a par value defined in terms of gold and declared to the Fund. There is provision for changes in these par values with the approval of the Fund and in certain circumstances countries are expected either to raise or lower the par values. We shall have more to say later on these changes in par values.

Certain features of the international monetary system derive directly from this undertaking. The first is that in order to give day-to-day effect to the undertaking, the monetary authorities of the member countries of the Fund must maintain working balances of assets which directly or indirectly may be used to purchase their domestic currency in their domestic markets for foreign exchange. If the demand for foreign currency in a country's exchange market exceeds the supply of it and pushes its price up toward the limit of the allowed range of fluctuation, then the authorities must be able to add to the supply of foreign exchange in the market from their own working balances. Accordingly, a principal form in which these working balances are held is the currency most commonly traded in that country's foreign exchange market. For a great many countries that currency is the United States dollar. As has been the tradition for centuries, countries hold a part, at least, of their foreign reserves in the form of gold. Gold is so generally acceptable among monetary authorities that it can readily be converted to US dollars. In any event, the United States undertakes to convert gold to US dollars and US dollars to gold on demand for monetary authorities. A third form in which authorities hold reserves is claims on the International Monetary Fund or on its members. Now let me take a few words to explain this rather technical idea and at the same time describe an aspect of this very important institution of the international monetary system. The traditional operations of the Fund concern the management of a pool of currencies and gold subscribed by its members. The subscription price or quota for each member is fixed from time to time by agreement. A quarter of the subscription is paid in gold and three-quarters in domestic currency. Now the purpose of the Fund or pool of currencies is to permit members to draw upon it, subject to limitations, when members need additional resources to use or have available for use in their exchange markets. A member draws from the Fund by purchasing other currencies from the pool with its own, upon an undertaking to repurchase its own later. As the Fund's practices have evolved, it has come to be accepted that members may draw from the fund virtually as of right such an amount as will bring the Fund's holdings of the drawer's currency up to 100 per cent of its quota. This is one form of claim on the Fund which members now count among their reserves. Another arises from loans to the Fund. In 1962 ten major industrial countries—the so called Group of Ten, which includes Canada—undertook, under specified conditions, to lend their own currencies to the Fund up to prescribed amounts to finance drawings on the Fund by members of the Group of Ten. Such loans constitute a claim on the Fund which may, in the case of need, be reimbursed by the Fund in convertible currency, in advance of maturity and thus may be included reasonably in the reserves of the lending country. There is provision in the Fund articles for individual members to lend to the Fund and there has been limited use of this provision outside of the General Arrangements to Borrow made with the Ten. Such loans would normally give rise to claims that might also reasonably be regarded as reserves.

I have been speaking of the traditional operations of the Fund that give rise to claims that countries regard as reserves. But this year there came to fruition as a result of long negotiation involving over 100 countries, a new form of claim destined, I believe, to play a growing and ultimately profoundly important role in the international monetary system. This is the much touted special drawing right or SDR. At the first of this year a total of about $3.5 billion of these assets was created. These claims are not strictly claims on the Fund, but claims on its members. There is no specific pool of currencies back of the special drawing rights. They are created simply by recording the rights in the books of the Fund in amounts proportional to members' quotas. Use of a drawing right consists in a member exchanging it with another member, designated by the Fund, for convertible currency. It is the solemn treaty obligation of participating members to make such exchanges of currency for rights up to prescribed limits, that gives the asset its value and acceptability.

I have said that the obligation to restrain the degree of fluctuation of exchange rates imposes upon countries the need to maintain reserves. We have been discussing the form these reserves take: currencies, especially the US dollar; gold; claims on the Fund and special drawing rights. Another important feature of the international monetary system derives from this obligation. This is the code of behaviour concerning the use of economic policy to influence the balance of a country's international transactions.

If the international monetary system is to avoid unnecessary changes in exchange rates in the interest of furthering the growth of international trade, persistent surpluses or deficits in the balance of payments of individual countries must be avoided. No country can endure indefinitely an increase or a decrease in its reserves. In conditions in which confidence in the stability of the exchange rate prevails, there are automatic stabilizing forces at work in exchange markets which tend to restrain or reverse exchange rate movements in any given direction. But normally these forces need to be supplemented by deliberate acts of policy. Principles of such policy action underlie certain of the Fund's Articles of Agreement. But in the course of the last quarter century the Fund has played a major role in articulating and developing these principles. The Fund has not been alone in this exercise, but it has had special reason to be concerned. It is called upon to approve par value changes. It is also required to exercise judgment in the granting of conditional credit, that is drawing or borrowing privileges beyond those referred to earlier that are exercised virtually as of right.

This then, in fairly brief terms is what the international monetary system is. It is the combination of treaties, institutions, assets, practices and policies which permits the meshing of national monetary systems. It is the function of the system to ensure that this meshing shall be orderly so that international commerce may flourish. In this fractious world it is a remarkable testament to the unifying force of a common interest in trade that this system, embracing 112 countries, exists and works. There is a power structure within it of course. The United States occupies a unique role. The nine major industrial trading nations around the rim of the North Atlantic plus the rising industrial giant of the East, Japan, form a central group of ten within it. They form a sort of sub-system not only because of their powerful common interest in trade, but also because they share in a general way a common approach to economic organization, policy and policy objectives. This sense of community has permitted these nations in the post-war era to give an essential leadership in guiding and developing the system.

## II  How does it work?

I shall discuss four aspects of this question: balance of payments equilibrium of individual countries; the equilibrium of the system as a whole, the special role of the United States and decision-making in the system.

## BALANCE OF PAYMENTS EQUILIBRIUM OF INDIVIDUAL COUNTRIES

The code of policy of which I have spoken envisages that Fund members will act to maintain equilibrium in their balances of payments so as to avoid unnecessary exchange rate adjustments. It also envisages that they will adjust exchange rates "to correct a fundamental disequilibrium." This code, partly written but mostly unwritten, is not easy to apply for a variety of reasons. An examination of these reasons will, I think, give us considerable insight into how the system works.

The first set of difficulties encountered in applying the code derives from the technical shortcomings of the art of economic policy-making. I do not wish to elaborate upon these matters here; they are common both to the domestic and international aspects of economic policy. Let me simply illustrate and pass on. If an economy, for example, is experiencing both an excess of aggregate demand and a deficit in its balance of payments the code of behaviour would direct that measures be taken to restrain the growth of demand. However, it is easier to state this rule than to apply it. Before applying it, authorities must have made an accurate appraisal of the economic situation and established its essential character. But the lags in economic information, the hazards of economic forecasting and the expected delays of reactions to remedial measures all militate against early and decisive responses to incipient disequilibria. The problem is real. The problem is recognized. But in the present state of the art, the problem persists.

I need here only refer in passing to a second difficulty in adopting adequate policies to correct payments adjustments. This is the difficulty that sometimes arises on the political front. A confident appraisal of a situation and a clear recommendation for action must receive political support to come into effect. International organizations may counsel, exhort and press but governments retain sovereign control of their economic policies. If governments choose to resist advice of their officials or of international bodies, because of disagreement with the advice or because the political timetable does not mesh conveniently with the required policy timetable, then the recommended policy action will be rejected or postponed.

We have also to recognize that even when the analysis of a situation is clear, the required response to policy may be difficult to achieve given the instruments available and the ranges through which they can be operated. Suppose, to take a very simple example, that a country has a surplus in its balance of payments deriving from a strong export demand and an inflow of capital and has at the same time a condition of inflation that is correctly analysed to derive from excess demand in the economy. It might be presumed that the best course would be to operate a contractionary fiscal policy to relieve the excess of demand and at the same time to opt for a relaxed monetary policy that would lessen the interest incentives to an inflow of capital. But this choice faces one with very fine judgments as to the degree to which to relax monetary policy so as to offset the effects of the fiscal policy. It also requires very delicate timing adjustments, for the flexibility of fiscal policy is less than that of monetary policy and the lags in effects are not the same for each. It may be possible to work out a combination of monetary and fiscal policies to adjust the payments imbalance and at the same time moderate the excess demand. But this example, less complicated than situations can in fact be, illustrates the point that even if a conjuncture is analysed essentially correctly, the cross-currents in the situation and the limitations of available instruments may sometimes make it exceedingly difficult, as a practical matter, to carry out an effective payments adjustment policy using domestic policy instruments alone.

Another set of factors creating problems in the application of the code for payments adjustment arises from the distribution among countries of responsibility for taking action. It is conceivable that a country may have achieved a position of dynamic equilibrium in its balance of payments and in its domestic economy only to find that its balance of payments is disturbed by events occurring in other countries with which it has close economic connections. If this is its analysis of the situation it may very naturally adopt the attitude that it is the responsibility of these other countries to take appropriate measures to eliminate the imbalances. Such an attitude may, however, result in a delay in action being taken at all and the development of a cumulative deterioration of the situation. Such an eventuality is especially likely should the country affected be small relative to a larger country generating the disturbance or should the origin of the disturbance be scattered over several countries. This theoretical example is of a rather purer form that one is likely to encounter in practice. Some analysts of the German surpluses that prevailed in the years immediately prior to the recent revaluation of the deutschemark argued that *that* payments imbalance was the result of failure of other countries, especially the United Kingdom and the United States, to adjust the deficits that had occurred in their payments positions.

This last example raises the question of the responsibility for action in its more traditional form, namely its distribution as between deficit and surplus countries. It is manifest that the pressure upon deficit countries to act to relieve payments imbalances is ultimately greater than upon surplus countries for the limits to the loss of reserves are more apparent and compelling than the limits that may exist to the accumulation of reserves. Moreover, in a growing world economy most countries are prepared to absorb some increase in reserves, especially if it is not too sudden and very large.

The code would suggest that surplus countries should pursue expansionary policies to the extent necessary to raise employment to high levels, reduce restrictions on imports and except in certain unusual circumstances seek to eliminate obstacles to the export of capital. The code would also suggest that deficit countries should seek to eliminate any excess demand in the economy, encourage the control of costs and remove impediments to exports of goods and services or to the inflow of capital.

Even if surplus and deficit countries both act in conformity with these general prescriptions, the consequences may not be adequate to restore equilibrium. A surplus country is not expected to pursue expansionist policies to the point of generating inflation nor is a deficit country expected to pursue policies of contraction to the point of generating excess capacity. There can be debate as to precisely how much inflation a surplus country should tolerate and how much excess capacity a deficit country should permit. But this is a debate about the precise meaning of fundamental disequilibrium. The Articles of Agreement of the Fund do not define this important concept. They merely declare that it is in conditions of fundamental disequilibrium that changes in par values are to be made.

The code provides for changes in par values as a means of adjusting payments imbalances, but the difficulty of giving a precise definition to fundamental disequilibrium is yet another of the difficulties of applying the code. I have spoken of fundamental disequilibrium in the balance of payments in relation to the degree of inflation or of excess capacity of the economy. But this is only one point of view on the meaning of the term fundamental disequilibrium, and as I have said the precise interpretation of it is debatable. Many experts prefer to think of fundamental disequilibrium as a structural feature of the balance of payments, in particular a tendency for current account, or even trade account imbalances to grow larger. The fact that I find there to be a good deal of mystique in this line of thinking, is not important in the present discussion. The important thing is that it adds to the confusion over the meaning of the term fundamental disequilibrium and therefore adds to the hesitancy of countries to use changes in exchange rates when such changes are necessary to assist in adjusting the imbalances we are concerned with here, namely persistent gains or losses of reserves.

Another important consideration that makes it difficult in practice to apply the code as it pertains to exchange rate adjustments is the reluctance of authorities to make such changes when they become necessary. This reluctance derives partly from the fact that a change in the rate favours some in the community and hurts others, and partly from the widespread feeling that a devaluation is a confession of failure of policy and is thus to be avoided.

There is one other impediment to the application of the code for payments adjustments which must be mentioned. Perhaps it might be called excess tolerance of imbalance. Let me explain. It is understood and accepted in the international monetary system that it takes time for policies that are designed to rectify imbalances to work. The Fund itself provides resources to deficit countries in need of accommodation during the period in which their policies are taking hold. Now this is a good system in principle and I do not attack it as such. Equally, it is often the case that when a country is losing reserves, speculation against that country's currency develops. The Fund's resources can be mustered on occasion to fight a speculative fire, but the practice has grown for central bankers, renowned for their flexibility and ability to act quickly, to club together to provide quick resources to meet such situations. The Federal Reserve System has worked out a very extensive network of currency swap facilities which can be activated on a phone call to help deal with such situations. The central bankers, especially those who meet regularly at the Bank for International Settlements in Basle have on several occasions in recent years provided special short-term facilities for one or other of the countries represented at these meetings whose currencies were under attack. Some very sophisticated techniques have been worked out. Canada has been both a borrower and a lender under some of these arrangements in recent years. These arrangements, too, fill a useful purpose and I do not condemn them as such. I think the question should be raised, however, whether the system may not in some instances have a tendency to be too tolerant of the persistence of payments imbalances. There is a risk that some surplus countries will be too ready to recycle funds back to deficit countries and deficit countries too ready to accept them. In practice, the decisions are always fine ones and almost invariably are taken in an atmosphere of crisis. The result in my judgment has sometimes been to produce too great a tolerance of imbalances and a failure to use the instrument of exchange rate adjustment in conditions of fundamental disequilibrium.

We have been speaking of how the system works in relation to the difficulties of applying the unwritten code governing the adjustment of payments imbalances of individual countries. I have referred to: difficulties of analysis, political difficulties, limitations of policy instruments, difficulties of assigning responsibility for remedial action, difficulty of defining fundamental disequilibrium, reluctance of authorities to make necessary changes in exchange rates, and excess tolerance of imbalance.

## THE EQUILIBRIUM OF THE SYSTEM AS A WHOLE

I turn now to the question of the equilibrium of the system as a whole, as opposed to that of any particular country. This question has to do with the total and the composition of the reserves in the system in relation to the aggregate demand for reserves. This question has been much debated lately and I propose to deal with it very briefly.

The demand of countries for reserves tends to grow as the volume of international business grows and as the variability of their individual positions increases. Both the growing volume of trade in goods and services and the increasing mobility of capital associated with developments such as that of the Euro-dollar market have contributed to the rising demand for reserves.

If the supply of reserves does not grow adequately to meet the rising demand for them, a disequilibrium in the system as a whole results. The evidence of this condition is to be found in a general tendency to adopt policies designed to produce or increase surpluses, an increased unwillingness of surplus countries to play a full part in adjusting payments imbalances and efforts to change the composition of reserve holdings.

It is a truism, of course, that there cannot be a general surplus in the system in which every country has a surplus on its official settlements account unless new reserves have come into the system without reducing any country's reserve position. There are not many ways in which this can happen. It can happen when gold moves into official holdings from new production or from private holdings. It can happen when central banks create simultaneously mutual credits in their domestic currencies in favour of each other. It can happen when the issue of SDRs is increased. It does *not* happen when the net increase in reserves in the system is in the form of official holdings of US dollars for these are properly reckoned as a debit to the US official settlements account.

Although it was probably prudent not to admit it officially at the time, it would now appear to be a plausible proposition that there was a growing disequilibrium of the system as a whole in the sixties. This was manifested both in the widespread wish of countries to augment their reserves, together with an unwillingness of surplus countries to take steps to adjust their surpluses and also in the general dissatisfaction of countries with the composition of their reserves, especially the rising proportion of US dollars in them.

The possibility of an eventual disequilibrium was recognized officially early in the sixties when studies were put in train to determine means of supplementing gold and dollars in reserves. In non-official quarters the speculation grew that a general disequilibrium was emerging that would have to be relieved by an increase in the price of gold. In the end the system adopted a two-tiered regime of pricing gold and created a new reserve instrument, SDRs.

With this instrument the international monetary system has the capacity to create reserves deliberately, in accord with an assessment of the over-all need of the system. The appearance of the SDR was a significant turning point in the history of the system. General disequilibrium may arise in the future because of an excess demand for reserves but if it does it will not be because of the lack of an instrument with which to effect an adjustment. It may also arise because of unwillingness of authorities to hold particular reserve assets in precisely the amounts in which they are available, and there may not yet be adequate means of avoiding that.

## THE UNIQUE ROLE OF THE UNITED STATES

It is apparent even to the most casual observer that the United States plays a unique role in the international monetary system. In giving some flavour of how the system works, one must pause to examine this unique role. Fundamentally, the position of the United States in the system derives from the pre-eminent political and economic power of the United States in the world today. That basic fact is obvious. We should note certain more or less technical manifestations and consequences of it.

We have already remarked the fact that the currency of the United States is, more than any other, the currency of the world. A large volume of world trade in goods and services is directly with the United States. Another important part is among countries which themselves have large trade with the United States and which even in trade with each other find it convenient to deal in US dollars. Added to this is the fact that the capital market of the United States is vast and highly developed and able to supply finance for trade among countries and for enterprise within countries. So widely used is the US dollar that active markets in dollars involving non-resident intermediaries—the so-called Euro-dollar and Euro-bond markets—have sprung up to effect transactions in dollars among non-residents of the United States and between non-residents and residents. Probably now even the vast technical resources of the United Kingdom capital market institutions, in their dealings with non-residents, deal more in $ US than in £ sterling. This is one technical manifestation of the unique role of the United States.

Another is related to it. The tie between gold and the US dollar is maintained by the United States. The United States is the only country in the world which undertakes as a practical matter to maintain an exchange value between its currency and gold. Other currencies tie to the dollar or to currencies that are themselves tied to the dollar. But the United States maintains the tie of the system to gold by its readiness to exchange gold for dollars and dollars for gold at fixed prices.

I would point out two consequences of the special place of the United States in the system. The first is that changes in the par value of the US dollar are virtually ruled out as techniques of adjustment of US payments imbalances. A change in the par of the dollar is a change in the price of gold. This can be accomplished; it is provided for in the Articles of Agreement of the Fund. But it is no routine operation. In fact, if the United States were to change its par, scores of other countries would wish to change their par values for they regard themselves as effectively tied to the dollar, not to gold. Of course frequent changes in par by the United States would be most disruptive of the entire system. Thus one of the consequences of the unique position of the United States is that other countries have par value changes available to them as instruments of adjustment whereas the United States does not except as a rare, once-for-all, highly exceptional act.

The other consequence of the special role of the United States is the tremendous importance to the rest of the world of domestic stability in the United States. This is a matter of degree; domestic stability of the United Kingdom or of Germany or of France, for example, is important to the stability of the system but the stability of the United States is vastly more important. Deflation in the United States with widespread unemployment would cripple the export markets of many countries directly and indirectly and give a great impetus to protectionism. Conversely, inflation in the United States damages the credibility of the United States dollar as the world's vehicle currency and menaces the domestic values of many other currencies. Thus because of the special predominant role of the United States in the world economy, the stability of the world economy and its monetary system depends in a very special way on the capacity of the United States to manage its domestic economic affairs well.

## DECISION-MAKING IN THE INTERNATIONAL MONETARY SYSTEM

Before leaving the discussion of how it works, I should like to make a few observations on decision-making in the international monetary system. There are two general classes of decisions to be discussed: independent decisions taken by national authorities concerning their own policies, and decisions taken jointly concerning the structure and operation of the system.

Decisions in the first category, of course, greatly affect the performance of the system. Our interest at the moment is in the way in which the view of the community as a whole is or may be brought to bear upon these essentially national decisions. What are the factors that impart a concern for international consequences of national decisions in the national decision-making process? One factor is fear of generating retaliatory action on the part of other countries. Such a fear may well be the result of past experience. Another factor is the existence of a code of behaviour which the country has helped to create and to which it subscribes. In fact, the code which we discussed earlier has been developed in considerable part out of fear of the consequences of mutual retaliation of the kind that broke out in the 1930s. Yet another factor is the knowledge that the international community has something to offer to the nation, especially if it encounters particular sorts of trouble and that accordingly it would be wise so far as possible to pursue policies generally acceptable to that community. Finally, a factor of very considerable importance and promise is the existence of occasions upon which nations are expected to explain, discuss and defend their policies before the international community or a segment of it. There are several such occasions in which Canada is involved of which the most important are the following. At least annually, the representatives of the International Monetary Fund visit Ottawa and consult with officials and Ministers over a period of about two weeks. During these visits the representatives of the Fund express views as to our economic policy and upon their return there is a discussion of their report in the Executive Board of the Fund. These consultations which the Fund holds with its members are a regular affair. Should a member of the Fund contemplate a drawing this would be the occasion for special consultations, and extensive drawings upon the Fund's resources are conditional upon the attainment of an understanding between the Fund and the member as to the economic policy to be pursued by the member.

As a member of the OECD (Organization for Economic Co-operation and Development) Canada's economic policy, like that of every other member, is discussed annually before the Economic Development Review Committee of that organization. But as far as Canada is concerned, perhaps a more important committee of the OECD is the so-called Working Party 3 of the Economic Policy Committee. This group has a limited membership (essentially the ten major industrial countries) and meets seven or eight times a year to review balance of payments developments and policies of the participating countries. It would be wrong to suggest that this body has powerful sanctions at its disposal. But on the other hand, one should not under-estimate the influence in policy formulation of the need to offer a convincing explanation of policy in such a forum.

Another body in which we participate and in which views as to policies and developments are exchanged is the Bank for International Settlements. We have for years attended meetings of central bank governors in Basle, even though we were not formally a shareholder in the Bank until this year.

It is in and through international bodies such as these that the international point of view is brought to bear upon national decisions affecting the international monetary system as a whole. One should not leave the impression that "international point of view" is clear and obvious and easily arrived at. Our discussion of the difficulties of applying the unwritten code of policy behaviour attests to that. As a general proposition one may say that a code is more easily agreed and applied, the greater is the harmony of objectives and experience of the nations comprising the international monetary system.

The other class of decisions on which I should like to comment are joint decisions concerning the structure and the operations of the system. These are the decisions about amendments to the Articles of Agreement of the Fund, Fund policy under the Articles, decisions of the Group of Ten to provide or extend the borrowing facilities of the Fund or ad hoc decisions, such as to establish a two-tiered price system for gold. With the exception of this last case there exists a formal structure of decision-taking. The Fund articles spell out the respective roles of the Board of Governors and the Executive Directors. The General Arrangements to Borrow between the Fund and the Group of Ten specify certain formalities of decision-taking. But the essence of the matter does not reside in these formalities.

The essence of the matter, I think, resides in the way in which a climate of opinion is formed and a consensus is developed.

The first step in the process is the expression of a view that is seen by some countries at least as having merit or force. This initial expression of view may very well come from outside of official circles. The views of Robert Triffin on the impending crisis of the international monetary system were a very powerful catalyst. So were the views of academic economists on the merits of various techniques for achieving greater flexibility of exchange rates important in initiating the official discussions now going on. All through the recent period in which the liquidity plans were the subject of official discussion, the writings and meetings outside the official sector had an important influence upon the official consensus which emerged.

Within the official sector the normal course is for discussions to take place in rather small groups first, and perhaps simultaneously in these groups. I refer to the Basle meetings of the central bankers, the meetings of the Deputies of the Group of Ten, informal meetings of the members of the IMF Board, meetings of financial officials from the EEC countries, for example. At the outset these discussions are exploratory, more like a seminar than a board meeting. It is helpful if some representatives put forward specific proposals for discussion, but it is not helpful at that stage if they take rigid positions on the matter. It is at this discussion stage that participants are all more or less equal. Because of this the smaller countries which have access to these groups have a golden opportunity. No one is inclined to count the speaker's chips before listening to him. It is also at this stage that staff members of international bodies may be able to present the more comprehensive suggestions that grow out of their experience and reflection. Any participant with a thoughtful constructive suggestion may have a hearing.

Gradually views begin to crystallize. Consultations begin with Ministers, on an individual basis and Ministers take up the discussions in the smaller bodies. Steering groups, formal or informal, start to assess the emerging consensus within the smaller bodies and to guide the groups toward the taking of a preliminary view before widening the discussion.

Some persons rather dislike the fact that small unrepresentative bodies in fact play such an important role in the formulative stages of new initiatives. The role of the Group of Ten in the development of ideas concerning the evolution of the Fund is questioned seriously by some. No doubt there are risks here. An organization may indeed be threatened if smaller cliques within it act irresponsibly toward other members. But as a practical matter it seems to me that there is an important place, probably an essential place, for discussions of new ideas and initiatives among smaller groups within the system if such ideas are to come to maturity and if the system as a whole is to advance.

## III   How may it evolve?

Let us turn now to the more speculative aspect of these reflections and consider how the international monetary system may evolve. I shall not try to climb to some lofty height in order to see over the mountains which hide the more distant future from view. Rather I shall try only to see as far as a work-a-day chap with his feet on the ground can see as he enumerates the problems within his limited range of vision and speculates as to how these might, for better or for worse, come to be resolved in fact.

Consider first, the role of gold in the system. There should be no misunderstanding on one point: gold is today very important in the international monetary system. It is so regarded throughout the system and it constitutes slightly over half of countries' international reserves. It is less important than it once was; two decades ago it comprised two-thirds of reserves. I feel sure that the role of gold will decline. One simple calculation will illustrate the possibilities. Should the composition of reserves change in no other respect save that same increase by $2 billion per annum, then in a little over two decades, gold would comprise only $^1/_3$ of reserves. It is not improbable that gold will become more valuable in private markets as the years pass, and gold may seep from the monetary system to the private sector. The orderly development of the international monetary system will accord gold a declining role just as has happened in national monetary systems. There seems to be no virtue in trying to hasten this process. Of course, should the system be rocked by deep crises of confidence a scramble back to gold would occur, for gold is the money of an unstructured system. Barring this unwanted sort of catastrophe, gold will be the old soldier of the system and will gradually fade away.

What about key currencies — are we liable to see new key currencies like the US dollar in the system? Key currencies are not created instantly. They arise in a natural way because of the extensive and widespread trade of the key currency country and because of that country's readiness to export capital and to provide banking facilities for its trade. Within the present international monetary system, that is excluding the communist bloc of the world, there is only one visible possibility for the development of a key currency and that would be the currency of an integrated Europe. European integration will have to proceed much further than it has at present for this to happen and it will have to embrace a more thorough-going political integration as well. An integrated monetary system requires the support of an integrated fiscal system. I am not prepared to speculate on the political development of Europe. There are two movements afoot; one is the lateral extension of the integration to additional countries, the other is its vertical extension. It is the latter which is essential to the emergence of a common monetary system. The key currency role for a European currency can only come after it becomes established as a common European currency and even that seems to me to be yet some way off. Certain it is that should another key currency emerge the problem of the multiplicity of reserves will be exacerbated.

In the sixties the problem of the multiplicity of reserves emerged as an unwanted rise in the proportion of US dollars in the holdings of certain large surplus countries. Their attempts to change the composition of their reserves through conversion of dollars to gold was worrisome because of the dispersal of a substantial portion of the US gold stock and the speculation to which this gave rise.

The problem of serious discrepancies between the demand for and supply of particular categories of reserves may not become acute because of certain adjustment features already built into the system. On the other hand, should it become acute there already exist suggestions for dealing with it that seem to be sufficiently in the line of evolution of the system as to have a fairly good chance of being acceptable.

The following are among the adjustment features already built into the system. Countries may sell gold to the market (though under the Washington agreement of March, 1968, such sales by a country should be regarded as a permanent reduction of its gold holdings). Countries may sell gold to each other and under certain circumstances may sell gold to or buy it from international monetary institutions. The United States, of course, continues to be prepared to buy and sell gold for monetary authorities of other countries. The United States is also entitled to use its SDRs to acquire US dollars from other authorities. Finally, the Fund is enjoined under its Articles in designating recipients of SDRs to promote a balanced distribution of SDRs among participants in the SDR regime.

There are two main classes of suggestion for meeting difficulties arising from disparities in the performance of countries for reserve assets. One is that a formal agreement should be concluded among countries for the international harmonization of the ratios among existing holdings or subsequent acquisitions of reserves. The other, in some ways less complicated, but certainly more far reaching is that countries should pool their existing reserve assets in a common account from which they would be credited with units of account. All countries then would hold their reserves in a common form and the question of harmonization would disappear. This is a logical extension of the line of evolution we have been following since the war.

I turn now to another aspect of the evolution of the system. Now that we have a means for deliberately creating reserves we are confronted with the problem of deciding how many to create. The world has had some experience of a similar kind already. Upon the establishment of the Fund itself it was necessary to decide upon the initial quotas. Since then there have been five quinquennial reviews of quotas. In addition, the initial decision as to the allocation of SDRs has been made.

My own feeling is that countries have a considerable tolerance for changes in their reserve positions and that in deciding upon any particular annual increment one can expect the system to accept without visible response any increments within a fairly wide range. One could expect, however, that the cumulative effect of fairly extreme increments always on one side of a range would become significant. It would seem to follow therefore that for a growing system, a policy of fairly steady increases of moderate dimensions would be what is called for in the absence of the knowledge and indeed the machinery for a finer tuning. The "monetarists" therefore have the day in terms of the international money supply if not the national money supply.

But even so, a problem remains, for if one is seeking moderate and regular increases in the total of reserves and one has direct control of only one of the several components of the total, one is confronted with the complex task of forecasting the movements of the components. Nonetheless, I remain optimistic that this aspect of managing the international monetary system will not prove too difficult or be the source of our most harassing problems in the near future.

I turn now to the future of the exchange rate system itself, certainly a vitally important aspect of the question of how the system may evolve. The subject is in fact *sub judice* at the moment as it is being discussed in the Fund and among member countries in other gatherings of officials. So I shall emphasize that I speak only for myself and in any event I shall be circumspect.

The present exchange rate system came into being with the Fund after the thirties and the depression and competitive devaluations that characterized that period. It is important to keep in perspective how it has served us. It has not prevented a vast growth of trade nor a greatly enhanced mobility of capital nor a tremendous expansion of living standards. It has not prevented a dramatic improvement in the processes of international discussion and collaboration on financial and economic matters. Why have we become concerned?

What has happened is that fairly recently — in the latter half of the sixties for the most part — we have had mounting inflation around the industrial world and we have had long delays in adopting exchange rate changes that markets recognized as inevitable. Consequently, there have been major surges of funds from the countries where the market felt devaluation was inevitable and toward countries where the market felt revaluation was likewise inevitable.

In the last annual report of the Executive Directors of the Fund it was stated that:

> In the Bretton Woods system, changes in par values were contemplated as one of the means of adjustment and elaborate provisions were written into the Articles of Agreement for them. Where countries — in deficit or surplus — can no longer maintain broad equilibrium over time in their external payments without having to incur undue unemployment or price inflation, it is wholly proper that these provisions should be used.[1]

I take it that the main issue in this domain today is how to accomplish exchange rate changes when they are needed in such conditions of fundamental disequilibrium, before the situation deteriorates to crisis proportions.

I believe it is a good thing that a debate around this subject has arisen. The very debate itself may well make it better understood that there are occasions on which changes in exchange rates are needed and that on such occasions it is no disgrace to make them.

Several suggestions have been made. Wider trading margins around the declared parity have been proposed. These might be helpful, but a widening of the margins of a degree that would not imply a basic change in the system would probably not deal with the big and important cases of fundamental disequilibrium.

Crawling pegs have also been suggested. I am convinced that the formulae for *automatic* adjustment of pegs which have been put forward are not satisfactory. Since cases of fundamental disequilibrium are, on my reading of history, comparatively rare events, and since an automatic formula will produce changes in the peg in all cases of disequilibrium, the formula will change the peg more often when it is not needed than when it is.

What we are left with then, is discretionary changes of exchange rates, be they crawls or otherwise. Different techniques may be applicable in different circumstances. A change of parity in a single step or a series of small changes of parity are possible techniques. A decision not to defend an existing parity but to review, after a period, the question of the appropriate level of the exchange rate to defend as a parity is another alternative.

In the evolution of the international monetary system I think we shall preserve the exchange rate system as envisaged in the Bretton Woods Agreements. I think that we shall improve our understanding and analysis of events however, and in so doing come to use this exchange rate system more effectively.

I come now to a final observation on the structure of the central institutions of the system themselves. This September the 25th Anniversary meeting of Fund Governors will take place. The history of the Fund over these past 25 years is an impressive history precisely because of the capacity the Fund has shown to adapt to the needs of the system. The Fund has shown a readiness to recognize that cases differ. The evolution of its policy in respect to reserve positions in the Fund, Fund borrowings, the requirement of gold subscriptions, stand-by agreements with potential drawers, currencies to be drawn by drawers, repurchases, compensatory financing of countries producing primary products and the SDRs, all of these policies and others attest to the resiliency of the institution that serves a world which recognizes its need of it. Some entertain starry-eyed dreams of a future Fund operating as a grand international central bank, issuing its own liabilities and conducting open market operations on its own initiative in the various capital markets of the world. From my ground-level stance, I cannot see such a Fund; it is beyond my horizon. I can see a widening of the membership of the Fund. I look forward, realistically, I think, to the day when the expansion of trade with countries of Eastern Europe, including Russia, will induce countries other than Yugoslavia which is already a member, to drop their objections to providing the information required of members and agree to join the Fund. Such a development will give us new opportunities and challenges. In the meantime, I believe the practices of international economic discussion and collaboration which we have learned to use and develop will continue to be cultivated. As this goes forward, the international monetary system, supporting commerce among nations, will increasingly serve as a unifying force in the world.

**Footnote**

1. International Monetary Fund, *Annual Report* (Washington, D.C., 1969), Chap. 2, p. 31.

## ROBERT M. DUNN, JR

# Canada's Experience with Fixed and Flexible Exchange Rates in a North American Capital Market

The difficulties that theory suggests as inherent in maintaining a fixed exchange rate in a world of highly mobile capital have been rather strikingly illustrated by Canada's postwar experience.

On two occasions since 1945, Canada has been virtually forced to choose between the continuation of a fixed exchange rate and the maintenance of control over the domestic money supply and, ultimately, over the economy. In both instances the government chose to abandon the exchange rate in favour of domestic economic stability. In the summer of 1950 and the spring of 1970, Canada experienced foreign exchange reserve inflows that were beyond the ability of the Bank of Canada to control or sterilize, and on both occasions the government felt that it would be impossible to choose a higher fixed exchange rate with any confidence that it could be defended. Both in 1950 and in 1970, large movements of foreign exchange were caused in part by the current or expected inflationary effects on the U.S. economy of military involvement in Asia. In 1950 the flows were largely speculative and followed the beginning of U.S. military operations in Korea, while the 1970 inflows were primarily the 'result of a large Canadian trade surplus which grew in part from the inflationary effects of four years of heavy U.S. expenditures in Vietnam. In both years, however, current or expected instability in the U.S. economy forced the Canadian government to abandon a fixed exchange rate if Canada was to avoid importing U.S. economic problems through the balance of payments.

The 1950 decision was expected by many to be temporary, but Canada remained with a flexible exchange rate for almost 12 years and provided economists with their only recent and prolonged example of a market-determined exchange rate for the currency of a major industrial country. The other experiences with floating exchange rates either occurred before the era of adequate statistics, or were too brief for serious study, or involved the currencies of underdeveloped countries whose statistics remain poor. The duration of the present float of the Canadian dollar cannot be predicted, but a decision to return to a fixed exchange rate soon would be a great disappointment to, among others, those many academic economists who have been waiting for eight years for another example of a major floating rate as a subject for further research.

## The 1950 Decision

The decision to free the exchange rate in the fall of 1950 followed two unsuccessful attempts to find an appropriate fixed parity. In 1946 the Canadian dollar was revalued from about U.S.$0.91 to U.S.$1.00 to reduce the effects on Canada of inflation in the United States and Europe. Widespread feelings that the Canadian dollar was overvalued at parity and fear of the effects of devaluations in Europe led to devaluation in the fall of 1949 to about U.S.$0.91. This change was widely regarded as excessive, and the combination of a booming Canadian minerals industry and the outbreak of the Korean War led the financial markets to the conclusion in mid-1950 that the Canadian dollar was seriously undervalued. A flow of speculative funds into Canada developed and continued through the summer. This flow became a flood in September, as Canadian foreign exchange reserves grew by almost $1 billion during the third quarter. The Bank of Canada attempted to offset the effects of the reserve inflows on the domestic money supply, but its efforts were overwhelmed by these inflows, and the government ended its defense of the rate on October 1, 1950.[1] The narrowness of Canadian financial markets made it virtually impossible for the Bank of Canada to sell government securities in the volume necessary to fully or even largely offset the effects of the reserve inflow. In addition, attempts to sell securities in anything approaching this volume would have increased Canadian interest rates, attracting even more money from the United States.

After the decision to free the exchange rate, the Canadian dollar appreciated rapidly during 1951 and reached U.S.$1.04 in 1952. It then fluctuated without any obvious trend between U.S.$1.00 and almost U.S.$1.06 until 1960. Day-to-day and week-to-week movements of the rate were almost universally small, and fears of a widely gyrating exchange rate which would depress foreign trade and capital flows turned out to be unfounded.

The movements of the exchange rate did not, however, provide Canada with the protection from externally generated business cycles that theory would predict. This was the result of Canadian monetary policy, which tended to lag events, and of a general lack of understanding of the relationship between a flexible exchange rate, monetary policy, and the business cycle. Canada was hit hard by the 1953-54 recession in the United States, primarily because the Bank of Canada lagged behind the Federal Reserve System in easing monetary policy.[2] This meant that the relatively high Canadian interest rates attracted undesirably large amounts of U.S. money, appreciating the Canadian dollar and reducing the Canadian trade balance.

Canada's experience in 1958-60 was made even worse by a still less appropriate monetary policy. In late 1958 the Bank of Canada overreacted to the potential inflationary effects of a large government deficit by imposing an extremely tight money policy in the face of high unemployment.[3] The Canadian money supply actually fell in 1959 and the recovery from the 1958 recession was completely stifled. The flexible exchange rate contributed to this outcome by protecting the monetary policy. High Canadian interest rates attracted large flows of funds from the United States, sharply increasing the exchange rate and greatly reducing the Canadian trade account. The loss of

**Chart 1.**
The Canadian Dollar, 1956-1970

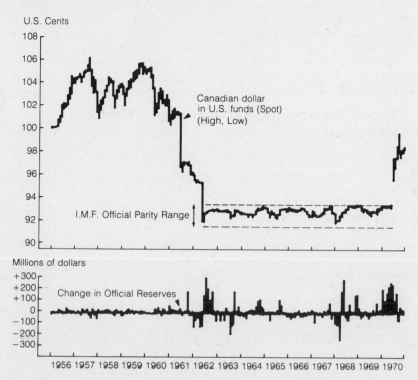

U.S. Cents

Canadian dollar
in U.S. funds (Spot)
(High, Low)

I.M.F. Official Parity Range

Millions of dollars

Change in Official Reserves

1956 1957 1958 1959 1960 1961 1962 1963 1964 1965 1966 1967 1968 1969 1970

**Source:** *Canada's Business Climate*, Toronto Dominion Bank, Winter 1971.

export and import competitive sales by Canadian firms deepened and prolonged the recession. Had fixed exchange rates been in existence, this inappropriate monetary policy would have been largely stymied by the effects of the capital inflows on the Canadian money supply. The high interest rates would have attracted funds from the United States, creating a large surplus in the Canadian balance of payments, which would have forced the Bank of Canada to increase the money supply by selling Canadian dollars in the exchange market. Under Canada's unusual exchange fund arrangements, the Canadian funds would have come from government balances at first, but the depletion of these balances by continuing large reserve inflows would have forced the Bank of Canada to create the necessary Canadian dollars for exchange market intervention.[4] The resulting increase in the money supply would have compromised or destroyed the original tight money policy and protected the Canadian economy from its consequences.

A change was made in the management of the Bank of Canada in 1961, and a program to reflate the economy began soon after. Unfortunately this program

included an attempt to bring the exchange rate down through public announcements that a lower rate was desired and that the exchange stabilization fund
would be used to encourage a decline. The government's rather unsubtle
attempt to manipulate the rate was far too successful; market confidence in the
Canadian dollar evaporated and speculators moved out of the currency in
volume. The exchange crisis of 1962 resulted, and the flexible exchange rate
was abandoned for a parity of U.S. 92.5 cents in May.[5] As can be seen in Chart
1, the Canadian dollar was then allowed to vary between U.S. 91.75 cents and
U.S. 93.25 cents until June 1, 1970.

## Research Conclusions from the 1950-62 Experience

As suggested earlier, Canada has provided economists with their primary
source of information on the actual workings of a flexible exchange rate
system. As a result the 1950-62 experience has been intensively analyzed by
economists working in the areas of international trade and finance, and a
number of issues have been covered.

(1) One of the most important questions about the Canadian experience—and a major concern of this study—is the impact of exchange rate
flexibility on the effectiveness of Canadian monetary policy. The Caves and
Reuber study uses an econometric model of the Canadian economy to deal
with this issue and concludes that during the 1950s the existence of flexible
exchange rates made monetary policy shifts at least six times as effective in the
short run as they would have been with a fixed exchange rate.[6] Over longer
periods monetary policy remained much more powerful with flexible than with
fixed exchange rates, but the relationship was somewhat less than six to one.
Although econometric studies of this type cannot be depended on for precise
results, this estimate does suggest the rough magnitude of the effect of exchange rate flexibility. In a separate econometric study of the Canadian
economy, Rudolph Rhomberg also reaches the conclusion that the effectiveness of Canadian monetary policy was greatly enhanced by a flexible exchange
rate.[7] His results suggest that, in a world of fixed exchange rates, monetary
policy will have almost no effects on domestic aggregate demand unless the
Bank of Canada succeeds in maintaining its desired change in the money supply
in the face of reserve flows caused by the change in relative interest rates. If the
Bank of Canada carries out an open market purchase at one time and then allows
the money supply to passively respond to the resulting foreign exchange reserve
flows, the original monetary policy shift will be almost completely destroyed.
Rhomberg also concludes that fiscal policy is somewhat stronger with fixed
than with flexible exchange rates when fiscal shifts are not accompanied by
parallel changes in monetary policy.[8]

(2) A second major topic of interest growing out of the Canadian experience
during 1950-62 was the apparent stability of the exchange rate and the role of
speculative capital flows as against the adjustment of the trade account as
sources of that stability. Most studies of the behaviour of the Canadian trade
account have suggested that the foreign trade elasticities of demand were rather
low, so that the trade account was not particularly responsive to modest shifts in

the exchange rate. The Rhomberg study, however, concluded that the Canadian elasticity of demand for imports was about unity and that the foreign elasticity of demand for Canadian imports was approximately two, so the elasticities totaled three, which is well above the minimum for exchange market stability suggested by the Marshall-Lerner condition.[9] It seems clear, however, that the primary source for stability in the exchange market came from outside the trade account. A number of studies have concluded that the primary factor was stabilizing speculative movements of short-term capital—that is, that exchange market speculators acted to resist sharp movements in the rate. They apparently sold the Canadian dollar when it was appreciating and bought it when it was falling, thereby reducing exchange rate movements.[10] The stabilizing behaviour of speculators was based on confidence in the existing exchange rate between the Canadian and U.S. dollars. This confidence could exist as long as the market had reasonable confidence in the policies of the Bank of Canada and as long as the government did not try to manipulate the rate. Such confidence is rather fragile and disappeared when the government tried to force the exchange rate down in 1961, leading to the exchange crisis of 1962.

It should be noted that, in addition to the stabilizing effects of private short-term capital flows, the Bank of Canada managed an exchange stabilization fund during the era of flexible exchange rates with the goal of moderating random day-to-day shifts in the market *without* resisting basic trends in the rate. The fund operated successfully on this principle by selling Canadian dollars when the rate rose sharply, and *vice versa*, until the 1961 decision to attempt to force the rate down. The operations of the stabilization fund were relatively modest in scope, however, so that it did not determine the stability of the market, but instead augmented other larger forces stabilizing the rate.

A further source of stability in the exchange market was the tendency of large inflows of funds for direct investment to be accompanied by large and offsetting increases in imports. This occurred because of the extremely high import content of Canadian investment expenditures (approximately 0.6 percent according to the Rhomberg study of the exchange market[11]). This meant that an investment boom in Canada that attracted large amounts of U.S. capital would also create a large Canadian demand for imports, balancing the payments accounts without a major exchange rate change.[12] When the Canadian economy was less expansive and investment expenditures declined, less money came in as direct investment *and* imports of capital equipment declined, meaning that the required adjustment of the exchange rate was again relatively modest. This historic importance of financial capital inflows and of imported capital goods in Canadian expansions has typically had a stabilizing effect on the overall Canadian balance of payments, reducing the cyclical pressures on the Canadian dollar in the 1950-62 period.

(3) Many businessmen and others have feared that a flexible exchange rate would greatly reduce the flow of foreign trade and capital by introducing a new element of risk in international transactions.[13] It was feared that exporters and importers would be discouraged from taking the risks implicit in using normal commercial credit arrangements in foreign trade when a flexible exchange rate introduced the possibility of unpredictable gains or losses for those holding uncovered positions in foreign exchange.

The first answer to this argument is that the forward market is always available for hedging such risks and that the introduction of flexible exchange rates can be expected to increase the size and breadth of this market. Although there may be modest transactions costs involved in arranging forward contracts, they are hardly a major hindrance. The second response to this argument is that there is no evidence that Canada's foreign trade or capital flows were significantly discouraged by the floating exchange rate. Between 1950 and 1962, Canadian exports grew from C$3,139 million to C$6,387 million, an increase of just over 100 per cent. Imports grew at a similar rate, rising from C$3,129 million to C$6,203 million. Although Canadian GNP grew slightly more rapidly than exports or imports, so that the percentage of Canadian GNP exported declined from 17.2 per cent to 15.8 per cent, the rapid growth of Canadian trade hardly suggests that a flexible exchange rate was a great barrier to international transactions.[14] It is impossible to know how Canadian trade would have behaved with a fixed exchange rate during the 1950s, but a doubling of trade in 12 years suggests that it was not seriously discouraged by flexible exchange rates.

International capital flows into Canada were also large during the 1950s, so foreign investors were apparently not discouraged by the flexible exchange rate system. Although, again, it is impossible to know how much might have been invested in Canada with a fixed exchange rate, total foreign investments in Canada rose from C$9.3 billion in 1949 to C$28.8 billion in 1962, and Canadian investments abroad rose from C$5.3 billion to C$10.2 billion during the same period.[15] In 1957 alone, American firms placed $678 million in direct investment funds in Canada, and in 1959 high Canadian interest rates attracted $437 million in new issues funds from the United States.[16] It hardly seems that either Canadians or foreigners were greatly discouraged from moving capital in or out of Canada by a floating exchange rate during the 1950s.

(4) The final issue is that of price stability. Some fear has been expressed that a flexible exchange rate would destabilize internal prices of traded goods. To the extent that the prices of major Canadian exports and imports are determined in the United States and fixed in U.S. dollars, Canadian dollar prices of these goods would seem to be forced to adjust constantly to changes in the exchange rate.[17] This conclusion assumes that the prices of traded goods can differ between countries only by transport costs and tariffs, and consequently assumes perfect competition. Under such circumstances, for example, the price of copper in Canada should equal the U.S. or U.K. price minus transport costs and tariffs, and the Canadian dollar price would obviously have to adjust to changes in the exchange rate to maintain this equality.

Canadian prices were not destabilized by the flexible exchange rate, however, because few if any traded goods markets are perfectly competitive. Firms and their customers in the imperfectly competitive markets of the real world have strong preferences for stable prices, and the market power of these firms provides means of maintaining such stability. Research on the Canadian experience concludes that it was common for firms involved in international trade to sell at two separate and rigid prices, one in Canada and one elsewhere.[18] Variations in the exchange rate within some range were absorbed in profit margins, and a combination of transport costs and the market power of large firms discouraged arbitrage. Since both suppliers and their customers preferred stable prices, firms in imperfectly competitive Canadian markets provided stable Canadian dollar prices despite the theoretical arguments that such stability should be impossible with flexible exchange rates.

The general conclusion of the research efforts into the Canadian experience of 1950-62 is that a flexible exchange rate system can be made to operate successfully if those setting monetary and other economic policies understand its implications. It is extremely important that monetary policy be set with allowance for its extra impact via the exchange market and the trade account and that the government not try to "talk" the rate up or down or to use the exchange stabilization fund to force the rate away from its market-determined trend. The possibilities for destabilizing private speculation in such cases are great, and consequently the exchange stabilization fund should be used solely for its intended purpose—to absorb day-to-day shifts in demand for foreign exchange without resisting fundamental market trends. Canada's widely discussed difficulties between 1958 and 1962 were not the result of inherent disadvantages of flexible exchange rates, but instead grew out of errors in monetary policy which were magnified by the operations of the exchange market. In addition, the government misjudged the effects on speculators of its attempts to manipulate the rate in 1961.

## The 1970 Return to a Floating Exchange Rate

As suggested earlier, Canada was almost forced off a fixed exchange rate in the spring of 1970 by a large inflow of foreign exchange which threatened to become massive and by the inability of the Canadian government to choose a higher fixed exchange rate with any confidence that it could be defended. An extremely strong trade balance and the beginnings of a speculative move into Canadian dollars had forced the Bank of Canada to purchase over $1 billion in foreign exchange in the spot market and an undetermined amount forward during the first five months of 1970. The government's Canadian dollar balances were at an extremely low level, and the defense of the 92.5 parity could have been continued only if the Bank of Canada was prepared to create the necessary Canadian dollars and lend them to the government to finance exchange market activities, thereby inflating the currency. The rate of reserve inflow was particularly heavy in May, and there was reason to fear that it would greatly increase when speculators became more active after the public announcement of the May reserve gains. Sterilization of the monetary effects of such inflows would have been impossible without raising interest rates and attracting still more foreign money. In addition, the narrowness of Canadian financial markets would have made it impossible as a practical matter for the Bank of Canada to sell the required volume of government debt without inviting chaos. 1950 repeated itself, and the government was again faced with the choice between controlling the exchange rate or maintaining a domestic monetary policy and, on June 1, 1970, it decided to let the rate go.

In addition to the monetary difficulties inherent in a continued defense of the 92.5 parity, the Canadian government probably doubted that the upward pressure on the exchange rate was temporary and consequently faced a long-term balance-of-payments adjustment problem. Since the mid-1960s, Canada's current account balance has been improving; and in early 1970 it began a remarkable surge that resulted in a C$2 billion gain over 1969 and the largest surplus on record—and the first since 1952. As the following tabulation shows, the dominant factor has been Canada's strengthening trade performance, mostly with the United States.[19]

| | Balances (receipts minus payments) in millions of Canadian $ | | | | | |
|---|---|---|---|---|---|---|
| | With all Countries | | | With the United States | | |
| | M'dise Trade | Services | Total Current Account | M'dise Trade | Services | Total Current Account |
| 1965 | + 118 | −1,248 | −1,130 | −1,041 | − 896 | −1,937 |
| 1966 | + 224 | −1,386 | −1,162 | − 993 | −1,024 | −2,017 |
| 1967 | + 566 | −1,065 | − 499 | − 655 | − 724 | −1,379 |
| 1968 | +1,376 | −1,436 | − 60 | + 249 | −1,041 | − 792 |
| 1969 | + 860 | −1,611 | − 751 | + 367 | −1,100 | − 733 |
| 1970 | +3,002 | −1,705 | +1,297 | +1,142 | −1,109 | + 33 |

**Source:** Dominion Bureau of Statistics.

Since the government was not prepared to inflate, the exchange rate provided the major available route towards payments adjustment.

A final and more modest reason for the decision to abandon the 92.5 parity on June 1, 1970, might have been the government's desire to avoid the large and politically embarrassing capital losses that would have resulted from a determined but unsuccessful defense of the existing parity. As the exchange rate has risen subsequently, the Canadian dollar value of Canada's previous holdings of U.S. dollars has declined proportionally, and the Canadian government has already taken a rather large capital loss (5 or 6 per cent of about $4 billion) on these reserves. The loss would have been much larger if Canada's foreign exchange reserves had been greatly inflated before Canada was finally forced off the 92.5 peg. The government might quite reasonably prefer to avoid a determined defense of the exchange rate unless it was certain that the defense would succeed.

The decision to float the rate rather than choose a new higher peg was based on the impossibility of determining a new rate with any confidence that it could be maintained. This was particularly true in the spring of 1970 because of the highly uncertain state of the U.S. economy. A 97 to 98 rate might have appeared reasonable at the time, but if the U.S. economy slipped into a recession of the 1958 variety, Canada might have been faced with rapidly declining exports and an exchange crisis. If, however, the U.S. economy were to resume its previous inflationary growth path, the resulting increases in the Canadian trade balance could make 97-98 too low and lead to a repetition of the events of early 1970.

A higher fixed exchange rate would also represent a potential threat to the Canadian economy. If the U.S. economy entered a recession, Canada would import that downturn through the trade account, as the combination of declining U.S. aggregate demand and the effects of the higher fixed exchange rate led to a sharp decline in Canadian exports. As suggested earlier, a flexible exchange rate breaks the linkage between the business cycles of the United States and Canada and provides Canada with incomplete but considerable protection from instability in the U.S. economy.[20] In light of these factors, the Canadian decision to float the exchange rate seems almost obvious, although it certainly did not appear so to the financial community in Canada or to the international central banking community on June 1.

As of the spring of 1971, the current state of the U.S. economy may well provide Canada with strong arguments for remaining with a flexible exchange rate. The Administration's "game plan" went through a rather dramatic change early in 1971, a change which suggests that the curbing of inflation in the United States no longer holds the first priority. The proposed Federal budget for fiscal 1972 is decidedly expansionary, and the Administration's controversial GNP forecast of $1,065 billion for 1971 would involve a very rapid recovery from the 1970 recession. Policy shifts intended to produce this recovery are being made despite continuing, though retarded, inflation in the United States and growing U.S. balance-of-payments problems. This would hardly appear to be a moment at which Canada would reasonably choose to tie its economy to the cyclical behaviour of the United States through a fixed exchange rate.

A policy of continued exchange rate flexibility for Canada is also supported by the findings of two recent reports on U.S. balance-of-payments policy. Haberler and Willett suggest that because U.S. official reserve liabilities now greatly exceed U.S. holdings of gold, the dollar is no longer convertible into gold in large amounts and consequently the world payments system is now on a dollar standard.[21] They then suggest that this situation relieves the United States of the necessity of even pretending to manage its domestic economic policies with the goal of balancing its international accounts. It is then argued that other countries must adjust to the U.S. payments situation, and can do so by simply building up their holdings of dollars indefinitely and trying to sterilize their effects on the domestic money supply, or by inflating to eliminate their surpluses, or by appreciating their currencies. This line of reasoning, which can also be found in a recent article by Lawrence Krause of the Brookings Institution[22], is becoming increasingly common in Washington and suggests that exchange rates will be used much more often in the future than they have in the past as an adjustment mechanism. The Canadian decision may be the beginning of a trend, despite the continuing opposition of the International Monetary Fund and others in international central banking to any form of exchange rate flexibility.

## International Concern over Canada's Action

One of the International Monetary Fund's primary arguments against flexible exchange rates is that one country's exchange rate seriously affects its trading partners, and as such is a matter of international concern which should not be left to the sole discretion of a national government. Further, since each country's exchange rate is also extremely important to its domestic economy, national governments are in fact unlikely to allow their exchange rate to be determined solely on the basis of market forces, but will instead use intervention and other techniques to manipulate the rate. This could be done most easily by having the central bank buy or sell foreign exchange in large amounts to force the market rate in the desired direction. Since this exchange rate is also of vital importance to its trading partners, these efforts to manipulate the exchange market are likely to cause injury abroad and encourage attempts at retaliatory intervention, with resulting chaos in exchange markets.[23]

There are two answers to this argument, one of which applies to Canada and one of which is more general. First, Canadian trade, however extensive, does not represent a significant part of any other country's GNP. About two-thirds of Canada's trade is with the United States, and Canadian exports to the United States amount to less than 1 per cent of U.S. GNP. It is inconceivable that Canadian efforts to manipulate a floating exchange rate could have any seriously disruptive effects on the U.S. economy and that therefore a Canadian decision to leave a fixed parity represents a threat to the United States.

If adopted by the world as a whole, however, flexible exchange rates without any binding agreements on government or central bank intervention policies might create the chaos foreseen by the IMF and threaten the maintenance of the liberalized foreign trade system which has developed since World War II. One possible answer would be for the countries floating their exchange rates to agree not to intervene in the exchange market, and for the International Monetary Fund, with significantly increased holdings of various currencies, to become the sole stabilization fund in the market and hence the only source of official intervention. The IMF balances would have to be arranged so that its stabilization activities did not affect government cash balances or the money supplies of various countries. If the IMF stabilization fund balances were placed in commercial rather than central bank accounts at the start, this problem would be solved. The IMF traders would be instructed to stabilize the rates from day to day, but not to resist underlying trends, and the governments would agree that all their foreign exchange needs would be met through direct transactions with the Fund, which could see to it that the needs were real and not intended to force exchange rates away from their market-determined level.[24] Each country would be freed from the demands of its balance of payments and able to pursue its own domestic economic policies, but would not be allowed to force its problems and instabilities on others through exchange rate manipulation. It should be noted that these arguments apply to large countries with broad exchange markets; it is not suggested that small or underdeveloped countries could successfully adopt flexible exchange rates.

In addition to the IMF's unhappiness with the Canadian decision of June 1, 1970, some of Canada's trading partners were also apparently disturbed, perhaps largely by a lack of prior consultation. Although consultation with important trading partners is commonly expected on major economic policy shifts which have international implications, such discussions involve large risks in the case of exchange rate changes. Once a decision has been made in this area, any delay in its enforcement greatly increases the risk of a massive and expensive speculative run. It is difficult to maintain absolute secrecy in such discussions, and if speculators even suspect that an exchange rate change is under consideration, they can move huge amounts of money which will impose large capital losses on the country which finally does change its rate. The rumours and apparent delay which surrounded the 1967 British decision to devalue are widely believed to have resulted in part from the consultation process and are also believed to have cost the British government untold millions in capital losses.[25] The Canadian decision was unusually successful in avoiding a prior speculative rush precisely because it was made quickly and without the risks inherent in widespread international discussions.

Lack of international popularity has been one cost for Canada of the 1970 decision to float the exchange rate. Historically Canada has been a major force in international cooperative ventures, and the government and the Bank of Canada may now feel quite uncomfortable in Canada's new role of an "outsider" in international central banking circles. In this instance, however, the demands of world opinion and financial orthodoxy conflicted directly with Canada's national interests and, if national sovereignty is to retain any meaning, the ultimate responsibility of those setting economic policies in Canada must be to the needs of the national economy rather than to the demands of world opinion. International cooperation can reasonably be expected in matters of limited importance, but the consequences for Canada of continuing a fixed exchange rate in the spring of 1970 were far too threatening for the opinions of those outside Canada to have been allowed to determine Canada's course. Canada's current role as a renegade in the world of international finance is undoubtedly unpleasant for many in Ottawa, but a premature decision to return to a fixed exchange rate that was quickly followed by balance-of-payments imbalances and serious restraints on Canadian economic policy could cost Canada a great deal more than international prestige.

## Preliminary Evaluation

At this writing (April 1971), it is still too soon to evaluate Canada's current experience with flexible exchange rates, but the improved understanding in Ottawa of how such a system works is obvious. An easing of Canadian monetary policy has been used to reduce an undesirably large increase in the exchange rate, and there have been no attempts to manipulate the rate through public pronouncements. The easing of Canadian monetary policy reflected domestic considerations, such as an unemployment rate of almost 7 per cent, but the intention of at least forestalling a further appreciation was alluded to in a recent statement by Governor Rasminsky. Canada's foreign exchange reserves rose quite rapidly during the summer of 1970 as a result of exchange market intervention by the Bank of Canada designed to reduce upwards pressure on the rate, but further purchases of U.S. dollars were small during the fall and winter. Canadian reserves totaled C$4.7 billion at year-end (C$4.8 billion on March 31, 1971). The exchange market activities of the Bank of Canada are analogous to the Bank's operation of the exchange stabilization fund during the 1950s.

Although an appreciation of the Canadian dollar was obviously expected when the rate was unpegged on June 1, the extent of the appreciation came as an unpleasant surprise to export and import competing industries and to the government. The forest product and other resource industries claim to have been particularly hard hit by the movement of the Canadian dollar from about U.S.$0.93 to over U.S.$0.99, and these effects are now described as spreading to other industries. The financial press has provided considerable support for their complaints.[26] The appreciation has forced Canadian exporters either to raise the foreign (U.S. dollar) prices, with a resulting loss of sales, or to maintain foreign prices at the cost of reduced Canadian dollar receipts and sharply reduced profits. Canadian firms which compete with imports are also put in a difficult position as U.S. exporters can either reduce their Canadian prices by the percentage of the appreciation with no loss of U.S. dollar receipts or maintain the Canadian dollar prices and absorb the effects of the appreciation as sharply improved profits, the existence of which could encourage greater U.S. advertising and promotional efforts in Canada.

The answer to the macroeconomic problem of unemployment caused by these effects of the appreciation is a set of Canadian fiscal and monetary policies which will restore full employment without regard to balance-of-payments effects, although expansionary policies will also tend to reduce the extent of the appreciation. A few particular industries may still be injured by the somewhat higher long-term equilibrium exchange rate, and this calls for a microeconomic solution of resource reallocation. Canadian export and import competing industries had a considerable competitive edge when the Canadian dollar was undervalued relative to the U.S. dollar and have now lost this advantage relative to the United States. The situation facing Canadian firms which export to Europe may have been made even more difficult by the appreciation, particularly if the European Community is expanded to include the United Kingdom and to allow associate membership for one or more Scandinavian countries.[27]

It should be noted that these problems of competitiveness resulted from the appreciation of the Canadian dollar rather than from the adoption of flexible exchange rates *per se*. These problems would consequently continue even if Canada returned to a fixed rate in the U.S.$0.98-1.00 range. The interests of these industries would probably be best served by a continuation of a flexible rate in the hope that it will float down at some time in the future, since it would be impossible for the Canadian government to peg it at a lower level now without a repetition of the problems of last spring. An attempt to significantly lower and then fix the Canadian exchange rate would produce a large balance-of-payments surplus for Canada, which would be followed by a movement of speculative funds into Canadian dollars. The Bank of Canada would again face the prospect of losing control over the money supply and ultimately over the economy. The fundamental goal of managing economic policy in the interests of the domestic economy rather than the balance of payments would then compel a return to a floating exchange rate, which would lead to an appreciation of the Canadian dollar to approximately its current level. Under a regime of free capital movements and relatively free trade, Canada cannot have a significantly lower exchange rate, either fixed or floating, except through inflation.

In closing, although the recent appreciation of the Canadian dollar has provided problems for particular industries, the potential benefits of a flexible exchange rate for the Canadian economy as a whole and for policy makers in particular, are sizable. It is now impossible for the Bank of Canada or the government to be forced to adopt domestically undesirable policies in the interests of the balance of payments, and this represents a major addition to Canadian economic independence. The potential benefits of flexible rates for Canada become real, however, only if the government and the Bank of Canada clearly understand the implications of a floating rate, and if monetary policy in particular is set with these implications in mind. The experience of the last 10 months suggests that Ottawa is aware of just how a flexible exchange rate system operates and that consequently Canada can expect a far more successful experience than in the 1950-62 period. This seems to be one of the happy but all too rare occasions when the advances of economic theory actually produce improvements in policy making.

### Footnotes

1. For histories of Canada's experience with a flexible exchange rate between 1950 and 1962, see Paul Wonnacott, *The Canadian Dollar, 1948-62* (Toronto: University of Toronto Press, 1965) and Robert A. Mundell, "Problems of Monetary and Exchange Rate Management in Canada," *National Banking Review* (September 1964), pp.77-86. Also see Donald Marsh, "Canada's Experience with a Floating Exchange Rate, 1950-62," in C. Fred Bergsten *et al.*, (eds), *Approaches to Greater Flexibility of Exchange Rates: The Burgenstock Papers* (Princeton: Princeton University Press, 1970), pp.337-44, and A. F. Wynne Plumptre, *Exchange Rate Policy: Experience with Canada's Floating Rate*, Essays in International Finance No.81 (Princeton: Princeton University Press, 1970). A somewhat more detailed treatment of this topic can be found in Leland B. Yeager, *International Monetary Relations* (New York: Harper and Row, 1966), pp.423-40. Virtually all of the students of Canada's history with a flexible rate conclude that the difficulties of 1958-62 were not the fault of the system, but instead grew out of a series of unfortunate or perhaps disastrous policy decisions in Ottawa.

2. Mundell, "Problems of Monetary and Exchange Rate Management," pp.82-4.

3. *Ibid.*, pp.79-80, and Richard E. Caves and Grant L. Reuber, *Canadian Economic Policy and the Impact of International Capital Flows*, Private Planning Association of Canada Series, "Canada in the Atlantic Economy" (Toronto: University of Toronto Press, 1969), pp.22-4.

4. The previously discussed Canadian system for the financing of foreign exchange inflows should be kept in mind. Although the Bank of Canada carries out the exchange market transactions, it does so only as an agent for the government, meaning that the government holds Canada's foreign exchange reserves. This also means that the government must finance these reserves by providing the necessary Canadian dollars. It is more typical for a central bank to hold foreign exchange reserves and for it simply to create the necessary domestic money to purchase foreign exchange inflows. In Canada, however, the government must provide the Canadian dollars, and foreign exchange inflows can represent a serious budgetary problem. If the government is finally forced to borrow from the Bank of Canada to finance reserve inflows, the net effect on the money supply is as if the Bank of Canada had merely created the local currency for exchange market intervention in the usual manner. Since the Canadian government's cash balances are seldom, if ever, large enough to finance major reserve inflows, the Bank of Canada must ultimately provide the necessary funds either by lending directly to the government or by easing general monetary conditions sufficiently for the government to borrow the necessary funds from the market.

5. Donald Marsh, a Canadian economist who is currently Assistant General Manager of the Royal Bank of Canada, has described the attempts to talk the rate down as the government's "open-mouth (or foot-in-mouth) policy." Marsh, "Canada's Experiences with a Floating Exchange Rate," p.341.

6. Caves and Reuber, *Canadian Economic Policy*, p.78.

7. Rudolph Rhomberg, "A Model of the Canadian Economy Under Fixed and Flexible Exchange Rates," *Journal of Political Economy* (February 1964), pp.22-4.

8. *Ibid.*, p.22.

9. *Ibid.*, p.11. The Marshall-Lerner condition demonstrates that if the Price elasticities of demand total less than one, the reaction of the trade account to the exchange can be perverse—that is, that a depreciation may worsen the trade account and *vice versa*. See Charles P. Kindleberger, *International Economics*, 4th ed. (Homewood, Ill.: Richard D. Irwin, Inc., 1968), pp.259-62 and 569-77, for a more complete analysis of this point.

10. Rudolph Rhomberg, "Canada's Foreign Exchange Market: A Quarterly Model," *IMF Staff Papers*, (April 1960), p.445, and Thomas L. Powrie, "Short-Term Capital Movements and the Flexible Exchange Rate 1953-61," *Canadian Journal of Economics and Political Science* (February 1964), pp.76-94. See also William Poole, "The Stability of the Canadian Flexible Exchange Rate," *Canadian Journal of Economics and Political Science* (May 1967).

11. Rhomberg, "Canada's Foreign Exchange Market," p.446.

12. Wonnacott, *The Canadian Dollar*, pp.128-29.

13. Scitovsky puts particular stress on an undesirable and large reduction in capital flows in arguing against flexible exchange rates within the EEC. Cooper brings up this point in arguing against flexible exchange rates in a broader context. See Tibor Scitovsky, *Economic Theory and Western European Integration* (Palo Alto: Stanford University Press, 1958), pp.78-80, and Richard Cooper, *The Economics of Interdependence: Economic Policy in the Atlantic Community* (New York: McGraw-Hill, 1968), p.233.

14. Dominion Bureau of Statistics, *Quarterly Estimates of the Canadian Balance of International Payments*, various issues, and *Canadian Statistical Review*, various issues.

15. Dominion Bureau of Statistics, *Quarterly Estimates* (third quarter 1968), Table V, p.20.

16. U.S. Department of Commerce, *Survey of Current Business*, balance-of-payments data, various issues. Many of the new issues purchased by Americans were denominated in U.S. dollars. This does not eliminate or reduce the exchange risk, however, but merely transfers it to the Canadian borrowers. If flexible exchange rates really inhibit capital flows, Canadian borrowers should have been unwilling to take the exchange risk inherent in selling U.S. dollar bonds in New York.

17. Ronald I. McKinnon, "Optimum Currency Areas," American Economic Review (September 1963), pp.717-25.

18. Robert M. Dunn, Jr., "Flexible Exchange Rates and Oligopoly Pricing: A Study of Canadian Markets," *Journal of Political Economy* (January/February 1970), pp.140-51.

19. The greatest single cause of Canada's C\$2.2 billion gain in trade balance with the United States between 1965 and 1970 has been a favourable shift in bilateral automotive trade of just over C\$1 billion (in these statistics), attributable to the 1965 Agreement. This leaves about a billion to increased exports, mainly of petroleum and of manufactured products that were influenced by U.S. inflationary pressures. (U.S. official statistics show even greater trade shifts in Canada's favour: U.S. \$2.5 billion total between 1965 and 1970, of which U.S. \$1.7 billion is automotive, the last figure being reduced to U.S.\$1.4 billion on the basis of transactions value).

20. This conclusion holds, of course, only if Canadian monetary policy is appropriate.

21. Gottfried Haberler and Thomas Willett, *A Strategy for U.S. Balance of Payments Policy* (Washington, D.C.: American Enterprise Institute, 1971).

22. Lawrence Krause, "A Passive Balance of Payments Strategy for the United States," *Brookings Papers on Economic Activity* No.3 (1970), pp.339-68.

23. *The Role of Exchange Rates in the Adjustment of International Payments* (Washington, D.C.: International Monetary Fund, 1970), p.42.

24. The IMF would not pass on the desirability of the government's intended use of the foreign exchange, since this would involve the Fund in basic foreign policy and military decisions which would obviously be unacceptable to national governments, but would merely ensure that the government buying or selling foreign exchange was not doing so solely in an attempt to manipulate the exchange rate.

25. The British are believed to have been forced to sell massive amounts of U.S. dollars to the exchange market in the days immediately preceding the devaluation of November 1967. Each of these dollars increased in value in terms of sterling by 15 per cent when the devaluation finally took place. To whatever extent the U.K. borrowed dollars to support the exchange market, or operated in the forward market by selling U.S. dollars for future delivery, the sterling value of these liabilities increased by 15 per cent. The British payments data show entries for "Adjustment for Forwards"

(defined as "arising from the fact that the pre-devaluation forward commitments of the Exchange Equalization Account were recorded as being settled on maturity at the new parity") as a minus £105 million in 1967 and a minus £251 in 1968. ("Balance of Payments," *Bank of England Quarterly Bulletin* (March 1970, Table 18, p. 99. These two items total over $850 million at the new exchange rate. An earlier and somewhat less expected devaluation would have saved the United Kingdom a great deal of money. See Samuel I. Katz' review of *The International Market for Foreign Exchange* in the *Journal of Economic Literature* (December 1970), pp. 1254-56.

26. See, for example, Bogdan Kipling and Bruce Little, "The Painful Problem of the Too-Strong Dollar," *The Financial Times of Canada* (March 15, 1971). The March and April issues of *The Financial Post* featured a number of articles on this subject, most of which were inspired by the announcements of very disappointing 1970 profits for Canadian export industries. One financial analyst is quoted as follows: "The Canadian dollar floats like a butterfly, but, from a profit point of view, it stings like a bee." *The Financial Post,* (April 3, 1971), p.3.

27. Although the Canadian dollar was undervalued relative to the U.S. dollar and other currencies with payments deficits before June 1970, it was not necessarily undervalued relative to the DM and other surplus currencies. The appreciation of the Canadian dollar, while correcting its position against the U.S. dollar, may have made it overvalued relative to the DM, etc., harming Canadian exports to the European Community and to other balance-of-payments surplus areas. Prospective British and Scandinavian participation in the European Community would further worsen Canada's export situation in Europe by eliminating its present advantage in the United Kingdom under Commonwealth Preferences and by providing Scandinavian exporters with a considerable advantage in selling forest products throughout the European Community in competition with Canadian firms. The answer to these problems is an appreciation of the DM and of other surplus currencies to at least partially return Canadian exporters to their previous competitive position in these countries.

## RONALD J. WONNACOTT and PAUL WONNACOTT

# Free Trade Between the United States and Canada

With free trade between the United States and Canada, there would be significant changes in the North American economy. In particular, free trade would increase the possibility of specialization and would lead to a greater exploitation of economies of scale. Because of the preponderant size of the U.S. economy, the advantage of free trade access to larger markets would be much more significant for Canadian than for American producers; therefore, the primary focus of this study has been on the changes that free trade would bring to the Canadian partner. This is not to argue that the effects on the United States would be trivial, particularly if subsectors of the economy are considered. However, the major changes would occur in Canada, with the benefits and risks being heavily concentrated there.

The evidence presented in this work indicates strongly that free trade in manufactured goods would yield substantial economic gains. The cost of North American tariffs to Canada was estimated at roughly 10.5 per cent of Canadian GNP. The cost to the United States is relatively and absolutely much smaller, amounting to a fraction of one per cent of GNP. All of this cost would not be eliminated immediately upon the adoption of free trade; there would be costs and strains of reorganization, with some firms facing acute problems. The pattern emerging from a period of rationalization cannot be precisely predicted, but the general outlines can be drawn.

Canadians would not become hewers of wood and drawers of water. Indeed, it seems unlikely that there would be any substantial shift in the Canadian employment mix between services, resources, and manufacturing, regardless whether or not resources were included with manufactured goods in the agreement. (To the limited extent that they enter international exchange, services are already freely traded; hence, tariff elimination would not affect this sector directly, and indirectly only insofar as changes in other sectors influenced the relative demands for services.)

The prospects for Canadian resources sectors are good. Since Canadian resources now receive less protection than U.S. resources, this Canadian sector might be expected to gain from free trade. An expansion in demand for Canadian resources is, however, unlikely to change the pattern of Canadian employment markedly, partly because the supply of resources tends to be inelastic, that is, dependent on the availability of rich ore bodies, etc. Furthermore, even limited tendencies toward the expansion of employment in resource materials would be counteracted by the rising supply price of labour resulting from the reorganization of Canadian manufacturing. It seems likely, therefore, that increased demand for resources will result more in rising wages than in increased employment.

Agricultural products raise special problems of analysis, both because of the widespread use of quotas and because the greatest natural markets of the United States and Canada are not one another (as they are for manufactured goods) but rather third countries. Therefore, this area has generally been excluded from the analysis.

Most of the specialization in Canada resulting from free trade would occur *within* manufacturing industries rather than *between* them. Because the competitive positions of Canadian industrial sectors do not vary widely it seems unlikely that any of the broad industrial groups examined in this study would disappear from Canada. Instead it is to be expected that specialization would occur in subindustries within each broad industrial group, with Canadian concentration drifting toward labour-intensive activities. However, major gains from free trade do not depend on this type of specialization; they depend primarily on the exploitation of economies of scale, defined broadly to include not only engineering economies but also managerial and organizational efficiencies associated with specialization and competition in a larger market.

It has often been contended in Canada that, with free trade, U.S. manufacturing would simply increase its output by 10 per cent, while Canadian industry would have to close down. This contention has been established as generally implausible, and it is particularly unlikely in growth industries. In these industries, new facilities are constantly being built. The question is: Where should these facilities be located? Canadian locations have major advantages. In particular Canadian labour costs are lower (and will continue to be in the foreseeable future, even though they can be expected to drift upward toward the U.S. level with free trade). Furthermore, contrary to common belief, transport and capital costs do not substantially offset this labour advantage because most Canadian industry lies either within or close to the North American industrial heartland. This potential strength of the Canadian competitive position would ease the major problems of production rationalization and marketing in the United States that Canadian firms would, with few exceptions, face. These same favourable cost conditions may induce U.S. producers who presently have no Canadian subsidiaries to expand in Canada rather than in the United States. It is even more likely that U.S. firms with existing Canadian subsidiaries would rationalize these facilities rather than write them off in favour of building new ones in the United States. Obviously every industry would not rush to Canada; any widespread movement would cause offsetting pressures in the form of rising Canadian costs as factor supplies became strained. There would, however, be a tendency for growth industries to expand in Canada.

In declining industries, the Canadian outcome would be less favourable. An American firm is unlikely to increase its facilities in Canada if it would involve closing down some of its U.S. facilities. Furthermore, the industry may be contracting not just relatively but also absolutely. In this case the obvious plants to eliminate will be those in Canada because the production aimed at a small market there would generally be inefficient in the new North American context. For rationalization to take place in Canada, wage (or other) operating cost advantages must be at least sufficient to cover costs of rationalization. By definition, declining industries face difficulties anywhere; but these difficulties would be even more severe in Canada.

Because Canada would become the area in North America where the greatest adjustments were taking place, it would be the area on which the pressures of both growth and decline would focus. There is a parallel conclusion: free trade would provide an additional impetus for particularly efficient (and fast growing) firms in any industry, but it would speed the demise of the inefficient. The relative sizes of the Canadian and U.S. economies imply that short-term reorganization problems would fall most heavily on Canada. However, these adjustment difficulties should not be exaggerated. In particular, Canada's small size means that it is not necessary for Canadians to compete with Americans all along the line; it is necessary only that they compete successfully in the production of a relatively limited number of products. The smaller the economic size of a country, the fewer are the lines of specialization required to balance trade and employ resources fully; hence, the easier it becomes to find subindustries in which competition may be successfully undertaken.

In order for Canada to take full advantage of the generally strong competitive position associated with its lower wage costs, several important conditions must be met in the period immediately following the establishment of free trade. One major requirement is sufficient flexibility and imagination by management to recognize and grasp the new opportunities for specialization opened up by freer access to the U.S. market. In short, it is essential that, in the face of a new set of circumstances, Canadian management not "die of shock" in exaggerated fear of possible injury from U.S. competition.

A similar onus would fall on the Canadian labour force. The lower wage is an advantage to Canadian locations only if Canadian workers are approximately as vigorous and diligent as their U.S. counterparts. We see no reason to doubt the high quality of the Canadian labour force. However, the free trade adjustment process would also require something extra of the labour force, namely, recognition of the need for, and vigorous cooperation in, major short-run changes. It is here that government adjustment assistance can be helpful. It is also important that the labour force cooperate in the period of adjustment by a degree of discipline and restraint in labour bargaining. It would, for example, be disastrous for the process of adjustment if Canadian unions were to take the long-run advantages of free trade as the basis for immediate insistence on wage parity with the United States. The long-run tendency for Canadian wages to rise toward U.S. levels under free trade requires vigorous expansion of industrial output. This expansion can be facilitated by short-run wage restraint.

Several limitations apply to any such study of free trade location pressures. Growth in selected U.S. areas (for example, Houston) has recently been heavily dependent on defense and space expenditures by the U.S. government. Canadian regions—and indeed many U.S. regions as well—can hardly expect an equal stimulus, although there is considerable scope for intercountry defense procurement. Amenities such as climate may also influence location decisions. Thus, Canada—like the industrial heartland in the U.S. North—may be at some disadvantage in the competition with California to attract and hold industry. In addition, there are certain market imperfections that can cause difficulty even for firms whose costs are competitive. Advertising and associated consumer loyalty make things difficult for the newcomer; although advertising is partly associated with the issue of economies of scale, it also involves something more. There seems, however, to be some general tendency to overestimate the significance of advertising in inducing "habit buying" because it is most important in the highly conspicuous sectors of the economy (consumer durables). Similarly, national preferences in purchases may provide some market imperfection. However, here, too, there would seem to be some tendency to overstate the difficulty. In part, past U.S. resistance to purchases from Canada has been associated with the problem of potential interruption of supply. This potential difficulty has, in turn, arisen from the possibility of tariff changes or reclassification, something which would be eliminated by free trade. In general, however, it cannot be maintained that economic forces will work out precisely as foreseen in any economic analysis.

The political significance of a bilateral free trade agreement cannot be foreseen with precision. There clearly would be some political implications: most obviously, each country would lose some degree of control over its commercial policy because it would commit itself by treaty not to impose tariffs on imports from the partner. Because it would cause an increase in trade across the common border, a free trade arrangement would tighten the already close economic ties between the two countries.

Yet paradoxically, Canada may become more dependent, yet less vulnerable. Specifically, Canada would be ensuring through such a treaty that U.S. tariffs would not be raised against Canadian exports, and this possibility is one of the major present sources of Canadian vulnerability. Moreover, freeing trade will have fewer critical implications for monetary and fiscal independence than does a fixed exchange rate. If a high degree of autonomy over these policies is judged a major objective in Canada, no commitment should be made to keep exchange rates frozen, for example, via a common currency arrangement. For similar reasons of autonomy, a free trade association is to be preferred over a customs union. The political case against fixed exchanges and a customs union draws support from economic considerations; a fixed exchange rate may not provide the authorities with sufficient scope to deal with balance-of-payments adjustments, whereas a customs union may not allow each partner to keep tariffs on third countries at as low a level as it would wish.

Because possible U.S. domination is a matter of concern in Canada, the initiative for any movement for free trade must come from Canada rather than the United States. In the final analysis, it must be the Canadian public who weigh the respective gains and losses from free trade. And public weighing of gains and losses is the purpose of the democratic process.

# Epilogue

## ATHELSTAN SPILLHAUS
# The Next Industrial Revolution

While I am not going to talk about population this evening, we all know that population is a central problem, and if we are "doers" then we must do the things the best way we know how for the population we have. Tonight, I am going to talk about what I call the next industrial revolution. Although we may not see it as a real constructive revolution, I think it has begun all around us here in Canada and the United States and will be everywhere in the world in the near future.

We must have this new industrial revolution, *even* if some of us have to invent it. The other industrial revolutions came along somewhat unplanned and certainly people were unprepared for the side effects of them. The first, which started in England, was magnificent. It was hailed as a way to ennoble man by substituting other forms of power for his muscles. But with that power came grime and smoke and the other things that were the side effects. However, the primary benefits were so worthwhile that the side effects were accepted for a long time or went unnoticed, but you might say that, with that industrial revolution, we also invented air pollution.

Then the existence of power had a second effect, it enabled us to mass produce things for people so that they could have more things to ease their lives. But by mass production, multiplying things to put in people's hands to give them an ease of living, we produced so many things that, after their use, there was more and more to throw away, and in this way we invented the solid waste problem.

Then a third revolution came about with the magnificent chemical revolution, the ability to tailor-make chemicals, pesticides, herbicides, fertilizers, the things that gave us an abundance of food. But here too came the side effects. They could selectively destroy elements of the biological system which were inimicable to man or to his food supply, but again with these new chemicals came an upsetting of the ecology—the word we have all learned to use, even if we don't understand it—and so we invented eutrophication and other new ways to pollute water.

Now, no balanced person regrets these discoveries in themselves. Without them we would not be living in the *ease* of the present century as contrasted to the *dis-ease* that existed before the first industrial revolution. But there is concern now for the steadily increasing poisoning and the spoiling of our environment which has caused some extremists to say, "stop doing what you're doing",... "stop increasing the production of things for people",... "stop making power because of the waste heat",... "stop using fertilizers''. Some conservationists, for example, wish to block the building of power plants because of the waste heat problem. Yet, the same people who would have us stop doing things for the peoples' benefit are just those who damn technology when shortage of power results in an overload and causes a brownout or blackout.

We must, I think, morally attempt to bring to all people as many things to ease their lives as modern science and technology are capable of providing; but at the same time, we must bring them, and I'm sure we can, a clean environment now that their rising aspirations insist on this. Hopefully, people will be willing to pay for it.

Man, of course, is the greatest polluter. The definition of a pollutant that I like is anything animate or inaminate that by its excess reduces the quality of living. In this sense man is also clearly the greatest pollutant because each one of us as one quantum in the great number of us does indeed, because of that great number, reduce the quality of each other's living. Now, to prepare you for this next industrial revolution, which I hope you will join me in planning, I suggest that we revise our vocabulary. For instance, there is no such person as a consumer. This is a word invented perhaps by Schools of Business or perhaps by Madison Avenue. It is over-used by advertisers. We consume nothing, whatever it be the food we eat, the automobiles we drive, or the hardware in our houses. We merely use things and, according to the Conservation of Matter, exactly the same mass of material is discarded after use. This is very simplistic but it is very important to remember that we consume nothing.

Thus, under our present system of mismanaging material after use, as the standard of living goes up, as the amount of things we use goes up, the amount of waste and consequent pollution must go up. In poor countries where things are scarce, there is very little waste, but the solution in any country is not the reduction of the Gross National Product or the lowering of the individual standards of living in order to reduce waste. I believe we must base this next industrial revolution, this planned one, on the thesis that there is no such thing as waste. Waste, as has been said many times, is simply some substance that we do not yet have the wit to use, or if we have the wit, our present economic system prevents our reusing it.

Industry and business, what we might call the private sector, has been asked to do only half its job. It performs magnificent feats of scientific, technological and manageriel skills to take things from the land, to grow them in the land, refine them, mass manufacture, mass market and mass distribute them to the so-called consumer—who is nothing but a user. But, after use, it is left to the public sector to dispose of this same mass of material. By and large, in our societies in North America, the private sector makes the things before use and for use and the public sector disposes of them after use. It is the public sector that has not done a very good job of this disposal. Yet now everybody points at industry—the private sector—which has done such a *good* job of providing the abundance of more and more new materials and it is because of this good job that the public sector can't keep up with its business of throwing the things away after use or what is euphemistically called ''disposing'' of waste.

But to continue the revision of our vocabulary, there is no such thing as ''disposal'' in the sense that the word has been used with regard to so-called waste. Disposal, as presently practised by the public sector, municipalities, city governments and the like, at least in North America, usually means grinding things fine, burning them, diluting them, and spreading them around in the hope that the taxpayers won't notice it. That's what we've been doing for centuries. It's very much like the lazy housewife who, when asked what she did with her garbage, said "I just kick it around until it gets lost." I think that we can no longer kick around our wastes till they get lost.

We don't need economists to tell us that spreading things around after use and then cleaning them up is more expensive than containing wastes at the source, separating them and, if possible, reusing them. Disposal in the true sense of the word connotes an arrangement. It is this kind of arrangement that I wish to talk about as the basis of this new industrial revolution. In other words, in this industrial revolution our industries must be encouraged to do the other half of their job, to close the loop back from the user to the factory. If industry itself takes on the job of closing this loop, hopefully, with the necessary subsidies and assistance from government and the necessary controls if it doesn't do it, then I think that in the design of articles for use the idea of reuse would be borne in the mind and incorporated in the original design. If, on the other hand, we continue to have the private sector design things up to the point of use and the public sector dispose of them, designs for reuse and reconversion will not easily come about.

The automobile is always used, at least in the southern part of North America, as a conspicuous scapegoat. Old cars are just abandoned and left to rust in acres of graveyards. We are now trying to compress them into chunks, but what do we do with the chunks of metal? In our economy we don't reuse them, and maybe it will take some time to tool up to reuse those chunks. This will be the truth of many other wastes. We are not prepared immediately to reuse them. In the meantime, I think we ought to still segregate them and compact them and keep them until the time when we do find out by changing our economies and also by advances in technology we can reuse and reconvert them.

I suggested that we might take these chunks of metal from compressed automobiles and, for instance, take them to our flat mid-Western plains, the middle of our countries. I have on previous occasions mentioned an area such as Kansas or Saskatchewan. I would call ours in Kansas the Alfred P. Sloan Memorial Mountain! But then I got all kinds of letters saying, "What do you want to send your junk to us for?" But I really thought I was doing them a favour because they need mountains. They could ski on them with artificial snow. They would be mountains of fairly pure iron and then when our economies change or iron ore becomes scarce, we could mine them. This would certainly be better than what we do now. Instead of concentrating this metal in one place, we allow it to rust, oxidize, and get spread around so that it is really not recoverable in any way.

Furthermore, in the remelting of automobile hulks it is very often the small amount of copper in the wiring and the motors—these motors which are distributed now all over the chassis—which when melted down, pollute the steel. If we were worried about that pollution of the steel through copper, then we would design automobiles with aluminum harness and ferrite magnets which would oxidize and come off as slag so that we would get a better grade of steel. This is just one tiny example of design for reuse and reconversion.

In our continent, the public is influenced by our vocal politicians' rhetoric and the mass media who point at industry as the chief villain that is ruining our environment. We have had an "Earth Day" down our way to clean up our world. Youngsters came out en masse for a very positive program. It only took the authorities about three days to clean up the mess after them! It is a good thing if there is a public awareness, and particularly among the young, about this problem.

But there is not much of an awareness of what positive steps need to be taken to cope with it. In the earlier days, people were willing to put up with the side effects because they needed the power, the food and the shelter that the former industrial revolution could bring them more importantly than a clean environment. But as industry and agriculture provided these things in abundance we now take them for granted and our aspirations have been raised. In recent years, people as a whole have begun to express a desire for a clean environment as well.

I have no doubt myself that this new need can be satisfied by imaginative private enterprise and industry without decreasing the supply of the other things that people need. It simply means that industry must take over the management of wastes as clean environment becomes one of the choices that people want and are willing to pay for.

Take, for example, the pride of a homemaker in having a spic and span house for her family. This legitimate pride has for a hundred years sold soaps and cleaning agents and was responsible for the soap operas on radio and TV. Immense sums are paid to satisfy the quite proper desire of these homemakers to have a clean indoors. I think we have just about arrived at the point where we can take this kind of pride outdoors and have outdoor soap operas and convince people that by paying a fraction more for the article they use they will be buying cleanliness and reuse of the materials as well.

We have, in this connection, to emphasize that a clean environment can't be "free". "Free" is a word that is used loosely for those things people expect to get which are not subject to the competitive pricing of supply and demand. Water has traditionally been a "free" thing. We have been conditioned to expect water to be delivered at a price far below the true cost. Yet food, which is even more fundamental to our living, is priced according to supply and demand.

The trouble with free things is that there is no feedback to or from the people. When water, garbage collection, sewage usage are hidden in inclusive taxes you get the wasteful use of water, wasteful packaging and overburdened sewers. The curious thing is that the human tendency of wanting to give things free doesn't really help people because it restricts rather than increases people's choices. For example, the thrifty person who is sparing of his water and his waste packing and other solid wastes does not have the choice to pay less in taxes and spend what he saves by his thrift for something he values more. We only have to think of how saturated the telephone system would become if telephone service was included in indirect payments instead of being paid for by direct payments. Why should we not have an industry that copes with our wastes, reprocesses them, and why should we not pay for our wastes and their reconversion by the bit, or by the amount we use?

In the economics of this recycling process—the cyclical conversion system toward which we must progress ultimately—costs per gallon, per kilogram, or costs per bit must really total the costs from any point in the cycle through the use of the product back to that point, i.e., the total cost of recycling. That is a little oversimplification because reuse may go into a totally different article from the original after use. But just as waste and water can no longer be a "political gift" I think we should understand that a clean environment cannot be a "political gift" in spite of what our politicians at least would like to have people believe. They are campaigning on the idea of giving people a clean environment and they are not telling people that really they have to pay for a clean environment. They all talk about recycling now. They have learned that word but with few exceptions we haven't even learned how to cycle yet.

Everything that we do to the resources on our earth is just a *conversion* process. Again, to get back to the semantics of conversion, we use different words for different parts of the conversion cycle. When we convert iron ore to iron we say we *smelt* or *refine* it. Then we convert the iron into something we use, we *manufacture* it—say to a car. Then we use that car and after use we let it rust, converting it into iron oxide or if we melt it down again we convert it back into iron. With food we convert land chemical substances with the help of the sun, the air and water into plants. We say we *grow* them. We use parts of these plants for food from which we extract energy and we use other parts for fibres. We convert them into different forms of organic matter which should return to the earth from whence it came. It is the old organic garden but now on a much bigger scale. Our conversion of water is generally merely the dirtying of it and the reconversion of water would be the cleaning of it. Conservation in the old-fashioned sense is no longer enough unless coupled to conversion. So you see that in terms of conversion and in the cycle of products there is no producer—only a converter, just as there is no consumer—only a converter.

If we move away from our customary treatment of wastes toward cycling and reconversion we will be investing our money and efforts in a new enterprise toward a *permanent* solution. When government and municipalities just spend more and more money in the old-fashioned so-called disposal of waste the money itself is wasted because it is not in the direction of the permanent solution. If we make synthetic materials by our technology that are not degradable by nature so that there is no natural way back, the loop to the earth is closed. Then we must, after use, unmake these things by that same technology. In fact, I would like to invert the words of the marriage ceremony in describing the problem of non-biodegradable synthetics. They are those things that man has joined together and let us not expect God or nature to put them asunder.

In other words, when we design things and put them together they must also be designed so that we can take them apart. Nerve gas, for instance, can be broken down into non-poisonous, perhaps even useful components and we should, before we ever synthesize something like that in any quantity, have a complete plan for breaking it down again.

Let's design the "off" switch before we turn on the "on" switch.

You see, conservation is not enough. In fact, too much conservation in the old sense of preserving old ecologies may be harmful. We should preserve these old ecologies in special places, in our outdoor museums and our preserves. We must also, if we are going to take care of the numbers of people we have, engineer new ecologies. We must develop engineering and ecological reconstruction and ecological inventing to preserve the qualities that we want in our environment. These qualities cannot necessarily continue to be supplied by the older ecologies which worked when there weren't so many of us. And ecological engineering, of course, is nothing new. It is just a term that has achieved popularity. All agriculture from the very beginning is ecological engineering. As soon as you clear the land from the mixed thickets that were on it and plant a single stand, you have essentially done a massive job of ecological engineering. You have engineered for the things that people need — the food.

But these new ecological systems also have to be built on the foundations of the old. Here again we have sometimes made mistakes. We have tried to transport temperate agriculture to the tropics and, of course, tropical areas are very different from the temperate latitudes. The main difference, I suppose, is that there is very little humus. In fact, once when I was introducing a chap, who described himself as a tropical agronomist, I introduced him as an agronomist without a sense of humus. Instead of merely transporting what we know from temperate latitudes, where the science of agriculture grew up, to the tropics we are now, more imaginatively, looking to the domesticating, husbanding and herding of the indigenous "wild" animals for meat — animals that are adapted by nature to the conditions.

But to come back to the reconversion business, governments are spending large sums of money to enforce mere punitive measures and this will not accomplish the permanent solution to which I am trying to move in suggesting the next industrial revolution. We will need, equally, to offer incentives to private industry to encourage them in the proper management and use of the by-products that we now call waste.

We've heard about lead in gasoline. But how did lead get into gasoline? People wanted lead for their high-compression, over-powered automobiles and industry gave it to them. Industry responds to people's needs. Now people don't want lead in their gasoline, and industry in various ways is responding to getting the lead out. I think this is the proper response.

The trouble is that we get awfully impatient. When an industry has been going in a certain direction for many years, it is rather hard for it to change overnight. Many industries are honestly doing things, though perhaps they may seem small, towards recovering and reusing their wastes. Platinum, for instance, is always recovered and reused. We must change our economies to make more and more reuse possible.

When we go to, say newspapers, at the other end of the scale, it is very hard to conceive of a way in our economies to collect newspapers, clean the print off them, and reuse them. But experiments are going on. In Beltsville, Maryland they are feeding pure cellulose with amino acids and other additives to cattle which the ruminants change into protein. I love to imagine a factory where old newspapers are going in one end and steaks coming out the other! Now that is the objective we are aiming toward.

We hear a great deal about waste heat these days. It is only waste heat because we waste it. More properly, it is the exhausts from power generators. It is extremely low-grade heat and difficult to utilize. It is not high enough in temperature to be practical for process heat, for space heating, for desalting sea water, or for any energy-intense industrial process. But there are uses for it. These again are in the experimental stage. One use that is coming to the fore is the use in fish farming or aquaculture where warm water is found to accelerate the growth and increase harvests of fish, shrimp, and other aquatic life. Also, experiments with warm water irrigation in agriculture to heat soil and extend the growing season are being tried in colder climates. These are the kinds of experiments that we need to foster because they are all steps in the direction of the permanent solution. We need massive experiments of this kind if we are going to really tackle the problem in the sense of the urgent constructive revolution that I think will be necessary to stop the further degradation of our environment.

It often seems to me that in some of these tremendous problems or challenges that we have ahead of us we are kind of half-expecting disaster and less than half planning for it. With all of our wonderful advances in science and technology, we deal woefully slowly and unimaginatively with the things for people's better living. We are timid to try new approaches. We whittle instead of making the massive, daring novel experiments which are possible. We often attack the wrong links in systems. For example, we have a huge problem in transportation for all people both here in Canada and in the United States, but what are we doing? We're building supersonic transports for the few. That doesn't solve the problem of how you get to the airport or back. The object of a transportation system is to get from where you are to where you want to go, and if you only improve the link in the middle, especially the link that serves the fewest people, it does not tackle the basic problem. This is quite apart from the fact, of course, that the SST, which may be a marvellous technological invention, reduces the choices of people who would like to be quiet.

I learned when I was in England recently of a new kind of pollution. They are building there an airplane which has a little engine and propeller in the front and a long light strut. It carries only two people but it is longer than our longest jet. This strut is for the purpose of carrying lights so that the airplane can flash advertising at night at 90 words a minute. This is optical pollution and I told them in Britain "Please keep it there! We have got enough of our own people creating that kind of a disaster!"

That art often precedes the science is nowhere more true than in the design of cities, in the relation of how cities must be developed if this recycling process is to come about. The city planners for many, many years have recognized the need for city folks to have open spaces, green spaces, access to the countryside and they did this from a sensitive assessment of the desires of people. The fact is that people want both the excitement, opportunity and choices that an intense living city can give them, but they also want an escape to a quiet restful countryside. But it actually follows that if you are going to recycle the foods and fibres and put them back on the land, you come to a technological reason for the coupling of the countryside and the city. You must have cities coupled to the rural areas. Otherwise, you cannot have the immense organic farms. This is the simple technological reason that reinforces the necessity of having cities in rural areas and rural areas near our cities. It is a buttress for what the planners have suggested for a long time. Furthermore, if you do have cities in rural areas then the waste heat could possibly be used to speed up the bacteriological and other processes of treating the organic wastes before they go back into the land so that we end up with a very nice arrangement—the power plants located close enough to the centre of use, to the people who need the power, but also close enough to the agricultural lands so that the waste heat may be used. It is a straightforward reason which tells us why we must not allow our individual cities, of the future at least, to grow physically too large because then it becomes, increasingly difficult to close the loop back to the land.

Many of the projects in this recycling or industrial urban/rural symbiosis that I have just described—where you pair different kinds of activities in order that by pairing their wastes you can get something useful out of it—are licked not because of a lack of scientific and technological know-how but because we just haven't grown-up enough institutional-managerial methods or political ways of doing things. Many of them are also licked by social or psychological or taboo reactions of people.

It was so that we might have places to experiment with agro-industrial symbiosis, with reconversion, with new integrated networks of service that I suggested sometime ago the building of new experimental places where we can test the technologies and their acceptance by people.

I really believe we need still to build limited physical-size cities, which means limited size of population, surrounded by land so that we can have full-scale experiments *with* people not *on* people. We need places where we can try out new transportation methods, where we can see if we can get clean industry, where we can see if we can get back to the original idea of a city which is to live, work or go to school all within a neighbourhood.

I have always thought that one of the things we need to experiment with, of course, is the question of mass transportation. The slogan used to be "a chicken in every pot" now it's "two cars in every garage". There's nothing wrong with the raised aspirations of people to have two cars in every garage; it multiplies people's choices. It means that the people can go in two different directions at two different times. In fact, if there are "N" people in a family ideally there should be "N" cars including safe cars for the children, so that "N" people could go "N" different places, at "N" different times. But how do we do it and preserve what people want in a car? A lot of schemes have been developed and can be categorized under what I call the private people-pod system of mass transportation.

Mass transportation as it is today fails for three reasons. There's an engine in the vehicle and that's expensive, there's a driver in the vehicle and he is expensive, and usually there's also someone taking the fares and he is expensive. If you can get rid of the driver, the engine, and the fare collector you begin to have the elements of a transportation system. You can reduce the size of the part down perhaps to the size of a private automobile and you're getting toward a mass transportation system which meets people's desires. We have mass transportation systems that have no driver, no engine in the moving part and which are for "free". They are elevators and escalators. Of course, they don't come "free". But I have always wondered why you can go vertically in an elevator and at a certain angle on an escalator for "free". At what critical angle do we have to begin to pay a fare? I think it is quite possible that in the intense cores of cities of the future we can have these private people-pod systems with traction in the track, computers guiding them and the fares paid by the business or services that they stop at, as elevators are paid for today. They could pass through buildings at the second-storey level so that the buildings could provide the supports and stations for the systems. Essentially they would be horizontal elevators.

In North America, while most people have sufficient of the physical things to live, there are many who do not have enough of the metaphysical or human services that make living human. We measure poverty in terms of the lack of human services to people more perhaps than in the lack of physical things. Poverty in this sense exists everywhere, but its dimensions are different. Until you provide the minimum standards to keep the body and soul together, food and shelter, fire which is power, people don't worry too much about the lack of other things. As soon as they get those, they properly worry about other lacks.

One other thing that will come about in the next industrial revolution, and we see it already, will be the entry of private enterprise into people-service fields. As we make more and more things with fewer and fewer workers in the automated factories, and continue to grow abundant food with fewer and fewer farmers, then if people are going to continue to work they are going to have to move into the business of people-service — education, health services and so forth — which are now dreadfully neglected, at least in my country. I think that we will see a continual enlargement of private business serving in the people business — bringing human services to all people. Could not a corporation run a school system? It certainly could do no worse than some that I have seen. Could not a corporation run a city and do a better job than the fragmented jurisdictions which, at least in my country, now mismanage our large municipalities and are continually perpetuated by a false interpretation of democracy?

I think that we will have some shocks in this next industrial revolution. We will wonder if we can any longer derive the primary source of funds for the management of the city from real estate taxes. Why shouldn't we derive these funds from the rental of three-dimensional space as in a hotel? A city on today's scale of population is nothing more than a large hotel. So that this next industrial revolution can only be accomplished by a radical revision of some of our economic traditions and even more difficult, the re-education of ourselves and our children toward a new sense of values and rewards.

One example: everyone of us accepts as part of the reward for his work now the pleasure of owning things. Yet one consequence of what I've said about the revision of our vocabulary is that we really own nothing. We've got to get used to the idea that we are no longer consumers and there is no longer ownership. We must replace the pleasure of usership for ownership. We already see it. This, too, is nothing new but it will be a hard thing for people to understand. We have rental cars, rental clothes. We have other euphemisms for ownership embodied in such devices as condominiums and time payment plans for even such simple things as household furniture. These are merely sales devices that are ingenious ways for capitalizing on everybody's innate desire for ownership. But if we face the fact that we are merely users, then somehow we must face the fact that we own nothing and that the reward for our labour must be to enjoy the use of things and human service for our mental and physical well-being and comfort.

And the shape of our cities will change with this industrial revolution. Winston Churchill once said, "we shape our cities and they shape our way of life". Indeed they do. It's the poor shape of our cities, the degradation of human beings by overcrowding, lack of good educational facilities, lack of economical mass transportation, which prevents them from fleeing, and which traps the poor and shapes their discontent. When we shape our cities, we should do this too in such ways that we can reshape them as people's desires change. Or in a sense of humility, as we admit that we haven't done a very good job.

Our present government policies to cure the ills of the cities are curiously in self-conflict. We continue to use the objectionable practice of zoning. Zoning is simply the admission of the failure of the city. Zoning comes about because industries and other places where people work are noisy and congested, and these areas are therefore zoned industrial. The parts around them become the area where those people who cannot afford the flight away to the suburbs and penthouses have to live. If we can use the power of our technology, through this next industrial revolution, to clean up the mess that technology has made and if we can create noiseless, fumeless factories then people can live, work, play and go to school all in the same neighbourhood and return to the essence of city life.

We have curious self-conflicts in government in my country, where it is heavily committed, and rightly so, to the integration of people with different coloured skins yet at the same time segregates people by income levels and by ages. Massive low-cost housing means simply that we segregate the poor from the rich. We have geriatric housing that segregates the old from the young. We have massive campuses outside of cities which again segregate the young from real life.

Well, ladies and gentlemen, I have attempted to describe in simple terms what I mean by the next industrial revolution. It is in essence the generating of a new industry, an industry as vast as our present productive industry, an industry managed and run with the scientific and technological, managerial and economic inputs of any ordinary productive industry, but it is an industry that will take things not to the user but from the user after his use and reprocess them and put them back to the manufacturer. This industry will not produce a product other than a clean environment. It will rather reprocess the things we call waste so that they may be reproduced in the factories into things we need. I think that this industrial revolution is on our doorstep. In fact, I think it is already going on and I talk to you in the hope that you will join me as being constructive revolutionaries that will shape it rather than letting it just happen and shape us.